Confrontation and Cooperation

Germany and the United States of America
The Krefeld Historical Symposia
Volume 2

Confrontation and Cooperation

Germany and the United States in the Era of World War I, 1900–1924

Edited by

Hans-Jürgen Schröder

BERG

Providence / Oxford

First published in 1993 by
Berg Publishers Inc.
Editorial Offices:
221 Waterman Street, Providence, RI 02906, USA
150 Cowley Road, Oxford, OX4 1JJ, UK

© Hans-Jürgen Schröder 1993

Library of Congress Cataloging-in-Publication Data
Confrontation and cooperation : Germany and the United States in the era of
  World War I, 1900–1924 / edited by Hans-Jürgen Schröder.
      p.   cm. — (Germany and the United States of America : v. 2)
    Includes bibliographical references and index.
    ISBN 0–85496–789–3
    1. United States—Relations—Germany. 2. Germany—Relations—United
States. 3. World War, 1914–1918—United States. 4. World War,
1914–1918—Germany. I. Schröder, Hans-Jürgen. II. Series.
E183.8.G3C625 1993
940.3'2443—dc20   93-19973
                                                                                   CIP

British Library Cataloguing in Publication Data
A *CIP* catalogue record for this book is available from the British Library.
ISBN 0–85496–789–3

Printed in the United States by E. B. Edwards Brothers, Ann Arbor, Mich.

Contents

Contents

Contents

PART V ISOLATION OR RECONSTRUCTION?

Preface

The Krefeld Historical Symposia have developed into an institution. Thanks to various initiatives of the City of Krefeld, historians from both the United States and Europe meet regularly to discuss historical dimensions of German-American relations. In June 1983, the first Krefeld Historical Symposium was held in commemoration of the tricentenary of the emigration of thirteen families from the City of Krefeld to the Colony of Pennsylvania. Its title was: "Religion and Society, Space and Time: A Comparative Approach to the History of the Eighteenth Century." Vice President George Bush was the most prominent visitor to come to Krefeld to celebrate this tricentennial. And his visit certainly contributed to also intensify public interest in the historians' debates.

In 1987, a second symposium was devoted to a comparative approach of "German and American Constitutional Thought: Contexts, Interaction and Historical Realities." It also marked the beginning of a new series: "Germany and the United States of America. The Krefeld Historical Symposia," published by Berg Publishers. Series editor is my colleague Hermann Wellenreuther.

The following essays are the results of the 1990 conference on "Germany and the United States in the Era of World War I" that concentrated on the years 1900 to 1924. American and European scholars discussed both the causes of German-American confrontation that culminated in American intervention against Germany in 1917, and the origins of close German-American cooperation in the 1920s.

Preparation and organization of the symposium could not have been realized without the already well-established team-work between the City of Krefeld and the various egg heads of the Academic Advisory Council for the Krefeld Historical Symposia. For their cooperation and support I would like to thank Erich Angermann, Herbert Eichmanns, Wilfred Esser, Reinhard Feinendegen, Norbert Finzsch, Eugen Gerritz, Rita Jakobs, Hartmut Lehmann, Friedhelm Kutz, Andrea Mania, Anja Rieger, Paul Günter Schulte, and Hermann Wellenreuther.

Needless to add that we all owe much to the symposium's participants. Most of them contributed to this volume. I would like to thank all of them for their cooperation and patience. They had to suffer from reminders to meet the deadline for submission of papers before the conference and also various editorial wishes after the conference. I hope that they enjoyed the time during the conference. The bibliography was compiled by Elisabeth Laube who also encouraged my involvement in both the conference and the publication project.

Again, we tried to attract the public's interest. Erich Angermann gave a public lecture on the historical dimensions of the year 1917 at a reception by the City of Krefeld at Burg Linn. The original German version was translated by Hermann Wellenreuther for publication in this volume. At the end of the conference, Helmut Rehmsen from the West German Broadcasting System moderated a panel of American and German historians on current problems in American-German relations. Although we had to compete with a soccer game, we had a marvellous audience which became actively involved in the discussion. The City Archives of Krefeld presented an exhibition on "Krefeld and America, 1900-1924," that was prepared by Wilhelm Stratmann. These various symposium activities were widely covered by the press. I would like to thank all journalists attending our meetings and press conferences for their interest and their articles.

Publication of the book was a transatlantic undertaking. Marion Berghahn and Robert Riddell of Berg Publishers have taken a lively interest in this volume, as did Ronn Smith who experienced some peculiarities of German academics while skillfully copyediting all manuscripts. I would like to thank him for his patience and cooperation.

As an historian one has always to be aware of the power of the purse. Fortunately, our sponsors did not use this power. I therefore gratefully acknowledge financial support by the Deutsche Forschungsgemeinschaft, the Fritz Thyssen Foundation and above all the City of Krefeld as represented by mayor Willi Wahl.

HANS-JÜRGEN SCHRÖDER

Introduction

The Past is Prologue: On the Significance of Twentieth-Century American-German Relations

Hans-Jürgen Schröder

In the twentieth century, American-German relations have oscillated between confrontation and cooperation. Within a quarter of a century the United States and Germany had been opponents in two world wars, and after both wars this confrontation was transformed into close cooperation, particularly in the economic sphere. The United States, which had been decisive in bringing about Germany's defeat in both wars, also took the lead in initiating the reconstruction of Germany and Europe. This policy of reconstruction was particularly impressive after World War II. The Marshall Plan became known as the most successful foreign aid program, and since its announcement the majority of the Germans have regarded it as a synonym for the beginning of the German *Wirtschaftswunder*.

Despite the United States' obvious importance for Germany and Germany's key role in Washington's policy towards Europe, however, both American and German historians were slow to discover American-German relations as a major field of research after World War II. Two reasons might be cited for this delay: Historians first wanted to document the Third Reich's responsibilities for the beginning of hostilities in 1939 and Nazi plans to dominate Europe and the world. The second reason is that in the period immediately following World War II, historical writing concentrated on the description of visible diplomatic actions rather than on the indirect and informal influences in the international system that are characteristic of American diplomacy.

Since the late 1960s research on American-German relations has intensified.[1] Historians have concentrated on the interwar period and the post-World War II years. Interest in the interwar years in particular reflects a shift in the methodological approach to the interpretation of international relations in both the United States and West Germany.

Notes to the Introduction can be found on page 7.

Since the late 1960s attention has increasingly focused on the role of domestic constellations in the formulation of a nation's foreign policy. In this context, economic factors have become more and more recognized as being of major importance when interpreting twentieth century international relations. This school of thinking, which tends to emphasize structural elements rather than personal factors, could be characterized by mentioning the names of two influential historians: William Appleman Williams[2] and Hans-Ulrich Wehler. Williams' influence in the United States is well documented by the vast amount of books published by his students. In the Federal Republic it was Wehler who contributed to the reception of the so-called Williams School during the 1960s. Wehler's research and publications about American imperialism must be mentioned in particular.[3] The debate within Germany as to whether Williams' approach could be regarded as a useful concept, not only for the interpretation of American foreign policy in general but also for a better understanding of the specific problems in American-German relations, had practical results, since this debate stimulated research on American-German relations during the twentieth century.

The generation problem has to be mentioned in this connection. Many German historians, having experienced the collapse of the Weimar Republic and the atrocities of the Third Reich, tended to present a rather idealistic view of American foreign policy. On the other hand, the so-called younger generation, which was influenced by the protest movements of the 1960s, was inclined to stress American self-interest and the materialistic side of United States foreign relations. These different approaches to the interpretation of American foreign policy have had a significant impact on the interpretation of twentieth century American-German relations, which have become a growing concern to historians in both the United States and Germany since the 1960s. Until recently, however, research has focused primarily on three areas: the United States and the Weimar Republic, Nazi Germany and the United States, and America's role in the reconstruction of West Germany after World War II.

Interpretations of American-German relations during the Weimar period have been closely connected with the problem of American isolationism. Did the United States retreat from Europe after World War I? Was American foreign policy during the Republican administrations from Harding to Hoover isolationist? Many historians still hesitate to accept the revisionists' rejection of any interpretation which might create the impression that American isolationism was the dominant force in Washington's policy towards Europe.

However, there has been a consensus among historians for a long time that United States financial involvement in Europe after World War I was considerable, despite an alleged American retreat from the Old World. In the context of American-German relations Werner Link, more than two decades ago, presented an epoch-making analysis of what he called the American stabilization policy in Europe.[4] Link's book is of central importance in explaining the origins and mechanisms of American-German cooperation that developed during the 1920s. His interpretation of American foreign policy follows the approach of William A. Williams and his students. By applying this interpretation to American-German relations after World War I, Link convincingly proves that Germany was of central importance for the United States, both as a market and as a partner in the struggle to establish a liberal world order.

The various steps of American stabilization policy as most clearly evidenced in the Dawes Plan of 1924 and the influx of American capital into Germany are extensively analyzed in Link's book. It is of central importance in explaining the origins and mechanisms of American-German cooperation of the 1920s, when Germany was the cornerstone of Washington's policy toward Europe. The empirical evidence presented by Link and others proves that Washington not only realized important economic goals, but that the American government was also in the position to decisively influence political developments in Europe.[5]

These political dimensions of American stabilization policy must be seen in the context of German foreign policy. For the Berlin government, close cooperation with the United States was essential for both economic and political reasons. The influx of American capital was vital for the reconstruction and stabilization of the German economy. This process of economic reconstruction was also defined in political terms. A strong economy in general and an active trade policy in particular were regarded as the most important levers for further German revisionist aims directed against the Versailles order. The Dawes Plan must be seen in this context, since it implied "The End of French Predominance in Europe," as Stephen Schuker has put it.[6] The German elites were convinced that their revisionist goals could only be achieved by close cooperation with the United States. Foreign Minister Gustav Stresemann had repeatedly stressed the key importance of the United States for Germany.[7]

The resulting German dependence on the United States offered Washington various opportunities to informally influence German economic and political decisions. The abortive Stresemann-Briand talks at Thoiry in 1926 and the failure of Aristide Briand's Pan-European Plan of May 1930 might be cited as examples. Due to the great dependence on Washington the Weimar Republic was even referred to as a "penetrated system."[8] However, American-German parallelism was brought to an end by the collapse of the Weimar Republic. Was the shift from cooperation to confrontation during the 1930s the result of Hitler's *Machtergreifung*? Or did long-established structural divergences between Washington and Berlin simply come to the surface during the Great Depression?

Although we need more information about the origins of the growing disharmony between the governments in Berlin and Washington, we have ample evidence of the various elements that intensified American-German conflicts from the mid-1930s onwards. An impressively large number of publications are available covering a broad spectrum of problems that shaped the Third Reich's relations with the United States: bilateral diplomatic as well as economic relations,[9] the United States as a factor in the strategic and political thinking of the Nazi elite,[10] National Socialist propaganda in the United States,[11] American reactions toward the prosecution of Jews in Germany,[12] and other challenges to the U.S. government's interests by National Socialist ideological, economic, and territorial expansion. The Nazi threat manifested itself dramatically in Berlin's policy towards numerous Latin American countries, which developed into an important zone of conflict between the United States and the Third Reich.[13]

Nazi domestic and foreign policies were regarded as challenges to the American model of a liberal world order. Given the close economic cooperation between the two states in the 1920s, it is no surprise that these challenges first became manifest in the economic sphere. German autarky and bilateral trade schemes, with Japan and Italy practicing similar methods, posed a threat to the Roosevelt administration's concept of an "indivisable world market."[14] This challenge to America's open-door concept was much more than a matter of foreign economic policy; for decision-makers in Washington, it was also of major political importance. German penetration into Latin America indicated that Nazi Germany's designs were not limited to Europe and that by the mid-1930s a American-German confrontation was emerging. This happened at a time when Nazi Germany pretended to still have working relations with the United States. However, this early confrontation between Berlin and Washington cannot be grasped by a purely bilateral interpretation of diplomatic relations. Therefore, a multilateral approach that takes into account economic elements as well is necessary for an overall interpretation of American-German relations. Such a multilateral approach offers new perspectives for the interpretation of American-German relations. The policy of appeasement is just one example.

Unlike London the United States government did not pursue a policy of appeasement. To the contrary, Washington tried to contain Nazi

Germany by economic means. These "Economic Aspects of New Deal Diplomacy,"[15] and the Hull trade agreements program in particular, were designed to improve America's foreign trade position. However, it was also used to bring about closer cooperation of the democratic countries by economic means. The Anglo-American trade agreement of November 1938 was a cornerstone of this economic containment strategy. It was developed before President Roosevelt stated on 15 November 1938 that the Nazi pogroms "had deeply shocked public opinion" in the United States and that he himself "could scarcely believe that such things could occur in a Twentieth Century civilization."[16] The inclusion of economic factors certainly helps to broaden the perspective for an interpretation of American-German relations.

The extent to which National Socialist expansion was regarded as a major threat to America's global interests is also reflected in Washington's postwar planning. One of the main problems was to deal with defeated Germany in a manner that would once and for all eliminate the danger of future German aggression. The most extreme approach, as suggested by Secretary of the Treasury Henry Morgenthau, had quickly become a historical episode. Less than two years after the defeat of the Third Reich, that part of Germany under the immediate control of the Western powers had again emerged as a cornerstone of American stabilization policy in Europe. There is general agreement that the reconstruction of West Germany has to be seen in the context of international relations, particularly in the context of growing East-West tensions. Germany was a major theatre in the cold war and needed special attention.

West Germany's vital role in Washington's postwar policy towards Europe is clearly evidenced in what came to be known as the Marshall Plan.[17] The conceptual preparations of the European Recovery Program could not neglect the fact that, due to the structure of the European economy, any long-lasting economic reconstruction of the West European countries was dependent on German participation in the Marshall Plan. This was clearly expressed in a State Department Policy Statement of 26 August 1948: "Our interest in Germany's relation to ERP arises from the importance of Germany's economic position in Europe. Germany is potentially one of the most important European suppliers of such acutely needed commodities as coal, mining machinery, and industrial equipment. At the same time she is potentially an important market for European goods. German economic recovery is therefore vital to general European economic recovery. On the other hand, German economic recovery is largely dependent on the economic recovery of other European countries since they are the chief markets for her goods. It is

U.S. policy that the fullest possible recognition be given this interdependence in order to achieve the greatest over-all benefits for the European Recovery Program."[18] This clearly expressed structural interdependence of economic developments in Europe and Germany has been an ongoing concern of American policy towards Europe since the beginning of the twentieth century. How could Germany's resources be used to benefit the world economy without threatening stability and peace? The Marshall Plan seemed to be the ideal answer. West German economic recovery was combined with Germany's integration into the West. While West German participation in the European Recovery Program was essential in containing Soviet expansion, Germany's integration into the West could be used to contain German nationalistic ambitions. This dual American foreign policy strategy has repeatedly been referred to as a policy of "double containment."[19]

Obviously, there are striking similarities between American stabilization strategies in Europe after both world wars.[20] In both periods Germany, within a few years, became the cornerstone of American policy toward Europe. And as in the 1920s, the problem of how to best stabilize Germany and Europe was primarily defined in economic terms. Both in the 1920s and after World War II, American stabilization policies in Europe formed the basis for extraordinarily close American-German cooperation in the political field as well. It is important to emphasize these continuities of the cooperative phases in American-German relations, and one might want to look with satisfaction at these successes. Nevertheless, it is also essential to further explore the causes of conflicts in the past. While we have excellent knowledge of the 1930s and the development that preceded Hitler's declaration of war on the United States in December 1941, many aspects of American-German relations during the two decades prior to American intervention in World War I are still terra incognita.

This was a central motive in bringing together American and European scholars working in the field to discuss American-German relations in the era of World War I. How did the German-American antagonism develop? How did the United States react to the German challenge? Why did Washington, after World War I, inaugurate a stabilization policy that brought about cooperation in the 1920s? For an historian, there should never be simple answers or even definitive solutions. And as intensive research on the 1930s has demonstrated clearly, the interpretation of American-German relations cannot be limited to a purely bilateral view. Thanks to the broad spectrum of contributors to this volume, it is possible to present a multiperspective of American-German relations in the era of World War I: the United States and Germany in the world arena, economic dimensions of diplomacy, cultural relations and German propaganda in the United States, the impact of the war on the economies in the United States and Germany and economic thinking in both countries, the German challenge to the Monroe Doctrine and economic confrontations in Latin America, Wilson's concept of a new world order in a revolutionary context, origins and elements of American-German cooperation after World War I.

An examination of American-German relations during the first seven decades of our century, for which the archival records have become available for empirical historical research,[21] is important not only to better understand developments during the past. Also, the past is prologue, but not in the sense that the future becomes predictable. Experiences of the past could help in recognizing potential frictions and areas of conflict between the two powers more quickly in the future. The diagnosis might also be a first step in curing potential problems in American-German relations, which could result from a shift of balances in the international system. This seems to be particularly important after the end of the Cold War, when dramatic changes in international relations have become the rule rather than the exception. As history shows, relations between the two powers since the beginning of the twentieth century have had far-reaching implications not only for Germany and the United States themselves, but for the international system as well. Stable American-German relations are therefore an important prerequisite for the stabilization of an international system, which is necessary to make the world safer for democracy.

Notes to the Introduction

1. For numerous references and reflections on German and American studies of each other's historical traditions see Hermann Wellenreuther, "Introduction: German-American Constitutional History – The Past and the Present," in Hermann Wellenreuther, ed., with the assistance of Claudia Schnurmann and Thomas Krueger, *German and American Constitutional Thought: Contexts, Interactions, and Historical Realities*, Germany and the United States of America, The Krefeld Historical Symposia 1 (New York/Oxford/Munich: Berg, 1990): 1–7.

2. William Appleman Williams, *The Tragedy of American Diplomacy* (Cleveland: World Publishing Co., 1959). Williams' publications are listed in the excellent *Festschrift* in honor of Williams: Lloyd C. Gardner, ed., *Redefining the Past: Essays in Diplomatic History in Honor of William Appleman Williams* (Corvallis, OR: Oregon State University Press, 1986).

3. Hans-Ulrich Wehler, *Der Aufstieg des amerikanischen Imperialismus: Studien zur Entwicklung des Imperium Americanum, 1865–1900* (Göttingen: Vandenhoeck & Ruprecht, 1974,

2nd ed., 1987), Wehler's numerous articles are listed in his bibliography. A summary of Wehler's views is presented in Hans-Ulrich Wehler, *Grundzüge der amerikanischen Außenpolitik, vol. 1: 1750–1900. Von den englischen Küstenkolonien zur amerikanischen Weltmacht* (Frankfurt/Main: Suhrkamp, 1983).

4. Werner Link, *Die amerikanische Stabilisierungspolitik in Deutschland 1921–32* (Düsseldorf: Droste, 1970).

5. See for example Frank Costigliola, *Awkward Dominion: American Political, Economic, and Cultural Relations with Europe, 1919–1933* (Ithaca, NY: Cornell University Press, 1984); William C. McNeil, *American Money and the Weimar Republic: Economics and Politics on the Eve of the Great Depression* (New York: Columbia University Press, 1986).

6. Stephen A. Schuker, *The End of French Predominance in Europe: The Financial Crisis of 1924 and the Adoption of the Dawes Plan* (Chapel Hill: University of North Carolina Press, 1976).

7. Manfred Berg, *Gustav Stresemann und die Vereinigten Staaten: Weltwirtschaftliche Verflechtung und Revisionspolitik 1907–1929* (Baden-Baden: Nomos, 1990).

8. Werner Link, "Der amerikanische Einfluß auf die Weimarer Republik in der Dawesplanphase (Elemente eines 'penetrierten Systems')" in Hans Mommsen et al., eds., *Industrielles System und politische Entwicklung in der Weimarer Republik* (Düsseldorf: Droste, 1974), 485–98.

9. See for example with numerous further references: Alton Frye, *Nazi Germany and the American Hemisphere* (New Haven: Yale University Press, 1967); Arnold A. Offner, *American Appeasement: United States Foreign Policy and Germany, 1933–1938* (Cambridge, MA: Belknap Press of Harvard University Press, 1969); Hans-Jürgen Schröder, *Deutschland und die Vereinigten Staaten 1933–1939: Wirtschaft und Politik in der Entwicklung des deutsch-amerikanischen Gegensatzes* (Wiesbaden: Steiner, 1970).

10. See especially Gerhard L. Weinberg, "Hitler's Image of the United States," *American Historical Review* 69 (1963/64): 1006–1026; Andreas Hillgruber, "Der Faktor Amerika in Hitlers Strategie 1938–1941," in Andreas Hillgruber, *Deutsche Großmacht- und Weltpolitik im 19. und 20. Jahrhundert* (Düsseldorf: Droste, 1977): 706–714.

11. See for example Arthur L. Smith, *The Deutschtum of Nazi Germany and the United States* (The Hague, Martinus Nijhoff, 1965); Klaus Kipphan, *Deutsche Propaganda in den Vereinigten Staaten von Amerika 1933–1941* (Heidelberg: Winter, 1971); Sander A. Diamond, *The Nazi Movement in the United States, 1924–1941* (Ithaca, NY: Cornell University Press, 1974).

12. Henry L. Feingold, *The Politics of Rescue: The Roosevelt Administration and the Holocaust, 1938–1945* (New Brunswick, NJ: Rutgers University Press, 1970); Saul S. Friedman, *No Haven for the Oppressed: United States Policy toward Jewish Refugees, 1938–1945* (Detroit, MI: Wayne State University Press, 1973); Arthur M. Morse, *While Six Million Died* (New York: Random House, 1968); Moshe R. Gottlieb, *American Anti-Nazi Resistance, 1933–1941: An Historical Analysis* (New York: KTAV Publishing House, 1982).

13. References are given in Hans-Jürgen Schröder, "Hauptprobleme der deutschen Lateinamerikapolitik 1933–1941," *Jahrbuch für Geschichte von Staat, Wirtschaft und Gesellschaft Lateinamerikas* 12 (1972): 408–433; Stanley E. Hilton, *Brazil and the Great Powers, 1930–1939: The Politics of Trade Rivalry* (Austin: University of Texas Press, 1975); Stanley E. Hilton, *Hitler's Secret War in South America, 1939–1945: German Military Espionage and German Counterespionage in Brazil* (New York: Ballantine Books, 1982).

14. Detlef Junker, *Der unteilbare Weltmarkt: Das ökonomische Interesse in der Aussenpolitik der USA 1933–1941* (Stuttgart: Klett, 1975); more recently the excellent study by Patrick J. Hearden, *Roosevelt Confronts Hitler: America's Entry into World War II* (DeKalb, IL: Northern Illinois University Press, 1987).

15. Lloyd C. Gardner, *Economic Aspects of New Deal Diplomacy* (Madison: University of Wisconsin Press, 1964).

16. Statement by Roosevelt, 15 November 1938, in Donald B. Schewe, ed., *Franklin D. Roosevelt and Foreign Affairs*, 2d ser., January 1937–August 1939, vol. I (New York: Clearwater Publishing Co., 1979), 83.

17. Most of the research on Germany and the Marhall Plan is presented in two recently

published essay collections: Hans-Jürgen Schröder, ed., *Marshallplan und Westdeutscher Wiederaufstieg. Positionen – Kontroversen* (Stuttgart: Steiner, 1990); Charles Maier, ed., with the assistance of Günter Bischof, *The Marshall Plan and Germany: West German Development within the Framework of the European Recovery Program* (New York/Oxford: Berg, 1991); updated German edition: Charles Maier/Günter Bischof, eds., *Deutschland und der Marshall-Plan* (Baden-Baden: Nomos, 1992).

18. Department of State Policy Statement, 26 August 1948, in *Foreign Relations of the United States 1948, vol. II, Germany and Austria* (Washington, DC: Government Printing Office, 1973), 1310.

19. Wilfried Loth, "Die doppelte Eindämmung: Überlegungen zur Genesis des Kalten Krieges 1945–1947," *Historische Zeitschrift* 238 (1984): 611–631, reprinted in Wilfried Loth, *Ost-West-Konflikt und deutsche Frage: Historische Ortsbestimmungen* (München: Deutscher Taschenbuch Verlag, 1989), 26–45; Wolfram F. Hanrieder, *Germany, America, Europe. Forty Years of German Foreign Policy* (New Haven, CT: Yale University Press, 1989), 4 ff.

20. Werner Link, "Zum Problem der Kontinuität der amerikanischen Deutschlandpolitik im zwanzigsten Jahrhundert" in Manfred Knapp, ed., *Die deutsch-amerikanischen Beziehungen nach 1945* (Frankfurt/New York: Campus, 1975), 86–131.

21. A good recent example on the 1960s is Adrian W. Schertz, *Die Deutschlandpolitik Kennedys und Johnsons: Unterschiedliche Ansätze innerhalb der amerikanischen Regierung* (Köln/Weimar/Wien: Böhlau, 1992).

PART I

The Globalization of the European System of Powers

1

From Anglophobia to Fragile Rapprochement: Anglo-American Relations in the Early Twentieth Century

Edward P. Crapol

In the 1890s the United States became a major world power. Just over a century after gaining its independence from Great Britain, it moved from a position on the semi-periphery to one at the center, or core, of the international system. This elevation to the elite status of core country meant that the United States had been transformed from a nation that specialized primarily in the production of foodstuffs and raw materials to one that led the globe in industrial production and controlled, along with other core nations such as Britain and Germany, the world's most technologically sophisticated, high-profit enterprises. The rapid development of American industrial power was accompanied by a spectacular increase in agricultural production, a more than doubling of the Gross National Product, a virtual sevenfold increase in exports, and an overall favorable balance of trade. In the late-nineteenth-century struggle for economic supremacy, the United States, as Paul Kennedy has observed, "seemed to have all the economic advantages which some of the other powers possessed in part, but none of their disadvantages." Goethe's earlier refrain, "Amerika, du hast es besser," still appeared to hold true at century's end.[1]

America's amazing industrial, agricultural, and commercial expansion forecast a major realignment in world power balances. Amidst its transformation to a global economic colossus, the United States challenged Great Britain for commercial and political dominance in the Western Hemisphere and the Pacific. These regional and global pretensions did not go unnoticed and rankled the United States's imperial rivals, especially Britain and Germany. In the late 1880s the German diplomat, Count Herbert von Bismarck, warned England's Lord Salisbury that the Americans "appeared now to interpret the Monroe Doctrine as though

Notes to Chapter 1 can be found on page 28.

the Pacific Ocean were to be treated as an American lake." Count Bismarck feared the United States planned "to bring under their exclusive influence not only Hawaii," but Samoa and the Tonga Islands as well to create "stages between the future Panama Canal and Australia." Salisbury, sharing the Count's concerns about American ambitions, advised him that "we must keep a sharp eye on American fingers." Despite these and other occasional concerns voiced over the next decade about the United States's imperial agenda, America's rivals were not able or chose not to prevent it from acquiring by 1900 a string of strategic bases and colonies in Puerto Rico, Cuba, Hawaii, Guam, Wake Island, Samoa, and the Philippines.[2]

However, the United States' climb to the top was not as effortless as it might first appear. In the two decades prior to their country's long-anticipated imperial and commercial success, when the nation was poised on the threshold of global power, a broad spectrum of Americans believed that Britain blocked the way to national destiny. Many dreamed of toppling Britain as the ruling monarch of the global marketplace, and they hoped that their nation at long last would break free of the British economic orbit. The commonly-held belief that Britain's vast economic and financial power had thwarted America's destiny for almost a century was shared by dirt farmers, sharecroppers, agrarian editors, and labor leaders as well as businessmen, industrialists, and politicians. This perception, and the anger and frustration it evoked, gave rise to the virulent Anglophobia and anti-British nationalism that pervaded the American consciousness in the 1880s and 1890s. Anglophobia, anti-British nationalism, and jealousy of British power proved to be deep-seated and resilient features of the American psyche; these traits and the emotions they sparked did not disappear entirely from the national consciousness "until the final displacement of British by American power."[3]

The late-nineteenth-century contest for commercial and industrial leadership triggered a worldwide scramble for markets and raw materials. Great Britain, the acknowledged leader at the start of this phase of the race for economic supremacy, faced strong challenges from Germany and the United States. Although the data on this global economic and industrial competition is incomplete, arguably it was the United States, and not Germany, as is often maintained, that presented the greater initial, and for that matter sustained, challenge to Britain's economic preeminence. Estimates for the period 1870–1913 place Britain's annual growth rate at 1.6 percent, Germany's at 4.7 percent, and the United States' at 5.0 percent. For the years 1873–1913, estimates for the growth rate pattern in manufactured goods are comparable: Britain's annual growth rate was 1.8 percent, Germany's 3.9 percent, and the United States' 4.8 percent. This widening disparity in growth rates relegated Great Britain, the world's workshop in 1870 with almost one-third of the globe's manufacturing production, to second place at century's end behind the United States, now the workshop of the world with 30.1 percent of manufacturing production, and a further drop to third place by 1910 when it was surpassed as well by its other major rival, Germany.[4]

America in these years also asserted control of its home market and ultimately broke free of the British economic orbit. Throughout the first half of the nineteenth century, the United States served as Britain's largest foreign customer and a major outlet for British manufactured goods. As late as 1860 Great Britain supplied 40 percent of America's imports and received over half of the total exports of the United States. However, by the end of the century, American industry asserted control of the home market, and in the decade between 1896 and 1905, Americans purchased only 7.5 percent of total British exports. The United States may have become less important as a market for British manufactured products, but it continued to be Britain's major source of wheat and cotton, and at century's end still furnished almost one-quarter of total British imports. By the early 1900s, that trade pattern also changed, as American manufactured goods began to flood the British market, and American capitalists, seeking to expand across the Atlantic, purchased a number of British firms. The British press and public momentarily panicked at the prospect of an American industrial and economic invasion of their isles.[5]

The reality of the loss of industrial preeminence hit home among British leaders in the late nineteenth century. William E. Gladstone, Joseph Chamberlain, Lord Salisbury, Arthur Balfour, and a host of others, closely observed the American industrial and trade phenomenon and readily perceived the nature of the American threat to their economic and commercial supremacy. Even before Britain's European isolation and the German challenge were fully visible on the horizon, Gladstone set the stage for future British policy by openly courting the United States. "The future of the world belongs to us," he predicted when discussing the necessity of Anglo-American friendship and cooperation. Chamberlain, more pessimistic perhaps about the future of the "weary Titan" staggering "under the too vast orb of its fate," scurried about for a policy that might preserve the English lead. After offering considerable resistance, especially to the United States' pretensions to hegemony in the Western Hemisphere, Salisbury only grudgingly acknowledged America's new position and power. Overall, however, British leaders patiently endured the excesses of this upstart rival, wisely accepting the assessment of Gladstone and Balfour that Britain's most favorable long-run course of action was to achieve a rapprochement with the United States. Chamberlain, for his part, ultimately went so far as to recommend publicly an alliance with the United States to secure "the bonds of permanent unity with our kinsman across the ocean."[6]

But prior to their nation's success in the war against Spain in 1898, the majority of Americans reacted unfavorably to any effort to secure closer ties with their national nemesis and chief economic rival. The United States may have gained ground in its economic competition with Great Britain by breaking the existing client-patron trade pattern and by establishing a favorable trade balance from the late 1870s onward. However, the United States remained a debtor nation with an overall balance of payments deficit, which, from the American perspective, still gave Britain the upper hand in the commercial race. America may have made impressive economic gains by the late 1890s, but Britannia's global power and economic influence remained the envy of her rivals. In the scramble with the other great European powers for Africa, Britain had secured Egypt, much of East Africa, and the southern African empire that was the personal handiwork of Cecil Rhodes. At the time of her Diamond Jubilee in 1897, Victoria as Queen Empress ruled a fifth of the globe. The Britain of Victoria also controlled three-quarters of the world's foreign investment and accounted for a fifth of the world's trade. At the turn of the century, Great Britain still appeared supreme.[7]

Appearances are sometimes deceiving, as Chamberlain and his contemporaries among the British elite realized full well. But Britain's apparent invincibility, and the widespread perception that its political and economic supremacy was insurmountable, frustrated countless Americans and fueled their Anglophobia. Americans of various political hues and affiliations claimed that Britain stymied their nation's realization of its global destiny. British naval actions and diplomacy in the hemisphere lent credence to such patriotic outbursts. England's role in the War of the Pacific, its show of force in the Corinto affair, its intransigence in refusing alteration of the Clayton-Bulwer Treaty, and its apparent territorial encroachments in the Venezuela boundary dispute, gave form and substance to the caricature, depicted in a political cartoon published during the Venezuelan crisis, of "The Real British Lion" as a gluttonous imperial pig, Union Jack grasped in its curly tail, astride the western half of the globe.[8]

Not all American commentators appealed to anti-British nationalism during the 1895–96 Venezuela dispute. Theodore Roosevelt, for one, saw the confrontation in strictly patriotic and nationalistic terms when he announced that "I have not the slightest feeling of hostility to England, only I want Americans to be Americans."[9] Perhaps the most explosive crisis in Anglo-American relations since the Civil War years, the Venezuelan controversy shocked elites on both sides of the Atlantic and sparked an arbitration movement designed to prevent such conflicts from leading to an Anglo-American war. The dispute involved the question of the boundary between Venezuela and British Guiana. Efforts dating back to the 1840s had failed to resolve the issue, and over the years the Venezuelans had expanded their territorial claims. The British, apparently willing to compromise initially, hardened their position after the discovery of gold in the disputed areas in the 1870s. The United States became involved in the squabble when Venezuela, citing the Monroe Doctrine, asked its northern neighbor for help in resolving the dispute.

The Grover Cleveland administration originally sought a diplomatic solution to the problem when Secretary of State Richard Olney sent a message to the British government requesting arbitration of the matter. Olney invoked the Monroe Doctrine in justifying the United States' right to interfere in the dispute and asked for a British response before Cleveland presented his annual message to Congress in early December 1895. In an unintentionally delayed reply that reached the United States after the president's annual message, Lord Salisbury rejected the applicability of the Monroe Doctrine and refused to arbitrate. An infuriated President Cleveland sent a special message to Congress declaring the Monroe Doctrine international law and calling for the United States to take responsibility for determining the true boundary line. With Congress's approval, the president proposed the creation of a commission to conduct an investigation and establish the boundary between Venezuela and British Guiana. Acknowledging that he was "fully alive" to the consequences of this action, Cleveland said the United States would honor the commission's boundary verdict and resist any British attempt to evade or violate the decision.

Cleveland's message ignited an outburst of anti-British nationalism among his fellow citizens that reverberated across the Atlantic and imperiled Anglo-American relations. Englishmen such as Joseph Chamberlain and James Bryce, members of an Atlantic community who frequently visited the United States and had many American friends, initially were as surprised and shocked at the Anglophobic outburst as were the majority of their less well-connected countrymen. However, Chamberlain, amid fearful talk of an Anglo-American war, quickly and rather astutely, came to understand what many others of his class dismissed as irrational American spread-eaglism. He wrote Lord Selborne shortly after Cleveland's special message reached England that many Americans "suspect us always of an assumption of superiority of which we are not conscious ourselves" and "they would not be sorry to prove that they are bigger and stronger and better than we are."[10] The Colonial Secretary may have identified and understood the psychological underpinnings of American anti-British nationalism, but he nonetheless recoiled in horror at the prospect of fratricidal war. Influential segments of both societies agreed. The transatlantic bellicosity quickly subsided as British and American sentiment favored the creation of some form of permanent arbitration system that would eliminate forever the possibility of an Anglo-American war.[11]

To some extent, of course, the entire episode was a contrived crisis designed primarily, if not exclusively, to revive Cleveland's sagging political fortunes and allow him to retain control of the Democratic party. But to interpret Cleveland's tough anti-British stance solely in a domestic political context would be incorrect. Whatever their domestic political motives, he and Olney also deliberately asserted, and sought Britain's acknowledgement of, the United States's hegemony in the Western Hemisphere. They succeeded when the Salisbury government backed down and ultimately accepted an American-sponsored arbitration of the boundary dispute. The British capitulation in the Venezuelan affair was not entirely prompted by Cleveland's toughness. The pressure of other diplomatic challenges in the Middle East and South Africa, including Kaiser Wilhelm's telegram to President Kruger of the Transvaal Free State congratulating him on the capture of the Jameson raiders, precipitated the British cabinet's decision to acquiesce to the United States. In the judgement of historian David Healy, Britain's decision to back down "was less the result of fear of the United States, whose armed forces were as yet no match for those of the British, than the result of a far-sighted decision to seek friendship with the rising power of the New World rather than implant a source of long-term hostility." London wisely decided that the disputed territory was not worth the enmity of the United States.[12]

Britain's acquiescence to the United States on the Venezuela boundary dispute apparently was a continuation of a longstanding British diplomatic pattern in Latin America. As one historian has noted, Anglo-American economic rivalry in the hemisphere was a reality, "but on the diplomatic level British policy toward Latin America stressed conciliation and cooperation with the United States rather than confrontation or conflict."[13] Perhaps a British policy of conciliation in Latin America was the norm prior to 1896. Nonetheless, a number of historians of Anglo-American relations traditionally have identified the settlement of the Venezuelan crisis as the key event that ushered in the great rapprochement between the two English-speaking nations that held sway from 1898 to 1914.[14] In this interpretation, the immediate step on the path to

Anglo-American reconciliation was the signing of the Olney-Pauncefote Arbitration Treaty in January 1897, an agreement that bound both nations to submit all future disputes to arbitration. True, the United States Senate gutted the treaty with amendments and then rejected it by three votes, but this display of residual Anglophobia did not stall the movement for reconciliation. The next step came during the Spanish-American War when Britain, although officially neutral, displayed a perceptible pro-American bias and worked to block a European proposal to intercede in the conflict on behalf of Spain. Among other things, Britain also aided America's war effort by selling it ships and coal in the Far East and by providing generous access to Hong Kong's facilities. For American leaders, including future president Theodore Roosevelt, the tangible British support for the United States war effort was a welcomed diplomatic adjustment. Writing his British friend, Arthur Lee, Roosevelt promised that "I shall not forget, and I don't think our people will, England's attitude during the Spanish War, and we all know it saved us from a chance of very serious complications."[15]

Such attitudinal changes in the thinking of the American political elite about Britian apparently were widespread at the turn of the century, particularly among those leaders who previously had been suspicious and resentful of British global power. Over the next three or four years, this "new spirit," as historian Bradford Perkins has dubbed the less anti-British, more conciliatory, official American outlook, led to a pair of formal agreements that cemented the Anglo-American rapprochement. The parameters of the nascent accord between the English-speaking powers were defined by the 1901 Hay-Pauncefote Treaty, which settled the long-festering isthmian canal issue by sanctioning America's unilateral right to construct and fortify a transoceanic waterway, and by the 1903 Alaska boundary agreement, which resolved a territorial dispute between the United States and Canada. These diplomatic agreements were accompanied by Britain's unilateral decision in the years 1904–06 to terminate its permanent, longstanding naval presence in North America, and for that matter in the hemisphere, by closing its North Atlantic naval facility at Halifax, relocating its West Indian squadron to a base in England, and effectively acceding to eventual American naval hegemony in the Caribbean. This fleet reorganization plan, which virtually guaranteed that the Caribbean would become an American lake, was designed primarily to scale down imperial defense obligations and shift British naval power to European waters. It was further recognition that Britain was overextended, as Prime Minister Henry Campbell-Bannerman conceded in 1903: "The truth is we cannot provide for a fighting Empire, and nothing will give us the power."[16]

The story of early twentieth century Anglo-American rapprochement is a familiar tale, a closely-studied diplomatic phenomenon frequently explained and at least partially understood in the context of Germany's threatening challenge to Britain's economic and naval supremacy. Apparently, Anglo-Saxon racism also played a role in encouraging the rapprochement. The doctrine of Anglo-Saxonism, based on the belief in the innate racial superiority of the descendants of the original Anglo-Saxon invaders of Britain and the preeminence of the civilization of English-speaking peoples, gained widespread public acceptance in both countries during the 1890s. Perhaps even more crucial to the emergence of the rapprochement was the fact that key figures in the American and British foreign policy elites, such as John Hay and Arthur Balfour, ascribed to the basic tenets of the Anglo-Saxon creed and preached the necessity of Anglo-Saxon solidarity. Balfour was unreservedly committed to the creed, as he confessed in 1900 to American diplomat Henry White: "I am, as you know, a most earnest advocate of harmonious cooperation between the two great Anglo-Saxon states." At this level among the foreign policy elite of both nations, Anglo-Saxonism may have been a positive influence in preventing war and in paving the way for a general easing of tensions between Britain and America. One historian, Stuart Anderson, has made the argument that "Anglo-Saxonism, as an intellectual construct, provided the primary abstract rationale for the diplomatic rapprochement" and has asserted that without the shared acceptance of this amorphous and pseudo-scientific racist doctrine the Anglo-American accord would not have occurred.[17]

Whether or not policy formulation in the two nations was meaningfully influenced by racial sentiments is debatable. But, as suggested earlier, the empirical side of the British story would appear to be fairly straightforward. Great Britain, pressed by Germany and unable to come to a broad diplomatic understanding with the Kaiser's government, found itself isolated on the European continent with its global economic supremacy steadily slipping away and its imperial reach badly overextended. In order to salvage their nation's deteriorating international position, and also to eliminate a possible future adversary, British leaders openly courted American friendship. As an initial gesture in the courtship, Britain gracefully removed its naval power from the Western Hemisphere and publicly applauded the Open Door policy in the Far East. Arthur Balfour, commenting on the full scope of the nascent Anglo-American partnership in Asia at the turn of the century, confided to American naval strategist Alfred T. Mahan: "We have not only the same ideas of progress, freedom, civilisation, religion, morality, but we have the same interests in peace and the open door." A few years later

Balfour wrote Henry Cabot Lodge: "I agree with you in thinking that the interests of the United States and that of ourselves are absolutely identical in the Far East, and that the more closely we can work together, the better it will be for us and the world at large."[18] In the meantime, however, for extra insurance in the Pacific against the encroachments of its European imperial rivals, Britain negotiated the 1902 Anglo-Japanese alliance. The agreement with Japan, which committed each nation to come to the aid of the other in the event it was attacked by two or more hostile nations, demonstrated the limits of Anglo-Saxon racism as a motive in diplomacy. Anglo-Saxonism did not prevent the British from signing a treaty with a distinctly non–Anglo-Saxon nation.

Britain's diplomatic objectives, according to this standard interpretation of early-twentieth-century British diplomacy, were clear: reduce the empire's naval and defense responsibilities in North America and Asia in order to provide protection for the home islands from the rising German naval threat. England's overall naval protection policy also included a move to end its isolation on the continent by negotiating the 1904 Entente Cordiale with France. The Anglo-French entente may have guarded Britain's continental flank, but equally importantly, the agreements that sealed the deal were imperialist bargains that stabilized Franco-British rivalries in West, Central, and North Africa, and in Asia and the South Seas.[19] Finally, no longer able to control and manage the international system as it had in the nineteenth century, Britain completely abandoned the "splendid isolation" of an earlier era with the 1907 Anglo-Russian entente.[20]

Some historians believe an American fear of Germany's ambitions in the Western Hemisphere and the Pacific also contributed to the evolving Anglo-American rapprochement. The McKinley administration was concerned that Germany had designs on a base in the Caribbean as a follow-up to its exercise in gunboat diplomacy against Haiti in late 1897. Theodore Roosevelt, normally wary of Britain's ambitions in the hemisphere, announced to Charles Arthur Moore in 1898 that "I feel most we should . . . beware of letting a foolish hatred of England blind us to our own honor and interests . . . Germany, and not England, is the power with whom we are apt to have trouble over the Monroe Doctrine." Germany's perceived practice of closing the door by restricting foreign trade in its possessions in Africa, Asia, and the Pacific upset American merchants and diplomats as well. It was German commercial and territorial acquisitiveness that fostered recognition of mutual Anglo-American interests in the Pacific and helped shape American imperial strategy in Samoa, Hawaii, and the Philippines.[21] Although recent scholarship suggests American fears of German territorial ambitions in the

Western Hemisphere and the Pacific, especially in the Philippines, were exaggerated, these suspicions undoubtedly played some role in determining American policies and actions.[22]

Important as perceived German threats to American interests may have been in promoting Anglo-American cooperation, in Britain's direct negotiations as well as its informal dealings with the United States during these years the dominant themes were those of acquiescence and appeasement. The British gave in to the United States at every crucial diplomatic juncture. One important sign of British capitulation to American power in the Western Hemisphere was a public and official acceptance of the Monroe Doctrine. In 1895 Lord Salisbury flatly rejected the 1823 doctrine and denied it had any standing in international law. Barely eight years later, in early 1903, his nephew and successor as prime minister, Arthur Balfour, proclaimed in an address at Liverpool that "[t]he Monroe Doctrine has no enemies in this country that I know of. We welcome any increase of the influence of the United States upon the great Western Hemisphere."[23] For historian Kenneth Bourne, the "appeasement" of the United States in the early years of the century was hardly a bolt from the blue, but rather the culmination of "a policy which Great Britain had long since adopted in the interest of her security."[24] To be sure, not all British leaders, particularly among the military, accepted the wisdom of appeasing the United States. In 1901 Admiral Sir John Fisher, who later served as first sea lord, doubted some mystical Anglo-Saxon affinity with this complaint: "Only a 1/4 of the population of the United States are what you might call natives; the rest are Germans, Irish, Italians, and the scum of the earth! all of them hating the English like poison."[25] Fisher's colleagues in the War Office initially shared his pessimism about the possibility of Anglo-American harmony, but by 1906 both Fisher and the War Office dismissed the possibility of a war with the United States and identified Germany as the only future foe Britain need fear.[26]

Agreeing with Professor Bourne was another expert on the nineteenth-century international system, historian Paul Kennedy, who viewed appeasement as one of the more constructive and positive features of British diplomacy in the roughly seventy-five year span from the mid-nineteenth century to the early 1930s. Of course, conceded Kennedy, appeasement has an extremely negative connotation as a method of conducting diplomacy because it "is inextricably associated in the historical consciousness with efforts of Neville Chamberlain's government to preserve peace with the dictators of the 1930s." If defined, however, as a reasonable and conciliatory method for settling disputes rationally through compromise, negotiation and the avoidance of bloody wars and conflicts, a policy of appeasement may be seen in a different historical light. In this context, appeasement was an optimistic and far-sighted policy that could serve a nation's long-term interests, as British diplomacy in the decade between 1895 and 1905 clearly demonstrated. In Professor Kennedy's view, Great Britain's willingness to appease the United States, beginning with its retreat on the Venezuela question and extending to the acceptance of the Monroe Doctrine and an American sphere of influence in the Western Hemisphere, represented a triumph for British diplomacy. A calculated appeasement of the upstart Americans avoided an "unnatural" war between the two Anglo-Saxon powers, and perhaps the ongoing success of this policy partially explained how a beleaguered and declining British Empire was able to survive as long as it did in the twentieth century.[27]

All of this may satisfactorily clarify British motivations and objectives in pursuing a rapprochement with the United States, but why did American leadership, and for that matter most of the American public, do such a dramatic turnaround? By all odds at the opening of the twentieth century the United States should have continued to be locked in fierce economic competition throughout the world with its national rival. A "new spirit" may have prevailed among members of the American foreign policy elite after Britain's strong support for the United States during the Spanish-American War. But that does not fully explain the quite remarkable transformation in the thinking of Americans in the decade or so prior to World War I about Great Britain, the national nemesis. A few years earlier, politicians, agrarians, businessmen, industrialists – a broad spectrum of American society – regularly had castigated John Bull and identified Britain as the major obstacle to the achievement of America's destiny. Why did anti-British nationalism rapidly dissipate? And why did American attitudes shift from Anglophobia to a rapprochement that virtually precluded the possibility of an Anglo-American war?

To begin with, after a false start or two on the isthmian canal issue and the hostility aroused by its Venezuelan debt collection escapade with Germany in 1902–03, Great Britain publicly and consistently appeased the United States. Britain's willingness to concede all points of contention between the two powers radically and steadily undermined anti-British nationalism. To be sure, some ambiguity remained in popular feelings about Britain, as evidenced by the American public's sympathy for the Boers in their unsuccessful struggle against British imperialism during the years 1899–1902. However, while the official position of the United States government on the Boer War was one of neutrality, the members of the McKinley and Roosevelt administrations were decidedly pro-British. Even Theodore Roosevelt, of Dutch ancestry, favored a

British victory as promoting civilization's march and the world mission of the English-speaking people.[28] Arguably in the years 1898–1906, when the Anglo-American rapprochement was being consolidated, the foreign-policy elite continued to be ahead of the general public in its pro-British sentiments. But in a very real sense it was the accumulated impact of Britain's appeasement policy, not the foreign-policy elite's cultural Anglophilia, that effectively removed America's bogeyman, neutralized the public's anti-British fears, and overcame years of national frustration stemming from the perception that the British lion stood in the path of America's global destiny. Appeasement proved a marvelous antidote to Anglophobia.

It cannot be overemphasized that Great Britain was ever the more ardent suitor in the reconciliation venture. The quest for rapprochement was a decidedly one-sided affair. With the exception of Secretary of State John Hay and possibly one or two others, American leaders did not seek a sweeping reconciliation with Britain. Rapprochement was a by-product of gaining American objectives in the Western Hemisphere and, to a lesser extent in the Far East. By no means would Theodore Roosevelt, either before or after he became president, yield on the issues of American ownership and fortification of an isthmian canal, or the settlement of the Alaska boundary, as the price of Anglo-American rapprochement. If Britain balked, as occasionally happened, Roosevelt and his supporters threatened action that clearly jeopardized any hope of Anglo-American harmony. Britain, guided by a clear vision of its long-range interests in global power balances, understood these were not idle threats and acquiesced on all counts. As Howard K. Beale observed in his study of Theodore Roosevelt: "Our expansionists were determined to have their own way and, under threat that we would take what we wanted anyway, in spite of resentment of our bad manners, Britain yielded everything as graciously as she could. Here was proof of how much she did want American friendship."[29]

While Britain's policy of conciliation and appeasement was central to the success of the rapprochement, a number of other factors also contributed to the United States' willingness to accept and support Anglo-American reconciliation. With the victory over Spain and the acquisition of an overseas empire that included the Philippines, Americans believed that they had finally joined the imperial club and were major international players. The exhilaration and pride felt by many, if not all, Americans over the United States' recently won imperial status was on display at the Pan-American Exposition in Buffalo, New York, subtitled "Pax 1901." Eight million people attended the Pan-Am exposition, which was dedicated to improving relations among the nations of the hemisphere and highlighted an agenda urging United States access to new markets and resources in Latin America. On the evening that opened the celebration of President William McKinley's visit to the fair, just days before his assassination, a spectacular fireworks display caught the expansionist spirit of the moment with this greeting emblazoned in the sky: "Welcome McKinley, Chief of Our Nation and Our Empire." Not only at the Pan-American Exposition, but throughout the land, Americans and their leaders were caught up in the happy diversions of empire. The commonly held belief that their nation had achieved a measure of imperial parity with Britain undoubtedly hastened the gradual demise of Anglophobia and led to the almost complete disappearance of any trace of American jealousy of British imperial success.[30]

Predictions by British and American leaders, in public discussion and private correspondence alike, that the dawning twentieth century would be the century of the English-speaking peoples appeared to be coming true. Pushing this speculative analysis further, Arthur Balfour claimed it was the dawning of an exclusively American century. In a 1902 letter to John Hay, he sounded a theme that was music to his American friend's ears when he accurately prophesied that the United States was "destined to be the mightiest of all English-speaking communities."[31] This budding convergence of British and American imperialisms was based, at least at the outset, on the belief in a joint imperial destiny and the conviction that Anglo-Saxon nations had a special duty to bring their laws, culture, and institutions to the rest of the world. For some Americans, this preoccupation with empire and imperial destiny reflected as well their pride and satisfaction in believing that the United States was now fully engaged in the world's work and carrying its share of the white man's burden. Anglo-American control of colonial or third-world areas, if not one of its primary goals, appeared to be an ancillary and long-range objective of Anglo-American entente.[32]

Doing the world's work was part of an imperial mindset that allowed Americans to act on the assumption that their control of colonial possessions, such as the Philippines, was a trusteeship, and that their imperial rule, which entailed the use of force when necessary, was in the best interests of the Filipinos and for the good of civilization. Americans originally adopted the concept of trusteeship from the British. The connection between empire and the trusteeship concept was clearly expressed by Lord Curzon in 1908: "In empire, we have not merely a key to glory and wealth, but the call to duty, and the means of service to mankind." In surveying the global scene and the role of the other major powers in the years prior to the outbreak of World War I, American leaders came to distinguish between "good" and "bad" imperialisms. Britain, and of course their own nation, the United States, were practitioners of the "good" and enlightened form of imperial control; Germany and Japan practiced "bad" imperialism, which was characterized by conquest and profit and ruthless exploitation of native peoples. Ultimately, even British imperialism, enlightened and beneficent as it was, became suspect when compared to the American variety of trusteeship. Many Americans perceived a marked contrast between Britain's alleged failure to prepare its colonies for eventual independence and British resistance to native nationalism on the one hand, and the United States self-proclaimed new departure in imperial trusteeship, which was aimed at preparing backward peoples for self-government and graduation to national independence on the other. American exceptionalism – the belief that the American empire was more enlightened than its counterparts and hence superior – was a prevailing assumption among the nation's new breed of colonial managers and proconsuls such as General Leonard Wood and William Howard Taft. Of course, even in their claims of exceptionalism, Americans were no different from their imperial rivals, all of whom also claimed their brand of imperial rule was the most enlightened and beneficial to the advancement of civilization.[33]

Perhaps one of the original cornerstones of the Anglo-American entente was this commitment to cooperative imperialisms intent on control of colonial or backward areas; but if so, it proved the foundation of a shaky edifice, undermined from the start by the reality of an ongoing competitive economic struggle for markets and resources between the two Anglo-Saxon powers. British-American competition prevailed in Asia, the Pacific, and the Western Hemisphere. Actually, in Latin America, and this was true of China as well, the United States and Great Britain had never stopped competing for economic predominance. In its public recognition of the Monroe Doctrine, Britain was willing to concede United States political dominance in Latin America, but certainly not economic monopoly. The British discovered that the United States, in managing its still unfolding Caribbean empire, pursued an exclusionary policy at odds with its open door stance in the rest of the world. When a nominally independent Cuba became an American protectorate under the Platt Amendment in 1903, it appeared an acceptable political arrangement to Britain as long as its merchants had equal access to the trade of the island. But the British ultimately failed in their efforts to insure equal access and attain an equitable commercial treaty with Cuba, which led business interests in Britain to fear for the future of the Open Door policy in Latin America. The "drive to hegemony" in the Caribbean, as historian David Healy has labeled the process that led to a closed sphere, was sustained in one form or another during the Taft and Wilson administrations. At the time of American entry into World War I in 1917, Great Britain had been displaced and United States economic hegemony in the Caribbean region was all but complete.[34]

During the years between 1898 and 1914, the Anglo-American relationship moved from one dominated by Anglophobia to one marked by rapprochement and an easing of tensions between the Anglo-Saxon nations. Britain's pragmatic decision to accede to American preeminence in the Western Hemisphere served as the basis for the new relationship. America's acquisition of an overseas empire and its rise to world power also smoothed the path for an Anglo-American entente. No longer did Britain loom as the national nemesis blocking America's global destiny. On the eve of the outbreak of World War I, the United States' per capita Gross National Product had surpassed Britain's, its population had reached 98 million people compared to Britain's 45 million, and it was not only the world's leading manufacturing nation, but it was also the globe's single greatest producer of raw materials. On a number of other critical indices of national power, it was apparent that the United States was overtaking Great Britain as the world's number one power.[35] From the American standpoint, the changing power relationship between the two nations was reassuring because support for the rapprochement always had been undergirded by the assumption that the United States would capture the laurels of leadership from Britain and become the senior partner in the Anglo-Saxon venture.

For all its apparent success, the Anglo-American rapprochement was a distinctly lopsided configuration in which one party made virtually all of the diplomatic concessions. Conceived, designed, and sustained by a British policy of acquiescence and appeasement, the new relationship was severely tested by American attitudes and actions in the years 1914–17, prior to United States entry into World War I. President Woodrow Wilson wished to insure American political and commercial dominance in the hemisphere and to establish American preeminence in world affairs. If his agenda endangered rapprochement, he would sacrifice Anglo-American harmony to further his nation's interests. Wilson planned to use Britain's financial dependence on the United States to accomplish his postwar objectives for an open-door world and unrestricted American economic expansion. As he wrote to his advisor, Colonel Edward House, in July 1917: "England and France have not the same view with regard to peace that we have by any means. When the war is over we can force them to our way of thinking, because by that time they will, among other things, be financially in our hands." To be sure, Anglo-American friendship survived the test of World War I, but Anglophobia did not disappear until the transfer of British power to American hands was complete.[36]

In retrospect, it was precisely the one-sided nature of the rapprochement that most clearly revealed its fragility and weakness. In the Western Hemisphere, Britain, occasionally unwillingly and usually grudgingly, learned to play by American rules. If Britain balked at further appeasement or at the acceptance of American hegemony, the new relationship was in jeopardy.[37] In practice, this fragile entente was riven predictably by contentious struggle for economic advantage in Latin America and Asia. Rapprochement had never led to formal alliance, as early backers of the entente on both sides of the Atlantic desired and as Chamberlain publicly bruited. Nor was there formal agreement on an international code of conduct, as some of its enthusiastic and optimistic supporters anticipated. What Great Britain and the United States had fashioned in the first two decades of this century was a workable, if fragile, rapprochement; what they had not yet succeeded in establishing was the "special relationship" that many commentators maintain has characterized Anglo-American relations since 1945.

Notes to Chapter 1

1. Thomas J. McCormick, *America's Half Century: United States Foreign Policy in the Cold War Era* (Baltimore, MD, 1989), pp. 1–24; Walter Russell Mead, *Mortal Splendor: The American Empire in Transition* (Boston, MA, 1987), pp. 11–12; Paul Kennedy, *The Rise and Fall of the Great Powers, Economic Change and Military Conflict from 1500 to 2000* (New York, NY, 1987), p. 243. See also: William Becker, *The Dynamics of Business-Government Relations: Industry and Imports, 1893–1921* (Chicago, IL, 1982); Mira Wilkins, *The Emergence of Multinational Enterprise: American Business Abroad from the Colonial Era to 1914* (Cambridge, MA, 1970).

2. Memo of Count Herbert von Bismarck, 24 August 1887, in E.T.S. Dugdale, *German Diplomatic Documents, 1871–1914* (London, 1928), 1:244. On the late nineteenth century American commercial and territorial expansion, see Edward P. Crapol and Howard Schonberger, "The Shift to Global Expansion, 1865–1900," in William A. Williams, ed., *From Colony to Empire, Essays in the History of American Foreign Relations* (New York, NY, 1972), pp. 135–202; Walter LaFeber, *The New Empire: An Interpretation of American Expansion 1860–1898* (Ithaca, NY, 1963); William A. Williams, *The Roots of the Modern American Empire: A Study of the Growth and Shaping of Social Consciousness in a Marketplace Society* (New York, NY, 1969); Charles S. Campbell, *The Transformation of American Foreign Relations, 1865–1900* (New York, NY, 1976); Robert L. Beisner, *From the Old Diplomacy to the New, 1865–1900*, 2nd ed. (Arlington Heights, IL, 1986); Michael H. Hunt, *Ideology and U.S. Foreign Policy* (New Haven, CT, 1987); David M. Pletcher, "Economic Growth and Diplomatic Adjustment, 1861–1898," in William H. Becker and Samuel F. Wells, Jr., eds., *Economics and World Power: An Assessment of American Diplomacy Since 1789* (New York, NY, 1984), pp. 119–71.

3. Christopher Hitchens, *Blood, Class, and Nostalgia: Anglo-American Ironies* (New York, NY, 1990), p. 292; Edward P. Crapol, *America for Americans: Economic Nationalism and Anglophobia in the Late Nineteenth Century* (Westport, CT, 1973).

4. Aaron L. Friedberg, *The Weary Titan, Britain and the Experience of Relative Decline, 1895–1905* (Princeton, NJ, 1988), pp. 25–26.

5. Harold G. Vatter, *The Drive to Industrial Maturity: The U.S. Economy, 1860–1914* (Westport, CT, 1975), pp. 29–32; United States Bureau of the Census, *Historical Statistics of the United States, Colonial Times to 1957* (Washington, D.C., 1960), pp. 550–53; B.R. Mitchell, *European Historical Statistics, 1750–1970* (New York, NY, 1976), pp. 571, 573; Edward P. Crapol, *America for Americans*, pp. 220–21; Vivian Vale, *The American Peril: Challenge to Britain on the North Atlantic 1901–1904* (Manchester, 1984). For a provocative discussion of the impact of the American export invasion, see Matthew Simon and David E. Novack, "Some Dimensions of the American Commercial Invasion of Europe, 1871–1914: An Introductory Essay," *Journal of Economic History* 24 (December 1964), pp. 591–608; David E. Novack and Matthew Simon, "Commercial Responses to the American Export Invasion, 1871–1914, An Essay in Attitudinal History," *Explorations in Entrepreneurial History* 3 (Winter 1966), pp. 121–47.

6. William E. Gladstone, "Kin Beyond the Sea," *North American Review* 127 (September–October 1878), pp. 179–212; Chamberlain quoted in *Literary Digest* 16 (28 May 1898), p. 634; see also Lord Charles Beresford's call for an Anglo-American alliance in *Literary Digest* 16 (30 April 1898), p. 511.

7. Paul Kennedy, *The Rise and Fall of the Great Powers*, pp. 224–32; David Dimbleby and David Reynolds, *An Ocean Apart: The Relationship Between Britain and America in the Twentieth Century* (New York, NY, 1988), pp. 30–31; Lance E. Davis and Robert A. Huttenback, *Mammon and the Pursuit of Empire, The Political Economy of British Imperialism, 1860–1912* (Cambridge, 1986); see also for a mild dissent from the view of imperial overstretch, Joseph S. Nye Jr., *Bound to Lead: The Changing Nature of American Power* (New York, NY, 1990).

8. *New York Evening World*, 1895, reproduced in Thomas G. Paterson, J. Garry Clifford, and Kenneth J. Hagan, *American Foreign Policy: A History*, 2nd ed. (Lexington, MA, 1983), p. 189.

9. Quoted in Howard K. Beale, *Theodore Roosevelt and the Rise of America to World Power* (Baltimore, MD, 1956), p. 89.

10. Chamberlain to Selborne, 20 December 1895, Joseph Chamberlain Papers, University of Birmingham, England.

11. Charles S. Campbell, *From Revolution to Rapprochement: The United States and Great Britain, 1783–1900* (New York, NY, 1974), pp. 182–83; Richard E. Welch, Jr., *The Presidencies of Grover Cleveland* (Lawrence, KS, 1988), pp. 180–92.

12. David Healy, *Drive to Hegemony: The United States in the Caribbean, 1898–1917* (Madison, WI, 1988), p. 35.

13. Joseph Smith, *Illusions of Conflict: Anglo-American Diplomacy Toward Latin America, 1865–1896* (Pittsburgh, PA, 1979), p. xiv.

14. For example, see Charles S. Campbell, *Anglo-American Understanding, 1898–1903* (Baltimore, MD, 1957); Bradford Perkins, *The Great Rapprochement: England and the United States, 1895–1914* (New York, NY, 1968); Robert L. Beisner, *From the Old Diplomacy to the New*, p. 143; Stephen R. Rock, *Why Peace Breaks Out: Great Power Rapprochement in Historical Perspective* (Chapel Hill, NC, 1989), p. 26.

15. Quoted in Beale, *Theodore Roosevelt*, p. 94.

16. Quoted in Archibald P. Thornton, *The Imperial Idea and Its Enemies: A Study in British Power* (London, 1959), p. 106.

17. Arthur J. Balfour to Henry White, 12 December 1900; Balfour summed up his efforts in behalf of Anglo-American accord in a 1 June 1905 letter to former American ambassador to Britain, Joseph Choate, Balfour MSS, British Museum, London; Stuart Anderson, *Race and Rapprochement: Anglo-Saxonism and Anglo-American Relations, 1895–1904* (Rutherford, NJ, 1981), p. 12. See also Reginald Horsman, *Race and Manifest Destiny: The Origins of American Racial Anglo-Saxonism* (Cambridge, MA, 1981).

18. Arthur J. Balfour to A.T. Mahan, 20 December 1899; Balfour to Lodge, 11 April 1905, Balfour MSS, British Museum, London.

19. Campbell, *Anglo-American Understanding*, and Perkins, *The Great Rapprochement*; see

also A.E. Campbell, *Britain and the United States: 1895–1903* (London, 1960), and an old classic, Parker T. Moon, *Imperialism and World Politics* (New York, NY, 1940 ed.).

20. Tony Smith, *The Pattern of Imperialism: The United States, Great Britain, and the late-industrializing world since 1815* (New York, NY, 1981), pp. 35–43; C. J. Bartlett, *The Global Conflict: The International Rivalry of the Great Powers, 1880–1970* (London, 1984), pp. 35–56.

21. Theodore Roosevelt to Charles Arthur Moore, 14 February 1898, in Elting E. Morison, ed., *The Letters of Theodore Roosevelt* (Cambridge, MA, 1951), 1:772; Norman A. Graebner, *Foundations of American Foreign Policy: A Realist Appraisal From Franklin to McKinley* (Wilmington, DE, 1985), pp. 346–55; Lewis L. Gould, *The Spanish-American War and President McKinley* (Lawrence, KS, 1982), p. 32; Nell Irvin Painter, *Standing at Armageddon: The United States, 1877–1919* (New York, NY, 1987), pp. 142–52.

22. Richard E. Welch, Jr., *Response to Imperialism: The United States and the Philippine-American War, 1899–1902* (Chapel Hill, NC, 1979), pp. 151–52; Melvin Small, "The United States and the German 'Threat' to the Hemisphere, 1905–1914," *The Americas* 28:3 (1972), pp. 252–70; Rock, *Why Peace Breaks Out*, pp. 38–40.

23. *The Times* (London), 14 February 1903; a few months earlier Balfour privately had written Andrew Carnegie that "the Monroe doctrine, to which we have not the smallest objection, (rather the reverse!)" would not be violated and complained "These South American Republics are a great trouble, and I wish the U.S.A. would take them in hand!" See Arthur J. Balfour to Andrew Carnegie, 18 December 1902, Balfour MSS, British Museum, London.

24. Kenneth Bourne, *Britain and the Balance of Power in North America, 1815–1908* (London, 1967), p. 410; see also Smith, *Illusions of Conflict*; Christopher Hitchens takes the opposite view of British policy in the nineteenth century, arguing that "the British fought tenaciously against the expansion of the United States across North America." See his *Blood, Class, and Nostalgia*, pp. 152–55.

25. Sir John Fisher to Lord Rosebery, 10 May 1901, in *Fear God and Dreadnought: The Correspondence of Admiral of the Fleet Lord Fisher of Kilverstone*, selected and edited by Arthur J. Marder, 3 vols. (London, 1952–1959), 1:190.

26. Bourne, *Balance of Power*, pp. 369, 405.

27. Paul Kennedy, "The Tradition of Appeasement in British Foreign Policy, 1865–1939," in Paul Kennedy, *Strategy and Diplomacy, 1870-1945: Eight Studies* (London, 1983), pp. 13–39.

28. For an overview of the American stance on the Boer War, see Thomas J. Noer, *Briton, Boer, and Yankee: The United States and South Africa, 1870–1914* (Kent, OH, 1978); for a discussion of maritime rights and the Boer War, see John W. Coogan, *The End of Neutrality: The United States, Britain, and Maritime Rights, 1899–1915* (Ithaca, NY, 1981), pp. 30–54.

29. Beale, *Theodore Roosevelt*, p. 109. Richard H. Collin, in his recent study of Roosevelt, agrees that "Britian would go to great lengths to keep America as her new ally in the world balance of power." See his *Theodore Roosevelt, Culture, Diplomacy, and Expansion: A New View of American Imperialism* (Baton Rouge, LA, 1985), p. 154.

30. For a discussion of the Pan-American Exposition and the importance of world's fairs to the creation of American empire, see Robert W. Rydell, *All the World's a Fair: Visions of Empire at American International Expositions, 1876–1916* (Chicago, IL, 1984).

31. Arthur J. Balfour to John Hay, 8 August 1902, Balfour MSS, British Museum, London.

32. Beale, *Theodore Roosevelt*, p. 148.

33. John M. Coski, "The Triple Mandate: The Concept of Trusteeship and American Imperialism, 1898–1934," Ph.D. diss., The College of William and Mary, (Williamsburg, VA, 1987), pp. 58–59; Stanley Karnow, *In Our Image: America's Empire in the Philippines* (New York, NY, 1989); Joseph A. Fry, "In Search of an Orderly World: U.S. Imperialism, 1898–1912," in John M. Carroll and George C. Herring, eds., *Modern American Diplomacy* (Wilmington, DE, 1986), pp. 1–20.

34. Warren G. Kneer, *Great Britain and the Caribbean, 1901–1913: A Study in Anglo-American Relations* (Lansing, MI, 1975), pp. 68–98; Healy, *Drive to Hegemony*.

35. Kennedy, *Rise and Fall of the Great Powers*, p. 243; Rock, *Why Peace Breaks Out*, p. 30; Alan Ned Sabrosky, "From Bosnia to Sarajevo: A Comparative Discussion of Interstate Crises," *The Journal of Conflict Resolution* 19 (March 1975), pp. 3–24; Tony Smith, *Pattern of Imperialism*, p. 150.

36. Wilson to House, 21 July 1917, quoted in D. Cameron Watt, *Succeeding John Bull: America in Britain's Place, 1900–1975* (London, 1984), p. 32; see also Edward B. Parsons, *Wilsonian Diplomacy: Allied-American Rivalries in War and Peace* (St. Louis, MO, 1978); and two articles by Kathleen Burk, "Great Britain in the United States, 1917–1918: The Turning Point," *The International History Review* (April 1979), pp. 228–45; and "The Diplomacy of Finance: British Financial Missions to the United States 1914–1918," *The Historical Journal* (1979), pp. 351–72.

37. For a discussion of the rapprochement that characterizes the improved relations of the period as "the myth of Anglo-American friendship," see Cedric James Lowe and Michael L. Dockrill, *The Mirage of Power*, vol. 1, *British Foreign Policy 1902–1914* (London, 1972), pp. 97–99.

2

The United States and Germany in the World Arena, 1900–1917

Ragnhild Fiebig-von Hase

When one studies the role of the United States and Germany in international relations at the beginning of the twentieth century, one is immediately confronted with the problem that the familiar picture of the global system before 1917 offers no suitable framework for an evaluation of the American position.[1] Traditionally, the world system is seen as a stratified system, determined by the power rivalries and imperialistic expansion of the European states, i.e., as a system dominated by the European center. Attention therefore concentrates on the European core. Here, as is commonly assumed, the relationships among the continental powers were regulated by the "balance of power" principle during the nineteenth century. England, which kept aloof from all alliances, acted as guarantor of the system and used its outstanding seapower to establish its worldwide Pax Britannica. Since 1898, however, Germany challenged this arrangement with its *Weltpolitik*, the fleet program of Tirpitz, and its increased hegemonic aspirations on the continent. Great Britain, realizing the threat to its leading position inherent in this policy, responded by concluding the entente with France and Russia, and by concentrating its fleet in the North Sea. As a result, the conflicts among the great powers, which had taken place primarily on the periphery of the system in the preceding years, were now concentrated dangerously in Europe itself. The European concert of powers lost its flexibility and changed to a dualistic structure in which Germany, Austria-Hungary, and Italy on the one side, and England, France, and Russia on the other, confronted each other. The principles of intimidation and deterrence with heavy reliance on military strength became the principal tools of diplomacy. Under the influence of the Anglo-German naval armament race, of the army increases on the continent, and of the dangerous determinism of fixed military war plans, there developed a climate of "cold" or "dry" war, which culminated finally in total war in August 1914. German policy-making certainly was at the center of this disastrous development.[2]

Notes to Chapter 2 can be found on page 60.

In this Eurocentric view, the United States obviously receives only marginal attention. However, it also must be said that American historiography contributed to this state of affairs with its conception of an isolationist tradition in American foreign policy,[3] as well as the attempt of the so-called revisionist school to explain American imperialism merely as a result of inner-American developments.[4] Thus, both sides did not encourage questions concerning transatlantic relations. The analysis of German-American relations remained a topic never really integrated into the study of international relations for the years before 1917.[5] This seems to be equally true for Anglo-American relations, although much more attention was given to them.[6] There developed a kind of circular argument: before 1917 the world system was Eurocentric because America abided by its isolationism, and America's foreign policy was isolationist because the country did not participate in the European alliance system. Scholars ignored the fact that during the nineteenth century England could guarantee the "balance of power" on the European continent only because it was not participating in continental coalitions and persisted in its "splendid isolation." Therefore, participation in the European alliance system does not seem to be a very useful characteristic for defining world power status and solving the given problem. On the American side of the Atlantic, the much-cherished belief in American abstinence from the evils of European power politics often lead to the neglect of the pragmatic basis of Washington's warning against alliances. Historians overlooked Washington's recommendation to combine a maximum of economic relations with European powers with a minimum of political commitments. The American *Staatsraison* required using the advantages given by its own "detached & distant situation" and avoiding entanglements in the European power struggle. But no sober American statesman cherished the illusion that the United States could be separated effectively from the developments of the European power system itself.[7] Therefore, could America's interests remain untouched by the revolutionizing of the European power structure after 1898?

In order to understand the United States' role in the global system, then, one must give up the perception of both American isolationism and Eurocentrism. The proposal to do this has already a weighty, albeit not vociferous, tradition. According to this view, leading statesmen and writers in the nineteenth century were already pointing to Great Britain, Russia, and the United States of America as the world powers. Europe was the most important center of the world-power system, Geoffrey Barraclough maintains, but it was certainly not the only one, and he stresses the importance of the United States and Japan as world powers.[8] In this paper, I assume that besides Europe, East Asia, and the Western

Hemisphere also were important centers of international activity. In addition, the network of relationships developing among the great powers with access to the North Atlantic – mainly Great Britain, Germany, and the United States – deserves increased attention. All these focal points of international action did not exist in isolation from each other, as the political and economic interdependence between states and regions was so far advanced that, as a rule, the political and economic events in one region had worldwide repercussions that touched the status of all great powers as well as the system as a whole. It seems appropriate to use this interdependence for defining world power: a world power is a state whose political and economic interests are not restricted to one geographical region, but which are spread out over the globe in such a way that they are affected by events in other regions and are also able to decisively influence those events themselves. Such a concept assumes that the world system cannot be adequately understood only in its political dimension as a system, constituted by political power rivalries. The economic aspects, as well as the linkage between the domestic and the external factors of foreign policy, deserve equal attention. Unfortunately, there is no theoretical framework that can help to structure and systematize empirical evidence under such aspects. Existing paradigms can only help to clarify certain aspects.[9]

These difficulties contribute to the extensive controversy over whether Germany and the United States can be rated as world powers at all for the period before World War I. Revisionist scholars accentuate German world-power ambitions[10] as well as the continuity of American global expansionism since the founding of the republic.[11] Historians focusing on diplomatic history are reluctant to consider the two countries as world powers before 1917 and emphasize their purely regional orientation.[12] But the revisionist approach, with its concentration on the domestic factors of foreign policy, can only demonstrate world power ambitions and explain their internal roots. It offers no analytical framework to evaluate the actual performance of both states in the world arena itself. Therefore, it cannot answer the question as to how, when, where, and by what means power was really executed in a way to justify the assignment of world-power status. On the other hand, the traditional view is characterized by a one-sided emphasis on political power as the moving factor of international relations and, as a logical consequence, stresses political and military questions as well as geostrategic considerations. It thus neglects the economic dimension of the world system and the important role economic exchange with foreign countries and economic foreign policy play for the welfare of a society, which has to be protected and promoted by the state as well. As German and American world interests were mainly economic, and while defense problems were centered regionally, the accentuation of regionalism or global designs seems to be the logical outcome of whichever methodological approach is adopted.

Stressing economic factors of international relations does not by itself imply economic determinism, as is so often maintained. On the contrary, it prepares the ground for a more flexible approach. It seems appropriate to remember that Max Weber's definition of power as "any chance to enforce one's will against opposition, no matter by what this chance is created"[13] encourages a very broad interpretation of the term. Power can be executed in the international system not only by political means, with military force behind it as a last resort, but also by economic and cultural influences. Such notions are applied by the *dependencia* theories and in Immanuel Wallerstein's model of the capitalistic world system.[14] But the categories set forth in these theories are highly debatable. They assume that the economic subordination of the less developed global regions to the industrialized Northern Hemisphere was and is sustained by the informal power relationships that are inherent in the international division of labor, which regulates the world economy. The crude dichotomy between the industrial center and the dependent periphery makes the model inapplicable for the relations between great powers.[15] Despite this reservation, the idea points to the fact that the role of a state within its international environment is determined not only by its internal socioeconomic development, but also by the power relationships set by the structure of the global economic and political system.[16] While the former represents the potential of what would be the "will" in Max Weber's definition, the latter can be understood as the setting in which the "opposition" organizes.

This paper is based on the hypothesis that Germany and the United States were world powers in 1900 according to the definition set forth above, as their political and economic interests were not confined to their respective geographical regions and their power potential sufficed to influence world events in a crucial way. There were certain inconsistencies in America's position. Although its economic interests were still primarily directed towards Europe, its policies, represented by the Monroe Doctrine and the concept of the "Open Door," pointed towards the Western Hemisphere and East Asia. In the German case, the global designs of *Weltpolitik* and the hegemonic ambitions on the continent far exceeded the country's economic and political potential. A different dynamic of American and German expansionism becomes evident: the architects of American foreign policy believed in the ultimate superiority of America's sociopolitical and economic structure, and they therefore relied primarily on the impulses emanating from the economy itself and the instruments of economic foreign policy to realize their objects. The main characteristic of German foreign policy, on the other hand, was the simultaneous use of economic strategies and the reliance on intimidation, i.e., using the heavily expanded military forces as an instrument of threat. The realization of the American as well as German aims implied restructuring the world-power system. But by resorting to military means, Germany chose the "revolutionizing" path,[17] while the United States believed that global evolution, if left unfettered, would work to the American advantage. Major misunderstandings about mutual political and economic aims did not exist either on the German or the American side. Instead, there was a clear perception that their interests collided almost everywhere on the globe. German-American antagonism existed almost continuously from 1889–90 up to the clash in 1917 because neither the aims nor the methods of German and American *Weltpolitik* could be harmonized.

I

Once one includes the economic dimension of the international system into the analysis, the hypothesis that Germany and America did not achieve world power status before 1914 appears to be untenable, as both countries were the most potent challengers of British economic world leadership. Both countries were overtaking Great Britain in industrial production not only quantitatively, but also qualitatively. America's share in world manufacturing output in 1913 was 32%, Germany's 14.8%, and England followed with 13.6%. Germany and the United States were leading in the new industries of mechanical and electrical engineering and chemistry. In world trade Germany surpassed the United States as a competitor of Great Britain, holding the second-rank position with a share of 13% against England's 14%; America following with 11%.[18]

Only the common rapid advance of economic development represented a common characteristic of both countries. Otherwise the differences are more marked. The United States' main strength was its high degree of economic autarky, which was brought about by an almost inexhaustible wealth of raw materials, the enormous capacity of the home market, and the coexistence of an extremely competitive agriculture with an efficient industry. In contrast, Germany lacked most of these advantages. By 1900 its agriculture was unable to compete in the world market, its raw materials were not sufficient to meet its industry's needs, and industry had outgrown both home and European markets. While the dependence of the American economy on foreign trade was relatively small, the conservation of German prosperity and growth depended more and more on the supply of raw materials from overseas – mainly from the United States and Latin America – and the sale of its industrial products on the world market. Dependence on foreign trade gave the German economy the necessary impetus to develop efficient instruments to handle this trade. German merchant houses, banks, and shipping lines spread their activities all over the globe, but primarily over Europe and the Americas. In contrast, American economic forces did not develop the necessary energies to build up a well-organized infrastructure for the transaction of foreign trade. Instead, American foreign trade was handled mainly by European agents, banks, and shipping lines.[19] Since the United States was still one of the world's debtor nations, the export surplus was essential to cover international financial obligations, while Germany could balance its foreign trade deficit only by its income from foreign investment and its activities in international services.[20] With its immense internal investment possibilities, surplus capital for foreign investment was scarce in the United States except during the few years preceeding the crash of 1907. Although this was also true for Germany in comparison to Great Britain and France, German participation in international investment undertakings before 1914 was much more visible.[21]

The American export surplus was produced by huge exports of raw materials and agricultural commodities that could be sold only on the European markets. Although exports of finished industrial products had grown considerably since 1898, the bulk of American exports in 1913 (68%) was still composed of raw and semi-finished products and bound for the European market (60%). The higher share of manufactures in exports was mainly the result of a more systematic cultivation of foreign markets by the emerging trusts. But, compared with its gigantic role in world production, American industry still resembled a dwarf in world trade in 1913. In contrast to this, in 1912, the share of finished industrial products in German exports was about two-thirds. Europe also was Germany's best market (76% in 1913). The outstanding importance of Europe in German as well as American exports reflected Europe's continuing central position in the world economy. Next in importance for German exports came the United States and Latin America; and for American sales, Canada and the northern Latin American countries. Asia's share in American and German export trade, although not unimportant, remained relatively small. The dream of a market in China simply did not materialize. It was the dream itself that counted, and the fear of being excluded from future opportunities motivated German and American expansionism in this part of the world.[22]

The same concentration on Europe and the Western Hemisphere can be observed in German and American investments. Europe absorbed the lion's share of German foreign investment (around 40% in 1913), while American export capital was attracted to the countries in its immediate neighborhood: Mexico, Cuba, and particularly Canada (together more than 70% in 1914). The regional aspect, therefore, was even more marked in American than in German foreign investment. Europe also received an astonishingly high share of American foreign investment (20%), while German capital engagement in the Western Hemisphere was even more pronounced (16% for Latin America and 15% for North America in 1914). East Asia followed as the next region of importance for both countries. This is another clear indication of the global orientation of German and American economic activities, although, again, it was more pronounced for Germany than for the United States.[23]

However, characterizing American economic engagement in Latin America as regionalism creates a misleading impression. American trade and investment were concentrated in the adjacent neighboring countries to such an extent and decreased so markedly further south that it seems more appropriate to identify them as "spillover" of home-market activities.[24] They were not the outcome of a consistent effort to open up new overseas markets and investment opportunities resulting from continuously pressing internal problems of overproduction and surplus capital. American economic influence dominated the northern part of Latin America, but the south was clearly the field of preponderant European activities. Here, Great Britain was leading, but Germany's strength increased considerably between 1890 and 1914. In South America, the United States was barely present economically, as there existed during that era almost no American merchant houses, or banks and relatively little American capital was transferred to this region. In addition, American products were primarily transported to these markets by British and German ships. Since Latin America was considered by Americans to be their natural domain of expansion, a kind of American backyard, this state of affairs created much discontent.[25] In contrast to the American inability to conquer these markets, South America became the most important region for Germany's overseas economic expansion. Nowhere in the world did German trade, banks, shipping, and capital work as successfully as in this part of the world.[26] Summing up, neither German nor American foreign economic activities were limited to their respective geographical region. For the United States, more was at stake economically in Europe than in the Western Hemisphere before 1914, and Germany's economic development and well-being equally depended on the transatlantic exchange. Therefore, a merely regional strategy of economic expansion could meet neither German nor American requirements. Economic regionalism made sense only as part of a greater global concept.

German and American performance in foreign economic activity was influenced by the structure of the world economy and its transformation, which was triggered by the ascendancy of both countries within this system. If contemporary observers in the United States and the German Empire around the turn of the century dreamed about an "informal empire," what they had in mind was the model of British domination over the world's economic development before 1870. This system was structured by the international division of labor between the European center, dominated by Great Britain as the most industrialized power, and the peripheral regions, which produced raw materials and agricultural products. The relationship between the two was asymmetrical. The advantages gravitated towards the industrial core because the dynamic impulses emanated from there. The peripheral economies, although in different stages of economic growth, depended more or less on the export of a few prime commodities, which could be sold only in the industrial center. The center handled world trade and had the capital at its disposal that was needed for the development of the periphery. The avenues of trade led from the periphery towards the European core, which rendered trade between peripheral regions difficult. British leadership in this system was based, at first, on its industrial priority, and then, after it had been challenged by German and American competition, on England's immense foreign investments and key position in world trade, transactions, financing, and shipping. The British navy stood as *ultima ratio* behind this economic power position, and protected both the "informal" and the formal empire.[27]

Germany's rise in the world economy took place within the European core and was, to a high degree, analogous to the British model. As was the case for Great Britain, the agrarian sector lost its international competitiveness, industry operated successfully in the world markets, an efficient infrastructure to handle foreign trade was developed, and capital exports to the peripheral regions took place. The big difference was trade policies, as extreme German protection contrasted with British free trade. Germany could make use of all the advantages the central geographical location offered within the existing system. It became not only the "economic powerhouse of Europe,"[28] but also the turntable of continental trade.[29] In addition, it could use the existing structure of world trade in order to expand worldwide.[30] German merchants, banking houses, and shipping lines began as junior partners of British establishments, thereby profiting from the existing global network. Then, in a second step, they emancipated themselves and competed with their former partners. This pattern characterized early German penetration into Latin America.[31]

American ascendancy within the world economy had to take a different course, since the country was geographically situated on the periphery of the old system. The great importance of British capital in its economic development, the composition and direction of American exports, and the handling of this trade by European agents were assets of the peripheral role of the country in the nineteenth century.[32] To attain a leading role in the world economy was therefore closely connected to overcoming the peripheral status and shifting the center of economic world activity and trade towards the West. At the turn of the century, this transformation had only partially taken place. The high degree of autarky and the rise of industry certainly symbolized the elements of emancipation from the existing system, and, as will be shown, even the exports of raw materials to Europe turned out to constitute an asset of American strength. However, the dependence of American export handling, financing, and shipping on European agents remained a serious weakness of the American position. The failure of American industry to conquer the Latin American markets from its British and German rivals has to be partially explained by this deficit. As long as the United States did not overcome the centripetal structure of world trade, only American trade with Europe fitted into the existing structure, not American exports to other peripheral regions like Latin America and East Asia. In contrast to the German experience, increasing trade with these regions was, for the United States, equivalent to swimming against the stream of well-established European trade connections – a task that necessitated extraordinary and coordinated effort.[33]

This comparison of the international conditions molding German and American ascendancy within the world-market structure helps to clarify Britain's behavior toward its two economic rivals. The "American export invasion" of Europe around the turn of the century clearly disturbed British observers.[34] But as long as American foreign trade as a whole still corresponded to the traditional international division of labor, and as long as the United States did not intrude in the sphere of international finance and shipping, thereby threatening the basis of British dominance, Great Britain's interests could be brought into harmony with the development of American economic power. Germany was a much more dangerous rival for England, precisely because its rise in the world economy threatened British preeminence in its heart: in industrial exports, shipping, banking, and foreign investment.

Still, the American and German ascendancy within the world economy cannot be explained solely as the result of the interplay of forces within the free market. An analysis of the economic foreign policies of both countries has to be added to fully evaluate their power potentials in the economic field. Again, a superficial overview creates the impression that American and German economic foreign policies developed along similar lines, as both countries combined an extreme form of protectionism with the idea of economic regionalism and with the concept of the "open door" in the rest of the world. High tariff walls and the creation of a regional preferential zone were supposed to shield not only the home market but also the region – *Mitteleuropa* in the German case, and Pan America in the American – from foreign competition. At the same time and inspite of all this, the rest of the world market was to be kept open for their own trade against foreign discrimination and tariff walls. This concept was extremely ambitious, representing an excessive economic nationalism, which certainly could be realized only with the help of sufficient economic or political power. The aim was to reinforce one's own economic independence and to enlarge one's own power base vis-à-vis one's rivals. While in the Anglo-American and Anglo-German relationship, British free-trade policy could at least mitigate the economic clashes that arose, the escalating American and German protectionism contributed decisively to reinforce the developing German-American economic antagonism. In this struggle, America turned out to be the more powerful of the two nations.

The impression of similar attitudes in German and American foreign economic policies vanishes however as soon as the internal discussion accompanying their formulation are analyzed. German protectionism was designed primarily to meet the demands of agriculture and was especially directed against the importation of American farm products. When the German agrarians saw their economic existence endangered by American food exports, which had flooded the European markets since the 1870s, they styled the *amerikanische Gefahr* into an economic "security dilemma" and demanded protection. They achieved their aim in alliance with heavy industry, which complained about British and, after 1900, about American competition. High grain tariffs were accompanied by sanitary decrees, the sole purpose of which were to keep American meat and livestock out of the German market. Agrarian protection remained the dominant characteristic of German economic foreign policies until 1914. This corresponded with the powerful position of the agrarian interests within the political structure of the empire.[35] Heavy industry also profited, as it could combine in cartels behind high tariff walls, monopolize the home market, and enforce exports through dumping practices. Suffering from increasing costs of living and production, consumers and manufacturers had to pay the bill, although the welfare of the nation depended more and more on the performance of the industrial sector and its exports. What export-oriented manufacturers demanded was a reduction of the existing tariff on food and basic materials, plus a foreign trade policy designed to open up foreign markets. They could not enforce this aim because their political position within the German Empire was not strong enough. The growing discrepancy between the sociopolitical power structure and the economic development of the empire, visible in foreign trade policies, constantly increased the difficulties of the ruling elite to legitimize its power. A suitable strategy to solve this dilemma was the promotion of economic expansion with its beneficial effects on national wealth. The insistence of the agrarians on high agricultural tariffs, however, left the government helpless in this respect, as these tariffs were the bargaining object in trade negotiations with all agriculturally oriented countries.[36] Another method of rallying public support was the designation of a common foe, and in this respect the United States proved to be a suitable object. Frightened by American protectionism, Pan-Americanism, and the appearance of American trusts on the European market after 1898, German manufacturers and heavy industry joined the agrarians in their warnings against the *amerikanische Gefahr*. Naturally, the devil was painted on the wall much blacker than he actually was, because stirring anti-American emotions now also fulfilled the political function of mobilizing the *Mittelstand* for the right-wing parties.[37] This explains why the years of intense internal political strife were at the same time the climax of anti-American tendencies in German economic foreign policies.

In contrast to the German development, American protection favored industry. It was directed originally against British competition, but then, after the turn of the century, more and more against the exceedingly efficient and aggressive German industrial rival. Industrial tariff barriers were raised considerably under Republican administrations in 1890, 1897, and 1909 – a development that reflected the predominant orientation of industry towards the home market. As was the case in Germany, high industrial tariffs encouraged the process of concentration in industry and the dumping practices of the trusts. On the other hand, midwestern farmers and southern planters demanded the return to free trade, which would reduce the cost of living and help to reopen the European markets essential for their exports. Republican tariff policies tried to soothe the farmers with the idea of reciprocity, which represented a weapon in tariff warfare and was used in negotiations with European countries to enforce tariff reductions or at least prevent discrimination against American products. This purpose to coerce concessions was even more evident in the maximum-minimum schedules of the Payne-Aldrich Act of 1909, which were directed primarily against Germany. Although the Democrats generally promoted free trade, tariff reductions in the Democratic tariff bills of 1894 and 1913 did not actually lead to a remarkable change. This demonstrated the strength of industry, whose interests in the home market could not be neglected by either party.[38]

The scene was thus set for the German-American economic antagonism. As American farm exports met heavy opposition from the German agricultural sector, American farmers objected to German agrarian protection; and while German industrial exports to the United States were resented by American industry, German industrialists protested against American tariffs. The outcome of this dispute as it evolved in the trade agreements between 1891 and 1910 that were negotiated by the two governments, demonstrated American strength. In all of these settlements, Germany had to concede more than it received. German industry depended heavily on sales in the American market as well as the supply of American raw materials, especially cotton and copper, and German shipping lines had much at stake in North Atlantic transportation.[39] Therefore, the Reich was not in a position to risk a tariff war with the United States. America, on the other hand, could just as well obtain its industrial imports and transportation services from Germany's rivals and could count on the strength of its almost monopolistic position in producing raw cotton and copper to strengthen its bargaining power. In the end, the United States had to concede only minor favors, while Germany had to grant its minimum tariffs on grain.[40] This shows that America managed to transform the symptoms of its former peripheral dependency into instruments of power, while the advantages of Germany's Eurocentric location turned out to be a source of weakness in the German-American relationship. In the transatlantic economic power struggle, the United States clearly was in a stronger position.

German and American regionalism combined economic and political motives, as Pan-Americanism was matched with the Monroe Doctrine, and *Mitteleuropa* with the idea of a continental European *Staatenbund*. Economically, both concepts failed before 1914 because the difficulties in reaching a consensus internally and of overcoming external opposition proved to be insurmountable. American regionalism culminated in 1889–90 in the ambitious plan of a Pan-American customs union and, when this failed, in the promotion of reciprocity treaties with the Latin American countries, which would create an inter-American preferential trade zone. This policy was not only designed to boost economic expansion, as revisionist historiography stresses,[41] but more specifically to wrest Latin American markets from Europe and remove European influence in

Latin American affairs. Two purposes could be pursued at the same time. First, expansion into Latin America as well as East Asia could bring relief to the economy, suffering under the last phase of the "Great Depression." In this it failed because the diverging interests within the economy prevented a consensus on the direction and means of expansion. While the eyes of the farmers, clamoring for enlarged export markets, were turned towards Europe, industry concentrated its hopes on the markets of the periphery, but lacked the necessary infrastructure to reach and exploit these markets. In addition, intense industrial interest in foreign trade was still a phenomenon apparent only in times of economic crisis. With the turning of the cycle, industry's attention was caught again by the enormous possibilities of the home market. At the turn of the century, Pan-Americanism and reciprocity with Latin America had lost most of its attraction.[42]

Second, the idea of an inter-American trade system originated from political motives. The absence of American economic interests in the southern Latin American countries, and their penetration by European economic influences, created a situation in which the political claim put forward by the Monroe Doctrine did not correspond to the economic reality. As Bismarck maintained angrily in 1898, the doctrine was a "preposterous assumption."[43] When the Latin American economies suffered under the depression of the 1890s and political instability created additional insecurity, the readiness of European governments to intervene for the protection of their "legitimate" interests intensified. Increased informal European control in the form of international financial receiverships threatened Latin American independence, as it had done in Egypt and many other countries. The Monroe Doctrine was in danger of being quietly undermined. To counteract this development, the American claim of preponderance in the Western Hemisphere had to be brought into congruity with economic facts by promoting American economic expansion. The problem was that the interests of the Latin American countries collided with this strategy. They welcomed the American initiative only as long as it gave them the chance to play off the United States and the European countries against each other. After all, their financial and commercial dependence on England, Germany, and France was too great to put European friendships at risk. The United States was therefore only partially successful in securing the Monroe Doctrine by economic, informal means.[44]

This state of affairs increased the importance of the Navy for the protection of the Doctrine. Again and again, President Theodore Roosevelt communicated this message to his audiences. By "taking" Panama, he rendered possible the building of the Panama Canal, which would be helpful for economic expansion, but even more so to strengthen America's military-strategic position in the all-important Caribbean Sea. After events in Venezuela and Santo Domingo had demonstrated that Latin American dependence on foreign capital created a wedge for European penetration and meddling, Secretary of State Elihu Root began to stress the financial side of the question. The greater increase of surplus capital in the United States before the crash of 1907 promised that the proper remedy for the intolerable situation could be found.[45]

President Taft and his Secretary of State, Philander Knox, followed this path under more difficult circumstances. The interest of American capital to engage in foreign investment had waned with the shock of the panic in 1907. Capital now demanded additional securities for such undertakings. If the American government insisted on such engagements, it had to pay the price by guaranteeing political and economic stability in the respective countries. Dollar diplomacy and intervention as exercised by the Taft administration in Central America, increased American financial and political influence in the Caribbean era. However, it proved extremely harmful for the American image in Latin America as a whole and estranged Great Britain. Capital also remained scarce for investment in China. The Taft administration had to signal its benevolent interest there in the same way as it had in Central America. The lack of sufficient American capital for foreign investment spurred the government's interest in currency-reform plans in Latin America, China, and even Persia. American management of these projects could help to increase the power of the dollar without requiring high American investments.[46]

Woodrow Wilson tried to avoid the mistakes of his predecessor and cultivated the friendship of the Latin American nations. At the same time, he clearly perceived the political danger inherent in European financial dominance over South and Central America. The entanglement of British and German capitalists in Mexican affairs heightened his perception of the potential threat. His Mobile address of October 1913 "verged on a declaration of economic war" against European financial control.[47] Still, a solution of the problem was not in sight under the existing economic and political power constellations. America failed to bring its hegemonic pretensions in the Western Hemisphere into alignment with economic reality before August 1914.

American regionalism was a reaction to European penetration into Latin America, which threatened the chances of future American economic expansion just as much as it challenged the widely enlarged security perimeter defined by the Monroe Doctrine. In the same way, German regionalism was a strategy to cope with problems arising from the changed international economic and political power distributions. *Mitteleuropa* plans had a long tradition and were not new ideas conceived during the discussion of German war aims after 1914.[48] Their revival since the 1870s has to be seen in connection with the grievances about the *amerikanische Gefahr*. The intrusion of American farm exports into the European markets, which touched off an upheaval in European trade relations, the development of the American industrial potential, and American counter-moves to European penetration in Latin America, created a new awareness about the transformation processes taking place within the global system and about the German role within it. Popular support grew for the theory that in the future only three world empires – Greater Britain, Russia, and Pan-America – would control the world's fate. Germany would become the "Portugal" of the future unless it broadened its economic and political power base in Central Europe, and thereby established itself as a fourth world power.[49] Around the turn of the century, agriculture and industry, as well as liberal and conservative politicians could easily agree that of the three empires rivaling Germany, the United States was the most dangerous economic foe.[50] They also agreed that Europe would have to unite to meet this challenge effectively. Essentially, *Mitteleuropa* was a strategy to counter the *amerikanische Gefahr*. The *Mitteleuropäische Wirtschaftsverein*, created in 1904 with the participation of almost all of the important German economic associations and of politicians from both the liberal and conservative parties, directed its energies chiefly against America."[51]

But the consensus on *Mitteleuropa* did not reach further than the designation of a common foe and the insight that Germany's bargaining position vis-à-vis the United States would be strengthened considerably by a united European front. Disagreement began among the diverging interests as soon as the details of such a regional concept were discussed. For the agrarians, the attraction of *Mitteleuropa* was restricted to the possibility of shutting out American competition from the European market with common tariff barriers, thereby restoring the old order. With Russian and Hungarian grain exports increasing, the most extreme group among them opposed even this concept and propagated the *geschlossene Handelsstaat*. Industry's interest in *Mitteleuropa*, on the other hand, was determined by its complaints about American tariffs, the "American invasion" of Europe, and Pan-Americanism. The combined energies of Europe were to be used to strengthen Germany's grip on the continental European markets, but even more as a weapon to enforce American tariff reductions and to impress on the Latin American states the necessity of complying with European demands. Closely connected with these disagreements was the question concerning whether *Mitteleuropa* was to become a customs union between Germany and Austria-Hungary or a preferential tariff zone including Belgium, Switzerland, the Netherlands, and the Scandinavian countries. The first was recommended by the more moderate agrarian Conservatives, who advocated monarchial solidarity with Austria, while industry's interest corresponded to the second alternative since it could create an impressive bargaining position against America.[52]

These difficulties in formulating a consensus – the "will" in Max Weber's terms – were surpassed by those that became apparent in the futile effort to overcome the "opposition." Although complaints about American trade policies were not restricted to Germany and European statesmen discussed more than once the *amerikanische Gefahr* and the necessity of coordinating a European defense front,[53] increasing political and economic tensions among the European powers prevented serious diplomatic negotiations on such a topic. It was America that profited most from European dissidence.[54] Realizing this, William II and German statesmen like Bismarck, Caprivi, Bülow, and Bethmann Hollweg shared the anti-Americanism of the majority of the German people and believed that only the unification of Europe could bring relief. But they also realized that such plans were utopian as long as the political landscape in Europe did not change.[55] The efforts to create a *Staatenbund* on the European continent, which ran parallel to the *Mittteleuropa* movement, should also be considered in this context. As was shown for the American case, regionalism recommended itself to Germany as a strategy for solving its continental security problems as well as its economic "security dilemma" vis-à-vis the United States. Therefore, German regionalism has to be interpreted in the context of transatlantic relations as well. It was an essential part of German *Weltpolitik*.

II

However, the German and American positions within the international system before 1917 were not determined only by the interplay of economic and political factors. The growing German-American antagonism cannot be explained simply as a result of economic tensions. The conflicting economic interests created an atmosphere of animosity and an increasing disposition to retaliate – but not more. The crucial point was Germany's decision to rely not only on economic means in this power competition, but to resort to military instruments as well. This step was taken with the Navy Laws of 1898 and 1900. The new, powerful battleship fleet was to be used as an instrument of *Weltpolitik*, as a means of compelling Britain and the United States to acquiesce in the Reich's ambitions for world power.[56] Reflecting the importance of Germany's transatlantic orientation and the existing anti-American animosities, the fleet propaganda gave high priority to complaints about the chaotic conditions in the Latin American republics and about the Monroe Doctrine, which stood in the way of a more energetic German policy towards these countries. But the naval program was also tied to German hegemonic aspirations in Europe and the *amerikanische Gefahr*.[57]

With the creation of the battleship fleet, the Reich added a new dimension to its defense policies. Whereas traditional German security planning had resticted itself to the European continent, the transatlantic relationship now had to be regarded as well. There was the army's task of defending Germany's geographical borders against France and Russia. To this was added the navy's duty to "defend" the Reich's expanding worldwide interests against possible British and American interference. The German security perimeter thereby gained global dimensions, and all world powers had to be considered as potential enemies. Under changing global circumstances, such far-reaching security commitments created immense problems of coordination, especially since they far exceeded the available military forces. The major weakness of German strategy can be easily recognized in naval-war planning which, after 1896–98, concentrated on the possibilities of a conflict with either Britain or the United States.[58] The constant strain on all available power resources created insecurity and contributed to the erratic image of German foreign policy before 1914.

The German decision to build a powerful battleship fleet started an upheaval in the military power distribution within the North Atlantic triangle. A new consciousness of possible dangers developed in Great Britain and the United States and caused major military and political rearrangements. The Anglo-German race in naval armaments became the outstanding feature of pre-World War I international development. Since both Great Britain and the United States were threatened by the German naval buildup, the arms race involved America as well.[59] The central characteristic of British and American foreign policy was now the endeavour to deter German global ambitions.

Since 1900, public expectations were high in Germany that the navy would radically enlarge the Reich's ability to promote *Weltpolitik* not only in Asia and Africa, but also in Latin America. In reality, Germany's freedom of action was restricted by the fact that the big fleet still had to be built before it could be used as a lever in political maneuvering. German foreign policy had to pass through a "danger zone" during which the possibility of a preventive strike by the leading seapower, Great Britain, had to be reckoned with. Therefore, the ultimate purpose of

naval building had to be veiled and foreign policy had to avoid any conflict with the other great powers. Under such circumstances, it was
advisable to cultivate British and American friendship and suppress internal anti-Americanism as well as Anglophobia. But such inactivity was
inconsistent with public expectations and the requirements of naval propaganda. The task of diplomacy was to find a way in which public
demands could be met while at the same time tensions with England and
the United States could be kept at a low level.[60]

Other complications arose as well. The ultimate success of *Weltpolitik*
depended on the continuation of the existing conflicts among the other
great powers, and German worldwide ambitions could easily trigger reconciliation among these powers. The crisis in Venezuela and South
Africa in 1895–96 was indicative of that risk: German efforts to utilize
Anglo-American tensions for overseas expansion encouraged the rapprochement between Great Britain and the United States.[61] On the
other hand, if Germany wanted to play off the powers against each other
and profit from their quarrels, it could not enter into an alliance itself,
but had to stick to a "policy of a free hand." Therefore, all indications of
German interest in an alliance, a detente, or friendship towards the English-speaking powers are to be evaluated with caution. German diplomacy was designed to gain time, to enlarge its own freedom of action by
secretly fostering existing conflicts among others and by creating vague
hopes of cooperation.

For the years from 1898 to 1914, three phases of German behavior
within the German-American-British relationship can be distinguished.

1. The years between 1898 and 1903 were characterized by increased
German readiness to risk conflict with the United States over Latin
American and East Asian affairs. At the same time, German diplomacy
tried to gain Great Britain's support against American expansionism.
This strategy failed during the Spanish-American War, and as a result of
its risky behavior with regard to the Philippines, Germany was confronted with a major German-American crisis. In 1902–03 Great Britain consented to cooperation with Germany during the blockade of the
Venezuelan coast. Since Germany's ultimate aim was to put Venezuela
under control of an international receivership dominated by German
banks, the intervention was a challenge to the Monroe Doctrine.
Because German and British economic interests suffered equally under
chaotic conditions in many Latin American countries, and an improvement of their relationship was highly desirable for both countries after
the frictions of the Boer War, cooperation in Latin American affairs corresponded to their interest. In addition, cooperation with England was
attractive to German political planners because it seemed to guarantee

American compliance with German ambitions, as the United States could not dare to stand up against the combined seapower of these two nations. But this plan failed when Great Britain retreated under the pressure of Roosevelt's diplomacy and public indignation at home. The Venezuela crisis became the second climax of the German-American antagonism before 1914 and signaled a parting of the ways: Germanophobia escalated dangerously in America and Great Britain, and the same was true of anti-Americanism in Germany. Anglo-German cooperation was no longer feasible, certainly not against the United States.[62]

2. Heightening tensions with Great Britain led to a reversal of Imperial policy towards America from 1904 to 1910, as the Kaiser and the Foreign Office hoped to use the American friendship as a counterweight to the growing Anglo-German antagonism. The Kaiser cultivated personal diplomacy with Roosevelt and encouraged German-American cultural ties. The Imperial government tried to attain German-American cooperation during the Russo-Japanese War and the Morocco crisis of 1905–06. It even offered military help during the Japanese-American crisis of 1907–08, and promoted a German-American-Chinese alliance in 1908. Internal anti-Americanism and *Mitteleuropa* plans were rigorously suppressed.[63]

But this courting of American friendship was superficial, and there was no real change in the ultimate aims of German *Weltpolitik*. The sudden enthusiasm for close cultural bonds and the increasing propaganda among German-Americans in the United States aimed at increasing German influence on American politics and the prevention of a further Anglo-American rapprochement.[64] German policy during the Russo-Japanese War was designed to direct Russia's energies towards East Asia, which would give Germany a free hand in Europe. When defeat by Japan removed Russia as a factor of continental power politics, the Imperial government tried to exploit this opportunity and force France to comply with German hegemonic ambitions on the continent. To accomplish this objective, a quarrel over Morocco was initiated and France was threatened with military aggression. But the latter was meant as a bluff, and Roosevelt's mediation services became urgent for German face-saving when France did not yield to German pressures.[65] The same kind of opportunism and miscalculation characterized the German endeavours to capitalize on American difficulties with Japan. German hopes concentrated on the idea that the developing American-Japanese conflict would involve Japan's ally, Great Britain, and destroy all chances of Anglo-American cooperation, drawing all great powers to the Pacific, thereby creating new chances for the realization of German plans in Europe.[66]

3. In September 1910 another change in German behavior towards the United States occurred under the impression of growing Anglo-American tensions over, on the one side, Taft's dollar diplomacy in Central America, his maneuvres in China, and the Panama Canal tolls controversy, and, on the other, repeated attempts to improve Anglo-German relations after Bethmann Hollweg became Chancellor. Realizing the futility of previous endeavours to activate American friendship for the promotion of *Weltpolitik* against England, Secretary of State Kiderlen-Wächter abandoned the long-cherished idea that Germany could profit from playing the East Asian card and refused further to support Taft's diplomatic initiative in Manchuria. Kiderlen believed that the much-needed improvement of Germany's position in the world and the breakup of the perceived "encirclement" could only be achieved by a rapprochement with Great Britain and a strengthened power position on the European continent. Regional strength had to be the basis of *Weltpolitik*.[67]

Not surprisingly, the new reversal of German policy towards the United States was accompanied by a reduced interest in East Asia, the revival of internal anti-Americanism, and a fresh interest in *Mitteleuropa* as a strategy to counter the *amerikanische Gefahr*.[68] New attacks on the Monroe Doctrine appeared in the German press.[69] The improvement of Anglo-German relations encouraged the government to adopt a more active policy in Latin America. Prince Heinrich and one of the impressive new German battle cruisers were sent to South America to boost German prestige and interests.[70] In Mexico, German recognition of the Huerta regime conflicted openly with President Wilson's intentions, but ran parallel to British policy. In 1914 the Imperial government defied Wilson in Haiti as German insistence on participation in the planned financial receivership in that country ran counter to Wilson's declared intention to eliminate European financial influence in Latin America.[71] Blatant cooperation against America was out of the question for the German and British governments after the debacle of 1902–03 and the growing estrangement during the following years. But they quietly coordinated their action in declining the American invitation to the Pan-American exposition at San Francisco, scheduled for the celebration of the opening of the Panama canal in 1915. In the United States this behavior was taken as an affront. Because this minimal Anglo-German arrangement encouraged new protests among American, British, and German public opinion, cooperation of the two powers proved again to be no longer feasible, especially if directed against the United States.[72]

The root of America's mistrust of Germany can be traced to the turn of the century and the beginning of *Weltpolitik* in 1896–98. The McKin-

o be an illusion.[82] Now the power elite of the Reic̶ op
̶itions for world power and continental hegemony its
the battlefields. In this respect the war was hailed as Ja
̶ortunities and new freedom of action. In the same v̶ V
the United States to the war demonstrated its inclina J
̶age of the disruption of the heretofore existing interna
̶prove its own position in the world arena, and secure its
̶nd military power in the Western Hemisphere. On the ̶
̶ican behavior was influenced by anxieties about the effect
̶n war on its own worldwide interests.

̶tely after the outbreak of the war in 1914, the question
̶merican relations did not play a decisive role in German polit
̶rations, as all energies were concentrated on the conduct o
̶ll, the fact that German economic war aims, centering on the
̶teleuropa, would radically change the economic relationship
̶e two countries was not lost sight of.[83] Hope prevailed that a
̶decisive German victory could be reached that would com-
̶t the pattern of international relations and thereby offer the
̶ to realize all existing aspirations. When this euphoric hope
̶to be an illusion, when the German advances came to a halt,
̶he dimensions of American help to the Allies were realized,
̶itung was confronted again with the problems of the transat-
̶le relationship. From this moment onwards, there was a con-
̶ng the Imperial government that it was highly desirable to
̶nd and America apart and to prevent the formation of ar
̶ween them, as this would mean America's entry into the war
̶was disagreement about the value that should be attached to
̶d the price that should be paid to accomplish it. Was it more
̶or winning the war not to endanger American neutrality, a
̶Hollweg and the Foreign Office maintained, or to fight Eng̶
̶ll available means even if this provoked the American entr̶
̶r, as the naval authorities under Tirpitz, supported by a wid̶
̶f the population, insisted.[84]

̶ispute, four misconceptions that had already determined Ge̶
̶ior toward the United States before 1914 played an importar̶
̶irst was the ill-conceived belief that it was possible decisive̶
̶e America's policies by propaganda. Stirring up the Germ̶
̶nd Irish-American elements of the population against e̶
̶ action amounted to an effort to carry the war into the ̶
̶self.[85] But not only potential internal American conflict̶
̶mentalized for the German war effort. In addition, ̶
̶endeavored to incite the existing American antagon̶

ley administration recognized immediately the potential threat to the Monroe Doctrine inherent in the two German Navy Laws. This led to a radical shift in American security planning, which was facilitated by Great Britain's tacit acceptance of the Monroe Doctrine in 1896. Since 1900, the newly created General Board, responsible for naval strategic planning, pointed out the possibility of a future German-American war. The cause of such a war, the Board believed, would be a German challenge to the Monroe Doctrine. As the Board warned, the alarming fact was that American naval strength and readiness for war was insufficient to defend the doctrine against a German assault. The Board's findings indicated that the Doctrine did not only fail to correspond to economic reality, but to military facts as well. The Navy's capability to deter German designs in Latin America was at least questionable. As a result, the McKinley and Roosevelt administrations endeavored to increase the Navy. Since inter-European power struggles served as an additional check on German ambitions, American interest in the European balance of power increased. Although they were not Anglophiles, American politicians, like Roosevelt and Henry Cabot Lodge, discovered the Anglo-American community of interest in stabilizing the existing European power structure.[73]

For the United States, England's cooperation with Germany during the Venezuela intervention had been a shocking experience, because the belief in British good-will had spread in Washington. All the careful preparations for the expected showdown with Germany proved to be in vain when Roosevelt suddenly found himself confronted with combined Anglo-German action. Only after the President had succeeded in driving a wedge between Germany and England, and England had signaled its readiness for a compromise, did American military preparations help to deter Germany. When Anglo-German cooperation crumbled, America again profited from European disunity and turned out to be the winner in the game of poker for influence and power in Latin America.[74]

With Great Britain and Germany drifting apart, and the theater of international activities moving to the Far East and Europe during the Russo-Japanese War and the Morocco crisis, the United States reached the zenith of its influence before 1914: Roosevelt's successful mediation efforts in 1905–06 were decisive in restoring peace in the Far East and preventing war in Europe. His readiness to involve himself sprang from the perception that Germany intended to "revolutionize" the European system and that it had a high chance of succeeding under existing circumstances. America's political interests and security were closely bound to the maintenance of the status quo in the Far East as well as in Western Europe, and therefore ran parallel to British endeavors to contain German ambitions. As a consequence of this, Roosevelt offered to informally cooperate with the Balfour government and this arrangement was renewed with the new Liberal government in Great Britain at the end of 1905. Despite all German efforts, Great Britain and France had carried the day in the European rivalry for American friendship.[75]

Germany's zeal to please the United States played into the hands of Roosevelt, who very clearly saw the tactical motives of German friendliness. Since 1907, tensions with Japan, created by California's opposition to Japanese immigration, growing American-Japanese competition for leadership in the Pacific, and antagonistic interests in China, confronted the American government with a serious "security dilemma" because the Navy was unable to simultaniously deter a German foe in the Atlantic Ocean and the Japanese in the Pacific Ocean. This dilemma was eased when German friendliness reduced the chances of a German-American war and the Navy could be sent to the Pacific on a so-called "good-will tour around the world" to impress the Japanese with America's military might. In 1908, the Root-Takahira agreement settled the conflict – at least momentarily. Berlin's efforts to profit from the tensions in the Pacific failed, but Washington profited from Germany's pro-American behavior. Again, the American and British interests in stabilizing the status quo, this time in the Pacific, ran counter to German hopes toward its destabilization.[76]

The legacy of the Taft administration in foreign relations was a deterioration of America's position as a world power. Taft and Knox miscalculated the degree of freedom that the Anglo-German antagonism created for American actions and alienated Great Britain. This led to a loss of prestige and influence in Europe. London declined Taft's informal offer of mediation during the second Morocco crisis as unwelcome meddling.[77] Then the Mexican troubles added a new dimension to America's security problems, as the American military forces proved incapable of coping with a serious challenge in Mexico, the Atlantic, and the Pacific. The General Board now uttered grave doubts about whether America could count on tacit support from Great Britain in case of a German-American war.[78] It is true that such pessimism reflected the tendency of military planning to consider the worst contingency. Nevertheless, the situation was politically disquieting. The more the relationships among the great powers were determined by military factors before 1914, the more it became important to support diplomacy with military might.

Wilson clearly recognized the necessity of consolidating America's international position with a realistic assessment of its own strength. Therefore, he terminated Taft's ambitious engagements in China and pressed Congress to repeal the Panama Canal Tolls Act. He thereby

ened the path for reconciliation w
support from Huerta in Mexico
pan during the newly aggravated A
Wilson pointed out to the Foreign
anuary 1914: A friendly British attit
foreign policy.[79] No such essential
between the United States and Ger
intentions was the naval question, a
States as it was for Great Britain. In
in the German navy and the Reich'
posals of armament reduction contr
intentions and friendship. German a
naval armament clashed during prepa
ference. German opposition to the ar
impression that the Imperial proclam
hollow. In this respect, American a
harmonized. Comparatively unprepa
weapons, the United States was natu
peacefully or at least in gaining time
American enthusiasm for arbitration
country's economic, political, and m
other hand, had based its whole secu
policy – on its first-strike capability,
by institutionalized arbitration. The si
as "militarism run stark mad" shortly
Colonel House's efforts at mediation i
were doomed consequently to failure
pitz fleet was so closely related to G
concessions concerning naval affairs
abandoning the aims and methods of
Germany's armaments policy had shift
fundamental change in policy was out
Kaiser. House went home as empty-l
years earlier.[80]

III

The beginning of the war in 1914 did
oncepts and strategies of German and
any's policy of "calculated risk," of u
strument, had failed during the Ser
perial government that Great Brita

turned out
that the am
realized on
up new op
reaction of
take advant
relations, in
economic a
hand, Ame
the Europe

Immedia
German-A
ical conside
the war. Sti
idea of Mii
between th
quick and
pletely ups
opportuniti
turned out
and when
the Reichsle
lantic triang
sensus amo
keep Engla
alliance bet
But there
this aim an
important
Bethmann
land with
into the w
spectrum o

In this
man beha
role. The
to influenc
American
pro-Britisl
ed States i
to be instr
diplomacy

Japan and Mexico – a behavior that corresponded to the Imperial diplomatic tactics of the prewar years. German attempts to reach a separate
peace with Japan and the Imperial meddling in Mexico, which climaxed
in the Zimmermann telegram, have to be interpreted in this context.
The aim was to engage America in the Pacific or in a war with Mexico
and thereby "turn its attention away from Europe," as Secretary of State
Jagow insisted already in the summer of 1915.[86] The third factor was the
expectation that Wilson's obvious eagerness to mediate among the fighting parties could be utilized to reach an end of the war that was advantageous to the Central Powers or even to draw the United States into the
conflict on the German side. American readiness for mediation was
exploited only when the war situation was advantageous to Germany.
This clearly resembled German behavior during the Morocco crisis of
1905. Germany's peace offer of December 1916 was a highly opportunistic diplomatic move initiated to either secure peace in a militarily
opportune situation, or to create a politically favorable situation for the
return to unconditional submarine warfare. At the same time, the German government wanted to stall Wilson's expected mediation.[87] German
diplomatic style certainly had not changed after 1914. The fourth factor
was the delusion about American readiness to fight and the decisive
impact American participation in the war would have on the outcome.
This miscalculation was nutured by the ostensible military unpreparedness of the United States for war on the European continent.[88] The false
perception of Germany's capability to bring Britain to its knees in naval
warfare in at least six months further increased the belief that America's
military help to the Allies was worthless because it would come too
late.[89] The larger these miscalculations grew and the more the illusion
about a military victory on the continental frontiers disappeared, the
more the readiness to play *va banque* and to risk war with America
increased. Finally, under growing internal pressures, even Bethmann
Hollweg's opposition to unrestricted submarine warfare collapsed when
the number of available submarines created the illusion that a victory
against England was within the reach of possibility.[90]

The immediate American reaction to war corresponded to the interests and concerns of the prewar years. It was characterized by an overwhelming mistrust of Germany, pro-British sympathies, and a strong
desire to keep the country out of the war. The policy of the Wilson
administration concentrated on five particular fields of action:

1. The interruption of the European economic relationship with Latin
America finally offered the chance for economic expansion into this
area. In pushing American trade and financial relations with Central and
South America, the government did not overlook the positive effects

that the increased economic engagement would have for American influence within the region and the standing of the Monroe Doctrine. Therefore, the task of stabilizing and influencing economic and political conditions in Latin America gained high priority in American decision-making.[91]

2. The government endeavored to protect the highly important American trade interests in Europe. This task required not only energetic protests against British blockade policies and German submarine warfare, but also strong efforts to overcome the still existing deficiencies of the American position in world trade. Concern about future American economic efficiency increased when news about European plans for an "economic war after the war," with *Mitteleuropa* on one side and the resolutions of the Paris Economic Conference on the other, reached the United States from the summer of 1915 onwards. This development greatly spurred American efforts to coordinate foreign trade policies and create the infrastructure necessary for successful economic expansion. Quite logically, such activities increased during 1916: the Shipping Bill passed Congress, the Federal Trade Act was amended to encourage American activities in foreign banking, the Tariff Commission was created to use the tariff more systematically as an instrument of protection and export promotion, and the belief that the Sherman Anti-Trust Act had to be amended in favor of combinations in foreign trade began to prevail. But the growing dependence of the Allies on American supplies and financial support contributed the most to America's now matchless economic might. The war accelerated immensely America's ascendancy to leadership in the world economy. The completion of American superiority in world trade and finance led immediately to grave frictions with England.[92]

3. The third element of concern was the growing internal frictions created by the multinational heritage of the country. In this respect the crude German propaganda activities among the German-Americans were particularly annoying. Woodrow Wilson's campaign to win the presidential elections of 1916 was influenced by intense efforts not to estrange the "hyphenated Americans," and the style of American neutrality before the election reflected the need to minimize such influences.[93]

4. Even more pressing was the American "security dilemma." As before 1914, the chaotic situation in Mexico contributed heavily to America's security problems. Mexican affairs could not be brought under control by Wilson's diplomacy nor military intervention. German activity in Mexico increased this problem and was therefore resented.[94] To this was added the problematic relationship with Japan. The war had cre-

ated a power vacuum in East Asia and Japan, no longer kept in check by its European competitors, exploited the situation and expanded aggressively into the mainland of China. Only the United States was left to contest Japan's bid for domination of the Pacific. But America's military might did not suffice to support its diplomacy in its efforts to deter the Japanese advances. As under Roosevelt, the Japanese challenge had to be met with a policy of appeasement at least until the end of the war. The Ishii-Lansing Agreement was concluded to avoid the danger of an entanglement in both oceans.[95]

The security problem, inherent in the situation in Mexico and the Pacific, preoccupied the General Board until the sinking of the Lusitania. From then on, preparations for the war with Germany were given top priority.[96] At this moment, German-American relations had reached a critical stage because unrestricted German submarine warfare was not only perceived as a threat to American honor and economic interests, but to American security as well. The latter relied on the prewar power distribution in Europe and the Atlantic, which was now endangered by Germany. Additional precautions were therefore taken. Since the summer of 1915, the State Department systematically brought all strategically important points in the Caribbean under its control. The Danish West Indies were bought from a reluctant Denmark. Haiti and Santo Domingo were put under American military command. A treaty with Nicaragua secured an option for a possible alternative canal route through this country for the United States.[97] This eliminated all possible weak spots in the American strategical position in the event that war with Germany would begin and take place in the Caribbean. In addition, increasing frictions with Great Britain over maritime rights heightened the American perception of possible future conflict. Finally, the decision of 1916 to build a navy "second to none" demonstrated the growing awareness of intense danger for the American international position.[98]

5. And finally, American concern was raised through the perception of how much the war endangered the whole structure of the international system and how important the European balance of power had been for American security and economic well-being. The prewar world system had created a maximum of protection for the United States against economic alliances in Europe, Japanese expansion in the Far East, and German as well as British threats to the Monroe Doctrine. It had combined these advantages with a minimum of American political and military commitment. Woodrow Wilson was not blind to this situation. His mediation efforts and his constant insistence on neutrality were motivated by the realization that after August 1914 only his own coun-

try was left with sufficient power and independence to intervene, to force the contending parties to accept a "peace without victory," and thereby to save the principle of balances in power relationships throughout the world. A repetition of the prewar armaments race had to be prevented, and a new system of collective security had to be created after the collapse of the old. Wilson decided to enter the war when the negative response to his mediation efforts in December 1916 indicated that his peace policy had failed. Neither of the contending war parties wanted to return to the status quo ante bellum. Now, the exhaustion of the Allies and the German return to unrestricted submarine warfare, brought a German victory within the reach of possibility. The aims that Wilson deemed essential for America's peaceful development could not be attained without direct involvement in the war.[99]

The decision did not come as a surprise. Germany and the United States were drifting apart throughout their ascendancy within the global system. Although the potential for conflict simmered constantly before 1917, it was not always visible. This does not mean that the clash in 1917 was determined by structurally given necessities, but rather that it would have needed serious and consistent efforts to counteract the deplorable development. Unfortunately, such measures were not taken into consideration by the United States, while in Germany the widely spread anti-Americanism was not overcome, since the endeavors by the German government to improve the relationship were only sporadic and mainly motivated by ad hoc tactical considerations of *Weltpolitik*.

Notes to Chapter 2

1. The following research is part of a larger project on German-American relations and the European balance of power before the American entry into World War I in 1917. I am indebted to the Deutsche Forschungsgemeinschaft, who sponsored the project. My special thanks go to Professor Erich Angermann, who contributed so much to the progress of this work with his constant encouragement and advice.

2. Only a few recent monographies can be quoted here: Theodor Schieder, *Europa im Zeitalter der Nationalstaaten und der europäischen Weltpolitik bis zum Ersten Weltkrieg*, Handbuch der europäischen Geschichte, 6 (Stuttgart, 1968), pp. 110–29; Wolfgang J. Mommsen, *Das Zeitalter des Imperialismus* (Frankfurt, 15th ed., 1987); C.L. Mowat, ed., *The Shifting Balance of World Forces 1898–1945*, The New Cambridge Modern History, 12 (Cambridge, 2nd ed., 1968), pp. 112–209; James Joll, *The Origins of the First World War* (London and New York, 2nd ed., 1992); René Girault, *Diplomatie européenne et impérialismes: Histoire des relation internationales contemporaines, I: 1871–1914* (Paris, New York, 1979); Paul M. Kennedy, *The Rise of the Anglo-German Antagonism, 1860–1914* (London, 1980); Paul M. Kennedy, *The Rise and Fall of the Great Powers* (New York, 1987), pp. 194–274; Klaus

ley administration recognized immediately the potential threat to the Monroe Doctrine inherent in the two German Navy Laws. This led to a radical shift in American security planning, which was facilitated by Great Britain's tacit acceptance of the Monroe Doctrine in 1896. Since 1900, the newly created General Board, responsible for naval strategic planning, pointed out the possibility of a future German-American war. The cause of such a war, the Board believed, would be a German challenge to the Monroe Doctrine. As the Board warned, the alarming fact was that American naval strength and readiness for war was insufficient to defend the doctrine against a German assault. The Board's findings indicated that the Doctrine did not only fail to correspond to economic reality, but to military facts as well. The Navy's capability to deter German designs in Latin America was at least questionable. As a result, the McKinley and Roosevelt administrations endeavored to increase the Navy. Since inter-European power struggles served as an additional check on German ambitions, American interest in the European balance of power increased. Although they were not Anglophiles, American politicians, like Roosevelt and Henry Cabot Lodge, discovered the Anglo-American community of interest in stabilizing the existing European power structure.[73]

For the United States, England's cooperation with Germany during the Venezuela intervention had been a shocking experience, because the belief in British good-will had spread in Washington. All the careful preparations for the expected showdown with Germany proved to be in vain when Roosevelt suddenly found himself confronted with combined Anglo-German action. Only after the President had succeeded in driving a wedge between Germany and England, and England had signaled its readiness for a compromise, did American military preparations help to deter Germany. When Anglo-German cooperation crumbled, America again profited from European disunity and turned out to be the winner in the game of poker for influence and power in Latin America.[74]

With Great Britain and Germany drifting apart, and the theater of international activities moving to the Far East and Europe during the Russo-Japanese War and the Morocco crisis, the United States reached the zenith of its influence before 1914: Roosevelt's successful mediation efforts in 1905–06 were decisive in restoring peace in the Far East and preventing war in Europe. His readiness to involve himself sprang from the perception that Germany intended to "revolutionize" the European system and that it had a high chance of succeeding under existing circumstances. America's political interests and security were closely bound to the maintenance of the status quo in the Far East as well as in Western Europe, and therefore ran parallel to British endeavors to contain German ambitions. As a consequence of this, Roosevelt offered to informally cooperate with the Balfour government and this arrangement was renewed with the new Liberal government in Great Britain at the end of 1905. Despite all German efforts, Great Britain and France had carried the day in the European rivalry for American friendship.[75]

Germany's zeal to please the United States played into the hands of Roosevelt, who very clearly saw the tactical motives of German friendliness. Since 1907, tensions with Japan, created by California's opposition to Japanese immigration, growing American-Japanese competition for leadership in the Pacific, and antagonistic interests in China, confronted the American government with a serious "security dilemma" because the Navy was unable to simultaniously deter a German foe in the Atlantic Ocean and the Japanese in the Pacific Ocean. This dilemma was eased when German friendliness reduced the chances of a German-American war and the Navy could be sent to the Pacific on a so-called "good-will tour around the world" to impress the Japanese with America's military might. In 1908, the Root-Takahira agreement settled the conflict – at least momentarily. Berlin's efforts to profit from the tensions in the Pacific failed, but Washington profited from Germany's pro-American behavior. Again, the American and British interests in stabilizing the status quo, this time in the Pacific, ran counter to German hopes toward its destabilization.[76]

The legacy of the Taft administration in foreign relations was a deterioration of America's position as a world power. Taft and Knox miscalculated the degree of freedom that the Anglo-German antagonism created for American actions and alienated Great Britain. This led to a loss of prestige and influence in Europe. London declined Taft's informal offer of mediation during the second Morocco crisis as unwelcome meddling.[77] Then the Mexican troubles added a new dimension to America's security problems, as the American military forces proved incapable of coping with a serious challenge in Mexico, the Atlantic, and the Pacific. The General Board now uttered grave doubts about whether America could count on tacit support from Great Britain in case of a German-American war.[78] It is true that such pessimism reflected the tendency of military planning to consider the worst contingency. Nevertheless, the situation was politically disquieting. The more the relationships among the great powers were determined by military factors before 1914, the more it became important to support diplomacy with military might.

Wilson clearly recognized the necessity of consolidating America's international position with a realistic assessment of its own strength. Therefore, he terminated Taft's ambitious engagements in China and pressed Congress to repeal the Panama Canal Tolls Act. He thereby opened the path for reconciliation with England. Great Britain withdrew its support from Huerta in Mexico and unofficially helped to placate Japan during the newly aggravated American-Japanese crisis in 1913. As Wilson pointed out to the Foreign Affairs Committees of Congress in January 1914: A friendly British attitude was indispensable for American foreign policy.[79] No such essential bonds of mutual interest existed between the United States and Germany. The test of Germany's real intentions was the naval question, and this was as true for the United States as it was for Great Britain. In this respect, the continual increases in the German navy and the Reich's negative attitude towards all proposals of armament reduction contradicted all affirmations of peaceful intentions and friendship. German and American attitudes concerning naval armament clashed during preparations for the Second Hague Conference. German opposition to the arbitration movement confirmed the impression that the Imperial proclamations of peaceful intentions were hollow. In this respect, American and German interests could not be harmonized. Comparatively unprepared for war in a world stockpiling weapons, the United States was naturally interested in solving conflicts peacefully or at least in gaining time before the outbreak of hostilities. American enthusiasm for arbitration, therefore, reflected exactly the country's economic, political, and military interests. Germany, on the other hand, had based its whole security concept – as well as its foreign policy – on its first-strike capability, an advantage which would be lost by institutionalized arbitration. The situation in Berlin was characterized as "militarism run stark mad" shortly before the beginning of the war. Colonel House's efforts at mediation in the question of naval armaments were doomed consequently to failure. Because the build-up of the Tirpitz fleet was so closely related to German global ambitions, German concessions concerning naval affairs would have been equivalent to abandoning the aims and methods of *Weltpolitik*. Although the weight of Germany's armaments policy had shifted to the army since 1913, such a fundamental change in policy was out of the question for Tirpitz and the Kaiser. House went home as empty-handed as Haldane had done two years earlier.[80]

III

The beginning of the war in 1914 did not lead to radical changes in the concepts and strategies of German and American global policies.[81] Germany's policy of "calculated risk," of using military strength as a political instrument, had failed during the Serbian crisis, and the hopes of the Imperial government that Great Britain could be kept out of the war turned out to be an illusion.[82] Now the power elite of the Reich believed that the ambitions for world power and continental hegemony could be realized on the battlefields. In this respect the war was hailed as opening up new opportunities and new freedom of action. In the same way, the reaction of the United States to the war demonstrated its inclination to take advantage of the disruption of the heretofore existing international relations, improve its own position in the world arena, and secure its own economic and military power in the Western Hemisphere. On the other hand, American behavior was influenced by anxieties about the effects of the European war on its own worldwide interests.

Immediately after the outbreak of the war in 1914, the question of German-American relations did not play a decisive role in German political considerations, as all energies were concentrated on the conduct of the war. Still, the fact that German economic war aims, centering on the idea of *Mitteleuropa*, would radically change the economic relationship between the two countries was not lost sight of.[83] Hope prevailed that a quick and decisive German victory could be reached that would completely upset the pattern of international relations and thereby offer the opportunity to realize all existing aspirations. When this euphoric hope turned out to be an illusion, when the German advances came to a halt, and when the dimensions of American help to the Allies were realized, the *Reichsleitung* was confronted again with the problems of the transatlantic triangle relationship. From this moment onwards, there was a consensus among the Imperial government that it was highly desirable to keep England and America apart and to prevent the formation of an alliance between them, as this would mean America's entry into the war. But there was disagreement about the value that should be attached to this aim and the price that should be paid to accomplish it. Was it more important for winning the war not to endanger American neutrality, as Bethmann Hollweg and the Foreign Office maintained, or to fight England with all available means even if this provoked the American entry into the war, as the naval authorities under Tirpitz, supported by a wide spectrum of the population, insisted.[84]

In this dispute, four misconceptions that had already determined German behavior toward the United States before 1914 played an important role. The first was the ill-conceived belief that it was possible decisively to influence America's policies by propaganda. Stirring up the German-American and Irish-American elements of the population against every pro-British action amounted to an effort to carry the war into the United States itself.[85] But not only potential internal American conflicts were to be instrumentalized for the German war effort. In addition, German diplomacy endeavored to incite the existing American antagonism with

Japan and Mexico – a behavior that corresponded to the Imperial diplomatic tactics of the prewar years. German attempts to reach a separate peace with Japan and the Imperial meddling in Mexico, which climaxed in the Zimmermann telegram, have to be interpreted in this context. The aim was to engage America in the Pacific or in a war with Mexico and thereby "turn its attention away from Europe," as Secretary of State Jagow insisted already in the summer of 1915.[86] The third factor was the expectation that Wilson's obvious eagerness to mediate among the fighting parties could be utilized to reach an end of the war that was advantageous to the Central Powers or even to draw the United States into the conflict on the German side. American readiness for mediation was exploited only when the war situation was advantageous to Germany. This clearly resembled German behavior during the Morocco crisis of 1905. Germany's peace offer of December 1916 was a highly opportunistic diplomatic move initiated to either secure peace in a militarily opportune situation, or to create a politically favorable situation for the return to unconditional submarine warfare. At the same time, the German government wanted to stall Wilson's expected mediation.[87] German diplomatic style certainly had not changed after 1914. The fourth factor was the delusion about American readiness to fight and the decisive impact American participation in the war would have on the outcome. This miscalculation was nutured by the ostensible military unpreparedness of the United States for war on the European continent.[88] The false perception of Germany's capability to bring Britain to its knees in naval warfare in at least six months further increased the belief that America's military help to the Allies was worthless because it would come too late.[89] The larger these miscalculations grew and the more the illusion about a military victory on the continental frontiers disappeared, the more the readiness to play *va banque* and to risk war with America increased. Finally, under growing internal pressures, even Bethmann Hollweg's opposition to unrestricted submarine warfare collapsed when the number of available submarines created the illusion that a victory against England was within the reach of possibility.[90]

The immediate American reaction to war corresponded to the interests and concerns of the prewar years. It was characterized by an overwhelming mistrust of Germany, pro-British sympathies, and a strong desire to keep the country out of the war. The policy of the Wilson administration concentrated on five particular fields of action:

1. The interruption of the European economic relationship with Latin America finally offered the chance for economic expansion into this area. In pushing American trade and financial relations with Central and South America, the government did not overlook the positive effects

that the increased economic engagement would have for American influence within the region and the standing of the Monroe Doctrine. Therefore, the task of stabilizing and influencing economic and political conditions in Latin America gained high priority in American decision-making.[91]

2. The government endeavored to protect the highly important American trade interests in Europe. This task required not only energetic protests against British blockade policies and German submarine warfare, but also strong efforts to overcome the still existing deficiencies of the American position in world trade. Concern about future American economic efficiency increased when news about European plans for an "economic war after the war," with *Mitteleuropa* on one side and the resolutions of the Paris Economic Conference on the other, reached the United States from the summer of 1915 onwards. This development greatly spurred American efforts to coordinate foreign trade policies and create the infrastructure necessary for successful economic expansion. Quite logically, such activities increased during 1916: the Shipping Bill passed Congress, the Federal Trade Act was amended to encourage American activities in foreign banking, the Tariff Commission was created to use the tariff more systematically as an instrument of protection and export promotion, and the belief that the Sherman Anti-Trust Act had to be amended in favor of combinations in foreign trade began to prevail. But the growing dependence of the Allies on American supplies and financial support contributed the most to America's now matchless economic might. The war accelerated immensely America's ascendancy to leadership in the world economy. The completion of American superiority in world trade and finance led immediately to grave frictions with England.[92]

3. The third element of concern was the growing internal frictions created by the multinational heritage of the country. In this respect the crude German propaganda activities among the German-Americans were particularly annoying. Woodrow Wilson's campaign to win the presidential elections of 1916 was influenced by intense efforts not to estrange the "hyphenated Americans," and the style of American neutrality before the election reflected the need to minimize such influences.[93]

4. Even more pressing was the American "security dilemma." As before 1914, the chaotic situation in Mexico contributed heavily to America's security problems. Mexican affairs could not be brought under control by Wilson's diplomacy nor military intervention. German activity in Mexico increased this problem and was therefore resented.[94] To this was added the problematic relationship with Japan. The war had cre-

ated a power vacuum in East Asia and Japan, no longer kept in check by its European competitors, exploited the situation and expanded aggressively into the mainland of China. Only the United States was left to contest Japan's bid for domination of the Pacific. But America's military might did not suffice to support its diplomacy in its efforts to deter the Japanese advances. As under Roosevelt, the Japanese challenge had to be met with a policy of appeasement at least until the end of the war. The Ishii-Lansing Agreement was concluded to avoid the danger of an entanglement in both oceans.[95]

The security problem, inherent in the situation in Mexico and the Pacific, preoccupied the General Board until the sinking of the Lusitania. From then on, preparations for the war with Germany were given top priority.[96] At this moment, German–American relations had reached a critical stage because unrestricted German submarine warfare was not only perceived as a threat to American honor and economic interests, but to American security as well. The latter relied on the prewar power distribution in Europe and the Atlantic, which was now endangered by Germany. Additional precautions were therefore taken. Since the summer of 1915, the State Department systematically brought all strategically important points in the Caribbean under its control. The Danish West Indies were bought from a reluctant Denmark. Haiti and Santo Domingo were put under American military command. A treaty with Nicaragua secured an option for a possible alternative canal route through this country for the United States.[97] This eliminated all possible weak spots in the American strategical position in the event that war with Germany would begin and take place in the Caribbean. In addition, increasing frictions with Great Britain over maritime rights heightened the American perception of possible future conflict. Finally, the decision of 1916 to build a navy "second to none" demonstrated the growing awareness of intense danger for the American international position.[98]

5. And finally, American concern was raised through the perception of how much the war endangered the whole structure of the international system and how important the European balance of power had been for American security and economic well-being. The prewar world system had created a maximum of protection for the United States against economic alliances in Europe, Japanese expansion in the Far East, and German as well as British threats to the Monroe Doctrine. It had combined these advantages with a minimum of American political and military commitment. Woodrow Wilson was not blind to this situation. His mediation efforts and his constant insistence on neutrality were motivated by the realization that after August 1914 only his own coun-

try was left with sufficient power and independence to intervene, to force the contending parties to accept a "peace without victory," and thereby to save the principle of balances in power relationships throughout the world. A repetition of the prewar armaments race had to be prevented, and a new system of collective security had to be created after the collapse of the old. Wilson decided to enter the war when the negative response to his mediation efforts in December 1916 indicated that his peace policy had failed. Neither of the contending war parties wanted to return to the status quo ante bellum. Now, the exhaustion of the Allies and the German return to unrestricted submarine warfare, brought a German victory within the reach of possibility. The aims that Wilson deemed essential for America's peaceful development could not be attained without direct involvement in the war.[99]

The decision did not come as a surprise. Germany and the United States were drifting apart throughout their ascendancy within the global system. Although the potential for conflict simmered constantly before 1917, it was not always visible. This does not mean that the clash in 1917 was determined by structurally given necessities, but rather that it would have needed serious and consistent efforts to counteract the deplorable development. Unfortunately, such measures were not taken into consideration by the United States, while in Germany the widely spread anti-Americanism was not overcome, since the endeavors by the German government to improve the relationship were only sporadic and mainly motivated by ad hoc tactical considerations of *Weltpolitik*.

Notes to Chapter 2

1. The following research is part of a larger project on German-American relations and the European balance of power before the American entry into World War I in 1917. I am indebted to the Deutsche Forschungsgemeinschaft, who sponsored the project. My special thanks go to Professor Erich Angermann, who contributed so much to the progress of this work with his constant encouragement and advice.

2. Only a few recent monographies can be quoted here: Theodor Schieder, *Europa im Zeitalter der Nationalstaaten und der europäischen Weltpolitik bis zum Ersten Weltkrieg*, Handbuch der europäischen Geschichte, 6 (Stuttgart, 1968), pp. 110–29; Wolfgang J. Mommsen, *Das Zeitalter des Imperialismus* (Frankfurt, 15th ed., 1987); C.L. Mowat, ed., *The Shifting Balance of World Forces 1898–1945*, The New Cambridge Modern History, 12 (Cambridge, 2nd ed., 1968), pp. 112–209; James Joll, *The Origins of the First World War* (London and New York, 2nd ed., 1992); René Girault, *Diplomatie européenne et impérialismes: Histoire des relation internationales contemporaines, I: 1871–1914* (Paris, New York, 1979); Paul M. Kennedy, *The Rise of the Anglo-German Antagonism, 1860–1914* (London, 1980); Paul M. Kennedy, *The Rise and Fall of the Great Powers* (New York, 1987), pp. 194–274; Klaus

Hildebrand, "Imperialismus, Wettrüsten und Kriegsausbruch 1914: Zum Problem von Legitimität und Revolution im internationalen System," *Neue Politische Literatur* 20 (1975), pp. 160–94 and 339–64; Klaus Hildebrand, "Zwischen Allianz und Antagonismus: Das Problem bilateraler Normalität in den britisch-deutschen Beziehungen des 19. Jahrhunderts (1870–1914)," in H. Dollinger et al., eds., *Weltpolitik, Europagedanke, Regionalismus* (Münster, 1982), pp. 307–31; Gustav Schmidt, *Der europäische Imperialismus* (München, 1985); Gregor Schöllgen, *Das Zeitalter des Imperialismus* (München, 1986).

   3. See for example: Samuel F. Bemis, *A Diplomatic History of the American People* (New York, 5th ed., 1965); Robert E. Osgood, *Ideals and Self-interest in America's Foreign Relations* (Chicago, 1953).

   4. William A. Williams, *The Tragedy of American Diplomacy* (New York, 2nd ed., 1962); William A. Williams, *The Roots of the Modern American Empire* (New York, 1969); Walter LaFeber, *The New Empire* (Ithaca, NY, 1963); Lloyd C. Gardner, Walter LaFeber and Thomas McCormick, eds., *Creation of the American Empire: U.S. Diplomatic History* (Chicago, 1973); Hans-Ulrich Wehler, *Der Aufstieg des amerikanischen Imperialismus* (Göttingen, 1974). An excellent resumé is Hans-Jürgen Schröder, "Ökonomische Aspekte der amerikanischen Außenpolitik 1900–1913," *Neue Politische Literatur* 17 (1972), pp. 298–321.

   5. Alfred Vagts, *Deutschland und die Vereinigten Staaten in der Weltpolitik* (New York, 1935); Hans W. Gatzke, *Germany and the United States, a Special Relationship?* (Cambridge, MA, 1980), pp. 27–51; Manfred Jonas, *The United States and Germany, a Diplomatic History* (Ithaca, NY and London, 1984), pp. 35–150; Ragnhild Fiebig-von Hase, *Lateinamerika als Konfliktherd der deutsch-amerikanischen Beziehungen, 1890–1903* (Göttingen, 1986); Reiner Pommerin, *Der Kaiser und Amerika* (Köln und Wien, 1986); Reinhard R. Doerries, *Imperial Challenge: Ambassador Count Bernstorff and German-American Relations 1908–1917* (Chapel Hill and London, 1989), i.e., the enlarged version of: *Washington-Berlin* (Düsseldorf, 1975).

   6. Charles S. Campbell Jr., *From Revolution to Rapprochement: The United States and Great Britain, 1783–1900* (New York, 1974); E.A. Campbell, *Great Britain and the United States, 1895–1903* (Glasgow, 1960); Max Beloff, "The Anglo-American Relationship: An Anglo-American Myth," in Martin Gilbert, ed., *A Century of Conflict* (London, 1966), pp. 151–71; Edward P. Crapol, *America for the Americans: Economic Nationalism and Anglophobia in the Late Nineteenth Century* (Westport, CT, 1972); Kathleen Burk, *Britain, America and the Sinews of War, 1914–1918* (Boston, 1985); Lloyd C. Gardner, *Safe for Democracy: The Anglo-American Respose to Revolution, 1913–1923* (New York, Oxford, 1984).

   7. Washington's farewell address, 19 September 1796, as cited in Victor H. Paltsits, ed., *Washington's Farewell Address* (New York, 1935), pp. 155ff; Erich Angermann, "To Steer Clear of Permanent Alliances: Neutralität, Parteipolitik und nationale Konsolidation in der Frühgeschichte der Vereinigten Staaten von Amerika," in Helmut Berding et al., eds., *Vom Staat des Ancien Regime zum modernen Parteienstaat* (München, 1978), pp. 133–44; Gordon A. Craig, "The United States and the European Balance," *Foreign Affairs* 5 (1976), pp. 187–98; Thomas A. Bailey, "America's Emergence as a World Power: The Myth and the Verity," *Pacific Historical Review* 29 (1961), pp. 1–16; some scholars plead for the years 1898 and 1899 as "some sort of watershed": Richard W. Leopold, "The Emergence of America as a World Power: Some Second Thoughts," in J. Braeman, Robert H. Bemmer, Everett Walters, eds., *Change and Continuity in Twentieth Century America* (Columbus, OH, 1965), pp. 3–34.

   8. Geoffrey Barraclough, *An Introduction to Contemporary History* (London, 1964), pp. 88–118; Geoffrey Barraclough, "Europa, Amerika und Rußland," *Historische Zeitschrift* 206 (1966), pp. 305–15; see also Alfred Vagts, "Die Vereinigten Staaten und das Gleichgewicht der Mächte," in Alfred Vagts, *Bilanzen und Balancen: Aufsätze zur internationalen Finanz und internationalen Politik*, Hans-Ulrich Wehler, ed. (Frankfurt, 1979), pp. 161–92.

   9. Charles S. Maier, "Marking Time: The Historiography of International Relations," in Michael Kammen, ed., *The Past Before Us: Contemporary Historical Writing in the United States* (Ithaca, NY, 1980), pp. 355–387; Gilbert Ziebura, "Die Rolle der Sozialwissenschaften in der westdeutschen Historiographie der internationalen Beziehungen," *Geschichte und Gesellschaft* 16 (1990), pp. 79–103; Ole R. Holsti, "Models of International Relations and Foreign Policy," *Diplomatic History* 13 (1989), pp. 15–43; John L. Gaddis,

"New Conceptual Approaches to the Study of American Foreign Relations: Interdisciplinary Perspectives," and Thomas J. McCormick, "Something Old, Something New: John Lewis Gaddis's 'New Conceptual Approaches'," *Diplomatic History* 14 (1990), pp. 405–32; "A Round Table: Explaining the History of American Foreign Relations," (especially the contributions of Akira Iriye, Thomas J. McCormick, Louis A. Pérez, Melvin P. Leffler, and Michael J. Hogan), *The Journal of American History* 77 (1990), pp. 93–180.

10. Fritz Fischer, *Griff nach der Weltmacht* (Düsseldorf, 4th ed., 1977); Fritz Fischer, *Krieg der Illusionen* (Düsseldorf, 2nd ed., 1970); Hans-Ulrich Wehler, *Das deutsche Kaiserreich 1871–1918* (Göttingen, 5th ed., 1983), pp. 182–212; Volker R. Berghahn, *Germany and the Approach to War in 1914* (London, 1973); Wolfgang J. Mommsen, "Domestic Factors in German Foreign Policy Before 1914," *Central European History* 6 (1973), pp. 3–43; for a comprehensive discussion of the German revisionist school and their critics, see Klaus Hildebrand, *Deutsche Außenpolitik 1871–1918* (München, 1989), pp. 99–106.

11. Williams, *Tragedy*; LaFeber, *New Empire*; Wehler, *Aufstieg*.

12. The most outspoken representative for Germany is probably Andreas Hillgruber, "Zwischen Hegemonie und Weltpolitik: Das Problem der Kontinuität von Bismarck bis Bethmann Hollweg," in Michael Stürmer, ed., *Das kaiserliche Deutschland* (Göttingen, 1979), pp. 187–204; Andreas Hillgruber, *Deutschlands Rolle in der Vorgeschichte der beiden Weltkriege* (Göttingen, 1979), pp. 9–67.

13. Max Weber, *Wirtschaft und Gesellschaft* (Tübingen, 1967), p. 28 (my own translation).

14. Dieter Senghaas, ed., *Imperialismus und strukturelle Gewalt* (Frankfurt, 2nd ed., 1973); Dieter Senghaas, ed., *Peripherer Kapitalismus* (Frankfurt, 1974); Immanuel Wallerstein, *The Capitalist World-Economy* (Cambridge, 1979).

15. Another major objection concerns the definition of the actors in the international system. There is the danger that the *dependencia*-theories and Wallerstein underestimate the extent up to which the states still shape the framework of global economic activities through economic foreign policies.

16. Ziebura, *Rolle*, pp. 94ff.

17. Hildebrand, *Imperialismus*; Volker R.Berghahn, *Rüstung und Machtpolitik: Zur Anatomie des "kalten Krieges" vor 1914* (Düsseldorf, 1973), p. 69.

18. Some of the more important statistical data are collected in Kennedy, *Rise and Fall*, pp. 200–02; David S. Landes, *The Unbound Prometheus* (Cambridge, 1969), pp. 193–358; W. Arthur Lewis, *Growth and Fluctuations, 1870–1913* (London, 1969), pp. 112–34; for the German case: Helmut Böhme, *Prologemena zu einer Sozial- und Wirtschaftsgeschichte Deutschlands im 19. und 20. Jahrhundert* (Frankfurt, 1973), pp. 96–110; Alan Milward and S.B. Saul, *The Development of the Economics of Continental Europe, 1850–1914* (London, 1977), pp. 17–70.

19. Before 1914, the share of exports in American Gross National Product remained always below 6.7%, while the German export quota varied between 13% and 17%, and the import quota climbed to 20%. Ragnhild Fiebig-von Hase, "Die deutsch-amerikanischen Wirtschaftsbeziehungen, 1890–1914, im Zeichen von Protektionismus und internationaler Integration," *Amerikastudien* 33 (1989), pp. 333ff; Fiebig-von Hase, *Lateinamerika*, pp. 89–194 and pp. 518–597, concentrates on developments in Latin America, but discusses also global aspects.

20. Statistical data in U.S. Department of Commerce, ed., *Historical Statistics of the United States, Colonial Times to the Present*, II (Washington, D.C., 2nd ed., 1977), Series U 1–25; Milward and Saul, *Development*, pp. 482ff.

21. Milward and Saul, *Development*, pp. 62ff; Milton Friedman and Anna J. Schwarz, *A Monetary History of the United States 1867–1960* (Princeton, NJ, 1963), pp. 142–49.

22. The statistical data were taken from *Historical Statistics*, U 317–334 and U 335–352; *Statistisches Jahrbuch für das deutsche Reich* 35 (Berlin, 1914), pp. 253ff and pp. 259ff; Paul A. Varg, "The Myth of the China Market, 1890–1914," *American Historical Review* 73 (1968), pp. 742–58; Michael H. Hunt, *Frontier Defense and Open Door* (New Haven and London, 1973); Werner Stingl, *Der Ferne Osten in der deutschen Politik vor dem Ersten Weltkrieg (1902–1914)* (Frankfurt, 1978), pp. 275–85; Ute Mehnert, *Die "gelbe Gefahr" als politisches*

Mittel der deutsch-amerikanischen Beziehungen in Ostasien, 1905–1909 (MS Köln, 1988), pp. 37–95.

23. Fiebig-von Hase, *Lateinamerika*, tables 2, 4, 24 and 25; see also table 2c in Wolfgang J. Mommsen, *Imperialismus: Seine geistigen, politischen und wirtschaftlichen Grundlagen* (Hamburg, 1977), p. 36.

24. An excellent demonstration of the "spill-over" of investment is Mira Wilkins, *The Emergence of Multinational Enterprise: American Business Abroad From Colonial Era to 1914* (Cambridge, MA, 1970), pp. 113–72.

25. Fiebig-von Hase, *Lateinamerika*, pp. 519–87.

26. Ibid., pp. 62–193.

27. A.G. Kenwood and A.L. Lougheed, *The Growth of the International Economy* (London, 2nd ed., 1979), pp. 90–115; Eric J. Hobshawm, *Industry and Empire: An Economic History of Britain since 1750* (London, 1968), pp. 134–53.

28. Kennedy, *Rise and Fall*, p. 211.

29. From 1899 to 1913, Germany's share of total exports of the industrialized countries to continental Europe grew from 22% to 31%, while Great Britain's share declined from 29% to 22%! Alfred Maizels, *Industrial Growth and World Trade* (Cambridge, 1963), pp. 92ff and pp. 430ff.

30. In 1913, Germany held 27.5% of world trade in manufactures, and thereby reached a position almost equal to Great Britain (30.6%), while the American share amounted only to 13%. Kenwood and Lougheed, *Growth*, p. 231.

31. For German expansion in Latin America: Fiebig-von Hase, *Lateinamerika*, pp. 62–193. For German penetration into the British position: D.C.M. Platt, *Finance, Trade, and Politics in British Foreign Policy, 1815–1914* (London, 1968), pp. 117–26.

32. Crapol, *America*; Edward P. Crapol and Howard Schonberger, "The Shift to Global Expansion," in William A. Williams, ed., *From Colony to Empire* (New York 1972), pp. 136–85.

33. Fiebig-von Hase, *Lateinamerika*, pp. 519–69; Burton I. Kaufman, "The Organizational Dimension of United States Economic Foreign Policy, 1900–1920," *Business History Review* 46 (1972), pp. 19ff.

34. F.A. McKenzie, *The American Invaders* (London, 1902); William A. Stead, *The Americanization of the World* (New York, 1901); David E. Novack and Matthew Simon, "Commercial Responses to the American Export Invasion, 1871–1914," *Explorations in Entrepreneurial History*, 2nd Series, vol. 3 (1965), pp. 136f.

35. James C. Hunt, "Peasants, Grain Tariffs and Meat Quotas: Imperial German Protectionism Reexamined," *Central European History* 7 (1974), pp. 311–31; Steven B. Webb, "Agricultural Protection in Wilhelmine Germany: Forging an Empire with Pork and Rye," *Journal of Economic History* 42 (1982), pp. 309–26; Fiebig-von Hase, *Wirtschaftsbeziehungen*, pp. 337–41; for the political influence of agriculture in Wilhelmine Germany: Hans-Jürgen Puhle, *Agrarische Interessenpolitik und Preußischer Konservativismus im Wilhelminischen Reich 1893–1914* (Hannover, 1966); Dirk Stegmann, *Die Erben Bismarcks* (Köln, 1976), pp. 20–31 and pp. 37–40.

36. Steven B. Webb, "Tariff Protection for the Iron Industry, Cotton Textiles and Agriculture in Germany, 1879–1914," *Jahrbücher für Nationalökonomie und Statistik* N.F. 192 (1977/78), pp. 336–57; Stegmann, *Erben*, pp. 59–97; Hans-Peter Ullmann, *Der Bund der Industriellen* (Göttingen, 1976), pp. 175–200.

37. Fiebig-von Hase, *Wirtschaftsbeziehungen*, p. 349.

38. Frank W. Taussig, *The Tariff History of the United States* (New York, 8th ed., 1931), pp. 251–446; Tom E. Terrill, *The Tariff, Politics, and American Foreign Policy, 1874–1901* (Westport, CT, 1973), pp. 141–217; Crapol, *America*, pp. 166–90; Fiebig-von Hase, *Lateinamerika*, pp. 587–612 and pp. 665–681; Fiebig-von Hase, *Wirtschaftsbeziehungen*, pp. 337–340.

39. Raw cotton was the most important article in German imports before 1914, its share amounting to 5.6% of the whole in 1913, while the share of copper was 3.1%. 77% of the cotton and 88% of the copper were of American origin. *Statistisches Jahrbuch*, p. 25; U.S. Department of Commerce, ed., *Economic Reconstruction: Analysis of Main Tendencies in the*

Principal Belligerent Countries of Europe (Washington, D.C., 1918), pp. 58ff. In 1900, the U.S. were third as recipients of German exports (9.2%), and in 1913 fifth (7.1%). The share of the North Atlantic route in German shipping was 24.1% in 1913. Fiebig-von Hase, *Wirtschaftsbeziehungen*, p. 333; Fiebig-von Hase, *Lateinamerika*, p. 179.

40. Vagts, *Deutschland*, pp. 187–205; Ludwig Prager, *Die Handelsbeziehungen des Deutschen Reiches mit den Vereinigten Staaten von Amerika bis zum Ausbruch des Weltkrieges im Jahre 1914* (Weimar, 1926), pp. 28ff and pp. 42–51.

41. See especially LaFeber, *New Empire*, and Wehler, *Aufstieg*.

42. Fiebig-von Hase, *Lateinamerika*, pp. 543–59, 589–93, 665–81.

43. Wolf von Schierbrand, *Germany: The Welding of a World Power* (New York, 1903), p. 54.

44. Fiebig-von Hase, *Lateinamerika*, pp. 590–604, and pp. 665–668.

45. Root declared in his address to the Committee on Appropriations of the House of Representatives in 1906 that "the whole trend of South American trade and social relations and personal relations subsist with Europe rather than with the United States. So that, while we occupy the political attitude of warning Europe off the premises in Central and South America under the Monroe Doctrine, we are comparatively strangers to them, and the Europeans hold direct relations with them." He expressed his expectation that the capital surplus in the U.S. would lead to a change. Cited in *Congressional Record*, 59th Cong., 1st Sess., (4 April 1906), p. 4819.

46. Dana Munro, *Intervention and Dollar Diplomacy in the Caribbean 1900–1921* (Princeton, NJ, 1964, reprint Westport, CT, 1980), pp. 160–268; Hunt, *Frontier Defense*, pp. 181–229; Charles Vevier, *The United States and China 1906–1913* (New Brunswick, NJ, 1955), pp. 113–207; Elisabeth Glaser-Schmidt, "Amerikanische Währungsreform in Ostasien und im karibischen Raum, 1900 1918," *Amerikastudien* 33 (1989), pp. 359–75.

47. Mark T. Guilderhus, *Pan American Visions: Woodrow Wilson in the Western Hemisphere 1913–1921* (Tuscon, AZ, 1986), pp. 17–20; Friedrich Katz, *The Secret War in Mexico* (Chicago and London, 1981), pp. 156–249.

48. Such plans were already important in the Prussian-Austrian power struggle before 1866. Helmut Böhme, *Deutschlands Weg zur Großmacht* (Köln, 1966), pp. 19–207. Georges Soutou simply neglects the discussion of the pre-World War I development in stating: "Le thème du Mitteleuropa économique ne fut certainement pas un thème gouvernemental avant 1914." Georges-Henri Soutou, *L'or et le sang. Les buts de guerre économique de la Première Guerre mondiale* (Paris, 1989), p. 23.

49. Böhme, *Deutschlands Weg*, pp. 595–604; Hans-Ulrich Wehler, *Bismarck und der Imperialismus* (Köln, 1969), pp. 109ff; Herbert Gottwald, "Gemeinsamkeiten und Unterschiede in der Mitteleuropapolitik der herrschenden Klasse von der Jahrhundertwende bis 1918," *Jahrbuch für deutsche Geschichte* 15 (1977), pp. 145–48; Peter Theiner, "'Mitteleuropa'-Pläne im Wilhelminischen Deutschland," in Helmut Berding, ed., *Wirtschaft und politische Integration in Europa im 19. und 20. Jahrhundert* (Göttingen, 1984), pp. 128ff; Fiebig-von Hase, *Wirtschaftsbeziehungen*, pp. 351–56.

50. In addition, of course, it was directed against Great Britain, but America was judged to be the more dangerous rival. For Julius Wolf, the founder of the *Mitteleuropäische Wirtschaftsverein*, it was perfectly clear that "America's superiority is a present fact, Britain's superiority a thing of the past." Julius Wolf, *Materialien betreffend den Mitteleuropäischen Wirtschaftsverein* (Berlin, 1913), pp. 17–30. The two catchwords, "*amerikanische Gefahr*" and "*britischer Handelsneid*" point into the same direction: America "endangered," Britain "envied" the German advances!

51. The *Mitteleuropäische Wirtschaftsverein* began its work with a memorandum, presented to the Imperial Government, demanding a stiff attitude against America in the forthcoming trade negociations and recommending a preferential central-European trade system. Ullmann, *Bund der Industriellen*, pp. 204–206; Willibald Gutsche, "Zur Mitteleuropapolitik der deutschen Reichsleitung von der Jahrhundertwende bis zum Ende des ersten Weltkrieges," *Jahrbuch für deutsche Geschichte* 15 (1977), pp. 87–92; Gottwald, *Gemeinsamkeiten*, pp. 151ff; Fiebig-von Hase, *Wirtschaftsbeziehungen*, pp. 354ff.

52. Ullmann, *Bund der Industriellen*, pp. 205ff; Gottwald, *Gemeinsamkeiten*, pp. 148ff; Fiebig-von Hase, *Wirtschaftsbeziehungen*, pp. 353ff.

53. See for example the discussions between William II and the Czar in 1896/97, discussions of the Kaiser with the French Ambassador in 1896, utterances of J. Meliné in the *République Française* in 1903, the discussion between President Loubet and the German Ambassador in Paris Radolin in 1903, and constant warnings from the Austria-Hungarian Minister of Foreign Affairs Goluchowski, especially in 1904. From Rumania, the German Minister informed the German Foreign Office about the sympathies of King Karl for a *Mitteleuropa*, directed against the United States. In 1906, the Russian Minister of Trade, Sergej Witte, warned Germany about the "*amerikanische Gefahr*" and declared that a united Europe was necessary against the "impertinent Monroe Doctrine." All the relevant reports are in Political Archive, Foreign Office, Bonn, America Generalia 13, Zusammengehen der europäischen Staaten gegen Amerika. These records were not filed there by accident. The organizational scheme of the Foreign office rather proves how closely related the questions of Pan-Americanism and *Mitteleuropa* were considered to be by the German government.

54. The political antagonism between Germany and France, for example, prevented the governments of the two countries from following the recommendations of the French Ambassador in Washington, Jean J. Jusserand, to cooperate against American demands in the trade negociations of 1909/10. As both countries individually were not strong enough to withstand American pressure, each one had to yield. Archives du Ministère des Affaires Étrangères, Paris, nouvelle série, Etats Unis 50 and 51, Relations et conventions commerciales avec la France, Jusserand to ministère, telegrams 11 January, 4 February and 5 February 1910.

55. Fiebig-von Hase, *Wirtschaftsbeziehungen*, pp. 354f; Vagts, *Deutschland*, pp. 40f; Fischer, *Krieg der Illusionen*, pp. 201–04 and pp. 368–73; Pommerin, *Kaiser*, pp. 25–29.

56. Volker R. Berghahn, *Der Tirpitzplan* (Düsseldorf, 1971), pp. 108–201; Volker R. Berghahn, "Zu den Zielen des deutschen Flottenbaus unter Wilhelm II.," *Historische Zeitschrift* 210 (1970), pp. 34–100; concerning the United States: Fiebig-von Hase, *Lateinamerika*, pp. 385–428.

57. In the parliamentary debates on the naval increases Friedrich Hammacher, the leader of the National Liberal Party, explained the function of the navy in future German-American relations rather bluntly, when he painted the bugbear of Pan Americanism on the wall, declared the "combination of all continental-European states as absolutely necessary . . . in the battle for economic survival" against America and Greater Britain, and assigned to Germany the "duty" to equip itself with the power instruments required to fulfill this task. In his eyes, the Navy Law was "an essential piece of future economic policy." *Stenographische Berichte über die Verhandlungen des Reichstages*, 9. Legislaturperiode, 5. Session (6 December 1897), p. 50.

58. Paul M. Kennedy, "The Development of German Naval Operations Plans against England, 1896–1914," and Holger H. Herwig and David M. Trask, "Naval Operations Plans between Germany and the USA, 1898–1913," both in Paul M. Kennedy, ed., *War Plans of the Great Powers 1880–1914* (Boston, 1979), pp. 171–198 and pp. 38–60; Fiebig-von Hase, *Lateinamerika*, pp. 472–506.

59. Fiebig-von Hase, *Lateinamerika*, pp. 755–63, 780ff, and 819–825.

60. Berghahn, *Tirpitzplan*, pp. 195–201 and pp. 380–415; Peter Winzen, *Bülows Weltmachtkonzept: Untersuchungen zur Frühphase seiner Außenpolitik 1897–1901* (Boppard, 1977); for German policy towards the U.S.: Fiebig-von Hase, *Lateinamerika*, pp. 418ff.

61. Fiebig-von Hase, *Lateinamerika*, pp. 632–42.

62. Vagts, *Deutschland*, pp. 1323–68; Fiebig-von Hase, *Lateinamerika*, pp. 846–1083, especially pp. 991ff.

63. An excellent resumé: Jonas, *United States*, pp. 73–91; Fiebig-von Hase, *Wirtschaftsbeziehungen*, pp. 354ff.

64. The real object of the Imperial interest in the university exchange program was revealed, when Harvard had sent Professor Schofield, a Canadian, to Berlin in 1907 and the Kaiser refused to receive him because he was not American. The Foreign Office uttered

displeasure and reproached Harvard with not complying to the terms of the exchange. National Archives, Department of State, RG 59, Numerical File 9687, Münsterberg to Roosevelt, 31 October 1907 and Tower to Root, 6 November 1907.

65. Heiner Raulff, *Zwischen Machtpolitik und Imperialismus: Die deutsche Frankreichpolitik 1904/06* (Düsseldorf, 1976); Barbara Vogel, *Deutsche Rußlandpolitik: Das Scheitern der deutschen Weltpolitik unter Bülow 1900–1906* (Düsseldorf, 1973), pp. 154–73 and pp. 201–31; *Die Große Politik der europäischen Kabinette, 1871–1914*, 19, 2 (Berlin, 3d ed., 1926), pp. 342ff and pp. 384–87, Bülow to Sternburg, telegrams 27 April, 5 May, and 30 May 1905.

66. Mehnert, "*Gelbe Gefahr*," pp. 145–72.

67. Ernst Jäckh, ed., *Kiderlen-Waechter: Der Staatsmann und der Mensch. Briefwechsel und Nachlaß*, II, (Stuttgart, Berlin, 1925), p. 115. The German Ambassador in Washington, Bernstorff, vehemently opposed this change of policy. Bundesarchiv, Potsdam, A. Zimmermann papers, Bernstorff to Zimmermann, 1 September and 1 December 1910. This led to angry reactions of Kiderlen. Kiderlen to Bernstorff, 10 July 1911, cited in Doerries, *Washington-Berlin*, 45. For Kiderlen-Waechter's influence on German efforts to reach a rapprochement with England: Fischer, *Krieg der Illusionen*, pp. 101–44; Stressing the Oriental question: Gregor Schöllgen, *Imperialismus und Gleichgewicht, Deutschland, England und die orientalische Frage* (München, 1984), pp. 287–316; Kennedy, *Anglo-German Antagonism*, pp. 446ff; Volker R. Berghahn, *Germany and the Approach of War in 1914* (London, 1973), pp. 90–98.

68. Fischer, *Krieg der Illusionen*, pp. 201–04 and pp. 326–59 passim.

69. Herbert von Dirksen, "Amerika den Amerikanern: Kritische Bemerkungen zur Monroedoktrin," in *Die Grenzboten* 71, 2 (1912), pp. 57–71; Daniel Fryman (i.e., Heinrich Claß), *Wenn ich der Kaiser wär* (Leipzig, 1912), p. 176; Walther Rathenau, *Zur Kritik der Zeit, Mahnung und Warnung* (Berlin, 1925), p. 271.

70. The detachment of the ship was initiated by Tirpitz, who actually wanted to send two of the newest German Dreadnoughts not only to South America, but to Mexico as well. The Chief of the *Admiralstab*, Pohl, opposed the project at first, but then consented, because the "general global situation seems to be opportune for such an undertaking." From London, the German chargé d'affaires Kühlmann reported that the detachment was seen with favor in England as a sign of detente. Bundesarchiv-Militärarchiv, Freiburg, RM 5/6101, Tirpitz to Wilhelm II., telegram 16 October 1913, Kühlmann to Bethmann Hollweg, 13 November 1913.

71. Katz, *The Secret War*, pp. 335–40; Thomas Baecker, "Deutschland im karibischen Raum im Spiegel amerikanischer Akten (1898–1914)," in *Jahrbuch für Amerikastudien* 11 (1974), pp. 182–86.

72. Bundesarchiv, Potsdam, No. O9.01.18401, Goetsch (F.O.) to Delbrück, 10 February 1913, Jagow to Lichnowsky, 14 May 1913, Lichnowsky to Foreign Office, telegram 17 July 1913 and 6 August 1913, Haniel to Bethmann Hollweg, 11 August 1913, Kühlmann to Bethmann Holweg, 15 August 1913; Hamburger Nachrichten, 5 September 1913.

73. Fiebig-von Hase, *Lateinamerika*, pp. 755–839, where I argue that American war planning against Germany can be understood only as a reaction to Germany's political and military moves in Latin America. Whether this was "defensive" or not depends on the evaluation of the Monroe Doctrine. Did the right of self-defense really justify the immensely inflated American security perimeter represented by the Doctrine, especially since it was not backed up materially? German operations plans against the United States concentrated in the same way on the "defense" of Germany's "legitimate" interests, not on outright aggression towards the United States. Against this interpretation see Holger H. Herwig, *The United States in German Naval Planning, 1889–1941* (Boston and Toronto, 1976), pp. 13–92.

74. Fiebig-von Hase, *Lateinamerika*, pp. 880–942, pp. 1003–13 and pp. 1027–69.

75. Roosevelt knew that the alternative to his mediation during the Morocco crisis would have been war. Ministère des Affaires Étrangères, Paris, Jules Jusserand papers, Roosevelt to Jusserand, 25 April 1906; Public Record Office, London, F.O. 800/116, Durand to Lansdowne, 27 June 1905, and F.O. 800/81, Edward Grey papers, Durand to Grey, 15

December 1905, Grey to Durand, 2 January 1906, and Durand to Grey, 26 January 1906.

76. Theodore Roosevelt, *The Letters*, Elton E. Morison and John M. Blum, eds., 6 (Cambridge, MA, 1951–1954), pp. 1510–14, Roosevelt to Knox, 8 February 1909; Charles E. Neu, *An Uncertain Friendship: Theodore Roosevelt and Japan, 1906–1909* (Cambridge, MA, 1967), pp. 163–80; Akira Iriye, *Pacific Estrangement, Japanese and American Expansion, 1897–1911* (Cambridge, MA, 1972), pp. 91–201; William Reynold Braisted, *The United States Navy in the Pacific, 1897–1909* (Austin, TX, 1958), pp. 191–239.

77. Public Record Office, London, F.O. 800/181, F. Bertie papers, Eric Drummond to Bertie, 6 September 1911, Bertie to Grey, 17 September 1911, Grey to Bertie, 20 September 1911, and Nicolson to Bertie, 21 September 1911.

78. Fiebig-von Hase, *Lateinamerika*, pp. 809ff.

79. Woodrow Wilson, *Papers*, Arthur S. Link, ed., 24 (Princeton, NJ, 1979), pp. 180–184, news report, 27 January 1914.

80. Doerries, *Imperial Challenge*, pp. 25–32; Jost Dülffer, *Regeln gegen den Krieg? Die Haager Friedenskonferenzen 1899–1907 in der internationalen Politik* (Berlin, 1981), pp. 292–99 and pp. 311–20; Jost Dülffer, "Limitations on Naval Warfare and Germany's Future as a World Power: A German Debate 1904–1906," *War and Society* 3 (1985), pp. 23–43; Roger Chickering, *Imperial Germany and a World without War* (Princeton, NJ, 1975), pp. 224ff; Merle Curti, *Peace and War* (Boston, 2nd ed., 1959), pp. 166–227; Roland Marchand, *The American Peace Movement and Social Reform, 1898–1918* (Princeton, NJ, 1972); Charles Seymour, ed., *The Intimate Papers of Colonel House*, 1 (Boston, MA and New York, 1926), p. 249, House to Wilson, 29 May 1914.

81. My research on the war years profited from the challenging ideas of Arthur S. Link, *Wilson*, Vol. 3–5 (Princeton,NJ, 1960–1965); Patrick Devlin, *Too Proud to Fight. Woodrow Wilson's Neutrality* (New York and London, 1975); Gordon N. Levin, Jr., *Woodrow Wilson and World Politics: America's Response to War and Revolution* (New York, 1968); Ernest R. May, *The World War and American Isolation, 1914–1917* (Cambridge, MA, 1959); Lloyd C. Gardner, *Safe for Democracy*; Fritz Fischer, *Griff nach der Weltmacht*; Georges-Henri Soutou, *L'or et le sang*, and many others.

82. Andreas Hillgruber, "Riezlers Theorie des kalkulierten Risikos und Bethmann Hollwegs politische Konzeption in der Julikrise 1914," in Andreas Hillgruber, *Deutsche Großmacht- und Weltpolitik im 19. und 20. Jahrhundert* (Düsseldorf, 1977), pp. 91–107.

83. Secretary of State of the Interior Clemens Delbrück's reaction to Bethmann Hollweg's war aims program of 9 September 1914 was typical in this respect. Delbrück maintained that the preconditions of Germany's economic foreign policy had changed with the beginning of the war. Now Germany was fighting for the "domination of the world market" and "only a Europe, united through a customs union, could effectively confront itself with the overpowering possibilities of production of the transatlantic world: we should thank god that the war offers us the occasion and the possibility to leave an economic system which is passing the peak of success." Delbrück to Bethmann Hollweg, 13 September 1914, printed in *Herrschaftsmethoden des deutschen Imperialismus, 1897/98 bis 1917*, Willibald Gutsche, ed., (Berlin, 1977), pp. 198ff. Later, Delbrück became again one of the more sober warners against the overestimation of Germany's power in its dealings with the United States and the follies of an anti-American economic foreign policy under wartime conditions.

84. Theobald von Bethmann Hollweg, *Betrachtungen zum Weltkriege*, 2 (Berlin, 1919/22), pp. 114–25; Fischer, *Griff nach der Weltmacht*, pp. 366–77; Karl E. Birnbaum, *Peace Moves and U-Boat Warfare* (Stockholm, 1958).

85. Doerries, *Imperial Challenge*, pp. 39–76; Link, *Wilson*, 3, pp. 20–43.

86. Katz, *Secret War*, pp. 327–78. For German endeavours to reach a separate peace with Japan: Akira Hayashima, *Die Illusion des Sonderfriedens: Deutsche Verständigungspolitik mit Japan im Ersten Weltkrieg* (München, Wien, 1982); Volker Ullrich, "Die deutschen Verständigungsversuche mit Japan 1914/1915," *Saeculum* 33 (1982), pp. 359–74. Both do not discuss the possible impact on American-Japanese relations. Auswärtiges Amt, Bonn, Politisches Archiv, R 16884, memorandum of Jagow, 10 May 1915.

87. Birnbaum, *Peace Moves*, p. 243; Doerries, *Imperial Challenge*, pp. 192–210; Fischer,

Griff nach der Weltmacht, pp. 369–97, the latter two with a critical position towards: Wolfgang Steglich, *Bündnissicherung oder Verständigungsfrieden* (Göttingen, 1968), which the author shares.

88. Fischer, *Griff nach der Weltmacht*, pp. 399ff.

89. On 31 January 1917, Secretary of State of the Navy Admiral von Capelle declared before the Budget Commission of the Reichstag that it would take the Americans one and a half years to get to Europe and even then, they would not arrive, because German submarines would sink them. "Therefore, America means zero militarily, and once again zero, and for a third time zero." Cited in Fischer, *Griff nach der Weltmacht*, p. 400.

90. In this context Kurt Riezler's, the chancellor's confidant's, remark of 10 January 1917 is important, when he reported that Bethmann Hollweg said "yes" to unrestricted submarine warfare, and then went on: "His personal position is favourable, he has always said no only *pro tempore* – has always stressed the increasing arguments *pro*. But he has not come around with a light heart. Despite all vows of the navy a jump into the darkness. . . . " Kurt Riezler, *Tagebücher, Aufsätze, Dokumente*, Karl D. Erdmann, ed., (Göttingen, 1972), p. 295 (emphasis by the author).

91. Guilderhus, *Pan-American Visions*, pp. 37–80.

92. Carl P. Parrini, *Heir to Empire: United States Economic Diplomacy, 1916–1923* (Pittsburgh, 1969); Burton I. Kaufman, *Efficiency and Expansion* (Westport, CT, 1974); William H. Becker, *The Dynamics of Business-Government Relations* (Chicago, 1982), pp. 138–56; Gardner, *Safe for Democracy*, pp. 114ff.

93. Doerries, *Imperial Challenge*, pp. 9–76 and pp. 141–92.

94. Robert Lansing, *War Memoirs* (Indianapolis, 1935), pp. 308–14; Katz, *Secret War*, pp. 253–524 passim; P. Edward Haley, *Revolution and Intervention: The Diplomacy of Taft and Wilson with Mexico, 1910–1917* (Cambridge, MA, 1970), pp. 250ff.

95. Gardner, *Safe for Democracy*, pp. 78–93; William R. Braisted, *The United States Navy in the Pacific, 1909–1922* (Austin, TX, and London, 1971), pp. 153–340.

96. National Archives, Department of the Navy, RG 80, General Board Proceedings, August 1914 to January 1917.

97. Charles C. Tansill, *The Purchase of the Danish West Indies* (Baltimore, MD and London, 1932); Munro, *Intervention*, pp. 307–16, pp. 333–62 and pp. 404ff; Hans Schmidt, *The United States Occupation of Haiti, 1915–1934* (New Brunswick, NJ, 1971), pp. 42–81. Critical towards the "German threat": Link, *Wilson*, 3, pp. 495–550. Especially Secretary of State Robert Lansing repeatedly stressed the threat of German penetration as a motive of American military intervention in the Caribbean: U.S. Department of State, *Papers Relating to the Foreign Relations of the United States: The Lansing Papers, 1914–1920*, 2 (Washington, D.C., 1939–1940), pp. 466–70, Lansing Memorandum, 24 November 1915, and Lansing to Wilson, 24 November 1915; Memorandum of Lansing, 11 July 1915, printed in: Lansing, *War Memoirs*, pp. 19–29.

98. Harold and Margaret Sprout, *The Rise of American Naval Power, 1776–1918* (Princeton, NJ, 1939), pp. 332–46; Arthur S. Link, *Woodrow Wilson and the Progressive Era, 1910–1917* (New York, 1954, reprint 1963), pp. 189ff; Edward B. Parsons, *Wilsonian Diplomacy, Allied-American Rivalries in War and Peace* (St. Louis, 1978), pp. 1–27; Devlin, *Too Proud*, pp. 501–24.

99. For neutrality and Wilson's mediation efforts: Link, *Wilson*, 3, pp. 191–231 and pp. 682–93, 4, pp. 101–41, and 5, pp. 165–289; Devlin, *Too Proud*; Ross Gregory, *The Origins of American Intervention in the First World War* (New York and London, 1971); Edward H. Buehrig, *Woodrow Wilson and the Balance of Power* (Bloomington, IN, 1955); Daniel M. Smith, *Robert Lansing and American Neutrality, 1914–1917* (Berkeley, 1958), pp. 145–65; Ernest R. May, *World War*.

3

Continentalism and *Mitteleuropa* as Points of Departure for a Comparison of American and German Foreign Relations in the Early Twentieth Century

Robert E. Hannigan

Some years ago, in researching American commercial diplomacy in the early twentieth century, I had the good fortune to come across evidence pointing to a significantly new view of the United States' bid for tariff reciprocity with Canada in 1911. The episode had been examined by historians before, but, as has so often been the case where the study of Canada by Americans is concerned, it had not been accorded any great significance, nor had it generally been connected to broader aspects of United States foreign relations – indeed, Canadian history and Canadian-American relations are subjects rarely studied in the United States. To the extent that any connection was ever made, moreover, this episode had just been seen as another example of Washington's efforts to promote the export of manufactured goods in this era. My research revealed that the bid for Canadian reciprocity had a more complex objective, and one that was perceived as integrally tied to the United States' position in the world as a whole. What struck me most, in fact, were the similarities with the concept of *Mitteleuropa*, which was important in Germany at roughly the same time.[1]

I have two objectives in this paper. One is to flesh out the particular notion of continentalism that arose in American policy-making circles in the early twentieth century (which embraced the United States' economic relations with Cuba and Mexico as well as Canada). Having done that, I think the similarities with *Mitteleuropa* will become clear. Secondly, it is my hope to use this issue of continentalism as a vehicle for also highlighting some of the key differences between German and American foreign policy during this period.

So far as the early twentieth century is concerned, when the concept of a new continental order has been discussed by historians, it has large-

Notes to Chapter 3 can be found on page 83.

ly, and not surprisingly, been the case of the Kaiserreich's quest for *Mitteleuropa*. First articulated in influential circles at the end of the nineteenth century, this idea took on much greater significance at the end of the first decade of the twentieth century when the problems confronting the German pursuit of *Weltpolitik* overseas, and of a navy capable of posing a serious threat to Great Britain's, began to seem more and more insurmountable – at least in the near term. Within this context it seems to me that most leaders in Berlin saw a new Central European order less as an alternative to *Weltpolitik* than as an intermediate step that would eventually allow the latter to be more successfully prosecuted. Thus, as Fritz Fischer demonstrated, in periods of optimism during the war, German aims still included the *Mittelafrika* idea plus objectives in what was then referred to as the Near East. The *Mitteleuropa* concept had appeal because it promised Germany a larger material base; because, if necessary, that base could be acquired and secured by the army, which gained in stature again as Tirpitz' promises seemed more and more unrealistic; and because its realization would also implicitly involve the creation for Germany of a position of unquestioned strategic dominance in Europe from which global interests and objectives could then be more effectively pursued. *Mitteleuropa* also appeared to offer some relief for the growing raw material dependency of the empire's economy, and it met a growing concern that the coming century would belong to much bigger states than Germany.[2]

One of these states, of course, was the United States. Having expanded rapidly and dramatically during the century after its birth, it controlled almost half of the entire continent of North America, including vast reservoirs of untapped natural resources and raw materials. German leaders envied the United States for its size and for the scale of its home market, and for this reason they were outraged by the hemispheric claims that Washington made under the rubric of the Monroe Doctrine. From Berlin's vantage point, the United States appeared as an already advantaged state that was greedily and unfairly blocking Germany's legitimate expansion.[3]

As has already been noted, however, the leaders of the great powers in this period took the long view. While American policymakers in the early twentieth century saw little to be gained by the United States adding to its territory (except in select areas), many nevertheless believed that it would be useful for America to solidify a still larger home economic base than it already had, and they hoped it could do so by pursuing reciprocity with its neighbors. It was out of this soil that a new continentalism grew, to be distinguished from earlier eighteenth- and nineteenth-century variants that had had territory as their objective, and that, likewise, had frequently focused on parts or all of Canada, Mexico, and Cuba.[4]

American exports of manufactured goods were expanding more rapidly with the adjacent markets of North America than with any other area of the world during the first decade of the twentieth century. This shift away from Europe was taken to confirm the emphasis that the United States' diplomacy was in this period placing on more distant, less developed areas of the world market, such as South America and China. But while the new continentalism was valued for the possible extension of the home market that it might bring, of even more significance, especially in the cases of Mexico and Canada, was the still greater supply of natural products and raw materials it might assure to United States industry and the American economy. The United States was consuming an ever increasing proportion of its own natural products, and the rising prices on these products in the early twentieth century seemed likely to threaten profit margins and to jeopardize America's competitive position globally. Indeed, as in Germany, one reason often given for encouraging exports was that the United States would in the future have to pay for greatly enlarged imports of natural products, including food. It was against this backdrop that decision-makers in America noted the booming growth of agriculture in western Canada during these years, the discovery of major new mineral deposits in the Laurentian Plateau, and the development of the east coast of Mexico as one of the most promising oil producing areas of the globe. American direct investment in these adjacent countries more than tripled in the decade after the Spanish-American War, focusing largely on mining and smelting, oil, and railroads in Mexico; on sugar, tobacco, and ranching properties in Cuba; and on railroads, timber, and mining in Canada. And American imports of natural products and raw materials from each of these sources were also growing rapidly. The purpose of creating a North American "commercial union" dominated by the United States was to solidify these trends.[5]

This view of the North American continent as one economic unit under American leadership was already being discussed in business and government circles beginning in the middle of the new century's first decade. Thus, Friedrich Katz, in his monumental study of the United States' (and other powers') involvement in Mexico during these years, cites New York banker James Speyer telling the German minister to Mexico in 1904, "In the United States there is a pervasive feeling that Mexico is no longer anything but a dependency of the American economy, in the same way that the entire area from the Mexican border to the Panama Canal is seen as part of North America."[6]

It was not until the advent of the Taft administration in 1909, however, that policymakers thought in terms of commercial policy initiatives that might guarantee and optimally rationalize these new trends. The revision of the United States tariff in 1909 paved the way. The tariff had become an increasingly problematic issue for the Republican party during the first decade of the twentieth century. Previously, the party's leadership had supported a policy of high protection for all producers in both agriculture and industry, but in the early years of the century, many medium-sized industrial constituents began to call for tariff changes that would give them cheaper raw materials and allow them to compete more effectively in world markets. Meanwhile, popular dissatisfaction with the existing tariff, the Dingley Act of 1897, rose steeply in tandem with the cost of living, and Republicans from midwestern agricultural states started criticizing high protectionism as the handmaiden of the trust movement that was so dramatically reshaping the contours of the American political economy. Roosevelt, who always viewed it first of all as a political issue, successfully avoided dealing with the tariff during his presidency, but no such option was available to Taft. He, moreover, favored a mild reduction of duties on some raw materials (the industrial rather than the agricultural revisionist position), both because he wished to assist smaller exporters and because he hoped that this would have a good effect on prices and Republican popularity. The Payne Bill that passed through the House of Representatives in the spring of 1909 conformed roughly with this approach, but under the impact of lobbying by heavy industry and other forces, uniform high protectionism staged a comeback in the Aldrich Bill that passed the Senate.[7]

Specialists in the Bureau of Trade Relations of the State Department sought at this point to inform both the secretary of state and the president about the implications each bill had for the United States' relations with its neighbors. Experts like Charles M. Pepper and John B. Osborne had been thinking in continentalist terms for the previous two or three years.[8] Revision of the tariff now raised the prospect that North American integration could be promoted by commercial policy, and both Taft and Knox were quickly converted to the cause. In a memo to the president entitled "The Open Door to Canada," Pepper was especially concerned about drawing Taft's attention to the consequences that American tariff policy might have on its relations with its huge northern neighbor. Although commercial ties had been increasing, and the American economic presence had been growing rapidly in Canada, Pepper pointed out that current Canadian industrial and commercial policy was designed to impede the kind of integration desired by the United States. It was official Canadian policy to build up its own industries and to foster a pattern of development between the eastern and western parts of the Dominion that would promote this. Moreover, since 1897 the Canadian government had begun a policy of discrimination in favor of imports from Great Britain, the greatest purchaser of Canada's natural products and its most important creditor. This, in turn, had heartened advocates of Tariff Reform and Imperial Preference in England, whom American observers still thought likely to succeed in the near future in their campaign to turn the British Empire in a protectionist direction – a development also feared by Germany. Pepper, in fact, believed that the participation of Canada would be vital to that program, which would, of course, affect American access to key markets far beyond North America. Pepper argued that the passage of a final measure along the lines of the Payne Bill, with its reductions on natural products and raw materials, would subvert all of these policies and have the effect of drawing the Canadian economy toward that of the United States. Instead of Canadian commercial channels running "from west to east and from east to west," this new American commercial policy would force what he defined as a "natural movement of trade" running from "north to south and south to north." On the other hand, he feared, passage of the Aldrich Bill would give "Canadians who want to keep as far away from the United States as possible . . . fresh encouragement."[9]

In the end, however, the rates of the House bill generally did not prevail in the Payne-Aldrich Act. Indeed, instead of drawing the two economies closer, the new American measure actually set the stage for a potential trade war between Canada and the United States. Non-British empire countries like France had bargained for, and received, tariff levies on their exports to the Dominion that were higher than those assessed on empire goods, but lower than Canada's general rates. Canadian authorities maintained that granting this benefit for free to the United States would amount to a surrender of Canadian commercial policy autonomy, but a penalty measure included in the new American act was designed to achieve precisely that result. Unless countries like Canada gave the United States their lowest rates, their exports to America were to be assessed at a rate 25 percent higher than otherwise would be the case.[10]

This was anything but the result Taft wanted. Early in 1910 he and Prime Minister Wilfrid Laurier agreed on a brief list of Canadian concessions that would allow the President to declare that Canada did not "unduly" discriminate against American trade.[11] What Taft did want was a reciprocity treaty with the Dominion that would see a lowering of tariff barriers between the two countries. He certainly hoped that this would address domestic American criticism of the Payne-Aldrich Act, but by this time he also was eager to pursue reciprocity as an instrument of continental integration. Within the State Department, the vision was laid out again in a planning memorandum of 23 May 1910, entitled "Trade Relations with Canada, Newfoundland, and Mexico." Pepper and Mack Davis, also of the Bureau of Trade Relations, wrote:

> Trade treaties of a reciprocal nature with a view to cheaper food products for consumers in the United States might be negotiated with Canada, New-foundland [at this point still separate from Canada] and Mexico on the basis of geography, that is the special relations resulting from contiguous territory. The Dominion of Canada is by far the most important, but the other countries also come within the sphere of a North American commercial policy. Newfoundland in the commercial sense is a prolongation of the New England coast, while Mexico, as relates to trade and industry, is an extension of the southwest.[12]

As much for political as economic reasons, a reciprocity treaty had been concluded between the United States and Cuba in 1902 in the aftermath of the first American occupation of that island.[13] Subsequently, reciprocity had faced great resistance in Congress, as was demonstrated when the Roosevelt administration, hoping to quell the dissatisfaction of New England businessmen, tried to promote a reciprocity treaty with Newfoundland between 1902 and 1905, but the Taft administration believed that times had now changed. (Republicans like Taft also continued to promote reciprocity as a policy that would preserve rather than undermine protectionism.)[14] Policymakers now hoped to negotiate reciprocity treaties with other adjacent states.

Friedrich Katz discusses the issue of reciprocity with Mexico in *The Secret War in Mexico*. In particular, he notes the great concern German officials had about this since the United States' position was that, under reciprocity, third states with most-favored nation treaties with Mexico would not be allowed to claim the same rates as the United States in the Mexican market. He concludes ultimately that the issue was not, in fact, of great interest in Washington because, "The U.S. government was far more interested in protecting American investments in raw materials and railways than in furthering exports to Mexico." Moreover, it would have been obvious that Mexico could not afford any reductions in its customs revenues.[15] As the example of Canada discussed below demonstrates, however, exports were far from the only objective of the reciprocity policy that the Taft administration sought to pursue, nor were reductions on other North American states' levies on manufactured imports seen as the key ingredient in expanding American sales in those markets. As Katz demonstrates in one of the many interesting sections of his study, during the first decade of the twentieth century, Porfirio Díaz actually had been in the process of revising the long-term policy he had pursued with regard to American involvement in Mexico's economy. Díaz had provided an extremely favorable climate for American investment in the late nineteenth century, but he and the *Científicos* who advised him had grown increasingly worried about its impact by about 1905. Such investment had not led to the degree or kind of Mexican development they wanted. Instead, increasingly large American firms had come across the border, and they had begun to dominate the economy and exert great influence politically. The Porfirian response was to look for European, and especially British, counterweights to American business power. After 1907 Díaz also began gradually to try to gain greater Mexican national control over the country's American-owned railways. He resented the preferences given to United States goods moving south over this network for the negative impact they were having on Mexican industrial development. Because the matter did not get very far, one can only surmise about the objectives that American officials hoped might be achieved by reciprocity. But it seems likely that, in addition to cheaper food and other natural products, they may have hoped that reciprocity could be used economically and/or politically as a mechanism for inducing a reversal in the current drift of Díaz' policies. The same arguments would have applied here as had been raised in connection with the Payne Bill's impact on Canada. Of course, there was no opportunity to follow up the Canadian negotiations with formal talks with Díaz. Within months Mexico was in the midst of revolution, the first phase of which was apparently supported by some elements of the American business community, although viewed more cautiously by Washington.[16]

Meanwhile, American authorities were quickly able to conclude a treaty with Canada by early 1911. Hoping that lower rates for Canadian natural products would yield political returns that would enable him to stay in power, Laurier had decided to respond favorably to Taft's initiatives. He resisted dramatic reductions on manufactured goods entering Canada.[17] But in Washington, these were not seen as essential, especially in what was only seen as the first of many future reciprocity accords. Knox and the State Department wanted as much as they could get, and they also recognized that such reductions on Canada's rates would assist the measure in gaining American political support. But their key objective was to draw the Dominion's economy toward that of the United States. A greater flow of natural products was seen by itself as ultimately assuring the dominance of the Canadian market for American manufacturers. The agreement reached on January 16 met this concern. It provided for a long list of natural goods that were to enter each country free of duty, and for lower duties on many processed food products and some manufactured goods.[18]

The Taft administration had great hopes for reciprocity. Historians generally have overlooked the initiative and what it signified, but Taft himself called the treaty "the most important measure of my Administration."[19] It was, to say the least, ambitious in its intent. First of all, reciprocity was seen as guaranteeing a long-term supply of natural products that would hold down prices in the United States. In his message accompanying submission of the agreement to Congress, the president discussed the measure from the perspective of one concerned about the growing competition of industrial powers for natural products and resources. Taft argued:

> We have reached a stage in our own development that calls for a statesman-like and broad view of our future economic status and its requirements. We have drawn upon our natural resources in such a way as to invite attention to their necessary limit. . . . We have so increased in population and in our consumption of food products and the other necessities of life, hitherto supplied largely from our own country, that unless we materially increase our production we can see before us a change in our economic position, from that of a country selling to the world food and natural products of the farm and forest, to one consuming and importing them [these were also among the concerns behind the interest in more efficient resource management in the United States in this period, often misunderstood as an interest in conservation]. . . . A farsighted policy requires that if we can enlarge our supply of natural resources, and especially of food products and the necessities of life, without substantial injury to any of our producing and manufacturing classes, we should take steps to do so now.[20]

Taft's envisioned economic annexation of Canada had obvious consequences for costs of production in the American market, for the United States' export trade, and, as the president told Theodore Roosevelt, for the Dominion's development and American industry's sales opportunities there. Commented Taft:

> [T]he amount of Canadian products we would take would produce a current of business between western Canada and the United States that would make Canada only an adjunct of the United States. It would transfer all their important business to Chicago and New York, with their bank credits and everything else, and it would increase greatly the demand of Canada for our manufactures. I see this as an argument against reciprocity made in Canada, and I think it is a good one.[21]

In fact, some American officials argued that the inevitable, although long-term, result would be the political annexation of Canada to the United States. Seeing the United States as already possessed of immense territory, and also viewing themselves in this period as beseiged by vast numbers of new immigrants whom they looked down upon and were not sure they could lead, American officials in the early twentieth century were generally not interested in acquiring populous new lands that they would have to govern directly. They were at this point, however, still prepared to make an exception for Canada if Canadians reached the point where they wanted to join the United States. Although they were often described as "bumptious provincials" and "spoiled children" – stereotypes strikingly similar to those many Europeans held of Americans in this period – Canadians were, in the racialist views held by officials in the United States, still seen as close enough to old-stock, "Anglo-Saxon" Americans in their background as to be easily assimilable. Although it was not a principal objective of reciprocity, formal Canadian annexation, if it ever came about, would also remove Great Britain from the continent and eliminate the disagreements Washington and London had had so frequently over the Dominion.[22]

Finally, reciprocity was not only intended to thwart the development of Canada into a core industrial state, the long-term goal that had guided Canada's National Policy since the 1870s. It was hoped that it would also pose insurmountable problems for British advocates of Imperial Preference. The President argued:

> [N]o such opportunity will ever again come to the United States. The forces which are at work in England and in Canada to separate her by a Chinese wall from the United States and to make her part of an imperial commercial band, reaching from England around the world to England again, by a system of preferential tariffs will derive an impetus from the rejection of this treaty. . . .[23]

It was, in fact, precisely such rhetoric as this, designed to overcome protectionist and agricultural opposition to the agreement at home, that ultimately doomed Taft's treaty. It passed both houses of Congress in the United States, but the arguments used in that debate just south of the border led to great apprehension in Canada. Canadian nationalism had long since been shaped, at least in part, in opposition to that of the United States, and Canadian fears of their own national growth being stunted and hemmed in, if not obliterated altogether, by their larger neighbor had grown enormously in the years since the Venezuela boundary dispute, the Dingley Tariff, and the Spanish-American War. Great bitterness had developed as a result of the Dominion's defeat over the Alaska boundary dispute, and, in fact, had been what had propelled many Canadians to support a commercial policy more oriented toward the British

Empire. It did not take long for the debate over reciprocity in the United States to arouse fundamental concerns about Canadian nationhood. As a result, with the strong support of industrial groups in the Dominion and of British interests, the opposition Conservative party successfully removed Laurier's Liberals from power in an election centered on the trade agreement. This defeat aside, it should be pointed out that the reciprocity treaty of 1911 nevertheless articulated a view of continental economic development that American policymakers and businessmen continued to aspire to, and that did, in fact, despite this measure's failure, still slowly but surely fall into place as the United States economy grew over the following years.[24]

Whether organized under a political imperium or around less formal economic spheres of influence, efforts to organize adjacent areas into an integrated economic unit, such as have been discussed here in the cases of Germany and the United States, need to be compared with other forms of international expansion pursued by the great powers in the early twentieth century. For starters, it seems clear to me that from the standpoint of economic policy, all of the activities of the powers at this time are best understood when placed within a world-system perspective such as that outlined by Immanuel Wallerstein.[25] In other words, whether the effort was to increase national territorial size or integration, or to raise tariffs, or to create a continental bloc, or to develop formal colonies overseas, or to benefit by less formal forms of dominion (and several powers pursued more than one of these approaches), all of these need to be understood in terms of how they affected the long- or short-term competitive position of that power in the world economy or world market *as a whole*, which is not to say that expansionist policies were not pursued for other purposes as well. The kind of world political and economic system that had come into being by the end of the nineteenth century all but mandated such striving. In the case of the principal world powers of the day, however, one would be hard-pressed to find leading groups that did not thrill at the prospect of eventually winning the prize of first place.[26]

Against this background, I think that the most instructive comparison to make is that between continental units and overseas colonies. From an economic standpoint, neither continental blocs nor overseas colonies were desired just for themselves, but rather for the advantages that they would yield a power economically and/or politically in the broader international arena. As a base of power within that global system, however, it is clear that there were advantages of both an economic and strategic sort to be obtained from a large unified bloc, advantages that would be especially apparent in time of war. And these, at least in some ways, were an extension of the kinds of advantages that physically larger and more populous nation states were already increasingly coming to have in the twentieth century. On several occasions, historian Paul Kennedy has revived and defended the thesis of Sir Halford Mackinder's 1904 lecture "The Geographical Pivot of History," where the latter argued (contra Mahan) that there was a geopolitical shift against maritime powers occurring in his lifetime, especially because of the railway. Kennedy writes:

> The "Columbian era" inaugurated by . . . Iberian adventures had given the west European maritime states an influence in world affairs out of all proportion to their actual size and population: now, with industrialization, with railways, with investment, with new agricultural and mining techniques, the power-balance was inexorably shifting towards the vast continent-wide nations such as Russia, the United States, perhaps Imperial Germany. . . . How could a small island [like England] compete in the long run with these modern Leviathans? How could the traditional maritime weapon of the blockade prevail against virtually self-sufficient nations such as Russia and the United States? How, even if the Royal Navy managed to preserve command of the seas, could the small British army hold Canada along its 3000-mile border with its southern neighbour, or check the creeping landward advance of Czarist imperialism across Asia? The latter, indeed, was the danger most evident to the late-Victorians, since the Orenburg-Tashkent and trans-Siberian railways posed threats to India and China respectively which no fleet of battleships could counter.[27]

Clearly, continental blocs had the potential of building on many of these same kinds of advantages.

There were many similarities between German and American foreign policy in the early twentieth century. Both nations were rising powers on the world stage, and they were the two great economic rivals for the position of industrial dominance that Britain had occupied toward the world during the nineteenth century. For their part at least, I know that American officials and others, recognizing these facts, studied with care German methods of industrial and military organization and of business-government coordination, although they did not feel that the overall political structure of Wilhelmine Germany was adequate to the needs of a twentieth-century state.[28] The pursuit of continentalism marks another point of comparison. Yet the episode with Canada described above also points to what I think is the fundamental difference in the roles played by Berlin and Washington in the international system at this time. This has to do with the relationship of these two powers toward the status quo, toward the basic organization of the globe in their day. For, unlike the case of Germany and its continentalism, the United States had no thought of carrying through forcibly on Canadian economic union or of embarking on the direct military challenge of Great Britain that that obviously would have entailed. America was well-positioned to wait for objectives that had a very good likelihood of coming its way in any event, and it was anxious to uphold, not undermine, global stability, although Canada undoubtedly continued to be viewed – as Theodore Roosevelt had put it – as a "hostage" for Britain's "good behavior" in the Western Hemisphere.[29]

It is generally thought normal for a rising power to be a power that also seeks to challenge the international status quo, yet this is not a formula that can be depended on. Even in the case of Wilhelmine Germany, we are talking about a state that wished to see preserved important aspects of the turn-of-the-century world order. Like all of the powers, Berlin wished to see order and stability prevail in the underdeveloped world, and it most certainly wished to see maintained the existing leadership of the great powers in the international system. In terms of its trade policy as well, Germany was often to be found on the side of the open door idea that Britain had championed relatively consistently throughout the nineteenth century. Yet the Kaiserreich also was determined to secure significant revisions in the prevailing international order, revisions that – along with a less clearly defined yearning for greater recognition and prestige – eventually led to war. These seem to have revolved principally around securing a larger amount of territory in the underdeveloped world and, eventually, near home. Its very restlessness in the early twentieth-century world may have put a greater premium on military approaches than might have been true otherwise (here, though, it seems to me that the case rests upon the degree to which one accepts the recent arguments about the evolution of Wilhelmine society put forward by David Blackbourn and Geoff Eley).[30]

The most distinguishing characteristic of America's rise as a world power in the early twentieth century has often been held to be its pursuit of non-colonial expansion. An even more important point, it seems to me, has to do with America's own relationship to the international status quo, which was much more consistent than that of Germany's. To cite Kennedy again, this time on England at the turn of the century:

> Britain was now a *mature* state, with a built-in interest in preserving existing arrangements. It is true that British statesmen, especially on the Liberal side, retained a belief in change; but what they had in mind was "progress," change for the better, the development of political and social and economic tendencies *on British lines* and not, of course, to Britain's detriment. The cold

and unrelenting alterations in the economic, colonial and strategic spheres from about 1870 onwards did not generally accord with such assumptions. This, in turn, increased the British preference for the *status quo*, even while they recognized that newer rivals would hardly be satisfied with a stabilization of that order.[31]

The United States was a rising, not established, power at the turn of the century, yet the above essentially describes its attitude toward the world order of that day as well. Washington policymakers wished to see the world order reformed, but this desire to a large extent grew out of their interest in seeing it stabilized, plus the common imperial urge to see affirmed and copied American ways of doing things. As I am arguing at much greater length elsewhere, a "search for order" describes not only American policy toward conditions in many countries in the underdeveloped world in this period, it also describes the overarching theme of the United States' posture toward the international system as a whole. This was, of course, also a theme of domestic politics in most of the industrial powers at the beginning of this century. But, while German leaders felt that the restoration of order at home required a disruption of order abroad, official American policy was largely symmetrical in both arenas.[32]

As were many of the methods employed. At home and abroad, the American political elite sought more efficient and effective methods than force. Force per se was certainly not glorified in this quintessentially middle-class culture in the way that it clearly seems to have been within at least important segments of German society. Yet one has to be very careful here, for force certainly was condoned (and combat romanticized), by many of those who led the United States, if employed in a cause held to be righteous.[33] And one would in fact be hard-pressed to find a power that used armed force outside its borders much more frequently than did Washington in the two decades prior to the Great War – as people in a considerable number of states in upper Latin America in particular could have testified.[34]

The theme of British-American relations illustrates the essence of the United States' posture toward the globe as it emerged as a world power in the early twentieth century. The five years after the Venezuela boundary dispute of 1895–96 witnessed a very loose but nevertheless significant coming together of these two states after more than a century of what was often considerable estrangement. Cultural factors and the creation of a transatlantic upper-class society certainly played a role, but the most important factor was the recognition on both sides that their interests would in many respects run, as Theodore Roosevelt put it, along "parallel lines" for the forseeable future. London saw itself as increasingly in need of friends, and at the very least it could not afford bad relations with a power whose policies did not seem in any way dramatically to constitute a threat to its own. Meanwhile, for Washington, the perception of London as a potential threat to the kind of order it wanted in the Western Hemisphere receded after Venezuela, just at the time Berlin was beginning to be viewed as a disturber there. British control of the seas came, instead, to be valued as a factor in the enforcement of the Monroe Doctrine, and for broader purposes. Policymakers in the United States came to value the order provided by the empire throughout so much of the globe, as well as its general commitment to the Open Door policy for trade. No alliance, as some had hoped, emerged over Pacific matters, and the United States proved insistent upon being the sole policeman itself of boundaries and trade policies in what it saw as its own, rather large, sphere. But a rough political alignment that was to have enormous consequences for twentieth-century world affairs had been formed.[35]

That was not all that was joined, however, although this is often the only aspect of British-American affairs in this period that is discussed by historians. On another plane, Britain and the United States would also continue a rivalry for first place within this order that they both were anxious to see stabilized and maintained, a rivalry the "final" outcome of which would still not be decided for several decades. The United States may have been a status quo power, but it was hardly one without further ambitions. Each of these states was approaching the existing world order from a different perspective. England was seeking to shore up arrangements it saw as providing the basis for its preeminence in the global system, while America's attachment was to a framework it believed over time would yield it first place. The United States was a confident power. It also did not believe it needed revisions in political boundaries; indeed, it recognized that behavior in that direction could undermine international stability. At the turn of this century, it accepted the essentials of the kind of global order that England had led in creating in the nineteenth century as both natural and just. And, on the basis of its industrial might, it looked forward to the time when what Theodore Roosevelt described as the "greatest branch" of the English-speaking peoples would lead that global order.[36]

One could look in a number of directions to examine this competitive aspect of British-American relations at the beginning of the twentieth century, but it was certainly on full display in North America. Not only did England and the United States contest for dominance in Canada, but the end of the Díaz period also set off several years of bitterness over British economic and political influence in Mexico, on both governmental and private levels.[37]

I think that the continentalist idea, finally, can help us to focus on even more than key aspects of early twentieth-century world affairs. There is certainly a good deal of utility in thinking about German and Japanese expansion in the 1930s and 1940s from this perspective. Two near continent-sized powers did come to dominate world affairs during much of the second half of this century, and I doubt that it is irrelevant also to consider and discuss the growing development of continentalist blocs today – i.e., the pursuit of continentalist trade pacts in North America, what the EC may become, etc. – from the perspective laid out above. From an economic and political point of view, there are certainly positive developments that can come from the kind of breaking down of barriers that continentalism involves, most especially where this is carried out on a basis of equality and respect among members. Yet this doesn't eliminate the need to be on guard against the development in the twenty-first century world of methods of global competition, among entities larger than ever before, that might rival or exceed the nightmares of the Cold War. The development of such gigantic and economically powerful competitors poses still other challenges from the standpoint of what continues to be the central international problem of modern times, the creation of peace, democracy, economic justice, and environmental stability for all people throughout all of the regions of the globe.

Notes to Chapter 3

1. Robert E. Hannigan, "Reciprocity 1911: Continentalism and American Weltpolitik," *Diplomatic History* 4 (1980), pp. 1–18.

2. My ideas about the concept of *Mitteleuropa* are based principally on discussions provided in the following works: Fritz Fischer, *Germany's Aims in the First World War* (New York, 1967); F. Fischer, *World Power or Decline* (New York, 1974); F. Fischer, *War of Illusions: German Policies from 1911 to 1914* (New York, 1975); Imanuel Geiss, *German Foreign Policy, 1871–1914* (Boston, 1976); V.R. Berghahn, *Germany and the Approach of War in 1914* (London, 1973); Paul Kennedy, *The Rise of the Anglo-German Antagonism, 1860–1914* (London, 1982); and James Joll, *The Origins of the First World War* (New York, 1984).

3. See, for instance, Holger H. Herwig, *Politics of Frustration: The United States in German Naval Planning, 1889–1941* (Boston, 1976), pp. 1–104.

4. A still useful overview of that earlier continentalism is Richard W. Van Alstyne, *The Rising American Empire* (Chicago, 1965). Also see Charles Vevier, "American Continentalism: An Idea of Expansion, 1845–1910," *American Historical Review* 65 (January 1960), pp. 323–35. The literature on American expansion in the eighteenth and nineteenth centuries is of course enormous.

5. U.S. Department of Commerce, *American Manufactures in Foreign Markets*, Miscellaneous Series, no. 11, 1913, pp. 1–12; Emory R. Johnson et al., *History of the Domestic and*

Foreign Commerce of the United States, 2 vols. (New York, 1915), 2:86–88; William C. Schluter, *The Pre-War Business Cycle, 1907–1914* (New York, 1923), p. 50; Harold U. Faulkner, *The Decline of Laissez-Faire, 1897–1917* (New York, 1951); Mira Wilkins, *The Emergence of Multinational Enterprise: American Business Abroad from the Colonial Era to 1914* (Cambridge, MA, 1970).

6. Friedrich Katz, *The Secret War in Mexico: Europe, The United States and the Mexican Revolution* (Chicago, 1981), p. 22.

7. Frank W. Taussig, *The Tariff History of the United States* (New York, 1923), pp. 361–408; Percy Ashley, *Modern Tariff History* (London, 1920), pp. 237–42; David W. Detzer, "The Politics of the Payne-Aldrich Tariff of 1909" (Ph.D. diss., University of Connecticut, 1970), pp. 4–28; William H. Becker, *The Dynamics of Business-Government Relations: Industry and Exports, 1893–1921* (Chicago, 1982), pp. 50–81; Robert H. Wiebe, *Businessmen and Reform: A Study of the Progressive Movement* (Chicago, 1968), pp. 56–60; John Braeman, *Albert J. Beveridge: American Nationalist* (Chicago, 1971), pp. 123–25; Kenneth W. Hechler, *Insurgency: Personalities of the Taft Era* (New York, 1940), pp. 92–93; Paolo E. Coletta, *The Presidency of William Howard Taft* (Lawrence, KS, 1973), pp. 69–74.

8. Gordon T. Stewart, "'A Special Contiguous Country Economic Regime': An Overview of America's Canadian Policy," *Diplomatic History* 6 (1982), pp. 345–46.

9. Charles M. Pepper, "The Open Door to Canada," undated memorandum, Philander C. Knox Papers, Library of Congress, Washington, D.C.; Taft to Pepper, 12 July 1909, William Howard Taft Papers, Library of Congress, Washington, D.C.

10. "Memorandum Respecting the Tariff Act of the United States, Approved Aug. 5, 1909," Knox Papers; Taussig, *Tariff History*, 403–04; Percy Bidwell, *The Tariff Policy of the United States* (New York, 1933), pp. 49–50; L. Ethan Ellis, *Reciprocity 1911: A Study in Canadian-American Relations* (New Haven, CT, 1939), pp. 7, 15, 35–40; Orville John McDiarmid, *Commercial Policy in the Canadian Economy* (Cambridge, MA, 1946), pp. 220–24.

11. Taft to Helen Taft, 19 March 1910, Taft Papers; Ellis, Reciprocity, pp. 44–45.

12. Memorandum by Charles M. Pepper and M.H. Davis, "Trade Relations with Canada, Newfoundland, and Mexico," 23 May 1910, Knox Papers.

13. David F. Healy, *The United States in Cuba, 1898–1902: Generals, Politicians, and the Search for Policy* (Madison, WI, 1963). On the subsequent integration of Cuba into the North American economy, see Jules Robert Benjamin, *The United States and Cuba, Hegemony and Dependent Development, 1880–1934* (Pittsburgh, PA, 1977) and Louis A. Pérez, Jr., *Cuba Under the Platt Amendment, 1902–1934* (Pittsburgh, PA, 1986).

14. On the Newfoundland effort, see Richard M. Abrams, *Conservatism in a Progressive Era: Massachusetts Politics, 1900–1912* (Cambridge, MA, 1964), pp. 111–13.

15. Katz, *Secret War*, pp. 80–84.

16. Katz, *Secret War*, pp. 21–27, 39.

17. Ellis, *Reciprocity*, pp. 44–45, 56; Donald Creighton, *A History of Canada: Dominion of the North* (Boston, 1958), pp. 432–36.

18. "Summary of Agreement Reached Jan. 16," Knox Papers; U.S., Congress, Senate, *Canadian Reciprocity*, Sen. doc. 787, 61st Cong., 3d sess., 1911, pp. 4–9.

19. Taft to W.O. Bradley, 27 February 1911, Taft Papers.

20. U.S. Congress, Senate, *Canadian Reciprocity*, v-vi. The classic study of American resource management in this period is Samuel P. Hays, *Conservation and the Gospel of Efficiency: The Progressive Conservation Movement, 1890–1920* (Cambridge, MA, 1959).

21. Taft to Roosevelt, 10 January 1911, Taft Papers.

22. Norman Penlington, *The Alaska Boundary Dispute: A Critical Reappraisal* (Toronto, 1972), p. 47; Roosevelt to J.H. Wilson, 12 July 1899 in Elting E. Morison, ed., *The Letters of Theodore Roosevelt*, 8 vols. (Cambridge, MA, 1951–1954), 2:1032; Pepper, "The Open Door to Canada," pp. 15–16. For background, see Donald F. Warner, *The Idea of Continental Union: Agitation for the Annexation of Canada to the United States, 1849–1893* (Lexington, KY, 1960); John Bartlet Brebner, *North Atlantic Triangle: The Interplay of Canada, the United States, and Great Britain* (New Haven, CT, 1945); Kenneth Bourne, *Britain and the Balance of Power in North America, 1815–1908* (Berkeley, CA, 1967).

23. Address before the Associated Press and the American Newspaper Publishers Associa-

tion, New York, 27 April 1911, in James D. Richardson, ed., *A Compilation of the Messages and Papers of the Presidents*, 20 vols. (New York, 1897–1914), 17:7975. On the "National Policy," begun under the Conservative Party but largely retained by the Liberals, see Peter B. Waite, *Canada, 1874–1896: Arduous Destiny* (Toronto, 1971); Robert Craig Brown, *Canada's National Policy, 1883–1900: A Study in Canadian-American Relations* (Princeton, 1964); Robert Craig Brown and Ramsay Cook, *Canada, 1896–1921: A Nation Transformed* (Toronto, 1974), pp. 18–21; McDiarmid, *Commercial Policy*, pp. 74–83, 155–79, 203–09; Creighton, *History of Canada*, pp. 345–94. For important perspectives on the Tariff Reform movement, see Bernard Semmell, *Imperialism and Social Reform: English Social-Imperial Thought, 1895–1914* (Garden City, NY, 1968), pp. 74–117, 150–56; Robert J. Scally, *The Origins of the Lloyd George Coalition: The Politics of Social Imperialism, 1900–1918* (Princeton, NJ, 1975), pp. 96–145. Paul Kennedy discusses Tariff Reform as an issue in Anglo–German relations. Interestingly, the British interpreted German commercial policy toward Canada at the beginning of the decade as an effort to block closer imperial relations, and Pan-Germans urged a European economic union under Germany's leadership as a way of responding to Tariff Reform and Imperial Preference. Many in England also saw the German fleet as aimed against Imperial Preference. See *The Rise of the Anglo-German Antagonism*, pp. 262–64, 314, 342.

24. Penlington, *Alaska Boundary Dispute*, pp. 33–34; W.M. Baker, "A Case Study of Anti-Americanism in English-Speaking Canada: The Election Campaign of 1911," *Canadian Historical Review* 51 (1970): pp. 426–449; Ellis, *Reciprocity*, pp. 88–186; Brown and Cook, *Canada, 1896–1921*, pp. 180–85. An interesting set of articles discussing subsequent Canadian-American economic and other relations is Ian Lumsden, ed., *The Americanization of Canada* (Toronto, 1970).

25. Wallerstein's framework is not without its problems, but I think this basic emphasis is extremely important. See, for instance, his *The Capitalist World-Economy* (Cambridge, MA, 1979).

26. See, for instance, Eric Hobsbawm's recent *The Age of Empire, 1875–1914* (New York, 1987).

27. This quote is from Kennedy's *The Realities Behind Diplomacy: Background Influences on British External Policy, 1865–1980* (1981), p. 34. See also his paper "Mahan versus Mackinder: Two Interpretations of British Sea Power" in Paul Kennedy, *Strategy and Diplomacy, 1870–1945* (1984).

28. This topic is discussed, for instance, in Burton I. Kaufman, "The Organizational Dimension of United States Foreign Economic Policy, 1900–1920," *Business History Review* 46 (1972): pp. 17–44.

29. Roosevelt to A.T. Mahan, 3 May 1897, Morison, ed., *Letters*, 1:607; Roosevelt to H.C. Lodge, 19 June 1901, Morison, ed., *Letters*, 3:97.

30. See *The Peculiarities of German History: Bourgeois Society and Politics in Nineteenth-Century Germany* (Oxford, 1984), wherein these authors question the long-held view that Germany's development took a dramatically different path than was the case in other western industrial capitalist states. Coming at this question from yet another perspective entirely is Arno J. Mayer, *The Persistence of the Old Regime: Europe to the Great War* (New York, 1981).

31. Kennedy, *The Realities Behind Diplomacy*, p. 69.

32. There are more broad studies of domestic affairs than there are of American foreign affairs for these years. For the former, see, for instance, Robert H. Wiebe, *The Search for Order, 1877–1920* (New York, 1967); James Weinstein, *The Corporate Ideal in the Liberal State, 1900–1918* (Boston, 1968); and Paul Boyer, *Urban Masses and Moral Order in America, 1820–1920* (Cambridge, MA, 1978). Two of the best overviews of American foreign policy for these years are Lloyd C. Gardner, "American Foreign Policy, 1900–1921: A Second Look at the Realist Critique of American Diplomacy," in Barton J. Bernstein, ed., *Towards a New Past: Dissenting Essays in American History* (New York, 1969) and Joseph A. Fry, "In Search of an Orderly World: U.S. Imperialism, 1898–1912," in John M. Carroll and George C. Herring, eds., *Modern American Diplomacy* (Wilmington, DE, 1986). I am currently at work on an interpretive history of American foreign policy in the period from the late 1890s to 1917.

33. Colonel House, for instance, noted that Woodrow Wilson told him that he considered war as an economic proposition ruinous, "but he thought there was no more glorious way to die than in battle." Coming from "the son of a minister," House was surprised. "It strengthened my opinion though as to his unusual courage both moral and physical." "From the Diary of Colonel House, 14 February 1913," in Arthur S. Link, et al., eds., *The Papers of Woodrow Wilson* (Princeton, NJ, 1966–), 27:113.

34. See, for instance, Lester D. Langley, *The Banana Wars: An Inner History of American Empire, 1900–1934* (Lexington, KY, 1983) and Stuart Creighton Miller, "*Benevolent Assimilation*": *The American Conquest of the Philippines, 1899–1903* (New Haven, CT, 1982).

35. For some of the issues between the two powers prior to 1900, see Edward P. Crapol, *America for Americans: Economic Nationalism and Anglophobia in the Late Nineteenth Century* (Westport, CT, 1973). There is an extensive literature on the British-American rapprochement. Some of the more central works are A.E. Campbell, *Great Britain and the United States, 1895–1903* (London, 1960); R.G. Neale, *Great Britain and United States Expansion: 1898–1900* (Lansing, MI, 1966); Charles S. Campbell, Jr., *Anglo-American Understanding, 1898–1903* (Baltimore, MD, 1957); Bradford Perkins, *The Great Rapprochement: England and the United States, 1895–1914* (New York, 1968); and Stuart Anderson, *Race and Rapprochement: Anglo-Saxonism and Anglo-American Relations, 1895–1904* (East Brunswick, NJ, 1981). The overall context from London's side has been discussed well in George Monger's classic *The End of Isolation: British Foreign Policy, 1900–1907* (London, 1963). On the American side, Theodore Roosevelt's correspondence in the years after the Venezuela boundary crisis is extremely illuminating. The quote cited here is from Roosevelt to H.C. Lodge, 19 June 1901, in Morison, ed., *Letters*, 3:97.

36. Roosevelt to Henry White, 30 March 1896, Morison, ed., *Letters*, 1:523. On the background for such "visions of national greatness," see, for instance, Michael H. Hunt, *Ideology and U.S. Foreign Policy* (New Haven, CT, 1987), pp. 19–45.

37. On this topic, Peter Calvert, *The Mexican Revolution, 1910–1914: The Diplomacy of Anglo-American Conflict* (Cambridge, MA, 1968) has now been superseded by Katz, *Secret War* (cf. pp. 161–67, 170–80). Other aspects of British-American competition in the early twentieth century are dealt with in Warren G. Kneer, *Great Britain and the Caribbean, 1901–1913: A Study in Anglo-American Relations* (East Lansing, MI, 1975) and Kathleen Burk, *Britain, America and the Sinews of War, 1914–1918* (Boston, 1985).

4

The Advantages of Cooperation: German-American Friendship as a Fundamental Principle of German *Weltpolitik* and Theodore Roosevelt's Big Stick Diplomacy

Raimund Lammersdorf

Let me point out immediately that I will confine myself to my own period – i.e., to the presidency of Theodore Roosevelt – both because I feel more comfortable in this period and because you will probably gain more from remarks substantiated by some primary research than from second-hand reading or speculation.[1]

From the beginning of the Roosevelt administration, the German government was convinced that the new president was friendly towards Germany, and it was decided to nurture this friendliness. To persuade the U.S. government and the American public of Germany's good intentions, the Kaiser wrote friendly letters, gave presents (like the statue of Frederick the Great), and sent his brother, Prince Henry of Prussia, on a good-will tour to America. More importantly, however, the Bülow administration consistently went out of its way through the next seven years to avoid any possibility of friction between the two countries and to enlist American support for German foreign policy goals. The Germans tried to convince President Roosevelt that Germany's interests and the interests of the United States were identical. This was believed to be true particularly in the case of the Open Door policy in China, where Berlin incited Roosevelt to neutralize the country during the Russo-Japanese War and then helped him to achieve peace. By his compliance to German suggestions, Roosevelt seemed to have helped Germany stop the development of an Anglo-Russo-French alliance to divide China. The Germans also were convinced that they had been successful in getting Roosevelt's help during the Moroccan crisis and the Algeciras conference.

Beyond direct help in their diplomacy, what Germany tried to gain

Notes to Chapter 4 can be found on page 92.

from American friendship was further isolation of Great Britain as part of their *Weltpolitik.* The developing Anglo-American rapprochement – one of several direct threats to this grotesque foreign policy concept – had to be stopped. German diplomats tried their best to avert this peril by sending Roosevelt dozens of memoranda meant to prove the evil ways of the British, whom they accused of planning to appropriate the Chinese Yangtse valley. Ultimately, the Germans were most successful in proving to themselves that the president was indeed suspicious of the British government.

As far as economic relations between Germany and the United States were concerned, the idea of a combined *Mitteleuropa* against the U.S. had long since been abandoned when the emperor, shortly after Roosevelt became president, wrote:

> Once we have created the ground on which for some time we could pursue or champion identical interests with the United States . . . we must together with the Americans inflict heavy losses on the British in this area, namely destruction of English world trade, their maritime commerce, etc., so that they will be forced to be on better political terms with us.[2]

In the interest of keeping the president's friendship, hence to gain major political advantages, any economic confrontation, like a tariff war, for example, was to be avoided by Germany at all costs. For the German foreign office, there was never any doubt that the trade policy had to serve the needs of the foreign policy.[3]

The British clearly realized that the Germans tried to outrank them in popularity. They never truly believed that the Germans would fully succeed in this since the Anglo-American rapprochement continued to progress steadily. That this growing friendship was helped along by a strong cultural and political affinity, especially in both government circles, is a well-known fact. But one often overlooks the conservative Balfour administration's certain unease with the American republic in general and the young president in particular. Foreign Secretary Lord Lansdowne and his protegée, Mortimer Durand, ambassador in Washington, found the Americans to be "excitable, and their patriotism is of a somewhat aggressive character. . . . " They thought President Roosevelt "a strange being" and constantly feared that he would be influenced by William II's "wild messages." Lansdowne once confessed: "Roosevelt terrifies me almost as much as the German Emperor."[4] Consequently, during the Anglo-German crisis of the spring and summer of 1905, they tried to keep the president from meddling in these strictly European affairs. His unavoidable interference during the Algeciras conference was considered counterproductive and discouraged.

During the first two years of the Roosevelt administration, there did emerge in the Far East a tentative cooperation against Russian expansion in Manchuria. But here, too, difficulties developed. Although Great Britain was interested in closer ties with America, there were other relationships – in particular, the Anglo-Japanese alliance – that were more important to the country. Thus the Far Eastern consensus evaporated over London's stubborn resistance against Roosevelt's demands to put pressure on its Japanese ally during the Portsmouth Peace Conference.

That Anglo-American relations did not deteriorate is evidence of how strong the cultural and ideological ties had already become. It helped, of course, that all major disagreements between them had been resolved and that other differences concerning foreign-policy issues were never too significant. Finally, the appointment of the liberal Edward Grey as the new foreign secretary, who supported a lot of Roosevelt's political ideas and finally removed Durand from Washington, harmonized transatlantic affairs.

As far as he was concerned, President Roosevelt welcomed Anglo-German competition for America's friendship. But because he considered Germany to be a potential adversary, particularly in Latin America, he encouraged closer ties with Berlin and welcomed all attempts at fostering a better relationship between the two nations. He realized that if he made the German emperor feel as if he had more to gain from American friendship than from an ill-advised adventure in the Western Hemisphere, the emperor was less likely to pose a threat. At the same time, the president enlarged the Navy, not as a reaction to the German naval program, but in order to encourage German friendliness. The fleet was built with no particular enemy in mind. It was not meant to deter a clear and present danger, but to keep other nations, like Germany, Japan, and Russia, from considering military options while dealing with the United States. In a sense, one could call this a policy of proto-deterrence that allowed for cordial relations with a potential foe.

President Roosevelt successfully exploited the wooing of Germany and Great Britain for his own foreign policy goals. He welcomed British wishes for cooperation in the Far East at the same time he ruthlessly exploited their willingness to compromise by insisting that they accept his solution to the Alaska-boundary dispute. He also was amused at Germany's attempts to gain his favor through fancy presents, but as long as William followed the Open Door policy in China, whatever his motives, he saw no reason why he shouldn't cooperate with the emperor. Although mildly suspicious about the emperor's tactics, Roosevelt genuinely welcomed Berlin's offers of help in the neutralization of China and during the Portsmouth Peace Conference.

The Kaiser has become a monomaniac about getting into communication
with me every time he drinks three pen'orth of conspiracy against his life and
power; but as has been so often the case for the last year, he at the moment is
playing our game – or, as I should more politely put it, his interests and ours,
together with those of humanity in general, are identical.[5]

President Roosevelt certainly did not accept Germany's constant
accusations against Great Britain. Neither could he believe that the Germans were trying to build a continental coalition against England. He
was, however, disturbed by what he saw as an unnecessary conflict
between civilized nations, calling it "as funny a case as I have ever seen
of mutual distrust and fear bringing two peoples to the verge of war." He
tried to mediate, but claimed it "perfectly hopeless to try to bring about
a better understanding between England and Germany. I attempted it in
vain."[6] Germany's provocation in Morocco, and finally the infamous
Daily Telegraph interview, worsened Roosevelt's image of the emperor,
but only to the point that he considered William a nuisance rather than a
danger.

At the end of his administration, Roosevelt looked back on his foreign
policy with satisfaction. "I do not believe that Germany has any designs
that would bring her in conflict with the Monroe Doctrine," he wrote in
a letter to the new Secretary of State Philander C. Knox. "The last seven
years have tended steadily toward a better understanding of Germany on
our part, and a more thorough understanding on the part of Germany
that she must not expect colonial expansion in South America."[7]

If one attempts to find a unified model based on a particular concept
of what constitutes a world power that would adequately describe the
position of the United States and Germany in the international system,
one would have to assume that basic aims, policies, and structures are
equally shared by all powers. This description pitches the United States'
and Germany's respective foreign policies against each other as if they
were structurally identical. But I do not think that this is the case. The
two countries were not working with the same rulebook of tactics and
strategies that would tell them how world powers had to behave. The
United States' contact with the world was based on a wholly different
concept, philosophy, and motivation.

The primacy of American domestic politics was one of the strongest
factors in American foreign policy. The voting public did not wish the
government to take an important role in the international system. Thus
the American involvement in Europe and elsewhere was, though often
forceful and significant, sporadic and inconsistent. Even when American
interests were obviously endangered, like when Russia tried to prohibit

American commerce in Manchuria in 1904, the public reaction against any foreign adventurism significantly dampened Roosevelt's willingness to intervene.

In contrast, the paramount importance Germany placed on its foreign policy is only too obvious. The German government spent vastly more energy, time, and resources on its diplomatic ventures, to which it tied the country's future. Also, compared to the Americans, German foreign policymakers acted almost autonomously or in a vacuum, if you like, free of most public interference. From this lack of democratic control, of course, an unrealistic, dangerous, and finally disastrous foreign policy emerged.

Instead of one unifying model, juxtaposing the genuinely different foreign policies of these disparate political entities will produce a much more varied and, to my mind, more convincing picture of their complex relationship. From this point of view, differences in German and American foreign policy are not just different dynamics in their otherwise similar expansionisms. Nor did they pursue the same goal of "restructuring of the world power system" on different paths. They did not perceive that their interests collided almost everywhere on the globe. Indeed, if anything, relations between Germany and the United States during the first decade of the twentieth century are characterized by major misunderstandings about each other's political goals.

Nor was there a continuous development of German-American antagonism from 1889 to 1917. I would suggest that this idea is the result of a teleologic vision of foreign relations developing inevitably towards World War I. Looking for explanations for the eventual enmity between Germany and America, one tends to overemphasize any conflict, disagreement, or competition as part of a continuum of bad relations. Industrial, economic, financial, political, and military competition can all be interpreted as part of worsening relations between Germany and other states, but we tend to forget the original vision of the decisionmakers and foreign-policy planners who could not see the brutal outcome of 1917. If we ignore this demarcation of what we in hindsight perceive to be an epoch, if we do not see every event before the United States' declaration of war as leading to it, we come across new and, to my mind, more coherent explanations of transatlantic relations at the beginning of the twentieth century.

Notes to Chapter 4

1. See my Ph.D. thesis "Anfänge einer Weltmacht: Transatlantische Beziehungen während der Präsidentschaft Theodore Roosevelts, 1901–1909 [Beginnings of a World Power: Transatlantic Relations during Theodore Roosevelt's Presidency, 1901–1909]," Freie Universität Berlin, 1991.

2. Metternich to Auswärtiges Amt, 29 October 1901, with marginal note by William II., Politisches Archiv des Auswärtigen Amtes (PA), Vereinigte Staaten 16 Bd. 1, secr.

3. See, e.g., Memorandum, 5 February 1906, PA Ver. St. 16 Bd. 18.

4. Durand to Grey, 15 December 1905, 2 and 26 January 1906, Public Record Office, London, PRO F.O.800 81; Percy Sykes, *The Right Honourable Sir Mortimer Durand: A Biography* (London, 1926), p. 299; Durand to Grey, 11 January 1906, Nr. 9, PRO F.O. 371 158, 2703; Lansdowne to Durand, 4 Febuary 1905, PRO F.O.800 144; Lansdowne to Balfour, 27 April 1905, British Library 49729.

5. Theodore Roosevelt to John Hay, 2 April 1905, Elting E. Morison, ed., *The Letters of Theodore Roosevelt* (Cambridge, MA, 1951–54), vol. 4, p. 1157.

6. Roosevelt to Hay, 30 March 1905 and Roosevelt to George von Lengerke Meyer, 22 May 1905, Morison, *Letters*, vol. 4, pp. 1150, 1157, 1189.

7. Roosevelt to Philander Chase Knox, 8 Febuary 1909, Morison, *Letters*, vol. 6, p. 1511.

Discussion

Since the papers of Edward Crapol, Ragnhild Fiebig-von Hase, and Robert Hannigan covered a broad spectrum of international problems during the two decades prior to World War I, it was no surprise that the discussion included a variety of questions as well. However, a set of issues was raised by most participants in the discussion: the origins and goals of German *Weltpolitik*, America's rise to world-power status, the tools of both American and German policy, the British-American rapprochement, the roots of German-American confrontations prior to World War I, and above all, the significance – or as some thought, the insignificance – of economic elements in international relations during the period under discussion.

Wolfgang Mommsen, in an extensive comment on all of the papers, welcomed the fact that, after approximately 50 years, the attempts of Alfred Vagts to interpret German-American relations not only in terms of diplomacy but also in terms of economic relations had found "a worthy continuation." However, he cautioned that economic rivalry and economic competition were seen as major factors in international relations, and then commented on the interrelationship of economics and politics. He challenged the idea that economic competition must necessarily have a negative influence on political relations. It seemed necessary to achieve "a clearer distinction between objective factors and the subjective presentation of things at the time." In addition, "economic progress of one nation need not necessarily mean economic loss of the other." In this context, Stephen Schuker mentioned that the United States did not have a coherent economic foreign policy prior to World War I. He argued that if "one tries to draw parallels between German *Weltpolitik* and American *Weltpolitik*, one can easily overloook the structural weaknesses" in American foreign policy. He generally warned not to overestimate economic factors either in American or German foreign policy: "But the phenomenon of German *Weltpolitik* before 1914 is that informal imperialism conducted by business and supported by international finance and formal imperialism are totally different, they operated on different levels." Whenever it came "to the crunch, the German Government always put politics first and trade second," Mommsen suggested in explicit agreement with Raimund Lammersdorf's contribution. When referring to the United States, Mommsen cited Max Weber's dictum that the main and most important result of the First World War was the economic world dominance of the United States, but he thought that this economic dimension had not been so important for the period before 1914. He also was "very sceptical" as to whether one could follow Robert Hannigan's approach in comparing American continentalism with the German concept of *Mitteleuropa*, since before 1914 Berlin had never envisaged territorial control of any European territory – either direct or indirect.

When comparing German and American imperialism, some participants (David Kennedy, Wolfgang Mommsen, Stephen Schuker) repeatedly pointed out that, prior to World War I, the United States still lacked the machinery to carry out an effective economic foreign policy. But Lloyd Gardner warned about carrying that argument "too far in the sense that there was no American historical association for the 1890s and that therefore there presumably was no American historical writing." Edward Crapol, Lloyd Garner, and Robert Hannigan made extensive comments on the evolution of American foreign policy before World War I. Lack of an organizational framework for the realization of overseas economic expansion should not be misunderstood as proof of a lack of interest either by businessmen or the federal government. The power elites' views were difficult to measure in terms of export figures, immediate economic benefits, or diplomatic treaties, it was admitted. But of course, there were not only visible diplomatic actions or commercial transactions that counted.

In this context, Crapol, Gardner, and Hannigan repeatedly stressed the conceptual visions of American policymakers for the future. What was very much at stake at the turn of the century was the future orientation of American foreign policy, the shaping of an international environment in a way that would best serve national interests. As Robert Hannigan put it: "I do not think that American foreign policy prior to World War I can be understood just in economic terms, and I think that economic concerns have to be filtered through the subjective viewpoint of the policymakers. On the other hand, economics was considered essential. And it was considered essential, as many policy makers felt, because America's status and prosperity would be based on it in the future." Hannigan thought it "very important to recognize that in the case of the United States, American policymakers were to a very large extent operating, prior to World War I, out of the feeling that the kind of world they wanted was threatened. It was a world that they considered natural and in their interests, and it was a world they felt was in jeopardy of being dramatically changed." Whether the United States "needed it the way it was at the moment or not, they wanted it that way for the future," and therefore "it is very important to look at these issues over time rather than in an absolute sense. This is in fact a very critical period in the evolution of America as a world power."

But why did an American-British rapprochement materialize at the turn of the century? And why did an antagonism develop between the United States and Germany? These questions stimulated a discussion on both the interrelationship of economics and politics and the potential importance of Latin America as a zone of conflict between the United States and European powers. If one concentrated only on the economic perspectives, one would expect a major confrontation between Great Britain and the United States, Edward Crapol argued. Because these countries were major rivals, one would expect that "they had been at loggerheads, but of course they were not." The simple explanation is that British leaders were willing to make concessions in Latin America, as was demonstrated by the outcome of the Venezuelan Crisis of 1895/96. British diplomats had already grasped the significance of the United States' rise to world power status. As Edward Crapol put it, "the British in the 1880s and the 1890s already see the handwriting on the wall."

While British leaders gradually prepared to comply with American wishes, especially in Latin America, this seemed to be different with Germany. London finally recognized Washington's interpretations and reinterpretations of the Monroe Doctrine, for example. Imperial Germany, on the other hand, never fully complied with Washington's expectations vis-à-vis Berlin and the Monroe Doctrine. This was repeatedly pointed out by Ragnhild Fiebig-von Hase: "Berlin and Washington were at odds about how to define the Monroe Doctrine." Germany was interested in having the Monroe Doctrine limited to territorial questions, but obviously the Americans were not prepared to have the Monroe Doctrine defined in such narrow terms. But was there any such thing as an economic Monroe Doctrine? And would an economic interpretation of the Monroe Doctrine imply the exclusion of economic activities by non-American powers?

Georges-Henri Soutou held the opinion that "the economic Monroe Doctrine did not have in mind to expel Europeans from Latin America." It was to make sure that the Americans would get "their fair share of Latin American trade, not really to expel the Europeans." This view was shared by Raimund Lammersdorf, who characterized Theodore Roosevelt's attitude towards Germany as basically friendly. President Roosevelt even encouraged German investments in Latin America as long as there was "fair competition."

But who should define the term "fair competition?" This was exactly the source of potential conflict. The Venezuelan crisis of 1902/03 demonstrated that Americans wanted to use an American definition. Obviously, the political dimensions of this problem had never been grasped by the Reich leadership – contary to the British government's decisions during the 1890s. Potential and actual German-American conflicts where intensified by false perceptions. Both countries "had difficulties with their images of each other and the judgement on the other's foreign policy" (Peter Krüger). This view was supported by Ragnhild Fiebig, who did not argue that economic clashes between great or world powers would immediately lead to political clashes or war. But she argued that "economic expansion into the peripheral regions of the world had political implications for the political position of a world power," and she expressed her conviction that it was German presence in Latin America "that really haunted the Americans."

Given the variety of problems discussed from differing perspectives it was no surprise that there was no consensus at the end of the session. However, it became quite clear that the impact of economic factors on the development of the German-American antagonism prior to World War I. Scholars of European history should remember the fact that the United States had become a world power by the turn of the century. This had significant impact on all European powers. Therefore, the nineteenth-century European power system cannot serve as a model for the twentieth century. The twentieth-century international system must be defined in global terms long before America's intervention in World War I. All papers included convincing arguments, as Gerald Feldman summed up, to better understand this transformation and its implications for the changing relationship between the United States, Germany, and Great Britain during the two decades prior to World War I.

PART II
Cultural Relations in Decline

5

Inventing the Enemy: German–American Cultural Relations, 1900–1917

Frank Trommler

German-American cultural relations have attracted considerable interest since the nineteenth century when a large number of American scholars and students visited German universities, which provided a model for the reform of the American college as a research university. For a long time historians viewed these relations as an indicator of a traditionally amiable encounter between two emerging nations; the relationship was not problematic as long as there was no real conflict of interest in their political or economic spheres. When this period came to an end in the late 1890s, however, cultural relations between the United States and the German Reich increasingly became an issue in its own right. After both nations embarked on imperialist ventures in the Far East and Latin America in the decades before and after 1900, a spirit of competition also entered the cultural sphere. From then on it became less opportune to consider the latter sphere as a mere indicator of political developments. The growing animosity between the two nations, resulting in the declaration of war in 1917, was preceded by a cultural alienation so intense that even the most skeptical of contemporaries were caught by surprise.

This paper will delineate the developments that led to that growing interest in cultural politics. It will situate those politics within the relations of the two countries and the confrontations of the war period. Due to the lack of scholarly studies, the problems will be addressed in a rather schematic fashion.[1] Three aspects seem to be crucial and deserve particular attention: (1) the official contacts of the two governments in the sphere of cultural relations; (2) the politization of the concept of culture as an important ingredient of the international confrontations in the period of imperialism; and (3) the role of the concept of culture for the identity and the fate of German-Americans and for the articulation of the American antagonism against imperial Germany in the period of World War I.

Notes to Chapter 5 can be found on page 122

The Emperor's Intervention and the Professors' Mission

The extensive cultural exchange between Americans and Germans before 1914 flourished without an established governmental network. As in most countries, these contacts originated in private, religious, or academic initiatives. It was not until 1920 that the German government overcame the traditional restrictions on its conduct of cultural politics, a domain of the individual German states, and established a *Kulturpolitische Abteilung* in the Foreign Ministry, which was to coordinate official cultural contacts with other countries.[2] Obviously, the effectiveness of cultural propaganda as part of foreign policy in the period of World War I was not lost on politicians and bureaucrats. Despite similar experiences, the American government did not establish an official program of international cultural cooperation until 1938 – a "latecomer in the field."[3] Its most momentous effect on Germany was felt, of course, after World War II, when the Marshall Plan was accompanied by a program of cultural reconstruction, which led to a period of close collaboration with the Federal Republic.

The lack of an institutional network for cultural exchange before World War I seems to account for the wildly differing evaluations of the few, yet broadly recognized, ventures. While the diplomatic services provided the main logistics, they did not necessarily provide the specific rationale beyond the usual declarations of international cooperation. Thus, the fact that Emperor Wilhelm II involved himself in several highly publicized initiatives after 1900 was prone to invoke both hostile speculations about German intentions and high praise for his generosity and foresight. The differences in the evaluations became apparent in the decades before 1914. The exchange programs for professors and students, for instance, which first were portrayed as an expression of the remarkable understanding between Wilhelm II and President Theodore Roosevelt, assumed a sinister quality at the outbreak of war when American journalists "revealed" them to be a part of a German masterplot to subvert American education. None of the official cultural initiatives before 1914, which generally showed Germany as the more active of the two governments, escaped the accusation of having been used for ill-meaning purposes.

Most of these ventures took place in the realm of universities and higher education, which had been a particularly fertile ground for cultural contacts in the nineteenth century. Yet, where the previous encounters had been motivated by academic interests through which participation in German *Bildung*, *Kultur*, and *Wissenschaft* provided important credentials for American elites, the new initiatives tended towards a symbolic mission that entailed a political concept of education and a prestige-based definition of culture.

The representative tone was set by the unexpectedly generous gift of copies and casts of masterworks of German art with which Wilhelm II endowed the newly created Germanic Museum at Harvard University in 1901. While the value of the portals of the cathedrals in Hildesheim and Freiberg was beyond doubt, their imposing white plaster casts in the Harvard museum objectified more than just great medieval art from Germany – namely, the claim that German art and culture ranked with the best examples of other countries. Kuno Francke, a professor of German literature and culture at Harvard, had initiated the founding of the Germanic Museum as well as the exchange professorships between Harvard and Berlin out of a strong sense of competition with the French, whose influence in art and literature had become dominant in the late nineteenth century.[4] Francke's proposition was eagerly accepted by Wilhelm II and Friedrich Althoff, the powerful *Ministerialdirektor* in the Prussian Ministry of Culture, who wished to counter the influence of France and Great Britain with first-rate artistic and intellectual presentations that would impress the American elites and instill in German-Americans a sense of pride of the achievements of their forefathers and the grandeur of the new Reich.[5]

The 1902 visit of the emperor's brother, Prince Heinrich of Prussia, was more clearly labeled a publicity stunt to enhance sympathy for the Germans, yet its high point – or at least what the German ambassador von Holleben hoped would be the high point – was also organized with academic decorum: the bestowal of an honorary doctorate by Harvard University. How academic it was can be ascertained by its description in a letter from Harvard's president, Charles W. Eliot: "We had lately a few days visit in the United States from Prince Henry of Prussia – a somewhat theatrical performance contrived apparently by Emperor William. It all went very well, the Prince being a simple, natural person who got used in a day to our troublesome democratic ways."[6]

A similar tone of bemused sarcasm can be found in the reaction to the ceremoniousness with which the exchange of professors between Harvard and the Berlin university was instituted in 1905. This time an American delivered the performance: the Harvard theologian, Francis Peabody. He carried a personal message from President Roosevelt to Wilhelm II, who honored him by attending his introductory lecture. It was the first time the German emperor had set foot in the Berlin university, which was about three hundred meters from his castle. When John Burgess from Columbia University, which instituted an exchange professorship shortly thereafter, lectured in Berlin in 1907, the Kaiser received him, as the Washington Evening Star reported, "very kindly." In fact, "the emperor hypnotized his guest." The paper remarked, however, that "hypnotizing distinguished visitors, even lecturers, is part of [the Kaiser's] business."[7] The realization that the idea for exchange professorships, which soon involved several universities (Cornell, Chicago, Wisconsin), was ascribed to the emperor himself might have added to the receptiveness of older American professors for this kind of treatment. Subsequently, some of those who had been students in Germany tried to mediate between Germany and the United States when the tensions mounted in 1914.

The only academic venture other than the student exchanges that reached beyond the idiosyncrasies of these prestige programs was the founding of the Amerika-Institut in Berlin by the Prussian Ministry of Culture in 1910. Its programmatic agenda, formulated by the Harvard professor Hugo Münsterberg, was to provide the basis for scholarly studies of the United States and its German element and to facilitate intensive contacts between American and German scholars.[8] However, while the institute enjoyed some acclaim under Münsterberg's initial directorship, it lost its momentum after his return to Harvard and never became a high-level research institute. Nor did it help to counteract the sagging reputation of German scholarship in the United States.

The lack of such an institute seems to have contributed to the diffuse, uninformed, and mostly self-serving academic diplomacy that marked the travels of German professors in the United States between 1904 and 1917. Received as envoys of a prestigious cultural tradition, scholars such as Hermann Oncken, Eduard Meyer, Erich Marcks, and Eugen Kühnemann used the podium for a presentation of their own version of American-German rapprochement,[9] which usually meant the improvement of American education and public life through an infusion of German culture. Who else but the academic leader was qualified to project the prestige of the German culture above the merely commercial and material machinations of this vast continent? How else but through spiritual symbols could the idealism of German *Bildung* be made manifest?

The equation of symbolism and education was tolerated when a German professor addressed an American audience, but only as long as he did not overstep his role as a guest. This equation lost its effect, however, when it appeared in the direct diplomacy of the German emperor – for example, in Wilhelm's offer to send a bronze statue of Frederick the Great to the land of the Bill of Rights. The Kaiser meant this gift to be an expression of thanks for the kind reception of Prince Heinrich and as a sign of the close relations of the two great nations.[10] Roosevelt, despite opposition from the Congress and the press, had to accept the unsolicited gift, and in 1904 placed it inconspicuously on the esplanade of the Army War College at the Washington Barracks Reservations. The Washington Evening Star summarized its bewilderment with the sarcastic suggestion that in return for the statue of Frederick, the United States might give Germany one of James Monroe. It "would be a neat exchange of compliments," the paper concluded, adding that "James Monroe smiling down from a lofty height upon the people of Berlin would be an edifying and perhaps a peace-preserving spectacle."[11] In view of the German government's unsuccessful challenge to the Monroe Doctrine in the Venezuela crisis, such a gift would have indeed been seen as a provocative gesture.

What was objectionable to the American public in these imperial undertakings was less the aristocratic and elitist spirit itself; moral symbolism and elitist rhetoric were, in fact, on the ascendency in the period of Roosevelt and Wilson.[12] The objections arose, rather, against the abrupt interventions of an individual authority who assumed the weight of a whole culture, a whole nation, in a minor piece of prestige politics, leaving the other side aghast as to its meaning. Of course, any contact with the German emperor brought immediate attention. Yet, at the same time, it exposed Germany to direct critique and transformed the nation into a mere appendage of an odd personality. Thus Wilhelm's attempt to harmonize relations with the United States through high-minded cultural gestures did not just fail, but became increasingly counterproductive as they created easy targets for criticism, which helped to crystallize a vague antagonistic sentiment against Germany and German culture. The statue of Frederick the Great is a case in point: "During the World War, the disposition of this statue furnished the theme for many speeches and attacks upon Germany."[13]

That there were established patterns of sentiments and animosities in the American public long before the anti-Kaiser feeling emerged should not be overlooked. Leading back to the stormy altercations in American relations with France, they add to the historical irony that permeates these high-level performances. The constellation had been quite different in 1870: France's star, personified in its emperor, Napoleon III, was at its nadir, and Germany's star at its zenith. Now the French were favored while Emperor Wilhelm II was "fearful and funny." As Bismarck and Napoleon III had widely personified the image of their people, now the Kaiser came to personify his people. The Germans were described as "arrogant," "power-mad," "militaristic and imperialistic," and "fond of vainglory and conquest." Norbert Muhlen observed: "If one took the editorials written about the French before 1870, they served with minor changes as editorials about the Germans in 1910."[14]

On the whole, the academic diplomacy of the professors did not fare better, as even Friedrich Schmidt-Ott, who oversaw the exchanges in the Prussian Ministry of Culture, conceded in his memoirs.[15] There were, of course, institutional obstacles; one-time lecturers and guest professorships, for example, rarely have long-term effects. Yet the main goal of renewing the sagging reputation of the German universities was not met. The enrollment of American students in Germany had continued to decline since the 1880's when French and British universities facilitated easier access for foreigners.[16] Increasingly, the German academic system was characterized for its authoritarianism and lack of democratic values. This critique reflected less the real state of scientific achievements and more the adjustment to the growing sense of competition in scholarship and science – an adjustment made easier by the rigidity with which German academics maintained their hierarchical thinking in both scholarship and academic life. A typical response was that of the famous psychologist William James to Hugo Münsterberg's design for the International Congress of Arts and Sciences at the World's Fair in St. Louis in 1904. Münsterberg had been able to lure the *crème* of German academics, people such as Max Weber, Wilhelm Ostwald, Adolf Harnack, Ernst Troeltsch, Karl Lamprecht, Ferdinand Tönnies, and Werner Sombart, to the New World. He conceptualized the Congress as a great interdisciplinary demonstration of the unity of knowledge.[17] James used well-established formulas in his criticism of the plan when he compared the German tendency towards artificial bureaucratization and authoritarianism with his own approach, which he called "unsystematic and loose."[18]

The encounter with America left certain traces in the work of some of the German participants. Lamprecht's, Weber's, and Sombart's observations continue to be an important source of information. However, the expected contacts between German and American academics, among them Woodrow Wilson and Frederick Jackson Turner, did not materialize. The best results lay in the attempts of German professors to stress mutual understanding; the worst, in their refusal to recognize Americans as equals. But even the best results did not make much of a difference. On the contrary, they veiled the fact that both communities were rapidly drifting apart.

Diplomats and German–American Leaders in Pursuit of Prestige

When Ambassador Theodor von Holleben responded favorably to Kuno Francke's proposal to establish a more official representation of German culture in America, he also considered his reaction as a means to intensify contacts with German-Americans. Holleben was aware that the new interest in culture, which originated in the political tensions between the United States and the German Reich during the Spanish-American War in 1898, was part of an attempt of German-Americans to counteract antagonism. Although a supportive role of the embassy was seen as an appropriate response, Holleben knew that involving German-Americans in the attempt to mend fences between Germany and the United States presented a precarious option. Assessing the effectiveness of German-American protests against anti-German politics, he concluded that they would be useful for Germany "only as long as they appeared completely spontaneous." This had happened in Chicago in March 1899 when German-Americans successfully protested the incessant vilification of Germany and German-Americans.[19] He warned, however, of the need to go further: "At the moment when it became apparent or the mere suspicion arose that Germany was inciting this movement, it would backfire badly."[20] The decision to use German-American protest potential for German politics nevertheless promptly backfired; Holleben obviously did not heed his own warning.[21] He pursued this option despite the realization that German-American leaders used culture not only to advance the public standing of their group, but also to gain personal recognition and inflate their own importance. In reality their commitment to German art and literature was tangential at best.[22]

Alfred Vagts, to whom we owe the most incisive study of American-German politics at the turn of the century, offers some clues concerning the predictability of diplomatic decisions in periods of tension. In his introduction to *Deutschland und die Vereinigten Staaten in der Weltpolitik*, Vagts points to the long-standing tendency of diplomats, especially those in the feudal tradition of Wilhelmine Germany, to determine their options under the auspices of honor, challenge, and response, often enhancing the intensity of conflicts in order to prove their own indispensability as mediators.[23] Vagt's assertion that the German envoys to the United States were engaged in influencing the voting patterns of German-Americans, although they did not think much of this group's ability to influence American politics, seems to be correct. Yet it is difficult to accept his subsequent statement that the diplomats, jealously guarding their monopoly on the power of reconciliation, dismissed completely the mediating potential of the German-Americans.[24] Each side, though, had its own agenda. The diplomats, responding in the spirit of increasing competition with the other European powers, France and Great Britain, crossed the line to the political utilization of cultural prestige. Enthralled by the American acclaim of German culture, they attempted to steer German-Americans in the political application of this prestige. German-

American leaders, in turn, learned to avail themselves of German officials in their attempts to bolster their own prestige both in and out of their communities. It seems more appropriate, therefore, to shift the focus of this analysis to the reciprocity of usefulness and exploitation.

The two most obvious objects of mutual interest were: one, the educational system in which German America was represented by hundreds of schools and an impressive program of German language instruction, and two, the university system, which had adopted many features of the German system and maintained an allegiance to the methods of German scholarship. In both cases certain steps by the German ambassador promised a rich yield in prestige for himself and his country. Since these steps implied German appreciation of American achievements, Holleben's involvement was not surprising. He valued the fact that his 1899 visit to Harvard's German department received much public attention as a symbol of Germany's recognition of American universities. When the University of Chicago invited him shortly thereafter, the official letter promoted the visit as a great opportunity for the American academy to express its gratitude to the Germans.[25] In his speech Holleben replied with the compliment that the encounter with American higher education had thoroughly cured him of any prejudice – Germans had no idea of the dedication with which American academics maintained the "*echt wissenschaftliche[n] Geist*"[26] in their work. During his 1901 visits to Johns Hopkins and Columbia, Holleben expressed the hope that, with this kind of recognition, a new era of American-German relations could commence. When Harvard bestowed honorary doctorates on him and Vice President Theodore Roosevelt, it honored in him "the representative of an old civilized people whose beginnings were closely intertwined with those of the American nation, the son of a nation whose scholars inspired the rest of the world."[27]

Louis Viereck proudly reported these events in his volume on the German-American school system, *Zwei Jahrhunderte deutschen Unterrichts in den Vereinigten Staaten*, which was written in New York and published in Braunschweig in 1903. Originally presented as part of the Report of the Commissioner of Education, United States Bureau of Education, for 1900–1901, the book was meant to encourage the recognition of the educational achievements of the German-Americans. Viereck emphasized that their work, especially the teaching of the German language, enabled German culture to exert a strong influence in the United States:

> German education does not just offer to the Americans the tool for acquainting themselves with the German language and literature; in the way it is prac-

ticed in the best educational institutions of the country, it makes a strong contribution to introducing the students more thoroughly into the German manner of thinking and to winning them over to the German cultural ideals.[28]

The success of German education in America was even more impressive because it had been attained without official assistance from Germany. While such an assessment could not overcome the strong skepticism of Germans – Holleben expressed his doubts whether the democratic tendencies in American schools could really serve as a basis for "a genuine German education"[29] – it strengthened the determination to consider German language instruction as an avenue of cultural influence.

The statistics on the teaching of German indeed looked impressive. In 1890, 10.5 percent of all public high-school students studied German, 5.8 percent French; in 1900, 14.3 percent German and 7.8 percent French; in 1910, about 24 percent German and 10 percent French. The general interest in foreign languages remained high until the war; in 1915 over 40 percent of the public and private high schools throughout the country were offering German (28 percent), French (11 percent), and Spanish (2 percent).[30] Traditionally, German language instruction was strongest in the Midwest, especially in Wisconsin, Missouri, and Kansas. Although the situation in universities and colleges looked less favorable, in 1910, of 340 such institutions, 101 required from one to four years of German or French or both for entrance; two-thirds of the 340 required some German or French for graduation. Of the 340 institutions, all but three taught German.[31]

Yet, as soon as German language instruction was viewed as a vehicle of cultural influence from Germany, it became a target of anti-German animosity. The relationship is obvious: as the instruction and use of the language was understood to be the most authentic and widespread display of German culture in the country, it helped to maintain the self-confidence of German ethnic groups and associations. However, as the language manifested the presence of the authentic "other" in everyday life, it provided a focus for the growing feelings of American nationalism. Of course, it took more than a decade to politicize the link between the study of German in American schools as a sign of culture and a good education and the demonstration of ethnic self-confidence. Nevertheless, once the manifestation of "the other" turned into a demonstration against the concept of America as a *Melting Pot*[32] – the title of Israel Zangwill's successful play of 1908 – the statistics on the dominating role of German in education could easily be turned into an indicator of the threat posed by the Germans. While education and language always had been sources of public apprehension, they now emerged as crucial paradigms of political confrontation.

The wartime use of these paradigms for anti-German propaganda would not have been as effective had it not been for the promotion of the concept of culture – i.e., German culture – in the declarations of ethnic pride. This promotion indicated more than simple resistance to the melting pot idea. As it received increasing support from the German Reich, primarily from the academic sphere, it challenged Anglo-American cultural leadership. Mobilizing the prestige of the fatherland culture for ethnic self-promotion signaled foreign interference, thus opening German-American politics to the accusation of disloyalty to the United States.

Seeking prestige was, without a doubt, the crucial motivation for the pursuit of culture by German representatives and German-American leaders. In the realm of academe, it coincided with the growing self-assertion of professors in the public discourse. As "active participation and leadership in politics, economics, and social reform became a professorial hallmark,"[33] the universities increasingly held the key to the definition of cultural – and to some extent political – prestige. Holleben's eagerness to exploit the contacts with elite institutions such as Harvard, Chicago, Columbia, and Johns Hopkins corresponded to the interest of their professors in furthering their own recognition. It was even suggested "that many academicians, particularly historians, were insecure about their new profession and eager to demonstrate the relevance of their work to major issues of the day."[34] The high prestige associated with German scholarship, and especially the constant promotion of the professor as a spokesperson for national issues in Germany, made the German connection attractive, though more in matters of repute than substance.

In this context the comparably important role of German professors who had become members of German America and increasingly engaged in advocating the German cause is hardly surprising. In "The German Influence on Education in the United States," which appears in his comprehensive assessment of 1909, *The German Element in the United States*, Albert Bernhardt Faust states that the volume does not have enough room for all of the names of Germans and men of German descent who occupy chairs at American universties. Emphasizing that "the German element is prominently represented in every field of intellectual activity,"[35] Faust points to prominent figures such as the historian H. E. von Holst; the Nobel laureate in physics, Albert A. Michelson; the president of Northwestern University, A. F. Ernst; the Germanist Kuno Francke and "one of the leading psychologists of to-day," Hugo Münsterberg – the latter two at Harvard University. A considerable number of these professors responded favorably to the recognition that they received from within the German Reich, others, such as Francke and Münsterberg, actively pursued a more direct commitment from the fatherland. That their collaboration seemed particularly attractive to German diplomats who looked for a more positive presence of Germany in American public opinion is even less surprising.[36]

The attractiveness of these academics also resulted from their peculiar standing within German America – itself a rather typical term of the ambition for ethnic self-reliance at that time. In order to project a leadership position in this community, they strongly criticized its political inefficiency and its failure to present German culture – i.e., *Kultur* – beyond the customs of everyday life and ethnic festivities. Hugo Münsterberg's assertation, "that the average German-American stands in some respect below the level of the average German at home,"[37] is indeed not very flattering. His explanation of the difference between the two illuminates the place where he sees he functions as a leader:

> On the whole the German-American masses of to-day show little of the German tendency of higher aims. They are surprisingly indifferent; their clubs and associations lack more and more the inspirations of earlier days, and they are satisfied to praise honesty as their peculiar German virtue instead of feeling it to be a matter of course. Alarmingly few men of individual power have grown up among those millions. What characterizes the German at home, the tendency to idealism and the desire for intellectual life, has evaporated; the artisan or farmer, whose highest wish at home would have been to send his son to the gymnasium, and perhaps even to the university, is here glad if his boy becomes a clever business clerk as quickly as possible.[38]

This was written in 1901, the year of the founding of the National German-American Alliance, which indicated that German-American groups had become interested in demonstrating a sense of national, though not openly political, representation. Münsterberg's intentions were directed, obviously, towards instilling in German-Americans the sense of idealism he found prevalent in Germany. His design for the Congress of Arts and Sciences at the St. Louis World's Fair in 1904 probably represents the most momentous expression of his "empirical idealism," which was to empower the concept of culture as an instrument for a higher organization of social and intellectual pursuits. Since German-Americans seemed to fail as mediators for this view of culture, Münsterberg implied, others had to take the lead. The claim, "that the German-Americans have done little to make the Germans understand America better, and perhaps still less to make the Americans understand the real

Germans,"[39] opened the door for many German-born academics, teachers, and journalists to assume the (fateful) role of mediators between the two countries.[40] In his study of the German professors as academic mandarins, Fritz Ringer has analyzed the crucial role of *Kultur* and idealism within German society. He also shows that the intensive promotion of *Kultur* as a higher principle increasingly reflected an attempt to counteract the loss of public influence.[41]

In contrast to Münsterberg's assumption, German-American leaders actually took up loftier aims after 1900. The constitution of the National German-American Alliance already indicated the organizational centrality of this commitment. As the contemporaries expressed it in the distinction of "stomach Germans" and "soul Germans,"[42] acculturation manifested itself in different ways such that the cultural and religious forms of allegiance became particularly prominent. Those German-Americans who had entered the middle class often tried to distinguish themselves through a higher – or German – cultural agenda. They tended to move away from those who confirmed their ethnicity in common customs and everyday leisure-time practices, like indulging in the magic of beer and *Gemütlichkeit*.

The first step towards the assertion of cultural factors had occurred in the 1880s and 1890s. This had been the time when American elites engaged in the "Search for a Usable Past,"[43] shifting the definition of the nation to a commemoration of the common history, where the individual ethnic history virtually disappeared in favor of the Anglo-Saxon heritage. After the American centennial of 1876 had set the tone, various ethnic groups – the Scotch-Irish and Irish as well as the Jewish, Polish, and German – responded with the founding of historical societies whose charge was to set the record straight and document the group's contribution to the history of the nation.[44] By suggesting in 1883 to celebrate a German Day as an annual public festival, Oswald Seidensticker, professor of German at the University of Pennsylvania, responded to Pennsylvania's colorful bicentennial celebration in Philadelphia in 1882. Subsequently, the celebration of German heritage since the days of General von Steuben had become the basis for a new ethnic awareness and pride. Whereas the average participant in the German Day festivities experienced their ethnic separateness by indulging in beer, singing, and *Gemütlichkeit*, the leaders invoked the great contribution of German-Americans to the history of the American nation. In this search for ethnic recognition through the reigning paradigm of history, many leaders also articulated a rallying point for German-Americans in their search for social recognition, especially as they ascended to the middle class.[45]

Drawing on the example of Cincinnati, G. A. Dobbert showed how upward social mobility weakened the ethnic ties of many German-Americans, who moved away from the traditional inner-city communities. He added, though, that many felt compelled to substitute for the lost community a spiritual one. Dobbert explains:

> That the latter was to be predicated on a common national ideology was self-evident. But in view of the Germans' still lingering differences, this ideology had to be kept purposely vague so as to make up in the intensity of its emotional pitch what it lacked in the logic of its definitions. To have done otherwise would have been to open the Pandora's box of all the Germans' old antagonisms.[46]

Whereas beer had no place in the constitution of the National German-American Alliance, which as the ethnic umbrella organization was heavily subsidized by the German-American brewing industry, history had a place. History was both vague and national enough to serve as the basis for ethnic bonding and social self-consciousness. Moreover, it could be publicly displayed in parades, floats, and speeches on German Day. German-American history could even legitimize the call for unifying this ethnic group because the struggle for its recognition affected a sizeable portion of non-Anglo-Saxon Americans. Equally important, German-American history demonstrated the superiority of this portion of ethnic America over the newly arrived immigrants from southern and eastern Europe, who at the turn of the century began to upset the established social and cultural self-perception of many Americans. Last but not least, history helped to compensate for the diminishing German immigration and the realization that the political weight of the group was shrinking.

From here the second step – embracing the idea of culture (*Kultur*) as an equally vague yet exclusively German concept of higher aspirations – followed with some consequence. It constituted a move from the position of inferiority vis-à-vis the Anglo-Saxons to a position of equality, even possibly superiority. The political significance of this step, however, only gradually became apparent, but more in the suspicious minds of critics than in the associations of German-Americans. Where history had provided a rationale for ethnicity as a mode of identification with America, the ethnic rationale of the identification with German culture received its momentum from the presence of another country. As a stimulus for attacks against these associations and a basis for exposing "the other" in the activities of the German-Americans, it increasingly symbolized a shift toward disloyalty. In the crassly worded polemics of Gustavus Ohlinger's influential treatise of 1916, *Their True Faith and Allegiance*: "The [National German-American] Alliance has simply made itself a part of the Teutonic battle line in the struggle against Anglo-

Saxon leadership which German historians have been predicting for so many years."[47]

In this vein, critics who attacked the challenge to Anglo-Saxon cultural dominance developed the thesis that German-Americans had been led astray by voices from the fatherland. This traditional culture of hard work and noisy festivities, recognized as a long-standing ingredient of American life, had given way to *Kultur* as the manifestation of Teutonic aggressiveness and the Pan-German claim for world leadership. As the critics pointed to the fact that the ethnic culture of the German-Americans would have disappeared quickly if it had not been for the intervention of German "agitators," they espied some of the real developments. In 1915 James Middleton was able to formulate it in one very long title: "Are Americans More German Than English? And Are German-Americans More German Than Americans? How The Tenacious German Culture (Not Kultur) Has Been Steadily Giving Way To The Americanizing Influence Of The Life Around The German Immigrants In The United States."[48] Middleton emphasized that the German-American culture had been vanishing when "Germanism" was, all of a sudden, professionalized by cultural agitators, ethnic associations, and German-American newspapers which had been resurrected through Germany's fight in the war. He added: "But the orator always attracts more attention than the millions whose business is not to stir up trouble but to earn a living and educate their children." Regarding the "revival of Teutonism," he concluded: "In the opinion of most observers, this represents merely a national sympathy of Germans with the German cause, and does not fundamentally affect their American allegiance."[49] What the author failed to consider was the extent to which cultural ideologies had instigated aggressiveness on the part of the Anglo-Saxon majority against German-Americans. This development came to fruition shortly after the United States entered the war on the side of the Allies.

The Role of Culture in the Invention of the Enemy

Before World War I, the cultural relations with the United States did not rank high in German public opinion. The fact that Kaiser Wilhelm II engaged in grand gestures that were intended to show off German sympathy and culture, generally confirmed the view that His Majesty's personal politics were a great asset in relating to this distant continent. In his use of the cliché of the American as an efficient engineer – "I need Americans" – the Kaiser certainly did not define Germany's relationship to the United States in cultural terms.

There were few serious critics of the imperial politics and optimism concerning America's positive attitude towards Germany.[50] Maximilian Harden, editor of *Die Zukunft* and the most prominent critic, considered Prince Heinrich's good-will visit a political failure with one exception: that it strengthened the political standing (*Machtposition*) of the German-Americans. Harden was aware that the ignorance of most Germans could lead to dangerous misunderstandings in the period of the Venezuela crisis. He had little sympathy for presenting the statue of Frederick the Great as a gift to this democracy. Similarly, the *Hamburger Fremdenblatt* considered the exchange program, with "a couple of professors there, a couple of professors here,"[51] an exercise in gratuity. The official exchange did not diminish the feelings of distance. While some interest in the United States developed in German universities after 1900, the dissertations and lecture courses concerned themselves with U.S. history, not the contemporary situation.[52] Münsterberg's two-volume work of 1904, *Die Amerikaner*, written with the express purpose of explaining the country to the Germans, remained the only comprehensive treatise on modern America. In it Münsterberg warned against underrating the continent, but shied away from directly confronting the problems of American-German relations. Also widely read was the travel diary, *Americana* (1906), in which Karl Lamprecht tried to convey an impression of the economic and cultural potential of that country. And yet, with as much insight into the peculiar culture as Lamprecht displayed, he did not yield in his condescension: "If the present American civilization disappeared: what would remain for posterity? Practically nothing. At the very least a new concept of the state and of human freedom."[53] Obviously, this concept did not count as culture. On the contrary, it constituted a threat to European culture: "It has to be expressed in no uncertain terms: vis-à-vis the old culture of the European population, both the Germanic and the Romanic, the Americans are still behind, and their political and military victory in the world, especially over Europe, would still represent at this moment a danger to the historical development of mankind."[54]

In contrast to Werner Sombart, who returned from America disillusioned with the future of *Kultur*,[55] Lamprecht was prompted to reconceptualize culture in political terms, making it an instrument of Germany's imperialist expansion. On the one hand, culture was to be used as a tool for colonializing backward nations, and on the other, to counter the intentions of Western nations to thwart Germany's quest for world power. In a 1913 letter to his former school mate, Chancellor Bethmann Hollweg, Lamprecht instigated a governmental statement concerning the importance of *auswärtige Kulturpolitik*. Bethmann Hollweg's *Runderlass* confirmed the notion that any economic expansion, particularly in

China, would have to be preceded by a policy of cultural penetration. Germany needed to utilize all of its resources, the statement read, "in order not to let other nations take a lead which could not be made up anymore."[56] Based on such a rationale, the definition of *auswärtige Kulturpolitik* reflected a strong commitment to imperialist expansion. At the same time, one could not overlook the compensatory role of cultural politics for the recent failures of German foreign policy. The spirit of international competition was essential. France, which for a long time had used its leadership in arts and culture in the battle for political power, provided the model.

In the compensatory use of *Kultur*, German-Americans did not fall far behind the Reich. The psychological stringency was similar: as the Kaiser engaged and rendered support in the pursuit of prestige, *Kultur* had to produce respect. Its politization did not result from a humanistic mission, but from a feeling of denigration from the side of "the other."[57] In the case of German-Americans, many of the most vocal elites "attempted to secure Yankee-American 'respect', based on admiration and fear of the Fatherland."[58] As they caused misgivings about the hierarchy of culture, the traditional English opposition against status-related *Kultur* gained new circulation in the United States.[59] In Germany, in turn, the suspicion grew that the United States as a country, which was dominated by low culture, presented a formidable challenge in the cultural as well as economic and military spheres.

Alfed Vagts' conclusion that both countries invented a viable enemy for internal and external power enhancement is also applicable in the realm of cultural relations. Vagts asserted: "It is probable that the American navy was even more active in this respect than the Germans, if only for the reason that the American navy needed the enemy, Germany, somewhat more than the German navy needed the enemy, America, especially after the Anglo-German antagonism had become fixed."[60] When applied to culture, the interpretation is that Germans invoked the threat of Americanism in order to bolster German *Kulturimperialismus*, whereas Americans determined that *Kultur* was the most explicit expression of the "German peril."[61]

How strongly the paradigmatic role of culture increased in the rhetoric of imperialist self-assertion can be ascertained in the anti-German polemics. Gustavus Ohlinger compared the German cultural influence with the effect of German acts of sabotage after 1914, and concluded that the activities of such men as Consul General Bopp, Boy-Ed, von Papen, Kaltschmidt, König, and von Igel "are insignificant when compared with the insidious and far-reaching [German] conspiracy against our education. . . . Bridges, canals, factories and ships are mere physical properties, easily replaced. Our public education, on the other hand, represents infinitely higher values."[62]

German *Kultur* and American Elites

Why did culture assume such a pivotal role for the formulation of national identity in a country that was not known for its strong aesthetic concerns or achievements? The explanation seems to lie precisely in the recognition of this deficiency vis-à-vis the European wealth of cultural artifacts and concomitant ideology. If in the nineteenth century American elites had not taken up the worshiping of high culture as a means of ennobling their lives, their feeling of betrayal during World War I would not have been expressed with such vehemence.

As Lawrence Levine has shown in his study on the emergence of cultural hierarchies in America, *Highbrow-Lowbrow*, the Germans played a growing part in the emerging concept of worshiping aesthetic culture as a way to enhance prestige. Germans had developed the most ritualized practice of transforming public spaces, such as concert halls, theaters, opera houses, and museums, into enclaves in which people were shamed, or forced, into behaving with passive decorum. They possessed the most intensive public ceremonialism of elevating art into a counter-sphere in opposition to the pressures of the market place. They had Beethoven's and Mozart's classical music, the most respected artistic phenomena in this sacralization, and, last but not least, Richard Wagner, the foremost expert in turning the stage into a temple. As middle-class Americans learned to embellish their social ascendency with cultural status symbols, the hierarchically minded Germans supplied a new set of such symbols that were comfortably distinct from those of the British. When in 1889 Theodore Thomas, one of the most prominent conductors of classical music, described his country house in New Hampshire, he mentioned busts of Shakespeare and Bach, an engraving of Mozart at the court of Vienna, another of Beethoven "under whom I sit, before a writing table," a picture of Goethe as an old man, a picture of Schiller's house and garden in Weimar, and pictures of Schubert and Schumann. "Here," Thomas wrote, "you have my *Glaubens Bekenntnis*."[63] It was a creed of participation in high culture, not in German cultural nationalism.

Concurrent with such statements were harsh critiques of American culture, litanies such as Charles Eliot Norton's assertation that "of all civilized nations," the United States was "the most deficient in the higher culture of the mind, and not in the culture only but also in the conditions on which this culture mainly depends."[64] This was in line with the requests for the censorship of mass culture, particularly "the music hall stuff,"[65] as the New York music critic, W. J. Henderson, called it. Courtenay Guild, who was elected president of Boston's Handel and Haydn Society in 1915, spoke with dismay of the new "talking machines," which substituted for attending concerts and helped to spread the "mania for dancing and syncopated time," which cultivated "a taste for a sort of barbarous sequence of sounds that is more worthy of savages than of civilization."[66]

At that time, however, a critic such as Thorstein Veblen, in *The Theory of the Leisure Class* (1899), had expressed his discomfort with "the regime of status." Sarcastically, Veblen reduced "leisure class culture" to the survival of ancient rituals of class discrimination and priestcraft. He loathed the combination of cultural arrogance and the feeling of inferiority toward the European cult of culture.[67] Other critics exposed the hostility against popular culture, which by now included film and gramophone, as a betrayal of American-based culture. When the focus shifted from popular culture to the hierarchical and undemocratic features of high culture, the German variation of culture became an easy target. Not surprisingly, even well-entrenched custodians of high culture joined the promoters of popular culture against elitism, especially since it was a Teutonic elitism that disregarded the lower sphere of the hierarchy. When these custodians of culture attached themselves to the Progressive movement, they felt comfortable with its well-heeled promoters,[68] who were committed to Woodrow Wilson's interest in "the constant renewal of society from the bottom,"[69] upon which the genius and the enterprise of America had always depended. With every revelation of the aggressive and, in the years before 1914, military features of German culture, they found it easier to bolster their own position and rescue their idealism by attacking the wrong elitism and compromised German idealism.

The often-quoted business interests were not at the heart of American interventionism on the side of the Allies, as Henry F. May observed in his ground-breaking study of 1959, *The End of American Innocence*, nor was a realistic sense of American interest in the Atlantic barrier or the balance of power. May points instead to the custodians of culture, "the beleaguered defenders of nineteenth-century tradition," as the driving force and asserts that those who were doubtful about the sanctity of the Allied cause were often those who had been involved, before the war, in some kind of intellectual revolt.[70] May summed it up as follows:

> For the custodians of culture the primary issue was not American interests, not neutral rights, not even the rescue of England and France. The ideals they wanted to defend abroad were to them the same as those they had long been defending at home. England, France and Belgium came to embody all they

believed in, Germany and her apologists all that they hated and feared. Their whole view of life and history seemed to lead toward this conclusion. If the war was not caused by the special wickedness of Germany, it would have to be accounted for in more general terms. This would suggest that all nineteenth-century civilization must be a sham and a failure.[71]

One should add that the Germans indeed compromised their ideology of *Kultur* with the growing militarism, and they contributed to the polemical split between the "good old" German culture and the contemporary deviation from it. The more successful the cultural ideology had been in shaping the mind of Americans, the more embarrassment these Americans tended to express. In one of the widely read examples of wartime propaganda, *Münsterberg and Militarism Checked*, Charles W. Squires emphasized in 1915:

> All must acknowledge the debt they owe to German *Kultur*. It was certainly no "self-deception" when all nations "went up" to Germany to learn its methods of social reform, its philosophy and its music. Such scholars as Humboldt, Helmholtz, Koch, Behring, Mommsen, Wundt, Harnack, and many others are cosmopolitan. There is no touch of provincialism about them. No one refuses them intellectual preeminence. There ought to be a way of making German intellectual power prevail without adding material dominion to it. But Germany is not satisfied with intellectual dominion. She must have the whole or none. It must be in the oft-repeated words of Bernhardi: "Empire or downfall (*Weltmacht oder Niedergang*)."[72]

Squires expressed this view after the manifesto of October 1914, in which ninety-three German intellectuals defended the "pure cause" of the fatherland against the lies of Western propaganda, stating the infamous line concerning the link between culture and militarism: "Without German militarism, German culture would have been extinguished from the face of the earth."[73] This manifesto confirmed the worst defamation of German culture, which had been articulated in response to the American publication of General Friedrich von Bernhardi's programmatic treatise, *How Germany Makes War* (1914). What Bernhardi had laid down in military terms – the necessity for a new concept of war that involved the whole society as never before – the German *Wehrverein* presented as the core of a new German *Geist* for which war would become "Kulturträger" and "Trostspender." Increasingly, the coming war was envisioned as the only way to rescue German *Kultur* from "westliche Zivilisation."[74]

Accordingly, in the flood of anti-German publications, *Kultur* was a most visible focus. Against Münsterberg's defense of the Reich in *The*

War and America (1914) and *The Peace and America* (1915), John Cowper Powys' *The War and Culture* (1914) and Charles W. Squires' *Münsterberg and Militarism Checked* (1915) received broad attention. Moreover, 1,225,000 copies of *Conquest and Kultur*, a pamphlet compiled by Wallace Notestein and Elmer E. Stoll for the Committee on Public Information, the American propaganda agency, were distributed in 1918; it was not an unusual number.[75]

Next to the motto "War and Culture," the most frequently used combination was "The Kultur of Kaisertum," as James W. Gerard, the last American ambassador to Germany, called a chapter in his autobiography, *Face to Face with Kaiserism* (1918). Choosing Kaiser and *Kultur* as the main targets was a logical outgrowth of the appropriation of German culture. Since Wilhelm II had maintained this appropriation as a crucial factor of Germany's commitment to war, propagandists had an easier time portraying the unholy triad of Kaiser, *Kultur*, and war as the incarnation of the enemy. Charles D. Hazen, author of one of the Committee's pamphlets, *The Government of Germany*, referred to it as "skinning the Kaiser and his system."[76]

In contrast to Germany, where the war was in easy reach of the populace, the United States had to import the war for the population. Thus, propaganda played a more important role in inducing the population to renounce its isolationism. "More than the other governments, the Wilson administration was compelled to cultivate – even to manufacture – public opinion favorable to the war effort. Lacking the disciplinary force of quick-coming crisis or imminent peril of physical harm, Wilson had to look into other means to rally his people: to the deliberate mobilization of emotions and ideas. Here, the Great War was peculiarly an affair of the mind."[77] In transforming the enemy from a mental obsession into a physical experience when war became a reality in 1917, German-Americans became the target of hysterical rampages in streets, schools, organizations, and private life. Consequently, the German-Americans suffered for their challenge of Anglo-Saxon leadership because they had come so close to it in their successful acculturation and were recognized as the only ethnic group that could present such a challenge through their organizational potential. At the same time, they suffered because the source of their additional strength, the German Reich, was too far away as to be immediately assaulted. On the side of the American elites, therefore, the long awaited declaration of war against Germany appeared as a welcome release: "Their feelings did not center in hatred, but in hope and exaltation. Instead of seeing the war as the doom of their culture, they believed it would bring about its revival: the war was a severe but necessary lesson in moral idealism."[78]

Yet the rampage of 1917–18 was not the only consequence of the propaganda focused on the Kaiser. The hostility of the population receded shortly after the target of the mental war had disappeared, the feudal structures had fallen, and democratization was under way. Thus, in an ironic twist of affairs, the focus on the Kaiser and his cultural war agenda proved to simplify the American reconciliation with Germany after 1919–20. Even the split within the definition of *Kultur* was soon to be overcome, reconstituting the American appreciation of German efficiency, intellectual energy, and engagement with modernity.

The price for this had to be paid by the German-Americans. Since they had made such an extensive use of Germany's cultural and political symbols in their play for ethnic unity and social acceptance, they became trapped by those symbols. Once the practice was prohibited, or had become obsolete with the disappearance of the Kaiserreich, the group disappeared as a viable factor in American politics.

Conclusion: Toward a Different Cultural Competition

What Randolph Bourne, untainted by the war fever, had found attractive in German culture in 1915, received a more thorough hearing in the 1920s and, again, after World War II. "We cannot seriously think merely of spewing everything German out of our mouths," Bourne wrote in his critique of the American hysteria, "American Use for German Ideals." "To refuse the patient German science, the collectivist art, the valor of the German ideals, would be simply to expatriate ourselves from the modern world."[79] Bourne even went so far as to qualify the American Progressive ideals as retrogressive:

> Whether we relapsed atavistically to our British roots, or because the incalculable energies of the German ideal really daunted us, we preferred to range our sympathy with the nations that were living on their funded nineteenth-century spiritual capital, rather than breaking new paths and creating new forms for a new time. Believing the Germans to be in error, we did not even feel a weakness for the tragic and heroic error as against the safe and fuddling plausibility.[80]

In his pursuit of the difference between *and* the reciprocity of the war fever in Germany and the United States, Bourne put the search for modernity into the center of the "real" competition. With astounding insight he described the German contribution to a culture of rational organization "in public buildings and domestic architecture of clean, massive and soaring lines, sculpture of militaristic solidity like the Leipzig and Bismarck monuments, endless variety of decorative and graphic art, printing and household design, civic art as embodied in the laying out of cities and squares and parks." Bourne added: "All this development has been of social art,"[81] – the first American formulation of what in Germany came to be called a culture of *Sachlichkeit*, which already pointed beyond the allegorical and ornamental mode of the Kaiserreich's official representation. On the German side, Moritz Julius Bonn located the real point of contention in American-German competition, which would remain central in developing modernity, as an expression of power. When Germany emerged as an adversary of the United States, Bonn concluded, the necessity arose for the Americans "either to prevent Germany from ruling the world or to imitate German organization."[82]

As the history of modernity has been written and rewritten since the 1920s, the difference between and the reciprocity of American and German technological productivity have become a crucial part of it. The reciprocity also encompasses the "second look" at the other nation which Bourne and Bonn defined under the auspices of modern productivity. What has been called the second discovery of America – the first being "that of the virgin land, nature's nation"[83] – was the realization that the United States had undergone a rapid technological transformation and, with the new century, had become the foremost industrial producer in the world. German industrialists and businessmen were among those Europeans who, in the decade prior to World War I, established the new concept of America as the model for industrial efficiency. The trip to America took the role of the nineteenth-century industrialist's journey to Great Britain, devoted to the competitor's look at the new technological organization through which the other country had achieved its industrial predominance. The title of Max Goldberger's 1903 assessment, "The land of unlimited possibilites,"[84] merged with the technological program of Taylorism into the new myth of Americanism, or Americanization.

The fascination with this "second discovery" of America held its own despite – or rather because of – the ruminations in German government and business circles concerning the "amerikanische Gefahr,"[85] and also despite – or rather because of – the outcry of the German custodians of high culture against the invasion of American popular, or low, culture into the country of Goethe and Beethoven. A famous witness of this "discovery" is Walter Gropius, who in 1911 was able to articulate the creative consequences of the encounter with the American working world. His visit to the monumental grain silos in the Midwest and his insights into the American forms of industrial rationalization inspired his architecture of functional *Sachlichkeit*. Although Gropius expressed the social significance of such architecture for Germany in nationalistic language, he credited the Americans with the invention of a truly modern monumentalism.[86]

In turn, Gropius, the founder of the Bauhaus in 1919, belonged to those Germans who figured prominently in the mind of Americans who engaged in the "second discovery" of Germany after World War I. This discovery was preconditioned on the disappearance of the Kaiser and his culture of feudal authoritarianism. Once the symbolic target of American enmity was removed, Germany could be seen in a different light. Already Thorstein Veblen's critical analysis of 1915, *Imperial Germany and The Industrial Revolution*, gathered arguments on German modernity beyond the narrow focus of Wilhelm's cultural and political mission.

Nevertheless, there is quite some irony in the fact that the "second discovery" of Germany as a quintessential modern nation which found its expression in the experimental spirit of the Weimar Republic, involved a conscious embrace of the features of high culture of German modernity. As Gropius had engaged in an "aesthetic filtering of American directness" (Adolf Behne) and raised the "anonymous ahistorical strength of American functional buildings through European culture,"[87] he was indeed welcomed in the United States in later decades as if he himself had invented the "international style" as a new icon of the modern world. In Tom Wolfe's sarcastic critique of the sell-out of American natural and authentic architecture to European modernism, Gropius appears as the "Silver Prince" who, after landing in the jungle, is surrounded by the natives, "who immediately bow down and prostrate themselves and commence a strange moaning chant. . . . "[88]

In conclusion, arguments concerning the relationship of productivity, organization, rationalization, and power make possible a different interpretation of the conflicts that occurred during the war period. They reveal a discourse in the early years of our epoch that has recently reemerged with renewed vitality. Endeavoring to understand the motivations for the German conflict in 1915, John Cowper Powys delineated a familiar pattern:

> The remarkable thing is, that this inspiring and formidable Idea, of a State-Machine, higher than the interests of which there is nothing in heaven or earth, is an idea which has brought under its spell every element in the German race. Even Professor Münsterberg's "Harnacks and Euckens and Haeckels" have succumbed to it; and the Social Democrats have given it their enthusiastic adhesion. Looking round the modern world to seek analogies for this German Idea in foreign nations Bernhardi rejoices to discover it in the spirit of modern Japan. It will be interesting to see in the future how far the

contact between Japan and her western allies, how far, in fact, the logic of the situation, in regard to this war of Ideas, changes and modifies this Japanese spirit which Bernhardi finds so analogous to the German one.[89]

The decline of cultural relations between the United States and Germany before 1917 was dependent on official political, diplomatic, and psychological investments. What was intended to be a bridge uniting the two nations turned out to be a justification for war, thus encouraging military confrontation. Yet, obsessed with the Kaiser's politics, most contemporaries overlooked the rise of new relational forms between the United States and Germany that converged in the competition for a more efficient modernity. As the United States, Japan, and Germany remained competitors in modernity throughout the century, research into the rise of these non-military forms of interaction provides important clues for subsequent political and cultural confrontations.

Notes to Chapter 5

1. The following works offer a valuable introduction to the topic from different points of view: Carol S. Gruber, *Mars and Minerva: World War I and the Uses of Higher Learning in America* (Baton Rouge, LA, 1975); Mona Harrington's "Loyalties: Dual and Divided," Philip Gleason's "American Identity and Americanization," Kathleen Neils Conzen's "Germans," in Stephan Thernstrom, ed., *Harvard Encyclopedia of American Ethnic Groups* (Cambridge, MA, 1980); Phyllis Keller, *States of Belonging: German-American Intellectuals and the First World War* (Cambridge, MA, 1979), more comprehensive is Keller's dissertation: "German-America and the First World War," Univ. of Pennsylvania (1969); Frederick C. Luebke, *Bonds of Loyalty: German-Americans and World War I* (DeKalb, IL, 1974); Henry F. May, *The End of American Innocence: A Study of the First Years of Our Own Time* (Chicago, 1964); Reiner Pommerin, *Der Kaiser und Amerika: Die USA in der Politik der Reichsleitung 1890–1917* (Köln/Wien, 1986); Günther Roth, *Politische Herrschaft und persönliche Freiheit* (Frankfurt, 1987), pp. 175–200 ("'Americana': Bildungsbürgerliche Ansichten und auswärtige Kulturpolitik im wilhelminischen Deutschland"); Alfred Vagts, *Deutschland und die Vereinigten Staaten in der Weltpolitik* 2 vols. (New York, 1935); Alfred Vagts, "Hopes and Fears of an American-German War, 1870–1915," *Political Science Quarterly* 54 (1939), pp. 514–35; *Zeitschrift für Kulturaustausch* 31 (1981). An extended bibliography in Arthur R. Schultz, *German-American Relations and German Culture in America: A Subject Bibliography, 1941–1980*, 2 vols. (New York, 1984).

2. Kurt Düwell, "Die Gründung der Kulturpolitischen Abteilung im Auswärtigen Amt als Neuansatz," in Düwell/Werner Link, eds., *Deutsche auswärtige Kulturpolitik seit 1871: Geschichte und Struktur* (Köln/Wien, 1981), pp. 46–71.

3. Ruth Emily McMurry/Muna Lee, *The Cultural Approach: Another Way in International Relations* (Chapel Hill, NC, 1947), pp. 208–29.

4. Kuno Francke, *Deutsche Arbeit in Amerika* (Leipzig, 1930), pp. 41–3; Friedrich Schmidt-Ott, *Erlebtes und Erstrebtes, 1860–1950* (Wiesbaden, 1950); Pommerin, *Der Kaiser*, pp. 258–65; Gerhard A. Ritter, "Internationale Wissenschaftsbeziehungen und auswärtige Kulturpolitik im deutschen Kaiserreich," *Zeitschrift für Kulturaustausch* 31 (1981), pp. 161–67.

5. Pommerin, *Der Kaiser*, pp. 260ff., 276.

6. Quoted in Pommerin, *Der Kaiser*, p. 111.

7. *Washington Evening Star*, 9 January 1909, quoted in Clara Eve Schieber, *The Transformation of American Sentiment Toward Germany, 1870–1914* (Boston/New York, 1923), p. 260.

8. Ritter, "Internationale," pp. 167ff.

9. Fritz T. Epstein, "Germany and the United States: Basic Patterns of Conflict and Understanding," in George L. Anderson, ed., *Issues and Conflicts: Studies in Twentieth Century American Diplomacy* (Lawrence, KS, 1959), pp. 284–314.

10. Pommerin, *Der Kaiser*, pp. 283–88.

11. Schieber, *The Transformation*, p. 253.

12. Roth, *Politische Herrschaft*, p. 187.

13. Schieber, *The Transformation*, p. 255.

14. Norbert Muhlen, *Germany in American Eyes: A Study of Public Opinion* (Hamburg-Wellingsbüttel, 1959), p. 20.

15. Schmidt-Ott, *Erlebtes*, p. 111.

16. Schieber, *The Transformation*, p. 256.

17. Hugo Münsterberg, "The Scientific Plan of the Congress," in Howard J. Rogers, ed., *International Congress of Arts and Sciences*, vol. 1 (London/New York, 1908), pp. 85–134. Cf. George Haines/Frederick H. Jackson, "A Neglected Landmark in the History of Ideas," *Mississippi Valley Historical Review* 34 (1947), pp. 201–20.

18. Keller, "German-America," p. 215.

19. Vagts, *Deutschland*, vol. 1, p. 587.

20. Quoted in Vagts, *Deutschland*, vol. 1, p. 588.

21. Cf. Emil Witte, *Revelations of A German Attaché: Ten Years of German-American Diplomacy* (New York, 1916), p. 195.

22. Quoted in Vagts, *Deutschland*, vol. 1, pp. 601ff.

23. Vagts, *Deutschland*, vol. 1, pp. vii ff.

24. Vagts, *Deutschland*, vol. 2, 1920.

25. Louis Viereck, *Zwei Jahrhunderte Deutschen Unterrichts in den Vereinigten Staaten* (Braunschweig, 1903), pp. 286–92.

26. Viereck, *Zwei Jahrhunderte*, p. 292.

27. Viereck, p. 293. Quoted from President Eliot's address.

28. Viereck, pp. viii.

29. Vagts, *Deutschland*, vol. 1, p. 602; Kurt Düwell, *Deutschlands auswärtige Kulturpolitik, 1918–1932: Grundlinien und Dokumente* (Köln/Wien, 1976), p. 288.

30. Edwin Zeydel, "The Teaching of German in the United States from Colonial Times to the Present," *The German Quarterly* 37 (1964), p. 357.

31. Zeydel, "The Teaching," p. 357.

32. Richard Conant Harper, *The Course of the Melting Pot Idea to 1910* (New York, 1980), pp. 288–331.

33. Jurgen Herbst, *The German Historical School in American Scholarship: A Study in the Transfer of Culture* (Ithaca, NY, 1965), pp. 162.

34. Stephen Vaughn, *Holding Fast the Inner Lines: Democracy, Nationalism, and the Committee on Public Information* (Chapel Hill, NC, 1980), p. 64; Richard Hofstadter, *The Age of Reform: From Bryan to F.D.R.* (New York, 1955), p. 154.

35. Albert Bernhardt Faust, *The German Element in the United States with Special Reference to Its Political, Moral, Social, and Educational Influence*, vol. 2 (Boston/New York, 1909), p. 232.

36. Cora Lee Nollendorfs, "Deutschunterricht in Amerika im Schatten des Ersten Weltkrieges: Öffentlich-offizielle Verfahrensweisen und gesellschaftliches Gebahren," *Zeitschrift für Kulturaustausch* 25 (1985), pp. 193ff.

37. Hugo Münsterberg, *American Traits from the Point of View of a German* (Boston/New York, 1901), p. 18.

38. Münsterberg, *American Traits*, p. 18.

39. Ibid.

40. The most informative studies are Melvin Small, "The American Image of Germany, 1906–1914," Diss. Ann Arbor (1965), and Phyllis Keller (cf. n. 1). On American *Germanistik* at that time cf. Henry Schmidt, "The Rhetoric of Survival: The Germanist in America from 1905 to 1925," in Frank Trommler/Joseph McVeigh, eds., *America and the Germans: An Assessment of a Three-Hundred Year History*, vol. 2 (Philadelphia, 1985), pp. 204–16.

41. Fritz Ringer, *The Decline of the German Mandarins: The German Academic Community* (Cambridge, MA, 1969), pp. 265 ff, 402ff.

42. Luebke, *Bonds of Loyalty*, pp. 27–56.

43. Henry Steele Commager, *The Search for a Usable Past and Other Essays in Historiography* (New York, 1967), p. 7.

44. Frank Trommler, "The Use of History in German-American Politics," in Charlotte Brancaforte, ed., *The German Forty-Eighters in the United States* (New York, 1989), pp. 279–95.

45. Willi Paul Adams, "Ethnic Leadership and the German-Americans," in *America and the Germans*, vol. 1, p. 156.

46. Guido A. Dobbert, "German-Americans Between New and Old Fatherland, 1970–1914," *American Quarterly* 19 (1967), p. 679. Cf. Kathleen Neils Conzen, "Political Myths and the Realities of Assimilation," in Clarence A. Glasrud/Diana M. Rankin, eds., *A Heritage Deferred: The German-Americans in Minnesota* (Moorhead, MN, 1981), pp. 127–30.

47. Gustavus Ohlinger, *Their True Faith and Allegiance* (New York, 1917), p. 43.

48. *The World's Work*, 31 December 1915, p. 141.

49. *The World's Work*, p. 147.

50. Gertrud Deicke, "Das Amerikabild der deutschen öffentlichen Meinung von 1898–1914," Diss. Hamburg (1956), pp. 227ff.

51. Hamburger Fremdenblatt, 4 January 1905, quoted in Deicke, "Das Amerikabild," p. 232.

52. Deicke, "Das Amerikabild," p. 234.

53. Karl Lamprecht, *Americana: Reiseeindrücke, Betrachtungen, Gesamtansicht* (Freiburg, 1906), pp. 32ff.

54. Lamprecht, *Americana*, p. 38.

55. Bernhard vom Brocke in *Deutsche auswärtige Kulturpolitik*, p. 145.

56. Quoted in Jürgen Kloosterhuis, "Deutsche auswärtige Kulturpolitik und ihre Trägergruppen vor dem Ersten Weltkrieg," in *Deutsche auswärtige Kulturpolitik*, p. 12.

57. Cf. Norbert Elias, *Studien über die Deutschen: Machtkämpfe und Habitusentwicklung im 19. und 20. Jahrhundert* (Frankfurt, 1989), pp. 61–158 ("Die satisfaktionsfähige Gesellschaft").

58. John R. Schedel, "A Rhetorical Study of Editorials in Wisconsin Newspapers During the Anti-German Movement, 1916–1918," Diss. Univ. of Nebraska (1982), pp. 341. Cf. Peter Frederick Stoll, "German-American 'Ethnicity' and 'Ego Identity'," Diss. State Univ. of New York at Albany (1984).

59. Raymond Williams, *Keywords: A Vocabulary of Culture and Society* (New York, 1976), pp. 81ff.

60. Vagts, "Hopes and Fears," p. 523.

61. Frederic Harrison, *The German Peril: Forecasts, 1864–1914; Realities* (London, 1915).

62. Gustavus Ohlinger, *The German Conspiracy in American Education* (New York, 1919), pp. 10–11.

63. Lawrence W. Levine, *Highbrow/Lowbrow: The Emergence of Cultural Hierarchy in America* (Cambridge, MA, 1988), pp. 140ff.

64. Levine, *Highbrow*, p. 215.

65. Ibid., p. 217.

66. Ibid.

67. Cf. John Higham, "The Reorientation of American Culture in the 1890's," in John Weiss, ed., *The Origins of Modern Consciousness* (Detroit, 1965), pp. 25–48.

68. Hofstadter, *The Age of Reform*, p. 144.

69. Quoted in Hofstadter, *The Age of Reform*, p. 225.

70. May, *The End of American Innocence*, p. 363.

71. Ibid., p. 366.

72. Charles W. Squires, *Münsterberg and Militarism Checked* (Toronto, 1915), p. 67.

73. Klaus Böhme, ed., *Aufrufe und Reden deutscher Professoren im Ersten Weltkrieg* (Stuttgart, 1975), p. 48.

74. George W.F. Hallgarten, *Imperialismus vor 1914: Soziologische Darstellung der deutschen Außenpolitik bis zum Ersten Weltkrieg*, vol. 2 (Munich, 1951), p. 264.

75. Cf. Vaughn, *Holding Fast*, pp. 62–82 ("The German Menace").

76. Quoted in Vaughn, *Holding Fast*, p. 67.

77. David M. Kennedy, *Over Here: The First World War and American Society* (New York/Oxford, 1980), p. 46.

78. May, *The End of Innocence*, p. 363.

79. Randolphe S. Bourne, *War and the Intellectuals: Essays, 1915–1919*, ed., Carl Resek (New York/Evanston/London, 1964), p. 50.

80. Bourne, *War*, p. 50.

81. Ibid., p. 49.

82. Moritz Julius Bonn, *Amerika als Feind* (Munich/Berlin, 1917), p. 38.

83. Thomas P. Hughes, *American Genesis: A Century of Invention and Technological Enthusiasm, 1870–1970* (New York, 1989), p. 295.

84. Max Ludwig Goldberger, *Das Land der unbegrenzten Möglichkeiten: Beobachtungen über das Wirtschaftsleben der Vereinigten Staaten von Amerika* (Berlin/Leipzig, 1903). Cf. Earl A. Beck, *Germany Rediscovers America* (Tallahassee, FL, 1968); John Czaplicka, "Amerikabilder and the German Discourse on Modern Civilization, 1890–1925," in Beeke Sell Tower, ed., *Envisioning America: Prints, Drawings, and Photographs by George Grosz and His Contemporaries, 1915–1933* (Cambridge, MA, 1990), pp. 37–62.

85. Vagts, *Deutschland*, vol. 1, pp. 345–425 ("Die amerikanische Gefahr"). Cf. Fritz Blaich, *Amerikanische Firmen in Deutschland, 1890–1918: US-Direktinvestitionen im deutschen Maschinenbau* (Wiesbaden, 1984).

86. Walter Gropius, "Die Entwicklung moderner Industriebaukunst," *Jahrbuch des Deutschen Werkbundes 1913*. See also his "Monumentale Kunst und Industriebau" (Typescript, Bauhaus Archiv, Berlin).

87. Winfried Nerdinger, *Walter Gropius* (Berlin, 1985), p. 10.

88. Tom Wolfe, *From Bauhaus to Our House* (New York, 1981), p. 42.

89. John Cowper Powys, *The War and Culture: A Reply to Professor Münsterberg* (New York, 1914), pp. 26ff.

6

The *Kultur* Club

Elliott Shore

Professor Trommler's compelling and nuanced treatment of the years of estrangement opens up a number of avenues for possible further inquiry. I would like to begin to get at one of those possibilities by focusing attention on a single World War I poster that, I believe, brings together a number of arresting images that complement Trommler's work. Let me first describe the poster, then make some brief comments on a few of Trommler's insights, and then attempt to take his analysis of German high culture a little bit lower into American life.

Enlistment posters that represent the enemy as nonhuman are a staple of modern warfare. One of the most striking of these images is found in the American World War I poster "Destroy this Mad Brute, Enlist," which takes to the logical extreme the image of the enemy as a threat to the nation. Foreshadowing the U.S. portrayal of the Japanese in World War II, this poster depicts the German as a gorilla with a huge, gaping mouth, striding onto the American shore, *pickelhaube* set at a rakish angle, with a bare-breasted woman writhing in his left arm. On the helmet is inscribed the word "Militarism," and the devastated wreckage of a European cathedral can be seen in the background. But what does the mad brute bear in his right arm? A mud and blood-encrusted club emblazoned "KULTUR."[1]

Frank Trommler's rich and suggestive essay on German-American cultural relations in the years leading to the publication of this poster gives us – for the first time, I believe – a way to understand how the image of *Kultur* as a bloodstained club wielded by an animalistic barbarian could stir the emotions of the average citizen. For although this poster is an elite creation, it was also, no doubt, an appeal that was probably successful beyond its designers' intentions because it played with a broader set of resentments and conflicts. Trommler's use of Lawrence Levine's *Highbrow/Lowbrow* formulation allows us to consider German culture not simply as a sophisticated domain separate and removed from everyday life, but as a weapon in the increasingly polarized relations among Americans in "the search for order."[2] That militarism and *Kultur*

Notes to Chapter 6 can be found on page 132.

came to be synonymous by 1917, I would suggest, was not just the result of an elite revulsion against the dismantling of ideals that they thought were represented by Mozart and Goethe. It also may have been propelled from below, from powerful resentment by those who would fight the war, directed not just at the German cultural foe, but the American one as well. I would like to speculate on how the lowbrows might be striking back, attacking the whole notion of a cultural sphere, German or not, separate from and above their understanding. To do this, I would like to move Trommler's analysis in the direction of an examination of the social implications of the culture of *Kultur* in precisely that period when new notions of ethnic identity, religious practice and values, gender relations, and modern industrial labor relations were being formed.

But before elaborating on this thesis, let me explore some of Trommler's fascinating insights. By focusing not just on the actual cultural treasures that came to America in this period but on such copies as the plaster casts sent to Harvard, he makes us see the importance of these exchanges as symbolic acts, valued precisely as a counterweight to French and English culture. And the apparent success of German cultural politics vis-à-vis the defeated neighbor France in the years after the Franco-Prussian War perhaps gave much impetus to the continuing use of this symbolic politics long after it started to backfire, when, as Trommler notes, the Kaiser started to exemplify and carry the weight of German culture on his authoritarian shoulders.[3]

As symbol, Trommler sees the notion of *Kultur* as "an exclusively German concept of higher aims," bringing with it an implicit sense of superiority to Anglo-Saxon culture and opening up both the German bearers of this tradition and the German-American supporters of this cultural politics to the attacks of elite critics, in whom it aroused "the traditional English opposition against status-related *Kultur*." I wonder, however, if Trommler's use of Raymond Williams' formulation is appropriate in this period for both the American highbrow and lowbrow, for although there is no doubt that such an opposition to German culture appeared within the elites, elite Americans still accepted some notion of culture as separate and apart, which was not a formulation appreciated by the lowbrow.

As a way into the argument, let me quickly relate what may be a familiar episode of high cultural relations during the war. This is the famous "Star Spangled Banner" incident. The Boston Symphony Orchestra stood at the pinnacle of American cultural achievement during this period. Having been among the first symphony orchestras to be created in the period of cultural consolidation at the end of the nineteenth century, it had always maintained a consciously highbrow profile.

Unlike the orchestras of Theodore Thomas in both New York and Chicago, which, at least in their early years, made some gesture in the direction of their audience, Henry Higginson's orchestra stood for only the classics since its founding in 1881, and left any concession to other tastes to the Boston Pops. Always led by European-trained, German-speaking conductors, Higginson's was the first professional orchestra in America, achieving artistic success chiefly through the control of the professional lives of its musicians according to rigid and binding labor contracts.

The World War I version of the orchestra was led by Karl Muck, an arrogant and brilliant musician – and a known sympathizer to the German cause, for which he was regularly castigated in the press. The attacks on him reached a crescendo when, on 30 October 1917, he did not play the national anthem to begin a concert in Providence, Rhode Island. Although he would start each subsequent concert with the familiar national song derived from an old drinking tune, and he would claim that he did not realize that the request had been made before the Providence concert (because he certainly would have honored it if he had known about it), it was enough of a symbolic act of refusal – at least as countlessly reiterated in the popular press – to lead ultimately to accusations of espionage. Muck was arrested on 25 March 1918 and interned until the war was over, even though he was not technically German, but a bona fide Swiss citizen with the papers to prove it.[4]

These contemporaneous images, of the barbarian clubbing America with culture and the arrogant conductor refusing to play the national anthem in old New England, stand at the end of a period that has fascinated American historians struggling to understand the transformation of the country and its culture from 1877 to World War I. As Trommler and Levine show us, the wresting of what would become the canon from the hands of everyone to establish it as a special elite preserve began at precisely that time in American history when the nation, fresh from the Civil War, was struggling to redefine itself. The industrial revolution unleashed powerful forces in society: the demand for women's rights, the formation of unions, the growth of social and political radicalism, the explosion of the popular press, the creation of hundreds of colleges and universities. At a time (1880) when England had four degree-granting institutions, Ohio alone had thirty-seven. This was a time when the role of religion was again questioned, when the social gospel and Christian socialism emerged, while the force of fundamentalism reformed. Race became a national issue and control of the nation's wealth and political future was up for grabs. Stirring this brew was yet another new wave of immigration, this time from southern and eastern Europe, which threatened to undermine the hegemony of the older English-, German-, and emerging Irish-Americans.

If looked at in the context that is being sketched much too briefly here, some of what Richard Hofstadter chose to call anti-intellectualism in American life starts to take on a more intelligible cast.[5] As colleges are being founded on the frontier, culture is being removed to a higher plane. And as journalism reaches out to a growing audience, Shakespeare is becoming the preserve of the elites. Read against this background, it makes sense that culture would become such a battleground for all segments of America. What might be at work when people clamored to hear the "Star Spangled Banner" from the nation's leading orchestra was not just a critique of the German sympathizer on the podium, but a sign of the anger with which that portion of the population most affected by the war was registering its protest against all forms of domination, not the least of which was the appropriation of classical music by the cultural and economic elites. The musical canonization that took place in the late nineteenth century was a thoroughgoing one that involved not just manners and decorum inside the hall, but what constituted classical music in general and how it was to be performed. This process repeatedly pitted the highbrow against the lowbrow. Italian opera – common music in many parts of America, influencing jazz in New Orleans and on the lips of workers in the streets of New York and New Iberia – was slowly and steadily degraded in favor of a German canon. At the same time, that canon was fixed in performance. No longer would popularizations of compositions be countenanced. The day was over when a Mozart could celebrate hearing his works being turned into dance music, for the guardians of the canon at the end of the century wanted to fix for all time a "pure" way of performing as well as an "appropriate" way of listening.[6]

One message that we can read in the poster associated the Germanization of culture with new elitist measures that would take the so-called canon away from the people. The fights in the cultural realm were reproduced again and again in this period, in almost all parts of American life. They even appeared in local class conflicts that resisted ethnic solidarity. In 1872, in Philadelphia, German-American furniture workers walked off the job to demonstrate for an eight-hour day, joining a strike begun by their colleagues at the Steinway Piano factory in New York City. These workers were admonished by the German-American factory owners to remember that they were Germans, and that the strike against their fellow countrymen struck a blow against ethnic and cultural solidarity. The strike leaders responded by exhorting their fellow workers to learn English, because their salvation lay not in obeying the dictates of their class and cultural superiors in the German community, reflected also in the derisive comments directed towards the workers in the German-American press, but, rather, lay in solidarity with their fellow, American workers. The appeal to communal solidarity would wear thinner and thinner when proposed from above, but in the same city of Philadelphia, fifteen years later, the same skilled workers would pull together against their fellow workers of other ethnicities when their own craft prerogatives were at stake.[7]

Both radical and deeply conservative reactions to the lead of the elite were clear in the political and the religious realm. A great wave of popular radicalism engulfed the country in this period, centered significantly not on the eastern seaboard, but in the midwest, south, and southwest, where the populist and socialist movements gained their greatest strength during this period of "democratic promise" by appealing to the intelligence of the common citizen. Almost exclusively peopled by self-taught men and women who published their ideas in countless periodicals and pamphlets, these movements gloried in homegrown solutions to economic and social problems. Such populist figures as Mary Ellen Lease and Senator William A. Pfeffer from Kansas were caricatured ceaselessly by the respectable press, while socialists like Eugene V. Debs, Mary Harris "Mother" Jones, and J. A. Wayland were cruelly lampooned as misguided and dangerous crackpots. The populist and socialist press, from whom many of the leaders of these movements emerged, denounced the moneyed elite and gloried in their own self-taught wisdom, caricaturing the puffed-up European-like fastidiousness and arrogance that they found in their urban critics.[8] The class enemy was also the cultural other.

The impulse for reform that came from above, manifested politically in that loose confederation of forces known as the Progressive movement, had a counterpart in the religious realm in the social gospel movement. The Progressives and the respectable religious leaders of the mainline movements wanted to reassert a kind of moral authority over their charges, and they disdained, or at least discouraged, autonomous labor organizations, attempting to lure back to the fold those who found their salvation elsewhere. This move was countered at every step by city and country Christians who held tent meetings in Kansas as well as in North Philadelphia in an attempt to assert the authority of the everyday worshipper against the domination of ritual in a hierarchical church.[9]

The main statement of the poster "Destroy this Mad Brute, Enlist" is simple and clear: to defend America from the barbarian – a typical message of patriotic appeals. But the specific linking of *Kultur* to a gorilla with a nude white woman struggling to be free from his grasp appeals to a whole set of contradictory impulses in American society, contradictions that I have tried to make clear in this comment. These are the ideas that fueled both the elite revulsion at German militarism and culture and the lowbrow reaction to it. The wrecked church, the striding military arrogance, and *Kultur* as a club vividly bring to life the complex emotional reaction to the connection between the war and German culture. But the two most obvious symbols remain unexplored: the gorilla and the woman. Here we see two of the most powerful images that our culture has to offer, and it is in this twin image, I would submit, that we might begin to find the common ground of both the lowbrow and highbrow in American life.

What seems to be at work is a classic example of displacement. Patriotic propaganda always functions to reconcile conflicting forces in the struggle against the common enemy. The internal struggle, the internal tensions of American society, are here displaced on a common, external enemy. But the language of the racial other and the role of gender in making the image a visceral one would have a powerful resonance in this period. Racist hysteria, fears of miscegenation, and rape are here conflated with high culture in a way not dissimilar to the program of the Societies for the Suppression of Vice, first made prominent by Anthony Comstock in 1872 in New York, and carried on with much greater success into the twentieth century in Boston. These societies made explicit the connection between the pornographic and the foreign while maintaining that purity had the protection of the family as its goal. This image embodies these fears. High culture, of any kind, encourages display, and is in this sense antithetical to American notions of moral propriety, a challenge to High Victorian notions of the respectable. The special tragedy of America is that race became the language of the displacement of these fears.[10]

Notes to Chapter 6

I'd like to thank Joan W. Scott, Nicholas B. Dirks, and Mary M. Steedly for their comments on this comment.

1. These posters were often icons of popular culture that sought to fix in the minds of their viewers a caricature of the enemy that would motivate their audience to acts of patriotic fervor. Picturing the foe as a rapist with animal-like features was a stock stereotype of both World War I and World War II posters published by Europeans, Americans, and Asians. Instead of portraying the German foe as a human with animal traits, this poster, which is reproduced in Sam Keen, *Faces of the Enemy: Reflections of the Hostile Imagination* (San Francisco: Harper & Row, 1986), p. 76, goes all the way. See also Shawn Aubitz and Gail F. Stern, "Ethnic Images in World War I Posters," *Journal of American Culture* 9/4 (Winter 1986); 83–98.

2. Here I am recalling Robert H. Wiebe's argument in *The Search for Order, 1877–1920* (New York: Hill & Wang, 1967).

3. See the works of Allan Mitchell, who has promised in the third volume of his trilogy to study in depth the effect of German culture on France after 1870. The first two works suggest the direction he is moving toward, *The German Influence in France after 1870: The Formation of the French Republic* (Chapel Hill: University of North Carolina Press, 1979) and *Victors and Vanquished: The German Influence on Army and Church in France after 1870* (Chapel Hill: University of North Carolina Press, 1984). I'd like to thank Joan W. Scott for pointing out the connection here between German policy in America and France.

4. The story has most recently been told by Alan Howard Levy, "The American Symphony at War: German-American Musicians and Federal Authorities During World War I," *Mid-America: An Historical Review* 71/1 (January 1980), 5–13. He brandished those citizenship papers on the stage of Carnegie Hall in January 1918. After the war, Muck went to Hamburg where he worked until his death in 1940.

5. I think that Hofstadter's work needs to be turned upside down, looking not just from the point of view of the intellectual, but from those who may have suffered from intellectuals. T.J. Jackson Lears has begun that work, but much more needs to be done. See Richard Hofstadter, *Anti-intellectualism in American Life* (New York: Knopf, 1966) and Lears, *No Place of Grace: Anti-modernism and the Transformation of American Culture, 1880–1920* (New York: Pantheon, 1981).

6. Levine's work is in many ways prefigured by the work of Barbara L. Tischler, whose *An American Music: The Search for an American Musical Identity* (New York: Oxford, 1986) identifies and elaborates upon what Levine would later make prominent. For a provocative elaboration of a similar argument for avant-garde music, which might be useful read against Trommler's concluding comments on the nature of the modern, see Susan McClary, "Terminal Prestige: The Case of Avant-Garde Music Composition," *Cultural Critique* 12 (Spring 1989), 57–82.

7. See Ken Fones-Wolf and Elliott Shore, "The German Press and Working-Class Politics in Gilded-Age Philadelphia," in Fones-Wolf, Shore, and James P. Danky (eds.), *The German-American Radical Press, 1850–1930* (Urbana-Champaign: University of Illinois Press, 1992).

8. Lawrence Goodwyn's work *Democratic Promise: The Populist Movement in America* (New York: Oxford, 1976) is the most fully developed consideration of the populists as a group of men and women whose political enthusiasm came from their own resources. For the socialists, see Nick Salvatore, *Eugene V. Debs: Citizen and Socialist* (Urbana: University of Illinois Press, 1982) and my *Talkin' Socialism: J. A. Wayland and the Role of the Radical Press in American Socialism* (Lawrence: University Press of Kansas, 1988). A contemporary manifestation of the construction of the politics of radical culture is a Midwest political/literary journal called *Foolkiller*, whose motto reads: "We prefer crude vigor to polished banality."

9. See Ken Fones-Wolf, *Trade Union Gospel: Christianity and Labor in Industrial Philadelphia, 1865–1915* (Philadelphia: Temple University Press, 1989).

10. For a full examination of the relationship between these twin images (and much else besides), see the monumental work of Donna Haraway, *Primate Visions: Gender, Race, and Nature in the World of Modern Science* (New York: Routledge, 1989). The King Kong image that this poster predates by a generation is explicitly examined in Haraway's work. On Comstock, see the work of Nicola Beisel of the University of Michigan, who skillfully interweaves the stories of the suppression of vice in Boston, Philadelphia, and New York with the work of Pierre Bourdieu and makes clear the linkages between the foreign other and the fear for the family. See her "'Morals Versus Art': Censorship, Class Reproduction and the Victorian Nude" draft in the possession of Nicholas B. Dirks.

7

Promoting *Kaiser* and *Reich*: Imperial German Propaganda in the United States during World War I

Reinhard R. Doerries

"We Tell the Truth" reads a wartime advertisement of the ill-famed journal *The Fatherland*, published by the colorful George Sylvester Viereck.[1] A thorough, scholarly investigation of the people and media employed to bring German truth to the American people during World War I has not been done yet, in spite of the fact that the bulk of the relevant archival material has been returned to Germany since the 1960s and American documents of the period are freely accessible. Certainly diverse, specific aspects of German propaganda have been scrutinized repeatedly in the larger context of German-American relations,[2] and some of the major propagandists have published their memoirs and views.[3] The lack of an overall appraisal has meant, however, that the question about the effects of the publicity still remains largely unanswered. That German propaganda did not, in the end, prevent the United States from joining the Allies, merely suggests its ineffectiveness as far as the final target was concerned. This failure does not by itself suggest anything about the influences positive or negative, upon various sectors of the American public. Nor should the final overall failure of German propaganda activities lead us to ignore the respective German operatives and their schemes in neutral America prior to 1917.

There is no shortage of informative studies on public relations and propaganda methods in general, and propaganda in its various forms has long been accepted as a part of the wider area of international relations. While the turn of the century was not characterized by an oversaturation of information on all levels of society as we know it today, there certainly were men and organizations concerned with what we would call public relations. Diplomats, in the course of their daily contacts and negotiations, were very much occupied with the image of the nation they represented, and the records clearly contain sufficient evidence to claim the existence of outright propaganda. The difference between propaganda

Notes to Chapter 7 can be found on page 158

campaigns prior to World War I and the far-flung media networks transmitting manipulated information at the end of the twentieth century would appear to be less the purpose than the state of the art. Wireless transmission of information was already possible and widely practiced, but the stations were relatively primitive, difficult to hide because of the size of the necessary equipment, and easily interfered with by unfriendly governments. Detection and sabotage, therefore, were much easier than in our own time, and entire campaigns were likely to grind to a halt if the relatively small number of wireless stations were put out of commission. Control of international sea lanes, the respective size of a nation's commercial fleet, the consular corps, and business representatives all played a more important part in the propaganda schemes of earlier wars.

When the "Guns of August" shattered the uneasy peace of 1914, both the entente and Central Powers almost immediately dispatched their operatives to North America.[4] The German government first intended to send the smooth Richard von Kühlmann, but then, for reasons not entirely clear, ordered the former Colonial Secretary Bernhard Dernburg to go to America.[5] We are still uncertain whether his mission was propaganda from the outset or whether, as is sometimes asserted, he took on the propaganda work after failing in his original task of placing a German War bond issue.[6] As it was, the Imperial Ambassador Johann Heinrich Count von Bernstorff, when he sailed for the United States, was accompanied not only by Bernhard Dernburg, but also by Geheimrat Heinrich F. Albert. The latter officially represented the German government's *Zentraleinkaufsgesellschaft*, but for much of his stay in the United States was also, in fact, deeply committed to propaganda activities, particularly after Dernburg's usefulness had come to an end during the noisy hullabaloo after the torpedoing of the British passenger liner *Lusitania* in the early summer of 1915.[7]

When they reached New York on 25 August 1914, the Germans did not have to begin quite from scratch. Both Count Bernstorff and his predecessor, Hermann Freiherr Speck von Sternburg, had had a special budget for propaganda, and both had retained at least one journalist.[8] Bernstorff, it should be pointed out, had acquired significant experience in the area of public relations during his tenure in London, and his fine relations with the American press before World War I, at least in part, may have been a consequence of that experience.[9] By contrast, Dernburg seems to have had no previous knowledge of influencing public opinion, and Albert, from all indications, appears to have been an extremely thorough, if not to say somewhat pedantic, largely commercially oriented man.[10] When they landed in New York, they found a propaganda organization hurriedly put together by Heinrich Charles, who had founded the German-American Chamber of Commerce in New York City just prior to the beginning of the war. Whether Charles' propaganda office, closed by the German diplomats and replaced with their own organization, was at the root of the initial problems of the German propagandists in the autumn of 1914 cannot be ascertained in retrospect. Closing down an existing office with all the accompanying controversy and adverse publicity, surely was not the smoothest approach to public relations efforts in America.[11]

Worst of all, the former Colonial Secretary was not one to take a back seat. Very soon after their arrival, Dernburg and Bernstorff were perceived, at least by some interested observers, to be working against each other. Whether the British fully understood this unpleasant development on the German side or whether they merely misrepresented the matter in order to damage the German Ambassador's position, is a matter open to speculation. When the British Ambassador, Sir Cecil Spring Rice, told President Woodrow Wilson's advisor, Colonel Edward M. House, on 20 September 1914, that Bernstorff was "thoroughly unreliable" and "sent to America because it was thought he could do no harm there," he was certainly twisting matters. When he added that "Dr. Dernberg [sic], for [sic] Colonial Secretary in Berlin . . . was a more important man to see" and that he had been sent to America "because of Bernstorff's known incompetency," he was evidently trying to confuse Colonel House.[12] Other than corresponding directly with certain officers in Berlin and thus bypassing the ambassador, Dernburg does not seem to have had major problems with Count Bernstorff. At least the documents do not contain evidence of serious disloyalty on the part of Dernburg. Instead, lack of organization, egotism, and tactlessness seem to have been at the root of the lack of cooperation.

Having shut down the publicity enterprise of Heinrich Charles, the Germans lost no time organizing a new press office. For no particular reason and in sharp contrast to the extremely careful operations of the British, they set up shop with considerable fanfare and engaged a colorful group of diverse talents. Since the complete minutes of the first business meeting of the new organization have been preserved, we are fully informed about the structure and the objectives of the undertaking. The meeting took place on 28 September 1914, on the premises of the Hamburg-American Line at 45 Broadway. It was attended by Bernhard Dernburg; Heinrich F. Albert; Anton Meyer-Gerhard, a former staff member of the Imperial Colonial Office; Julius P. Meyer, Director of the Hamburg-American Line in New York; Frederick F. Schrader, a man of some voice among politically active German-Americans; A. Rau, an associate of George Sylvester Viereck; a man called Clausen (probably

Matthew B. Claussen of the Hamburg-American Line in New York); and Karl A. Fuehr (a former interpreter at the German Consulate General in Yokohama). Dernburg outlined the following aspects of the planned operation: (1) The preparation of the material to be disbursed, (2) ways of distributing the material, (3) the financial side of the enterprise, and (4) the content of the material to be distributed. Those present agreed that the material needed would come from German and British newspapers reaching the United States, from information collected by the staff of *The Fatherland*, from the Imperial Embassy in Washington, and, of course, from articles to be written by themselves. The propaganda material was to be prepared in an office rented for Karl A. Fuehr in the Townsend Building at 1123 Broadway. Dernburg proposed that a special commission, consisting of Albert, Viereck, and Claussen, should be responsible for "control over the material." Dernburg further underlined that the funds needed for the operation were not coming from the Imperial Embassy but, in fact, were private donations from friends of Germany. When Viereck estimated his costs for preparing the material at about $500 a week, and Claussen proposed to employ 8 to 10 persons for his press office at a cost of $700 a week, Dernburg promised that Albert would pay each of them $500 per week. Concerning the tenor of the texts, the German operatives apparently agreed with Dernburg that all polemics should be avoided. Topics such as brutality of soldiers, the violation of Belgian neutrality, Serbia in general, and German militarism were not to be handled.

The minutes of this meeting are of importance for a number of reasons. They confirm without any doubt that the official German representatives organized an official propaganda office in the fall of 1914. Claims that the Imperial Embassy was not underwriting the operating costs are a clear misrepresentation of the facts. The minutes also show that Dernburg, already at the end of September, less than a month after his arrival, had been given control over German propaganda in the United States.[13]

Bernstorff, who forwarded these minutes to Berlin, leaves no doubt as to the financial base of the planned operation: "Mr. Dernburg is now dedicating his time exclusively to the press, which lightens my load, and I have given him the necessary means for the [press] office." While numerous messages from the Imperial Treasury demonstrate that the operations of Dernburg and Albert were being financed from German government accounts, it is not entirely clear whether all funds used were made available by Berlin or whether the relatively small German bond issues placed in the United States were also employed to acquire additional funds. The Secretary of the Imperial Treasury, in fact, already on

11 August 1914, had told the Foreign Office: "Funds for possible personal expenses of Mr. Dernburg as well as for such expenses, which become necessary due to a respective influence upon the American press, would be taken from the Imperial accounts. . . . The press expenses in the end would be accounted for in the secret account."[14]

As if to underline the importance of the work of the press office in New York, the ambassador himself attended some of the meetings, and it is difficult to believe that he was not rather fully informed about the operations.[15] His controversy with Dernburg, in fact, suggests that the two men repeatedly saw each other and possibly disagreed on some major procedures. Whatever Bernstorff and Dernburg may have shared by way of a certain liberal political stand, there also seem to have been insurmountable differences. The ambassador was a very sensitive individual, given to diplomatic negotiations and, in general, holding or at least exhibiting a tolerant view of his opponents. By contrast, Dernburg, a large hulk of a man and gifted with a booming voice, appears to have been inclined to force issues. Diplomatic tact does not seem to have been one of his major characteristics. If Bernstorff saw pacifism in America as a political sentiment to be recognized and delt with, Dernburg explained American pacifism as part of the "effeminacy of feeling of a nation that has not seen a war for more than 50 years."[16] Particularly revealing are the notes jotted down by Oswald Garrison Villard, the publisher, after he had lunch with Bernstorff on 15 May 1915. It was shortly after a German submarine had torpedoed the luxury liner *Lusitania* in the Irish Sea, sending 1,198 civilians, including 124 American citizens, to their death. Bernstorff told Villard confidentially that he had been to see Lansing "and offered to make Dernburg go. There were few things he could do in this emergency, but he thought he could do that and help relieve the stress and remove a cause of offence in this way." The ambassador felt that Dernburg had done well in writing articles, but that his nervousness had gotten the better of him when he had started to give interviews. He would have sent Dernburg home months ago if it had not been for the demands from German-American groups who clamored for action. In other words, Dernburg was permitted to continue his appearances because the ambassador felt organized German-Americans would misinterpret the recall of the rambunctious propagandist.[17]

While Dernburg certainly was a major obstacle to a less noisy and, therefore, possibly more effective campaign in the United States, he was not the only operative lacking the skills required of a successful public-relations man. Few of those who wrote articles and brochures, addressed Americans at public and private meetings, and advised German officials in Berlin about America had experience in publicity work or knew

America well enough to appraise public opinion and cultural traditions. Among those who either were called upon by the Germans to assist in the American propaganda work or who volunteered their services were the Harvard professor of psychology Hugo Münsterberg; Edmund von Mach, the art historian at the Bradford Academy in Cambridge; the American journalist James F. J. Archibald; the German economist Moritz Julius Bonn; the American journalist William Bayard Hale; the German professor of philosophy Eugen Kühnemann; and Kuno Meyer, the Celtic studies expert from Berlin, on leave of absence from his minister of culture and with false papers from the German Foreign Office declaring him to be a businessman.[18]

Possibly because academics tend to leave behind a written record, their activities in Germany and the United States during these turbulent years are well documented and have been scrutinized repeatedly, most thoroughly on the American side by Carol Gruber in her study inspired by Richard Hofstadter at Columbia University and entitled *Mars and Minerva: World War I and the Uses of the Higher Learning in America*,[19] and on the German side by Klaus Schwabe in his 1958 dissertation supervised by Gerhard Ritter at Freiburg and entitled *Wissenschaft und Kriegsmoral: Die deutschen Hochschullehrer und die politischen Grundfragen des Ersten Weltkrieges*.[20] While this is not the place to take a closer look at American university professors and their leanings towards one side or the other during the war, a brief consideration of German academics in the service of the Imperial propaganda organization should be included. From the records it is evident that most of the German academics either volunteered for the work or followed an invitation from official circles. Some of them already had demonstrated a real interest in America prior to the war. Others were called upon because it was hoped that their academic reputation would lend a certain strength to their political expressions. Again others, like Moritz Julius Bonn, just happened to be in the United States and stayed, not having gone there for this type of work, but also certainly not having been forced into it.

One of the most vociferous academics on the German side was Hugo Münsterberg, the Harvard psychologist who had come from Germany in the 1890s. Not one to underestimate his own grandeur and influence, he participated in almost all aspects of German propaganda, from the bumptious efforts of George Sylvester Viereck and his *Fatherland* to the more sophisticated plan of winning the former president and political activist Theodore Roosevelt for the German side. "I am regrettably the only German, who has long lasting intimate contacts to the leading men of the country . . . ," he informed the Imperial Chancellor in Berlin. And a short while later he reported: "I took on the task on my own responsibility, knowing well how hopeless it seemed. From intimate knowledge of his (TR's) character I knew that, if I could just build him a bridge, his conceit and ambition would not overlook it."[21] There can be no doubt that Hugo Münsterberg was a German agent who was privy to most German propaganda plans in the United States and who cultivated close contacts with other German operatives on every level. Robert Lansing referred to him as "a German subject, in fact an agent of the German Government," and when he died in 1916, his family approached the German Foreign Office for financial assistance.[22]

Another representative of academia who served as German propaganda agent was Eugen Kühnemann, whose masquerade as a German businessman has already been mentioned. He went to the United States in September 1914 and stayed until May 1917. Later, he proudly publicized that he had traveled 107,000 miles, spoken in 137 different towns and cities, in some of them several times, visited 36 states in the course of his work, given 121 speeches in English and 275 in German, and addressed more than 200,000 people altogether. How well his propaganda efforts were received by his audiences is another question. Even the German Military Attaché, Captain Franz von Papen, generally not known for his diplomatic acumen, wrote to the War Ministry in Berlin that while Kühnemann's message, "An deutschem Wesen muß die Welt genesen," was important, the way he chose to deliver it to U.S. audiences was damaging to Germany's interests. Kühnemann's very personal report on his activities, *Deutschland und Amerika*, is a fascinating documentation on the cultural differences between American and German culture, and the author's biting and often unjust comments on Americans and their society should not deter the modern reader from recognizing the documentary value of these memoirs. Most notably, Kühnemann often slips out of the superficial language of propaganda and allows us to see his very personal views. It may be more than coincidental that one of the more reserved and intelligent voices of German-America, Kuno Francke, was befriended by this paid messenger of German culture.[23]

Not all academic warriors fighting the propaganda battle in America were doing as well as Kühnemann. Karl Oskar Bertling, for instance, whom the Germans had brought over from the Amerika-Institut in Berlin, was so thoroughly unsuccessful that already two months after his arrival the German ambassador wrote to the Imperial Chancellor requesting permission to send him back: "[Bertling] is driven by the best of intention, but he has no experience in journalistic matters. Also his ability to appraise people is rather small. . . . I would ask Your Excellency to be allowed to send him back. Circumstances being what they are, we will have to drag him through with us."[24] In the end, Bertling was arrested following the American declaration of war in the spring of 1917 and taken to Fort Oglethorpe in Georgia, where a number of other German agents, such as Felix Armand Sommerfeld, were housed after 1917.[25]

Numerous academic personalities inside Germany also actively supported the Imperial German propaganda apparatus. The connections between Kuno Meyer and his brother, the highly reputed ancient historian and later *Rektor* of the university in Berlin, Eduard Meyer, are evident.[26] Others, such as the theologian Adolf Deißmann, the zoologist and philosopher Ernst Haeckel, the Jena philosophy professor Rudolf Eucken, the theologian Adolf von Harnack, the historian Friedrich Meinecke, the historian Hans Delbrück, and the philosopher and psychologist Wilhelm Wundt, have not received much attention in the literature on the war, but their emotional public statements often became known abroad or found their way into print across the Atlantic. Some of them, in fact, explicitly wrote for American readers.[27] Thus Eduard Meyer, in August 1914, felt inclined to tell Americans that German revenge was unavoidable in Belgium as a consequence of the attacks on German soldiers by the "verwilderte Pöbel Belgiens." His reassuring vow to Americans: "There is on earth no army that is more humane than the German army."[28] "An Appeal From Eucken and Haeckel," published in *The Independent* in New York in September 1914, instructed American readers: "Great Britain is fighting for a Slavic, semi-Asiatic power against Teutonism; she is fighting not only in the ranks of barbarism, but also on the side of wrong and injustice. . . . England was envious of Germany's greatness. . . . Upon England alone rests the monstrous guilt and the responsibility in the eye of world history."[29] Adolf von Harnack, the theologian, speaking from the elevated pulpit of his professional reputation, thrashed America and President Woodrow Wilson with the indictment: "What then has democratic pacifism of America, praised by Wilson as the saving strength of the world, in reality done since the beginning of the war? . . . It has committed the greatest crime of the world's history, as has been said rightfully; for it has made possible the war of lies as well as England's starvation war against us. . . . From a genuine democratic republican to a deceitfully embellished imperialist! – this is the course of development Wilson has gone through, and with him many an American regrettably has abandoned his better wisdom, yes, indeed, disavowed earlier ideals."[30] One of the high points of German professorial intervention in the undisciplined hubbub of war propaganda was the much publicized manifesto in October 1914 by ninety-three scholars and members of the German intelligentsia, among them such names as Gustav von Schmoller, Eduard Meyer, Walter Nernst, Hans Thoma,

Franz von Stuck, Ulrich von Wilamowitz-Moellendorff, and Adolf von Schlatter. Addressing the *Kulturwelt*, the German intellectuals protested against "the lies and libel with which our enemies try to sully German's clean institutions in this difficult battle for existence forced upon it." The manifesto, in the end supported by almost all professors in Germany, may have been a true expression of the mental state of German intellectuals, writers, and artists; outside Germany it merely contributed to the growing cultural estrangement of the Germans from the rest of Europe and North America. Reactions were sharp, and no lesser person than the well-known New Historian James Harvey Robinson appraised the manifesto as "the sign and seal of the success of German *Kultur* in making all her subjects accept the Kaiser and his decisions in exactly the same unquestioning and dutiful spirit in which the Jesuit accepts the organization of the Roman apostolic church and the decrees of its head."[31]

If the voices emanating from Germany were ill suited to win American public opinion for the Kaiser and his state, the German diplomats and agents in the United States had little more to recommend them to the man on the street. From the very beginning, the German operatives split their energies between a string of different campaigns directed at ethnic groups, such as German-Americans, Irish-Americans, American Jews, Austro-Hungarians, and even such an unlikely group as the Indians in America. Further targets of Imperial propaganda were the Catholic Church, and expectedly, the German Lutherans, who early in the century were still divided into numerous synods. Whether the German propaganda scheme actually included efforts among America's Black population must remain a matter of speculation until more substantial research has been done. Aside from what would appear to be incidental leads, the usual sources have not revealed persuasive evidence of German activities in this direction.

Moreover, German propaganda was not confined to lectures and articles in the press. Existing organizations and political groups were influenced, and new organizations were founded, to press for the maintenance of American neutrality and, by the same token, prevent all support for the war efforts of the entente. Many of the individuals involved were or became what can only be described as German agents; others were Irish revolutionaries, labor radicals, Hindu revolutionaries, or Jewish activists. Some of those working for the Germans were paid for their services; many others, however, were driven by hatred for such lands as Great Britain or Russia. When Count Bernstorff and his staff realized that the regular ethnic media they were supporting did not reach a large sector of the American population, they decided to purchase American newspapers. That most German propagandists also became involved in

143

or associated with various projects often referred to as *Propaganda der Tat* diminished and, in some cases, destroyed their effectiveness. All too often their names appeared in the press in connection with illegal acts or campaigns that could easily be associated with disloyalty to America.[32] The demise of the Privy Counselor Heinrich Albert on a Manhattan subway on a sultry summer day in 1915, with the subsequent sensationalist press coverage of German activities in the neutral United States, may serve as one of the more spectacular examples of irresponsible action by a German agent.[33]

German-Americans certainly were the largest ethnic group addressed by the Kaiser's agents. While a number of scholars have scrutinized German-American reaction to World War I, and much has been made of the imagined or real sufferings of this ethnic group as a consequence of the U.S. entry into the war on the side of the Allies, we still lack a full-scale investigation based on the mass of documentary evidence now available for several years. The question concerning the degree of assimilation of the Germans in America prior to World War I cannot be covered here, and it could even be argued that the degree of ethnic maintenance among German-Americans may not be of immediate relevance for an evaluation of the German propaganda campaign.[34] Neither the German intelligence service nor its German-American operatives appear to have been able to comprehend ethnicity as a social or political force. More significant in this context might be an investigation of the numerous German-American associations and institutions in order to determine whether they represented a cross-section of German-American political feeling, or whether they were mere vehicles for the political views of a number of individuals who, in fact, did not represent the majority of German-Americans. To the uninitiated observer, German-America, if such designation is justified at all in view of the different generations and their varied interests, offered a picture of turbulent excitement. Most evident were the relief campaigns for those suffering from the war, in East Prussia for instance, but the war-bond drives and the low-brow celebrations of patriotic sentiment were equally visible. "German-American newspapers sold pictures of the Kaiser, official German casualty lists, 'War Albums,' American and German flags, watch-fobs, souvenir spoons of the Kaiser, the Kaiserin and General Paul von Hindenburg, new war postcards from Germany, and 'Iron Cross' watches, and contributed part of the proceeds to the relief fund for German widows and orphans."[35]

Whether German agents and a few German-Americans of influence were the prime agitators behind such spectacle, or whether many German-Americans were genuinely moved and eager to express their sympa-

thies for the German cause, must remain an open question. Without doubt, however, the agents employed existing organizations ranging from the powerful National German-American Alliance to smaller regional and local groups. Political, cultural, and religious associations were of equal interest to the Germans, and even Jewish and Roman Catholic organizations, hardly known for their closeness to official circles in Imperial Germany, were not excluded from the propaganda campaign.

What most German propagandists, with the exception of the ambassador, do not seem to have comprehended was the absence of German-Americans and their activities from the mainstream of American political life. Contrary to the American Irish, they had little official clout in Washington, and their attempts to gain recognition were often marked by disunity. Within the existing political parties they wielded no political influence comparable to that of their American Irish contemporaries.[36] Eugen Kühnemann, the German propagandist, explained in his memoirs the German political ineptitude this way: "The old German state was a state of officials and officers. Our kings, our officials, and officers had created it. The people were only governed masses. They were used to see and leave the public life of the state in the hands of the professionals. They had no part. With these habits they came to the new world. . . . The Germans continued to live as apolitical beings, according to their custom."[37]

Among the German ethnic organizations, one of the most vociferous was the National German-American Alliance, which united and represented a large number of state and local German associations. Members of the state associations were also members automatically of the National Alliance, and independent members could only come from those few states that did not have associations.[38] While it may be accurate, as has been asserted, that the National Alliance was not in the main a politically but rather a culturally motivated organization, its activities on all levels certainly also sought to shape what it understood to be German-American political opinion. Examining the development of the National Alliance, it is difficult to overlook the connections to the *Alldeutsche Verband* (Pan-Germans) and the goals of that association, namely to establish close ties to the *Auslandsdeutsche* and to strengthen the *Deutschtum im Ausland* for the benefit of the fatherland.[39]

During the years of American neutrality, the National Alliance organized numerous public demonstrations during which speakers clearly representing the German viewpoint, demanded an end to the arms shipments to the Allies. Also, it was no secret that the National Alliance supported German agents, such as Eugen Kühnemann, who spoke at their mass meetings and was an honorary member of their Wisconsin state chapter. As often in time of crisis and under pressure from political interest groups, the campaign was not always characterized by tact and good taste, not to mention political acumen. In the final analysis, the German-American, Harvard professor Kuno Francke may well have been correct when he charged that the National Alliance tended to exacerbate Americans and, in fact, to increase "the bitterness against Germany." Hexamer, for his part, did not even pretend to be civil when he slanderized the American government: "We have never yet had such a miserable, weak-kneed government as now. . . ."[40] The end of the possibly most influential of all German-American associations came in 1918, when the Senate passed a bill revoking the charter of the Alliance because of "its disloyal and disgraceful career."[41]

In contrast to the already existing Alliance, other vehicles of propaganda had to be organized by the Germans after August 1914. Undoubtedly many of those who cooperated knew what they were doing, but it is worth remembering that propaganda and intelligence organizations tend, at times, to produce lists of people who, for various reasons, are considered useful for certain tasks. The appearance of a person on lists of this nature by itself represents no proof of the individual's involvement. One such organization was the German University League, whose members – according to Rudolf Pagenstecher there were 700 in 1915 – had studied at German universities. In the words of Carol S. Gruber, their "expectation" was "that intellectual and professional indebtedness to Germany would lead American professors naturally to sympathize with German aims in the war." The reasons for their failure to gain a stronger foothold in American academic circles may be less their own propagandistic incompetence or their evident misreading of U.S. public opinion than the firm British foundation of the American educational system and the highly developed intellectual independence of American academics.[42] Nevertheless, the German University League members are often thought to have had some influence, and Arthur S. Link refers to "a number of Americans of the old stock who took up the cudgels for Germany" and then names such well-known academics as the influential historian John W. Burgess, the professor of philosophy George Stuart Fullerton and the admiral and historian French E. Chadwick.[43]

One actual contribution of the German University League was the funneling of pro-German articles from American academics into George Sylvester Viereck's journals *The Fatherland* and *The International*, the latter acquired by Viereck already in 1912. Niel Johnson's description of Edmund von Mach, one of the organizers of the University League, as "the most prolific and provocative pro-German propagandist in World War I" may be somewhat overstating the case, but undoubtedly von

Mach had access to the German representatives and became a go-between for them and sectors of the American academic world.[44] Whether a large number of university professors were inclined to give consideration to what appeared to be blatant propaganda is another question. At least some of those addressed by the Germans openly attacked the German cause and found public channels to vent their opposing views, in a way thus pulling the rug out from under the German campaign.[45]

Other organizations connected with the German propaganda effort were, for instance, Labor's National Peace Council, the American Truth Society, and the Friends of Freedom for India. Labor's National Peace Council and its prime movers were so obviously German instruments that important American labor leaders, notably Samuel Gompers and his American Federation of Labor, were not inclined to lend them their support. The organization had been founded by Franz Rintelen, the still mysterious German naval agent who, in this, worked closely with David Lamar, the ill-famed "Wolf of Wall Street." While campaigning for an end of American shipments of arms to the Allies, the fomenting of strikes in the ammunition industry appears to have been one of the more urgent activities.[46] In 1915 the Imperial ambassador described such interference in the American arms industry as follows: "The method of inducing strikes differs from case to case. Largely it is labor leaders who are outfitted with the necessary means by our confidential agents. These agitators, who are totally ignorant of the origin of the funds they receive, are assisted by helpers who by pointing out the economic situation incite the workers on their way home from work or in the saloons to want to improve their lot."[47] The American Truth Society, actually founded shortly before World War I, was an Irish-American group led by the well-known but also controversial Jeremiah O'Leary. It was typical of a number of joint efforts of German propagandists and Irish-Americans. Such well-known German agents as George Sylvester Viereck, F.F. Schrader, and the Ridders of the *New Yorker Staats-Zeitung* were among its members.[48] The Friends of Freedom for India was one of several organizations that supported anti-British Indian groups in Germany and the United States. In the course of the war, German diplomats and agents not only established close relations with Hindu groups in the United States, but also brought numerous Indians from Germany and elsewhere to America and supported the rather ineffective revolutionary activities of the Hindus against the British. That such paramilitary actions were planned in and, in some cases, started from the neutral United States was not appreciated in Washington and later led to a complicated series of legal proceedings against the captured Asians and their German associates.[49]

Of considerable interest are the propaganda activities among American Jews. With the exception of Egmont Zechlin's *Die deutsche Politik und die Juden im Ersten Weltkrieg*, written, however, without research in any of the numerous respective American archives and thus limited in its usefulness, we have to this day no complete and reliable study of this phase of Imperial German propaganda.[50] The Germans entered the fray among the various Jewish groups and directions hoping that Jewish animosity towards Russia could be turned into pro-German sentiment. But even if such considerations may have had some promising aspects, the apparent urgency with which the Germans tackled this rather sensitive area of propaganda, and the evident lack of information in Berlin about the significant differences between the various Jewish activists and leaders, caused from the outset a poor selection of agents, created false expectations in German military and political circles, and, worst of all, tended to be counterproductive in the socially and culturally disunited Jewish ethnic groups in the United States. It remains an enigma how Berlin could have imagined penetrating the politically active and urbane Jewish leadership with the unimpressive agents dispatched to New York.

The so-called German Committee for the Liberation of the Russian Jews, founded by several leading German Jews and heavily supported by the German government, had a dual mission. While American Jewish public opinion was to be influenced in favor of Germany, the Germans also counted on Jewish support for their expansionist plans in Eastern Europe. The Committee was going to work "for a peace . . . that brings freedom to the suppressed peoples of Western Russia."[51] The agents Isaac Straus, Arthur Meyrowitz and S. M. Melamed may have looked like a good propaganda team, well suited to spread German ideas in American cities; the truth is that Berlin had ignored the strong religious-cultural diversity among American Jews and had made no effort to scrutinize the target before unleashing this phase of the war of words. Not surprisingly, the Imperial emissaries soon found themselves carried away by the swift undercurrents of diverse opinion inside the Jewish ethnic group. The quarrels finally reached such embarrassing staccato that at least one German agent, namely Meyrowitz, was paid a monthly salary just to be quiet and stay out of things. Isaac Straus, by the same token, created such unrest among New York Jews that the influential Warburgs wrote angry letters requesting an end to his activities.[52]

If the Jews from Russia were not always convinced of the sincerity of the German declarations, the Jews of German descent, still a powerful force among America Jews, remembered the rampant anti-Semitism that characterized Imperial Germany, and their willingness to serve Imperial interests was clearly not unlimited. All in all, one is not astonished to find that American Jews neither joined the German propaganda machine in appreciable numbers nor volunteered to offer their financial resources to buttress the German war effort. German militarism, even exhibited in the propaganda denying its existence, and past and current anti-Semitism did not lend itself to attract Jews of German or Russian descent. One of the more expressive examples of the political opinion of influential American Jews of German descent is a letter written to the German Foreign Office by Jacob Schiff, chief of the powerful American Jewish Committee, in 1915. In Schiff's words: "The sympathies of a majority of American Jews, who are in the main of Prussian origin, decidedly are on the side of Germany but I cannot but state that a good number of Jews, especially those born in this country, whose parents came here from Germany many years ago, do not completely share this sympathy, because the members of this younger generation, very much convinced of their human dignity, cannot forget that Germany has been the breeding ground of anti-Semitism and that this irresponsible movement has spread out further from Germany . . . a new spirit would have to be raised systematically in the German people, which naturally has to be initiated by the government, so that the harm which anti-Semitism has wrought will first of all be completely banned and, in the course of time, the virus which in this connection has gone into the blood of the German people will be completely eradicated."[53]

As already pointed out, when the Germans realized that they were not reaching vast sectors of the American public, they decided to purchase newspapers as pliable vehicles for their propaganda. In fact, early in the war they had become involved in the financial rescue of some tottering newspapers and journals. Almost from the beginning German money was funneled into such floundering enterprises as George Sylvester Viereck's *Fatherland* and Herman Ridder's *New Yorker Staats-Zeitung*. *The Fatherland* could have addressed American readers of other than German descent because it was published in English. Its message, however, was so evidently German propaganda that it is difficult to imagine most American readers being hoodwinked. Whether the German investment in what Carl Wittke has called "perhaps the most outspoken German propaganda sheet in America" paid any dividends, seems at least doubtful. When Count Bernstorff realized the uselessness of further payments to *The Fatherland*, "for this publication too has proved a failure," it was too late. There was no way to withdraw support from Viereck.[54]

Another weekly journal on the Imperial payroll was Marcus Braun's *Fair Play*. This gentleman persuaded the German embassy to subsidize his journal, and when Bernstorff tired of meeting his demands, he resorted to threatening the Germans with unfavorable publicity. The ambassador felt a great relief when he was able to extricate himself from this unpleasant and unrewarding relationship.[55]

A particularly difficult move for the Germans was the acquisition of a daily paper. The first engagement was with the well-known German-American *New Yorker Staats-Zeitung*, published in New York since 1834 and in considerable financial straits by 1914. Surviving documents indicate that already in October 1914 its owner, Herman Ridder, received a financial boost of $20,000, paid by Adolf Pavenstedt of Amsinck & Co. Barely two months later the German ambassador was requesting permission from Wilhelmstrasse to make another payment to the Ridders. Explaining the need of financing a debt of $550,000, Bernstorff told the German government that "[the paper's] collapse would be most disadvantageous to our interests." Bernhard Dernburg had been able to come up with half of the sum from German businesses in New York, but the other half was to be taken on by Berlin. When the Foreign Office displayed no particular interest in financing the Ridders' family newspaper, Bernstorff quickly trimmed his request to $200,000 and informed his superiors in Berlin that action was necessary "since otherwise [there is] danger of [the] paper going into hands that try to move the Germans here in another direction." Undersecretary Zimmermann seems to have understood the urgency and replied: "Agreed." The full extent of German control of this New York paper can be seen in Bernstorff's correspondence with the Foreign Office, occasioned by Herman Ridder's death in the late fall of 1915.[56]

If dealing with the Ridders was not an easy matter,[57] acquiring an English-language daily in New York turned out to be a difficult undertaking. Keeping the acquisition of the *New York Evening Mail* secret was one thing, but paying for it quite another, especially if every sizeable financial commitment had to be approved by the Berlin authorities. Beginning in the autumn of 1914, those involved in this drawn-out transaction, besides Count Bernstorff, were the Freiburg economist Gerhart von Schulze-Gaevernitz; an American businessman, Hermann Sielcken; Albert Ballin, from the Hamburg-American Line; Edward E. Rumely, a German-American with numerous contacts in Germany; Heinrich F. Albert; Bernhard Dernburg; the German Foreign Secretary Gottlieb von Jagow; and a number of law firms and banks.[58] In the end the paper was bought with funds from various sources, with Edward Rumely acting as strawman holding the firm. First Bernhard Dernburg and later Heinrich Albert supervised the business in order to guard German interests. The final payment from Bernstorff to Rumely was made by the New York law firm Hays, Kaufmann & Lindheim, it is difficult to believe, in April 1917, long after the ambassador had left the United

States. Incidentally, even some of the highly confidential correspondence between Schulze-Gaevernitz and Rumely was transmitted through the German embassy in Washington, and it may be safely assumed, therefore, that such messages were picked up by British intelligence and later deciphered. Whether the Germans were able to fully enjoy their acquisition seems at least doubtful. During the war, the paper was forced to keep a somewhat neutral line in order to avoid detection. After the war Rumely found himself in court facing legal problems arising from his collaboration with the Germans and their agents. Considering that the German government had consented to the acquisition under the condition that the paper would be equally useful after the end of the war, the complex transaction, in the long run, appears to have been a costly failure.[59]

Other attempts to purchase newspaper influence reportedly involved the *New York Sun* and the *Washington Post*. Apparently the *Washington Post* was not up for sale,[60] and the *Sun* was acquired ultimately by other interests, though negotiations in this case produced enough documentation to supply American investigators with information to create difficulties for the New York lawyer Samuel Untermyer, a contact of the German agents in this connection. The price of the deal, $2,000,000 plus another $500,000 for getting this paper back into shape, was not cheap, and Count Bernstorff, for reasons unknown, was certain that no one would suspect German ownership.[61]

Although many of these financial transactions have been public knowledge since the American trials of the post-1917 period, several authors still insist that German-language newspapers in the United States could not be bought.[62] The historical evidence seems to indicate, instead, that the six to seven figure outlays for German- and English-language press propaganda brought only minimal results. American public opinion, including the majority of Americans of German, Irish, or Jewish descent, was not particularly taken by the Imperial German viewpoint as it was presented by the Berlin emissaries and their American collaborators. Even if German agents in the United States had refrained from sabotage and other illegal activities, it is doubtful whether the efforts in the press could have seriously affected American public opinion.

One of the lesser known aspects of German propaganda is the work among the churches. In the case of the Roman Catholic Church, the Germans were faced with a rather curious situation. It was not very long ago that German Catholics had earnestly tried to assert themselves against what, to them, had appeared as an overburdening Irish influence. They had lost the fiercely fought battle against the Irish, and their movement, known as Cahenslyism, was an unpleasant memory for many non-German Catholic leaders in America.[63] But if Catholics were to be approached, leaving out the Irish would have been impossible. More-over, even if the British ambassador in Washington, Sir Cecil Spring Rice, exaggerated the new degree of cooperation between Irish and Germans,[64] especially in the Catholic hierarchy, there can be no doubt that Irish and Germans, at least on the organizational level, had moved much closer to each other in the early years of this century.[65] In the course of the war, intensified anti-British feelings among Americans of German and Irish descent, particularly more recent immigrants, led to common demonstrations and other group actions.[66]

Was it German Catholic spectacles such as the annual convention of the *Deutsch-Römisch-Katholischer Central-Verein*, which opened in Pitts-burgh in August 1914 with "Die Wacht am Rhein" and "Deutschland über Alles," that convinced German diplomats and agents that the Catholic Church was receptive to German propaganda?[67] Including the privately sharply anti-Catholic Bernstorff, they were certainly aware of the possible advantages of winning the Catholic Church for the German viewpoint. A report reaching the German Foreign Office from the U.S. through Schulze-Gaevernitz in April 1915 suggested that "the Catholic Church if she could be induced to exert her Power from Rome could exert a tremendously strong influence in this Country." The Schulze-Gaevernitz contact then put it more bluntly: "[I]t must be borne in mind that Germany victorious with Catholic Belgium and Austria added would be preponderately a Catholic Country, which would mean that the Great European Empire would throw glory upon Rome."[68] The ambassador himself also thought it worthwhile to remind Rome of the Russian-Orthodox danger after the fall of Constantinople, particularly, he added in his report to the Foreign Office, in view of the high birth rate of the Russians.[69] Whether such proposals led to concrete action and whether any measurable results were achieved inside the American Catholic Church, is difficult to ascertain.[70] Most likely, the majority of German diplomats and agents lacked personal connections to the Catholic hierarchy, and even those working among the American Irish were more inclined to cooperate with revolutionaries and dock workers than with their priests and bishops. Also, it should not be forgotten that British propaganda had made much of the excessive brutality that had accompanied the German invasion of Belgium,[71] and the large-scale deportation of Belgian civilians for forced labor in Germany in late 1916 must have reinforced the picture of hardship inflicted upon Catholic Belgians by what, in the eyes of a Catholic, must have appeared to be Protestant Prussians.[72] In fact, the news of the deportation of Belgians to Germany in late 1916 and early 1917 became a major factor in defeating German propaganda, comparable only to the original violation of Belgium in 1914. Lord Bryce once again lashed out against the Germans, and the American liberal journalist and lawyer Brand Whitlock, working with the American relief mission in Brussels, published a scathing pamphlet entitled *The Deportation*.[73]

That all sides would meddle in the appointment of American bishops does not seem very surprising. Whether such efforts, including those proposed by Count Bernstorff and apparently followed up by the well-connected *Zentrum*-politician Matthias Erzberger and his contacts to the Vatican, had any part in decisions affecting the structure of the Catholic hierarchy in the United States, and whether such interference had some indirect influence on American public opinion, is quite another question.[74] Surely Cardinal James Gibbons, Archbishop John Ireland, and Archbishop George Mundelein, the latter appointed in 1915 in Chicago, were not accessible for the political hacks of the two propaganda machines directed from London and Berlin.[75]

On the side of the Protestant churches, the picture is more complicated. Most of the evidence, though often very circumstantial and not indicative of any interference by German agents, does appear to suggest pro-German feelings in many of those churches and parishes where German culture was still a factor of some influence. If one accepts the thesis that German ethnicity in the United States was generally receding at the end of the nineteenth century, one would surmise that the remaining centers of German culture were either hold-outs of another era, such as the Missouri Synod, or churches with a high number of first-generation German immigrants. Furthermore, if German-Americans as an ethnic group did not achieve political influence commensurate with their numbers, it is not surprising that their churches as a rule were not very proficient participants in American political life either.[76] The noisy engagement demonstrated under emotional stress and in time of crisis does not necessarily suggest political influence and, in some cases, seems to have been motivated less by German patriotism than by well-worn arguments over such topics as prohibition[77] or even traditional internal German differences of class and regional culture.

Observing the German churches from this perspective and taking into account their generally apolitical role in American society, one might be tempted to explain the patriotic voices of 1915 by pointing to statements such as Wilhelm Löhe's call to German Lutherans in North America back in 1845: "Do not surrender yourself nor your children to the foreign nation! . . . for truly a German, who is not German, is a punished man on earth because all privileges given to him by merciful God before the nations will be taken from him. . . ."[78] This may be the key to an understanding of church leaders like Walter Rauschenbusch, the American-born son of an emigrated German, converted Baptist pastor and himself one of the eminent figures in the American Social Gospel movement. His much publicized outcry, "Be Fair to Germany: A Plea for Open-Mindedness," of November 1914 unreservedly defends Berlin's position and indeed sees the German attack on Belgium as a mere consequence of Britain's despicably reckless imperialist policy. Whether he was, as Arthur S. Link has called him, "perhaps the most influential apologist in the United States" may be open to question, but there can be no doubt that such views, especially when emanating from the immigrant church, contributed to the general hypocrisy and hostility vented on German-Americans in wartime America.[79] When Franz A. O. Pieper, the successor of Carl F. W. Walther in the Missouri Synod, wrote in *Der Lutheraner* about the war "in which Germany must fight for its life," or when the *Lutheran Witness* introduced Field Marshall Paul von Hindenburg as a Christian soldier, one wonders if it was not the voice of Wilhelm Löhe rather than admiration for the Kaiser's Germany that spoke. One also wonders what meaning the photos of Wilhelm II or German battle scenes could have had for German-American farmers toiling in North Dakota or Nebraska. As in the case of politicians and professors, it seems plausible that the noise was made by relatively few but heard by many and misinterpreted as the opinion of German-America. Walter Rauschenbusch, G. C. Berkemeier, Friedrich Bente, and their fellow theologians may have been voices of German-America, and the German press office in New York surely registered them this way; that, in fact, such voices represented only a small segment of Americans of German descent could not be read from their published statements.[80] That parish members did not rebel against pastors who preached loyalty to and offered prayers for the Kaiser and fatherland may have had other reasons than general agreement with such views. From Hermann Hagedorn we know that pastors such as Fritz O. Evers of Zion Lutheran Church in Philadelphia, who wore a German helmet on the occasion of a Red Cross benefit at his church, was not a typical German-American, and, in fact, that many a German-American may have shuddered when confronted with such primitive excesses of nationalism. There is much to indicate that it was only those born in Germany who felt the thrill reflected in the letters of Hermann Hagedorn's father from wartime Germany: "We speak the truth. Our reports from the front are the truth, and nothing but the truth. Every word issued by our Supreme Army Command or our government is purest truth!!!"[81]

Those selling what was purported to be "the truth" found their engagement increasingly unrewarding as the war progressed from what appeared to be a European event to a conflict that had gotten out of control and would, sooner or later, engulf the United States. Whether the sinking of the *Lusitania* in May 1915 was the hiatus, or whether it was rather a chain of occurrences including the torpedoing of passenger liners, the rejection of Woodrow Wilson's offers of mediation, the underground war of intelligence agents inside neutral America, and such master strokes of diplomatic incompetency as the Zimmermann Telegram,[82] which caused the German propaganda machine to sputter and eventually experience a total breakdown, is largely a question of weighing the relative importance of these events within the respective historical context. However one may assess the political climate in the United States during the years from 1914 to 1917, the tragedy in the Irish Sea undoubtedly played havoc with German propaganda. With the death of those American civilians on board the *Lusitania*, German "frightfulness" had touched America in a way that the Foreign Office, Bethmann Hollweg, and even the German navy may not have fully registered.[83] The flow of warnings from the German ambassador in Washington apparently did not penetrate the armor of Imperial self-confidence.

Well before the torpedoing of the great liner, German propaganda had had its difficulties in reaching Americans, and, however the political wisdom of the Boston Brahmin Henry Cabot Lodge may be appraised, the Senator's reaction to Friedrich Bente's appearance on the Hill may not be so far removed from mainstream American political opinion: "The German-American propaganda has become pretty bad. We had them before the Foreign Relations Committee the other day on the question of prohibiting the export of munitions of war, when a man from Lutheran Theological Seminary in St. Louis, named Bente, addressed us. . . . He had an accent so strong that you could tumble over it, and he proceeded to lecture us on Americanism, patriotism, what true Americanism was and what the opinions of George Washington were. Some of us are not hyphenates – we are just plain Americans – and the wrath of the members of the Committee, Democrats and Republicans, was pleasing to witness."[84] Surely Cabot Lodge and not a few Americans of all political persuasions must have been delighted to see the chief of German propaganda, Bernhard Dernburg, become so offensive that the British had to be asked to grant safe conduct for his journey home before the Americans arranged for his expulsion.[85]

The poorly organized propaganda network he left behind was taken over by Heinrich Albert, who was already overburdened with the complex assignments of buying up war material and managing the finances of almost all German operations in the United States. The finicky administrator was no more qualified than his predecessor to direct the propaganda apparatus in an increasingly hostile American environment against what appears to have been an infinitely more elegant and professional public-relations machine directed by Charles F. G. Masterman, from Wellington House in London, and his capable head for American operations, Sir Gilbert Parker. Of course, the British had a language advantage that was, in turn, closely connected to a cultural advantage.[86] The former was a given fact and a formidable barrier for the German agents. The latter was equally a fact by 1914, but one that the Germans, through their conduct of foreign policy and the aggressive staccato of Pan-German barks across the Atlantic, had helped to erect.[87] In contrast to the massive early propaganda onslaught of the Germans, the British established and renewed discrete ties to leading American professionals, who in turn would pass on the British viewpoint almost coincidentally[88] and certainly without the "sledge-hammer type of appeal" of such representative Germans as Bernhard Dernburg,[89] Eugen Kühnemann, or Kuno Meyer and their German-American friends, such as Charles Hexamer, G. C. Berkemeyer, or Hugo Münsterberg.

Foremost among those who were specifically hired to face the British foe in the battle for the minds was the well-connected American journalist William Bayard Hale, known to the Foreign Office since the undiplomatic pronouncements of Wilhelm II in an interview with the American in the autumn of 1908. Being on the payroll of both the German embassy and William Randolph Hearst, Hale was contracted by the Germans until June 1918 and drew a salary of $15,000 per annum.[90] Miss von Schmidt-Pauli, a young German woman apparently with connections to the Hamburg-American Line and to Matthias Erzberger, was another German agent who came to the United States in 1914 to make pro-German speeches. Her hectic activity was cut short in early 1915 when she contracted a serious illness and was forced to enter a hospital.[91] James F. J. Archibald was yet another journalist who was retained by the German embassy for lectures and other activities. His usefulness to the Germans ended rather abruptly when Czech and Slovak moles in the German and Austrian embassies told their British organizer, Naval Attaché Captain Guy Gaunt, that Archibald was about to take a trip to Europe. British intelligence arranged to meet Archibald on his way and confiscated sensitive documents he was carrying for the Austrian ambassador Constantin Dumba. Needless to say, the British were pleased to supply the Americans with a set of photographs of the papers.[92] Others, such as members of "the friendly inclined press," were sent to Europe to produce pro-German news for American readers. Edward Lyell Fox and Albert Dawson went on such errands for the Germans and were outfitted with recommendations and funds from the Hamburg-American Line office in New York.[93] The number of German agents and their free movement between the United States and the continent indicate that it was not for lack of material that Germans lost the war of words. The lists of officers and sailors traveling on neutral ships and transporting mail and material are further evidence of a constant flow of messages between Germany and New York. Because many of these men were American citizens, their messenger service was relatively safe from British interference.[94]

In retrospect, much of the propaganda the Germans produced for American consumption probably did not address the average American, the proverbial man on the street. The Foreign Office and the Washington embassy clearly lacked a concept and competent operatives to move about smoothly in the United States. One could take the view that working conditions in America were such that even a well-planned German propaganda campaign would not have been able to reach American public opinion. This, however, can be easily countered by pointing to the long tenure of the ambassador in Washington and his knowledge of the specificities of American political life. Explaining the ineffectiveness of much of the German propaganda efforts may be rather more complicated and should take into consideration a number of European and American influences. Besides lacking a concept, the Germans in the United States were forced to work in a climate that was constantly influenced by at least two other fields of activity, namely the troublesome submarine war and the accompanying destruction of American lives as well as the widely publicized sabotage campaigns of German agents. The threat to American security was perceived to be so real, it must be recalled, that Washington was forced to develop a functioning intelligence service to replace a handful of Treasury agents, and that the American president, early in the war, ordered the telephones of the German embassy and others with German connections to be tapped. Finally, we now know that British intelligence broke German codes relatively early in the war, and thus was able to read much of the coded German cable traffic between Washington and Berlin. The awareness of the British of numerous German activities, and the close and often publicized linkage between those active in public relations and those planning sabotage, negotiating with the ousted Mexican dictator Victoriano Huerta, outfitting Indian revolutionaries, or fomenting strikes, could have been almost insurmountable obstacles even for an expert propaganda team. The German team, however, was short on experts, and its members, by their own undertakings in neutral America, seemed to confirm the worst prejudices about German "frightfulness" in wide sectors of the American public.

Notes to Chapter 7

1. Advertisement on back page of Bernhard Dernburg, *Germany and the War* (New York: The Fatherland, no date).

2. For instance in Jürgen Möckelmann, *Deutsch-amerikanische Beziehungen in der Krise: Studien zur amerikanischen Politik im ersten Weltkrieg* (Frankfurt: Europäische Verlagsanstalt, 1967), pp. 11–15, 19–24. Reinhard R. Doerries, *Washington-Berlin 1908/1917* (Düsseldorf: Schwann, 1975), particularly chapter 2. For a completely revised and expanded English edition see Reinhard R. Doerries, *Imperial Challenge* (Chapel Hill: The University of North Carolina Press, 1989), chapter 2.

3. For instance George Sylvester Viereck, *Spreading Germs of Hate* (New York: Horace Livewright, 1930). Eugen Kühnemann, *Deutschland und Amerika: Briefe an einen deutschamerikanischen Freund* (München: C.H. Beck/Oskar Beck, 1917). M.J. Bonn, *So macht man Geschichte* (München: Paul List, 1953). Bernhard Dernburg, *Von beiden Ufern* (Berlin: Kronen-Verlag, 1917). Heinrich F. Albert, *Aufzeichnungen* (Berlin: W. Büxenstein, [1948]). Karl Boy-Ed, *Verschwörer?* (Berlin: August Scherl, 1920).

4. Cf. James D. Squires, *British Propaganda at Home and in The United States from 1914 to 1917* (Cambridge: Harvard University Press, 1935), pp. 45, 48. On Sir Gilbert Parker, the British propaganda chief for the United States, see Viereck, *Spreading Germs of Hate*, pp. 5–6, 126–27, 129. Dennis J. McCarthy, "The British," in Joseph O'Grady, ed., *The Immigrants' Influence on Wilson's Peace Policies* (Lexington: University of Kentucky Press, 1967), p. 87. M.L. Sanders and Philip M. Taylor, *British Propaganda during the First World War, 1914–1918* (London: Macmillan, 1982), pp. 168ff.

5. Cf. Kühlmann's own comment in Richard von Kühlmann, *Erinnerungen* (Heidelberg: Lambert Schneider, 1948), p. 421.

6. Cf. Harold D. Laswell, *Propaganda Technique in the World War* (New York: Peter Smith, 1938), p. 149.

7. Arthur S. Link, *Wilson: The Struggle for Neutrality, 1914–1915* (Princeton: Princeton University Press, 1960), pp. 378–79.

8. In 1909, the journalist paid by the Germans was J.D. Whelpley. Another smaller sum went to a Dr. A.D. Jacobson. Bernstorff to Bülow, 15 April 1909, and Bernstorff to Bethmann Hollweg, 4 April 1910, vol. 1, Vereinigte Staaten von Amerika 2, secr., Politisches Archiv, Auswärtiges Amt (AA). Whether J.D. Whelpley is identical with the "competent English observer," cited by James D. Squires, *British Propaganda at Home and in The United States from 1914 to 1917*, p. 49, or the "Special Agent, G2, SOS, AEF" reporting to Chief Intelligence Officer, Base Section No. 3, SOS, AEF, in September and October 1918, could not be ascertained. A. Campbell Turner to Edward Bell, 5 October 1918, Box 200, RG 59, National Archives, Washington, D.C. (NA).

9. On Bernstorff's public relations work in London (1902–1906) see Doerries, *Imperial Challenge*, pp. 7, 236–37. Otto Hammann, *Zur Vorgeschichte des Weltkrieges* (Berlin: Reimar Hobbing, 1918), pp. 113–14. Cf. correspondence between Lucien Wolf and Bernstorff (1903–1907), David Movshowitch Collection, Yivo Institute, New York. For Bernstorff's success, see Link, *Wilson: The Struggle for Neutrality, 1914–1915*, p. 35.

10. Bernhard Dernburg as a young man had been in the United States for a banking internship. While he was generally thought to be a man of considerable abilities, tact and diplomatic finesse apparently were not among them. Heinrich Schnee, *Als letzter Gouverneur in Deutsch-Ostafrika* (Heidelberg: Quelle & Meyer, 1964), pp. 82–83. Frederic W. Wile, *Men around the Kaiser* (London: William Heinemann, 1914), pp. 180–81. Among Dernburg's publications are *Search-Lights on the War* (New York: The Fatherland, 1915); *German Resources and the War* (Chicago: Germanistic Society, 1914); *Germany and the War* (New York: The Fatherland, no date). Heinrich F. Albert seems to have been driven by the desire to meddle in almost every aspect of German activities in the United States. To him goes the doubtful distinction of having left to the Americans a nearly complete record of his activities. Curiously enough, Bernstorff informed the U.S. Government only in June 1915 that Albert was Commercial Attaché to the embassy.

11. At the outbreak of the war, Heinrich Charles had been approached by the German Minister Haniel von Haimhausen and asked to organize German propaganda. With the support of the former German consul in New York, Paul Siegfried Horst Falcke, he had set up office. From all indications, however, he did not get along with either the leading Germans in New York or the ambassador and his staff after they arrived in the early fall of 1914. Heinrich Charles to Otto Wiedfeldt, 19 May 1922, Roll 21, T 290, NA. Ecker to Huldermann, 28 September 1914, and 2 June 1915, Hamburg-Amerika Linie, New York, HAPAG Archiv, Hamburg.

12. Diary entry of Colonel House, 20 September 1914, in Charles Seymour, ed., *The Intimate Papers of Colonel House*, vol. 1, (London: Ernest Benn Ltd., 1926), p. 33. Text deleted by Seymour is found in *The Diary of Edward M. House*, vol. 5, Yale University Library, pp. 164–65.

13. The minutes of this crucial meeting of the German propagandists are an enclosure to Bernstorff to Bethmann Hollweg, 4 October 1914, vol. 20, Vereinigte Staaten von Amerika Nr. 2, AA.

14. Bernstorff to Bethmann Hollweg, 4 October 1914, vol. 20, Vereinigte Staaten von Amerika Nr. 2, AA. Imperial Treasury to Foreign Office, 11 August 1914, vol. 1, Weltkrieg 10, secr., AA. It should be pointed out that the press account was soon used to spend large sums for so-called insurrection purposes, that is for intelligence operations including sabotage and the organization of armed rebellions in various parts of the world. Cf. Undersecretary Zimmermann to Imperial Chancellor, 21 October 1914, vol. 3, Akten des Auswärtigen Amtes im Grossen Hauptquartier 1914–1916 24, AA.

15. Minutes of the meeting on 5 November 1914, vol. 21, Vereinigte Staaten von Amerika Nr. 2, AA.

16. Report by Dernburg, 31 August 1914, vol. 1, Weltkrieg 10, Secr., AA.

17. Notes by Oswald Garrison Villard, O.G. Villard Papers, Houghton Library, Harvard University. Since German officials and agents insisted on reporting on their work to friends and relatives in Germany, and since the Intelligence Division of the British Admiralty Staff had become very efficient in the business of intercepting German mail from the United States, the British were likely to be well informed on the German problems in the United States, enabling them to adjust their own efforts accordingly. Cf. George von Skal to Maximilian Harden, 15 December 1915, 2847, FO 371, Public Record Office, London (PRO), here translation, from which British intelligence could learn that "the fact that for a time B[ernstorff] could accomplish but little here was mainly due to the presence of your friend (?) B[ernhard] D[ernburg] . . . . This man was regarded by the Americans – and even by many Germans – as the real Ambassador. His immense vanity, his desire to come to the front, his tactlessness, and the qualities which he himself with a certain pride described as 'truthfulness and openness,' did a very great deal of harm."

18. Zimmermann to Bernstorff, 28 October 1914, vol. 1, Weltkrieg 11k, AA. Falcke to Bethmann Hollweg, 7 December 1914, vol. 3, Weltkrieg 11k, AA.

19. Carol S. Gruber, *Mars and Minerva* (Baton Rouge: Louisiana State University Press, 1975).

20. Klaus Schwabe, *Wissenschaft und Kriegsmoral* (Göttingen: Vandenhoeck & Ruprecht, 1969).

21. Münsterberg to Bethmann Hollweg, 24 September 1915 and 7 December 1915, vol. 2, Vereinigte Staaten von Amerika Nr. 16, AA.

22. Lansing to Wilson, 9 December 1914, quoted from Link, *Wilson: The Struggle for Neutrality, 1914–1915*, p. 162. Phyllis Keller, *States of Belonging* (Cambridge: Harvard University Press, 1979), pp. 79–80, on the accusations of Frederic William Wile against Münsterberg. Cf. also the insinuations against Münsterberg in Emil Witte, *Aus einer deutschen Botschaft* (Leipzig: Zeitbilder, 1907), pp. 172–83. Count Montgelas of the German Foreign Office saw to it that the request of the Münsterberg family was not fulfilled. Vol. 46, Vereinigte Staaten von Amerika Nr. 16, AA. Münsterberg's so-called American war diary, *Amerika und der Weltkrieg* (Leipzig: Johann Ambrosius Barth, 1915) may serve as an example for his views during 1914/15. This publication unites two previous U.S. publications: *The War and America* (September 1914) and *The Peace and America* (April 1915). Christian

H. Freitag, "Die Entwicklung der Amerikastudien in Berlin bis 1945 unter Berücksichtigung der Amerikaarbeit staatlicher und privater Organisationen" (Freie Universität Berlin,
Dissertation, 1977), p. 63, surprisingly refers to Münsterberg as "an experienced propagandist abroad."

23. Eugen Kühnemann, *Deutschland und Amerika*, here especially p. 13. Kuno Francke,
Deutsche Arbeit in Amerika (Leipzig: Felix Meiner, 1930), p. 54. Papen to Ministry of War,
30 November 1914, vol. 16, Vereinigte Staaten von Amerika Nr. 5, AA. In December
1914 at the Tivoli Theater in Seattle, Kühnemann said: "In regard to the so-called German
atrocities. It is an evident fact that in no army in the world are there so many good-hearted and highly civilized men as in the German army; and for this simple reason, because the
German army is the people in arms, and that same good-hearted, loyal and highly civilized
people, which the Germans are, is the same in arms. . . . Therefore, atrocities are more
improbable, not to say more impossible in the German army than in any other army in the
world." *The Seattle German Press*, vol. 1, Nr. 44 (14 December 1914), pp. 1–2.

24. Bernstorff to Bethmann Hollweg, 19 December 1914, vol. 21, Vereinigte Staaten
von Amerika Nr. 2, AA.

25. Freitag, "*Die Entwicklung der Amerikastudien in Berlin bis 1945*," pp. 65–66. Following his release Bertling beginning in 1920 directed the Amerika-Institut in Berlin.

26. Concerning the famous Meyer brothers, see for instance Eduard Meyer, *Nordamerika
und Deutschland* (Berlin: Karl Curtius, 1915), p. 58 (Eduard reports on Kuno's propaganda
work in the United States); p. 57 (Eduard maligns Kuno Francke for not having supported
Hexamer's National Alliance); and p. 45 (Eduard predicts that the Democrats will win the
elections in 1916). *Irische Blätter*, vol. 1 (1917), p. 232, published by George Chatterton-Hill
at the Karl Curtius Verlag in Berlin: "Professor Kuno Meyer, who in late 1914 traveled to
the U.S. to make propaganda for the German side, was active largely in Irish circles. In all
parts of the Union he spoke to crowded and enthusiastic gatherings where the common
interests of Germany and Ireland in the battle against albion were emphasized. . . ." Eduard
Meyer as *Rektor* of the university in Berlin in March 1920 recognized Wolfgang Kapp as
chancellor when the latter attempted a coup (Kapp-Putsch). *Mitteilungen aus dem Verein zur
Abwehr des Antisemitismus*, vol. 30, Nr. 6 (30 March 1920), p. 45.

27. Eduard Meyer, *England* (Stuttgart: J.G. Cotta, 1915, and Boston: Ritter & Co.,
1916); *Weltgeschichte und Weltkrieg* (Stuttgart: J.G. Cotta, 1916); *Nordamerika und Deutschland* containing an article by the New York theologian Thomas C. Hall who sympathized
with the Irish cause and decided to stay in Germany; *Der amerikanische Kongress und der
Weltkrieg* (Berlin: Karl Curtius, 1917). Shortly after the defeat of Germany Eduard Meyer
added another title to this list: *Die Vereinigten Staaten von Amerika* (Frankfurt: Heinrich
Keller, 1920), bristling with attacks on Woodrow Wilson, Bethmann Hollweg, and Bernstorff and speaking for the Mexican dictators Porfirio Diaz and Victoriano Huerta. Adolf
Deißmann, *Der Krieg und die Religion* (Berlin: Carl Heymann, 1914). Rudolf Eucken, *Die
sittlichen Kräfte des Krieges* (Leipzig: Emil Gräfe, 1914). Friedrich Meinecke, *Die deutsche
Erhebung von 1914* (Stuttgart: J.G. Cotta, 1915). Hans Delbrück, *Über den kriegerischen
Charakter des deutschen Volkes* (Berlin: Carl Heymann, 1914). Wilhelm Wundt, *Deutschland
im Lichte des neutralen und des feindlichen Auslandes* (Bologna: Nicola Zanichelli, 1915). Oskar
Fleischer, *Vom Kriege gegen die deutsche Kultur* (Frankfurt: Heinrich Keller, 1915).

28. Meyer wrote this specifically for the United States right after the beginning of the
war. It appeared instead in *Weltgeschichte und Weltkrieg*.

29. "An Appeal from Eucken and Haeckel," *The Independent*, 79 (28 September 1914),
p. 439.

30. Adolf von Harnack, *Wilsons Botschaft an die deutsche Freiheit* (Gotha: Friedrich
Andreas Perthes, 1917), quoted from Ernst Fraenkel, ed., *Amerika im Spiegel des deutschen
politischen Denkens* (Köln: Westdeutscher Verlag, 1959), p. 241.

31. Exhibit "Romain Rolland Weltbürger zwischen Frankreich und Deutschland,"
University Library Bonn, 29 April – 31 May 1969. Catalog: Klaus Dahm, ed., *Romain Rolland* (München: Süddeutscher Verlag, 1967). The most thorough study of the views and
activities of German professors during World War I remains Schwabe, *Wissenschaft und
Kriegsmoral*. Robinson here quoted from Gruber, *Mars and Minerva*, p. 67. Richard O'Con-

nor's suggestion that the declaration of the German professors was largely directed against the United States is incorrect.

32. German sabotage projects cannot be covered within the limited frame of this essay. The author is presently preparing a full-scale study of German intelligence activities in the United States during World War I. Previous publications concerned with sabotage are for instance Henry Landau, *The Enemy Within* (New York: G.P. Putnam's Sons, 1937); W. Reginald Hall and Amos J. Peaslee, *Three Wars with Germany* (New York: G.P. Putnam's Sons, 1944); and the recent journalistic treatment by Jules Witcover, *Sabotage at Black Tom* (Chapel Hill: Algonquin Books, 1989).

33. Heinrich Albert claims that his briefcase containing highly sensitive papers was stolen from him by the Secret Service while he took a nap on the subway. *Aufzeichnungen* (Berlin: W. Büxenstein, no date), p. 73. In fact, Albert probably fell asleep, left the train in a hurry, and forgot his briefcase. Frank Burke, a U.S. Secret Service agent shadowing Albert on that day, could not pass up the opportunity. Cf. Landau, *The Enemy Within*, p. 100. This is also the version given by W.G. Sickel and J.P. Meyer of the Hamburg-American Line in New York to their chief Albert Ballin in Hamburg, 19 August 1915, HAPAG NY, HAPAG: "Dr. Albert one evening about three weeks ago was taking to his home with him a leather mappe containing quite a large quantity of his confidential papers which he left on an elevated train." Ballin commented on this report in the margin: "Das ist aber auch leichtsinnig." Frederick C. Luebke, *Bonds of Loyalty* (DeKalb: Northern Illinois University Press, 1974), p. 139, agrees with this version, but then speaks of "the theft of the portfolio by an official agent of the United States government." Much of the material from the briefcase was later published in the press, confirming that Germany's top representatives were deeply involved in questionable clandestine activities in neutral America.

34. For the complicated acculturation process of Germans in America prior to World War I see my study *Iren und Deutsche in der Neuen Welt* (Stuttgart: Franz Steiner, 1986).

35. Carl Wittke, *German-Americans and the World War* (Columbus: The Ohio State Archaeological and Historical Society, 1936), p. 31.

36. Bernstorff, *Deutschland und Amerika: Erinnerungen aus dem fünfjährigen Kriege* (Berlin: Ullstein, 1920), p. 20. Cf. Doerries, *Imperial Challenge*, pp. 21–22. Some members of the German propaganda crew such as Münsterberg were aware of the political impotence of the Germans as an ethnic group, but this realization does not seem to have affected their activities in the United States. Cf. Hugo Münsterberg, *The Peace and America* (Leipzig: Tauchnitz, 1915), p. 161. Cf. also Consul Rohe, New Orleans, to Bethmann Hollweg, 8 June 1914, vol. 16, Vereinigte Staaten von Amerika 13a, AA.

37. Kühnemann, *Deutschland und Amerika*, p. 47. Cf. Witte, *Aus einer deutschen Botschaft*, p. 258.

38. The National Alliance was founded in 1901 in Philadelphia. Its German name was Deutsch-amerikanischer Nationalbund der Vereinigten Staaten von Amerika, and its president was Charles J. Hexamer of Philadelphia. The second and third national conventions were held in Baltimore and Indianapolis. The last meeting took place in Chicago in November 1917. Hexamer and other leaders resigned and elected S.G. von Bosse as president. John Goebel, *Der Kampf um deutsche Kultur in Amerika* (Leipzig: Dürr'sche Buchhandlung, 1914), p. 145, estimates membership at approximately 2,500,000.

39. Ernst Ritter, *Das Deutsche Ausland-Institut in Stuttgart 1917–1945* (Wiesbaden: Steiner, 1976), pp. 9–10, argues that there was "no dependence" on the *Alldeutsche Verband* "as American war propaganda claimed." Ritter also asserts that the National Alliance was not strong enough to withstand the "psychologizing and moralizing allied propaganda." Carl Cesar Eiffe, *Früchte deutscher Arbeit* (Leipzig: Dieterich'sche Verlagsbuchhandlung Theodor Weichert, 1910), pp. 94ff., reports about his founding an "alldeutscher Verein" in 1898 in Iowa. Eiffe asked the *Alldeutsche Verband* for books for a library for the German *Vereine* and later published articles about the National Alliance in the *Alldeutsche Blätter*.

40. Clifton J. Child, *The German-Americans in Politics, 1914–1917* (Madison: University of Wisconsin Press, 1939), pp. 30–31. Kuno Francke, *Deutsche Arbeit in Amerika: Erinnerungen* (Leipzig: Felix Meiner, 1930), p. 68. Cf. J.P. Tumulty to Woodrow Wilson, 6 August

1915, in Arthur S. Link, ed., *The Papers of Woodrow Wilson*, vol. 34 (Princeton: Princeton University Press, 1980), p. 116. Georg von Bosse, *Dr. C. J. Hexamer* (Stuttgart: Chr. Belser, 1925), p. 89. German text: "Wir haben noch nie eine so erbärmliche, knieweiche Regierung gehabt, wie jetzt." The Chicago branch of the National Alliance told Wilson that the United States "owes it to the many millions of Teutonic descent not to force upon them the terrible choice between long remembrance of the old fatherland and beautiful, loyal love of our glorious republic which they have always demonstrated in the past." Andrew J. Townsend, "The Germans of Chicago," in *Jahrbuch der Deutsch-Amerikanischen Historischen Gesellschaft von Illinois*, vol. 32 (1932), p. 77.

41. Quoted from John J. Appel, *Immigrant Historical Societies in the United States, 1880–1950* (New York: Arno Press, 1980), p. 314.

42. Gruber, *Mars and Minerva*, pp. 47, 20–24. For a list of names deemed suitable by the German propagandists for a request for their signature see enclosure to J.P. Meyer to Huldermann, 23 September 1914, Hamburg-Amerika Linie, New York, HAPAG Archiv, Hamburg.

43. Link, *Wilson: The Struggle for Neutrality, 1914–1915*, pp. 24–25. On Burgess, see also Hans-Ulrich Wehler, *Der Aufstieg des amerikanischen Imperialismus* (Göttingen: Vandenhoeck & Ruprecht, 1974), pp. 55–60.

44. On *The International* and von Mach, see Niel M. Johnson, *George Sylvester Viereck: German-American Propagandist* (Urbana: University of Illinois Press, 1972), pp. 15–16, 29–30. Von Mach was close to Münsterberg and until 1915 held a position as professor of art history at Bradford Academy in Cambridge. He is the author of *What Germany Wants* (1914), *Germany's Point of View* (1915), and *Sir Edward's Evidence* (1915). Doerries, *Imperial Challenge*, pp. 48, 264.

45. Cf. the reaction of one angry American university official in *The New York Times*, reported in Falcke, *Vor dem Eintritt Amerikas in den Weltkrieg*, p. 166.

46. For Labor's National Peace Council see *Brewing and Liquor Interests and German and Bolshevik Propaganda*. Report and Hearings of the Subcommittee on the Judiciary. United States Senate, vol. 2 (Washington, D.C.: Government Printing Office, 1919), pp. 1571ff.

47. Bernstorff's report (presumably to Foreign Office in Berlin), 3 November 1915, vol. 16, Vereinigte Staaten von Amerika Nr. 5, AA.

48. Doerries, *Imperial Challenge*, pp. 76, 164. Another American Truth Society was organized in Munich, and one of its main supporters, the controversial Thomas St. John Gaffney, in his *Breaking the Silence* (New York: Horace Liveright, 1931), pp. 27–30, reports that it tried to counter British propaganda. For O'Leary's own viewpoint, see *My Political Trial and Experiences* (New York: Jefferson Publishing Co., 1919).

49. For an abbreviated treatment of the connections between German agents and the Hindus and some of their activities, see Doerries, *Imperial Challenge*, pp. 146–55. Of special interest are the memoirs of the Indian leader Har Dayal, *Forty-four Months in Germany and Turkey* (London: P. S. King, 1920).

50. Egmont Zechlin, *Die deutsche Politik und die Juden im Ersten Weltkrieg* (Göttingen: Vandenhoeck & Ruprecht, 1969). See also Nachum Orland, "Reichsregierung und Zionismus im Ersten Weltkrieg," in *Saeculum* 25 (1974). Relevant information may be gained from Franz Oppenheimer, *Erlebtes, Erstrebtes, Erreichtes* (Düsseldorf: Joseph Melzer, 1964); Max Isidor Bodenheimer, *So wurde Israel* (Frankfurt: Europäische Verlagsanstalt, 1958); Kurt Blumenfeld, *Erlebte Judenfrage* (Stuttgart: Deutsche Verlags-Anstalt, 1962).

51. Justizrat Max Isidor Bodenheimer to Diego von Bergen in the Foreign Office, 16 September 1914, vol. 1, Der Weltkrieg 11, adh. 2, AA.

52. Max Warburg to Arthur Zimmermann, 19 July 1916; Felix Warburg to Max Warburg, 18 June 1916; Max Warburg to Arthur Zimmermann, 2 October 1916, all in vol. 6, Weltkrieg 11, adh. 2, AA.

53. Jacob H. Schiff to Arthur Zimmermann, 19 October 1914, vol. 2, Weltkrieg 11, adh. 2, AA.

54. Bernstorff's report, 27 October 1916, vol. 25, Vereinigte Staaten von Amerika 2, AA. Falcke, *Vor dem Eintritt Amerikas in den Weltkrieg*, pp. 36–37. Wittke, *German-Americans and the World War*, p. 23. Of interest is the involvement of the German socialist Louis

Viereck, George Sylvester's father, as "European representative" of *The Fatherland*.

55. Re: Marcus Braun see George Barany, "The Magyars," in Joseph P. O'Grady, *The Immigrants' Influence on Wilson's Peace Policies* (Lexington: University of Kentucky Press, 1967), pp. 151–53. Barany reports how Braun, after U.S. entry into the war, "stressed the traditional friendship of Magyars toward England and France and their dislike for Germany and Austria." See also Doerries, *Imperial Challenge*, pp. 52–53.

56. For details of this relationship, see Doerries, *Imperial Challenge*, pp. 51–52, 265–66. Photographic reproduction of check to *New Yorker Staats-Zeitung*, made out by Adolf Pavenstedt, 12 October 1914, in John P. Jones and Paul M. Hollister, *The German Secret Service in America* (Boston: Small, Maynard & Co., 1918), opposite p. 230. See especially Bernstorff to Bethmann Hollweg, 6 November 1915, vol. 4, Vereinigte Staaten von Amerika 2, AA.

57. The Ridders had another go at it during the Nazi period, and the results, at least as far as family publicity was concerned, were not better than in World War I. Cf. Louis Nizer, *My Life in Court* (Garden City: Doubleday & Co., 1961), pp. 288ff.

58. Bernstorff to Foreign Office, 22 and 24 March 1915; Zimmermann to Bernstorff, 28 March 1915; Schulze-Gaevernitz to Zimmermann, 16 March 1915; all vol. 1, Vereinigte Staaten von Amerika 2, secret, AA.

59. Clipping, *Boston Globe*, 20 November 1922, Daniel F. Cohalan Papers, Irish Historical Society, New York. Foreign Office to Imperial Finance Ministry, 27 December 1919, secret; Minister of Finance to Treasury, 19 January 1920, secret; both vol. 1, Vereinigte Staaten von Amerika 6, AA. Rumely to Schulze-Gaevernitz, 22 March 1915, Box 243, RG 59, NA. For further details on acquisition of *New York Evening Mail* see Doerries, *Imperial Challenge*, pp. 53–55.

60. Bernstorff wrote to the Foreign Office on 27 October 1916, vol. 25, Vereinigte Staaten von Amerika 2, AA, that he was very sad about the death of the owner of the *Washington Post*, John R. McLean, who had "given a quite anti-English character to his paper." His death, in Bernstorff's view, was a loss for Germany. To fill a part of the void left by McLean the Germans gave financial assistance to Theodore Lowe and his *National Courier*, a weekly in Washington.

61. Bernstorff to Bethmann Hollweg, 27 March 1916, vol. 1, Vereinigte Staaten von Amerika 4, secret, AA. *Brewing and Liquor Interests and German and Bolshevik Propaganda*, p. 1861. Albert, *Aufzeichnungen*, pp. 49–50.

62. For such incorrect information, see for instance Wittke, *The German-Language Press in America*, p. 238. Theodore Huebner, *The Germans in America* (Philadelphia: Chilton, 1962), p. 146.

63. On Cahenslyism, see Doerries, *Iren und Deutsche in der Neuen Welt*, pp. 280ff. Reinhard R. Doerries, "Zwischen Staat und Kirche: Peter Paul Cahensly und die katholischen deutschen Einwanderer in den Vereinigten Staaten von Amerika," in Alexander Fischer and others, eds., *Russland-Deutschland-Amerika* (Wiesbaden: Steiner, 1978).

64. Spring Rice to Sir Edward Grey, 12 February 1916, 2793, Fo 371, PRO.

65. See for instance treaty between the Ancient Order of Hibernians and the National German-American Alliance on 22 January 1907. Doerries, *Iren und Deutsche in der Neuen Welt*, p. 11.

66. Even a memorial mass for "dead Catholic soldiers" without specification of whether they had been Irish-Americans or German-Americans could "be made a great demonstration." John Devoy to Jeremiah O'Leary, 15 October 1915, Maloney Collection, New York Public Library, New York.

67. James Hennesey, *American Catholics* (New York: Oxford University Press, 1981), pp. 224–225.

68. Rumely to Dernburg, November 1914, quoted in clipping, *Boston Globe*, 20 November 1922, Daniel F. Cohalan Papers, Irish Historical Society, New York.

69. Bernstorff to Foreign Office, 27 February 1915, vol. 6, Vereinigte Staaten von Amerika 13a, AA.

70. Falcke, *Vor dem Eintritt Amerikas in den Weltkrieg*, p. 98, mentions German propaganda among Catholics but then confesses his ignorance of any specific measures taken.

71. One of the most aggressive pieces of British propaganda was the *Report of the Committee on Alleged German Outrages* usually referred to as the Bryce Report of 1915, appearing soon after the Germans torpedoed the *Lusitania*.

72. Cf. Archbishop John Ireland's reply in January 1918 to the question whether he still expected an allied victory. He could not imagine that the Central Powers were meant to win because "it would be a victory of injustice and Lutheran principles." Quoted from James H. Moynihan, *The Life of Archbishop John Ireland* (New York: Arno Press, 1976), p. 271.

73. Doerries, *Imperial Challenge*, pp. 201–02. M.L. Sanders and Philip M. Taylor, *British Propaganda during the First World War* (London: Macmillan, 1982), pp. 144–145. Stephen Vaughn, *Holding Fast the Inner Lines* (Chapel Hill: University of North Carolina Press, 1980), p. 64.

74. Bernstorff report, 16 August 1916; Erzberger to von Bergen, 14 October 1916; both vol. 6, Vereinigte Staaten von Amerika 13a, AA.

75. Gerald P. Fogarty, *The Vatican and the American Hierarchy from 1870 to 1965* (Stuttgart: Anton Hiersemann, 1982), pp. 207–08. Fogarty reports the British Foreign Office intervening in the appointment of Mundelein to the See of Buffalo because of his German descent.

76. Townsend, *The Germans of Chicago*, p. 119.

77. The American theologian Thomas C. Hall who allowed himself to be used for German propaganda in one of his speeches in Bremen in 1916 went so far as to suggest that German-Americans had no other common political interest than the engagement for their beer on Sunday. T.C. Hall, *Das Deutschtum in der amerikanischen Politik* (Bremen: Bremer Gesellschaft, 1916), p. 13.

78. Wilhelm Löhe, *Zuruf aus der Heimat an die deutsch- lutherische Kirche Nordamericas* [sic] (Stuttgart, 1845), pp. 29–32.

79. Reinhard R. Doerries, "Walter Rauschenbusch," in Martin Greschat, ed., *Gestalten der Kirchengeschichte*, vol. 10, part 1 (Stuttgart: W. Kohlhammer, 1985), pp. 180–81. Arthur S. Link, *Woodrow Wilson and the Progressive Era, 1910–1917* (New York: Harper Torchbook, 1963 [first publ. 1954]), p. 146.

80. Alan N. Graebner, "The Acculturation of an Immigrant Lutheran Church: The Lutheran Church – Missouri Synod, 1917–1929" (Columbia University, New York: Ph.D. [Pol.Sc.] Dissertation, 1965), pp. 33 ff. F.A.O. Pieper succeeded C.F.W. Walther as president of Concordia Seminary in St. Louis and president of the Missouri Synod. G.C. Berkemeier was an important voice of Lutheran German-America. Bente was editor of *Lehre und Wehre* and very outspoken for the German cause. Frederick C. Luebke, *Bonds of Loyalty* (DeKalb: Northern Illinois University Press, 1974), p. 104.

81. Hermann Hagedorn, *The Hyphenated Family* (New York: Macmillan, 1960), pp. 225–26. David L. Scheidt, "The Role of Linguistic Transition in the Muhlenberg Tradition of American Lutheranism" (Temple University, Philadelphia: Ph.D. [Theology] Dissertation, 1963), pp. 130ff.

82. For detail concerning the Zimmermann Telegram see Barbara W. Tuchman, *The Zimmermann Telegram* (New York: Viking Press, 1958) and Friedrich Katz, *The Secret War in Mexico* (Chicago: University of Chicago Press, 1981), pp. 350–78.

83. Otherwise the heavy-handed censorship in wartime Germany would hardly have permitted the press to jubilate over the dead of the passenger liner. Cf. Doerries, *Imperial Challenge*, pp. 293–94.

84. Henry Cabot Lodge to Theodore Roosevelt, 22 February 1915, in *Selections from the Correspondence of Theodore Roosevelt and Henry Cabot Lodge, 1884–1914* (New York, 1925), here quoted from Graebner, "The Acculturation of an Immigrant Lutheran Church," p. 41. On 4 February 1915, Bente had already seen President Wilson and argued for an arms embargo. Wilson seems not to have been impressed. Link, *Wilson: The Struggle for Neutrality, 1914–1915*, pp. 169–70.

85. After the sinking of the *Lusitania* Dernburg instructed Americans in Cleveland that the torpedoing had been a justified measure. The tasteless comments marked the end of his public relations career and he departed before he was expelled. Frank P. Chambers, *The*

War Behind The War 1914–1918 (London: Faber and Faber, 1939), pp. 203–05. Doerries, *Imperial Challenge*, pp. 43, 262–63.

86. Masterman had been Financial Secretary to the Treasury and Chancellor of the Duchy of Lancaster. The office established by him in 1914 stayed at Wellington House until Lord Beaverbrook heading the Ministry of Information in 1918 closed it down. Sir Gilbert Parker, a Canadian by birth, knew North America well and directed the American operation from England until 1917, when he went to the United States. His United States assistant for propaganda was the Glasgow professor William Macneil Dixon. In June 1917 Lord Northcliffe came to the United States and opened the British Bureau of Information in New York. The period of shying away from publicity had ended. For detail see James D. Squires, *British Propaganda at Home and in The United States* (Cambridge: Harvard University Press, 1935).

87. Cf. Armin Rappaport, *The British Press and Wilsonian Neutrality* (Stanford: Stanford University Press, 1951), p. 10, who specifically mentions that "friction [had] characterized German-American relations" and then lists "rival colonial ambitions in the Pacific and the Caribbean, . . . Samoa, and . . . the affair at Manila Bay . . . too, the 'blood and iron' character of Bismarck's Empire. . . ." Vaughn, *Holding Fast the Inner Lines,* p. 64, mentions as factors increasing "anti-German sentiment" the Zabern affair, the Delbrück law, and Friedrich von Bernhardi's *Deutschland und der nächste Krieg* (1912), which carried an unmistakable German message to the United States. It was translated in 1914 and received wide attention in Britain and America. Cf. Robert S. Osgood, *Ideals and Self-Interest in America's Foreign Relations* (Chicago: University of Chicago Press, 1953), p. 131.

88. Cf. Report by Harry E. Brittain (probably 1915) after a seven-months tour of the United States, 2591 B, FO 371, PRO.

89. Z.A.B. Zeman, *A Diplomatic History of the First World War* (London: Weidenfeld and Nicolson, 1971), p. 169.

90. Hale himself denied receiving pay from Bernstorff. *New York Times* clipping, 4 February 1916, 2848, FO 371, PRO. W.G. Sickel and J.P. Meyer, 14 January 1915, to Albert Ballin, Hamburg-Amerika Linie, New York, HAPAG, Hamburg. Bernstorff to Foreign Office, no Washington date, Stockholm, 6 June 1916; memo by Philip Baron Mumm von Schwarzenstein, 4 July 1916; both vol. 5, Die Presse in New York, AA. Bernstorff to Foreign Office, 7 July 1916, vol. 19, Weltkrieg 18, AA. Concerning the 1908 interview and consequences, see Doerries, *Imperial Challenge*, p. 21.

91. J.P. Meyer to Albert Ballin, 12 December 1914 and 1 February 1915, Hamburg-Amerika Linie, New York, HAPAG, Hamburg.

92. Doerries, *Imperial Challenge*, p. 115. Patrick Beesly, Room 40 (New York: Harcourt Brace Jovanovich, 1982), pp. 228–29.

93. Bernstorff to Foreign Office, 2 and 5 June 1916, translations, Box 205, RG 59, NA. J.P. Meyer to Huldermann, 19 November 1914, and 18 February 1915, Hamburg-Amerika Linie, New York, HAPAG, Hamburg.

94. Scandinavian, American, and other vessels were used for such purposes. In some cases the messengers were employees of the German shipping companies. Cf. J.P. Meyer to Huldermann, 19 November 1914, Hamburg-Amerika Linie, New York, HAPAG, Hamburg.

8

German Imperial Propaganda and the American Homefront in World War I: A Response to Reinhard R. Doerries

Jörg Nagler

Professor Doerries's stimulating and detailed examination of Imperial German propaganda efforts in the United States during the American period of neutrality dramatically demonstrates that German propagandists did not understand the complexities of American society. In this article, I will amplify the reasons for the failure of German propaganda, suggest further lines of inquiry into this subject, and examine the effects of German propaganda on American society.

Any assessment of German propaganda must look thoroughly at the prevailing social, political, and cultural forces that shaped American society in the World War I era. Propaganda is successful only when it takes these factors into consideration. It is thus not the organizational but the conceptual dimension that primarily forms the precondition for a successful modification of public opinion. A discussion of propaganda should concentrate on including the overall American political and cultural context in which Imperial propaganda operated. Although this context was mentioned in the beginning of Professor Doerries's paper, the reader would like to know more about those sectors of the American public that were inclined to believe the information disseminated by German propagandists and thus influenced in the war of words.

When we look for reasons for the failure of Imperial propaganda, we need to differentiate between internal and external factors. In addition to Professor Doerries's well considered arguments, let me suggest some alternative reasons for this failure. Internally, an overarching plan seemed to be missing, Berlin lacked a coordinating office similar to the Wellington House in London, and the propagandists lacked the information necessary for public relations activity among almost every possible audience. Moreover, there was insufficient information about the American side, almost no individual access to relevant American leaders, especially politicians, and insufficient information about the British side. The Ger-

Notes to Chapter 8 can be found on page 173

man propagandists also lacked adequate information about their own propaganda policy. In other words, the German propagandists were, in historian H.C. Peterson's words, "deaf, blind, and dumb,"[1] which is not an ideal starting point for effective propaganda, and largely because of external factors, they were always forced to be on the defensive in their work.

Although British intelligence was unable to intercept all of the information coming out of Imperial Germany, the British slowed down the flow of information tremendously. Thus, British news received by the U.S. media was always "fresher," and the Germans usually had to react to it. Another factor – and I think the most relevant one – was that the British established a link between a smoothly functioning intelligence apparatus and their propaganda efforts in the United States. They were able, thus, to implement both negative and positive propaganda.

The British employed negative propaganda in the sense that they were able to disclose German propaganda activities through intercepted mail, broken codes, etc., and they accumulated evidence that was then provided to the Americans. Because the British maintained anonymity, the American public never learned about these activities. The positive propaganda efforts of the British are well known and need not be treated at length here, [2] other than to emphasize that their approach was fundamentally different from their German counterparts. The British avoided the boisterous and vociferous public profile of their competitors; they firmly believed in gaining personal access to leaders as a means of shaping public opinion; and they had the advantage of a very well organized and well coordinated office in London, although they avoided the establishment of an office in the United States, which would have provoked animosity from the American public.

Internal conceptual, organizational, and individual blunders in the German propaganda effort prompted countermeasures from the American side, which then diminished the effectiveness of the German operations. A particular and fateful problem was the employment of many German academics, who felt compelled to instruct the American public about "the truth." This kind of *Oberlehrer* approach was not intended to reach the man on the street – in fact, it rather repelled him. It also demonstrated a symptomatic lack of understanding of American political civic culture and increased antagonistic feelings toward the perception of German *Kultur*, a term British propagandists were able to define with negative connotations and exploit for their own propaganda purposes.

One of most fateful factors leading to the failure of German propaganda in America was the intermingling of the war of words with that of actual deeds, expressed through *Propaganda der Tat*. I think that Professor

Doerries underestimates the impact of this kind of propaganda in his assessment of the failure of German propaganda. In the American mind, propaganda came to be equated with espionage and even sabotage. It became a synonym for alien subversiveness – a trauma and a nightmare in American history since the eighteenth century – with dramatic impact for German-Americans. Their legitimate struggle for neutrality was now interpreted as an Imperial German effort to influence American affairs through this "fifth column" of disloyal Americans of German descent. Since loyalty became the primary psychological touchstone for national cohesiveness, which aimed at transcending ethnic heritage, the presumed disloyalty on the part of the substantial number of German immigrants loomed as a potential threat to national security. The projection of a distant German menace onto the internal "fifth column" (or alien) reflected increasing nativism and helped to foster a irrational xenophobia that would explode after America's entry into the European war. This xenophobia threatened the cultural and often even the economic survival of German-Americans, especially since everything German, and *Kultur* in particular, had become synonymous with barbarism, militarism, authoritarianism, and the urge for world hegemony. In other words, German values appeared to be the antithesis of American values. This can even be seen in the ridiculous name-changing campaign of 1917 and 1918, when "German" was replaced by "Liberty" (as in "Liberty measles") because even the word "German" was charged with sinister meanings.

Although we are partly aware of the harassment of German-Americans after America entered World War I, we have overlooked the more than half a million German immigrants who were not naturalized and thus stigmatized as enemy aliens. Lacking the constitutional rights granted to American citizens, these people became the victims of governmental control and arbitrary action. Many who felt the American government's "firm hand of stern repression"[3] found themselves charged with German propaganda activities, and some were subsequently interned for the duration of the war. It is at this point that my own interests mesh with those of Professor Doerries. I have found that some of these internees were indeed connected with the Imperial propaganda efforts,[4] and they were willing to cooperate with the authorities, especially in the so-called Overman Committee investigation, begun in September 1918 and conducted by the Senate Judiciary Committee, into the alleged connection between American brewing interests and German propaganda.[5] One internee has left us a thorough description of the policy and personnel of the German Information Service.[6] According to one of the principal investigators, this internee became one of the most important sources for the compilation of the report.[7]

Disclosures of the various legal and illegal activities of the Imperial German government coincided with the preparedness campaign of 1915 and 1916, which had not only a military dimension but implicitly attempted to homogenize American society and prepare the home front to resist internal threats. Such threats were most likely to come, it was alleged, from outspoken, pro-Central Power, hyphenated groups like the German-Americans, who many viewed as the vehicle for German propaganda.[8] This movement was led by such advocates of immigration restriction as Senator Henry Cabot Lodge and Representative August P. Gardner. In a motion picture entitled *Battle Cry of Peace*, released in late 1915, an unprepared America is invaded by aggressors who are made to look German.[9] There is no doubt that the German menace, represented by the *Propaganda der Tat*, helped to solidify political and social consensus in American society against Germany and German-Americans. On the other hand, anti-German propaganda in the Anglophile media provoked counter-reactions among some German-Americans who felt inclined to promote cultural superiority, thus hindering the efforts of the Imperial German propagandists who wanted to avoid *Kultur* as a means of propaganda.[10]

After World War I, the U.S. government used the surveillance and control of German propaganda during the period of neutrality as a pretext for investigations concerning "foreign propaganda." This also made more palatable the control of radicals during the Red Scare, when anti-subversive committees in Congress uniformly singled out "propaganda" as their target. The progenitor of these committees was the Overman Committee of 1918/19, cited above.[11]

The exposure of Heinrich Albert's activities illustrates how disastrous were the blunders of the propagandists. According to Wilson's adviser, Col. Edward Mandell House, these revelations brought the two countries to the brink of war.[12] I would have liked Professor Doerries to devote more attention to the degree of awareness and level of information Wilson and his administration had concerning various German propaganda activities and about subsequent American intelligence countermeasures. Early in 1915, for example, Wilson, who was undoubtedly disturbed by the German propaganda,[13] had ordered a thorough investigation of the activities of the German propagandists and spies.[14] This was the reason why Secret Service agents placed Albert under surveillance. Although Albert's disclosed activities were still legal in an American framework, they indicated the broad spectrum of efforts by a foreign power to influence American public opinion and affairs. The documents, which were published in the *New York World* with Wilson's approval,[15] increased already prevalent anti-German feelings in the

American public.[16] When Albert mentioned to American journalist William B. Hale his consternation concerning the publication of these documents – he considered his papers to be private! – Hale replied: "But Herr Geheimrat, this is a World War!"[17] I think the Albert incident, including Albert's reaction, is symptomatic of the amateurish character, even naiveté, of the Imperial propaganda effort. It also gives an impression of the tragicomic ambience of these German soldiers in the war of words.

The single successful attempt to acquire an American daily newspaper in order to mold American public opinion deserves a brief comment. Research in the manuscript collection of Dr. Edward Aloysius Rumely does not support Doerries's statement that he was a mere "straw man" for German propaganda. Rumely was indeed very active in promoting a pro-German course; to cite one example, he distributed much propaganda material on his own initiative. But Rumely did not accept uncritically any contribution by German or German-American authors, and he even returned a manuscript to Karl A. Fuehr of the German Information Service for revision. A fervent supporter of the dwindling Progressive party, Rumely entertained a close relationship with Theodore Roosevelt, whom he favored for the Republican presidential nomination in 1916. When Rumely was criticized by German-Americans for a less-than-fervent stance in favor of the German cause, he made it very clear that he supported only genuine American interests, and not suggestions from those who Roosevelt termed "professional German-Americans," those who were committed exclusively to narrow ethnic interests.[18] He thus expressed the same concern as Roosevelt about the hyphenated mentality in America, which had to be counterbalanced through the famous anti-hyphenate campaign of 1915/16.[19]

In his unpublished autobiography, Rumely claims that he approached Bernhard Dernburg with the idea of buying an American daily newspaper in order to counterbalance the British-dominated American press.[20] Both the publisher and famous muckraker S. S. McClure,[21] and Rumely had tried to buy other American daily newspapers before acquiring the *New York Evening Mail*.[22] In short, it seems to me that a successful project of the German propaganda apparatus, i.e., the purchase of a daily American newspaper, was originally the idea of an American. No wonder the editorials were more balanced than the German purchasers intended.[23] Rumely – who had an academic background in Germany and was a member of the *German University League*[24] – was indeed pro-German and well-connected in Germany, but he also was American enough not to become a "straw man" for the German propaganda interests to the detriment of American interests.

I'd like to respond to Professor Doerries's call for more research on the question of German propaganda among American blacks with some further insights, especially since a thorough investigation would show what stance the German propagandists took on race. How did they resolve the dialectic between the "inferior race argument," used to condemn the British and French for using black troops against white Europeans,[25] and appealing to blacks in the United States as potential allies. According to American intelligence sources, the German propaganda machine had a separate unit for "American race problems" that was intended specifically to appeal to blacks in the South. Evidently, this branch collected information regarding the mistreatment of blacks, such as lynching, and wrote articles that were distributed to newspapers. Although the "field work" was conducted by Consul von Reiswitz, who was stationed in New Orleans, the actual propaganda work was conducted from Mexico by von Eckhardt, who employed Mexicans and "halfbreeds." As in many other cases, this effort blurred the distinction between propaganda and illegal activities and directly attempted to stir up conflict.

German propaganda claimed that if Germany won the war, blacks in the South would become equal to whites. It also claimed that France always sent black soldiers to the front lines. Even the Civil War provided ammunition for the German propagandists: English support for the South demonstrated support for white supremacy.[26] The major argument made by German propagandists, however, was that once the United States entered the European war, blacks would not only face social and economic injustice, but also would face racism in a white man's army.[27] As in many other cases these activities among blacks amplified the suspicion about the existence of a Pan-German conspiracy. It was this suspicion that was partly responsible for the anti-German hysteria of 1917 and 1918. In 1917, for example, a rumor swept the South that a German plot for a black insurrection was about to be implemented.[28] Also, the so-called race riot in East St. Louis on 2 July 1917 was allegedly fostered by German propagandists and spies.[29]

The more one analyzes the social, political, and cultural conditions of the United States in the World War I era, the more one tends to agree with Doerries's view "that working conditions in America were such, that even a well planned German propaganda campaign would not have been able to reach American public opinion." These conditions included pro-British bias among the highly influential East Coast elites; progressivism, with its crusading spirit of high moral and ethical sensibilities, which set the stage for the tremendous uproar that greeted stories of atrocities committed by German soldiers against civilians; the preparedness campaign of 1915/16, which included a strong dose of nativism; and anti-German and pro-Ally associations, such as the National Security League. Professor Doerries's argument that Count Bernstorff's long tenure and intimate knowledge of American political life counterbalanced these conditions is weak, since Bernstorff was rarely able to control the propaganda efforts of his own men. Although David Hirst, in his dissertation on German propaganda, concludes that America's period of neutrality might have been shorter without the efforts of the German propagandists,[30] one could easily turn the argument around and say that without these efforts, America's period of neutrality might have been even longer.[31] But this provocative statement should be taken as it is intended – as a starting point for further discussion.

Notes to Chapter 8

1. Horace C. Peterson, *Propaganda for War* (Norman, OK: University of Oklahoma Press, 1939), 137.

2. For British propaganda in the United States during World War I see M.L. Sanders and Philip M. Taylor, *British Propaganda during the First World War, 1914–1918* (London: Macmillan, 1982), 167–207.

3. Woodrow Wilson in his War Message to Congress, 2 April 1917, cited in *The Papers of Woodrow Wilson*, ed. Arthur Link (Princeton, NJ: Princeton University Press, 1983), 41: 526.

4. There were a few former German propagandists who were connected with the Information Service among the approximately 2,500 persons incarcerated as allegedly dangerous civilian enemy aliens in two internment camps during the war. These included eccentric poet and translator Dr. Hanns Ewers, Dr. Isaac Straus, and P.A. Borgemeister, New York banker and confidential secretary to Heinrich Albert. On Ewers see 9–16–12, sec. 4, Justice Department, RG 60, National Archives, and Hanns H. Ewers to A. Mitchell Palmer, 8 April 1919, Records of the Adjutant General's Office: Prisoners of War and Alien Enemies in the United States, Alphabetical Files, Record Group 407, National Archives; on Straus 9140–2755–155, MID, NA; on Borgemeister see "Enemies within the United States: The Government's Treatment of Enemy Aliens, Spies, and Seditionists," *Current History: A Monthly Magazine of the New York Times*, 7, No. 1, part 1 (October 1917): 22.

5. See *Brewing and Liquor Interests and German Propaganda: Hearings before a Subcommittee of the Commitee on the Judiciary, United States Senate, 65 th Congress, Second and Third Sessions*, 2 vols. (Washington: Government Printing Office, 1919).

6. Georg L. Byram to U.S. Attorney General, 9 January 1918, 10972–5–17, Record Group 165 (Military Intelligence), National Archives, hereafter abbreviated as MID, NA. The informant was Dr. William Othmer. He appears in the files of the MID under the pseudonym of "Dr. Williams," see 9140–7166/34, MID, NA. Dr. Othmer was paroled from internment by arrangment of the Justice Department and was put in the custody of the MID in June 1918. He conducted two investigations of "enemy activities" among Lutheran clergy in Baltimore, Harrisburg, Pennsylvania, New York, and Philadelphia.

7. Captain George B. Lester to Major Wrisely Brown, Military Intelligence Division, 31 December 1918, 10992–5–43, MID, NA. According to his own statement, Dr. Othmer

had delivered more than 60 pages to Captain Lester in November 1918 describing in detail the activities of the German propagandists, see Memorandum for Mr. Henry A. Uterhardt by Othmer, 5 July 1919, 10972–5–49, RG 165, MID, NA.

8. For the preparedness campaign, see Kennedy, *Over Here: The First World War and American Society* (New York and Oxford: Oxford University Press, 1980), 36–40; Harry N. Scheiber, *The Wilson Administration and Civil Liberties* (Ithaca, NY: Cornell University Press, 1960), 2–5; Frederick C. Luebke, *Bonds of Loyalty: German Americans and World War I* (DeKalb: Northern Illinois University Press, 1974), 158–59, 167, 169; John Higham, *Strangers in the Land: Patterns of American Nativism*, 2nd ed. (New York: Atheneum, 1969), 199–200, 202.

9. See Ronald Fernandez, "Getting Germans to Fight Germans: The Americanizers of World War I," *The Journal of Ethnic Studies* 9 (1981): 60. A year later, movie director Thomas Dixon portrayed alien invaders into America as obvious German forces, see Richard Wood, ed., *Film Propaganda in America: A Documentary History. World War I* (New York: Greenwood Press, 1990), xxi.

10. Dernburg himself expressed in one of the business meetings of the German Information Service that the term *Kultur* should be strictly avoided in the propaganda campaign, see *Brewing and Liquor Interest*, vol. 2, 1391.

11. See Frank J. Donner, *The Age of Surveillance: The Aims and Methods of America's Political Intelligence System* (New York: Knopf, 1980), 49, 386.

12. "It [the publication of the papers] may, in my opinion, even lead us into war, but I think the publication should go ahead. It will strengthen your hands enormously. . . . The people will see things as those of us that know the true conditions have long seen them, and it will make it nearly impossible to continue the propaganda." Col. Edward Mandell House to Woodrow Wilson, 10 August 1915, *Wilson Papers*, 34 (1980), 158.

13. Scheiber, *The Wilson Administration and Civil Liberties*, 6–7.

14. George Sylvester Viereck, *Spreading Germs of Hate* (New York: Horace Liveright, 1930), 71, quotes from *The Saturday Evening Post*. On Viereck see *Phyllis Keller, States of Belonging: German-American Intellectuals and the First World War* (Cambridge, MA: Harvard University Press, 1979), 119–188.

15. See William Gibbs McAdoo, *Crowded Years: The Reminiscences of William Gibbs McAdoo* (Boston: Houghton Mifflin, 1931), 328–30, Arthur S. Link, *Wilson: The Struggle for Neutrality* (Princeton: Princeton University Press, 1960), 555–56.

16. *Wilson papers*, vol. 34 (1980), 158–59, f.n. 1.

17. Viereck, *Spreading Germs of Hate*, 72. Viereck compared the disclosure of the Albert portfolio with "the loss of the Marne," see *Spreading Germs of Hate*, 74. On Alberts activities in general, see the highly interesting and revealing Bureau of Investigation file, OG 174, Bureau of Investigation, RG 65, National Archives.

18. Robert Kann to Rumely, 13 June 1916, Rumely Mss., Manuscripts Department, Lilly Library, Indiana University, Bloomington, Indiana, henceforth abbreviated as L L.

19. For the anti-hyphenate campaign see Higham, *Strangers in the Land*, 198–201.

20. Rumely Autobiography, 2 vols., bound, Rumely Mss., Manuscripts Department, Lilly Library, Indiana University, Bloomington, Indiana. This is also supported by the statement of Bureau of Investigation chief Bruce Bielaski, see *Brewing and Liquor Interests*, vol. 2, 1450.

21. Interestingly enough, McClure later worked for the Committee on Public Information, for which he prepared essays on German espionage in America and other related subjects, see Stephen L. Vaughn, *Holding Fast the Inner Lines: Democracy, Nationalism, and the Committee on Public Information* (Chapel Hill: University of North Carolina Press, 1980), 77.

22. S.S. McClure to Rumely, 30 January 1915, Rumely Mss., LL. This letter was later used as evidence in the trial against Rumely.

23. See *The Gravest 366 Days: Editorial Reprints from the Evening Mail* (New York: New York Evening Mail, 1916).

24. The German University League to Rumeley, 22 January 1915, Rumely Mss., LL. The 1920 trial against Rumely revealed his activities, see "Conspiring To Commit Offense Against United States" (three bound proceedings of the trial, Rumely Mss., LL).

25. Dernburg in *New York Times*, 6 September 1914; David Wayne Hirst, "German Propaganda in the United States, 1914–1917" (Unpublished diss., Northwestern University, 1962), 99.

26. See *Brewing and Liquor Interests*, vol. 2, 1574 (Bielaski testimony), and 1784–1785.

27. See Othmer (alias "Dr. Williams") file, 9140–7166–34, MID, NA.

28. See Kennedy, *Over Here*, 29.

29. See enclosure in letter from Woodrow Wilson to Joseph Patrick Tumulty, 5 July 1917, *Wilson Papers*, 43 (1983), 103.

30. Hirst, "German Propaganda," 248.

31. In this context Count von Bernstorff's remarks made in retrospect are revealing: "If I am questioned, I shall say that if we made a mistake in the United States, it was that we dealt too much in propaganda rather than too little." Quoted in *Official German Documents Relating to the World War*, trans. under the supervision of the Carnegie Endowment for International Peace, 2 vols. (New York: Oxford University Press, 1923), 1, 927.

9

The War on German Language and Culture, 1917–1925

Paul Finkelman

During and after World War I, German-Americans were the targets of official harassment, political suppression, police brutality, and mob violence. This repression was rooted in the hostility to foreigners that reemerged in the late nineteenth century as nativist organizations, such as the American Protective Association, began agitating for an end to non-Anglo-Saxon immigration.[1] Even before the rise of this new xenophobia, conservative Americans had been appalled by the labor radicalism and socialism espoused by many immigrants.

Germans and Radicalism: Prelude to Repression

Long before World War I, German immigrants and their children gained a reputation for radicalism, anarchism, and violence. After being expelled from Germany and imprisoned in England, Johann Most brought his brand of anarchism to America in 1882. He soon "pulled the scattered fragments of the social revolutionary movement together, giving it new energy and a more sharply defined sense of purpose."[2] His German language periodical, *Freiheit*, published in New York City, symbolized the importance of German immigrants to the new labor and social radicalism of the era.

Most was the first of several Germans publicly associated with radicalism. Rev. Robert Reitzel left his position as a pastor in the German Reformed Church and in 1884 founded the paper *Arme Teufel* in Detroit. Carl Nold, a young immigrant, spent five years in prison after the Homestead steel strike.[3] Six of the eight men tried for the Haymarket riot were German-American anarchists.[4] When five were sentenced to death and another to a long imprisonment, one commentator noted that "the enemy forces are not American," but "rag-tag and bob-tail cutthroats of Beelzebub from the Rhine, the Danube, the Vistula, and the Elbe."[5] Other Germans became leaders of individual union movements,

Notes to Chapter 9 can be found on page 197.

like William Trautmann, a brewery union organizer who became the secretary-treasurer of the Industrial Workers of the World (IWW) and translated the writings of Karl Marx into English.[6] Thus, by the time the United States entered World War I there was already a climate favorable to repression based on the assumption that German radicals threatened American society.[7]

The position of German-Americans was further undermined by the vast majority of German-Americans who, while not supporters of the Kaiser, nevertheless wanted the United States to remain neutral and not enter the war against Germany. Finally, revelations of "widespread German sabotage, intrigue, and plotting against American neutrality"[8] in the years immediately before the war led to the stereotyping of all German-Americans as spies or enemies.[9]

German–American Opposition to the War

German-American opposition to the United States's entrance into World War I came from three different sources. Unfortunately, most American superpatriots, blinded by war fever, were incapable of understanding the not so subtle differences between these groups of German-Americans. Thus, superpatriots lumped them together and concluded that all opponents of the war sympathized with the enemy.

In 1914 most German-Americans "were either indifferent to the war in Europe or actually hostile to the German government and its goals."[10] German-Americans, after all, had abandoned Germany for the United States. Most "thought of themselves as Americans totally loyal to American democratic ideals. . . . In the German-American's view, his cultural heritage created no special loyalty for the German Imperial Government, nor did it inhibit his capacity for patriotic citizenship in his adopted homeland."[11] However, this did not mean German-Americans were anxious to fight against their friends and relatives in their former homeland. Few faced the family crisis of the singer Ernestine Schumann-Heinck "who had sons in both the German and American armies,"[12] but for German-Americans immigrants and their children, the prospect of fighting against their relatives was disturbing. Even the Chicago *Tribune* thought German-Americans should not be sent to the front "to drive bayonets into the breast of [their] blood brother unless that brother is invading the country."[13]

Not surprisingly, before 1917 German-Americans strongly favored a non-interventionist policy. After the United States entered the war most German-Americans agreed with the *Cincinnati Volksblatt* that "To support the United States is a duty."[14] But, many Americans could not forgive their earlier opposition to the war and their continuing hostility to aiding Great Britain.

While most German-Americans accepted the war and conscription,[15] two groups – religious pietists and socialist radicals – did not. Mennonites, Amish, Dunkards, Hutterite Brethren, and other pietists retained their pacifist values.[16] Their rejection of modern garb and technology, as well as their continued use of the German language, made them particularly vulnerable in their opposition to military service. After being drafted some Mennonite conscientious objectors were denied adequate food, beaten, or tortured in army camps.[17] Over 130 German-American pacifists were court-martialed and jailed, mostly in Fort Levenworth, where some died from poor treatment. By contrast, Canada granted Mennonites conscientious objector status, even though that nation lacked a bill of rights, a guarantee of religious freedom, or separation of church and state. Where the federal and state governments failed to act, the mob took over. Some Amish in Ohio were forced to buy Liberty bonds. In South Dakota, Liberty Loan committee members confiscated farm animals from Hutterites and sold them to purchase bonds, while in Illinois "patriots" desecrated Mennonite churches. In Kansas members of a mob forcibly cut off the beards of some Mennonites while others were whipped and/or tarred and feathered.[18]

German radicals, along with socialists and anarchists from other ethnic groups, opposed the war because they believed it was a capitalist plot, in which working men would die to further the imperial goals of England and Germany. The prominence of German Leftists, like Milwaukee's Victor Berger, led many Americans to the erroneous beliefs that most Germans were socialists and allied with the Kaiser in an attempt to undermine the American war effort. Socialist opposition to the war, tied to the visibility of German-Americans and other immigrants in labor and socialist organizations, gave conservative forces an excuse to launch a general crackdown on the American Left. This helped lead to the destruction of the Left as a viable political force.[19] Many Americans believed, as former President Theodore Roosevelt did, that the "German Socialists in the United States, who for years have been the leaders in the American Socialist Party, have in this war shown themselves not only disloyal to the United States but traitors to humanity and to democracy, and tools of the unscrupulous militaristic autocracy of the Hollenzollerns." Roosevelt claimed that during the war socialists had become "the enemies of America, and the tools of German militaristic brutality."[20]

People of German ancestry were not the only Americans to oppose the war. Woodrow Wilson, after all, had been reelected in 1916 on the slogan "he kept us out of war." In April 1917, six Senators and 50 members of the House voted against the declaration of war. This contrasts sharply with the unanimous Senate support for World War II and the single symbolic dissent in the House. Perhaps an even greater contrast was the 98 to 2 vote in the Senate in favor of the Gulf of Tonkin Resolution in 1964.

The divided sentiments about the war in Europe help explain the domestic crusade against German culture during and immediately after the war. Americans had to be convinced that the war was just and necessary. Indeed, "the Wilson administration was compelled to cultivate – even to manufacture – public opinion favorable to the war effort."[21] The administration did so by bringing an "unparalleled missionary fervor"[22] to the war effort both at home and abroad. Part of this effort was a massive propaganda campaign against Germany, Germans, and German culture. An article in the popular magazine *McClure's* declared "we are at war with Germany, the German people, and everything connected with Germany." The article, written by a soldier, urged Americans to "wipe out the German-language press in the United States . . . and make this an America for Americans."[23] Clergy were equally militant. The evangelist Billy Sunday offered a simplistic analysis of the war: "I tell you it is Bill against Woodrow, Germany against America, Hell against Heaven. . . . All this talk about not fighting the German people is a lot of bunk." The mainstream Rev. Dr. Newell Dwight Hillis of Brooklyn's Plymouth Congregational Church urged Americans to "consider the sterilization of 10,000,000 German soldiers and the segregation of the women," to insure "that when this generation of German goes, civilized cities, states and races may be rid of this awful cancer that must be cut clean out of the body of society."[24]

The need to switch from neutrality to support for the war led to excessive patriotic attacks on Germans. In this context hyperbolic denunciations of the German government and the Kaiser are perhaps understandable. Thus, a reference to Kaiser Wilhelm as "Bill the Butcher" seems little more than a crude bit of wartime propaganda. But if the Kaiser was a "butcher," what did this make those who carried out his orders? One article explained "The Satanic Kaiser stalks gloomily among his hordes of Satan-whelps, calls upon God to help him in his nameless crimes, and urges his faithful imps to still greater deeds of brutality."[25] Such propaganda made the German people, at best, into unwitting servants of the devil. This propaganda at least had the virtue of allowing that Germans might cease to be "Satan-whelps" or "faithful imps," if they were educated to appreciate democratic values and taught to reject the Kaiser. "Whelps" and "imps" after all, might grow up to be better adults.

But many commentators were not satisfied with simply attacking the Kaiser and the German political system. To justify the carnage of World War I, propagandists on both sides of the western front painted their enemies as hopelessly less than human. "We are fighting for humanity," Theodore Roosevelt proclaimed,[26] implying that Germans were not within the pale of humanity. Thus, calling Germans "whelps" implied they were animals, and calling them "imps" implied they were other-worldly creatures. Other propaganda followed this line, referring to the Kaiser as the "werewolf of Potsdam."[27] The Committee on Public Information's support for movies with titles like *The Prussian Cur*, *Wolves of Kultur*, and *The Kaiser, the Beast of Berlin* exemplifies the semi-official process of dehumanizing the Kaiser and his people.[28] This recalled the response to the Haymarket riot, when one commentator referred to German radicals as "Europe's human and inhuman rubbish."[29] In the 1890s the American Protective Association and other nativist groups began referring to German immigrants as "huns."[30] During the war propagandists revived this epithet, which conjured up images of a blood-thirsty, anarchistic, and cruel barbarian. Billy Sunday said of Germany that "no nation so infamous, vile, greedy, sensuous, bloodthirsty, ever disgraced the pages of history."[31] "The Prussian," a professor in Nebraska declared, "is a moral imbecile, an arrested development, a savage in civilization's garb, and even the garb he has stolen." Professor Vernon Kellog at Stanford declared the Germans "unclean, unclean."[32]

The United States entered the war late, but quickly made up for lost time with articles arguing that Americans had to reject their "good-natured and somewhat sentimental" attitudes in order to fight Germany. It was "not only foolish but positively dangerous" to make a distinction between the German Government and the German people because "if it is a perilous thing to underestimate one's opponent physically, it is at least equally hazardous to overestimate him morally. And this is precisely what we are doing when we sentimentalize over the poor deluded, naturally sweet-tempered and generally angelic Hun and weep about the way his Government forces him to do things entirely out of keeping with his kindly disposition." After detailing the alleged atrocities of the German army, this article concluded "it is time we stop sentimentalizing over the Hun, and realize . . . [it is] congenial to him to perform such barbarous cruelties that beside his deeds those of the Huns of old appear white and shining. . . . We are at war, not with a mere government, but with a nation of moral perverts, a nation which exalts in torture, admires murder, and has no faintest conception of the meaning of the word of honor."[33] Rev. Newell Hillis asked, "Shall this foul creature that is in the German saddle, with hoofs of fire, trample down all the sweet growth in the garden of God?" The Germans were barbarians who, according to Hillis, "slaughtered old men and matrons, mutilated captives in ways that can only be spoken of by men in whispers, violated little girls until they were dead, and committed atrocities, the worst of which cannot even be named." A Presbyterian minister summed up: "German devilishness is instinct with the genius of Hell." Indeed, "made in Germany" was synonymous with "made in Hell."[34]

The Domestic War on Germans and German Culture

If the German people were "moral perverts" and "barbarians" who had no sense of honor and had been "made in Hell," then it was logical to assume that German-Americans could not easily overcome their genetic and cultural propensities for evil. The scholar Lyman Abbott assured Americans that "Fourteen centuries have not made any improvement in his character. Time is no cure for sin."[35]

Americanization might make Germans into better people, but this could be accomplished only by making them into Americans and destroying their remaining vestiges of German culture. The logical result of this thinking was the conclusion, reached by many Americans during the war, that German culture was evil and dangerous and had to be eliminated before it could contaminate American culture. German culture was the culture of barbarians and huns. The war at home led to the repression of Germans and anything German. Thus, Theodore Roosevelt could "emphatically protest against" discrimination of German-Americans, but at the same time talk about the "Hun within our gates" who he thought "should be hunted down without mercy." After all, he thought, their "Kultur" could "be translated as culture only in a pathological sense. German 'Kultur' is precisely analogous to a 'culture' of cholera germs."[36]

With nearly three-quarters-of-a-century hindsight, the American response to World War I seems almost incomprehensible.[37] On the homefront hostilities were directed not so much at the Kaiser's Germany, but at people of German ancestry and at German culture. As one author succinctly put it in a wartime article, "There is a slogan in this war that says, 'if you can't fight over there, fight over here.'"[38] The war on German culture was the fight over here.

President Woodrow Wilson helped lay a foundation for the war-era repression of German-Americans. In his annual message to Congress in 1915, Wilson complained of "citizens of the United States . . . born under other flags but welcome under our generous naturalization laws to the full freedom and opportunity of America, who have poured the poison of disloyalty into the very arteries of our national life." He asked for new legislation because "such creatures of passion, disloyalty, and anarchy must be crushed out."[39]

Wilson's attack on hyphenated Americans was, in part, a function of his desire to avoid direct confrontation with any of the Central Powers belligerents. It was easier, and safer, to "draw attention away from the German government and focus it upon disloyal foreign-born Americans."[40] While not naming any particular nationality, everyone knew that Wilson had German-Americans in mind. Wilson's biographer notes that when the president "denounce[d] those citizens of foreign birth, obviously German Americans" his "voice became almost emotional as he called for legislation to save the nation's honor and self-respect." The British ambassador happily reported that "the passage in the President's speech denouncing the disloyal action of the hyphenated citizen was greeted with great applause and is now the predominant element in the present situation."[41] Wilson's 1916 campaign, with its emphasis on eliminating "hyphenated-Americans" was anti-German in spirit. While German-Americans supported Republican Charles Evans Hughes, "Wilson made it his policy throughout the campaign openly to repudiate the vote of the German-Americans."[42] Except for southern Democrats rejecting the votes of Afro-Americans, this is an almost unique example of a major party rejecting the votes of a powerful ethnic group on a large scale.[43] The Democratic party's campaign text-book for 1916 "stressed the fact that 'agents of the German-American Alliance and other such organizations worked day and night'" for the Republican candidate, "'promising German support'" for Hughes' campaign.[44] This tactic made German-Americans a domestic enemy even while Wilson was campaigning on his success at keeping the nation "out of war." Thus, by the time he asked for a declaration of war, Wilson had primed the United States for a crusade, not only against Germany, but against German-Americans.

In his war message, Wilson continued to set a tone of repression. In his penultimate paragraph, Wilson warned that disloyalty among German-Americans would "be dealt with with a firm hand of stern repression."[45] Wilson's statement, which he probably meant as little more than a warning to hyphenated Americans with pro-German sympathies, was received by "an explosion of applause" from the Congress,[46] and, as events would soon demonstrate, by an enthusiastic public.

Some of the responses were truly horrifying. The April 1918 lynching of Robert Prager in Collinsville, Illinois heads any list of wartime attacks on Germans. Prager was a German-born socialist falsely accused of disloyalty and hording explosives.[47] There were countless examples of other German-Americans being beaten, tarred and feathered, and humiliated or intimidated. In Detroit a mob took a German-American from his home in the middle of the night, cut his hair, and carried him to the Detroit River in which the mob threatened to throw him. In San Jose, California a German-American was tarred and feathered and then chained all night to a canon in a park. The burning of German books, including Bibles, that took place throughout the country did not physically harm anyone, but its intimidation factor must have been great. In Milwaukee dachshunds were killed by rock-throwing patriots.[48] Many individuals lost their jobs,[49] or freedom, because of their ancestry or their unwillingness to placate superpatriots.

The American Defense Society declared German music to be "one of the most dangerous forms of German propaganda, because it appeals to the emotions and has power to sway an audience as nothing else can." With attitudes like this, it is not surprising that German music quickly fell out of favor. The city of Pittsburgh prohibited the playing of Beethoven. Opera companies in New York and Chicago stopped performing works in German.[50]

Musicians and conductors of German ancestry were particularly vulnerable. Many concert halls barred violinist Fritz Kreisler because he was allegedly an officer in the Austrian army. He went into temporary retirement for the last year of the war. Dr. Karl Muck, a Swiss citizen of German birth and the conductor of the Boston Symphony Orchestra, nearly lost his position because he refused, on aesthetic grounds, to begin his concerts with the "Star Spangled Banner," and because he insisted, also on aesthetic grounds, on playing music by German composers. The trustees of the Symphony backed Muck, but may have felt some sense of relief when federal authorities arrested him. Muck was not arrested for seditious activities. After an enormous investigation, the Justice Department arrested him for "sending obscene materials through the mail." The "materials" were love letters, which were "affectionate but neither personally lewd nor politically seditious." After intense questioning, Muck, despite his Swiss citizenship, submitted to internment at Fort Oglethorpe, Georgia, as an enemy alien. Muck's Cincinnati counterpart, Ernst Kunewald, who was in fact a German citizen, suffered a similar fate.[51]

The litany of silly things Americans did to purge the nation of German cultural and linguistic influences seems almost endless. Hamburgers became "liberty steaks," frankfurters became "victory sausages," and sauerkraut became "victory cabbage." Mindlessly, a physician in Massachusetts began calling German measles "liberty measles." Berlin, Iowa changed its name to Lincoln, while East Germantown, Indiana became Pershing. Banks, hotels, and other businesses with "German" in their names soon found new identities. Vigilantes, meanwhile, defaced statutes of Schiller, Beethoven, Heine, and other icons of German culture. In Texas the governor tried to fire all aliens on the faculty of the state university, while the College of the City of New York reduced "by one point the credit value of each course in the Department of German." The Poetry Society of America expelled George Sylvester Viereck, and "except for a short reference his name disappeared from *Who's Who in America*. . . ." More serious was the defacement of numerous Lutheran and Mennonite churches, and the physical assaults and intimidation on German clergy.[52]

Language and Americanization

Authorities were especially concerned with protecting young children from the contamination of anything German. In Columbus, Ohio public school teachers pasted "in school music books blank sheets of paper covering 'The Watch on the Rhine' and 'The Lorelei.'" New Jersey's superintendent of schools banned all German songs while "in California, the state board of education directed that all pages in music textbooks that contained German folk songs be cut out." Montana banned a history textbook which stated that "Christianity advanced from the Rhine to the Elbe." Apparently these patriotic watchdogs "believed that any identification of Christianity with the Germans was un-American."[53]

The most important aspect of the control of culture and the protection of children concerned attempts to limit the teaching of foreign languages, particularly German, in the nation's schools.[54] Connected to this was the desire to eliminate private schools, especially those connected to churches.

Such goals were, of course, not new in American history. Opposition to Catholic schools first emerged in the mid-nineteenth century.[55] Conflict over foreign language education and parochial schools re-emerged in the 1880s – at precisely the same time immigration from Central, Eastern, and Southern Europe began to rise dramatically and "foreign" doctrines, like socialism and anarchism, began to capture the minds of some American workers. In 1889 Illinois passed the Edwards Law, which required mandatory education in English. Also in 1889 Wisconsin's Bennett Law required that children attend a school within "the city, town or district" they lived in and that all "reading, writing, arithmetic and United States history" be taught "in the English language."[56] This threatened German Catholic and Lutheran schools in the state, which often drew students from more than one school district. It also hurt the many German language schools in Wisconsin.[57] From 1886 through 1888, nativist members of the school board in Indianapolis, Indiana attempted to suspend the teaching of German in the public schools and in 1890 these nativists succeeded in prohibiting all German language education before the sixth grade. The school board acted in spite of a law requiring schools to provide German language instruction "whenever the parents or guardians of twenty-five or more children in attendance at any school . . . shall so demand. . . ."[58]

The Wisconsin law, similar laws in Illinois and Michigan,[59] and the Indianapolis school board's action reflected the larger movement designed to "Americanize" foreigners.[60] This movement did not quickly become popular.

In Wisconsin German-Americans showed that, despite their language preference, they were "Americanized." Part of the attack on the Bennett Law was phrased in the traditional American context of personal liberty and religious freedom, which the German-Americans argued they favored and the English-Americans opposed.[61] The Wisconsin German-Americans also proved adept at coalition politics in their response to the Bennett Law. The attack on German language education managed to unite two previously bitter foes: the German Lutherans and the German Catholics. The traditionally Republican German Lutherans rejected the Grand Old Party because it supported English language eduction. "The Republicans were buried by" what one Wisconsin politician called "the Lutheran land-slide." This Democratic sweep in the 1890 state elections led to the repeal of the Bennett Law in the following year.[62] In Illinois the Edwards Law led to massive statewide Democratic victories, including the election of the German-born John Peter Altgeld as the state's governor. In the campaign Altgeld successfully "persuaded thousands of voters that the Republicans were responsible for the law." Following his election the legislature repealed the "Edwards Law."[63] In Indianapolis supporters of German language education won a narrow victory in the 1890 school board elections, followed by a more substantial victory before the Indiana Supreme Court, which found that the board's decision to terminate language education violated state law. The court ruled that the purpose of the 1869 amendment to the Indiana School Law "was to compel the teaching of physiology and history of the United States, and to withdraw the German language from a list of purely optional languages that might be taught at the discretion of the trustees, and place it conditionally in the list of required studies." By the turn of the century, enrollment in German had nearly tripled in Indianapolis from 1890, when the board had tried to eliminate courses in the subject.[64] By 1903 only 14 states required education in English. Some of these laws allowed education in foreign language beyond the primary grades.[65]

The defeat of this early English language movement showed the power of German-American voting, especially in the Midwest, but the movement also revealed the desire of many Americans to force immigrants to conform to the language and customs of their new home. When the war made the German-American community more vulnerable to political demagoguery, and at the same time less politically potent, nativists were able to achieve the hegemony in education and language that they had been striving for since the late 1880s.

World War I and the German Language

The superpatriotism of World War I stimulated the attack on education in foreign languages and, more importantly, the teaching of foreign languages. The end of the war did not end the demand for instruction only in English. Former President Theodore Roosevelt set the tone, declaring "We must have in this country but one flag, the American flag, and for the speech of the people but one language, the English language." He advocated night schools for every adult immigrant "and if after, say, five years he has not learned English, he should be sent back to the land from whence he came."[66] The American Legion, organized in 1919, made forcing immigrants to learn English one of its major goals. The American Bar Association joined the crusade two years later.

Perhaps the best example of the assault on language came from Gustavus Ohlinger, who identified himself as "Captain, U.S.A." Ohlinger believed that the very nature of the German language undermined the Americanization of immigrants. "No man of German descent can become thoroughly American while retaining allegiance to the German language; no man of any race can become American at heart until he seeks to make the English language not merely the language of his business, but also of his fireside."[67]

The results of this campaign against foreign language education were enormously successful. On the eve of World War I, only 17 states required instruction in English. By 1923 this number had grown to 35 states.[68]

While foreign languages in general were under assault, German was the major target during and after war. During the war the National Security League urged a total ban on teaching both German language and German literature. By the end of the war 16 states had prohibited the teaching of German.[69] "Much of the repressive activity of the state councils [of national defense] came to center on the elimination of the use of the German language."[70] Theodore Roosevelt, a scholar in his own right who also had been president of the American Historical Association, supported a ban on teaching German, while a professor at Johns Hopkins University declared that German was "a barbarous tongue" with no cultural or commercial value.[71]

The large German-American population in the West and Midwest led to an intense effort to suppress the German language. In South Dakota the legislature prohibited all foreign language education before the ninth grade.[72] This law simply legitimized the action of South Dakota's State Council for National Defense, which had already "ordered that all teaching of the German language during the period of the war be discontinued in all the schools and educational institutions of the state." In July 1918 the South Dakota Council prohibited the use of German in telephone conversations. The Washington Council for National Defense was less authoritarian and simply requested that the state Board of Education prohibit German language education. The Board complied with this request. The Governor of Montana likewise prohibited the German language in his state's schools, while in Iowa the Governor banned the use of German in any public place.[73] Shortly after the declaration of war, the Nebraska State Council for National Defense verbally assaulted the Lutheran churches of the state for continuing to worship in German, on the grounds that the language "had been a potent preventative means against the Americanization of the people who came under such influence." In April 1918 the Nebraska legislature condemned, but did not prohibit, the use of foreign languages in the state's private schools.[74] While framed in general terms, this resolution was aimed at Nebraska's German speaking Lutheran schools. Indianapolis, which had taught German in the primary grades for decades, abolished such classes during the war. The resolution that achieved this result also declared that the city's school board "subscribes to the belief that the public schools should teach our boys and girls the principle of one nation, one language, and one flag, and should not assist in perpetuating the language of an alien enemy in our homes and enemy viewpoints in the community."[75] After the war was over, Ohio specifically prohibited the teaching of German in elementary schools, while numerous other states required that all instruction be conducted in English.[76] Indiana, which had once required German in high schools, now flatly prohibited the language in all schools.[77]

Louisiana led the nation in its wartime paranoia of the "enemy language." The state's wartime prohibition on teaching German in any public or private school in the state, at all levels from elementary schools to universities, was the most extreme in the nation until Indiana passed similar legislation in 1919.[78] But beyond this, Louisiana also prohibited the display or use of any "sign, insignia, name, designation, title, phrase, circular, or other form of advertisement or description, written, printed or appearing in the German language or that of any of its allies, or derived from any such language." Furthermore, the law prohibited "the sale or disposal in any manner of books, magazines, and papers printed or appearing in the German language or the language of any of its allies."[79]

Where states did not act, localities and students did. School districts throughout the nation began eliminating German from their curriculum. Meanwhile, throughout the country, high school students stopped studying German during the war. In Seattle a newspaper indicated the tone of the movement with the headline, "Speech of Hated Hun Forbidden."[80] This movement was astonishingly successful. In 1915 nearly 25 percent of all high school students in America studied German.[81] At that time 28 percent of all high schools, public and private, offered German, while only 11 per cent offered French. In California alone, 72 per cent of all high schools taught German.[82] During the war the California State Board of Education asserted that the German language "disseminates the ideals of autocracy, brutality and hatred," while in Iowa a politician argued that "ninety percent" of the German language teachers in the state were "traitors."[83] Such ideas and statements had a profound affect on American education. During World War I, thousands of school districts dropped German from their curriculum, never to return to it.[84] By 1922 less than 1 percent of all American high school students studied German.[85]

The Wilson administration gave mixed signals about the study of German. President Wilson thought the idea of eliminating German language study "childish," although did not say so in public. Privately George Creel, the head of America's main propaganda agency, the Committee on Public Information (CPI), apparently privately agreed with Wilson.[86] In public, however, Creel supported the bans on teaching German. On 19 March 1918, the United States Commissioner of Education, Philander P. Claxton, published a letter in the *Official Bulletin*, a daily newspaper published by the CPI, criticizing the movement against teaching German. In response to a "wave of indignation" against Claxton's letter, Creel stated that "if he had seen the letter he would never have allowed it to be published in the *Bulletin*."[87] Samuel B. Harding, a history professor on leave from Indiana University to work at the CPI, "believed that the German language was but a means of Germanizing the United States."[88] The *New York Times*, along with most other papers, urged that German language education be diminished or eliminated altogether.[89]

Not all Americans reacted to the study of German with such hostility. Although the *New York Globe* argued that "ignorance of the language and customs of our enemies harms us, not them," such an enlightened view was rare. *The Manufacturers' Record*, a Baltimore periodical, agreed that studying German might be useful, "provided there is no ulterior motive behind such teaching." However, the paper believed that supporters of teaching German did not take their position because of the language's "intrinsic value, but rather as part of a persistent political propaganda intended to wean the people of this country away from their Anglo-Saxon and Anglo-Celtic origins and ideals and divide the national interest and national sympathy."[90]

Even if all school administrators had agreed with the practical and enlightened view of the *New York Globe*, it seems unlikely that German would have remained the most studied foreign language in the nation. Where schools did not drop the language from their curriculum, students simply stopped studying the language. The "American Students Boycotting German" story in the *Literary Digest* carried the revealing subheading: "French and Spanish are Crowding out the Enemy Tongue."[91]

With no one learning German, it took little effort to remove German books from the schools and libraries. Book burnings were common, as schools, libraries, and book stores disposed of their German language texts.[92] The public library in Columbus, Ohio sold its German collection for scrap paper. The Cincinnati library cancelled its German language newspapers and removed all German books from its shelves.[93] If this could occur in Cincinnati, where German-Americans were the largest and "most thoroughly organized" ethnic community in the city,[94] it is not surprising that libraries across the nation took similar actions.

Even after the war, the attack on German culture and language continued. In 1919 Captain Ohlinger argued that a "German Conspiracy" still threatened American education. He noted that the "thousands of young men who during the past forty years have entered German universities . . . fell into the goose-step of *Kultur*, without realizing whither the march was directed." Ohlinger urged that "instruction in the German language . . . should never again be permitted in the elementary or high schools" because, in part, the German language was incompatible with American values. He argued that it was impossible to "render into the Kaiser's language the second paragraph of the Declaration of Independence" because there were "no equivalents for such expressions as 'liberty,' 'pursuit of happiness,' 'the consent of the governed.'" Ohlinger acknowledged the value of the "treasures of German literature," but only when "the associations of the German language with the atrocities of the war" had "been effaced" could Americans "return and bring our tribute to Schiller, Goethe and Lessing, well knowing that those great spirits, if present with us today, would require that we do that very thing."[95]

Meyer v. Nebraska: A Bit of Sanity in a Crazy World

In 1919 Nebraska prohibited instruction in any "private, denomination-al, parochial or public school," except in English. Furthermore, the law prohibited the teaching of any modern foreign language until "after a pupil shall have attained and successfully passed the eighth grade. . . ."[96] A year later Nebraska added a 27th section to its bill of rights, making English "the official language of the state" and providing that it be the language of instruction in "the common school branches . . . in public, private, denominational, and parochial schools."[97]

In 1920 authorities charged Robert T. Meyer, a teacher in a Lutheran school, with violating this statute by teaching biblical studies in German to 10-year-old children during a special hour and a half recess period that the school had instituted after the adoption of this law.[98]

Although this law proscribed all foreign language education, it was aimed at the state's large German-American population. The law's pur-pose was clearly described by the Nebraska Supreme Court, which upheld its constitutionality:

> The salutary purpose of the statute is clear. The legislature had seen the bane-ful effects of permitting foreigners who had taken up residence in this coun-try, to rear and educate their children in the language of their native land. The result of that condition was found to be inimical to our own safety. To allow the children of foreigners . . . to be taught from early childhood the language of the country of their parents, . . . was to educate them so that they must always think in that language, and, as a consequence, naturally inculcate in them the ideas and sentiments foreign to the best interests of this country.[99]

By a seven-to-two vote, an odd coalition of justices on the United States Supreme Court rejected this law. In the minority were the rela-tively liberal Justice Oliver Wendell Holmes, Jr. and the extremely con-servative George Sutherland. The majority opinion, written by the extraordinarily conservative James C. McReynolds, was supported by the very liberal Louis D. Brandeis. In his opinion of the court, McReynolds, who was notorious for his bigotry and anti-Semitism, showed a remarkable sensitivity to minorities. He was also able to defend minority rights on grounds that were compatible to economic and social conservatives. McReynolds conceded the inherent value of all Ameri-cans speaking the same language. He appeared to agree with the "desire of the [Nebraska] legislature to foster a homogeneous people with American ideals, prepared readily to understand current discussions of civic matters." He also agreed that the "unfortunate experiences of the late war . . . were certainly enough to quicken that aspiration."[100] For

McReynolds, the goals of the legislature seemed laudable enough; the question was the constitutionality of the methods.

McReynolds found three problems with the Nebraska law. First, it seemed overly broad. It prohibited the teaching of all modern foreign languages before the eighth grade. But was this reasonable? The Justice noted that the "Mere knowledge of the German language cannot reasonably be regarded as harmful. Heretofore it has been commonly looked upon as helpful and desirable."[101] Therefore, was it reasonable to now proscribe it? McReynolds did not directly confront this question because it was easier to strike down the law.

The Justice found that the Nebraska law unconstitutionally deprived foreign language teachers of their liberty to make a living, which was in violation of the Fourteenth Amendment. In a sense this was simply an application of the substantive due process and freedom of contract doctrines used to strike down protective labor legislation in earlier cases, such as *Lochner* v. *New York*.[102] However, McReynolds also hinted that the Fourteenth Amendment might protect non-economic substantive rights as well:

> While this court has not attempted to define with exactness the liberty thus guaranteed [by the Fourteenth Amendment], the term has received much consideration, and some of the included things have been definitely stated. Without doubt, it denotes not merely freedom from bodily restraint, but also the right of the individual to contract, to engage in any of the common occupations of life, to acquire useful knowledge, to marry, establish a home and bring up children, to worship God according to the dictates of his own conscience, and, generally, to enjoy those privileges long recognized at common law as essential to the orderly pursuit of happiness by free men.[103]

McReynolds further found that "it is the natural duty of the parent to give his children education suitable to their station in life."[104] He thus concluded that the Fourteenth Amendment protected the parents' right to educate their children, subject to the "reasonable" police power of the state. Prohibiting the teaching of a foreign language was, in this context, unreasonable.

The unreasonableness of the statute did not stem solely from the inherent value of learning a foreign language. It also reflected the dangers that could result from the overregulation of education. Quoting from Plato's *Republic* and describing education in ancient Sparta, McReynolds showed how a society might undermine the parent-child relationship in order to ensure the proper education of all children. The ancient Greek models, he conceded, would "submerge the individual and develop ideal citizens," but such a system was also "wholly different from" the "ideas touching the relation between individual and state" in the United States.[105] In essence, McReynolds saw the Nebraska law as leading to a totalitarian state which could undermine basic American liberties. While not explicitly stating the point, the McReynolds decision showed that in fighting against German "tyranny," Americans were creating their own, home-grown, system of tyranny and oppression, which violated the guarantees of the Constitution.

In a companion case, the Supreme Court struck down similar legislation from Ohio. The Court also struck down an Iowa statute that flatly prohibited the teaching of German in any school to children of any age. Even Justices Sutherland and Holmes concurred in finding the Iowa act unconstitutional.[106]

Two years after *Meyer*, in *Pierce* v. *Society of Sisters*, the court struck down an Oregon law banning private schools. Again the Court relied on economic, property, and substantive due process arguments to find the law in violation of the Fourteenth Amendment.[107] This law had been actively supported by a revived Ku Klux Klan, which focused its hate against Catholics, Jews, and immigrants as well as blacks. Governor Walter Pierce, who signed the bill, had been elected with strong Klan support.[108] Opposition to the law predictably came, not just from Catholics, Jews, and blacks, but also from German-American Lutherans, who "bristled at the bill not only because they had parochial schools to defend but also because they knew that their way of life was threatened."[109]

By 1925 German-Americans had retained the right to educate their children in their own schools and teach them to speak their mother tongue. However, by this time the repression of the war period and the push for Americanization had taken its toll. In Ohio, for example, with its huge German-American population, only five high schools still taught German.[110]

Along with language education, the German language press had been devastated. No German publications had actually been closed down during the war, although "some lost second-class mailing privileges or, in a few cases all use of the mails." But government suppression was unnecessary to destroy the German language press. Vigilantes did their part, as Boy Scouts in Cleveland "burned bundles of the *Wachter und Anzeiger*." Throughout the country advertisers succumbed to patriotic boycotts of German language publications and newsstands refused to carry them. "Circulation fell accordingly," and many publications simply folded.[111] In 1910 there were 3,391 German language publications in the nation, but by 1920 there were only 1,311.[112] Many of the surviving publications "were not newspapers, but lodge, church, and craft organs." German dailies dropped from 53 to 26.[113] The collapse of the German-

American press can be measured by comparing it to other ethnic presses. While German publications decreased by over 60 percent every other language group publication increased. Yiddish publications nearly tripled, from 321 to 808; those in Italian more than doubled, from 245 to 584; Polish publications more than quadrupled, from 212 to 906; and Greek publications grew by 10-fold, from 10 to 102.[114]

During the war the German churches also suffered from the war on language. Many German churches no longer conducted their services in German. In St. Louis, for example, 70 percent of the Lutheran churches used German in 1914, but by 1929, only about 25 percent conducted their services in German.[115] German theater was virtually destroyed, and many German Lutheran and Catholic schools closed their doors or cut back their programs. But most important, neither significant numbers of young German-Americans nor other school children had been taught German for nearly a decade.

Conclusions

Both the short- and long-run results of this repression are ironic. In the short run, most of the actions and measures aimed at individual Germans were successful. They stifled labor radicals, muffled opposition to the war, and in general made life more difficult for German-Americans. This hostility caused the lynching of one German immigrant and led to the terrorizing of thousands of German-Americans during the "war to make the world safe for democracy."[116] On a larger scale, the short-term effects of the repression helped lead to the destruction of the American Socialist movement and the I.W.W.

In the long run, this repression affected American culture in unexpected ways. By mid-century, American labor had achieved many of the early twentieth century "radical" goals, such as the eight hour day, the minimum wage, and a ban on child labor. At the same time, German-American labor leaders, such as Walter Reuther, became models of respectability on the national scene. Similarly, Americans remembered the repression of World War I with embarrassment. During World War II there was little hostility to German-Americans and often sympathy for recent German immigrants, many of whom were viewed as refugees from Nazi oppression rather than potential spies. With leaders of the army and navy named Eisenhower and Nimitz, it was hard to conceive of German-Americans as a group threatening the war effort.

Nor was vigilantism a threat to Americans of German or Italian descent during World War II. Americans learned from their mistakes in World War I, and they were more capable of distinguishing between nationality and national loyalty. The horrible exception to this was the internment of nearly 120,000 Japanese-Americans during World War II. Japanese-Americans were needlessly and unfairly denied their liberty. Yet, even this racially motivated nightmare was influenced by the experience of World War I. Part of the official rationale for the internment of Japanese-Americans was to protect them from potential mob violence.[117]

During World War II the government also avoided the massive suppression of freedom of speech and the press, which had been so common in World War I. Moreover, the Supreme Court overturned the convictions of pro-Nazi activists where the defendants had done nothing more than speak, publish their ideas, or talk to Nazi saboteurs.[118] In more recent times, the repressive free speech precedents of the World War I period have been rejected, even by relatively conservative jurists.[119]

While the suppression of free speech was successful during World War I, only to be repudiated at a later date, the World War I suppression of German culture, especially the teaching of German, had a more twisted history and a more lasting effect.[120] During and after the war, the study of German almost disappeared from American schools. In 1948, for example, only 43,000 students, less than 1 percent of American high school students, studied German. This was the same percent studying the language twenty-five years earlier. In 1948, five times that many students studied French and ten times as many studied Spanish.[121] Today, nearly three-quarters of a century after the World War I, and nearly half a century after the end of the World War II, German remains a rarely studied language in American high schools and universities.[122]

This long-term result is ironic, because the only major civil liberties victories before the Supreme Court in this period concerned the right of parents to educate their children in private schools and in foreign languages. *Meyer* v. *Nebraska* was the first modern Supreme Court civil liberties victory. While it gave parents the right to educate their children in German, few took advantage of this right. The second major civil liberties victory centered on an Oregon statute prohibiting parochial and private education. Although this law affected many different Americans, it was aimed especially at foreigners in general and German-Americans in particular.[123] Parochial and private education have, of course, remained strong since that decision, but few Americans have taken advantage of their right to have their children study a foreign language from an early age.

While these court victories insured that German-Americans might continue to teach their children their mother tongue in their own schools, in the long run the war on German culture in America was successful. Under fear of repression, German churches and schools began to switch to English during the war. After the successful appeal in *Meyer* v. *Nebraska*, German-Americans knew they had the right to teach their children German, but the incentive had already disappeared.[124]

One long-term result of the war was the disappearance of German-Americans as a distinct ethnic group in many parts of the nation. In the late nineteenth century, Germans "were indisputably the second largest group" in New York City, outnumbered only by the Irish. At that time Germans "account[ed] for perhaps a third of the population." At the beginning of the war, one-fourth of New York City's population was of German birth or had at least one German-born parent. Yet by 1963 sociologists would not include Germans as a major ethnic group in New York. "The Germans as a group are vanished. No appeals are made to the German vote, there are no German politicians . . . and generally speaking no German component in the structure of the ethnic interests of the city."[125] Part of the disappearance of a distinct German-American community in New York City and elsewhere was the decline in the use of the German language. Indeed, language may have been more important to the maintenance, and then the disappearance, of an identifiable German community than with other groups. Unlike Italian, Irish, or Jewish immigrants, Germans did not share a common religious tradition. Nor was there any kind of identifiable political tradition or goal common to most of them – such as Irish independence or Zionism. Since language was a key to maintaining a community, the war on language was particularly effective.

Beyond the German-American communities, war hysteria seriously undermined the tradition of German language training, and the ties to German universities that had developed before 1914.[126] Even today American students are more likely to have the opportunity to study Spanish or French, than German. The gap, however, between the first two and German is enormous. In 1982 over one and a half million students studied Spanish and over 800,000 studied French, but only 266,000 studied German. Until 1965 German ranked fourth, following Latin, as the language of choice among students in public schools.[127] When students in non-public schools are counted, it still remains fourth among all students today, and may drop further in the future, as the teaching of other languages, such as Russian, Japanese, Korean, Chinese, and Hebrew, continues to grow. This may be the greatest legacy of the World War I repression.

Notes to Chapter 9

1. David H. Bennett, *The Party of Fear: From Nativist Movements to the New Right in American History* (Chapel Hill: University of North Carolina Press, 1988), 171–182. John Higham, *Strangers in the Land: Patterns of American Nativism, 1860–1925* (New York: Atheneum, 1967), 194–233. Anti-immigrant sentiment in the United States first emerged with the adoption of the Alien Acts of 1798. In the 1840s and 1850s hostility to immigrants led to the formation of the American, or Know-Nothing Party.

2. William O. Reichert, *Partisans of Freedom: A Study in American Anarchism* (Bowling Green, OH: Bowling Green University Press, 1976), 375.

3. Reichert, *Partisans of Freedom*, 367–73.

4. Defendants August Spies, Adolph Fischer, George Engle, Michael Schwab, and Louis Lingg were born in Germany. Oscar Neebe was born to German immigrant parents in New York City, but was sent to Hesse Cassel for his primary education and did not return to the United States until he was fourteen. Samuel Fielden, the seventh defendant, was an English immigrant. Only Albert R. Parsons was born in the United States. See generally Philip S. Foner, ed., *The Autobiographies of the Haymarket Rioters* (New York: American Institute for Marxist Studies, 1969). All eight were convicted of killing seven policemen and wounding more than 70 others in the riot. German-born John Peter Altgeld, the first foreign born governor of Illinois, pardoned the three Haymarket prisoners who were not executed (Neebe, Schwab, and Fielding), an act that was used by his opponents "to beat at Altgeld's head for the rest of his life," and unfairly tainted him as a socialist. Ray Ginger, *Altgeld's America: The Lincoln Ideal versus Changing Realities* (New York: New Viewpoints, 1973), 61–88, quoted at 85.

5. Quoted in Higham, *Strangers in the Land*, 54, 55.

6. Melvyn Dubofsky, *We Shall Be All: The History of the Industrial Workers of the World*, 2nd ed. (Urbana and Chicago: University of Illinois Press, 1988), 108.

7. Higham, *Strangers in the Land*, 217–222.

8. Arthur Link, *Wilson: Confusions and Crises, 1915–1916* (Princeton: Princeton University Press, 1964), 56.

9. Reinhard R. Doerries argues that the failure of German propaganda in the United States paved the way for American entrance into the war, along with such events as: the large amount of German spying and sabotage in the country; the unrestricted submarine warfare and the sinking of neutral ships; and "The rape of Belgium, a harsh German military regime in the occupied territories, the deportation of forced labor from Belgium, and the sinking of passenger liners and commercial ships carrying civilians. . . ." Doerries, "Empire and Republic: German-American Relations Before 1917," in Frank Trommler and Joseph McVeigh, eds., *America and the Germans: An Assessment of A Three-Hundred-Year History*, 2 vols. (Philadelphia: University of Pennsylvania Press, 1985), 2:10. However, none of this explains or justifies the repression of German-Americans, whose only "crimes" were their ancestry, the language they spoke, or the faith they followed.

10. Frederick C. Luebke, *Bonds of Loyalty: German Americans and World War I* (DeKalb: Northern Illinois University Press, 1974), 88.

11. Luebke, *Bonds of Loyalty*, 50–51.

12. Carl Wittke, *German-Americans and the World War* (Columbus: Ohio State Archaeological and Historical Society, 1936), 184.

13. Quoted in Wittke, *German-Americans and the World War*, 160.

14. Quoted in Luebke, *Bonds of Loyalty*, 229

15. Luebke, *Bonds of Loyalty*, 228–31; Wittke, *German-Americans and the World War*, 160–61.

16. Many suffered tremendously for their pacifist beliefs. They were harassed and beaten by mobs and often jailed for refusing to serve. See generally, Luebke, *Bonds of Loyalty*, 256–59, 289–90; Wittke, *German Americans and the World War*, 159–60.

17. On the treatment of Mennonites, see J. S. Hartzler, *Mennonites in the World War: Or Nonresistance Under Test* (Scottsdale, PA: Mennonite Publishing House, 1922), Chapter 10:

"Some Experiences in Camp," 122–34. One Mennonite inductee reported: "We were cursed, beaten, kicked, and compelled to go through exercises to the extent that a few were unconscious for some minutes. They kept it up the greater part of the afternoon, and then those who could possibly stand on their feet were compelled to take cold shower baths. One of the boys was scrubbed with a scrubbing brush, using lye on him." Ibid., 123.

18. Wittke, *German Americans and the World War*, 159–60, 191. Luebke, *Bonds of Loyalty*, 257–59, 274, 289. H.C. Peterson and Gilbert C. Fite, *Opponents of War, 1917–1918* (Madison: University of Wisconsin Press, 1957), 121–38, 262–64; Hartzler, *Mennonites in the World War*, passim.

19. In 1912, for example, Eugene V. Debs, the Socialist candidate for president, won almost 900,000 votes. By 1918 he would be in jail for his opposition to war and the draft. *Debs v. United States*, 249 U.S. 211 (1919). The Socialist party gained electorial strength during the war. This was "apparently attributable to the party's emergence as the rallying point for opposition to the war." David M. Kennedy, *Over Here: The First World War and American Society* (New York: Oxford University Press, 1980), 70. David A. Shannon, *The Socialist Party of America* (New York: Macmillan, 1955), Chaps. 4 and 5.

20. Theodore Roosevelt, *The Foes in Our Own Household* (New York: 1917), reprinted in *The Works of Theodore Roosevelt: National Edition* (New York: Charles Scribner's Sons, 1926), vol. 19:41, 97.

21. Kennedy, *Over Here*, 46.

22. Stephen L. Vaughn, *Holding Fast the Inner Lines: Democracy, Nationalism, and the Committee On Public Information* (Chapel Hill: University of North Carolina Press, 1980), 83.

23. *McClure's Magazine* (July 1917), quoted in Erik Kirshbaum, *The Eradication of German Culture in the United States, 1917–1918* (Stuttgart: Hans-Dieter Heinz, Academic Publishing House, 1986), 62–63.

24. Sunday and Hillis quoted in John F. Piper, Jr., *The American Churches in World War I* (Athens, OH: Ohio University Press, 1985), 11–12. A minority of churchmen took a different view. Harry Emerson Fosdick prayed "O God, bless Germany! At war with her people, we hate them not at all. . . . Our enemies, too are sons of God and brothers for whose sake Christ died." Ibid., 63. For other examples of ministers attacking Germans in ungodly language, see George Sylvester Viereck, *Spreading the Germs of Hate* (New York: Horace Liveright, 1930), 194–98.

25. *The Liberty Bell*, quoted in Luebke, *Bonds of Loyalty*, 244.

26. Roosevelt, *The Foes in Our Own Household*, 19.

27. Sean Dennis Cashman, *America in the Age of the Titans: The Progressive Era and World War I* (New York: New York University Press, 1988), 503–04. Viereck, *Spreading the Germs of Hate*, 194–95.

28. James R. Mock and Cedrick Larson, *Words That Won the War: The Story of the Committee on Public Information, 1917–1919* (Princeton: Princeton Univ. Press, 1939), 151.

29. Quoted in John Higham, *Strangers in the Land: Patterns of American Nativism, 1860–1925* (New York: Atheneum, 1967), 54, 55.

30. Bennett, *The Party of Fear*, 174–75.

31. Cashman, *America in the Age of the Titans*, 504. Many nativists, like Sunday, were also prohibitionists, and this further made them hostile to German-Americans who were usually "wets." During the debate over the Eighteenth Amendment, Wayne H. Wheeler, a leading prohibitionist, argued that "The liquor traffic is the strong financial supporter of the German-American Alliance. The purpose of this Alliance is to secure German solidarity for the promotion of German ideals and German Kultur and oppose any restriction or prohibition of the liquor traffic. Its leaders urge its members to vote only for those who stand for Germanism and oppose prohibition." Quoted in Charles Merz, *The Dry Decade* (Seattle and London: University of Washington Press, 1970, reprint of 1931 edition), 27.

32. Viereck, *Spreading the Germs of Hate*, 189–90.

33. Louise Maunsell Field, "Sentimentalizing the Hun," *Forum* 58 (1917), 307–312, reprinted in David F. Trask, ed., *World War I at Home: Readings on American Life, 1914–1920* (New York: John Wiley & Sons, Inc, 1970), 83–86. Not surprisingly, World War I poster propaganda also represented German soldiers as brutish "huns," beastly men,

and apes. On "posters depicting the common enemy," the "Germans (or Huns) were represented by grotesque, animal-like features and hulking frames." Shawn Aubitz and Gail F. Stern, "Ethnic Imagines in World War I Posters," *Journal of American Culture*, 9:4 (Winter 1986), 85. For examples, see pictures of posters in Sam Keen, *Faces of the Enemy* (New York: Harper & Row, 1986), "Beat Back the Hun With Liberty Bonds," [Showing a brutish looking soldier with blood dripping from his fingers and his bayonet], p. 39; "Destroy this Mad Brute: Enlist" [Showing an ape wearing a German spiked helmet and carrying a bloody club reading "Kultur" in one hand and a semi-naked woman in the other, walking away from the continent "America"], p. 76. Germans as apes are also portrayed on non-American posters, pp. 113 and 147. Elliott Shore, of Princeton University, brought this volume to my attention. See also the pictures in Vaughn, *Holding Fast the Inner Lines*, 63, 87, 165–67 and in Aubitz and Stern, "Ethnic Imagines," 89–95.

34. Viereck, *Spreading the Germs of Hate*, 194, 196.

35. Viereck, *Spreading the Germs of Hate*, 195.

36. Roosevelt, *Foes in Our Own Household*, 19:35; Roosevelt, *The Great Adventure* (1917), reprinted in *The Works of Theodore Roosevelt*, vol. 19, quoted at 19:327.

37. It also may have been forgotten by well-educated Americans. In *University of California Regents* v. *Bakke*, 438 U.S. 265 (1978), Justice William Brennan argued that affirmative action was justified where previously legal classifications had been "drawn on the presumption that one race is inferior to another or because they put the weight of government behind racial hatred and separatism." Ibid., at 357–58. Brennan then contrasted the situation of non-whites with other ethnic American s under the affirmative action program at the University of California at Davis, using German-Americans to illustrate his point. "The program clearly distinguishes whites, but one cannot reason from this a conclusion that German-Americans, as a national group, are singled out for invidious treatment. And even if the Davis program had a differential impact on German-Americans, they would have no constitutional claim unless they could prove that Davis intended invidiously to discriminate against German-Americans." Ibid., at 359n. Justice Brennan is apparently unaware of the massive repression of German-Americans during World War I and the many laws that "put the weight of government behind . . . hatred and separatism." Unless one accepts the artificial distinction between "race" and "ethnicity," it is clear that by these standards German-Americans might indeed have a claim to affirmative action. I do not mean to suggest that we need an affirmative action program for German-Americans, since in the long-run this repression has not prevented them from becoming part of the mainstream of American society. Rather, this aspect of the *Bakke* case illustrates the shortness of the historical memory of the World War I repression. See also, Stephen Gottlieb, "Strife in the Carolene Garden," 57 *University of Detroit Journal of Urban Law* 919 (1980), at 926.

38. *McClure's Magazine*, quoted in Kirshbaum, *The Eradication of German Culture*, 45.

39. Woodrow Wilson, "Third Annual Message," Delivered to a Joint Session of Congress, 7 December 1915, in *A Compilation of the Messages and Papers of the Presidents* (New York: Bureau of National Literature, n.d.), 17:8114.

40. Harry N. Scheiber, *The Wilson Administration and Civil Liberties, 1917–1921* (Ithaca: Cornell University Press, 1960), 7.

41. Link, *Wilson: Confusions and Crises*, 36, the British ambassador is quoted at 29–30. This volume also details the growing estrangement between the United States and Germany immediately before the war and after hostilities broke out, but before the United States became a belligerent. For a shorter summary, see Vaughn, *Holding Fast the Inner Lines*, 61–82. See also, Clara Eve Schieber, *The Transformation of American Sentiment Toward Germany, 1870–1914* (New York: Russell and Russell, 1973, reprint of 1923 edition).

42. Clifton James Child, *The German-Americans in 1914–1917* (Madison: University of Wisconsin Press, 1939), 143. See also Higham, *Strangers in the Land*, 199. Theodore Roosevelt actively supported the attack on hyphenated Americans. He wrote in 1916: "I do not believe in hyphenated Americans. I do not believe in German-Americans or Irish-Americans; and I believe just as little in English-Americans. I do not approve of American citizens of German descent forming organizations to force the United States into practical alliance with Germany because their ancestors came from Germany. Just as little do I believe in

American citizens of English descent forming leagues to force the United States into an alliance with England because their ancestors came from England." Roosevelt argued that "For an American citizen to vote as German-American, Irish-American, or English-Americans is to be a traitor to American institutions. . . ." Roosevelt, *Fear God and Take Your Own Part* (New York: 1917), reprinted in *The Works of Theodore Roosevelt*, 18:281–82, 394.

43. This of course excludes strictly nativist parties, like the American Party of the 1850s or local elections, where inter-ethnic politics has led to one party attacking an ethnic group affiliated with another party.

44. Child, *The German-Americans in Politics*, 140.

45. Woodrow Wilson, "War Message," Delivered to a Joint Session of Congress, 2 April 1917, in *Messages and Papers of the Presidents*, 17:8232.

46. Kennedy, *Over Here*, 14.

47. See generally, Donald Hickey, "The Prager Affair," *Journal of the Illinois Historical Society* 62 (Summer, 1969), 117–34. Ironically, some of those involved in the lynching were themselves Americans of German ancestry who were "quite willing to suppress any hints of 'un-American' activity" in order "to prove their own loyalty and show their own dedication to the war effort and the capitalistic system." Ibid., 134. The extent of German-American acquiescence in, or collaboration with, anti-German hysteria is an important, but apparently neglected, aspect of the war on German culture. See also Luebke, *Bonds of Loyalty*, 226–27.

48. These events are described in Paul Murphy, *World War I and the Origin of Civil Liberties in the United States* (New York: W.W. Norton, & Co., 1979), 128–32; Luebke, *Bonds of Loyalty*, passim; and Peterson and Fite, *Opponents of War, 1917–1918*, passim. Alan Howard Levy, "The American Symphony at War: German-American Musicians and Federal Authorities During World War I," *Mid-America: An Historical Review* 71 (January 1989), 5. German-Americans were not the only victims of patriotic violence. In Montana the IWW organizer Frank Little was tortured and then lynched. Dubofsky, *We Shall Be All*, 392. The pacifist clergyman Herbert S. Bigelow was dragged from a podium in Cincinnati and severely whipped, and throughout the country lesser-known people were whipped, tarred and feathered, run out of town, or in some other way intimidated. See James R. Mock, *Censorship 1917* (Princeton: Princeton University Press, 1941), 33–38 and Murphy, *World War I and the Origins of Civil Liberties*, 128–32.

49. Wittke, *German Americans and the World War*, 159; Luebke, *Bonds of Loyalty*, 244–45; Viereck, *Spreading the Germs of Hate*, 166, 186–87.

50. Murphy, *Origin of Civil Liberties*, 128–32; Luebke, *Bonds of Loyalty*, 248–49; Wittke, *German-Americans and the World War*, 183.

51. Carl Wittke, *German-Americans and the World War*, 183; Luebke, *Bonds of Loyalty*, 248–49; Murphy, *Origin of Civil Liberties*, 128–32; Alan Howard Levy, "The American Symphony at War: German-American Musicians and Federal Authorities During World War I," *Mid-America: An Historical Review* 71 (January 1989), 5–13, quoted at 12.

52. Murphy, *Origin of Civil Liberties*, 128–32; Luebke, *Bonds of Loyalty*, 248–49; Wittke, *German-Americans and the World War*, 183–93; Higham, *Strangers in the Land*, 215; Viereck, *Spreading the Germs of Hate* 187, 165–66; Kirshbaum, *The Eradication of German Culture*, 135. Some German clergy were publicly whipped, although the usual form of intimidation was to make them publicly kiss a flag or perform some other "patriotic" act.

53. Murphy, *Origin of Civil Liberties*, 128–32; Luebke, *Bonds of Loyalty*, 248–49; Wittke, *German-Americans and the World War*, 183. Ironically, "*Die Wacht Am Rhein*" was written by the composer Carl Wilhelm, in 1854, while residing in the city of Krefeld, where this paper was initially read. Wilhelm Buchner, ed., *Lieder und Gesänge für eine Singstimme mit Begleitung des Pianoforte von C. Wilhelm* (Leipzig: Beitkopt & Harte, n.d.), 102. Lewis Paul Todd, *Wartime Relations of the Federal Government and the Public Schools, 1917–1918* (New York: Teachers College of Columbia University, 1945), 75.

54. For a short and very useful history of German language education in the United States, see Edward H. Zeydel, "The Teaching of German in the United States From Colonial Times to the Present," *German Quarterly* 37 (September 1964), 315–92.

55. Sidney E. Ahlstrom, *A Religious History of the American People* (New Haven and Lon-

don: Yale University Press, 1972), 560–63.

56. Paul Kleppner, *The Cross of Culture: A Social Analysis of Midwestern Politics, 1850–1900* (New York: The Free Press, 1970), 158.

57. Kleppner, *Cross of Culture*, 159–60. The Irish Catholic hierarchy in the midwest supported such laws as a way of undermining German Catholic priests. Ahlstrom, *A Religious History of the American People*, 562.

58. Francis H. Ellis, "German Instruction in the Public Schools of Indianapolis, 1869–1919, Part II," *Indiana Magazine of History* 50 (1954), 262–70. *Indiana Acts of 1869, Special Session* 40.

59. Richard Jensen, *The Winning of the Midwest: Social and Political Conflict, 1888–1896* (Chicago: University of Chicago Press, 1971), 123; David Tyack, Thomas James, and Aaron Bennett, *Law and the Shaping of Public Education, 1785–1954* (Madison: University of Wisconsin Press, 1987), 68.

60. Battles similar to those in Indianapolis also took place in Madison, Wisconsin and Cincinnati, Ohio. Ellis, "German Instruction in the Public Schools of Indianapolis," 270–71.

61. William F. Whyte, "The Bennett Law Campaign in Wisconsin," *Wisconsin Magazine of History* 10 (1927), 373.

62. Kleppner, *Cross of Culture*, 161–70, quoted at 167; Louise Phelps Kellogg, "The Bennett Law in Wisconsin," *Wisconsin Magazine of History* 2 (1918), 3–25.

63. Jensen, *Winning of the Midwest*, 220–21; Ginger, *Altgeld's America*, 73–75, quoted at 74.

64. Ellis, "German Instruction in the Public Schools of Indianapolis," 270–76; *Board of School Commissioners of the City of Indianapolis* v. *The State, ex rel. Sander* 129 Ind. Rep. 14 (1890), quoted at 21. Starting in 1907 German was mandatory in all Indiana high schools. *Laws of Indiana, 1907*, 324.

65. Tyack, et al., *Law and the Shaping of Public Education*, 171, 68.

66. Roosevelt, *Foe of Our Household*, 39, 46.

67. Gustavus Ohlinger, *The German Conspiracy in American Education* (New York: George H. Doran Co, 1919), 108.

68. Tyack, et al., *Law and the Shaping of Public Education*, 171–73.

69. Tyack, et al., *Law and the Shaping of Public Education*, 174; Viereck, *Spreading the Germs of Hate*, 187–88.

70. William J. Breen, *Uncle Sam at Home: Civilian Mobilization, Wartime Federalism, and the Council of National Defense, 1917–1919* (Westport, CT.: Greenwood Press, 1984), 81.

71. Peterson and Fite, *Opponents of War*, 195.

72. *South Dakota Laws, 1918*, ch. 41, 42, excerpted in U.S. Judge Advocate General's Department (Army) *Compilation of War Laws of the Various States and Insular Possessions* (Washington: GPO, 1919), 147.

73. *Report of the Superintendent of Public Instruction of the State of South Dakota*, quoted in Todd, *Wartime Relations of the Federal Government and the Public Schools*, 72; Peterson and Fite, *Opponents of War*, 195–96; Breen, *Uncle Sam at Home*, 82.

74. Breen, *Uncle Sam at Home*, 82.

75. Ellis, "German Instruction in the Public Schools of Indianapolis, 1869–1919, Part III," *Indiana Magazine of History* 50 (1954), 373–74.

76. *Meyer* v. *Nebraska, Brief and Argument of State of Nebraska*, 25, 28, 24, reprinted in Philip B. Kurland and Gerhard Casper, eds., *Landmark Brief and Arguments of the Supreme Court of the United States: Constitutional Law* (Arlington, VA: University Publications of America, 1975), 21:725, 728, 724. Wittke, *German Americans and the World War*, 179. The best introduction to the history of these laws is William G. Ross, "A Judicial Janus: *Meyer* v. *Nebraska* in Historical Perspective," *University of Cincinnati Law Review* 57 (1988) 125–204.

77. In 1907 Indiana had made German a required course in the state's high schools. *Laws of Indiana, 1907*, 324. At this time German was taught in elementary as well as secondary schools in Indianapolis. These classes were conducted entirely in German. Francis H. Ellis, "German Instruction in the Public Schools of Indianapolis," 359. This law was amended

twice in 1919, first to prohibit German in elementary schools and then to prohibit it in all schools. *Laws of Indiana, 1919*, 50; 822–23.

78. *Louisiana Acts, 1918*, No. 114, p. 188, excerpted in U.S. Judge Advocate General, *Compilation of War Laws*, 47.

79. *Louisiana Acts, 1918*, No. 177, p. 333, quoted in U.S. Judge Advocate General *Compilation of War Laws*, 39.

80. Peterson and Fite, *Opponents of War*, 196.

81. Patricia Dandonoli, "Report on Foreign Language Enrollment in Public Secondary Schools," *Foreign Language Annals* 20:5 (October 1987).

82. Zeydel, "The Teaching of German in the United States," 356.

83. Todd, *Wartime Relations of the Federal Government and the Public Schools*, 73.

84. Dandonoli, "Report on Foreign Language Enrollment in Public Secondary Schools."

85. Tyack, et al., *Law and the Shaping of Public Education, 1785–1954*, 170. This did not happen in England, where German was taught "in only eight fewer secondary schools in 1917–1918 than in 1911–1912." Kirshbaum, *The Eradication of German Culture*, 45.

86. Mock and Larson, *Words That Won the World*, 214.

87. Breen, *Uncle Sam at Home*, 82.

88. Stephen L. Vaughn, *Holding Fast the Inner Lines*, 51.

89. See *New York Times*, 5 April 1918.

90. *Globe* and *Manufacturers' Record* quoted in "American Students Boycotting German," *Literary Digest*, 56 (30 March 1918), 29.

91. Peterson and Fite, *Opponents of War*, 196, citing "American Students Boycotting German," *Literary Digest*, 56 (30 March 1918), 29, 44, 46–50, 52, 54–55, 58, 61–64, 70, 72–74.

92. Peterson and Fite, *Opponents of War*, 196.

93. Wittke, *German Americans and the World War*, 182; Luebke, *Bonds of Loyalty*, 253.

94. Zane Miller, *Boss Cox's Cincinnati: Urban Politics in the Progressive Era* (New York: Oxford University Press, 1968), 35.

95. Ohlinger, *The German Conspiracy in American Education*, 106, 107, 108, 109. It is worth noting that Ohlinger published this book after the war was over and the Kaiser was no longer in power.

96. *Meyer v. Nebraska, Brief and Argument for the Plaintiff in Error*, 1–2, reprinted in Kurland and Casper, *Landmark Briefs*, 675–76. The best introduction to the history of the law itself, and to the litigation in Nebraska on the law is William G. Ross, "A Judicial Janus: *Meyer v. Nebraska* in Historical Perspective," 125–204.

97. Legislative Drafting Research Fund of Columbia University, *Constitutions of the United States: National and State* (Dobbs Ferry, NY: Oceana Publications, 1990), Binder 3. At the same time Nebraska changed its constitutional provisions on the ownership of property. Both the 1866 and 1875 Constitutions provided "No distinction shall ever be made by law between resident aliens and citizens in reference to possession, enjoyment, or descent of property." In 1920, in the wake of World War I, this provision was amended to read as follows: "There shall be no discrimination between citizens of the United States in respect to acquisition, ownership, possession, enjoyment, or descent of property. The right of aliens in respect to acquisition, enjoyment, and descent of property may be regulated by law."

98. *Meyer v. Nebraska, Brief and Argument for the Plaintiff in Error*, 1–2, reprinted in Kurland and Casper, *Landmark Briefs*, 675–76. Ross, "A Judicial Janus: *Meyer v. Nebraska* in Historical Perspective," 125–204.

99. 107 Neb. 657, quoted in *Meyer* v. *Nebraska*, 262 U.S. 390, at 397–98 (1923).

100. *Meyer* v. *Nebraska*, at 402. He did not, however, indicate what those "unfortunate circumstances" were.

101. *Meyer* v. *Nebraska*, at 400.

102. *Lochner* v. *New York*, 198 U.S. 45 (1905).

103. *Meyer* v. *Nebraska*, at 399.

104. *Meyer* v. *Nebraska*, at 400.

105. *Meyer v. Nebraska,* at 401–02.

106. *Bartles v. Iowa; Bohning v. Ohio; Pohl v. Ohio,* 262 U.S. 404 (1923).

107. *Pierce v. Society of Sisters,* 268 U.S. 510 (1925).

108. Kenneth P. Jackson, *The Ku Klux Klan and the City, 1915–1930* (New York: Oxford University Press, 1967), 205–06; David M. Chalmers, *Hooded Americanism: The History of the Ku Klux Klan* (New York: New Viewpoints, 1981), 88–90.

109. Tyack, et al., *Law and the Shaping of Public Education,* 184.

110. Zeydel, "The Teaching of German in the United States," 362.

111. Carl Wittke, *The German-Language Press in America* (Lexington: University of Kentucky Press, 1957), 265, 271, 243, 273.

112. Joshua Fishman, *Language Loyalty in the United States* (The Hague: Mouton & Co., 1966), 60.

113. Wittke, *The German-Language Press in America,* 265, 271, 243, 273. See also La Vern J. Rippley, "Ameliorated Americanization: The Effect of World War I on German-American in the 1920s," in Trommler and McVeigh, eds., *America and the Germans,* 2:224; the statistics are based on those gathered by Ayer's *Newspaper Annual.* "Although Ayer's reports are neither complete nor always accurate" they do show trends and are the best statistics available. Wittke, *The German-Language Press in America,* 244.

114. Fishman, *Language Loyalty,* 60. Robert E. Park, *The Immigrant Press and Its Control* (New York: Harper & Bros., 1922) citing different sources provided a similar story, although with different statistics. According to Park, in 1900 there were 747 German publications. The next largest groups were Scandinavian (128 publications), French-Canadian (44), Bohemian (44), Polish (41), Spanish (41), and Italian (36). In the next twenty years, 379 new German publications began, far more than for any other ethnic group. Had all publications stayed in operation there would have been 1,126 different German publications in the country, instead of the 278 that Park found had survived the war. Meanwhile, most other ethnic papers held their own, or grew in numbers during this time. Scandinavian and French-Canadian papers had a slight decrease in numbers, to 112 and 41, but the numbers of Bohemian (51), Polish (76), Italian (99), and Spanish (102) publications all rose. Ibid., 317.

115. John A. Hawgood, *The Tragedy of German-America* (New York and London: G.P. Putnam's Sons, 1940), 300.

116. See generally, Luebke, *Bonds of Loyalty* (DeKalb: Northern Illinois University Press, 1974).

117. United States Department of War, *Final Report: Japanese Evacuation from the West Coast, 1942* (Washington: G.P.O., 1943), 43–44. Roger Daniels, *Concentration Camps USA: Japanese-Americans and World War II* (Hinsdale, IL: The Dryden Press, 1971), 28. In a documentary film, "Japanese Relocation," produced by the Office of War Information in 1942, Milton Eisenhower explained how the relocation was designed to protect the Japanese-Americans from vigilantes.

118. See Paul Murphy, *The Constitution in Crisis Times, 1918–1969* (New York: Harper and Row, 1972), 225–32. See also *Viereck v. United States,* 318 U.S. 236 (1943); *Hartzel v. United States,* 322 U.S. 680 (1944); *Cramer v. United States,* 325 U.S. 1 (1945); and *Keegan v. United States,* 325 U.S. 478 (1945) for examples of the convictions of Nazi sympathizers being overturned by the United States Supreme Court, and *Baumgartner v. United States,* 322 U.S. 665 (1944) overturning a denaturalization order of a German-American citizen who had become a Nazi after be became a naturalized United States citizen.

119. The first three supreme court decisions on free speech were *Schenck v. United States, Frohwerk v. United States,* 249 U.S. 204 (1919), and *Debs v. United States,* 249 U.S. 211. The first involved an Eastern European Jewish immigrant who was the secretary of the Socialist party in Philadelphia. The second was the prosecution under the Espionage Act of 1917, of persons associated with the *Missouri Staats Zeitung,* a German paper published in Kansas City, Missouri. Only after the Supreme Court upheld these two convictions did it review, and uphold, the conviction of a native born citizen of Anglo-Saxon ancestry, the leader of the Socialist Party Eugene Victor Debs. The precedents in these cases were overturned in *Brandenburg v. Ohio,* 395 U.S. 444 (1969).

120. The very fact that this paper was initially given at a conference in Krefeld, West Germany, that was held in English is, in part, a legacy of World War I.

121. Zeydel, "The Teaching of German in the United States," 368.

122. While anecdotal evidence is often suspect, a high school counselor in a medium sized city in upstate New York explained in the spring of 1990 that German was not taught because it was a "dead language."

123. *Meyer* v. *Nebraska*, 262 U.S. 390 (1923); *Pierce* v. *Society of Sisters*, 268 U.S. 510 (1925).

124. For a variety of reasons the study of German probably would have declined somewhat without the war. Even before the war, fewer Americans were attending German universities than a few decades earlier. This coincided with the "replacement of Teutonic cultural models with enthusiasm for French elegance and English flair toward the end of the [nineteenth] century." Most important of all was the beginning of the "disintegration in German-American ethnic coherence" which began before the war. Christine Totten, "Elusive Affinities: Acceptance and Rejection of the German-Americans," in Trommler and McVeigh, *America and the Germans*, 2:193. Indeed, because German-Americans were among the oldest ethnic group in the nation, it was likely that there would be some falling off in the study of German by third- and fourth-generation German-Americans. But none of these trends would have by themselves led to the changes that resulted from the war and its aftermath.

125. Daniel P. Moynihan and Nathan Glazer would note in *Beyond the Melting Pot: The Negroes, Puerto Ricans, Jews, Italians, and Irish of New York City* (Cambridge: The M.I.T. Press and Harvard University Press, 1963), 311. Similarly, as late as 1970, German-Americans made up the largest foreign-born group in Chicago, but they had no visible presence in the political or ethnic structure of the city.

126. In 1982 only 21.3 percent of American public secondary school students took a modern foreign language. This contrasts with the 35.9 percent rate in 1915. In 1982 only 2.1 percent of public secondary school children studied German, while in 1915 24.4 percent studied that language. Dandonoli, "Report on Foreign Language Enrollment in Public Secondary Schools."

127. Statistics for 1960 and 1965 show German ranking a far distant fourth behind Spanish, French, and Latin in number of American students enrolled in all schools.

Foreign Language Enrollment for Public and Private Students, 1960, 1965

	1960	1965
TSE	11,847,783	16,400,985
TFLE	2,775,152	4,494,212
Spanish	1,037,320	1,833,960
French	853,342	1,586,852
Latin	678,928	626,199
German	62,130	373,771
Russian	10,051	32,027

TSE=Total Student Enrollment
TFLE=Total Foreign Language Enrollment

ACTFL, *Foreign Language Education: Volume I, An Overview* (Skokie, IL: National Textbook Co., 1973), 417.

Foreign Language Enrollment for Public School Students

	1960	1965	1982
TPSSE	8,649,495	11,611,197	12,879,254
TPSFLE	1,867,358	3,067,613	2,740,198
Spanish	933,409	1,426,822	1,562,984
French	744,404	1,251,373	857,984
Latin	654,670	591,445	169,580
German	150,764	328,028	266,901
Russian	9,722	26,716	5,702

TPSS= Total Public School Student Enrollment
TPSFLE= Total Public School Foreign Language Enrollment

Dandonoli, "Report on Foreign Language Enrollment in Public Secondary Schools," 459.

Discussion

The detailed discussion on American-German cultural relations that was chaired by Hartmut Lehmann clearly demonstrated the importance of cultural dimensions for an overall interpretation of German-American relations. According to the problems dealt with in the papers presented by Reinhard Doerries, Paul Finkelman, Elliott Shore, and Frank Trommler, the following issues were debated extensively: methods of German propaganda and their effectiveness, American reactions to German propaganda and espionage activities, the problem of perception, nativism in the United States, anxieties in Germany about the Americanization of German life.

In his response (an extended version of which was sent to the editor after the conference) to Jörg Nagler's comment, Reinhard Doerries dealt with the organizational dimension of German propaganda: "The 'conceptual dimension' of German propaganda mentioned but not elaborated by Nagler may be of interest, but it is doubtful whether the Germans had a concept, and the documents of *Wilhelmstrasse* reveal no evidence other than of a German interest in manipulating the opinion of various ethnic groups. The scope of the paper was a clear limit to my comments on such groups, but details have been published elsewhere [cf. Reinhard R. Doerries, *Imperial Challenge* (Chapel Hill, NC, 1989), pp. 39ff]. I cannot tell why Nagler would think that I 'underestimate' the 'impact' of sabotage upon U.S. public opinion. To the contrary, my paper states that the involvement of most German propagandists in the so-called *Propaganda der Tat* 'diminished and in some cases destroyed their effectiveness.' . . . 'Espionage,' cited by Nagler as another deterrent to effective propaganda, did not play a significant role during U.S. neutrality, and thus was not a major concern of the American public or the government. Concerning the 'many' who in Nagler's view felt the American government's 'firm hand of stern repression', it needs to be said that Nagler's use of this quote from Wilson's address before Congress on 2 April 1917, could be misleading. Wilson speaks of 'the millions of men and women of German birth and native sympathy who live amongst us and share our life' and makes it clear that 'friendship' is the feeling of Americans toward them because 'they are, most of them, as true and loyal Ameri-

207

cans as if they had never known any other fealty or allegiance.' Only 'the few who may be of different mind and purpose,' in his words, 'will be dealt with with a firm hand of stern repression.' Wilson knew well what he was saying at this exceedingly important occasion."

Doerries then addressed to what extent Americans had been aware of various German intelligence activities: "Nagler's query concerning the degree of awareness of the German intelligence activities is legitimate. Replies to the question, however, are varied and often connected with a specific aspect of German actions in neutral America. Thus we know that Washington was informed about the passport forgeries in late 1914, about the German connections to the Mexican dictator General Victoriano Huerta, about the mission of the naval agent Franz Rintelen, and a number of other aspects. I have, in my paper, mentioned the organization of an American intelligence service and the decision of the White House to tap German official telephones in the U.S. More detail on this and other counterintelligence measures was not possible in this conference paper. Concerning the person and role of Rumely, I state that he acted as 'a straw man holding the firm.' Nagler's interesting information about the man's possible motivations does not call for a revision of my statement. Nagler's response to my suggestion that serious further research would have to be done before any conclusion on German intelligence work among American Blacks, regrettably fails to expand our knowledge on this matter. The German propaganda against the French use of colonial troops is well known, but did not play a significant part in the American propaganda war. The activities of Reiswitz and von Eckhardt are also known, but the evidence about an organized campaign among American Blacks is still rather inconclusive. My paper contains no 'argument' that Count Bernstorff 'counterbalanced' the disadvantageous conditions under which German propaganda was brought to the U.S. Instead, I emphasized that Bernstorff 'had acquired significant experience in the area of public relations' in London and that he had maintained good relations with the American press prior to 1914. Moreover, I suggested that while one could take the view that even a well-planned German propaganda campaign at that time would not have reached the American public, one might counter by pointing to Bernstorff's long tenure and knowledge of American political life."

Potential "success" of any German propaganda activities in the United States was doubted by various participants. Paul Finkelman rejected the "notion that if the German propaganda people had done it differently, had they been better, had they been smarter – somehow the result might have been different." He raised the question whether German propagandists "would have been better off doing nothing at all." If "they really understood America they would have understood that there is nothing they can do", since the "Germans are trying to sell a product that no one in America will ever want to buy." Some participants referred to what they called the "realities" of German politics, e.g., German actions in Mexico, German military needs, and the sinking of the *Lusitania*. Nevertheless, Ragnhild Fiebig-von Hase wondered "whether German propaganda was really unsuccessful." The Kaiser had tried to mobilize German-Americans, and this might have complicated Wilson's domestic situation during the election campaign of 1916 by "cautioning" the President on the issue of American intervention. Did German-Americans have to "pay" for this after April 1917?

There is no doubt that German propaganda and German espionage contributed to the harsh treatment of German-Americans once the United States had entered the war. But why had the government and the people responded in an irrational way? This question led to an extensive discussion on nativism and xenophobia. Paul Finkelman suggested that one should not hesitate to speak of elements of xenophobia, which "does not have to be expressed in a sort of death rate. But if you look at the harassment, the extreme harassment, and especially of enemy aliens . . . who were interned, and not only interned but surveyed and controlled, they had to leave their jobs. The Justice Department files express it. This is a very severe xenphobia we are talking about."

Frank Trommler put the problem of growing nativism during World War I into the broader framework of the United States' rise to world-power status and the development of American exceptionalism. He thought it "highly interesting that at that moment nativism came back as part of the self-definition of the United States. I think one should also see when trying to understand this nativism, why it was so outrageous, especially for foreign observers or for other certain immigrant groups. It was the period in which the American dream was still seen as the utopia and the hope for Europeans and other peoples of the world, especially in Eastern Europe." And when Wilson developed a "new exceptionalism", this too was "turned against the nineteenth-century concept of culture, and the Germans became the target." This Wilsonian exceptionalism was, as Frank Trommler put it, also an expression of the "founding years of America as a world power in cultural terms."

Paul Finkelman added that natitivism did not end with the end of hostilities, because "what we get after the war are the immigration acts of 1921 through 1925 and the closing down of the borders. Yes, the New Deal coalition can bring all of the immigrants into the Democatic Party, but the cost is that no one else can come into the country. Of course, this is particularly tragic with the rise of fascism in Europe. Literally millions of people might have been saved had America not had the kind of immigration laws that are in part the result of what I think has been accurately described as the whipping up of hysteria against foreigners." Jörg Nagler stressed what he called the "keyword" continuity. He saw a continuity in American history since the eighteenth century of using alien influence, or alien subversiveness, to "quell domestic unrest" or to "manage American society."

Although the discussion was primarily devoted to Wilson's policies and American reactions to German actions, the issue of anxieties in Imperial Germany concerning the potential Americanization of German life was raised repeatedly. Gerald Feldman thought it important to pay attention "to the way in which America is received in Germany and the relationship between the desire to peddle *Kultur* and the desire to avoid *Amerikanisierung*, at the same time wanting to take advantage of what Americans have demonstrated to be superior at. Ironically, after both world wars, many Germans regarded the Americanization of German life as being of key importance in regaining world-power status for Germany."

PART III

Economic and Social Change

10

American Political Culture in a Time of Crisis: Mobilization in World War I

David M. Kennedy

"War is the health of the state," the radical American journalist Randolph Bourne proclaimed in 1918. That judgement, denatured a bit after being stripped of much of the polemical point that the pacifistic Bourne gave it in wartime, has echoed ever since in history books as a description of World War I's transformative effect on American state and society. In the Crisis of 1914–18, so the argument runs, the exceptionally ramshackle, disarticulated, laissez-faire course of American political-economic development (or underdevelopment) was decisively deflected onto an evolutionary path toward the universal modern model of a corporatist, integrated social organism, complete with the apparatus of an active, interventionist bureaucratic state.

Much of the persuasive power of Bourne's observation is owed to its use by a subsequent generation of reformers – notably Herbert Hoover and Franklin D. Roosevelt – as they sought to legitimize the extraordinary expansion of the state that they undertook in the face of the crisis of the Great Depression. Hoover invoked the example of the War Finance Corporation to justify the greatest of his political-economic innovations: the Reconstruction Finance Corporation. New Dealers often spoke about "America's wartime socialism" as providing a fund of experience upon which they could credibly draw in the quest for resources with which to fight the Depression. Among scholars, William E. Leuchtenburg has probably done the most to propagate this image of the war as the antecedent for the state-building programs of the New Deal, notably in a widely cited article entitled "The New Deal and the Analogue of War" and in his description of the War Industries Board as a body with "sweeping authority" and "dictatorial powers."[1]

But it is the argument of this paper that this assessment of the war's effects in the United States is vastly overdrawn. Its durability in the face of abundant contradictory evidence is ascribable, no doubt, to a number of factors: to the politically legitimizing role it played a decade or so after

Notes for Chapter 10 can be found on page 226.

the armistice, as noted above; to the natural inclination of historical writers to identify turning points, and to find them in dramatic events like war; and, especially, to an unfortunately mistaken disposition to use the benchmarks of *European* history to gauge the evolution of American society and institutions.

World War I serves much more plausibly as a pivotal event in European than in American history. In Europe it shattered empires, revolutionized states, toppled governments, mortally wounded some political institutions (like the British Liberal party), and breathed life into others (like the British Labor party, not to mention the Nazi party). Nothing remotely similar can be said about the United States. The very rhetoric used by Europeans to reflect on the war's meaning as early as the moment of its ending in 1918 should provide some clue as to the war's wholly different dimensions in the scales of European and American history. Winston Churchill, staring at the crowds in Northumberland Avenue as the bells of London signaled the armistice on 11 November 1918, mused on the war's "fifty-two months of gaunt distortion. . . . [F]ifty-two months of making burdens grievous to be borne and binding them on men's backs. . . ."[2] Adolf Hitler, recuperating from a gas attack at a military hospital in Pomerania, brooded about "the sacrifices and starvation . . . the hunger and thirst often of months without end . . . the death of two millions."[3] Nothing comparable to these somber, emotionally freighted observations can be found in the entire library of contemporary American reflections about the war's scale and significance.

The United States, after all, entered the war late, reluctantly, and with some notable reservations. And the fighting always remained mercifully distant from American shores. For those reasons, if for no other, the amplitude of the war's impact was necessarily less than it was in Europe. Perhaps the most significant fact about the U.S. Congress' declaration of war was the date on which it was issued – 6 April 1917. By that time, what Americans persisted in calling "The European War" had been raging for two-and-one-half years. The sinking of the *Lusitania*, which many in America and elsewhere regarded as a sufficient *casus belli*, had occurred nearly two years earlier. The German declaration of unrestricted submarine warfare was more than two months old. This hardly adds up to the picture of a nation aggressively seeking to enter the war or eager to make transformational use of it. As the journalist Mark Sullivan put it: "The war did not come to America as it came to Europe. . . . It was not in the shape of violence of any sort that the war . . . came to us. Its coming took a form hardly physical at all; it came as newspaper despatches from far away, far away in distance and even farther away in spirit."[4]

Even as a belligerent, the United States displayed marked reluctance fully to enter the fray. Woodrow Wilson's disenchantment with what he could perceive of the Allies' war aims compelled him to maintain a formal political aloofness from his co-belligerents. The United States, therefore, would not fight, strictly speaking, as one of the "Allies." Rather, the anti-Central Powers coalition would be known after April 1917 as the "Allied and *Associated* Powers," a cumbersome nomenclature that awkwardly but unmistakeably testified to Wilson's attenuated belligerency. Similarly, Wilson refused, with only partial and grudging exceptions, to heed British and French importunings to amalgamate American troops into Allied units, despite the pressing need for men, especially after the commencement of the German offensive in the spring of 1918. As a result, no sizeable American force took the field until the St. Mihiel battle in September 1918, just sixty days before the war's conclusion.

In some tellingly important ways, in short, the United States was not a full-fledged participant in World War I. Its relation to the armed conflict of 1914–18 closely paralleled its relation to the international system as a whole in the early twentieth century. It stood on the periphery, a marginal player of some considerable potential influence, but in actuality a nation that remained economically self-absorbed and disorganized, politically inexperienced, and culturally provincial, even isolationist. A few numbers can summarily capture this point: the period of American belligerency lasted nineteen months, its active military engagement less than two months; American battle deaths totalled fewer than 55,000; Britain's were nearly 1,000,000, while France, Germany, and Russia each suffered losses well in excess of 1,000,000. And all those states, with the qualified exception of Russia, were lashed to the wheel of war for more than four years.

Some further numbers, utilizing the crude but suggestive index of federal government expenditures as a percentage of Gross National Product, will help to frame an understanding of the war's impact on the political economy of the United States. American GNP in 1916, the last full peacetime year, was $48.3 billion; the federal government's budget in that year was about $713 million – or about 1.4 percent of GNP. To be sure, government activity would account for almost 22 percent of GNP in 1919, the year of the war's maximum fiscal impact. That governmental share of national product was huge in historical terms, probably dwarfing even the claims of government during the Civil War; and of course it was unarguably enormous in relative terms, representing almost a sixteenfold increase in government's economic share in the span of three years.

But of more interest than this undeniably large temporary surge in the government's economic presence is the long-term effect of the war experience. Here, I believe, the evidence is clear. The war did nudge the federal budget onto a permanently higher plateau, from an average of about $700 million in annual expenditures in the years just before the war, to an average of about $3 billion through the decade of the 1920s, though as much as half of that increase is attributable to inflation. In the more revealing terms of share of GNP, by 1928, the last full pre-Depression year, the federal budget accounted for not quite 3 percent of GNP – a doubling from the prewar percentage, to be sure, but still a very modest figure in absolute terms.[5] And the war's formal institutional legacy was also minimal, as most war agencies were frankly conceived as emergency measures and almost immediately dissolved at the time of the armistice.

To these quantitative measures may be added some qualitative considerations. It has been frequently remarked that the war overtook the United States in the midst of a prolonged and unusually agitated period of economic and social reform, customarily referred to as the "progressive era." No issue was more central to the politics of this Progressive era than the debate about the government's proper relation to the economy. Progressives had labored for a generation by 1917 to redefine the social and economic role of the state. Thus, the war figures in many conventional accounts either as an event that provided the opportunity to bring that effort to some kind of culmination, or as an exogenous blow that disrupted the evolution of reform. Progressives themselves were divided over this very issue. Some, like John Dewey, believed in "the social possibilities of war" and welcomed belligerency as a kind of solvent that might cut through the cake of custom and render fossilized institutions malleable – including the institution of government itself. Others, like Woodrow Wilson, were more skeptical; they could see the corrosive effect of war on the social structures of all the belligerent states in Europe and feared its impact in America, especially its impact on the meager but precious progressive achievements of the preceding decade. "Every reform we have won," Wilson told an associate in 1914, "will be lost if we go into this war. We have been making a fight on special privilege. We have got new tariff and currency and trust legislation. We don't yet know how they will work. They are not thoroughly set."[6]

Beyond this uncertainty lay another and more enduring confusion about the proper strategy for progressive reform itself. Progressives divided into two broad camps, notoriously represented in the presidential campaigns of Theodore Roosevelt and Woodrow Wilson in 1912. Roosevelt Progressives, heavily Republican, welcomed economic giantism in the form of large corporations. To contain and channel the huge power of those bodies to socially productive use, they favored active and continuous government interventions in the marketplace. Powerful regulatory bodies, they believed, could exert a kind of micro-economic, socially beneficial discipline over the capitalist economy. Wilsonians, concentrated in the Democratic party with its historical strains of rural populism, were more fearful of big corporations and advocated a far more limited style of state activism. They would confine government power to a few macroeconomic matters, like the regulation of the money supply and, especially, vigorous enforcement of the antitrust laws.

Both wings of Progressivism, of course, represented challenges of a sort to the traditional doctrines of laissez-faire. Yet both schools of Progressive political thought also shared a willingness to settle for what Richard Hofstadter once called "ceremonial solutions" to political and economic problems. They were content, in short, to embrace psychologically comforting but substantively empty reforms of a capitalist system that was sufficiently functional – and powerful – to discourage schemes for truly radical reordering. The Progressives, in sum, stood in relationship to American capitalism as America stood in relation to the war and to the world geopolitical system: potentially disruptive, but whether from basic contentedness, indifference, or ideological innocence, only weakly motivated to play a dramatically reformist role.

What's more, Woodrow Wilson, as the leader who presided over the American mobilization effort, belonged to that wing of the Progressive movement that was, in any event, most wedded to Jeffersonian doctrines of atomized political and economic power, and therefore least disposed to seize upon the war crisis as an opportunity to aggrandize government. A biographer has accurately described Wilson's Secretary of War, Newton D. Baker, in terms that could be easily generalized to his entire administration: "During the war he was seldom among those who saw the conflict as an opportunity to increase the control of the federal government over the life of the nation, and he opposed the creation of new agencies that might place more power permanently in federal hands."[7]

It is in this dual context, then, of the war's relatively feeble impact on America and the Progressives' weak and even contradictory reform agenda that the war's political-economic implications must be understood. An examination of five areas in which the state did of necessity expand its presence in wartime will draw out some of these implications. The areas are: military conscription, agricultural policy, industrial mobilization, finance, and the manipulation of public opinion.

The very name that the Wilson administration employed to describe conscription is richly emblematic of the ideology of voluntarism that informed all the government's efforts in wartime mobilization: Selective Service. The operational techniques of the Selective Service System in the war illustrates an important and often overlooked connection between the theory of minimal government and the practice of officially sanctioned emotional provocation, occasionally to the point of near-hysteria, that sometimes violently convulsed American society in the World War I years.

Conscription was, in the nature of the case, frankly and unambiguously coercive; as such, it represented a dramatic violation of traditional American principles of individual liberty. Wilson's advisers knew that the Union's experiment with a forced draft in the Civil War had been disastrous. The Civil War draft provided fewer than 6 percent of Union troops and provoked bitter resentment, including a bloody riot that rocked New York City for four days in the summer of 1863. This was not a comforting precedent. Nevertheless a draft in 1917 seemed preferable to the alternative of relying on volunteers. Raising a sufficiently sizeable force of volunteers would take time; at least as troubling, it would necessitate a vigorous campaign to whip up patriotic emotion among a people who, as Mark Sullivan observed, regarded the war as "far away in distance and even farther away in spirit." Coaxing millions of men to volunteer for the armed services, Walter Lippmann warned the President, would require "a newspaper campaign of manufactured hatred that would disturb . . . the morale of the nation." Conscription, on the other hand, however distasteful, was "the only orderly and quiet way to accomplish what may be the necessary result."[8]

But in practice, ironically enough, the administration of the Selective Service law managed to be orderly only by not being quiet. Their study of the Civil War experience, and their knowledge of their countrymen's ignorance and indifference about "The European War," bred deep doubts about the workability of a draft that gnawed at Wilson and Baker and Selective Service System administrator Enoch H. Crowder. One Missouri Senator starkly predicted that the streets of America would run red with blood on registration day, 5 June 1917. Accordingly, the administration did its utmost to make conscription look like something else – to wrap it in a mantle of voluntarism and localism that would mask the necessarily coercive hand of central government. Wilson first adopted the transparent fiction of presenting the draft as simply a mechanism of "selection from among a nation which has volunteered in mass."[9] Crowder tried to perpetuate this myth after the war, when he recollected that "conscription in America was not . . . drafting of the unwilling. The citizens themselves had willingly come forward and pledged their services."[10] But to insure that this mass volunteering went smoothly, the administration arranged for propaganda speakers, marching bands, and flamboyant newspaper and magazine advertisements to urge men to do their duty by registering for the draft. The hoopla that attended a registration drive in September 1918 was described by Mark Sullivan, himself no stranger to the techniques of the publicist, as "a propaganda and publicity campaign of a magnitude never seen before or since in this country."[11] Crowder pointedly drew the contrast between these manpower mobilization techniques and those of the hated statist regimes of Europe when he said that "we were attempting to do voluntarily in a day what the Prussian autocracy had been spending nearly fifty years to perfect."[12] To further insure the success of the draft registration campaign, Wilson added an appeal for "every man, whether he is himself to be registered or not, to see to it that the name of every male person of the designated ages is written on these lists of honor."[13] Here were dramatic instances – and in their sources instructive ones – of the government-sponsored emotionalism and officially sanctioned vigilantism that were characteristic features of the entire mobilization effort.

Among the worst features of the Civil War system, said Crowder, was its administration by uniformed military officers, a policy that "bared the teeth of the Federal Government in every home within the loyal states."[14] Crowder now applied his considerable administrative and political genius to avoiding that naked display of governmental authority. He and Secretary Baker hit upon the device of administering the draft through local, civilian boards. The boards, Crowder explained, would have the appearance, at least, "of local self-government," though their substantive purpose was quite different. As Crowder later candidly conceded, the local boards "became the buffers between the individual citizen and the Federal Government, and thus they attracted and diverted, like local grounding wires in an electric coil, such resentment or discontent as might have proved a serious obstacle to war measures, had it been focused on the central authorities. Its diversion and grounding at 5,000 local points dissipated its force, and enabled the central war machine to function smoothly without the disturbance that might have been caused by the concentrated total of dissatisfaction."[15]

This brief recital of the history of the Selective Service System contains in microcosm all the elements that informed mobilization policy in a variety of sectors. Uncertainty about their countrymen's enthusiasm for the war, and acute consciousness of the powerful grip that the values of individualism, localism, voluntarism, and laissez-faire held in American political culture, led policy-makers to avoid the appearance – and, as we shall see, even the substance, insofar as possible – of centralized, coercive authority. In place of that authority they substituted appeals to patriotism, public relations campaigns, propaganda, and vigilantism. The important point is that these techniques did not constitute instruments of formal state power, but substitutes for it.

Wartime agricultural policy provides a further case in point. As in many other sectors, mobilization measures were entrusted to a new agency – in this instance, the Food Administration – rather than placed in the hands of existing departments. This reliance on a newly created government body is especially revealing in the case of agriculture, since the Department of Agriculture was arguably the most well-developed "modern" bureaucracy in the American government.[16] But when even this institutionally sophisticated bureau proved inadequate to the demands of wartime, the Wilson administration's response was not to strengthen it but to summon into being a new body, explicitly understood to be an emergency creation with only a limited lifetime.

The Food Administration's methods also faithfully reflected the markedly tentative revision of laissez-faire doctrine and the conscious preference for voluntarism that pervaded all aspects of mobilization. Food Administrator Herbert Hoover neither requisitioned crops nor imposed production quotas in his effort to boost agricultural production. He relied instead on high prices, partly supported by the government – but in greater part supported by hungry (and resentful) Allies – in order to induce American farmers to produce more foodstuffs. To control the profiteering of middlemen, Hoover later reflected, "no attempt was made to fix prices . . . by European methods. The economic policy of the administration was therefore to stabilize prices and reduce speculative profits by purely commercial pressures and business methods as distinguished from legal regulations."[17] Most famously, Hoover refused to dampen domestic consumption by resorting to rationing, despite the urgent pleadings of the Allied governments who had themselves by 1917 long since imposed food rationing on their own peoples. Instead, Hoover orchestrated a monstrous propaganda campaign to persuade housewives voluntarily to observe "wheatless Wednesdays" and "meatless Mondays," and even to induce apple-munching children to be "patriotic to the core." Half a million persons carried this campaign from door to door. "The significance of this broad campaign," the Food Administration explained, "is far deeper than may appear at first thought." It is indeed typical of the whole program of the Food Administration, in its insistence upon cooperation rather than coercion, upon the compelling force of patriotic sentiment as a means to be tried before resort to "threats and prosecutions."[18]

The policy of voluntarism found not only one of its exemplary practitioners in the person of Food Administrator Herbert Hoover, but its chief philosopher. Before he returned to the United States in 1917 to take up his position in the Wilson Administration, Hoover had spent virtually all of his adult life outside the United States, amassing a modest fortune in various mining ventures in Asia, Africa, and Latin America. Like any observant traveler, he found that his experience abroad gave him a new sensitivity to the distinguishing characteristics of his native culture. Significantly, Hoover used Europe as a foil against which to define his sense of American uniqueness, even though he had less personal familiarity with Europe than he did with other regions. In a sense, Hoover thus took his place in a centuries-old discussion of American national identity defined in relation to the old Mother Continent, a discussion that already included such eminent contributors as John Winthrop, Thomas Jefferson, Voltaire, Raynal, Goethe, de Tocqueville, Mark Twain, and Henry James.[19] Like those other observers, Hoover frequently invoked myths and stereotypes, but the egregious distortions in his analysis rendered it no less consequential. They served, rather, to highlight the power of cultural paradigms in shaping even the prosaic details of economic policy.

In testimony before the Senate Committee on Agriculture in June 1917, Hoover explicitly contrasted his intended methods with what he took to be typical practices in the Old World: "The food administrations of Europe and the powers that they possess," he warned, "are of the nature of dictatorship, but happily ours is not their plight. . . ." His methods, he explained, would be "based on an entirely different conception from that of Europe. . . . Our conception of the problem in the United States is that we should assemble the voluntary effort of the people. . . . We propose to mobilize the spirit of self-denial and self-sacrifice in this country."[20]

In 1922 Hoover codified his thinking on this general subject into a little book, *American Individualism*. Its theme was that the peculiarly *American* variant of individualism was not isolating and selfish, but altruistic and communal. It fed a mutualistic, spontaneously cooperative ethos that rendered unnecessary and inappropriate in America what Hoover regarded as the noxious growth of state power, which he took to be the sad fate of Europe. In the course of developing this thesis, Hoover dwelt affectionately on the very term that had been appropriated to describe the military draft: "The ideal of *service*," he claimed, constituted a "great spiritual force poured out by our people as never before in the history of the world."[21]

The repeated appearance of that word, "service," in connection with American war mobilization should give the analyst pause. It signified, I believe, the self-conscious passage of Americans between individualistic and collective eras – between eras of laissez-faire and statism – and their reluctance wholly to abandon the former or wholly to embrace the latter. The very ambiguity of the word, connoting both individual autonomy and social obligation, captured the conflicting values that marked this historical passage. And Hoover's ascendancy in wartime to the status of heroic philosopher of this cultural moment – "the only man who emerged from the ordeal of Paris with an enhanced reputation," said John Maynard Keynes; "the biggest figure injected into Washington life by the war," said Louis Brandeis; "he is certainly a wonder and I wish we could make him President of the United States," said Franklin Roosevelt – can be taken as symbolic of the kind of transient resolution of this conflict of values that marked the war years.[22]

Perhaps the most extensively studied wartime agency has been the War Industries Board. Though an older literature portrayed the Board as a powerful center of iron-fisted command over the industrial sector of the economy, more recent scholarship, especially the work of Robert Cuff, has severely qualified, perhaps even nullified, that judgement.[23] To be sure, the appearance of *any* agency even nominally charged with regulating the industrial sector in the United States was a striking novelty. The food and agricultural sector of the economy had begun to explore close institutional relationships with the state well before World War I, as evidenced by the passage of the Meat Inspection Act in 1906 and the creation of the agricultural extension service in 1914. The transportation sector had been subject to at least modest regulatory control since the passage of the Interstate Commerce Act in 1887. Even the financial sector had begun to move into the penumbra of governmental power with the Federal Reserve Act of 1914. But American manufacturers had been notoriously resistant to any form of government oversight or orchestration. Indeed, government intervention in the industrial sector prior to 1914 almost exclusively took the form of antitrust legislation, itself designed not to concert, but to fragment yet further the centers of administrative control in this part of the economy.

Despite the appearance of novelty and of a dramatic breakthrough for an anti-laissez-faire point of view in the creation of the War Industries Board, the Board, in practice, conformed to the model already sketched for conscription and food policy. Its formal powers were few. It had scant and dubious legal authority until it came under Bernard Baruch's direction and was given statutory definition in the spring of 1918, just months before the war's end, and it operated both before and after that time under a cloud of uncertainty about its constitutional standing. President Wilson deliberately refused to invest the Board with the kind of sweeping powers that legend incorrectly ascribes to it. It had no authority to enter into contracts, for example, a responsibility that remained where it had always been, with the War and Navy Departments. Nor could it dictate prices; what limited price-fixing activity Wilson permitted he assigned to a separate committee chaired by Robert S. Brookings.

As the Board's official historian, Grosvenor Clarkson, later described it, all the WIB's directions to industry "took the form of negotiations. . . . Compliance was based as much upon the compulsion of reasonableness and the pressure of opinion as upon fear of governmental power." In one revealing instance, Bernard Baruch was called upon to persuade a recalcitrant lumber supplier to provide a quantity of building materials at a price the Board wanted. If he failed to agree with Baruch's terms, the WIB chairman cooly informed the supplier, "you will be such an object of contempt and scorn in your home town that you will not dare to show your face there. If you should, your fellow citizens would call you a slacker, the boys would hoot at you, and the draft men would likely run you out of town."[24]

That statement surely attests to Baruch's willingness to flex his muscle. It was not for want of its chief's personal appetite for power that the WIB tread so carefully in 1917 and 1918. But like the dog that did not bark in the Sherlock Holmes story, "Silver Blaze," what is remarkable about Baruch's outburst in this case is what he did *not* threaten: to commandeer the needed supplies, or to take legal reprisals if they were not forthcoming. He relied here, as elsewhere, not on the majesty of the laws or the unimpeachable authority of the state, but on bluff and bluster, on cajolery, and on the threat of bad publicity and public humiliation. Here again, the deliberate manipulation of public opinion appears less as an instrumentality of state power than as an index of its effective absence.

Suffice it to say here that an analagous, though not precisely identical, case can be made for the methods of war financing employed by the Wilson administration. Though the American government financed a higher proportion of the war through current taxation than did most other belligerent governments, it was still compelled to borrow heavily in the money markets. Given the historical antipathy to national indebtedness, the government tried to sell war bonds at below-market rates (3.5 percent in the case of the first loan issue in the spring of 1917, at a time when market interest rates were running at 4 percent; later loan issues carried higher interest rates). This meant, among other things, that the private banks that had traditionally absorbed big war-funding issues could not be expected to take a keen interest in buying bonds on purely economic grounds; neither, for that matter, could the general public.

To make up for the economic bond-buying incentives that it was unwilling to provide, the government was thus compelled to supply psychological incentives. These took the form of mammoth bond-selling campaigns that Senator Warren G. Harding accurately labeled "hysterical and unseemly."[25] Secretary of the Treasury William Gibbs McAdoo, like Baker and Crowder a careful student of the Civil War, believed that Lincoln's Treasury Secretary, Salmon P. Chase, had made a "fundamental error" because he "did not attempt to capitalize the emotion of the people." In contrast McAdoo explained, "We went direct to the people, and that means to everybody – to business men, workmen, farmers, bankers, millionaires, schoolteachers, laborers. We capitalized the profound impulse called patriotism."[26] McAdoo became the impresario of a circus-like round of monster bond rallies, poster campaigns, and speeches by "Four-Minute Men" in schools, churches, and movie theaters. During a second loan drive later in 1917, McAdoo himself exemplified the kind of tactics employed in the bond-selling campaigns before a crowd in California: "Every person who refuses to subscribe or who takes the attitude of let the other fellow do it, is a friend of Germany and I would like nothing better than to tell it to him to his face. A man who can't lend his government $1.25 per week at the rate of 4 percent interest is not entitled to be an American citizen."[27]

Several common strands run through these various aspects of American war mobilization. Taken together, they weave a fabric of distinctive pattern that signifies the peculiar character of American war-making in 1917–18. This pattern shows the uncertain, attenuated commitment of the United States to the Allied cause; the pervasive anxiety that public support for the war effort might be wanting; the persistent Progressive hesitancy – especially among Wilson's fellow Democrats – to make a truly radical break with the laissez-faire tradition; and the consequently large reliance not on formal state power but on propaganda, public relations, and an aroused patriotism to accomplish the necessary tasks of organizing the economy and disciplining the society for large-scale modern warfare.

It is in this context that the claim can be made for the Committee on Public Information as the most characteristically American war mobilization agency. The CPI, significantly enough, was virtually the first war agency created after the congressional declaration of war on 6 April 1917. It was established by executive order on April 14, and was from its inception headed by the boundlessly energetic, muckraking journalist George Creel. To his new position Creel brought the moral passion of a Progressive reformer, and an advanced expertise in all the most sophisticated techniques of a public relations specialist. And like his colleagues Crowder and Hoover, Creel boasted of the weakness of his formal power and made the familiar comparisons with the Old World. "We had no authority," he declared in his postwar memoirs, "yet the American idea *worked*. And it worked better then any European *law*."[28]

Though officially dedicated only to providing factual information about the war, the CPI inexorably developed into a massive instrument for cultivating and playing upon the full range of public emotions. In speech and print, in music and film, in art and dramatizations, it harped on three themes: that the purposes of American belligerency lay less in a concrete defense of American interests than they did in protection of the abstract ideal of democracy against the threat of "autocracy"; that the menace of autocracy took the subhuman form of bestial "Huns" (among the CPI's most notorious films was one entitled "The Kaiser, the Beast of Berlin"); and that any questioning of the American war effort was to be equated with disloyalty to the United States itself. The overarching purpose of the CPI, of course, was to create and sustain a popular mood of enthusiasm for the war that would minimize any necessity for the formal, statutory enforcement of such policies as conscription, food conservation, industrial coordination, or war financing. This, in Creel's language, was "the American idea," pointedly contrasted with "European *law*."

The CPI may be taken as the summary example of the style of American war mobilization: the appeal not to the authority of the state or to the concrete discipline of felt necessity, but to high abstractions like "democracy" and "loyalty" as well as to base emotions like hatred and fear. The consequences of officially nurturing those emotions are infamously documented in the sorry record of anti-radical and anti-foreign hysteria, vigilantism, and violence that stained the history of World War I-era America.

Less well documented is the linkage that connects those regrettable domestic effects of American belligerency to their causes in the overall context of mobilization, and in the still larger context of modern American political culture. Contrary to much mythology, the hyper-agitated atmosphere of wartime American society was not due to popular enthusiasm for the war, nor even, simply, to the war's perturbation of a social system already irritated by a generation of reform, rapid urbanization, and massive immigration – though all those factors played an undeniable role.

The principal explanation for American wartime hysteria, I believe, is to be found in the Wilson administration's willful avoidance of formal instrumentalities to effect its mobilization program, and by its consequent heavy reliance on the deliberate stirring of emotion. To this explanation must be added considerations of some enduring features of American political culture, evident before, during, and after World War I.

"The great object of terror and suspicion to the people of the thirteen provinces," Henry Adams wrote of the founding eighteenth-century circumstances of American society, "was power; not merely power in the hands of a president or a prince, of one assembly or several, of many citizens or few, but power in the abstract, wherever it existed and under whatever form it was known."[29] That fear has run like an electric current through American life. It has pulsed from Andrew Jackson, who considered government to be "an engine of oppression to the people," through all the World War I administrators who paradoxically prized and protected the weakness of the government agencies they were called upon to lead, down to Ronald Reagan, who repeatedly declared that "Government is not the solution to our problem. Government is the problem."

From Alexis de Tocqueville to Werner Sombart to Jean-Francois Revel, European observers have made a point of "American exceptionalism," especially regarding hostile attitudes toward the state and the anemic development of formal political institutions. The American experience in World War I tends powerfully to confirm this judgement. When Woodrow Wilson shattered isolationist precedent and took his countrymen into the distant European War, he and they went about the task in a typically American way, in a way charted over three centuries of insulated experience that had deeply molded the character of the republic. In the last analysis, they could do no other.

Notes to Chapter 10

1. William E. Leuchtenburg, "The New Deal and the Analogue of War," in John Braeman, et. al., eds., *Change and Continuity in Twentieth-Century America* (New York, NY, 1966), pp. 81–143; Leuchtenburg, *The Perils of Prosperity* (Chicago, IL, 1958), p. 39.

2. Winston Churchill, *The World Crisis, 1916–1918* (New York, NY, 1927), vol. 2, p. 275.

3. Adolf Hitler, *Mein Kampf* (New York, NY, 1939), p. 203.

4. Mark Sullivan, *Our Times: The United States, 1900–1924* (New York, NY, 1924), vol. 5, p. 2.

5. *Historical Statistics of the United States* (Washington, D.C., 1975), pp. 224, 1104.

6. Quoted in Ray Stannard Baker, ed., *Woodrow Wilson: Life and Letters* (New York, NY, 1927–39), vol. 5, p. 77.

7. Daniel R. Beaver, *Newton D. Baker and the American War Effort, 1917–1918* (Lincoln, NE, 1966), p. 6.

8. Lippmann to Wilson quoted in Beaver, *Newton D. Baker,* p. 26.

9. Ray Stannard Baker and William E. Dodds, eds., *The Public Papers of Woodrow Wilson* (New York, NY, 1925–27), vol. 5, p. 39.

10. Enoch Crowder, *The Spirit of Selective Service* (New York, NY, 1920), p. 125.

11. Sullivan, *Our Times,* vol. 5, p. 312.

12. *Second Report of the Provost Marshal General* (Washington, D.C., 1919), p. 28.

13. Baker and Dodds, eds., *Public Papers,* vol. 5, p. 39.

14. Crowder, *Spirit of Selective Service,* p. 78.

15. *Second Report of the Provost Marshall General,* p. 277.

16. For an elaboration of this point in the context of New Deal agricultural policies, see Theda Skocpol and Kenneth Finegold, "State Capacity and Economic Intervention in the Early New Deal," *Political Science Quarterly* vol. 97, no. 2 (Summer 1982), pp. 255–278.

17. William Clinton Mullendore, *History of the United States Food Administration, 1917–1919* (Stanford, CA, 1941), introduction.

18. Mullendore, *History*, p. 221.

19. For an extended analysis of this discussion, see Antonello Gerbi, *La disputa del Nuovo Mondo: Storia di una polemica, 1750–1900* (Milano, Italy, 1955).

20. Quoted in Mullendore, *History*, pp. 52–53.

21. Herbert Hoover, *American Individualism* (Garden City, NY, 1923), pp. 28–29.

22. Descriptions of Hoover quoted in Arthur M. Schlesinger, Jr., *The Crisis of the Old Order* (Boston, MA, 1956), pp. 80–82.

23. Robert D. Cuff, *The War Industries Board: Business-Government Relations during World War I* (Baltimore, MD, 1973).

24. Grosvenor Clarkson, *Industrial America in the World War: The Strategy behind the Line, 1917–1918* (Boston, MA, 1923), pp. 177, 94, 99.

25. *Congressional Record*, Senate, 65th Congress, 1st sess., vol. 55, part 4, 8 June 1917, p. 3325.

26. William Gibbs McAdoo, *Crowded Years* (Boston, MA, 1931), pp. 374–79.

27. McAdoo quoted in a letter from Hiram Johnson to C.K. McClatchey, 21 November 1917, Johnson Papers, Bancroft Library, University of California, Berkeley.

28. George Creel, *How We Advertised America* (New York, NY, 1920), p. 24. Emphasis in original.

29. Adams quoted in Grant McConnell, *Private Power and American Democracy* (New York, NY, 1967), p. 33.

11

War Economy and Controlled Economy: The Discrediting of "Socialism" in Germany During World War I

Gerald D. Feldman

The events of the past few years in central and eastern Europe and, indeed, in the western world as well, have made it patently obvious that, however it may be characterized, the twentieth century has not turned out to be the century of socialism of which its proponents dreamed nor even the century of state planning anticipated by technocrats. While the levels of state interventionism, monetary steering, welfarism, and "corporatism" of various kinds certainly have increased over the century in capitalist societies, there have been powerful impulses toward deregulation and decontrol and even social demontage after World War I and more recently. Capitalism has certainly become more organized, but whether one can speak meaningfully of the development of an "organized capitalism" is another matter.[1] Needless to say, it is important not to confuse the discrediting of socialism with the vindication of capitalism, and exactly what is meant by "socialism" is far from easy to say. Nevertheless, I think that it is fair to argue that what has been identified as "socialism," whether it has taken the form of the actual ownership of the means of production and distribution or substantial state interference with privately owned means of production and distribution, has been repeatedly discredited. This has been the case especially with respect to its utter failure to satisfy basic consumer needs.

World War I Germany is an especially important illustration of this phenomenon since the experience with the so-called controlled economy, or *Zwangswirtschaft*, produced an especially virulent and broadly-based hostility toward government controls. Yet, important elements of the controlled economy were viewed by many socialists and social reformers as steps in the direction of socialism or a substantial change in the nature of capitalism. Both the controls and the hostility continued on

Notes to Chapter 11 can be found on page 250.

into the early years of the Weimar Republic and contributed mightily to the fatal tarnishing of that regime in the eyes of significant elements in the population. As is well known, the chief reason for this is that the system failed miserably, and one of the functions of this paper will be to explore certain aspects of its failure. Another will be to make some suggestions about how and why the discrediting of socialism in World War I Germany may have left a legacy of danger for German capitalism as well.[2]

I

In thinking about socialism and capitalism in wartime Germany, it is important to recognize that war does not constitute a normal economic environment and cannot be considered a fair test of any economic system. This abnormality of war economics received some theoretical recognition during the war itself, when the economist and sociologist Franz Eulenburg tried his hand at a "Theory of the War Economy."[3] According to Eulenburg, the war economy, while leaving modes of production, property relations, and the profit motive intact, nevertheless produces major changes and distortions in the national economy. The first of these is the distortion in the consumption of goods, since the determination of demand by private consumption, insofar as purchasing power will allow, is replaced by the demand of a war machine whose characteristics are entirely different from those of the private consumer. In contrast to the private consumer, who is moved to produce in order to consume, the military consumer produces nothing. Also, private consumption uses up goods in a gradual and reasonably predictable manner and thus permits the appropriate and timely repair and renewal of the productive apparatus. The military consumer uses up goods practically as rapidly as it receives them and shows little concern for the reproduction of the productive apparatus. Even without increasing his prices, the businessman who produces for military purposes has a higher profit and can justify more rapid amortization of his plant and equipment because of the rate of military consumption. While some effort is made to correct this situation through systematic attempts to save raw materials and labor, such efforts can never make up for the extent of wartime consumption and therefore do not have the benefits of similar strivings in a cyclical downturn in peacetime. Naturally, military consumption takes place at the expense of private consumption, which is reduced both quantitatively and qualitatively. An especially crucial point in Eulenburg's conception, however, is that the phenomena just described are dynamic, that the balance between supply and demand is not simply reduced from one level to another, but is perpetually being disturbed by the continuation of the war and thus threatens to produce increasing national impoverishment.

The second major economic disturbance generated by the war economy, according to Eulenburg, is to the free market and prices. The breakdown of international trade and the isolation of national markets are of themselves factors that change supply and demand relationships, but the most important influence is that of what is today known as demand-pull inflation, namely, money chasing an inadequate supply of goods for the war economy. Not only does the price of daily necessities rise, but those articles that are of poorer quality increase relatively in price to those of greater quality. The result is a general rise in the level of prices and a reduction in the purchasing power of money. Price controls may dampen such tendencies, but they cannot be carried too far without driving the available goods from the market. Even without errors on the part of the purchaser in choosing from whom to purchase, and even without deliberate exploitation and profiteering on the part of the producer or merchant, a situation is created in which "the buyer knows no upper price limit"[4] when it comes to military purchasing or to buying vital necessities, and "the holder of certain means of production has a dividend fall into his lap, which in no way has anything to do with improper actions or arises in some [deliberately] unfair way, but is rather the simple consequence of the altered structure of the market."[5] Profiteering, in a sense, is the essence rather than the excrescence of the war economy.

Thirdly, the war economy interrupts what Eulenburg calls the circulation process, that is, the process of capital accumulation and economic growth. Production is reduced through the removal of large numbers of workers from industry and the low priority given to maintenance and new plant construction. Consequently, there is an increasing undercapitalization of the economy despite savings made by war industries or by individuals unable to find goods to purchase. In a very literal sense, the war economy turns the purposes of normal economic life upside down: "While the wealth of a land is composed of the sum of useful things which serve the promotion of human welfare, nothing of this kind is to be found in the expenses for war."[6] The only check on this process is a bitter one indeed, namely, that a war economy "is only possible for a certain amount of time and threatens to come to an end because of its own exhaustion."[7]

The monetary inflation is the final disturbance for which the war economy provides a "unique experiment." Eulenburg views it as "merely the external expression of the self-generated purchasing power and demand produced by the Reich through its credit. . . . It is the consequence of the entire economy of indebtedness with which the war is being fought."[8] Hence it veils the unproductive activity of the war economy that has all the symptoms of an economic crisis and yet gives the appearance of an economic boom. Full employment and rising prices accompany diminishing national productivity and depreciation of the currency. The visible evidence of currency depreciation, rising prices, may follow from the less apparent phenomenon of its oversupply, but the two processes do not have to operate in tandem either with respect to tempo or incidence. They depend on the pace of war contracting and the way in which its effects spread through the interconnections between and among the various sectors of the economy. Thus, the willingness of the military to grant high prices to encourage conversion to war production and to foster high levels of military production lead to a similar generosity with respect to raw materials and wages. The merchants and businessmen involved are permitted to charge high prices for their services as well as to increase the salaries of their employees. The workers and employees can then increase their demand for food and such consumer goods as are available.

As Eulenburg was already able to note at a relatively early period of the war, however, not everyone was equally advantaged by these developments. Different groups were differently affected by the wartime inflation. Those already in possession of factories and plants producing for the war effort, or those with efficient agricultural holdings, were in a position to make a good profit because pricing policies in the war economy were almost invariably based on the costs of the least efficient producer. Also, certain classes of workers, namely, those skilled workers producing for the war effort, gain relative to those working in less favored industries. Much less happily situated were those living on fixed incomes – officials, white collar workers, pensioners – and those living on fixed investments. The latter were being "proletarianized."

While such redistributional effects of wartime inflation seemed clear enough, their macroeconomic implications were by no means so transparent. Obviously, the value of property, both landed and industrial, was increasing greatly in nominal terms, but so were the costs of purchasing or reproducing them again. One thing was certain, however, the real national wealth had diminished during the war, thus demonstrating that "the national economy can be impoverished in war and yet become richer in nominal terms."[9] Ultimately, what Eulenburg was arguing was that the war economy was potentially a form of national economic suicide.

This is a useful perspective from which to view the controlled economy and war socialism just as it is valuable in assessing the less controlled and more profitable economic sectors. It suggests the high level of economic and social vulnerability created by the war itself, especially for those whose task it was to service the war economy in the status of auxiliaries, that is, of producers and distributors of consumer goods, to its most important purpose of producing the engines of war themselves.

II

Agriculture and the distribution of foodstuffs and other basic consumer items were the most important of the areas to fall into the auxiliary category. The prewar protection of German agriculture at the expense of the German consumer had been the source of endless socialist and liberal criticism, and had been defended as a necessary means of maintaining Germany's vital interests in peace and war as well as of preserving two of her most important "productive" strata by the conservative groups influencing government policy. Whatever the benefits of protection, they did not include making Germany self-reliant in foodstuffs even before the war, let alone after 1914. The blockade created a situation in which imports were severely restricted, while labor and material shortages were bound to reduce the productivity of German agriculture. All this would have been bearable if the war had been short, and the initial measures to deal with the problem were based on that expectation. Although the Bundesrat had extensive powers to control prices and undertake other measures under the Enabling Act, its initial actions in the realm of price ceilings, regulation of production, and rationing were slow and unsystematic. Ironically, the first initiatives came from the agricultural organizations themselves. Their leaders, wishing to combat speculation and avoid unpleasant political accusations, urged the imposition of price ceilings on wheat and rye at the end of October 1914 and later extended this request with respect to all cereal grains. They continued to favor price ceilings until the spring of 1915, before the increasing differences between the prices they proposed and those actually imposed made them realize that public pressure was turning the ceilings into an instrument of "consumer" rather than "producer" interests.[10]

The situation was made all the more irritating because they had turned down the alternative approach, recommended by the coal industry leaders, Hugo Stinnes and Alfred Hugenberg, in September 1914, that a corporation be established to buy up two million tons of wheat so as to insure the supply for 1915 by reducing the amount then on the market and driving down consumption by increasing the price. The Stinnes-Hugenberg argument, which was one that Stinnes was to repeat for almost a decade, was that the high prices would guarantee the supply and could be covered by increased wages if necessary. This argument was rejected by the agrarian leaders at the time with the claim that such prices could not be paid by the lower middle class, and that the price ceilings agriculture proposed would prove most adequate to the situation. Increasingly, however, agriculture became the chief target of what was to become known as the controlled economy (*Zwangswirtschaft*).

This was because the piecemeal approach to prices, production, and distribution of foodstuffs did not work. The peasantry have never been quite as "backward" as urban-centered historians have claimed. Especially where they were engaged in diversified farming, as in the Rhenish-Westphalian region, they were quick to react to market signals. Price ceilings on one crop led them to concentrate on another, and where price ceilings on food crops began to make production for the human market less profitable, they used those crops as fodder for their animals until controls on such use forced the great pig slaughter of the spring of 1915. The end result was that the entire production of German agriculture came under government control. Not only were the prices controlled, but also the use to which agricultural products could be put and the customers to whom the crops could be sold. Wheat, for example, had to be sold to the War Wheat Corporation (*Kriegsgetreidegesellschaft*), which monopolized the sale of German domestic wheat production as well as such foreign imports as came into the country. Farms were subjected to searches and the confiscation of hidden or unreported production.

Unfortunately, these measures in no way insured that the urban population would receive the food supplies it needed. Nearly all the measures came too late. Thus, bread rationing was not introduced until January 1915 in Berlin, and later than that in the rest of the country. The price ceilings were not introduced in any coordinated manner, so the later a price ceiling was issued, the higher the price relative to its predecessors and the more the farmers favored production of the crops last placed under control. Most important, it was clear by 1916 that Germany was suffering from an absolute shortage of foodstuffs as well as declining production due to labor shortages, insufficient fertilizer, and equipment problems. The farmers found their profit margins inadequate and were increasingly hostile to the controlled economy, while the urban population complained about the inadequate supplies and high prices. The result was a growing black market, especially in those areas where the urban population could easily get to the countryside and purchase items at the source. At the end of May 1916, an effort was made to pacify the complaints about the chaos in the regulations and the inadequacies of distribution through the creation of a War Food Office (*Kriegsernährungsamt*). The new organization was intended to centralize the management of the food supply as well as insure that those doing heavy industrial labor for the war effort would get enough to eat. Unfortunately, the combination of actual food shortage combined with the effects of past policies set real limits on what the new agency could do either about the situation or about the increasing hostility between city and country. At the same time, the creation of special categories of 'hard working' and 'hardest working' (*Schwer- und Schwerstarbeiter*) laborers who were entitled to extra rations produced tensions among the workers as well as between the blue collar workers and other consumers.[11]

Certainly no one could be sanguine about the effects of the methods employed against the farmers. It was impossible to "enlighten" them, especially in the context of the unavoidably more forceful techniques being used to bring them into line. The often successful night "inspections" of small mills and farms to check for false production reports and hidden stores "produced much bitterness among the people on the countryside," while the use of informers, so helpful in getting information about illegal cattle and pig slaughters, was "so poisonous and demoralizing in its effect as to make authorities doubt whether the advantages were greater than the disadvantages."[12] The certain consequence of all government attempts to control the food supply, and to do with inadequate personnel, was to stir the resentment of the peasantry against what the historian Robert Moeller has properly called an "affirmative action program for the consumers."

Even the very traditional respect of the farmers for the army was undermined in the spring of 1918 when soldiers were sent out to the countryside to confiscate fodder for military purposes and thereby starve the work animals. The agricultural workers, already in short supply, were demoralized as well. If the farm workers were unable to follow the model of their urban counterparts, who went out on strike and demonstrated for higher wages and lower working hours, they could simply go to bed and report themselves "sick," and they began to do so.[13] Thus was threatened a harvest which strangers were going to take anyway to feed other strangers at prices that farmers deemed unsatisfactory. From the perspective of the farmers, the attitude of the workers and the authorities was nothing but hypocritical. The workers were being supplied from the black market by the large firms and municipalities with the collusion and even the approval of the authorities. As for the workers, "on the one side they demand the strictest suppression of black marketeering, even in the big industries, but on the other side gladly benefit from the black market supplying of food through the plants and set the condition that the supplying of the workers ought under no circumstances to be reduced because of the fight against the black market."[14]

The peasants were not the only subjects of the controls placed on prices and the distribution of food and other vital necessities. The war marked the beginning of a decade of hell for the German retailer. Panic buying on the part of consumers was already evident in July 1914, and some retailers unquestionably took advantage of the situation to raise prices as well as to hold back their goods in the expectation of higher prices. It did not take long for public outrage to express itself or for the authorities to take measures. The latter, however, often created more problems than they solved because of their typically decentralized character. Price ceilings and other regulations against holding back goods were issued by the twenty-odd Acting General Commanders responsible for internal security under the 1851 Prussian Law of Siege or by local civilian authorities using authority granted under the Law on Price Ceilings issued on 4 August 1914. As usual, the isolated price ceilings proved to be a primitive approach to a complex problem that made things worse, especially when they seemed to be inspired by medieval notions of a just price. They drove goods to those districts where there were no controls or where they were least obnoxious. Gradually, therefore, important articles of daily consumption became subject to centralized price ceilings by the Bundesrat, and the number of such items swelled to 763 by the end of 1916. The results were not very satisfactory, however, because the controlled items either disappeared into the black market, reappeared in stores as "foreign goods," or were packaged or reworked in some manner so as to make them sellable at a higher price.[15]

The stuff of which much of the controversy with the retailers was made, however, was not the price ceiling regulations, but rather the Bundesrat decree of 23 July 1915 against excessive prices, that is, against profiteering (*Preistreibereiverordnung*). The concept of excess profit introduced by the decree was a more flexible standard than the price ceiling because it made profiteering a function, not of charging more than an allowed price, but rather of making an "excess profit" on "objects of daily use." The courts then defined this to mean that "no one shall earn more on his goods than he did in peacetime."[16] Not only were violators of these provisions threatened with fines and even imprisonment, but also those who sought to manipulate the market situation by holding back goods for speculative purposes or engaging in other unfair practices. While these may have been conceptual steps forward in the battle against profiteering – or a return to the "moral economy" of a bygone age with their bans on forestalling and engrossing – they created a whole new set of complications by requiring some form of expert judgement to determine what constituted a justified price and profit for the host of items on the market.

This was one of the tasks of the Price Examination Agencies (*Preisprü-fungsstellen*) created under a decree of 25 September 1915. These new institutions were charged with determining the appropriateness of prices in the various districts in which they were set up, assisting the authorities in controlling prices, issuing regulations for retailers, and providing the public with information. All municipalities with over 10,000 inhabitants were required to set up such agencies, half of whose membership was to be composed of producers, wholesalers, and retailers, and the other half of which was to be composed of independent experts and consumers. Each agency was to have a non-partisan chairman. The decree also provided for the establishment of a network of price examination agencies at the district, provincial, and state levels, with a center in Berlin. Until the fall of 1916, this central headquarters was the Reich Examination Agency for Food Prices. Then it was placed under the National Economy Section (*Volkswirtschaftliche Abteilung*) of the War Food Office. By this time, there were over a thousand price examination agencies in Germany, the most important and active of which were located in the industrial districts.

The above mentioned decrees were by no means the only important regulations dealing with the selling of food and other vital necessities issued during the first years of the war. There were regulations requiring the public display of all prices in retail stores as well as the placing of accurate information on packaging. Particularly important were the regulations issued with the object of controlling the entry into the business of selling goods of daily use as well as provisions for excluding from such business not only those violating the regulations, but also those engaged in the "chain-trade" (*Kettenhandel*), that is, introducing an unnecessary number of middlemen into the distribution of goods with the object or effect of raising the price.

This flood of organization and regulation was a response to the rising tension between consumers and retailers that accompanied the already mentioned tension between city and country. The peasantry, however, had the advantage of some measure of distance from the consuming public as well as the possibility of covering up their delinquencies more effectively. The retailer lived among his customers, and his place of business was where the consumer actually faced the realities of shortages and rising prices. Thus, the shopkeeper and merchant were the objects of immediate hostility and suspicion.

Furthermore, the hostility was organized. At the end of 1914, a host of civil service, labor, and white-collar organizations joined with various housewife organizations to form the War Committee for Consumer Interests (*Kriegsausschuss für Konsumenteninteressen*), which later teamed up with other consumer groups to form a Working Community of Consumer Organizations. Its board of directors included such prominent Social Democrats as Deputy Robert Schmidt, who had a trade union background, August Müller, the Business Manager of the Central Association of German Consumer Cooperatives, and Siegfried Aufhauser, the head of the socialist white-collar Federation of Technical Employees (*Bund technischer Beamten*). Other members were the Christian trade unionist Adolph Giesberts; the liberal feminist, Dr. Gertrud Bäumer; and the prominent academic social reformers, Professors Waldemar Zimmermann and Ernst Francke. Francke and the Society for Social Reform he represented were prominent in providing advice to the civilian and military authorities, and August Müller became a member of the Advisory Board of the War Food Office in May 1916. The War Committee for Consumer Interests, therefore, was well placed to influence the government and the price examination agencies as well as to provide information to the public and disseminate its point of view very widely.

The latter function was performed by a newsletter, "Consumer Economics in the War" (*Verbraucherwirtschaft im Kriege*), which was sent out twice weekly in 1916 and also supplied material for the press. The content of an issue of this two-page publication is a good illustration of the goals and style of the organized consumer propaganda. Thus, the issue of 24 November 1916 provided eight items for its recipients.[17] The first contained information on a petition to the War Food Office calling for price ceilings on horsemeat that, "because of the shortage of other kinds of meat is very much sought, especially by those doing heavy labor, but which, because of the absence of price ceilings, has become monstrously expensive, often five times its peacetime price. . . ." There followed a critical commentary concerning the recent confiscation of foodstuffs at the Berlin railroad station and post offices, apparently of goods sent by farmers to their relatives in the city. While the effort to equalize consumption was laudable, the authors of the article wished to remind the public that the recipients of these packages "are in no way only rich families, but often those who are suffering severely from the needs of the time" and that, since these surpluses normally would never be freely surrendered by the farmers, "one should view their import into the cities sympathetically."

The articles that followed had a much harsher tone. One severely criticized the city of Nuremberg for retreating from its efforts to centralize the making of sausage after the meat dealers had deliberately delivered inferior meat so as to prove that good sausage could only be made by individual butchers. Another attacked the inadequate punishment of a canned goods producer whose meat products only contained 10 percent meat and who had overstated his daily production costs by 240 marks. This individual had been fined only 2000 marks, the equivalent of seventeen days worth of his unjust profit. The compilers of the issue turned next to a matter of particular concern, namely the arguments of those who claimed that higher prices were the best means of getting the farmers to follow the regulations. The authors hoped that Field Marshall von Hindenburg's recent appeal to the farmers to do their duty would be supported through a cessation of arguments for high prices.

There followed two articles that touched upon another major theme of interest to the consumer, namely, the disappearance of certain goods from the market and the availability of others only at extremely high prices. The authors wanted to know why cooking oil had not been available for months and why it had suddenly reappeared at astronomical prices. They also wanted to know what happened to the skimmed milk upon which the people were counting after whole milk had disappeared from the market. Was it being turned into cheese in order to increase the profit, or was it being fed to the animals? The publication then concluded with a lengthy poem, "For the Album of the Profiteer!" which concluded by declaring that "You are worse enemies of your country/ than are the Russians, Britains and Frenchmen."

Such poetic flights of fancy, as well as articles of the character described above, were common in the urban and trade union newspapers throughout the war. Little wonder, therefore, that retailers felt constantly on the defensive. In the early months of the war, they argued that the price increases were largely the consequence of military purchasing and panic buying by the municipalities. Somewhat gingerly at first, and then with much more vehemence, they attacked the purchasing policies of the municipalities, which, they argued, often bought up stores of low quality food at excessive prices and thus created a situation in which the retailers looked like profiteers because they charged higher prices for better quality products. They claimed, not entirely without evidence and reason, that municipal purchasing would have been more effective and efficient if the advice of experienced local merchants had been employed, but they were most insistent that they could ultimately do a better job of procuring and selling food than the municipalities. At the same time, they pointed out that it was the municipalities themselves that had promoted the rise of profiteering merchants by permitting new persons unable to pursue their old occupations because of the war to enter the retail trades. Lastly, the retailers contested the capacity of their old enemies, the consumer cooperatives, to do a better job of food procurement and keeping prices low. They protested what appeared to be a growing preference being shown toward the cooperatives by the authorities.[18]

The greatest concern of the retailers, however, was that they were being singled out, not only for public disapproval but also for actual sanction by the authorities. It was indeed something quite new for this once respected part of the Mittelstand to find itself increasingly on the wrong end of the law. Unhappily, there was much to justify a growing feeling of paranoia. In July 1915, for example, the Acting Commanding General of the First Bavarian Army Corps issued a decree threatening a year in prison to anyone who offered to sell or to pay for food at prices which were "inappropriately high" or "unjustifiably high." The same penalty threatened anyone who withheld food "without sufficient cause." The Acting Commanding General in Münster, Egon Baron von Gayl, enthusiastically proposed to copy the order with some additional touches of his own, such as compelling those convicted under the decree to pay the costs of publishing the judgement in three newspapers chosen by the court. Not surprisingly, the Münster Chamber of Commerce strongly protested the proposed decree. They pointed out that the language was fuzzy. At its worst, it was an invitation to denunciations; at its best, it compelled retailers to fear loss of freedom and reputation. Indeed, the flood of regulations piled troubles upon troubles for the retailers. While the requirement that they place their prices on display seemed reasonable enough, it encouraged consumer groups to go about comparing prices without regard to quality distinctions and launch complaints against retailers. Retailers were hauled into court without prior investigation and, even if acquitted, "being charged in itself tends, not only to damage the honor of the retailer but also to leave him tarnished in the eyes of the consumers, which naturally makes itself felt in his business and unfavorably influences his economic existence."[19]

Efforts by retailer organizations to persuade the authorities to compel those making accusations of profiteering to the press to identify which group they were actually accusing – producers, wholesalers, or retailers – and to prevent accusations until there was an independent investigation by the Chamber of Commerce, were rejected by General von Gayl in unsympathetic language: "The newspapers are consistently striving to serve the interests of the population, and the criticism of the excesses in the food trades, where these have developed at the present time, cannot be denied them."[20] In the course of 1916, a new and particularly unwelcome development alarmed the retailers, namely, the decision of certain large industrial firms to buy food and then sell it below cost to their workers. Not only did this threaten the economic life of the retailers by taking away business, but it also strengthened the impression that the retailer prices were excessive. The lack of solidarity especially irritated the retailers, who thought that employers had every reason to join with other entrepreneurs "for the defense and maintenance of their independence against state socialist efforts which are spreading very widely."[21]

Yet, matters only became worse, and the fight against profiteering was more complicated than the war against black marketeering, which contributed substantially to the breakdown of respect for law and authority during the war. When the head of the Saxon Price Examination Agency, Professor Obst, reviewed the previous two years of activity by the agencies in December 1917, he came to the sad conclusion that "the results do not stand in relation to the effort expended."[22] He blamed this, on the one hand, on the unhappy wording of the existing legislation and, on the other hand, on the profit seeking of commerce and industry and their hostility to the Price Examination Agencies. While changes in the wording of the legislation were subsequently undertaken so that the War Profiteering Decree of 23 July 1915 appeared in revised form in a Decree Against Price Gouging (*Preistreibereiverordnung*) of 8 May 1918, the basic sources of tension were in no way eliminated and the new regulations were indeed to generate endless new problems.

The July 1915 decree sought to impose a profit standard that was "just" or "appropriate" (*angemessen*), and placed under penalty those who sought to gain an "inappropriate profit for items needed for pursuit of the war effort or items of daily necessity after taking into consideration the total circumstances, especially market conditions."[23] The fundamental paradox of both the old and the new decree was that they maintained the principle of private profit for merchants while placing the determination of what a legitimate profit was in the hands of the authorities. The principles under which such determinations were to be made were anything but clear, and the result was extraordinary confusion and an increasing uncertainty as to what the law actually was. Obviously, the merchants had every interest in defining the range of products under control as narrowly as possible, but both the network of price examination agencies and the courts tended to expand the list of items under control in the most extraordinary way. In April 1918, for example, the German Association of Toy Makers contacted all the chambers of commerce to complain that not only toys but even Christmas tree decorations had fallen under the anti-profiteering regulations.[24]

As might be expected, the biggest headaches involved the question of what constituted an "appropriate profit." In general, this was defined as the costs, including some allowance for salary and sometimes even for risk. The net profit was defined as the difference between these costs and the selling price and, in the interpretation of the courts, was not to exceed the net profit earned in peacetime. The trouble was that the experts consulted by the courts found it impossible to adequately compare peacetime and wartime costs or peacetime and wartime net profits, especially for new products never sold before the war. The most grotesque aspect of the measurement of net profits, however, was the tendency of the courts to think in absolute rather than in relative terms, so that, as one of the countless *gravamina* from retail organizations pointed out: "It is also incomprehensible why the merchant, who in peacetime made a net profit of 20 pfennig on an item with a value of perhaps 2 marks should now, when the same item costs 8 marks, also make only the same 20 pfennig profit on this 8 mark item."[25]

What ultimately threw the entire effort to determine a just price into total disarray, however, was the erroneous belief of the merchants that the Decree of July 1915 left them free to base their prices on the market price. The courts ruled, however, that the market price was only one factor in price formation and that, under wartime conditions of shortage, "emergency market conditions" (*Notmarktlage*) often existed and that traditional price determination, when applied to such markets, constituted an abuse for which a merchant could be fined, have his goods confiscated, his business closed, and even go to jail. While the Decree of 8 May 1918 sought to remedy this ambiguity by omitting all reference to market conditions in the determination of an appropriate profit, market conditions could be subsumed in the "consideration of the total circumstances," and this left matters as uncertain as ever.[26]

The effort by a committee of Price Examination Agencies and the retail price specialist in the War Food Office, Professor Julius Hirsch, who was to exercise great and considerably more sensible influence on postwar economic policy, to set up national price guidelines for such individual items as school supplies, wood, ground black pepper, and cocoa beans, and then to illustrate the problems of determining costs by the example of the "calculations for sauerkraut in a factory that also sells vegetables and pickles," suggest that by 1918 the price examination effort was firmly committed to the achievement of the impossible and that the potentiality for conflict between the retailers and the authorities would find its limit only in the actual number of items sold on the market.

The regulations concerning excess profits did not exhaust the sanctions of the Decrees of 1915 and 1918, which also contained injunctions against hoarding in order to raise prices, collusion to raise prices, incitement to raise prices, and middleman operations that unnecessarily raised prices. The question of whether sales between and among merchants were legitimate efforts to promote economical distribution or were speculative ventures was, of course, extremely difficult to determine and necessarily provided further challenges for the authorities and the courts.[27]

It should not be thought that the retailers and wholesalers were totally unsympathetic to all these regulations. They had always supported restrictions on those allowed to engage in merchandising and marketing, and they persistently argued that the real problems stemmed from the "illegitimate" rather than the "legitimate" merchants. Thus, in Oldenburg, the retailers sought to use the black market as an excuse to petition for the banning of door-to-door peddlers, noting that many war disabled were seeking to make a living in this manner and fearing that "the public would buy from the war disabled out of sympathy for them."[28] This particularly ugly example was part of a general pattern of resentment to be found among Germany's retailers over their disadvantaged position in the war economy. They asked why the civil servants and workers were allowed to get regular cost of living increases, and why industry, craftsmen, and farmers had to be encouraged by profits, while retailers were denied the right to exceed their prewar profit rates despite the fact that they were unable to sell as much as in peacetime. They viewed the supplying of food to the workers by the factories and municipalities, and the favor shown to consumer cooperatives, as threats to their existence from large-scale capitalism, on the one hand, and creeping socialism, on the other.[29]

What was viewed as a veritable socialization of those sectors of the economy producing for daily consumer needs, especially the production and sale of foodstuffs, was by no means greeted with universal approval among those who dealt with economic questions. The maverick socialist economic writer, Richard Calwer, was particularly critical about the unreality of some consumer demands:

> When one follows the public discussions of food profiteering during the war, then one is struck by two things: on the one side, one tries to find who is guilty for the fact that there are excessively high prices, and to be sure, if possible, a whole economic group, like the farmers, the merchants, the retailers, the banks, the industrialists, even at times portions of the consuming public itself. That purely objective reasons could bring about a sharp increase in prices is something that one does not want to grant in his anger over rising prices. On the other side, one cries out, in the knowledge that one is powerless, for strong help, which in such cases ever and always means the authorities and the state. Like the child who, when it cannot help itself, calls for mother and father, so the consumers call for Father State when there are high prices.[30]

If Calwer fought against unrealistic consumer expectations, Friedrich Bendixen, speaking for the hard-pressed merchants of his native Hamburg, took an extreme free market position and argued that allowing prices to reach their natural levels would lead to greater production and bring demand into line with supply. He was extremely skeptical of the usefulness of what he labeled "fortress communism": "We decree that when we have a reduced supply which cannot satisfy the usual demand, the market is disturbed and the increased prices are artificial and harmful to the common good. We destroy the clock because the hour which it shows displeases us just when we most desperately need a measure of the time."[31]

Bendixen's optimism that Germany could manage to feed itself if free economic forces were allowed free rein was not shared by all economic liberals. His friend, Kurt Singer, was convinced that the food deficit was so great that uncontrolled prices would lead to the speculative holding back of food and prevent the supplying of the poorer classes.[32] There was one point that Bendixen made, however, which was incontestably true, and that was that the war socialism did not extend to the entire economy: "It exists for the nation's food supply. For the second part of our war needs, for armaments, weapons and munitions, it does not exist."[33] Bendixen sought to use this argument to demonstrate that productivity depended on a free market. What he failed to recognize, however, was that the war had created two markets, and that their status was by no means the same. Richard Merton, a leader of Germany's metals business who was then serving as adjutant to the head of the German field railways, General Wilhelm Groener, spelled out the problem in a memorandum for his chief of October 1916. Merton confirmed that the food supply regulations had a "socialist" character and hurt farmer initiative. If the inadequacies of the system were unquestionable, however, Merton shared Singer's view that the food supply simply was inadequate in absolute terms and required market control. The free market had become an unacceptable alternative because it would alienate the urban masses upon whose labor and morale military production depended.[34]

III

Merton was to achieve a certain notoriety for singing a different tune in July 1917 when, as adjutant to General Groener, now head of the War Office, he felt compelled to address the problems created by the orgy of profit making and wage increases that followed the launching of the Hindenburg Program and the passage of the Auxiliary Service Law of 5 December 1916. The new weapons and munitions program had led to an abandonment of all restraints on prices in the war production effort, while the law was the consummate expression of inflationary logrolling in that it permitted unrestrained wage increases to be traded off for uncontrolled price increases. Just as Merton had argued for the necessity of retaining the compulsory economy for foodstuffs three-quarters of a year earlier, so now he came to the conclusion that the war required firm intervention in the military production sector as well.

He expressed these views in a memorandum "On the Necessity of State Intervention to Regulate Employer Profits and Worker Wages" of July 1917.[35] Merton began by bluntly pointing out that the accomplishments of those producing for the war had very little to do with patriotism and love of country. They were largely motivated by the quest for profit, and the longer the war lasted, the more producers were taking advantage of the booming market for military production. Not only had the appetite of industry increased with the eating, but its huge profits and exploitation of the situation had spilled over into the labor market, where wages were being bid up constantly by competing employers, while differences in wage levels were being created between the industries producing for the war effort and those producing peacetime products. Many of these differences had nothing to do with productivity, but were simply a function of the vagaries of the wartime economy: "The workers know that their power has grown without limit, and the employers, especially the short-sighted ones or those who are to be viewed only as war industrialists and have no concern with the future development of the peacetime economy – and both together constitute a majority – can in large measure protect themselves against the increasing wage demands by increasing the prices of their products as they will, while the state, which is the final customer, can do nothing else under the present circumstances than agree to every price demanded of it."

Merton was particularly alarmed by a phenomenon which was to become one of the hallmarks of business practice in the inflation and which he correctly recognized to be undermining business morals, namely, the abandonment of firmly contracted prices in favor of arrangements in which either the price was left open or additional charges were allowed once all the cost increases occurring between the time an order was placed and the date of delivery had been calculated. Not only did this practice destroy every incentive to keep costs down, but because profits were calculated on the basis of a fixed percentage of costs, it also actually encouraged the disregard of cost increases. Merton placed the chief blame for these practices upon the producers of coal, iron, and steel, that is, the raw materials producers in heavy industry. He noted that the heavy industrialists were particularly reluctant to make long-term delivery contracts at firm prices, and thereby were forcing the manufacturers to abandon the practice of charging stable prices themselves.

Merton proposed that these problems be attacked by a virtual ban on further price increases for heavy industrial products on the grounds that heavy industrial profits were high enough already. This would make it possible to insist on stable pricing policies by all producers for the war effort. Indeed, he went so far as to argue that existing contracts should be revised toward this end. Most radical, however, was his proposal that legal measures be taken to put an end to the exploitation of the war economy by employers and workers. He urged increasing the war profits tax to the point where "no war profits actually can be made" and the passage of a law permitting the War Office to take over the management of any company where this appeared the only means of settling differences over prices and wages.

Both Groener, to whom the memorandum was addressed and who thought it a splendid program that would produce happy political results, and Merton were sent packing in August 1917, and no serious efforts to control industrial profits and wages were undertaken for the duration. Nevertheless, the memorandum did come to the attention of the officials of the Reich Office of the Interior and to its head, Karl Helfferich, who had already demonstrated himself to be one of the staunchest opponents of controls on profits and wages. Helfferich and his aides subjected the memorandum to vigorous criticism, and their comments are most revealing of the State's role in reinforcing the pattern of social development triggered by the war and sustained in the Weimar Republic.

These officials in no way shared Groener's sanguine expectations concerning the potential impact of the program. They thought that it would produce "endless political battles"[36] and that the left would try to use the situation to participate in employer profits. Repeatedly, they warned against taking away the material incentives they considered essential to war production, declaring that "it probably will be impossible to maintain production at the unconditionally necessary high levels with reduced wages and lowered profits." Lastly, they were frankly critical of further state intervention, commenting that the proposed legislation was destructive of "every private initiative, a social state pure and simple," and that the easiest way of interpreting the proposal was that "the War Office takes German industry under its compulsory authority, when and how to be determined by the War Office."[37] These marginalia finally became the basis of a lengthy memorandum, probably by Helfferich himself, in which the author insisted, on the one hand, that "with pure ethical attitudes and enthusiasms one can in no way bring a war economy to its height" and that high profits were necessary and, on the other hand, that the most important and productive industrialists wanted to remain "masters in their own house" and would never cooperate in becoming "civil servants of the economic state."[38]

These arguments for monetary incentives and for unfettered entrepreneurial initiative had by now become traditional, and Helfferich certainly believed them. There probably was more to be said for his claim that neither the personnel nor the skills were available to master the technical problems involved in assessing prices and wages throughout the country and revising existing contracts. His most compelling arguments, however, were the political ones, and they were also the most revealing because they demonstrated how much the price–wage spiral was a function of the powerlessness of the state in the face of the social and economic forces unleashed by the war economy:

> In view of the previous experience one cannot expect that the factory owners will voluntarily change in any substantial way their views about taking advantage of the boom and the appropriateness of war profits. In the numerous and very detailed negotiations last year concerning the limitation of the prices for coal and iron, the two pillars of our economic life, the intransigence of the interested parties with respect to price decreases made itself apparent. Despite the high dividends, royalties, write-offs, etc., they are convinced that the prices and profits stand in proper relationship to the risk and consider further price increases, not reductions, to be justified. Should, however, the factory owners be prepared to restrain themselves voluntarily under the Damocles Sword of the law, then the workers would only yield on the question of substantial wage reductions under direct and strong compulsion. This is demonstrated by the wage conflicts during the war. . . .[39]

Helfferich was convinced, however, that the labor leaders would use every opportunity to get the plants under War Office control, and that the government would find itself in the impossible position of trying to determine what actually constituted proper prices and wages. Just as he had warned that a law intended to provide plebiscital acclamation for total mobilization would end up with a legislative product based on parliamentary logrolling and increased labor power, so now he warned that the Auxiliary Service Law debate had provided "foretaste of the conflicts to be expected" if a law on profits and wages were presented to the Reichstag.

The extent of Helfferich's cynical skepticism was really quite extraordinary. The old utilitarian argument for the free market had been that the pursuit of self-interest would serve the common good. Helfferich's argument, however, was that the free market was necessary because the alternative would require "a sum of unselfishness, sense of obligation, subordination"[40] that was not to be found in human beings. Above all, as he made clear in the conclusion, these qualities were not to be found in German industrialists. He warned with incredible frankness that a tax

247

that wiped out war profits would not only damage Germany's war effort, but would also constitute a heavy liability for Germany's military future:

> The German Empire would, after the introduction of such a tax, not be able to conduct a new war in the foreseeable future unless it was completely on the basis of a nationalized economy. For one should not overlook the fact with respect to high war profits that the employers almost without exception have run extraordinarily great dangers. They have done so in the hope that they would be compensated with a reward for their risk, and they would not act the same way in a new war if they have to pay out their profit in full.[41]

IV

This statement casts a rather bizarre light on governmental views of industrialist patriotism, in some quarters at least, and the next war was to prove that businessmen could be "inspired" to run more formidable risks for less profit. At the same time, the invaluable protection provided by Helfferich and others, and the sheer unwillingness of the government to engage in the kinds of price controlling and surveillance that had made such a mess of the consumer sectors of the economy, should not be taken to mean that the war industrialists did not face irritating state intervention and did not fear a continuation of wartime "socialistic" measures in the future. The system for the control and distribution of raw materials created under the guidance of Walther Rathenau and Wichard von Moellendorff at the beginning of the war was viewed with considerable distrust, even if it was being managed by the industrial interests themselves, and the Rathenau-Moellendorff proposals that their model be used as the basis for a restructuring of the postwar economy that would involve a measure of central planning and *Gemeinwirtschaft* was viewed with genuine horror. They were also extremely unhappy about the government's interference in labor relations on the side of labor and the endless irritations created by government incompetence in the management of the consumer economy. In the last analysis, however, Germany's industrial and commercial leaders were far more exercised during the war about the planned economy schemes of Walther Rathenau and Wichard von Moellendorff than they were about the Marxist visions of the Social Democrats. In the last two years, they devoted increasing effort to find institutions and mechanisms to orchestrate the demobilization and transition to a peacetime economy in such a way as to prevent planned economy and other 'socialist' schemes from being effectuated.[42]

In this struggle against the perpetuation of war socialism, the dissatisfactions of farmers and merchants with the *Zwangswirtschaft* and its all-too evident failures were a powerful tool of mobilization against "socialist" ideas. In the mounting crescendo of attacks on the perpetuation of economic controls, industrialists could join with merchants and craftsmen in what appeared to be a common front. The high point of such efforts probably was a large meeting at the headquarters of the Hamburg-America Line in Hamburg on 15–16 June 1918, to which 160 Reichstag deputies came on the invitation of the Hamburg commercial interests who had organized the event. The tone of the assemblage was set by the Hamburg-America Line's President, Albert Ballin. Ballin attacked the "dangerous intention of driving the national economy and the world economy into the barrack square."[43] The agitation against state interference was sufficiently strong to paralyze the Reich Economics Office, which had been created in the fall of 1917 to deal with such questions. No program for the transition to a peacetime economy ever really was developed. In fact, the leadership of the new office, Baron von Stein and his Undersecretary, Heinrich Göppert, were basically committed to the restoration of a free market economy as rapidly as possible. The Socialist undersecretary in the RWA dealing with food questions, however, made an important qualification to this policy. Agrarians and merchants would have to wait for their liberation:

> Many people in Germany believe that the end of the war will also be the end of the price examination and antiprofiteering agencies. A dissemination of this view, not to mention its implementation, would however be fateful for the German people. On the day when peace comes, a ruined national economy will lay before us. The conditions which could develop within the Reich cannot yet be foreseen. . . . Under all circumstances, everything must be done to bring the prices of articles of daily use into conformity with the purchasing power of the people. It will be the task of the government to undertake a reduction of the price level and an adjustment to the existing levels of income with all its energy. All special interests will have to be set aside. Only the general interest counts. If we do not succeed in this, then there will be internal conflicts with unpredictable consequences. Here, in the dismantling of the wartime conditions, lies the great important tasks for the price examination agencies in the future.[44]

After much delay, these tasks were finally elaborated upon in September 1918 by Dr. Zahn, an eminent statistician and president of the Bavarian Price Examination Agency, and Dr. Thiess, of the War Food Office, both of whom advocated the continuation and even strengthening of price controls and regulation during the transition to peacetime conditions with the argument that they were absolutely necessary to prevent excessive profiteering and difficulties for the consumer during the time when other wartime controls and restraints were being eliminated. That is, the decontrol of production and distribution would, in their view, necessarily lead to rising prices, which had to be controlled. Indeed, they thought that particular attention would have to be paid to cartel and syndicate prices since the organized power of such bodies placed them in a good position to raise prices unjustifiably as well as prevent their natural decline. The proposals of Zahn and Thiess addressed themselves to what was to be a repeated problem in the coming period, namely, the prevention of decontrol measures leading to unbearable shocks to the consumer or outright exploitation. At the very best, the adjustment of demand and supply on the liberated market would lead to a preliminary period of price increases before the hoped for sufficiency of supply would drive prices down. The object of continued price controls, therefore, was to cushion this process.[45]

The incentive to "cushion" the process was made all the greater by the outcome of the war, and the alliance between industry and labor in the *Zentralarbeitsgemeinschaft*, of which August Müller was one of the most important midwives, promoted a goodly measure of decontrol in the industrial sector and maintained the price-wage tradeoffs that had characterized the wartime period. The *Zwangswirtschaft* in food products, clothing, and rents, however, was retained, thus insuring a perpetuation of the daily discrediting of "socialism" and creating a deep antagonism of farmers, retailers, houseowners, and the Mittelstand more generally and nurturing their resentments against the ability of organized capital and labor to escape the controls imposed on other classes. There was good reason for the Nazi slogan "the public good before the private good" ("*Gemeinnutz vor Eigennutz*") to be so appealing.

Notes to Chapter 11

1. On organized capitalism, see Heinrich Winkler, ed., *Organisierter Kapitalismus: Voraussetzungen und Anfänge*, Kritische Studien zur Geschichtswissenschaft, 9 (Göttingen, 1974). For my somewhat skeptical views, see pp. 150–54.

2. This essay relies heavily on themes developed at much greater length in my forthcoming book, *The Great Disorder: Politics, Economics, and Society in the German Inflation, 1914–1924* (Oxford, 1993), and I shall keep references to a minimum.

3. Franz Eulenburg, "Zur Theorie der Kriegswirtschaft," *Archiv für Sozialwissenscaft und Sozialpolitik* 43 (1916/17), pp. 349–96. It is not irrelevant that Eulenburg produced what was for many years the most important analysis of the social consequences of the inflation, see Franz Eulenburg, "Die sozialen Wirkungen der Währungsverhältnisse," *Jahrbuch für Nationalökonomie und Statistik* 122 (1924), pp. 748–94.

4. Eulenburg, "Zur Theorie der Kriegswirtschaft," p. 369.

5. Eulenburg, "Zur Theorie der Kriegswirtschaft," p. 376.

6. Eulenburg, "Zur Theorie der Kriegswirtschaft," p. 392.

7. Eulenburg, "Zur Theorie der Kriegswirtschaft," p. 393.

8. Franz Eulenburg, "Inflation. Zur Theorie der Kriegswirtschaft," *Archiv für Sozialwissenschaft und Sozialpolitik* 45 (1919), pp. 477–526, quote on 504. This important article was finished at the end of 1918.

9. Eulenburg, "Inflation. Zur Theorie der Kriegswirtschaft."

10. For useful discussions of the controlled economy in agriculture that form the basis of the account given here, see Martin Schumacher, *Land und Politik: Eine Untersuchung über politische Parteien und agrarische Interessen 1914–1923*, Beiträge zur Geschichte des Parlamentarismus und der politische Parteien 65 (Düsseldorf, 1978); Jens Flemming, *Landwirtschaftliche Interessen und Demokratie: Ländliche Gesellschaft, Agrarverbände und Staat 1890–1925*, Forschungsinstitut der Friedrich-Ebert-Stiftung. Reihe: Politik und Gesellschaftsgeschichte (Bonn, 1978); Robert G. Moeller, *German Peasants and Agrarian Politics, 1914–1924: The Rhineland and Westphalia* (Chapel Hill, 1986).

11. On these institutions see Gerald D. Feldman, *Army, Industry and Labor in Germany, 1914–1918* (Princeton, 1966; new printing by Berg Publishers, New York, Oxford, Munich, 1992), pp. 97–116.

12. Meeting of the Price Examination Agencies, 15 December 1917, Geheimes Staatsarchiv Kulturbesitz Merseburg, HB, Nr. 1032, Bl. 370.

13. Report of the Acting Commanding Generals, 15 June 1918, Bayerische Hauptstaatsarchiv München, Abt. IV, MK, l Mob zu 4, Allg. U.-A. 2, Bd. 2.

14. Report of 15 October 1918, (cf. n. 13), Bd. III.

15. Most of the account of the regulations and development of price controls discussed here is based on Hans Geithe, *Wirkungen der Lebensmittelzwangswirtschaft der Kriegs- und Nachkriegszeit auf den Lebensmitteleinzelhandel* (Halle, 1925), pp. 11ff.

16. Geithe, *Wirkungen der Lebensmittelzwangswirtschaft*, pp. 17ff. and Carl-Ludwig Holtfrerich, *The German Inflation 1914–1923: Causes and Effects in International Perspective* (Berlin & New York, 1986), p. 82.

17. Verbraucherwirtschaft im Kriege, Bd. l, Nr. 67/68, 24 Nov. 1916, in Hauptstaatsarchiv Hannover, Frauenverein.

18. See the host of chamber of commerce protests for the 1916–1918 period in the Rheinisch-Westfälisches Wirtschaftsarchiv, Köln, 5/28/1, 5/20/10, 3/10/14, 3/10/18.

19. Reichsdeutschen Mittelstandsverband to Handelskammer Münster, 9 August 1915, Rheinisch-Westfälisches Wirtschaftsarchiv, Köln, 5/28/1.

20. Petition of 4 August l915, ibid.

21. Petition of 19 September 1916, Rheinisch-Westfälisches Wirtschaftsarchiv, Köln, 3/10/16.

22. Meeting in Dresden of 15 December l917, Geheimes Staatsarchiv Kulturbesitz Merseburg, HB, Nr. 1032, Bl. 370.

23. Max Alsberg, "Wirtschaftsstrafrecht. Besonders die strafrechtliche Bekämpfung des Sozialwuchers," in Gerhard Anschütz, et. al., eds., *Handbuch der Politik* (Berlin and Leipzig, 1921), vol. 4, pp. 143–59, quotation on 150.

24. Deutscher Spielwarenverband an die deutschen Handelskammern, 8 April l918, Rheinisch-Westfälisches Wirtschaftsarchiv, Köln, 5/28/1.

25. Verein der Kaufmannschaft zu Münster an die Handelskammer für den Regierungsbezirk Münster, 10 September 1917, Rheinisch-Westfälisches Wirtschaftsarchiv, Köln, 5/28/1.

26. Alsberg, "Wirtschaftsstrafrecht," p. 150.

27. Alsberg, "Wirtschaftsrecht," pp. 150ff.

28. Kleinhandelsausschuss Sitzung, Handelskammer Oldenburg, 12 March 1918, Niedersächsisches Staatsarchiv in Oldenburg, 265/147.

29. See the host of documents from the Chambers of Commerce in ibid., 265/147; Rheinisch-Westfälisches Wirtschaftsarchiv, Köln, 5/28/1, 5/28/10, (Münster); 3/10/14, 3/10/18 (Koblenz).

30. Quoted in a speech of 8 November 1915, Rheinisch-Westfälisches Wirtschaftsarchiv, Köln, 5/28/1.

31. Kurt Singer, ed., *G.F. Knapp/F. Bendixen: Zur Staatlichen Theorie des Geldes. Ein Briefwechsel (1905–1920)* (Tübingen, 1958), p. 23.

32. Singer, *Briefwechsel*, p. 174 (n. 1).

33. Singer, *Briefwechsel*, p. 17.

34. Feldman, *Army*, pp. 114ff.

35. The Merton Memorandum is printed in Wilhelm Groener, *Lebenserinnerungen: Jugend, Generalstab, Weltkrieg*, ed. by Friedrich Freiherr Hiller von Gaetringen (Göttingen, 1957), pp. 520–25, from which the quotes and discussion below are taken.

36. Marginal comment on Groener's covering letter by Geheimer Regierungsrat Mathies, Bundesarchiv Potsdam, Reichwirtschaftsministerium, Nr. 3410, Bl. 3.

37. Marginalia to the Merton Memorandum, Bundesarchiv Potsdam, Reichwirtschaftsministerium, Nr. 3410, Bl. 6–8.

38. Unsigned and undated memorandum, Bundesarchiv Potsdam, Reichswirtschaftsministerium, Nr. 3410, Bl. 15–21, quotes on Bl. 17–18.

39. Bundesarchiv Potsdam, Reichwirtschaftsministerium, Nr. 3410.

40. Bundesarchiv Potsdam, Reichwirtschaftsministerium, Nr. 3410, Bl. 18.

41. Bundessarchiv Potsdam, Reichwirtschaftsministerium, Nr. 3410.

42. For excellent analyses, see Friedrich Zunkel, *Industrie und Staatssozialismus: Der Kampf um die Wirtschaftsordnung in Deutschland 1914–1918*, Tübinger Schriften zur Sozial- und Zeitgeschichte, 3 (Düsseldorf, 1974) and Hans Gotthard Ehlert, *Die wirtschaftliche Zentralbehörde des Deutschen Reiches 1914 bis 1919*, Beiträge zur Wirtschafts- und Sozialgeschichte, 19 (Wiesbaden, 1982).

43. Quoted in Ekkehard Böhm, *Anwalt der Handels- und Gewerbefreiheit*, Staat und Wirtschaft. Beiträge zur Geschichte der Handelskammer Hamburg, 179.

44. Speech of 15 December 1917, Geheimes Staatsarchiv Kulturbesitz Merseburg, HB, Nr. 1032.

45. September 1918 meeting of the Price Examination Agencies, Geheimes Staatsarchiv Kulturbesitz Merseburg, HB, Nr. 1032.

12

"Zwangswirtschaft" and "Socialism": Critical Remarks on Gerald D. Feldman's Contribution

Norbert Finzsch

I will not question the empirical evidence of Gerald Feldman's contribution. However, it does seem fitting to shed light on the methodological and conceptual framework of Feldman's main arguments, which point to an implicit equality between "socialism" and "war economy." Does the author really imply a virtual identity of both forms of economy?

In my comment I would like to concentrate firstly on a comparision between the Russian and German experiences as perceived by Lenin, secondly the problem of how to bring into balance production and demand in a controlled economy, and finally, I want to draw attention to those groups in the German society that suffered most from the kind of economic policies adopted in Germany during the War.

It may be very interesting to look both at Lenin's remarks pertaining to the New Economic Policy (NEP) and Evgenij Preobrazenskij's work on the new economy, which belong to about the same epoch as Eulenburg's essays on the war economy. Both theorists had gone through similar experiences as the German writer. I do not think Professor Feldman would raise protest against this procedure, since he clearly perceives the parallels between war economy and war socialism, although he does not explicitly equate the two concepts.[1]

War socialism or war communism, as it was labeled somewhat imprecisely, constitutes only one stage in the development of a state socialist economy. The renunciation of the hitherto moderate line of "one foot in socialism" led to a focus on the expropriation of industries in a grand style in the middle of 1918. The Russian society, which had been characterized until then by having access to private property, was about to be transformed into a classless communist society in one big leap. Workers' control in the factories was abolished, administration and management were centralized and tightly controlled. Economic and political disaster

Notes to Chapter 12 can be found on page 256.

directly followed these measures. Productivity plunged severely. Whereas Russia had produced 4.2 million tons of steel in 1913, it produced only 200,000 tons in 1920. In 1921 war communism had to be discounted as a total failure. What followed was the New Economic Policy (NEP), which was denoted by Lenin without much ado as a return to a state capitalist variation of socialism.[2] NEP turned out to be very successful, at least economically. A market economy and stable currency were restored. The peasants could sell their products on the free market again.

By 1925 the Russian economy had reached its prewar level of productivity. Most of the factories had been reprivatized; only the so-called command posts remained under state control. A new class of entrepreneurs and speculators – the "NEP-men" – emerged as a result. In this case, the *homines novi* were a result of the turning away from war communism.

For the purpose of analytical clarity of concepts, it is essential to point out the difference between capitalist war economy and war socialism. One must not forget that the only kind of practical socialism the world knew during those years was the Russian variation. Consequently, socialist Russia is a legitimate paradigm to probe one's analytical framework.

Eulenburg, without being a Marxist, was influenced – perhaps against his will – by Marxist terminology. Referring to a capitalist war economy, he stressed the fundamental differences by pointing out, as Feldman quotes, that "(the) modes (*sic!*) of production, property relations, and the profit motive (stayed) intact." He proceeded by saying that this kind of capitalist economy produced changes and distortions. The essence of capitalism, however, remained what it was; only on the surface were certain forms altered. In other words, war economy was an anomaly. Among the changes and distortions, he particularly mentioned the uncontrolled waste of consumer goods, which prohibited an increase in fixed capital.[3]

At least in theory, Preobrazenskij digressed from this conception in his description of a socialist economy. Also in a planned socialist economy there would be the problem of adapting production to demand. But this problem could be solved, according to the Russian theorist, "a priori, ante factum, in the consciousness of the regulation organs of society. Not prices on the market after production, but the columns of numbers of socialist bookkeeping before production, will sound the alarm. This anticipation constitutes the first characteristic trait of the new socialist mode of production that differs from the old one."[4]

I will not delve into the problem of demand-pull inflation here; the similarities between both systems are too obvious to be commented upon. In order to finance the costs of the civil war, the Bolsheviks simply increased the production of money in the mints. In 1922 the ruble had declined to 1:200,000 of its prewar value; here one can easily perceive the German and the Russian experience along the same lines. The similarities do not stop here, however. In the areas of the "circulation of capitals," the comparison between Germany and Russian is worthwhile. This concept – which was, by the way, created by Karl Marx, not by Eulenburg[5] – is applicable to socialism in its Soviet provenance and, some might argue, to socialism in general. What happened was a permanent under-capitalization, as was also the case in Germany between 1914 and 1918, if for different reasons. The state of affairs in the *Kombinate* in East Germany is evidence enough of this theory.

That German peasants had to suffer severely under the "controlled economy" (*Zwangswirtschaft*) during World War I cannot be denied. The question remains, however, whether this group nevertheless sympathized with socialism as a political doctrine. Election results for the Social Democrats on the flatland before 1914 indicate a lack of support for the Social Democratic Party on the side of the farmers. It did not take the war to make socialist politics anathema to agrarians.[6]

As to the tensions between city and country, this is a recurring pattern of German politics during the Kaiserreich and had to do only mediately with the war. The middleman as a questionable figure, both morally and economically, haunted German history ever since Johannes Eck wrote two treatises of interest at the beginning of the sixteenth century. The middleman is the standard villain, often disguised as a Jewish travesty, and the modern polemics against the "controlled economy" only had to take up the old, and only too familiar, *topos*. The 1915 ordinance to fix prices (*Preistreibereiverordnung*) is, ironically, reminiscent of the discussions of the moral economy and the bread riots of the eighteenth century. Both relied on the concept of a "just price" and a "justifiable profit," in contrast to an excessive profit. Certainly the very obscure definition of the word "justifiable" (*angemessen*) in the context of 1915 and the theoretically unclear meaning of the word "profit" in the ordinances between 1915 and 1918 indicate the reemergence of pre-modern concepts in this area.[7] The question may be asked as to why, with a controlled economy in wartime, Germany did not return to traditional economic values and ideas. It was especially the articles in the consumers' journals that pointed to a mode of production that reintroduced the values of the Middle Ages during which the guilds had a say.

Another group that suffered under war production was the middle-class retailers. Traditionally they belonged to a group that saw its interest best served by the "ghetto party" Social Democrats, especially after the election of 1890. Within this group, the combination of agitation against

Zwangswirtschaft and socialism is very plausible and merits further investigation. At the contemporary level of discussion of the history of political parties and elections, it remains unclear how profoundly conservative arguments and/or effects of long-term trends in modernization have influenced voting behavior.[8] I would have liked to have read some quotations out of the "host of documents" from various Chambers of Commerce that prove that *Zwangswirtschaft* was indeed perceived by the retailers as "creeping socialism."[9]

Notes to Chapter 12

1. Page 233 of his paper.

2. Wladimir I. Lenin, "Die Neue Ökonomische Politik und die Aufgaben der Ausschüsse für politisch-kulturelle Aufklärung," in *Lenin, Ausgewählte Werke in sechs Bänden,* Band 6 (Frankfurt am Main, 1971), pp. 369–418.

3. Feldman, p. 234.

4. Evgenij A. Preobrazenskij, *Die Neue Ökonomik*, Moscow 1926, here quoted from the first German edition (Berlin, 1971), p. 68. My translation.

5. Karl Marx, *Das Kapital*, first volume; Marx Engels, *Werke* (MEW), vol. 23, p. 162.

6. Heinrich Best, "Politische Modernisierung und parlamentarische Führungsgruppen in Deutschland, 1867–1918," in *Historical Social Research*, vol. 13 (1988), pp. 5–74, here pp. 21, 63–74.

7. Feldman's paper, pp. 236ff.

8. Gerhard A. Ritter, *Die Deutschen Parteien 1830–1914*, (Göttingen, 1985), p. 49. Best, *Politische Modernisierung*, statistischer Anhang, pp. 63–74. Heinrich Best, "Recruitment, Careers, and Legislative Behavior of German Parliamentarians, 1848–1952," in *Historical Social Research*, vol. 23 (1982), pp. 20–54.

9. Footnote 29 in Feldman's paper.

Discussion

The session on "Economic and Social Change under Duress" was chaired by Carl-Ludwig Holtfrerich. The papers by Gerald Feldman, Norbert Finzsch, and David Kennedy stimulated a lively discussion on the impact of World War I on both the American and German economies: the managing of the war economies, the extent of state intervention, the problem of how to find a definiton for what was regarded as socialism in Germany or the United States, the possibilities of a comparative analysis.

In his written remarks on Norbert Finzsch's comment, Gerald Feldman emphasized that "Mr. Finzsch has done a splendid job of raising the most serious and conceptual problems . . . of reminding us that the 'real' and 'true' socialism practiced in revolutionary Russia was something quite different in both theory and practice from war socialism. It is a dangerous business for the historian to let his or her own analysis blend with perceptions of contemporaries." After "conceding the point that sharper analytical distinctions are needed or should be maintained," Feldman nevertheless inisted that the approach taken in his paper is "a fruitful one," especially "in the light of the long-term history of socialism in our century. A good argument can be made that socialism and communism — if I may sin by blurring distinctions once again — have been discredited above all by their failures in the realm of distribution, but this has been the problem of all controlled economies from the First World War to the present time. For consumers, the common denominators have been *Mangelwirtschaft* and *Versorgungsschwierigkeiten*. In this context, I am not entirely convinced that the controlled economy in Germany and its problems are fully explained by the persistence of tradition attitudes, a return to pre-modern forms, and 'moral economy' notions. Those elements certainly are there, but they have an entirely different meaning in a modern industrial society at war. One can also argue that communism is rooted in certain primitive Christian notions and that it, of course, shares many of the pre-modern attitudes with respect to profit, interest, and the role of middlemen entertained by anti–capitalist ideologies on the right. This has limited value in explaining its actual history. Perhaps, in the last analysis, the fundamental issue in all these societies has been and is the willingness to accept the market and to use price incentives. That is what England did in the First World War, much to the advantage of both agriculture and labor. A major problem in Germany was that many capitalists were quite prepared to see other groups 'socialised' when it was to their advantage. The lack of solidarity shown by the industrial employers especially irritated the retailers who, to provide Mr. Finzsch with at least one explicit reference to anxiety over creeping socialism from September 1916, thought that industrial employers had every reason to join with retailers 'against the widely spreading state socialist efforts.'" (Reichsdeutscher Mittelstandsverband, Landesausschuß Rheinland und Westfalen to the Handelskammer Koblenz, 19 September, 1916, in: *Rheinisch-Westfälisches Wirtschaftsarchiv Köln 3/10/16.*)

State intervention in both the United States and Germany was the central issue of the detailed discussion. What did it mean for the war efforts? How did it influence economic and social developments in both countries during the war? What kind of consequences did state intervention during the war have for post-World War I developments?

Stephen Schuker thoroughly agreed with David Kennedy's point "that the expansion of the Federal Government in World War I in the United States took place within the volontarist tradition." He argued, however, "that the expansion of the Federal Government itself creates new facts no matter what ideology is used to justify it."

In her comments on David Kennedy's paper, Joan Hoff-Wilson warned about overreacting to a set of historiographical works that do and did perhaps overemphasize the First World War as a watershed. She suggested that although structural changes might have been minimal, experience during the war did have a "tremendous impact" on the thinking of individuals and groups of businessmen. She emphasized that the split between the American business community was much more discernable in the course of the war and immediately following it – the distinction between what the bankers and the large manufacturers in the United States perceived to be in the best interest of the country was quite different from what the small manufacturers thought to be in the best interest of the United States economically from both the financial and commercial point of view. Joan Hoff-Wilson stressed this evolutionary change in the mentality. "There were important segments of the business community that came out of the war thinking differently about the economic position of the United States in the world."

Lloyd Ambrosius suggested that during the war there developed what he called "a strange mixture" between the private sector and the state to explain why the Federal Government of the United States could afford to be less coercive than the Imperial German government. In America "the state does not have to be so directly coercive if it can tie into private networks and get them to do what they want to do." In the case of Wilson, "the Red Scare is an obvious example of hysteria where people experience oppression, but the Red Scare was officially sanctioned and officially encouraged by Wilson, which he specifically encouraged on his Western tour when he was trying to sell the idea of a League of Nations." Wilson had been successful in manipulating public opinion.

As to the postwar period, various participants of the discussion emphasized different developments in the United States and Germany. Lloyd Gardner pointed out "that one of the reactions in America to state intervention in the economy was like they had touched a hot stove. They did not want to touch it again."

When looking at the German side, Stephen Schuker felt "that *Zwangswirtschaft* never really ends in Germany. That although it is cut back in the stabilization crisis of 1924, it is defeated only temporarily. The Weimar Republic, even in the later 1920s, remained a socialist state – or perhaps it is better to use Peter Krüger's phrase of an anti-liberal state, a state in which people do not believe in the free market." Carl-Ludwig Holtfrerich commented on the different attitudes of industrialists in both countries towards monopoly and cartellization. After the war, German industrialists had wanted to get rid of the controlled economy as soon as possible, but "American industrialists took a different viewpoint." Some of them "wanted to keep some of the achievements of the controlled economy." While cartels had been legalized in Germany in the 1890s, and industry could well organize itself, this kind of organization was open to American industry only when exemptions from the antitrust laws were legalized during the war. "And that aspect they wanted to keep for the American economy after the war," Holtfrerich emphasized.

During the debate on state intervention, there emerged consensus that socialism was used as a scapegoat by those who opposed state regulation of the economy. From a historical perspective, Elliot Shore argued, it is quite obvious that socialism was failing by 1912, "yet it is perceived as not having failed." It is even "perceived as something to be afraid of." Therefore, state intervention could be labeled as socialism in order to effectively discredit those activities of the state. In Germany, as Gerald Feldman argued, many deficiencies of the German *Kriegswirtschaft* were labeled as *Mangelwirtschaft*. For many Germans, state intervention obviously had not brought about the desired results, and this contributed to the "discrediting of socialism." Gerald Feldman thought it significant that in Germany, as in the United States, "forms of state intervention you liked" were not socialist, "but any form of state intervention you do not like become socialist."

Werner Link raised the question of whether there were common experiences of the war economies in the United States and in Germany. He particularly referred to the relationship between government and business corporations, where both had been forced to cooperate under external pressures. Once these external pressures had disappeared, it was quite obvious that "things developed differently in the United States and in Germany." In the United States the tendency was to find the "road back to normalcy against state intervention," external pressures having disappeared. Germany, on the other hand, had to face the situation of a vanquished nation, which had to cope with a variety of external pressures during the early 1920s: reparations, occupation of the Ruhr, etc. Did these different experiences also produce different mentalities as far as the acceptance of state intervention was concerned?

Link's comparative approach was taken up by David Kennedy in his concluding statement. David Kennedy cited Churchill, who characterized the time span from roughly 1914 to 1945 as the period of a second Thirty Years War. "Europe feels the effect of this almost from the outset, but the United States does not really feel the effects until some place midway through the period, probably the Great Depression." This explains the First World War, David Kennedy argued, as the palest, most minimum kind of rehearsal in the United States for the kind of social, economic, political, and industrial processes and changes it took on by the 1930s and 1940s. "I think that will be my answer to Professor Link's question about the simliarities between the two experiences." They might have been "assimilated to one another over the thirty year period, but the timing is different, the sequence is different." There was consensus that a comparative approach as suggested by Werner Link and other participants of the discussion is important and certainly needs further exploration.

PART IV

Imperialism and Revolution

13

The United States, the German Peril and a Revolutionary World: The Inconsistencies of World Order and National Self-Determination

Lloyd C. Gardner

The election of 1800, a Republican newspaper appeared to believe, "would fix our national character and determine whether republicanism or aristocracy would prevail. Moreover, the solution of this problem in America might perhaps turn the suspended balance in favor of liberty or despotism throughout the world."

Joseph Charles, *The Origins of the American Party System*[1]

Gore Vidal, the iconoclastic chronicler of American history, has reached the World War I era and its aftermath in his newest novel, *Hollywood*. Vidal is surprisingly sympathetic to Woodrow Wilson, skeptical about the nature of American democracy and the crusade the president was about to embark upon, but seeing Wilson, the person, as genuinely committed to bettering the conditions of international life. Vidal paints the scene in the House of Representatives the night Wilson asked for a war declaration this way:

As if he had anticipated what wildness he was provoking around the campfire, Wilson moved swiftly to high, holy ground. . . . "[We] fight thus for the ultimate peace of the world, and for the liberation of its peoples, the German peoples included; for the rights of nations great and small and the privilege of men everywhere to choose their way of life and of obedience. The world must be made safe for democracy."[2]

Wilson was serious, Vidal implies, about the compatibility of self-determination and world order: "the privilege of men everywhere to choose their way of life and of obedience." He sympathized with the plight of the submerged, yet he frequently felt the need to emphasize obedience over choice. He was convinced, for example, that industrial

Notes to Chapter 13 can be found on page 278.

nations had both the obligation to lead, and the right to expect compliance from the less "advanced" countries of the world. He saw nothing wrong with his own formulation of the basic problem: how to teach less endowed peoples to elect good men. Thus he espoused a double-standard: industrial nations and the rest of the world. Obviously, race played a fairly significant role in such thinking about both national questions and international issues.

From the White House he preached sermons to the world, and he defined individuals and nations in black and white, but he understood the complexity of the matter, i.e., that self-determination and world order could be both complementary and contradictory. And if he did not have the answers to these paradoxes, he was aware of the fate that awaited a non-comprehending stand-pat conservatism in a world swept by firestorms of war and revolutionary tides. "The conservatives do not realize," he said on the way to the Paris Peace Conference, "what forces are loose in the world at the present time. Liberalism is the only thing that can save civilization from chaos – from a flood of ultra-radicalism that will swamp the world. . . . Liberalism must be more liberal than ever before, it must even be radical, if civilization is to escape the typhoon."[3]

How could liberalism become radical and still remain liberalism? How were liberals to work their way between self-determination and world order, without falling into the abyss of chaos or giving up freedom for the sake of "civilization"? If one is looking for an entry point into the complex subjects we are considering here, a good place to begin is with the very familiar, and then branch outward. The House/Wilson relationship has been studied from many angles, for example, but perhaps not adequately from the perspective of what historian Bernard Semmel has called "social imperialism."[4] Professor Semmel has elucidated the intellectual climate in Europe and England from the turn of the century to World War I, the impact of social Darwinism, the rise of the socialist challenge, and elite comprehension of the changes these intellectual forces wrought on imperial and foreign policies.

Nineteenth-century liberalism stressed self-determination at home and abroad; twentieth-century liberalism would stress government intervention and world order. When the Great Depression finally erased old certainties, Walter Lippmann pondered the meaning of the dramatic changes. To meet demands that they take control of economic affairs, Lippmann wrote, national leaders everywhere were acting out new roles. "They will enormously increase the scope of government and greatly intensify the dependence of the individual upon government." Questions settled by the marketplace in the nineteenth century would now become the subject of government-to-government arrangements.

The effort by states to manage the commerce of the world would reshape as well the older questions of diplomacy, boundaries as well as tariffs, the balance of power as well as industrial strength.[5]

The chief preoccupation of the future would now become the attempt to sort out the division of labor in the world economy. Writing privately to a friend, Lippmann put the question this way:

> The great difficulty in seeing into the future, to my mind, lies in trying to decide whether or not the die is cast for a world of more or less self-sufficient, or at least isolated economic empires, or for a truly international world with international markets. All our conclusions depend upon which premise we adopt and I don't know that any one of us is yet able to decide that fundamental question. . . .[6]

Actually, it could be argued, these were the very questions facing American leaders much earlier, if still in veiled fashion. Colonel House's crucial role during the war as Wilson's alter ego is well-known to historians. Wilson used the phrase to describe their relationship, and later observers have found no reason to doubt it. House was, in a very real (if informal) sense, the first National Security Adviser.

Like the later holders of that trusted position – McGeorge Bundy and Henry Kissinger being the prime examples, of course – House controlled the flow of information to the White House. Whether receiving powerful visitors at his residences in Massachusetts and New York, sitting with the president in the White House, or carrying out secret diplomatic missions, House provided a useful, private channel through which information passed to and from Wilson. Given his position, the presidential adviser was able to filter and fit the information thus transmitted into an agreed framework – and policy was made.

It was not this simple, of course. Wilson did not depend upon House for ideas or for carrying all his ideas into action. He did, however, look to him often for confirmations of various sorts. When House provided Wilson with the assurances he wanted, this meant he was also able to influence affairs in subtle ways that the president may or may not have been entirely aware of, and may or may not have entirely wished to know. I suggested immediately above that the relationship operated from an agreed framework, but they did not approach that common ground from exactly the same direction. Each man represented, in fact, a major tendency in American thought about how to deal with the increasingly complex and contradictory world everywhere around them, whether close to home in Mexico, across the Atlantic, or as far away as China.

Looked at casually, the differences may seem only a matter of degree, and, of course, that is so. It was not yet the stark dilemma that Lippmann described. Nor was it the lesser case that the objectives or means for achieving their desired objectives were always seen to be in opposition. But it is into that span, however narrow and however disguised (at least sometimes) from themselves, that a wedge was driven that reflected the tensions in liberal thought before and during the Great War.[7] Finally, one must take into account that House and Wilson spoke of relations between the great and small powers in Europe quite differently than they did about relations between the white, industrial, urban nations, and the colored, agricultural, rural peoples Eric Wolf describes as those "without a history."

Still, Wilson approached the problem of a framework for understanding imperialism and revolution from a point of view not unlike that offered by the British theoretician John A. Hobson, in that while they both saw evidence that imperialism emanated from the capitalist system (thereby producing the distortions of nineteenth-century liberalism that affected both the metropolis and the colony), both – as believing liberals – also saw imperialism as a choice rather than a circumstance of the economic system.

A nation could not be said to be truly "self-determined" if the special interests (monopolies, and what would later be called the military–industrial complex) dominated foreign and domestic policy. It was necessary, therefore, to sever the links between the special interests and government policy through a powerful act of will (a reaching for the higher good) that would also coincide with economic good sense. Wilson's first Secretary of State, William Jennings Bryan, talked incessantly about what he called the "economic value of righteousness." Imperialism, he would assert, actually blocked the development of overseas trade and investment and destroyed the potential for self-determination at home and abroad.

President Wilson, Bryan told a newspaper reporter early on in the Administration, did not intend to curtail foreign investment because he opposed "Dollar Diplomacy." Quite the opposite. "The preceding administration attempted to till the field of foreign investment with a pen knife; President Wilson intends to cultivate it with a spade."

> Many rich fields are awaiting development – the development of Central America and South America is still in its infancy – and our nation is the nation to which our sister republics to the south . . . naturally look for such assistance as they need. . . . Why should they not look upon the United States as the great clearing house of their natural wealth?[8]

Wilson used the same language in talking about Mexico's future in 1918. Their country, he told Mexican newspaper editors, was a "wonderful storehouse of treasure." Once the war ended and fair dealing and justice became the rule throughout the world, Mexico would prosper as never before, "because so soon as you can admit your own capital and the capital of the world to the free use of the resources of Mexico, it will be one of the most wonderfully rich and prosperous countries in the world."[9]

He could guarantee this happy outcome because, as a result of the Great War, "the influence of the United States is somewhat pervasive in the affairs of the world." At the opposite pole from this kind of "disinterested service" America offered the world was the enemy, German imperialism. Thus the Great War was not just a struggle with the Kaiser's drive to world power, but in Wilson's mind the turning point in history when, as in 1800, American liberals believed their nation and the world stood suspended between "liberty or despotism."

Of course German imperialism would have to be defeated on the battlefield, but when it was swept away, with it must go the European domination of the world order. This was especially so after the Bolshevik Revolution raised the question of whether there was any role at all for "liberalism" in the future, but it is well to keep in mind in this regard that Wilson's first military intervention in Mexico in 1914, ostensibly to prevent the landing of German arms to resupply the dictator Huerta, had been undertaken to forestall a British move to protect oilfields in the Tampico area.[10]

While he waged war on Germany, therefore, the menace was all of European imperialism, a reflection of the dominance of the old order. "Under your instruction," Wilson told the teachers of America in 1918:

> children should come to see that it was the high logic of events and the providence of God that the United States and Germany, the one the most consistent practitioner of the new creed of mankind and the other the most consistent practitioner of the old, should thus meet in battle to determine whether the new democracy or the old autocracy shall govern the world, and under your instruction the children should be made to understand the stern duty and the supreme privilege which belong to the United States of being chief interpreter to the world of those democratic principles which we believe to constitute the only force which can rid the world of injustice and bring peace and happiness to mankind.[11]

Henceforth, if Wilson's vision were realized, "democratic principles," and not entangling alliances and secret treaties, would rule the world. And this was because "the high logic of events and the providence of God" had put the United States in a position to be the "chief interpreter to the world" of those principles. What he aimed at, then, was a world order somehow purified by the elimination of the power of imperialist forces in each nation, and one, therefore, that would allow nations the greatest degree of self-determination consistent with liberal ideas and institutions.

Colonel House early on had projected the key role for Wilson in the peacemaking process. House had insisted that the European nations would have to come to him (though later than he expected) to put the world back in order. He regretted rather more – in fact, a lot more – than Wilson would the decline of European prestige brought about by the war in what would later be called the "Third World." "I told him," House recorded in his diary of a conversation with German Chancellor Theobold von Bethmann Hollweg, "western civilization had broken down, and there was not a market-place or a mosque in the East where the West of to-day was not derided. He admitted this, but said the fault was not Germany's."[12]

House's ruminations on this occasion, and indeed his thoughts throughout his diplomatic activities, reflect an American variation not on Hobson, but on Karl Kautsky and super-imperialism. There are indications in House's political novel, *Philip Dru: Administrator*, which he published anonymously in 1912, that the Colonel was familiar with Karl Marx's theories, and that Dru's "revolution" was a proposed alternative to socialism. Perhaps Dru was more reflective of House's secret preference for TR's "New Nationalism" over his friend's "New Freedom," for both the national and international policies Dru pursued when he became "Administrator" of the United States, replacing a hopelessly corrupt regime under the "old" Constitution, stress order and cooperation among corporate bodies.

As the nation moved to the center of world affairs, neither the Wilson/Hobson reformist approach nor the House/Kautsky variations turned out to be a viable policy for the United States, and the tension between the two stood out all the more clearly in the aftermath of the Bolshevik Revolution.

In House's novel, no sooner had Philip Dru overcome the old order and put things to right in the United States, replacing the defunct elected government with a non-political regime run by experts and technicians, than he must face a revolution in Mexico, where, "in spite of repeated warnings," adventurers "had obstinately continued their old-time habit of revolutions without just cause, with the result that they neither had stable governments within themselves, nor any hope of peace with each other." What is there for Dru to undertake but an intervention to persuade the would-be revolutionary leader the error of his ways? During a truce on the battlefield, Dru tries to explain why he cannot be allowed to succeed:

> Our citizens and those of other countries have placed in your Republic vast
> sums for its development, trusting to your treaty guarantees, and they feel

much concern over their properties, not only to the advantage of your people, but to those to whom they belong.[13]

This achievement is capped, logically enough from House's viewpoint, by an informal entente among the industrial nations to cooperate in the development of the rest of the world. Before be became convinced, as did Wilson, that "high logic" required the United States to enter the war against Germany and the Central Powers, House believed Berlin's ambitions could be converted, à la the outcome in *Philip Dru*, to the general good. England should be less intolerant of German ambitions, the colonel told a friend even before Wilson entered the White House, and its leaders should be encouraged "to exploit South America in a legitimate way," not only by developing the resources of the continent, but by sending "her surplus population there . . . such a move would be good for South America and would have a beneficial result generally."[14]

On the eve of the war, House undertook the first of his several diplomatic missions to Europe on behalf of President Wilson. He informed Kaiser Wilhelm that Wilson believed that because the United States was a disinterested party, it was in a position to "compose the difficulties here."[15] To Wilson he wrote, however, that the British had become too absorbed in the social events of the season, a social Darwinist commentary, of course, in this critical time, while, "In Germany, their one thought is to advance industrially and to glorify war."[16]

But he was not completely discouraged. "I proposed, when I go home," he recorded of a talk with Sir Cecil Spring-Rice, "that I take up with the President the formation of a definite foreign policy in regard to financial investments in the undeveloped countries of the world, particularly South America."

> My plan is that if England, the United States, Germany and France will come to an understanding concerning investments by their citizens in undeveloped countries, much good and profit will come to their citizens, as well as to the countries needing development. Stability would be brought about, investments would become safe, and low rates of interest might be established.[17]

Apparently intrigued by House's definition of Wilsonian internationalism, Spring-Rice suggested (perhaps with an inner smile) that the problem would be to convince the United States – meaning Wilson – that concessions were not usurious, and did not produce a tendency toward political control of an area. After all, although the ambassador did not mention it on this occasion, Wilson had firmly rejected further American participation in the China Consortium on precisely those grounds. The Consortium was a six-power group formed for the purpose of making loans to China. When asked whether he would "request" American bankers to participate, Wilson had responded, "The conditions of the loan seem to us to touch very nearly the administrative independence of China itself, and this administration does not feel that it ought, even by implication, to be a party to those conditions."[18]

Yet House did not shy from presenting the plan he had in mind to Wilson, even suggesting that only such an agreement between the money-lending nations would guarantee that the "waste places of the earth" could be developed under reasonable conditions. He did add that he had warned leaders in the countries he had visited that "usurious interest and concessions which involve the undoing of weak and debt involved countries, would no longer be countenanced." British liberals were enthusiastic about the idea, he told the president. It would do away with much of the international friction that "such things cause," and it would be a step towards bringing about stability "in those unhappy countries which are now misgoverned and exploited both at home and abroad."[19]

House had obviously taken Spring-Rice's admonition to heart, and phrased his suggestions accordingly. Yet his greatest fear in the early months of the war remained that France and Russia would seek to rend Germany in twain, thereby foreclosing an agreement along the lines he had imagined, perhaps forever. The possibility of Russian dominance on the European continent did not appeal to either House or Wilson. Berlin had been riding for a fall, he confided to his diary, but it was to London's and Washington's interest that German integrity be preserved, stripped, of course, of its military and naval power. He would, he further confided, seek to "persuade the president to this course."[20]

The question they felt they had to face was whether Germany's resort to arms permitted of any "solution" *except* an Allied "victory." Thus Wilson and House faced the same dilemma as did Churchill and Lloyd George in the prewar years, when, it became apparent, the reform program at home would constantly be held hostage to the fear of foreign aggression. Whether the German menace was real or not, conservatives would always be able to divert attention from the social agenda at home, and channel the nation's energies into defense, unless that threat was removed once and for all.[21]

Wilson was thinking about such things, certainly, when he told Spring-Rice only a month after the war began that, "Everything that I love most in the world is at stake." If the Central Powers succeeded, "we should be forced to take such measures of defense here as would be fatal to our form of Government and American ideals."[22] In this regard, House felt it was a great pity that the men around the Kaiser were all so bloody minded. His plan would have succeeded, he had convinced himself, but for their fears, and German militarism would have been re-channeled into productive outlets.

Talking with Spring-Rice once again, House wondered if, "I might have been the immediate although unconscious cause of this war." Sir Cecil had made the suggestion, but House eagerly picked it up, stretching it out to the idea that the war party had been frightened at the near success of the House mission to prevent war, and decided that they must take advantage of the Archduke's murder to precipitate matters, "believing they were coming to the end of the past, and that it was, as Sir Cecil explained it, 'now or never'."[23]

Still, and with an inkling here of the later hope that the "war party," including the Kaiser, could be somehow separated from the German "nation," House continued to press the idea that – probably through Wilson's mediation – the warring sides could be brought together to negotiate a peace that would not leave Russia in a dominant position. "If Germany and Austria are entirely crushed," House noted their agreement, "neither of us could see any way by which Russia could be restrained. He [Wilson] thought I should bring this strongly to Sir Edward Grey's attention."[24]

The two men went back and forth on the question of whether, and to what degree, Germany had to be defeated. Departing from his usual (if gradually receding) hope that the Germans were somehow salvageable for his plan, House expressed a fear that the Kaiser would hold America to accounts if Germany won the war. He has it in mind, House suggested to the president, to declare that the Monroe Doctrine extended only to the equator. "He [Wilson] replied that the war was perhaps a God-send to us, for if it had not come we might have been embroiled in war ourselves."[25]

All the more remarkable, then, that when House undertook his mission in the early months of 1915, a mission to encourage the warring nations to invoke the president's mediation, he returned to the prewar plan for Germany to develop South America. Now, of course, it was being offered by House as compensation for major German concessions in any peace negotiations. When he told Wilson about the conversations he had had with German officials, however, the colonel made it appear that the proposals had all come from them. Yet he did not hide his continuing interest in a great power trusteeship over the "waste places of the earth," as he had often referred to the undeveloped areas:

> I also pointed out that in the future there would be far less segregation of interests throughout the world than there had been in the past, that inter-

communication had become so general that a new and better outlet for expansion would probably take place.[26]

Berlin's inauguration of submarine warfare – viewed from this framework – allowed Wilson the opportunity to press a Hobsonian interpretation onto German behavior that coincided with his fundamental interpretation of the causes of imperialism, and gave House the opportunity to continue the search for an "acceptable" Germany to play its role "throughout the world" after the war.

"In the event of war with Germany," House wrote the president at the height of the *Lusitania* crisis,

> I would suggest an address to Congress placing the blame of this fearful conflict upon the Kaiser and his military entourage and I would exonerate the great body of German citizenship stating that we were fighting for their deliverance as well as the deliverance of Europe.[27]

House added that he thought such an approach would have a fine effect on German-Americans, but that was really a minor consideration. The first submarine crisis passed, but by the end of 1915 it was apparent that "neutrality" was fast becoming an untenable position. House devised the instructions for his next mission to Europe. The plan was for the colonel to seek Allied agreement to a set of principles on which to end the war and establish a just peace. If the Central Powers refused to parley on the basis of these principles, the United States would enter the war.

Wilson undercut the new House plan by adding the key word "probably" to the promise to enter the war, but Sir Edward Grey, the British Foreign Secretary, well understood what was at stake. After all, House had explained it perfectly clearly. "I told him if we failed to come to a better understanding with England and failed to help solve the problems brought about by this war properly," House reported to the president, "it would be because his government and people could not follow you to the heights you would go."[28]

In effect, both the Allies and the Central Powers were being asked to trust American judgment and statesmanship in bringing about a new world. The key for House was that if this second plan came into force – military intervention on the Allied side – it would come at a moment when neither side in Europe had a chance for a decisive victory, and American intervention would be as much to protect a future German role as it would be to defeat German militarism. "My thought was," he wrote Wilson of his talks with British leaders, "that England might give Germany a freer hand in Asia and look to Africa as her sphere of influence."[29]

As it became clear that Allied statesmen had no intention of "inviting" an intervention, House revealed still more clearly his concern for a post-war concert of nations. "The impression grows," he complained to Sir Edward Grey, "that the Allies are more determined upon punishment of Germany than upon exacting terms that neutral opinion would consider just."[30] That being the case, House and Wilson agreed that the president should begin at once to define American war aims unilaterally – aims that would be imposed on both sides.

The result was the conception of a "League to Enforce Peace." One curious aspect of this development in American diplomacy during the summer of 1916 was Secretary of State Robert Lansing's private dissent from what he feared was a House/Wilson convergence on a plan that would not really eliminate the German menace. Historians have often seen Lansing as the unheeded voice of "realism" in Wilson's cabinet. It is interesting, therefore, to see Lansing worrying about the president's lack of sensitivity to the ideological questions posed by the war. Wilson did not seem to grasp the full significance of the situation, Lansing complained. "That German imperialistic ambitions threaten free institutions everywhere apparently has not sunk very deeply into his mind. For six months I have talked about the struggle between Autocracy and Democracy, but do not see that I have made any great impression."[31]

House was to blame, he thought, with his schemes for Wilson's mediation to end the war. (Actually, and without understanding it fully, Lansing had grasped the difference between House's approach and Wilson's as yet nebulous design for a league of nations.) He would play along with these ideas, Lansing wrote privately, but only because he thought they would not amount to anything. Ironically, House also worried that the president might miss the point by going to war with the Allies over violations against American commerce.[32] The point, as House consistently saw it, was to construct a new concert of powers.

There was great peril, consequently, in the president's "Peace Without Victory" speech in January 1917. But this was because House had now concluded that diplomatic intervention, without either side being defeated, would only repeat the frustrations he had faced in trying to "talk sense" to the Kaiser in 1914 and to Sir Edward Grey in 1915 and 1916. Each was surrounded with a coterie of chauvinists at home and importuning allies, and therefore unable to respond to Wilsonian overtures.

What separated House from Lansing, on the other hand, was the colonel's conviction that either diplomatic or military intervention must result in an outcome that would force both warring sides to accept American conceptions of world order. Crushing Germany completely was not enough, and in any event was not wise given future problems. One could not rest secure, as Lansing suggested, with the simple notion that the war was between democracy and autocracy. "I am not at all afraid of Germany after the war," he wrote Wilson, "unless, indeed, England is put out of commission, but it is conceivable that we might have trouble with England in the event she is victorious."[33]

Germany's resumption of submarine warfare put an entirely new face on matters, though the Zimmerman Note and the Russian Revolution clinched the question of war or peace. Up until the actual time Congress responded to Wilson's request for a declaration of war, American war aims – and House's plans – were entirely theoretical. The emphasis was bound to be different now. The great change, of course, was that Wilson's views, not those propounded by House on his behalf, determined American policy. The president's first initiative in wartime diplomacy actually predated his request for a declaration of war. On 8 February 1917, Lansing sent a message to the American Embassy in London that had been drafted by Wilson. The import of the message was that the president was interested in maintaining a "channel" to the Central Powers even if the United States should go to war.

For this reason, the United States did not wish to break with Austria. A recent Allied statement of war aims had, unfortunately, set forth objectives that meant the virtual dismemberment of the Austro-Hungarian Empire. If Wilson could give the Austrians assurances that this would not happen, the message went on, he could "in a very short time force the acceptance of peace upon terms which would follow the general lines of his recent address to the Senate [the Peace Without Victory speech] regarding the sort of peace the United States would be willing to join in guaranteeing."[34]

Rejecting Wilson"s overture, the new British Prime Minister nevertheless insisted that only by being an active participant in the war could the president achieve his goals. "We have no policy of sheer dismemberment," said Lloyd George, "but we must stand by the nationals of our allies, such as the Roumanians, the Slavs, the Serbians and the Italians."[35] This clever bit of diplomacy managed to reject Wilsonian aims while offering assurances of ultimate redemption. But more than that, it pointed to the difficulty of pursuing a policy of "self-determination." Wilson had argued the Austrian point, as he would many others, on the grounds of national self-determination. It seems not to have occurred to either House or Wilson that there might be several different claims of "national self-determination" overlapping from one disputed territory to another.

If Wilson's hope for a peace based on "self-determination" was thus flawed at the outset, aside from anything Lloyd George had said about

Allied claims, House had yet another variation of his plan to pursue. A combination of American military might and diplomatic pressure on the Allies still could turn things in the right direction. The March revolution in Russia had already changed prospects for Wilsonian diplomacy. Like Lenin and the Bolsheviks after he came to power, House believed that a great deal hinged on what happened in Germany. If the "liberals" in Germany could overthrow the Kaiser, the war could end on a triumphant note for American policy and a new world order could be established that would not result in the overweening dominance of either side.

Everything was balanced delicately on this thin hope. "Unless we can break down Germany from within," House wrote the president on 19 July 1917, "I am afraid of what may happen in France and Russia before the year ends."[36] That was the dilemma. If Germany did not have its revolution, the situation inside the Allied nations might deteriorate – and another form of revolution that would be less hospitable to "liberalism" and American objectives might appear. And, of course this is what happened with the Bolshevik Revolution.

The German "peril" now, i.e., after the Bolshevik Revolution, could not be "cured" by internal revolution. And this left the emphasis completely upon a world order imposed by the victors. The League of Nations, as Wilson's Progressive opponents at home would argue, would resemble a new version of the Concert of Europe, a military alliance to enforce the terms of the Treaty of Versailles. It will always be a question as to whether Wilson could have won the day for his original vision had the Russian situation stabilized before the October Revolution and the German "revolution" occurred sooner. Probably not.

Yet that should not obscure the impact of the Bolshevik triumph on the shape of the peace treaty and the League of Nations. It can be argued, for example, that Lenin's challenge to Wilsonian liberalism – his insistence that capitalism, old style or reformed "liberal" capitalism, was the enemy, not the army in the opposite trench – required that the president differentiate (along Hobsonian lines) between "good" capitalist nations and "bad" ones. If there was to be any room for liberalism, such a distinction had to be made, and in the context of a war it was all the easier to do so. The irony, of course, rests in the way that such a choice promoted the very ends both Wilson and House feared most.

As early as 4 December 1917, Lansing described the Bolshevik regime as "class despotism" that differed from autocratic monarchy only in that the latter was exercise of sovereign authority by an individual, while the former was excercised by a group of individuals. "Upon despotisms of every nature the people of the United States have looked invariably with disfavor as subversive of the rights of man, and hostile to justice and liberty."[37]

Thus Lansing reversed Lenin's accusation. Despotisms of the Right or the Left were equally repugnant. Germany would have to be punished, or the crucial distinction between liberalism and despotism would break down. And, after the Bolshevik Revolution, there was a new fear about what kind of revolution would occur in Germany. For months Wilson had been insisting, most recently in his response to the Pope's appeal for a negotiated peace, that he could not deal with the Kaiser's unrepresentative government. But what was there to say now?

The congratulations the American radical, Max Eastman, editor of the banned publication, *The Masses*, sent to Wilson about his response to the Pope, for example, took on a less favorable aspect after Lenin's success in toppling the provisional government. Eastman had written:

> Now you have declared for substantially the Russian terms – no "punitive damages," no "dismemberment of empires," "vindication of sovereignties," and by making a responsible ministry in Germany the one condition of your entering into negotiations, you have given a concrete meaning to the statement that this is a war for democracy. The manner in which you have accomplished this – and apparently bound the allies to it into the bargain – has my profound admiration.[38]

The new "Russian terms" were hardly like those advanced by the leaders of the provisional government when they had sought to end the war before they themselves were overwhelmed, but tampering with the established order was now a much more dangerous thing, especially when the Bolshevik example of revolution was a powerful counter-attraction to Wilsonian liberalism.

The changing mood was evidenced in a number of ways. Even at the time he delivered the Fourteen Points speech – in large part a response to the Bolshevik appeals and the revelation of the secret treaties – Wilson was drawing new distinctions unlike those, at least in emphasis, he had made earlier. He had made the Fourteen Points speech, he told Ambassador Spring-Rice, to call Germany's bluff and to get a new statement of German war aims, in the hope that it would force the issue in the Russo-German peace talks – meaning, apparently, that both the Germans and the Russian government were, in effect, collaborating in the promotion of German imperialist ambitions.

But then he went on. He had always thought the United States would enter the war, he said, in sharp contradistinction to his views in late 1916 and early 1917,[39] but the country had had to be united first. And finally this:

Speaking of the British Empire he said Germany wholly failed to understand that such an empire was entirely different from the German conception of Empire, and was a union of free peoples acting on free impulses.[40]

Self-determination now became a celebration of Allied virtues – or much closer to it than Wilson had ever come before. A few months later, Wilson told another British agent, Sir William Wiseman, about his fears for the future. "He foresees grave danger after the war from forces of anarchy which had been let loose. The submerged classes, lacking discipline and restraint, will tend to excess."[41]

In this statement were justifications both for assigning Germany war guilt, and for checking revolutionary forces in Central and Eastern Europe. Revolution came in Germany, but it was now a cause of concern to Wilson more than a prayer answered.[42] Secretary of War Newton D. Baker put it this way in a letter to Wilson a few days before the armistice in Europe. Baker wondered if Wilson should not issue a statement expressing the hope that the peoples of the defunct Austro-Hungarian empire would:

> observe orderly processes in these revolutionary days and refrain from acts of violence in order that their candidacy to admission in the family of nations will not be blemished at the outset by disorders which would tend to throw doubt upon their capacity for self-government in the eyes of the nations whose ordered civilizations have made this era of freedom possible for them. . . . There may be people in those countries in large numbers who have so little comprehension of us as to believe that they would gain favor with us by killing their kings.[43]

The British Ambassador in Paris awaited Wilson's arrival in Europe to begin the peace negotiations with some trepidation about all that talk of Freedom of the Seas and a League of Nations. Everything would stand or fall on the success of the League, Wilson told Lord Derby, but he had not meant to imply that Great Britain or the United States should give up their navies. Instead, "we should between us do the whole of the marine policing of the world." And what about those "various weird creatures" the president had wanted to see? Colonel House told Derby, "the whole of that was dropped. . . . " The British diplomat was delighted that Wilson did not intend to lead the European left or seek the aid of socialists for his program.[44]

In London, Wilson confided to the King that Germany should not be eligible for membership in the League of Nations until after a probationary period had elapsed. Near the end of the peace conference, Robert Lansing wrote a private note to himself on the erosion of Wilsonian principles at Paris. "The honesty and faith of the President have been taken advantage of in every way. He has been led into a net . . . until I fear that he is so entangled in the meshes that he can never extricate himself."[45]

This was not all there was to the story. The delicate balance that House and Wilson sought to strike, first between the warring alliances, and then between self-determination and world order; or between liberalism and reaction, and then between a victor's peace and the League of Nations, faced long odds from the beginning. Wilson had set a high standard for the peacemakers and himself. "A supreme moment of history has come," he wrote on the night of the armistice. "The eyes of the people have been opened and they see the hand of God is laid upon the nations. He will show them favor, I devoutly believe, only if they rise to the clear heights of His own justice and mercy."[46]

Wilson invoked the Christian diety in Paris as well. "Why," he asked his fellow peacemakers, "has Jesus Christ so far not succeeded in inducing the world to follow His teachings in these matters? It is because He taught the ideal without devising any practical means of attaining it. That is the reason why I am proposing a practical scheme to carry out His aims." The French Premier, Georges Clemenceau, slowly opened his eyes to their widest and swept them around the room, noted Lloyd George, "to see how the Christians gathered around the table enjoyed the exposure of the futility of their Master."[47]

But Wilson's "practical scheme" had to straddle too many contradictions, even if his critics had not kept America from joining the League. His successors avoided the dilemmas until another war forced them to rethink the entire range of problems and their solutions.

Notes to Chapter 13

1. (Williamsburg, VA, 1956), p. 6.

2. (New York, 1990), p. 45.

3. "Conference on *George Washington* with Wilson," 10 December 1918, notes by Charles Seymour, copy in Wilson Collection, Princeton University, Princeton, NJ.

4. Bernard Semmel, *Imperialism and Social Reform: English Social Thought, 1895–1914* (New York, 1968).

5. "Ten Years: Retrospect and Prospect," *Foreign Affairs Quarterly* 11 (October 1932), pp. 51–53.

6. Lippmann to William Allen White, 22 April 1931, in John M. Blum, ed., *Public Philosopher: Selected Letters of Walter Lippmann* (New York, 1985), p. 288.

7. Arno Mayer, *Wilson versus Lenin: Political Origins of the New Diplomacy* (Cleveland, 1964).

8. *St. Louis Post-Dispatch*, 19 April 1913.

9. Quoted in Lloyd C. Gardner, ed., *Wilson and Revolutions: 1913–1921* (Philadelphia, 1976), pp. 66–69.

10. Lloyd C. Gardner, *Safe for Democracy: The Anglo-American Response to Revolution, 1913–1923* (New York, 1984), pp. 59–60.

11. "A Message to Teachers," [28 June 1918], in Arthur S. Link, et al., eds., *The Papers of Woodrow Wilson*, vol. 48 (Princeton, NJ, 1985), pp. 455–56.

12. Charles Seymour, *The Intimate Papers of Colonel House*, 4 vols. (Boston and New York, 1926–1928), vol. 2, p. 142. (Hereafter, *Intimate Papers*.)

13. *Philip Dru: Administrator* (privately published, 1912), p. 280.

14. Diary Entry, 27 January 1913, *The Papers of Colonel House*, Sterling Library, Yale University, New Haven, Connecticut. (Hereafter, *House Papers*.)

15. Diary, 1 June 1914, *House Papers*.

16. House to Wilson, 17 June 1914, *House Papers*.

17. Diary, 21 June 1914, *House Papers*.

18. Diplomatic Circular, 19 March 1913, in United States, Department of State, *Papers Relating to the Foreign Relations of the United States, 1913* (Washington, D.C., 1920), pp. 170–71.

19. House to Wilson, 26 June 1914, *The Papers of Woodrow Wilson*, Library of Congress, Washington, D.C. (Hereafter, *Wilson Papers, LC*)

20. Diary, 6 August 1914, *House Papers*.

21. This point is well-developed by Richard Shannon, *The Crisis of Imperialism, 1865–1915* (London, 1976 ed.), p. 428.

22. Spring-Rice to Grey, 3 September 1914, *The Papers of Sir Edward Grey*, Public Record Office, London, England, FO 800/84.

23. Diary, 21 September 1914, *House Papers*.

24. Quoted in Arthur S. Link, *Wilson: The Struggle for Neutrality* (Princeton, NJ, 1960), p. 205. For Wilson's initial toying with the idea, see Wilson to Walter Hines Page, 10 November 1914, *The Papers of Ray Stannard Baker*, Princeton University Library, Princeton, NJ.

25. Diary, 25 November 1914, *House Papers*.

26. House to Wilson, 11 April 1915, *Wilson Papers*.

27. House to Wilson, 3 June 1915, *House Papers*.

28. House to Wilson, 7 January 1916, *Wilson Papers*.

29. House to Wilson, 15 January 1916, *Wilson Papers*.

30. 11 May 1916, Seymour, *Intimate Papers*, vol. 2, pp. 278–80.

31. "The President's Attitude Toward Great Britain and its Dangers," September 1916, *The Papers of Robert Lansing*, Library of Congress, Washington, D.C. (Hereafter, *Lansing Papers*.)

32. Diary entry, 17 November 1916, *House Papers*.

33. House to Wilson, 20 December 1916, *Wilson Papers*.

34. Lansing to American Embassy, 8 Feburary 1917, *Lansing Papers*.

35. Walter Hines Page to Lansing, 11 February 1917, *Lansing Papers*.

36. House to Wilson, 19 July 1917, *Wilson Papers*.

37. Robert Lansing, untitled memorandum, 4 December 1917, Wilson Collection, Princeton, NJ.

38. Eastman to Wilson, 8 September 1917, Wilson Collection, Princeton, NJ.

39. On 4 January 1917, Wilson told House, "There will be no war. This country does not intend to become involved in this war. We are the only one of the great white nations that is free from war to-day, and it would be a crime against civilization for us to go in." Seymour, *Intimate Papers*, vol. 2, 412.

40. Spring Rice to Balfour, 9 January 1918, *Papers of the Foreign Office*, Public Record Office, London, England, FO 115/2432.

41. "Notes on Interview, etc.," 1 April 1918, *The Papers of Arthur Balfour*, British Museum, London, England, Add. 4947.

42. The standard work, of course, is Klaus Schwabe, *Wilson and the German Revolution* (Chapel Hill, NC, 1986).

43. Baker to Wilson, 2 November 1918, Wilson Collection, Princeton, NJ.

44. Derby to Balfour, 24 December 1918, *Balfour Papers*.

45. "The Weakening of Principles by Compromise," 15 April 1919, *Lansing Papers*.

46. Handwritten Note, 11 November 1918, Wilson Collection, Princeton, NJ.

47. David Lloyd George, *Memoirs of the Peace Conference*, 2 vols. (New Haven, CT, 1939), vol. 1, p. 142.

14

The German Challenge to the Monroe Doctrine in Mexico, 1917

Laura Garcés

"In general, Americans have not looked for Mexico in Mexico; they have looked for their obsessions, enthusiasms, phobias, hopes, interests – and these are what they have found. In short, the history of our relationship is the history of a mutual and stubborn deceit, usually involuntary though not always so."

OCTAVIO PAZ, *Mexico and the United States*

An American Dilemma: Mexico, 1913–1917

In January 1917, as Wilson prepared himself to declare publicly his desire for a "peace without victory,"[1] he had already elaborated a rationale for the European war, a rationale that fit neatly with his interpretation of events in Mexico, and which in fact built upon it. In his perspective, each of these events gave meaning to the other, and both reflected the general course taken by civilization in modern times. Much stigmatized for wanting a "peace without victory" by the growing ranks of Americans who indicted Germany, Wilson's paradoxical stance originated in his conviction that the European war was a fundamental social, political, and religious revolution.[2] Conceiving the European war as shattering the old order to "make the world safe for democracy," Wilson vehemently refuted the notion of victors and vanquished because it rested on the postulates of *Realpolitik* and represented, therefore, no more than a rearrangement within the old order. Proposing that "the nations should with one accord adopt the doctrine of President Monroe as the doctrine of the world," Wilson called for an end to "entangling alliances, which would draw them into competition of power, catch them in a net of intrigue and selfish rivalry, and disturb their own affairs with influences intruded from without."[3]

This comprehension of the European war as a revolution and the

Notes to Chapter 14 can be found on page 302.

direct reference to the Monroe Doctrine allows us to draw a parallel with Mexico, which had once represented "Wilson's laboratory, his great experiment."[4] While inconclusive attempts at achieving stability and the outright hostility manifested by Mexico towards the United States had tempered Wilsonian enthusiasm for the cause of the Mexicans by 1917, Wilson had gone to great lengths to understand the revolutionary turmoil that rocked the neighbor to the south. And until increasing tensions with the Central Powers had turned Europe into the number one problem, the Wilson administration had been very absorbed by Mexico. If the rationale it gave to events in Mexico between 1913 and 1915 differed somewhat from the conclusions it was to reach in 1916/17, this rationale nonetheless provided the basics of its understanding of Mexico and of that nation's dealings with foreign powers.

One of these basics was that Mexico, in a sense, didn't really exist at all. There, on the southern border of the United States, in a very strategic position, a mass of miserable, ignorant people lived and died without having taken charge of their destiny. Some policymakers in Washington, among them Leon Canova, head of the State Department's Mexican Affairs Division, had persistently continued to advocate intervention in Mexico for the protection of American lives and interests. They had consistently favored a strong regime for Mexico to force law and order onto the generalized chaos. But Wilson's initial attitude, shared by many, including William Jennings Bryan, his secretary of state until June 1915, had been moved by the distress of the Mexican people, and been totally geared, in the beginning, to encourage change in Mexico in favor of a genuinely representative government.

The official line followed by the Wilson administration until 1917 has been much explored.[5] Suffice it to note here the basic consensus which, since 1913, had underlain the different perspectives held in Washington on Mexico. Whether paternalistic or contemptuous, the basic understanding of Mexico had been founded on a common distinction between "civilized" and "backward" nations. Even Wilson's more confident and sympathetic perspective of 1913 had been flawed from the outset by his tendency to relate the American and the Mexican experiences and to distinguish "good" from "bad" revolutions.[6] A certain vision of history drawn from the American experience had thus early permeated the perspectives of the Wilson administration on Mexico. Wilson's advocacy of non-intervention had been based on the conviction that the North American revolution had succeeded because it had not suffered, in contrast to France, from outside interference.[7]

But Wilson was not the only one to draw these parallels. The whole attempt to foster reconciliation among the constitutionalist factions in

1915 had been based on the idea that the latter could be brought together as different parties in a representative government. And parallels with the American experience had been traced on occasion. In August 1915, at a meeting between the American Secretary of State and Pan-American delegates, Robert Lansing had compared the Mexican situation to the American Civil War, and associated the conflicts among constitutionalists to quarrels that were "not based on any great principle, but along personal lines," which impeded the achievement of the revolution. "The result," he asserted, "is that the revolution itself, while it is represented by all these factions combined, is unable to accomplish its purpose, unable to restore a stable and responsible government in Mexico. . . . "[8] In January 1917, when no progress had been made along these lines, Wilson's enthusiasm was deflated, and skepticism on the resolution of the problem began to prevail in Washington. In May 1917 Senator Albert Beveridge reiterated the vision of Mexico as a backward nation by pointing out a "fatal defect" in the American perspective of Mexico. "It assumes," he wrote, "that the inhabitants of Mexico are a people. But this is not true. . . . Such a tangle of human elements cannot, of course, be called a people. . . ."[9]

European Challenges to the Monroe Doctrine in Mexico, 1913–1917

In the ardent pursuit of resolving the question in the good tradition of Anglo-Saxon law and procedures, Mexico's character had been forgotten. The long-range forces that Francisco Madero's coup had unleashed in 1911 were lost to sight.[10] Instead, two notions had come to dominate the Wilson administration's thinking on the Mexican imbroglio: first, that the contentions among the Mexicans themselves were largely based on personal rivalries, and second, that foreign instigators of intrigue would delight in stepping in to reap the harvest from the troubles afflicting this strategic spot, which was endowed with great economic potential. These premises had led the North Americans to overlook the social dynamics at work in Mexico; to misinterpret the fierce nationalism of Victoriano Huerta, Venustiano Carranza, or Pancho Villa as subservience to some foreign power hostile to the United States. From the start, as historian Lloyd Gardner notes, Wilson's understanding of Mexico had been shaped by his perception of European political dynamics: "Latin America was . . . a mirror-image of Europe – although a distorted one. European imperialism produced the injustices that led to revolution; Latin American revolution produced intervention and imperialism."[11]

Thus, the discussion of Mexican events had increasingly assumed the tone of a debate on European instigated anti-Americanism. The Wilson administration failed to understand "that whoever became President in Mexico would inevitably be drawn into an anti-American position."[12] When repeated assurances of the United States' friendship for Mexico awoke hostility instead of amity, the Wilson administration had been dismayed. In the course of 1913/14, for example, as Huerta incurred the increasing wrath of the United States, Carranza had been looked upon as a lesser evil. Clearly, he had been accepted with reluctance since the beginning, as an element to be "digested."[13] After a Pan-American Conference that included the United States, Argentina, Brazil, Chile, Guatemala, and Uruguay, convened on 3 August 1915 had had to admit Carranza's undeniable military superiority over his opponents, the Wilson administration extended de facto recognition to the Constitutionalist leader on 19 October 1915.[14] This gesture, however, expressed the reservations with which the United States accepted him, and did not mark the beginning of a Mexican-American dialogue.[15] Since repeated professions of American disinterestedness and continued attempts at securing cooperation from the Mexicans did not seem to succeed, chances were, it was argued in Washington, that Mexico had ulterior motives, or rather that, intentionally or not, it was carrying out the plans of other hostile powers driven by economic ambitions.[16]

Worried since 1913 that the Monroe Doctrine did not cover indirect attempts by European powers at control through economic means, the Wilson administration had considered broadening it in a manner that marked a significant break with earlier interpretations. In October of that year, Wilson had pinpointed the problem as he believed it posed itself in modern times. In a conversation with Colonel House, he asserted that "in former years the Monroe Doctrine had been aimed at preventing any political control of Latin America by European nations," but "financial control was equally reprehensible, and more likely in the modern world."[17] This conception, a direct projection of the progressive indictment of the "special interests' ambition and greed," was originally intimately linked to the perception of Huerta as the tool of British interests. In a memorandum written in June 1914, Lansing had questioned in a similar way the relevance of the Monroe Doctrine in modern times: "Should a new doctrine be formulated declaring that the United States is opposed to the extension of European control over American territory and institutions through financial as well as other means. . . . ?"[18] A new interpretation which envisaged protecting the nations of the hemisphere against the encroachment of foreign business and financial interests had thus early emerged to inspire American perceptions of Mexico.

The main economic challenge to the Monroe Doctrine in Mexico at the beginning of Wilson's presidency had been Great Britain, not Germany,[19] and the determination with which Wilson had concentrated on ousting Huerta and pressuring the Mexicans into representative government was, in fact, a direct, if mainly tacit, confrontation with Great Britain. Traditional and main obstacle to U.S. ambitions in the Western Hemisphere, Great Britain had progressively scaled down her ambitions since the 1890s, but still remained, at the beginning of Wilson's presidency, the main economic competitor of the United States in Mexico. Tension between London and Washington had gradually eased after London had weighed the friendship of the United States against the value of its interests in Mexico. And many unrelated events had intervened early to facilitate this decision without Ambassador Sir Cecil Spring-Rice feeling touchy about his country stepping down: the settlement of the Panama Canal tolls controversy in a way that satisfied Great Britain,[20] and of course London's need of U.S. support in the European war. Prompted by feverish British admonitions and loud partisan outcries in the United States, the Wilson administration's diplomacy had shown, in the course of 1915, that it started to view the nation's survival as hinging on Allied victory.[21] More immediately, the search for a resolution of Mexican domestic problems seemingly had confirmed Washington's suspicions that these were related to an evil outgrowth of European imperialism. Indeed, the Wilson administration began to hunt for evidence of the intimate connections between German ambitions in Europe and the Mexican revolution.

By 1915, in the context of the deteriorating relations between Germany and the United States caused by the U-boat offensive and the discovery of conspiracies plotted by the Central Powers in the United States, the threat to the United States in Mexico, as Washington had come to perceive it, had shifted from Great Britain to Germany. As early as October 1915, Lansing had resolved that the United States should not intervene in Mexico because such a decision would divert Washington's attention away from the European scene and would, therefore, serve German interests.[22] Although Great Britain "pursued the sharpest and most aggressive policy in that country during the war,"[23] a policy geared even to the overthrow of the Carranza government, Washington's feeling of vulnerability stemmed from the fact that Mexican intractability was perceived as the sign of the Central Powers' hatred for the United States. After Huerta's defeat, which in Washington had been largely construed as Great Britain's demise, Carranza had increasingly appeared to incarnate the European threat, although from then on the peril was understood in Washington to be German-induced. His obduracy only rendered him more suspect. During 1915, and especially 1916, reports on the progress of the civil war had often presented Carranza's contempt and hostility for Washington as inspired by Germany.[24] Among the most alarming rumors was Carranza's alleged aim of recovering Texas and California, as well as the drawing up of the San Diego plan, completed in February 1915, which had envisaged an uprising of Mexican-Americans and blacks in Texas, New Mexico, Arizona, Colorado, and California.[25]

The suspicion that Mexican leaders were, in fact, conniving with Germany had continued to deepen in the course of 1916.[26] And before Pancho Villa's raid on Columbus, New Mexico, which occurred on March 9, some attack across the United States border had been feared or expected.[27] Rumors as to another possible offensive or conspiracy against the United States had not abated after the Pershing expedition had been despatched to capture Villa.[28] The latter had been suspected on occasion of being the agent of the Germans, and this suspicion also had been at the basis of concerns over Carranza's strength to subdue his rivals.[29] General Pershing's expedition, which started on March 15, had of course greatly offended Mexican pride, leaving Carranza no option but to protest this violation of Mexican sovereignty.[30] The U.S.-Mexican commission to settle the border conflict, convened between 6 September 1916 and 15 January 1917, was unable to reach agreement. Carranza's representative insisted upon unconditional withdrawal of American troops, while the U.S. commissioners wanted the Mexican government to commit itself to protect foreign lives and interests, failing which the United States would reserve for itself the right to re-enter Mexico.[31] The withdrawal of the troops commanded by John Pershing between 28 January and 5 February 1917 did not do much to ease Mexican-American relations, which, if at a precarious standstill, had reached no common ground.[32] There was "admitted failure to agree on the principal points at issue,"[33] and the Mexican-American joint commission was dissolved on January 16 without reaching an understanding. The *New York Times* then reported that "the administration's future policy in dealing with Mexico . . . contemplates dealing with the de facto government on a strictly formal basis rather than on an altruistic basis."[34] This formal basis entailed the lowering of lofty ideals to the level of immediate concerns that loomed in the background during much of 1917, among them Villa's continued hostility and fears of further attacks across the border.[35]

Despite the withdrawal of the Pershing expedition, fear of Germany in Mexico lingered on in 1917. Many in Washington continued to think that the Mexican president was an agent of the Germans. A Foreign Relations Committee report, issued by Senator Albert Fall as late as 1920, asserted strongly that "Carranza and all his followers were pro-German during the war."[36] Oblivious perhaps of Carranza's tottering strength in 1917, of his need to subdue his opponents and to lead a coherent movement, the report stated that "the Carranza government was pursuing a war against the United States during the period immediately prior and subsequent to Carranza's recognition by this country," and that German Minister "Von Eckardt was on such terms with Carranza that he could convey the Zimmermann note to Mexico . . . [which] was exactly the old 'plan of San Diego'."[37]

But Carranza and Villa were not the only ones to inspire American suspicions for their allegedly pro-German position. Alvaro Obregón and Francisco Murguía, the leaders of Carranza's armed forces, as well as Manuel Peláez, another one of his opponents, and the strong man who controlled the oil fields, were also singled out for their friendliness with Germany and even suspected of being the latter's agents.[38] Almost everything unfavorable observed in Mexico was seen as the fruit of German conspiracy: the anti-American if not outright pro-German tone of the press;[39] the peace initiative itself proposed by Carranza to other neutral countries in February;[40] Carranza's subsequent refusal to align himself to the United States; the strikes that erupted during spring and summer against American and Allied properties;[41] and even the expressions of independence in the drafting of the Mexican constitution.[42]

War or Peace? Zimmermann's Telegram and Carranza's Neutrality

The Zimmermann telegram of 19 January 1917 did much to reinforce and crystalize the feeling of German-instigated Mexican hostility. Forwarded to Washington by Ambassador William Hines Page from London on February 24,[43] the Zimmermann telegram did not strike Washington with extraordinary surprise, since rumors about German plots in Mexico had extensively occupied the State Department as early as 1915. Commenting on the cable after its disclosure, *The New York Times* observed that "no doubt exists now that the persistent reports during the last two years of the operations of German threats not alone in Mexico, but all through Central America and the West Indies are based on fact."[44] Publicly, Mexican officials displayed sympathy for the Allies. As early as November 1916 Carranza's aide, Luis Cabrera, had issued a reassuring statement: "The foes of the United States will certainly assume to be friends of Mexico and will try to take advantage of any sort of resentment Mexico may have against the United States. Mexico, nevertheless, understands that in case of conflict between the United States and any other nation outside America, her attitude must be one of continental solidarity."[45] After the publication of the Zimmermann telegram, the

Mexican chargé d'affaires in the United States, Ramon De Negri, formally denied that his government had been involved in the plot.[46] On March 3, General Cándido Aguilar, Minister of Foreign Relations, formally denied that Germany had proposed the formation of an alliance hostile to the United States.[47]

Nevertheless, the Zimmermann telegram prompted Washington to verify Mexico's position directly with Carranza. In a telegram to Henry P. Fletcher, who would present his credentials as the new U.S. Ambassador to the Mexican President on March 3, Under Secretary of State Frank Polk instructed that General Carranza be approached to make some statement on the subject.[48] On March 10 Fletcher cabled back, noting, on the one hand, Carranza's desire to be accommodating, and on the other, his reluctance to make any commitments: "In answer to my direct question as to his attitude in case Germany should propose an alliance he said that Mexico desires to avoid becoming involved in the war . . . but he avoided saying directly that such a proposition would be rejected. . . . While both he and Minister for Foreign Affairs were very careful and guarded in their utterances, I gathered that their sentiments inclined somewhat toward Germany."[49]

Frustration over this issue did not subside, as subsequent discussions with Mexican authorities were unable to clarify the latters' position with respect to actual or potential alliance proposals by Germany. General Aguilar remained as reluctant to state Mexico's position as Carranza had been when questioned by Fletcher in March: "He stated that the German Minister had made no proposition of alliance to him and he did not believe he had done so to the First Chief. . . . He said . . . that [the German Minister] may have written to the First Chief, but he did not believe he had done so. . . . "[50] Further discussion with Carranza yielded no further results.[51] The latter remained friendly but distant, displaying in his public statements his will to remain free from both Washington and Berlin. While he spoke in May at the National University of the "good and noble Germany" who had never bothered Mexico, the evasiveness he had just manifested in responding to Germany's offers of a loan in April made a point that few at the time understood.[52]

Carranza's noncommittal attitude in regard to the Zimmermann telegram was clearly linked, in Washington's perception, to the proposal he had extended on February 11 to pressure the European powers into concluding peace. Addressing, among others, the United States, Argentina, Brazil, and Chile, Carranza proposed an agreement to prohibit the exportation of munitions and foodstuffs to the belligerents in Europe.[53] Since such a move would have benefited mainly the Central Powers, it tended to be interpreted in the United States as "evidence of German influence in Mexico."[54] Referring to Carranza's evasive answer on the subject of an alliance with Germany, Fletcher thought that the "First Chief wishes [to] withhold categorical statement to that effect in the hope of inducing our Government to accept his peace proposals or a peace conference of neutrals."[55] Prepared by Robert Lansing in mid-March, the Wilson administration's answer politely declined the Mexican proposal.[56] Washington never wholeheartedly relied on Mexican neutrality – in Lansing's words "We could in the circumstances count on Mexico being an unfriendly neutral, if she remained neutral. . . . "[57] – and seeked further assurances from Carranza that Mexico would not become a "base of hostile acts toward the United States."[58]

How justified were American concerns about German influence in Mexico? Clearly, Germany's interest in Mexico stemmed less from economic ambitions than from the latter's strategic value, but as historian Friedrich Katz observes, "Germany's notion that it could dominate Mexico was based on a gross overestimation of its own strength, on a similar underestimation of the strength of the Americans, and a complete ignorance of the dynamics of the Mexican revolution.[59] Moreover, Germany's diplomacy vis-à-vis Mexico was vacillating because of internal conflicts over the contradictory temptation to play the Mexican card against the United States while not wanting to provoke the latter's hostility.[60] Although real, Germany's influence was in no way proportionate to American concerns.

More realistic was Mexico's position and its practical diplomacy. Rumors since 1915 alluding to plots concerning the secession of the south-western U.S. states could only frighten Washington more than raise expectations in Mexico. "A German offer of Texas, New Mexico, and Arizona to Mexico could only be viewed with skepticism by Carranza. . . . ." Carranza came to the conclusion "that Germany would never be in a position to insure adequate supplies of arms and ammunition to the Mexican army," and that "the repossession of Texas, Arizona, and New Mexico would be a permanent source of conflict with the United States and would have to lead to a new war."[61] The continued threat that Germany was able to pose to the United States in Mexico was made possible by Carranza's skillful playing of the two powers' interests against each other. The proposal made in the Zimmermann telegram was never clearly refuted vis-à-vis Germany, while Mexico tantalized the United States with denials and declarations of solidarity and continued to negotiate with Germany on issues of lesser importance than a war alliance. Among these issues were the wireless station Germany wanted and succeeded in building in Mexico, the base for German U-boats on Mexico's coast that did not materialize, and a loan from the German government that in the end fell through. Nevertheless, German attempts at influencing Mexico continued through various means: bribery, propaganda campaigns against the United States through the press, a campaign directed at certain groups unfavorably disposed towards Carranza, such as the Catholics.[62]

Reappraising Priorities in the Light of the World War

U.S. perception of German hostility induced a temporary rapprochement between Washington and London on the subject of Mexico. "The Mexican situation is full of difficulties and dangers," read a memorandum written by House and Sir William Wiseman at the beginning of March 1917, and concurred in by President Wilson, "chiefly on account of German intrigues which will try to create bad feeling between the United States and Britain. Here again, Great Britain must play the prominent part on account of her large interests and the big Canadian interests in Mexico. Careful handling of this situation should avoid all difficulties because the aims of the United States and Great Britain are identical, namely: to restore order and protect foreign lives and interests."[63] This association with Great Britain regarding Mexico was affirmed after U.S. entry into World War I. Fearing in April a possible move of the Mexican government to prohibit the export of oil, Lansing saw "no way but to occupy the territory with troops or else to allow the British to do so, even though it would be a technical violation of the Monroe Doctrine."[64] Wilson showed himself adamantly opposed to such an option unless "the most extraordinary circumstances of arbitrary injustice on the part of the Mexican government" compelled the United States to intervene. Noting the predominantly British influence in the oil region, Wilson went on to add that "there is absolutely no breach of the Monroe Doctrine in allowing the British to exercise an influence which anti-American sentiment in Mexico for the time prevents our exercising."[65]

This tacit understanding with Great Britain amounted to a recognition of a shift in interests. War in Europe and failure to resolve Mexican differences led the Wilson administration to scale down its ambitions. Stability, rather than a resolution of the situation that many thought hopeless, was now the aim of the Wilson administration. "It was no time to break with this impossible old man," wrote Robert Lansing in his Memoirs. "We had to swallow our pride and to maintain as good relations as possible with the de facto Government in Mexico."[66] In a confidential despatch to Robert Lansing, George C. Carothers proposed that the United States serve as intermediary between the different opposing factions.[67] Washington was well aware of Carranza's dire need of funds to defeat his opponents. In August, echoes that Carranza's forces were not even trying to capture Villa in Durango were attributed to a lack of materials.[68] Yet the pursuit of stability in Mexico was undermined by the distrust which the Wilson administration had developed during the past years. Hence its reluctance to assist Carranza. The American embargo on the export of arms and ammunition that subsisted until July increased the latter's difficulties, but was viewed by some as desirable because of the "practical impossibility of obtaining arms and ammunition for filibustering expeditions."[69] "Rigid restrictions on the exportation of gold, machinery, foodstuffs, and other goods," which lasted until the end of the year, created a situation in which "Mexico was selling products to the United States but could not touch the earnings or convert them into imports."[70] In 1917 bad crops and the widespread destruction brought about by the continuing civil war accentuated Mexican difficulties.[71] The arms embargo betrayed the aloofness with which Washington watched Carranza's struggle to subdue his rivals: Villa, whom the Pershing expedition had not been able to capture, Emiliano Zapata, who held firm ground in the South, and other strong rivals, such as Peláez in the oil-rich Huasteca Veracruzana, and Esteban Cantú in Baja California. Washington's dealings with Carranza during 1917 were marked by ambivalence. On the one hand, Washington wanted to see stabilized the Mexican situation, but on the other hand, it was reluctant to assist Carranza, through funds and arms, in attaining this goal.[72]

Much debated in the course of 1917, the possibility of a United States public or private loan to Carranza's government was repeatedly discarded. Washington was placed in a dilemma, clearly expressed in a report from the Office of Naval Intelligence in September 1917. Arguing that "it is evident that the situation as to internal peace in Mexico can not clear up unless a loan is made enabling the Mexican government to place a much larger army in the field," the report, nevertheless, concluded: "It is believed that even the success of a loan would not help matters as such a loan would place available a large amount of money for the disbursement of which those now in power would fight among themselves and additional revolutions might ensue. The Mexican government is apparently moved by the right intentions and is desirous of bringing about order but it is doubted that the small number of really able men in the Government can control the irresponsible majority."[73]

The idea of using a loan as a powerful leverage on Carranza was nevertheless contemplated. Robert Lansing and Chandler Anderson, among others, favored resorting to dollar diplomacy to enforce stability.[74]

So did Leon Canova. To bolster Carranza's regime and to "crystalize . . . professions of friendship into a substantial, convincing and material form," Canova proposed that the United States guarantee an issue of Mexican bonds, provided many strenuous conditions were met. Besides giving the United States a decisive weight in the allocation of funds as well as the responsibility of rehabilitating the railroads, the extension of this guarantee depended on the modification of certain decrees, laws, and constitutional provisions "that are onerous and unjust to foreigners." This foresaw that the United States would appoint to the Mexican government one or more commissioners as financial advisors, "empowered to scrutinize all customs and other receipts, as well as expenditures," and "that the Mexican government . . . maintain a border patrol which shall be capable and adequate to prevent border raids from the Mexican side into United States territory." Canova saw many advantages to the plan he proposed. "The strategic effect," he wrote, "will be immediately to make an ally of the Mexican government, and of the Mexican people, and it will completely paralyze German influence in Mexico. . . . The political effect," he went on to emphasize, "would be far-reaching, for it would immediately nullify that which, from our standpoint, is Carranza's principal defect, and that is, his anti-American policy . . . for the Mexican people would then realize that by acts, and not by words alone, we are their friends." Canova finally noted that American assistance would strengthen Carranza's hold on the country.[75] Assistance of the U.S. government failed to materialize. In August, however, the Wilson administration finally decided not to block negotiations for a loan from U.S. bankers on the condition that Carranza would provide guarantees to protect "valid vested interests."[76] Moreover, the abdication even of neutrality was a precondition that some demanded in Washington for extending a loan to Mexico.[77] But Carranza gave no guarantees and received no money.

The ambiguity in Washington's relations with Mexico came out even in the manner used to address the Mexican government, leaving Carranza until September in a kind of diplomatic no-man's land. During the first months of the year, the Wilson administration denied de jure recognition to Carranza, even after the latter's May 1 inauguration as President of Mexico, an inauguration which Fletcher, the American ambassador, would attend. "As to whether Fletcher's presence would be a formal recognition of the de jure character of the government," wrote Robert Lansing, "I think that the words 'de facto' may be employed before and after the inauguration in such a way as to indicate that we consider the character of the Government has not changed by the ceremony of inauguration. . . ."[78]

As implicit in the wavering attitude of the United States, it was not affinity but apprehension that led both countries towards an uneasy rapprochement in 1917. From Washington's perspective, the desire to help Mexico financially was closely related to the belief that poverty could breed pro-German sentiments if Berlin's propaganda succeeded in directing the people's discontent against the United States.[79]

From Washington's point of view, however, other prominent obstacles had to be overcome if the Mexican government wanted financial assistance. When the commissioners for the settlement of disturbances on the border had suddenly urged the withdrawal of the Pershing troops, it was because they felt that the anti-American feelings aroused in Mexico as a consequence of this expedition had to be quieted to allow the settlement of more essential questions.[80] The commissioners had indeed pressed for Fletcher to be sent to Mexico as more ominous developments awaited to be tackled.

These developments concerned the coming into effect of the 1917 Mexican constitution. While the civil war continued despite Villa weakening, yet constantly managing to elude the grip of Carranza's forces, the constitutional convention in Querétaro had been busy reaching a compromise between divergent aspirations since November 1916. Promulgated on February 5, the Constitution provided a common ground, which Smith characterizes as a "unifying national mystique" for the government to build on.[81] The more radical wing had managed to push through provisions calling for agrarian and labor reform, and they formulated explicit measures for the nation to regain control over its economy. Viewed from the angle of Mexican-American relations, the principal object of contention was Article 27, which declared subsoil resources Mexican property. This did not represent a radical break with the past; it only applied traditional Spanish law to the newly discovered oil and coal resources. As explained in February 1917 by the Mexican News Notes, "the so-called and misunderstood 'nationalization' of the petroleum measures of the Republic is merely their inclusion in the category of minerals that have for all time been thus nationalized. Under the Spanish crown, and following that under succeeding governments, all mineral resources except coal and oil were declared to be the property of the nation and have always been treated as such. These were omitted merely because their existence was not known until long after the Spanish domination ended."[82] Other points of contention were Article 33, which, based on the Calvo Doctrine, stipulated that private foreigners residing in Mexico as well as foreign business operating in that country would be subject to Mexican laws like all Mexicans and could not invoke diplomatic status or preferential treatment.[83] Finally, the very liberal labor code outlined in Article 123 forebode troubles ahead for foreign interests.[84]

The new constitution, which was to go into effect on 1 May 1917, provoked an uproar among American interests in Mexico, and of course much concern among policymakers in Washington.[85] While Carranza's earlier statements had announced clearly such an evolution, it marked a distinct break from the Díaz regime, which, as early as 1885, had given subsoil rights to foreign owners of the land.[86] As early as February 1917, the Mexican Minister of Foreign Affairs, General Aguilar, "distinctly stated that it was not the intention of the de facto Government to give a retroactive effect to its decrees nor to the constitution and laws made in pursuance thereof."[87] But this did not quiet the fears in Washington. "The reservation of rights improperly impaired by the new constitution" was one of the reasons for not extending de jure recognition to Carranza.[88] Consideration in depth of the new Mexican constitution would have brought out the fragility of Carranza's position. In a conversation with Fletcher in February, Aguilar had "intimated that the new constitution contained provisions of a progressive and advanced character which the Government might find difficulty in carrying into immediate effect."[89] The Wilson administration could not have been unaware, for instance, of Carranza's precarious relationship with labor.[90] The spontaneous reflex of Washington was, however, to relate the nationalist stance of this constitution more to German intrigues than to domestic politics in Mexico,[91] and this despite the fact that Carranza disclosed to foreign interests in 1917 both his "plans to rewrite offensive sections of the new Constitution" and his inability to control the government's policy.[92]

As in preceding years, Washington had difficulty in discerning where exactly the threat emanated from and who, in Mexico, was really Germany's agent. Consequently, it continued during 1917 to vacillate between the Mexican leaders to whom Washington should give its support and who might be the agent of Germany: Obregón, who had emerged as a new *caudillo* in the summer of 1915, following his successful fight against Villa;[93] Peláez, who controlled the oil fields and who had assured foreign companies of his support; or Carranza, who struggled during the whole year to subdue his opponents? In March, House seemed inclined to believe, like the British, that "active support" should be given to "some other factor than that of Carranza," sensing that the Mexican leader would probably not heed Washington's advice.[94] Chandler Anderson and Frank Polk feared that Wilson would offer recognition to Carranza as the only means of bringing the latter to resist German influence.[95] Yet other echoes hinted at Carranza's favorable dispositions towards the United States,[96] and insisted on the need to help him subdue his opponents.[97] All in all, confusion persisted on this issue. In April 1917 Wilson confessed his frustration to Lansing: "I do not know what to make out of the despatches from Mexico. It is by no means clear . . . which is the anti-American party, Carranza's or that which is forming under the leadership of disaffected military men."[98]

Because of the uncertainty surrounding the motives of Carranza, the Wilson administration wavered in the support it gave the latter, and often favored other strong leaders openly or tacitly opposed to the Mexican president. Allegations that Carranza was preparing to oust Cantú, who ruled Baja California, was, for instance, a cause of concern.[99] The proximity of California made it imperative, in the eyes of Canova, that Cantú's stronghold be permitted to remain.[100] The latter had emerged from the Federal collapse as the dominant figure of the region and had refused to surrender to Carranza.[101] Geared to his immediate concern of remaining in control and not motivated by long-term ideological considerations, Cantú was "very well disposed in every way toward Americans and American investments" and "display[ed] none of the usual Mexican attitude of intolerance towards Americans." The "absolute tranquility" reigning in his part of Mexico made even vice and gambling appear acceptable: "both Americans and Mexicans . . . [gave] him credit for using the revenues derived from the gambling privileges for the betterment of his territory in public improvements and such."[102]

A strong element the United States and Great Britain were prepared to bank on at the beginning of 1917 was Manuel Peláez, leader since late 1914 of one of the landlord rebellions that had broken out in response to the threat represented by Carranzismo and firmly in control of the oil district in 1917.

"Rebel chieftain of no particular convictions," Peláez had seen "a chance to curry favor with the Americans."[103] Seizing the opportunity of gaining Washington's support, Peláez declared that Carranza was preparing to occupy the oil fields with the ultimate aim of turning them over to Germany. The oil companies also saw Carranza's attempt to gain control over the region as German-instigated.[104] As a result, a representative of the oil business would confide to President Harding in 1923, that "untold sums" had "been expended by the oil interests to nourish discord in Mexico."[105] The oil district was a source of serious concern for Washington and London: first, implementation of Article 27 in this region could severely harm economic interests, and without control of the rich subsoil of this region the constitution could not be put into effect;[106] second, many feared possible German attempts at sabotage, and the strikes which broke out during the summer in the area were attributed to Germany.[107] Rumors that Carranza was planning to overthrow the resistant Peláez naturally alarmed Washington. Thus, Consul Claude Dawson reported on 15 April 1917, that "verbal information from a

Laura Garcés

trustworthy source . . . confirms local opinion that attempts on oil fields will be made by Germans, or Carranza troops dominated by them, in the guise of restoring constitutional authority."[108] Those who favored Manuel Peláez in Washington believed that he was an asset for the United States – "not a bad man," thought Carothers. "The logical man to save the oil fields."[109] More enthusiastically, a representative of the oil interests thought Peláez "a splendid type of Mexican."[110] Indeed, Peláez was generally favored by business interests since he did not prejudice them, but, on the contrary, showed himself eager to levy taxes and extract from them the necessary income to stay in control of the area.[111] Thus, widely circulated rumors as to Carranza's desire to regain control over this strategic area occasioned some torment in the Wilson administration. After having raised the possibility of a German or Carranzista sabotage in the region, Dawson warned "that the status quo must be maintained in the southern oil fields and that to change to de facto control now would be calamitous."[112] This concern continued to occupy the minds in Washington during a large part of the year. At the beginning of September, Dawson again reported on a probable move by Carranza into the oil fields, adding that "the present status," which did not injure foreign interests, "should be maintained."[113] Alluding in October 1917 to the possibility of a move by Carranza against Peláez, Canova wrote in a note to Polk "that something should be done to deter the Mexican authorities from their purpose to proceed against Peláez at the present time."[114]

U. S. support for Peláez was not, however, unconditional. Until the end of the year, it remained unclear to some what side the Mexican supported. Commenting on the shipment of ammunition to Ciudad Victoria, which seemingly indicated "a probable intent to attack Peláez from the North," a Navy report, dated September 1917, was uncertain about the latter's position: "such attack, if Peláez is involved in German plot, would only hasten the destruction of oil-well property, but if Peláez is not involved in such plot, it would cause him to make heavy demands upon oil men in order to raise and equip troops, and in the event he were defeated he might cause destruction of oil wells."[115] Was Peláez to be designated "the big man of Mexico out of gratitude" if he supported a possible U.S. intervention, or was he to be pressed "to come to terms with the provisional government"?[116] The threat of sabotage in the oilfields by Carranza or Germany never materialized and the United States was spared the decision to intervene.[117]

A Circular Path

Little progress was made in American-Mexican relations in 1917. The cooling off of tensions to the relief of both parties was mainly the fruit of

296

constraining outside circumstances. Both nations were absorbed in their respective wars: Carranza against Villa and the widening rifts that sapped his movement and the United States in the European war. Carranza was moved by American pressure in August 1917 to declare that this clause would not be retroactive, that is to say, that it would not apply to properties exploiting the subsoil before February 5, but he essentially would maintain his nationalistic position in 1918 and 1919.[118] He eventually accepted a further compromise in applying Article 27 by stating that ownership of a property's subsoil could be obtained by special government authorization. "At this juncture," historian Ramon Ruíz remarks, "a delighted President Wilson extended Carranza de jure recognition. By 1918, the two leaders had worked out a *modus vivendi*. Carranza refused to modify the nationalistic character of Article 27 or to settle accounts with foreign investors; but, all the same, he left undisturbed the titles of Americans to property in Mexico, including the holdings of the petroleum companies."[119]

At the end, just as in the beginning of 1917, when the Pershing forces had withdrawn because "the stubborn, proud Mexican had seemingly outwaited and outmaneuvered the stubborn, proud American President," there was no alleviation of tension other than that induced by practical necessity.[120] The problem of securing safety and order on the Mexican-American frontier had not been resolved. In November, Villa and a thousand men had attacked Ojinaga, in the proximity of Texas, causing Lansing to urge Fletcher to communicate with "appropriate Mexican authorities and impress upon them the urgent necessity of providing adequate protection against border raids and attacks."[121] Peláez's hold on the oil fields was growing more precarious by the day. Companies feared cessation of production, and relations with Peláez began to deteriorate. Rumors also had it that Peláez might set fire to the oil wells in a desperate attempt to cause a U.S. intervention if government forces attacked.[122] In the last months of the year, the overthrow of Carranza was held as a distinct possibility.[123] Poverty in Mexico was increasing, due not only to international conditions but also to bad crops, and some Americans continued to interpret this as a good sign: "Some of the Mexicans," remarked Consul General Philip C. Hanna in January 1918, "are coming to their senses and . . . instead of boasting, blowing as to how easily they could whip the United States, proper fear and respect is taking hold of them which is a very good indication – and it is my candid opinion that a feeling of respect for the United States intermingled with a goodly amount of fear, will tend to greatly improve general conditions in Mexico, and that the careful handling of food supplies will have much to do in ending the nonsense of some Mexicans, and causing that proper appreciation and respect from the Mexicans which have long been due us."[124]

Pressure, however, had been inconclusive, and points of discord remained. Carranza could not agree to the conditions of the loan the United States proposed to extend to him, and the Wilson administration was unable to draw Mexico firmly into its ranks against the Central Powers. The Mexican government's cautiousness, when faced with German proposals of an alliance, was more induced by a realistic assessment of its vulnerability to its powerful neighbor than by pan-American solidarity, which U.S. diplomacy, ironically enough, had discouraged in the eyes of the Mexicans. Wilson's messianic efforts to moralize the Mexicans and promote democracy had contributed by 1917 to steering much of the Mexican revolutionary fervor into a contest between rival factions eager to attract American favors and capital. And Washington's diplomacy did lead Mexico to seek an arrangement with powers hostile to the United States. There were other ominous implications. By refusing to deliver arms to Carranza during a large part of the year, the Wilson administration weakened the hold of a regime relatively favorable to Washington; by putting restrictions on the delivery of food, it worsened the fate and accentuated the plight and the desperation of the Mexican people. It therefore unleashed a formidable amount of anti-Gringoism.

Conclusions

The inconsistencies both in European and in American diplomacy vis-à-vis Mexico can be explained tentatively by the misunderstandings that shrouded communication about Mexico within the United States, Great Britain, and Germany, and between each of these powers and Mexico. The power rivalry in Mexico in 1917 can thus be seen, beyond the mere events, as the pursuit of different strategies in parallel, none of which could possibly succeed because, however hard they tried to adapt to prevailing conditions, they never were in concert with Mexico. Rather than responding to the Mexican situation, Great Britain and the United States, as well as Germany, oriented their strategies on past fears and domestic pressures. The German political and military establishment, gnawed as it was in 1917 by dissensions over U-boat warfare, was trapped since the beginning of the year in the quandary of how to silence the open conflict that broke out after the disclosure of the Zimmermann telegram. Hence, Zimmermann's drive, until his resignation in August, to seal the much decried alliance with Mexico and to succeed in the strategy he had defended earlier.[1185] More generally, Berlin's diplomacy with respect to Mexico must be evaluated in the context of the wavering diplomacy conducted vis-à-vis the United States since the spring of 1916. The Wilhelmstrasse could not have been unaware of the fact that the conclusion of a financial deal with Mexico, tied to political and economic conditions, would arouse enormous antagonism in the United States and weaken the extended peace initiatives, thereby ensuring the United States on its path to confrontation.

Great Britain's Mexican diplomacy can be assessed in a similar manner. Obsessed since the turn of the century with her declining greatness, and concerned about pulling the American giant to her side, Great Britain was, in fact, expressing her fear of German vigor and ambition. The influence of the British Foreign Office on the American interpretation of events is well known. But if the effort of Great Britain to draw the United States into the camp of the Allies was eventually successful, tacitly since the House-Grey memorandum of 1916 and formally with the intervention of the United States in the war in April 1917, this strategy had direct implications on Great Britain's position in Mexico. With regard to the defense of her interests in that country, Great Britain had lost in 1917 whatever margin of maneuver she possessed in earlier years. For while the United States was ready to associate with her efforts of assisting Peláez in 1917, Wilson strongly opposed in August 1918 the intervention to protect oil interests that the British contemplated.[126]

The United States misunderstood the nature and the depth of the Mexican revolution. Mesmerized by the hostility and resentment Mexican leaders had for the United States, the Wilson administration tended to focus its attention more on personal rapports than on the social and political conditions in Mexico, which thus exaggerated the power of the revolutionary leaders. This was not prompted in the least by a desire to identify among the Mexican leaders one who could be considered responsive to the concerns of the U.S. government and a reliable counterpart in dealing with foreign interests. While prepared to sign financial agreements with foreign governments and interests, the latter were in reality tremendously limited in their choices. They were occupied less with long-term plans than with immediate military and economic necessities.[127] Hardships did force them to seek help from foreign countries, but long-term alliances with European powers, as manifested clearly by Carranza in 1917, would have brought unnecessary complications to a government entirely absorbed in closing the widening gaps within its ranks. Surely, frightening the gringos could stir up popularity, and no Mexican leader could afford to ignore this, not even such opposing characters as Carranza and Peláez.

Another, greater misunderstanding had been, since the beginning, to believe that a compromise would be possible between the different factions that were in reality pursuing incompatible aims. The era following the long *Porfiriato* was one struggling with the twofold and complex need to contain and channel the revolutionary outbursts throughout the country. Carrancismo, disliked and viewed with distrust in Washington by the Wilson administration, was in fact the "'self-criticism' of Maderismo, refined and tempered in the furnace of 1913–1914. . . . Alternatively, it was the 'hawkish' Maderismo of 1912 grown to maturity."[128] Although aware of Mexican poverty and social inequalities, and conscious that the revolution originated in these conditions, the Wilson administration had contributed to the deterioration of the situation from the start by refusing to recognize Huerta, and later Carranza.[129] In 1917 it had continued to worsen the plight of the Mexican government by holding the latter responsible for all property losses incurred by the United States and demanding compensation, even when the destruction had occurred as a direct consequence of the fighting and not on the initiative of the Mexican government.[130] Worse, the pressure brought to bear on Carranza's government by the conditions attached to a potential American loan, and the restrictions placed on the exportation of food and machinery that threatened to provoke disturbances in Mexico, were anything but conducive to the maintenance of stability.[131] By refusing its help, the Wilson administration led Carranza into seeking economic agreements with other powers.[132]

At the same time, paradoxically, the United States overestimated from the start the influence it could bring to bear on Mexican politics. By its constant appeals to cooperation among constitutionalist factions, it overlooked both the profound personal rivalries which characterized the *caudillos* and the clashing nature of their political programs. In showing commiseration or contempt for the chaotic conditions ruling this neighborly land, the U.S. government demonstrated a lack of awareness about the Mexican, and more generally, Latin American culture: chaos and sharp conflicts did not necessarily show, as Knight observes, "evidence of an aimless, unprincipled revolution."[133] It also misunderstood the heterogeneity within Carranza's movement and the local factors that determined the struggle.[134] The more the Wilson administration pressed Mexico for signs of cooperation, the more the latter recoiled. The more it professed its desire to serve and insisted in qualifying its interventions as helpful and friendly actions towards the Mexican government, the sterner Carranza became, the more resolved in his anti-Americanism, and the more popularity he seemed to attract.[135] In short, Washington failed to understand fully that Mexico's resistance stemmed from its nationalism. The pursuit of a different course was understood as evidence of hostility, a traditional, almost automatic assumption of American ideology. Had the Wilson administration grasped the catalytic property of anti-Americanism among the Mexicans, had it understood that the latter "were not anticapitalistic *per se*, although they could use the rhetoric when it supported their goals," and that "most wanted to control – not eliminate – foreign enterprises,"[136] it could have bolstered Carranza's leadership much earlier, thus securing for itself long sought Mexican favors.

The role of Mexican diplomacy vis-à-vis the United States and the European powers should not be overlooked. On the one hand, Carranza's obduracy in dealing with the United States certainly contributed to the economic pressures he had to suffer and to his difficulty in gaining control over his opponents. On the other hand, this was to be expected given his natural desire to be respected internationally and domestically as the head of a sovereign country. Perhaps Carranza took upon himself too many risks at the same time. Desirous of preserving independence from foreign powers, he needed all the domestic backing he could muster and would, perhaps, have benefited from accepting as reality the undeniable strength of some individuals, such as Manuel Peláez, in certain areas. By departing from Madero's call to national conciliation, by believing that "victory never comes by halves and that for it to be complete it is necessary to destroy the enemy," he was, perhaps, attacking foes on too many fronts.[137] Nevertheless, he was able to steer a course clear from both Germany and the United States.

Attributed to Benito Juárez, the traditional Mexican maxim "say yes, but never say when" proved to be a sounder precept to follow than economic ambitions or yearnings for worldwide democracy.[138] Of course, neither the Americans nor the Europeans had much of a feel for the Latin reliance on the virtues of *mañana*. While Mexico was ultimately left out of the game, superseded by developments in Europe, Carranza essentially maintained Mexican independence at the cost of economic losses. The Wilson administration ultimately proved to be of help in this process. By incessantly countering Carranza's struggles to bring the country out of chaos, it helped the latter regain a sense of identity sorely tried in the revolutionary turmoil, as well as a new, if fragile, national composure. Despite the deadlock, therefore, some progress had been accomplished. In this sense, to paraphrase Diaz' famous exclamation, was it perhaps after all that Mexico was nearer to God than to the United States?

Much of the reason for the deadlock that imprisoned Mexican-American relations in 1917 has to be looked for in considerations that go beyond both the clash between opposing personalities and the turns, fortunate or not, of political negotiations. It is buried, perhaps, in mutual incomprehension, in the fear bred by the deep-seated conviction of incompatibility these neighboring countries share. This is why there was to be a continual readaptation of the Monroe Doctrine to fit changed conditions. It is ironical that, formulated to defend the Western Hemisphere from intrusion, the Monroe Doctrine was, on the contrary, to perpetually recreate that threat it sought to fence off. In this sense, Calvert's remark about the Taft administration having acted "less as upholder of the Roosevelt corollary than as its prisoner" can be extrapolated to the Wilson administration as well.[139] The nationalist stance of the Mexican constitution shows that North American attempts to enlarge and enforce the Monroe Doctrine were paralleled by similar efforts on the part of Mexico to resist these attempts and shield itself off from outside intrusion. Surely, these perspectives were not unrelated; they nourished and reinforced each other. Moreover, Wilson's understanding of Mexico as the theater of European corruption also played a major role in affirming his determination to proclaim a Monroe Doctrine for the world. In the evolution of this perspective, Mexico essentially played the role of catalyst, not that of an interlocutor.[140] After having been looked at from Washington with eyes wary of a British, and then a German, peril, Mexico was soon to be watched in another light, – as the incarnation of a socialist threat.[141] There could be no resolution to a dialogue that had never really begun. As noted by Octavio Paz: "From the historical point of view, the end of the Monroe Doctrine means a return to the beginning. Our continent is open to the expansionism of powers from other continents just as it was in the sixteenth century."[142]

Notes to Chapter 14

1. "An Address to the Senate," 22 January 1917, in Arthur S. Link, David W. Hirst, John E. Little et al., eds., *The Papers of Woodrow Wilson*, 67 vols., (Princeton, 1966–1992), 40: 536.

2. Laura Garcés, *La mondialisation de la doctrine Monroe à l'ère wilsonienne*, (Lausanne, Payot), 1988, 71–81, discusses various factors that account for the particular meaning Wilson gave the European war, namely his presbyterian *Weltanschauung* which undoubtedly influenced his interpretation of world events as the theater of confrontation between "evil" and "right," his evolutionist vision of history, and the compelling impulse of his own rhetoric in which he was trapped. Klaus Schwabe, *Woodrow Wilson, Revolutionary Germany, and Peacemaking, 1918–1919, Missionary diplomacy and the Realities of Power*, (Chapel Hill, 1985), 69, makes an interesting remark on this point with respect to Germany. Wilson's intellectual background is well-analyzed by Henry W. Bragdon, *Woodrow Wilson, The Academic Years*, (Cambridge, MA., 1967).

3. "An Address to the Senate" (cf. n. 1), 539.

4. Lloyd C. Gardner, *Safe for Democracy, The Anglo-American Response to Revolution, 1913–1923*, (New York, 1984), 61.

5. Arthur S. Link, *Woodrow Wilson: Revolution, War, and Peace* (Arlington Heights, IL.), 1977; N. Gordon Levin, Jr., *Woodrow Wilson and World Politics* (New York, 1968); Gardner, *Safe for Democracy* (cf. n. 4), are three important different approaches.

6. This point is very well discussed by Gardner, *Safe for Democracy* (cf. n. 4), 61–62. Calvert mentions the influence of "constitutionalism" on the Wilson administration's outlook on Mexico, and notes the irony that two individuals as opposed in their views as Henry Lane Wilson and Woodrow Wilson should have placed so much faith in selecting a "right" leader for Mexico, which evidently would not have sufficed to cure that nation's problems: Peter Calvert, *The Mexican Revolution, 1910–1914, The Diplomacy of Anglo-American Conflict*, (Cambridge, 1968), 293–94. Michael Hunt, *Ideology and U.S. Foreign Policy*, (New Haven, 1987), comments on the North American stereotyped views of the *Latinos*, 58–62, and on Wilson's paternalism, 108–09.

7. Cf. Gardner, *Safe for Democracy* (cf. n. 4), 61–62.

8. "Conference made at the office of the Secretary of State, between the Ambassadors of Brazil, Argentina, and Chile, and the Ministers of Uruguay, Guatemala, and Bolivia, 5 August 1915," *State Department Records Relating to Internal Affairs of Mexico, 1910–1920*, 812.00/15714 – 1/2, NA, RG 59. Same idea expressed in "Continuation of the Conference on Mexican affairs, Biltmore Hotel, New York City, 11 August 1915," 812.00/15754 –1/2; "Robert Lansing to Woodrow Wilson," 6 August 1915, 812.00/15715 –1/2 A: "I said . . . that the factions of the revolutionists, which were now quarreling, were joint possessors of the sovereignty; that personal ambition and personal greed were the causes of the factions. . . ."

9. "George Creel to Lansing," 31 May 1917, *State Department Records* (cf. n. 8), 812.00/21353.

10. The origins of the Mexican revolution, much debated among high caliber historians, cannot be addressed here. Ramón Eduardo Ruíz, *The Great Rebellion, Mexico 1905–1924*, (New York, 1980), 9 f., makes an interesting comment on the decisive role of the *Porfiriato* in the outbreak of the revolution in that it encouraged the people to have new aspirations. James D. Cockcroft, *Intellectual Precursors of the Mexican Revolution*, (Austin, 1968), examines the contribution of Mexican intellectuals to the Revolution. François-Xavier Guerra, *Le Mexique, De l'Ancien Régime à la révolution*, (Paris, 1985), focuses on the discrepancy between the theoretical, mainly European, references of Díaz's regime, and the totally different social and economic reality of Mexico as a major factor in the outbreak of the Revolution. Alan Knight, *The Mexican Revolution*, (Cambridge, 1986), vol. 2: *Counter-Revolution and Reconstruction*, xi, sees the Revolution as a "genuinely popular movement and thus an example of those relatively rare events in history when the mass of the people profoundly influenced events." Knight tends to underemphasize the role of foreign powers in the revolution and argues for instance, 70, that Huerta himself, not foreign pressure, brought about his downfall. He states, 68, that "American policy had less direct impact on Mexico than has often been supposed." Friedrich Katz, *The Secret War in Mexico, Europe, the United States and the Mexican Revolution*, (Chicago, 1981), 5, brings out the role of outside rivalries and sees the Mexican revolution as originating "in the convergence of three developments on the eve of revolution, each initiated early in Diaz's reign and brought to near completion towards its end: the expropriation of the free-village lands in central and southern Mexico; the transformation of the country's northern frontier into 'the border,' that is, its political and economic integration into the rest of the country, as well as into the U.S. sphere of influence; and the emergence of Mexico as the focal point of European-American rivalry in Latin America."

11. Lloyd C. Gardner, "Woodrow Wilson and the Mexican Revolution," in Arthur S. Link, ed., *Woodrow Wilson and a Revolutionary World, 1913–1921*, (Chapel Hill, 1982), 22.

12. Calvert, *The Mexican Revolution* (cf. n. 6), 290.

13. "Wilson to Lansing," 11 August 1915, *State Department Records* (cf. n. 8), 812.00/15753 – 1/2. In April 1917, Wilson would speak of Carranza as a "pedantic ass": "Wilson to Lansing," 9 April 1917, quoted in Charles C. Cumberland, *Mexican Revolution,*

The Constitutionalist Years, (Austin, 1972), 397. Note the initial American preference for Villa in spite of his more radical position: Arthur S. Link, *Woodrow Wilson and the Progressive Era, 1910–1917,* (New York, 1954), 129; Howard F. Cline, *The United States and Mexico*, (Cambridge, 1967), 170–171, mentions the early influence of Fuller on Wilson in this respect. Katz, *The Secret War in Mexico* (cf. n. 10), 149–151.

14. Josefina Z. Vazquez, Lorenzo Meyer, *Mexico Frente a Estados Unidos, Un ensayo historico, 1776–1980*, (México, 1982), 130; Cline, *The United States and Mexico* (cf. n. 13), 172–173 comments on Woodrow Wilson's evolution from his earlier, more confident position.

15. This reluctance did not only apply to Mexico, but also to other Latin American nations as noted by Cline, *The United States and Mexico* (cf. n. 13), 174.

16. Concerns about the threat of business and financial circles represented a spontaneous projection of progressive concerns as insightfully developed and analyzed by Calvert, *The Mexican Revolution* (cf. n. 6), 295, 296–97.

17. Quoted in Gardner, *Safe for Democracy* (cf. n. 4), 56.

18. "Present Nature and Extent of the Monroe Doctrine and its Need for Restatement, Memorandum by the Counselor for the Department of State," 11 June 1914, *Papers Relating to the Foreign Relations of the United States, The Lansing Papers, 1914–1920*, vol. 2, 464.

19. Katz, *The Secret War in Mexico* (cf. n. 10), 50–62.

20. Arthur S. Link, *Woodrow Wilson and the Progressive Era* (cf. n. 13), 90–93, gives a concise explanation of this matter settled in June 1914.

21. This is apparent for instance in the evolution of American mediation efforts: Garcés, *mondialisation de la doctrine Monroe* (cf. n. 2), 284–288.

22. Quoted by Katz, *The Secret War in Mexico* (cf. n. 10), 302. Same idea in "Philip C. Hanna to Robert Lansing," 3 February 1916, *State Department Records* (cf. n. 8), 812.00/17260; Clarence C. Clendenen, *The United States and Pancho Villa, A Study in Unconventional Diplomacy* (Port Washington, 1961), 297, asserts that Wilson concurred in this idea.

23. Katz, *The Secret War in Mexico* (cf. n. 10), 461.

24. Cf. for instance Leon Canova, "Memorandum of Conditions Existing at Tampico, Mexico, on About the 15th of May, 1916*," Frank L. Polk MSS*; "Joseph Tumulty to Frank L. Polk," transmitting a letter addressed to President Wilson by David Lawrence of the *New York Evening Post*, 2 June 1916, *Frank L. Polk MSS*; "Senator Works to Robert Lansing," 30 June 1916, *State Department Records* (cf. n. 8), 812.00/18499; "John R. Silliman to Robert Lansing," 8 August 1916, 812.00/18934. Robert Lansing, *War Memoirs*, (Indianapolis, 1935), 308–311, mentions German intrigues in Mexico and Central America. The Central Powers' plottings and sabotage attempts in the United States in 1915 contributed to intensify Washington's fears and suspicions about German activity in Mexico: Katz, *The Secret War in Mexico* (cf. n. 10), 328 sq.; Arthur S. Link, *Confusions and Crises, 1915–1916*, (Princeton, 1964), 55–61.

25. Katz, *The Secret War in Mexico* (cf. n. 10), 339–344, explains that Carranza used this movement (originally sponsored by partisans of Huerta) to pressure the United States into recognizing him. Although Katz notes "that there is no evidence . . . in German archives" that Germany was involved in this plot, he asserts that "that fact is hardly conclusive since not all plots of this kind were recorded in the documents preserved in German archives." Knight, *The Mexican Revolution* (cf. n. 10), 345–346, 376–377, tends to minimize the influence of foreign powers in Mexican initiatives, arguing, 346, that "at times, it seems, adherents of the *Weltpolitik* thesis are won over less by hard evidence than by the perennial attraction of conspiracy theories, allied to the somewhat patronizing assumption that the key determinants of events lay outside Mexico: in the White House, the Wilhelmstrasse, or the offices of Standard Oil."

26. Leon Canova, "*Confidential Memorandum* for Use at the Conference with the Secretary and the Counselor," *State Department Records* (cf. n. 8), 812.00/17271–1/2; "U.S. Consul in Veracruz to Robert Lansing, 22 March 1916, *State Department Records* (cf. n. 8), 812.00/17713; "Assistant Attorney General of the Justice Department to Robert Lansing," 17 June 1916, 812.00/18503; "Parker to Robert Lansing," 23 June 1916, 812.00/18560;

"Rodgers to Robert Lansing," 28 June 1916, 812.00/18607; "Garrett to Robert Lansing," 28 June 1916, 812.00/18608.

27. "Robert Lansing to the American Consul, Brownsville, Texas," 25 February 1916, *State Department Records* (cf. n. 8), 812.00/17309; "Leon Canova, *Confidential Memorandum* for use at the Conference with the Secretary and the Counselor," 14 February 1916, 812.00/17271.

28. "John R. Silliman to Robert Lansing," 8 August 1916, transmitting a copy of a letter addressed to him from Sr. G. M. Seguin, Mexican Consul in Eagle Pass, Texas, dated 7 August 1916, which announces the formation of a new revolutionary movement, called *legalista*, aiming at fomenting U.S./Mexican friction, *State Department Records* (cf. n. 8), 812.00/18934; "Garrett to Robert Lansing," 12 June 1916 on a possible incursion of Mexican officers into Texas, 812.00/18394; "Garrett to Robert Lansing," 13 June 1916, 812.00/18418; "Johnson to Robert Lansing," 12 June 1916, 812.00/18397; "Covarrubias (former Secretary of the Mexican Legation under Romero) to Robert Lansing," 7 August 1916, on Carranza's desire to recover Texas and California, 812.00/18990.

29. "Marion Letcher to the Secretary of State, Probable Understanding of Germans in Chihuahua with Villa," 20 January 1916, *State Department Records* (cf. n. 8), 812.00/17144; "Weekly Report of general conditions along the Mexican border, based on weekly reports of January 15, 1916, from the local military commanding Officers and upon information received from all sources to date," 812.00/17152; "William Gibbs McAdoo to Robert Lansing," 25 January 1916, 812.00/17178.

30. A concise evaluation of this expedition can be found in Cline, *The United States and Mexico* (cf. n. 13), 176 sq., who also develops Wilson's delicate position in view of increasing tensions over U-boat warfare, and of the 1916 elections. Katz, *The Secret War in Mexico* (cf. n. 10), 461, explains how the Pershing expedition led Carranza to seek an understanding with Germany. On Carranza's obduracy in his dealings with the U.S. during the Pershing expedition, cf. Link, *Confusions and Crises* (cf. n. 24), 281 sq.

31. Katz, *The Secret War in Mexico* (cf. n. 10), 311–312; Robert Freeman Smith, *The United States and Revolutionary Nationalism in Mexico, 1916–1932*, (Chicago, 1972), 60–61; Cline, *The United States and Mexico* (cf. n. 13), 182.

32. *New York Times*, 3 January 1917. Cf. Carranza's official response, 6 January 1917; and his counter-proposal "which asked permission for Mexican troops to cross into the United States in pursuit of raiders provided such a right were granted the United States by Mexico," 16 January 1917. Arthur S. Link, *Wilson, Campaigns for Progressivism and Peace, 1916–1917*, (Princeton, 1965), 333 sq. gives an account of the Mexican-American negotiations and of Wilson's decision to withdraw.

33. *New York Times*, 16 January 1917.

34. *New York Times*, 21 January 1917.

35. "Carothers to Lansing," 25 March 1917, *State Department Records* (cf. n. 8), 812.00/20732; "Baker to Wilson," 16 February 1917, *Papers of Woodrow Wilson* (cf. n. 1), 42: 236–37.

36. United States Senate, "Affairs in Mexico," Senate Reports, 66th Congress, 2d Session, 1 December 1919–5 June 1920, vol. B, (Washington, 1920), 53. Cf. also United States Senate, Committee on Foreign Relations, *Investigation of Mexican Affairs: Preliminary Report and Hearings*, 66th Cong., 2d Sess., 2 vols. (Washington, 1920), vol. 1, 1240, 1311, 1322–23; vol. 2, 2899, 2982. Allegations about Carranza's connections with Germany in 1917 are abundant: "Jones to Lansing," 12 April 1917, *State Department Records* (cf. n. 8), 812.00/20788; "Carothers to Lansing," 15 April 1917, 812.00/20808; "Baker to Lansing," 1 May 1917, 812.00/20868; "Fletcher to Lansing," 3 December 1917, 862.20212/836.

37. Senate, "Affairs in Mexico," 66th Congress, 2d Session, 1 December, 1919–5 June 1920, vol. B, (Washington, 1920), 53–54. Senate, *Investigation of Mexican Affairs* (cf. n. 36), vol. 2, 3241. On concerns over Germany's desire to capitalize on Mexican hostility for the United States after American intervention, cf. "William P. Blocker to Lansing," 30 July 1917, *State Department Records* (cf. n. 8), 812.00/21177; "Baker to Daniels," 18 August 1917, 812.00/21205. Rumors of a possible Mexican attack in other Central American

countries continued in 1917: "Robert Lansing to Woodrow Wilson," 8 October 1917, *Papers of Woodrow Wilson* (cf. n. 1), 44: 331.

38. On Villa: "Funston to Baker," 26 December 1916, *State Department Records* (cf. n. 8), 812.00/20199, mentioning an understanding between Villa and the Germans to invade the oil district; "McAdoo to Polk," 22 December 1916, 812.00/20208; "McAdoo to Polk," 4 January 1917, 812.00/20256 1/2; On Murguía: "Cobb to Lansing," 7 August 1917, 862. 20212/571; "Cobb to Polk," 13 August 1917, 812.00/21186; "Cobb to Lansing," 23 August 1917, 812.00/21231; "Cobb to Lansing," 18 September 1917, 812.00/21294; "Cobb to Lansing," 12 November 1917, 862.20212/782; "Lansing to Fletcher," 7 December 1917, 862.20212/818; On Obregón: "Pittsburg to Daniels," 14 April 1917, 812.00/20872; On Peláez: "Dawson to Lansing," 8 October 1917, 812.00/21371; "Lansing to Fletcher," 23 October 1917, 812.00/21411 a.

39. "Lansing to Fletcher," 22 August 1917, *State Department Records* (cf. n. 8), 862.20212/580 a, mentioning possibility of placing an embargo on the shipment of paper, and Fletcher's answer advocating control but against strict embargo: "Fletcher to Lansing," 28 August 1917, 862.20212/581; "Fletcher to Lansing," 6 September 1917, 862.20212/599; "Coen to Lansing," 9 September 1917, 862.20212/625; "Cobb to Lansing," 28 August 1917, 862.20212/638. The different measures planned to counter this German propaganda in Mexico are well summarized in *Papers of Woodrow Wilson* (cf. n. 1), 44: 91, n 1.

40. *New York Times*, 15 March 1917, 17 March 1917.

41. "Hanna to Lansing," 18 August 1917, *State Department Records* (cf. n. 8), 862.20212/545; "Dawson to Lansing," 23 August 1917, 862.20212/591.

42. *New York Times*, 15 March 1917.

43. "William Hines Page to Robert Lansing," 24 February 1917, *State Department Records* (cf. n. 8), 862.20212/69. This telegram announced that Germany intended to begin unlimited U-Boat warfare on February 1. In the event America did not remain neutral, Germany proposed an alliance to Mexico promising "substantial financial support and an agreement . . . for Mexico to reconquer its former territories in Texas, New Mexico, and Arizona." It also proposed that following the outbreak of war with the United States a proposal of alliance be made to Japan. The circumstances in which this telegram was conceived, and its details, are very well-analyzed by Katz, *The Secret War in Mexico* (cf. n. 10), 350–78. This essay chooses to deemphasize its impact and to situate it in the continuity of the apprehensions plaguing U.S.-Mexican relations since 1915.

44. *New York Times*, 1 March 1917.

45. Quoted in *New York Times*, 1 March 1917. Katz, *The Secret War in Mexico* (cf. n. 10), 461, relates this attitude to "German plots on Huerta's behalf, about which he was well informed."

46. *New York Times*, 2 March 1917; cf. also *New York Times*, 3 March 1917.

47. *New York Times*, 4 March 1917.

48. "Frank L. Polk to Henry Fletcher," 26 February 1917, *State Department Records* (cf. n. 8), 862.20212/70A.

49. "Henry Fletcher to Robert Lansing," 10 March 1917, *State Department Records* (cf. n. 8), 862.20212/89. Henry Fletcher had been designated Ambassador in February.

50. "Henry Fletcher to Robert Lansing," 13 March 1917, *State Department Records* (cf. n. 8), 862. 20212/119.

51. "Henry Fletcher to Robert Lansing," 13 March 1917, *State Department Records* (cf. n. 8), 862. 20212/119; *New York Times*, 3 March 1917. Other prominent Mexicans, such as Obregón, adopted just as dexterous a position in dealing with the Americans on this sensitive issue as noted by Katz, *The Secret War in Mexico* (cf. n. 10), 523: "Obregón's statements show that he was skillfully exploiting the great powers' contradictions without taking one side or another. What was at stake . . . was not the desire to collaborate with Germany, but the limits of such cooperation. For Carranza, Aguilar, and Obregón, the limits were fixed at the point where American intervention became a danger." Washington's misperception of Mexican sensitivity with regard to independence led it to mistake the issue for a struggle between a pro-German Carranza and a pro-American Obregón. On this cf. "Lansing to

Fletcher," 2 April 1917, *State Department Records* (cf. n. 8), 862.20212/ 173 a; "Fletcher to Lansing," 4 April 1917, 862.20212/177. Mexican attempts at maintaining independence also go to explain why the U.S. had difficulty in identifying the allegiance of Mexican leaders who appeared to shift constantly between a pro-American and a pro-German position. On Obregón's pro-German and Carranza's pro-Allied positions, cf. "James W. Keys to Lansing," 3 August 1917, F.W. 812.00/21220; on Villa as pro-German, cf. "Cobb to Lansing," 5 September 1917, 812.00/21259; on Cantú, having switched from a policy favorable to the U.S. to a pro-German orientation, cf. "Carothers to Lansing," 25 March 1917, 812.00/20732. It is this tendency to associate Mexican actions and intentions with foreign influences, and the inability to draw a firm conclusion as to the Mexican position precisely because the latter was not primarily determined by the preoccupation of carrying out the plans of other powers, but by nationalist considerations, which brought U.S. diplomacy vis-à-vis Carranza into a self-defeating quandary (between the will to stabilize his government by giving him the necessary material means, and to withhold such aid to pressure him into a perfect alignment with the United States).

52. Cited by Cumberland, *Mexican Revolution* (cf. n. 13), 396, who concludes, however, that Carranza's sympathies lay with the Germans.

53. *New York Times*, 1 March 1917.

54. *New York Times*, 1 March 1917, 2 March 1917. Cf. Mexico's refutations of such a charge: "Lansing to Wilson," 7 March 1917, enclosing a dispatch from Fletcher, dated 21 February 1917, *Papers of Woodrow Wilson* (cf. n. 1), 351. It is interesting to note that similar proposals emanating from the Vatican were also linked to German influence: "Thomas N. Page to Lansing," 20 March 1917, *Papers of Woodrow Wilson* (cf. n. 1), 42: 433–435.

55. "Henry Fletcher to Lansing," 10 March 1917, *State Department Records* (cf. n. 8), 862. 20212/89. Fletcher tried to use the issue of lifting the arms embargo to pressure Carranza into making a public statement on the Zimmermann telegram: "Fletcher to Lansing," 13 March 1917, 862.20212/119.

56. "Lansing to Wilson," 14 March 1917, *Papers of Woodrow Wilson* (cf. n. 1), 42: 404; "Wilson to Lansing," 14 March 1917, *Papers of Woodrow Wilson* (cf. n. 1), 42:404–406.

57. Lansing, *War Memoirs* (cf. n. 24), 308, 314 (U.S. apprehension with regard to Mexican neutrality came from concerns about Mexican oil), and 315 on Mexico's assurance that Mexico would not place an embargo on oil. 316: Lansing also noted the disappointment caused by Argentina and Chile's neutrality, and the "disquietude caused by the action of Mexico, Ecuador and Argentina each of which attempted to organize conferences of the Latin American Republics to consider the question of neutrality and its enforcement."

58. "Lansing to Fletcher," 21 April 1917, *Papers of Woodrow Wilson* (cf. n. 1): 42, 116. On March 17, however, Mexico issued "an absolute declaration of neutrality, asserting in definite terms that it is the determination of Mexico to devote its affairs to keeping any country on this continent from taking part in the European war": *New York Times*, 18 March 1917.

59. Katz, *The Secret War in Mexico* (cf. n. 10), 441, and 62 sq. on Mexico's strategic importance for the Germans. Brígida von Mentz, *México en el siglo XIX visto por los Alemanes*, (México, 1980), provides an interesting view on the shaping of the German vision of Mexico during the nineteenth century.

60. Katz, *The Secret War in Mexico* (cf. n. 10), 62–63: "The total failure of [German maneuvers] was matched only by their clumsiness and vacillation, for German policy wavered constantly between the desire to use Mexico as an anti-American instrument and the fear of antagonizing the United States because of Mexico," cf. also 71: "Germany . . . underestimated the strength and determination of the United States to put Europe in its place as far as Mexico was concerned." Knight, *The Mexican Revolution* (cf. n. 10), 614, note 438, remarks that "German policy is more notable for its internal fragmentation than for its direct impact on events in Mexico."

61. Katz, *The Secret War in Mexico* (cf. n. 10), 364.

62. Katz, *The Secret War in Mexico* (cf. n. 10), 429, 430; "Silliman to Lansing," 9 August 1917, *State Department Records* (cf. n. 8), 862.20212/548; "Silliman to Lansing," 25 September 1917, 862.20212/668; 416 sq. on German intelligence in Mexico, and 433 sq., on

the Allies' awareness of Germany's undercover activities in Mexico, thanks to British breaking of the German secret code; 397, 399–403, on the question of a German loan to Mexico.

63. "Sir William Wiseman to Sir Cecil Spring-Rice," 6 March 1917, *Papers of Woodrow Wilson* (cf. n. 1): 42, 348. W.B. Fowler, *British-American Relations, 1917–1918, The Role of Sir William Wiseman*, (Princeton, 1969), 19–24, comments on this memorandum and on Wiseman's role in furthering Anglo-American association at this time.

64. "Lansing to Wilson," 11 April 1917, *Papers of Woodrow Wilson* (cf. n. 1), 42: 37.

65. "Wilson to Lansing," 19 April 1917, *Papers of Woodrow Wilson* (cf. n. 1), 42: 96. Gardner, *Safe for Democracy* (cf. n. 4), 204–206, comments insightfully on this evolution and on Wilson's position.

66. Lansing, *War Memoirs* (cf. n. 24), 308; Cline, *The United States and Mexico* (cf. n. 13), 171. The failure of the Pershing expedition to capture Villa also contributed to discourage the U.S. from intervention in Mexico as noted by Friedrich Katz, "Pancho Villa and the Attack on Columbus, New Mexico," *American Historical Review*, vol. 83 (1978), 130. Note that the British and American positions in regard to Mexico evolved in opposite directions after 1917, the first more aggressive aiming at Carranza's downfall and the second geared to promoting stability: cf. Katz, *The Secret War in Mexico* (cf. n. 10), 460.

67. "Carothers to Lansing," 30 May 1917, *State Department Records* (cf. n. 8), 812.00/20966–1/2, noting, however, that Carranza will never succeed in the long-term. Carothers' proposal aimed at diminishing the power of the military, which he considered "almost unanimously pro-German" and reconciling "the civil faction . . . composed of the intelligent men of the country, who realize the folly of such a policy. . . ." This vision shows how the American understanding of Germany influenced its perception of Mexico. Carothers continued to advocate the same position towards the end of the year: "Carothers to Lansing," 18 October 1917, 812.00/21383. Lansing betrayed a similar perspective: "Robert Lansing to Woodrow Wilson," 18 April 1917, in *Papers of Woodrow Wilson* (cf. n. 1), 42, 92–93: "It appears to me that the military party in the Mexican government is controlling its policies and that that party is intensely pro-German or at least anti-American. Whatever may be Carranza's personal views I do not think that he will strong enough to resist the pressure of the element hostile to us. . . ."

68. "Homer C. Coen to Robert Lansing," 27 August 1917, *State Department Records* (cf. n. 8), 812.00/21235.

69. Cline, *The United States and Mexico* (cf. n. 13), 181; "John Pershing to Hugh Scott," 1 May 1917, *Papers of Woodrow Wilson* (cf. n. 1), 42: 226.

70. Smith, *The United States and Revolutionary Nationalism in Mexico* (cf. n. 31), 113–114.

71. Douglas W. Richmond, *Venustiano Carranza's Nationalist Struggle, 1893–1920*, (Lincoln, 1983), 121–124, comments on Carranza's efforts to deal with the food shortage.

72. Cf. Wilson's vehement refutal of a statement made by Edmund E. Martinez, a representative of the Mexican Federation of Labor, according to which, in an interview with Wilson in July, the American President had promised to lift the arms embargo and assist in the coining of money: "Frank Polk to Wilson," 6 August 1917, *Papers of Woodrow Wilson* (cf. n. 1), 43: 378–79; "Wilson to Polk," 7 August 1917, *Papers of Woodrow Wilson* (cf. n. 1): 381; and Gompers' account of this interview: "Samuel Gompers to Woodrow Wilson," 13 August 1947, *Papers of Woodrow Wilson* (cf. n. 1) 43: 449–450.

73. "Navy Department, Office of Naval Intelligence to State Department," 17 September 1917, *State Department Records* (cf. n. 8), 812.00/21349.

74. Smith, *The United States and Revolutionary Nationalism in Mexico* (cf. n. 31), 109–110.

75. "Canova to Lansing, In re Mexican Policy. Recommendation as to what the United States can do to rehabilitate Mexico, and Reasons Therefor," 18 June 1917, *State Department Records* (cf. n. 8), 812.00/21170.

76. Quoted in Smith, *The United States and Revolutionary Nationalism in Mexico* (cf. n. 31), 113. Cumberland, *Mexican Revolution* (cf. n. 13), 397. Cf. "Wilson to Lansing," 7 August 1917, *Papers of Woodrow Wilson* (cf. n. 1), 43: 384–385. On August 8, Fletcher was instructed to tell Carranza among others, that such a loan would unlikely be granted unless the government was prepared to give certain guaranties in regard to foreign property, 384, n. 1.

77. Smith, *The United States and Revolutionary Nationalism in Mexico* (cf. n. 31), 113, mentions Fred I. Kent of the Federal Reserve Board; Katz, *The Secret War in Mexico* (cf. n. 10), 470.

78. "Lansing to Wilson," 25 April 1917, *Papers of Woodrow Wilson* (cf. n. 1), 42: 130–131; also "Lansing to Fletcher," 28 April 1917, *Papers of Woodrow Wilson* (cf. n. 1), 42: 154–155.

79. "Homer C. Coen to Robert Lansing," 27 August 1917, 812.00/21235; Smith, *The United States and Revolutionary Nationalism in Mexico* (cf. n. 31), 110, also notes the fear that "British and French business interests might use Mexico's financial problems to force a unilateral settlement (which might be detrimental to U.S. interests) or even to help a counter-revolutionary movement overthrow Carranza before the end of the war."

80. Smith, *The United States and Revolutionary Nationalism in Mexico* (cf. n. 31), 60–61; cf. Cline, *The United States and Mexico* (cf. n. 13), 182.

81. Smith, *The United States and Revolutionary Nationalism in Mexico* (cf. n. 31), 73. Cf. 71 sq. for a clear presentation of the main lines of the constitution. Vazquez, Meyer, *Mexico Frente a Estados Unidos* (cf. n. 14), 133–134, comments on the heterogeneity of the *carrancista* coalition divided between a group of *renovadores*, who supported Carranza's position and did not break too much away from the old constitution, and the *jacobinos* who favored drastic changes; cf. Katz, *The Secret War in Mexico* (cf. n. 10), 318–319, for a analysis of the respective successes achieved by both groups: if on the whole, the radicals managed to impose their view calling for deep social and economic changes, Carranza more often than not refused to proceed to a redistribution of land. As noted by Vazquez, Meyer, *Mexico Frente a Estados Unidos* (cf. n. 14), 139, The Calvo Doctrine was the one constitutional provision which Carranza continued to insist upon, while he was never eager to press neither for the implementation of labor legislation nor for agrarian reform; on the same subject, cf. Daniel James, *Mexico and the Americans*, (New York, 1963), 193.

82. "Mexican News Notes," February 1917, *State Department Records* (cf. n. 8), 812.00/20729.

83. Smith, *The United States and Revolutionary Nationalism in Mexico* (cf. n. 31), 27–28, explains the origins of the Calvo Doctrine, and, 82–84, comments on Carranza's application of the doctrine; James, *Mexico and the Americans* (cf. n. 90), 193, enumerates other articles of nationalist intent (Art. 9, forbidding foreigners from taking part in Mexico's political life, Art. 32, giving general preference to Mexicans over foreigners with regard to government concessions and employment, Art. 33, providing for the expulsion of undesirable foreigners, who showed themselves reluctant to follow the law.)

84. Vazquez, Meyer, *Mexico Frente a Estados Unidos* (cf. n. 14), 139.

85. Smith, *The United States and Revolutionary Nationalism in Mexico* (cf. n. 31), 88 sq. On June 24, Carranza ordered that the basic prohibitions of the constitution had gone into effect on February 5, the day of the Constitution's publication: Cumberland, *Mexican Revolution* (cf. n. 13), 394. Lorenzo Meyer, *Mexico and the United States in the Oil Controversy, 1917–1942*, (Austin, 1972), 48–49, goes back on the origins of American concerns in 1915 and 1916. Echoes of these concerns can be found in "Judge Helbert Haff to Robert Lansing," 5 May 1917, *State Department Records* (cf. n. 8), 812.00/21233.

86. Ruíz, *The Great Rebellion* (cf. n. 10), 397–98, notes that this tradition of Spanish colonial law, which had been altered by Díaz, had gradually been reestablished since Madero's administration. The latter had begun an attempt to recover this right by levying a tax on crude petroleum, a measure which the constitutionalists continued before deciding on the setting up of a commission (March 1915) to study the problem; cf. also Cumberland, *Mexican Revolution* (cf. n. 13), 251; Meyer, *Mexico and the United States in the Oil Controversy* (cf. n. 85), 48; Smith, *The United States and Revolutionary Nationalism in Mexico* (cf. n. 31), 44–47, summarizes the debates in Washington between 1916 and 1917 following the attempt to assert Mexican control over the oil industry. For archival sources indicating concern, cf. "Leon Canova to Robert Lansing," 5 July 1917, enclosing memorandum dated 14 June 1917, *State Department Records* (cf. n. 8), 812.00/21171.

87. "Lansing to Wilson," 7 March 1917, enclosing a dispatch from Fletcher, dated 21 February 1917, (cf. n. 54); cf. "From the Diary of Chandler Parsons Anderson," 8 March

1917, *Papers of Woodrow Wilson* (cf. n. 1), 42: 365–67, on the necessity of protecting American rights in Mexico against the retroactive application of the constitutional provisions; cf. also "From the Diary of Chandler Parsons Anderson," 10 March 1917, *Papers of Woodrow Wilson* (cf. n. 1), 42: 385–387.

88. "Lansing to Wilson," 25 April 1917, (cf. n. 78); this was also the fear expressed by certain business interests: "From the Diary of Chandler Parsons Anderson," 8 March 1917, *Papers of Woodrow Wilson* (cf. n. 1), 42: 364; "From the Diary of Chandler Parsons Anderson," 10 March 1917, *Papers of Woodrow Wilson* (cf. n. 1), 42: 385–87;

89. "Lansing to Wilson," 7 March 1917, enclosing a dispatch from Fletcher, dated 21 February 1917, (cf. n. 57).

90. Richmond, *Venustiano Carranza's Nationalist Struggle* (cf. n. 79), 124–129, gives an overview of Carranza's efforts to control labor since 1915 while acceding to some of the latter's demands, whereas Jean Meyer, "Les ouvriers dans la Révolution mexicaine: les bataillons rouges," *Annales*, 25 (1970), 30–53, fundamentally questions the existence of a labor movement with a class consciousness in Mexico at that time, arguing that workers tended to rally around *caudillos* and were primarily motivated by nationalism.

91. Vazquez, Meyer, *Mexico Frente a Estados Unidos* (cf. n. 14), 135; Gardner, *Safe for Democracy* (cf. n. 4), 68–69; Katz, *The Secret War in Mexico* (cf. n. 10), 512 stresses the "utter groundlessness of the charge that Germany was controlling Mexico," citing, for instance, Eckardt's extremely negative reaction to the Mexican constitution of 1917.

92. Knight, *The Mexican Revolution* (cf. n. 10), 489, 642, n. 1223.

93. "James W. Keys to Lansing," 3 August 1917, *State Department Records* (cf. n. 8), F.W. 812.00/21220.

94. "Thomas Beaumont Hohler to Lord Hardinge," 23 March 1917, enclosing a memorandum of conversation with Colonel House in New York on March 9, *Papers of Woodrow Wilson* (cf. n. 1), 42: 459. On the controversial point of knowing how important Mexico's oil was for the allies during the war, Cumberland, *Mexican Revolution* (cf. n. 13), 391, note 91.

95. "From the Diary of Chandler Parsons Anderson," 10 March 1917, *Papers of Woodrow Wilson* (cf. n. 1), 42: 385–87. Link, *Wilson, Campaigns for Progressivism and Peace, 1916–1917* (cf. n. 32), 337, discusses the difference between Wilson's attitude, more favorable to granting recognition to Carranza because of German intrigues in Mexico, and the position defended by Anderson, Polk, and Lansing who wanted to make recognition dependent upon the conclusion of a treaty protecting American rights and property against retroactive application of art. 27.

96. "Baker to Wilson," 5 April 1917, enclosing a despatch from Pershing, dated April 5, 1917, *Papers of Woodrow Wilson* (cf. n. 1): 42: 545–546.

97. "David Lawrence to Woodrow Wilson," 27 January 1917, *Papers of Woodrow Wilson* (cf. n. 1) 41: 43–44.

98. "Woodrow Wilson to Robert Lansing," 19 April 1917, *Papers of Woodrow Wilson* (cf. n. 1), 42: 95.

99. "Polk to Fletcher," 28 September 1917, *State Department Records* (cf. n. 8), 812.00/21270.

100. "Canova to Auchincloss," 12 September 1917, *State Department Records* (cf. n. 8), 812.00/21260.

101. Knight, *The Mexican Revolution* (cf. n. 10), 210.

102. "Sloane Gordon to Canova," 6 September 1917, *State Department Records* (cf. n. 8), 812.00/21257; "Carothers to Robert Lansing," 25 March 1917, 812.00/20732, noting that Cantú's allegiance has shifted since 1916 from the U.S. to Germany.

103. Meyer, *Mexico and the United States in the Oil Controversy* (cf. n. 85), 45; Cumberland, *Mexican Revolution* (cf. n. 13), 251. Knight, *The Mexican Revolution* (cf. n. 10), 199–200, discusses the landowners' attempts to "colonize the revolution" and distinguishes two different trends: "while some landlord revolts after 1914 were clearly, ideologically conservative, in that they resisted the radical change (including land reform) implied by the revolution, there were many in which this element was secondary or absent, and where the rebels . . . represented a collective, parochial protest against revolutionary invasion, control

and centralisation." On Peláez, cf. 201–202, and on the nature of his relations with the oil companies, 386–388.

104. Meyer, *Mexico and the United States in the Oil Controversy* (cf. n. 85), 45.

105. Cited in Ruíz, *The Great Rebellion* (cf. n. 10), 399.

106. Cumberland, *Mexican Revolution* (cf. n. 13), 390–391.

107. Meyer, *Mexico and the United States in the Oil Controversy* (cf. n. 85), 45.

108. "Claude Dawson to Lansing," 15 April 1917, *State Department Records* (cf. n. 8), 862.20212/233.

109. "Carothers to Lansing," 25 March 1917, *State Department Records* (cf. n. 8), 812.00/20732. Katz, *The Secret War in Mexico* (cf. n. 10), 463, develops the subject of British support to Peláez, and the consequent deterioration of relations between Carranza and London. One of the three British plans envisaged between March and June 1917 to overthrow Carranza banked on Peláez as the central element in an anti-Carranza coalition, 466.

110. Senate, *Investigation of Mexican Affairs* (cf. n. 36), vol. 1: 840.

111. Knight, *The Mexican Revolution* (cf. n. 10), 386–387; Ruíz, *The Great Rebellion* (cf. n. 10), 399. Certain representatives of the oil companies later claimed that they had insisted that Carranza drive Peláez out: cf. for instance Senate, *Investigation of Mexican Affairs* (cf. n. 36), vol. 1, 281.

112. "Claude Dawson to Lansing," 15 April 1917, *State Department Records* (cf. n. 8), 862.20212/233.

113. "Dawson to Lansing, Effort to be made by Mexican government to control the oil region now dominated by General Peláez," 6 September 1917, *State Department Records* (cf. n. 8), 812.00/21272. "William W. Canada to Robert Lansing," 14 September 1917, 812.00/21273, sends a warning to the same effect.

114. "Canova to Polk," 19 October 1917, *State Department Records* (cf. n. 8), 812.00/21330.

115. "Canova to Polk," 26 September 1917, transmitting a report from USS Annapolis to Opnav, Washington, dated 25 September 1917, *State Department Records* (cf. n. 8), 812.00/21303. On Peláez's refutations of being involved in a German plot, cf. "USS Annapolis to Opnav., Washington," 26 September 1917, 812.00/21304.

116. "Canova to Polk," 26 September 1917, transmitting a report from USS Annapolis to Opnav, Washington, dated 25 September 1917, *State Department Records* (cf. n. 8), 812.00/21303.

117. Knight, *The Mexican Revolution* (cf. n. 10), 387. Note however that the relations between Peláez and the United States as well as the oil companies eventually deteriorated as Carranza gained ground in the Huasteca. On this point, cf. Meyer, *Mexico and the United States in the Oil Controversy* (cf. n. 85), 51; Knight, *The Mexican Revolution* (cf. n. 10), 387–388.

118. Cumberland, *Mexican Revolution* (cf. n. 13), 394–395.

119. Ruíz, *The Great Rebellion* (cf. n. 10), 398.

120. Cline, *The United States and Mexico* (cf. n. 13), 183.

121. "Lansing to Fletcher," 15 November 1917, *State Department Records* (cf. n. 8), 812.00/21453.

122. "Dawson to Lansing," 10 November 1917, *State Department Records* (cf. n. 8), 812.00/21455; note that some favored sending forces in view of an imminent *carrancista* campaign for possession of the oil fields: "Canova to Polk," 8 January 1918, 812.00/21651, while others feared that a U.S. intervention would cause the Mexicans to unite against the foreign intruder: "USS annapolis to Chief of Naval operations," received 10 January 1918, 812.00/21649.

123. "Ferris to Fletcher," 20 October 1917, *State Department Records* (cf. n. 8), 812.00/21417; "Dawson to Lansing," 13 October 1917, 812.00/21381, writing that Carranza's move against Peláez is prompted by fear of a revolutionary uprising; "USS Annapolis to Chief of Naval Operations," 23 November 1917, 812.00/21498 on a possible move of Peláez against Carranza.

124. "Hanna to Lansing," 3 January 1918, *State Department Records* (cf. n. 8), 812.00/21633.

125. He did succeed to some extent in laying the blame of the telegram's disclosure on Bernstorff, a blame which brought American fears of German infiltration to their culmination and promptly backfired on Germany: cf. *New York Times*, 1 March 1917: On Berlin's desire to avoid a break with Mexico "which would have completely discredited . . . Zimmermann who was still in office at that time," cf. Katz, *The Secret War in Mexico* (cf. n. 10), 398. Cf. also *ibid.*, 460, where Katz notes the widening divergencies between the intelligence service of the General Staff which "advocated an aggressive policy aimed at provoking U.S. intervention, while the business interests, with the increasing support of the Foreign Office, pursued the opposite aim of keeping the United States out of Mexico in the hope of converting Mexico into an object of German economic expansion."

126. Fowler, *British-American Relations* (cf. n. 38), 211–212.

127. Knight, *The Mexican Revolution* (cf. n. 10), 5: "The personal, the immediate, the contingent, thus overrode the dictates of ideology."

128. Knight, *The Mexican Revolution* (cf. n. 10), 104, quoting Córdova, *Ideología*.

129. Calvert, *The Mexican Revolution* (cf. n. 6), 301, enumerates the consequences of non-recognition: "financial starvation, exacerbating the revolutionary temper by its burden on the lower classes; the arming of the Constitutionalists, which encouraged a devastating civil war; and armed intervention itself, to end all hopes that non-recognition might be regarded as being a safe alternative to war."

130. Smith, *The United States and Revolutionary Nationalism in Mexico* (cf. n. 31), 91.

131. Smith, *The United States and Revolutionary Nationalism in Mexico* (cf. n. 31), 112–114. "George Sammerlin to Robert Lansing," 17 July 1917, 812.00/21150, NA, RG 59.

132. Cline, *The United States and Mexico* (cf. n. 13), 181, mentions Carranza's purchase of arms with the Japanese after Wilson's ban on arms exports in 1916.

133. Knight, *The Mexican Revolution* (cf. n. 10), 49–50.

134. A good illustration of this is the manner in which the different regions related to the agrarian problem as developed by Knight, *The Mexican Revolution* (cf. n. 10), 186–187: "While in Morelos *agrarismo* dictated the character of the civil war, in the north the civil war dictated the character of *agrarismo*. Committed to a long, conventional war, the northern leaders needed a continuous supply of men and resources; they could not halt cash-crop production; and they would not jeopardise their mass armies by exposing them to the lure of land distribution. So, throughout the North, confiscated estates were often kept intact, and worked for the good of the cause, either directly or through commercial contracts. In Sonora, this was evident from the early days of the Constitutionalist revolution, and it proceeded in typically efficient, Sonoran fashion, with no hint of popular agrarianism." 199, Knight also notes the opposition to centralization.

135. Katz, *The Secret War in Mexico* (cf. n. 10), 309, remarks that the Pershing expedition had been a bitter, if ironic, illustration of this. "The farther the punitive expedition penetrated in Mexico, the less disposed many of Carranza's soldiers were to fight Villa. As war with the United States came to seem more and more imminent, they wanted to concentrate on repelling the foreign invaders." It is interesting to note how much support Villismo drew during the Pershing expedition considering that, in contrast to Zapatismo, for instance, Villismo "was remote, diffuse, ideologically vague. . . .": Knight, *The Mexican Revolution* (cf. n. 10), 284.

136. Smith, *The United States and Revolutionary Nationalism in Mexico* (cf. n. 31), 76. Cf. also 79.

137. Córdova, *Ideología*, cited by Knight, *The Mexican Revolution* (cf. n. 10), 180.

138. Cited by Robert A. Pastor, Jorge G. Castañeda, *Limits to Friendship, The United States and Mexico*, (New York, 1988), 24.

139. Calvert, *The Mexican Revolution* (cf. n. 6), 289. This does not imply agreement with Calvert's statement, 303, that "what distinguished" Taft and Wilson was "the personal feeling he gave to the matter" which does not address the issue of Wilsonian messianism. In a similar sense, 299: "In 1917, as in 1914, [the President] found himself leading his country to war to uphold his word, and taking refuge in the meaningless phrases of Fourth of July rhetoric." This assertion, insightful to the extent that it denotes the hold of ideas on Wil-

son's thought, does not address the essential issue of knowing why what is characterized as "meaningless" provided such a powerful rationale for action. The question raised by Schwabe, *Woodrow Wilson* (cf. n.2), 8 – "Does an ideologically conceived missionary foreign policy not tend to obscure the real issues at stake in a given set of international negotiations?" appears to overlook the fact that ideology determines the awareness of "real issues at stake," and that it cannot be discarded as a superfluous, "neutral," factor.

140. Garcés, *mondialisation de la doctrine Monroe* (cf. n.2), 203–226.

141. Gardner, *Safe for Democracy* (cf. n. 4), 209; Senate, *Investigation of Mexican Affairs* (cf. n. 36), vol. 1, p. 829; vol. 2, p. 2820.

142. Octavio Paz, "Latin America and Democracy," in Octavio Paz, Jorge Edwards, Carlos Franqui et al., eds., *Democracy and Dictatorship in Latin America*, (New York, 1982), 13.

15

German Economic War Aims Reconsidered: The American Perspective

Georges-Henri Soutou

The American perception of German economic war aims gradually evolved during World War I. Initially rather benign and practicing a kind of moral equivalence, it tended to equate Germany's aims with those of the Allies. Slowly, however, the opinion emerged that Germany's prewar economic policy contradicted the practices of air trade even more than did the commercial practices of the Allied powers. As a result, Germany's main war aim, the creation of a politically and economically closely knit Mitteleuropa, appeared to be a dangerous breach of world order, even more serious than the economic aims of the Allies as defined by the Allied Economic Conference of June 1916. The harsh economic terms of the Brest-Litovsk and Bucharest treaties, in March and May 1918 respectively, convinced President Woodrow Wilson that Germany was the major threat to the restoration of a fair economic world order. He then became ready to support at least some of the objectives of Paris and London, and fully concurred in the preparation of the severe economic terms of the Treaty of Versailles, even if, in the long term, his views were still different from those of the Allies.

While it is not possible to discuss the American war aims in detail here, there existed a relationship between their development and the evolving perception of Germany's motives. Until 1916 American foreign economic policy relied on bilateralism. Its aim, as expressed by the Underwood Act of 1913, was to conclude bilateral trade agreements based on reciprocity. Every concession from the high tariff was to be paid by each country separately and American concessions to one country would not be extended automatically to another. In other words, Washington did not practice – but of course benefited freely and unilaterally from – the most-favored-nation clause, a prominent feature in the tariff laws and trade agreements between the major European partners of the United States.

Note to Chapter 15 can be found on page 321.

During the first part of World War I, the United States practiced a kind of economic Monroe Doctrine, with Washington trying to use the war to replace European interests in the Western Hemisphere with American trade and capital. But another trend, particularly favored by New York bankers in cooperation with Great Britain and the Allies, supported a worldwide trade policy, as opposed to a hemispheric one. When he decided to enter the war, President Wilson swung to the side of the pro-European forces of American economy and finally adopted the Open Door policy. In his view, this policy was the best way to promote both peace and democracy, as well as secure American interests in the postwar world. In this move from bilateralism and a hemispheric trade policy to multilateralism and the Open Door, Wilson was influenced to a large extent by his changing perception of German war aims.

The German trade policy towards the United States before the war was altogether benign – and understood as such in Washington. At the time of the German-American trade agreement of 1910, Berlin intended to grant the United States the benefit of the most-favored-nation clause in case Germany concluded more advantageous agreements with other countries. But in 1911 Washington granted special bilateral terms to Canada, which thus prevented Berlin from extending the most-favored treatment to the United States in the same year that it made with Sweden and Japan. As a result of this and other factors, the State Department decided in April 1914 that the bilateral trade policy of the Underwood Tariff was not in the American interest, and that a multilateral policy (i.e., the Open Door) should be adopted. This considerable change would not be completed before 1917, however.

One cannot say that a real trade rivalry existed between Germany and the United States before 1914. When Paul Warburg, brother of the Hamburg banker Max Warburg, consulted his European colleagues in 1913 about the creation of the Federal Reserve System, German bankers hoped that the United States would establish a strong currency, thus preventing the recurrence of monetary crises that had frequently crippled the world economy since the end of the nineteenth century. A strong American economy was seen in German banking and industrial quarters as essential to the well-being of world trade. The obsession with and hostility to American economic power was evident in *Alldeutsch* circles and for those publicists who supported a central European trade association in competition with Russia, the British Empire, and the United States. This was not the policy of either the German government or German industry and finance before 1914. In September 1914, however, Chancellor Theobald von Bethmann Hollweg accepted the concept of *Mitteleuropa*, which was based on a customs union of European countries around Germany. Bethmann Hollweg did not adopt the concept for economic reasons – he knew that the European market was already too small for Germany and that other countries would impose higher tariffs against Germany – but for political reasons. In his view, *Mitteleuropa* was the only way Berlin could control the European continent and the unstable Austrian Empire. For Bethmann Hollweg, no other way could secure the Reich against the combined hostility of England, France and Russia. On the other hand, the bureaucracy, the bankers, and most of the industrialists adamantly opposed *Mitteleuropa*, fearing the reaction of the other markets, which were far more important to them.

In 1914 President Wilson did not hold Germany solely responsible for the war. He certainly did not believe that Berlin presented an economic threat, even if he felt that the German political system needed to be radically reformed. In 1915 and 1916 Wilson and the American public opposed the prospect of *Mitteleuropa*, but did not think that it was more dangerous for American interests than the preferential tariff policy which discriminated against both Germany and the neutrals, that the Allies began discussing at the end of 1915. The January 1916 session of the National Foreign Trade Council deemed both the German and the Allied projects as equally dangerous for the United States. Washington's tendency was, first, to devise a belligerent tariff policy that would counteract the tariff barriers expected to be erected around the two European blocks, and second, as noted above, to retreat into a kind of economic Monroe Doctrine.

This situation began to change in 1916, however. Allied economic aims for the United States were seen as less dangerous than those of Germany. New York banking circles and the new Federal Reserve Board, particularly with Benjamin Strong of the New York Reserve Bank, played a major role in this evolution. They had already established a cooperative relationship between the City and the British government in the autumn of 1914, a time of great difficulties for the American external account. During the spring of 1916, Strong went to Paris and London to lay the foundation for the central banks' cooperation with the Banque de France and the Bank of England. An Atlantic system for the postwar period was gaining support, especially in comparison with the Western Hemisphere trade system still favored by a majority in Washington. Also, an important section of the American economy now supported the Allies and considered cooperating with them after the war, even if only to enable them to repay their war loans. Strong and the Federal Reserve Board were not strictly anti-Germany, but their orientation ran counter to the German interests.

Another contributing factor in the evolving American perception of

German motives was the inquiry of the Federal Trade Commission, published in June 1916. This thorough inquiry, which had taken one year to complete, focused on the effects of foreign trusts and trade practices on American exports. It broke the ground for the preparation of what would eventually become the Webb-Pomerene Act. Its main conclusion was that if all European countries indulged in unfair trade practices – i.e., producers' cartels, special deals between bankers, industrialists, railway and shipping companies, etc. – the major culprit was Germany. This view can now be disputed, but at the time it was instrumental in persuading the American public that Germany was more averse than the Allies to the principles of American free enterprise and the antitrust component of President Wilson's New Freedom.

The Federal Trade Commission's conclusions seemed to be confirmed by the decision of the German chemical industry, made in January 1916, to build a cartel after the war. (This cartel was the origin of IG Farben.) The American chemical industry asked immediately for new protective taxes. Wilson readily agreed to these new taxes because he felt that the cartel was contrary to fair–trade practices and because the American economy was heavily dependent on German chemicals. Fiscal 1917, voted on 7 September 1916, included heavy protection for the chemical industry. The German chemical companies in America were liquidated in 1917, and in 1919 the United States agreed with the Allies to take over German patents. In this instance American policy became more and more anti-German, thus aligning itself with British and French aims out of both a national interest and growing suspicions about Germany.

Fiscal 1917 also included an anti-dumping provision. One fear in Washington was that Germany was accumulating goods in order to flood the American market and sell them at cut-price rates after the war. President Wilson took this fear – which in fact was unfounded – very seriously and linked it with the new protective tax for chemicals. The anti-dumping provision was important because it was of a general nature; it departed from the bilateral philosophy of the Underwood Act in providing all foreign producers equal access to the American market; thus, it was the first step on the road to the Open Door policy and a multilateral trade system.

It is not irrelevant that President Wilson's conversion from the Underwood Act to the Open Door policy was closely linked to his growing fear of Germany's trade practices. It is also not irrelevant that during the autumn of 1916 he ceased to support Secretary of the Treasury William McAdoo's attempt to strengthen relations with Latin American countries through trade agreements. Wilson was now gradually moving towards involvement in European affairs and a transatlantic trade policy, abandoning his defensive, Monroe Doctrine-like policy of 1914–15. The United States was about to assert its role in the world.

The June 1916 Allied Economic Conference in Paris, which promoted a trade block against Germany and the neutrals after the war, caused much fear in Washington. In most parts of the political and industrial world, the response would have been to step up the preparation of a hemispheric trade alliance, which would have protected the American markets from the expected offensive of Germany and the Allies. But Wilson adamantly refused to follow this track. Although he was convinced of the danger of an economic partitioning of the world, he reacted on the offensive rather than the defensive: America would transcend the nascent partition of the world by promoting those "American principles" the President extolled before the Senate on 22 January 1917. Those principles, which Wilson explained comprehensively for the first time in his speech to the "League to enforce Peace" on 26 May 1916, included both a League of Nations, to serve as a permanent international forum of discussion, and commercial freedom for all countries and guarantees against all forms of trade war or trade exclusion after the war. Wilson stated quite clearly what he meant by those guarantees, which for him ranked in importance with the League of Nations to protect peace in the future, in a document he wrote on 7 February 1917. Although this was a step towards the Open Door policy, access to the multilateral world of equal opportunities would not be granted automatically, but only to countries that would have been admitted to the League of Nations after the war and which would abide by its principles. As Wilson moved from a policy of active mediation in the war to participation on the side of the Allies, his perception of Germany's relationship to the League of Nations and what was to become the Open Door changed. He felt that Germany's acceptance into the League would not be automatic, but would depend on its conforming to the new international principles and on becoming more democratic. Only then would Germany be granted equal economic treatment.

In the summer of 1917, France suggested that the Allies should use their control of raw materials to hasten victory and, after the war, keep Germany in check. The British fully endorsed this so-called economic weapon. Although Wilson's response was more ambiguous, contrary to popular opinion it was not wholly negative. On August 27, in response to the Pope's peace address, the President stressed that the United States, rejecting all economic leagues, wanted equality of access for all, including the Reich, on condition that it accept a world order founded on the equal status of all countries. In October and November 1917, Wilson considered publicly endorsing the Open Door. This momentous turn of

American foreign economic policy was closely linked to what was perceived as the German problem, and can be seen in the discussions that took place around this time. The chairman of the new Tariff Commission, Robert Taussig, wanted to extend the Open Door policy to all countries, including Germany. Colonel House, however, wanted to exclude the Reich, at least until it had reformed itself and accepted the new world order. President Wilson followed Colonel House's suggestion. On November 12, in an important speech to the American Federation of Labor, the President stressed that Germany was determined to control *Mitteleuropa* in order to dominate world economy, and that this was a danger to free enterprise. The Allies and the United States would have to take defensive measures against the Reich. Wilson's point of view on Germany had thus radically changed since the beginning of the war, but – and here he differed with Great Britain and France – he was ready to cease any discrimination against Germany as soon as it reformed itself and accepted the League of Nations.

As is well known, the Open Door was included as the third point in the Fourteen Points of 8 January 1918. It was one of the major principles of future peace. Although Germany would be granted the benefit of Open Door only when it reformed itself, President Wilson opposed the Allies' view that the "economic weapon" should be used to control the Reich indefinitely.

Wilson's pessimistic view of Germany's intentions became even bleaker after the Brest-Litovsk and Bucharest treaties in 1918. Both of these treaties included important economic sections that were thought by the Allies to be even harsher than they actually were in their attempt to build an economic fortress in Europe. In fact, Germany's intention was not to permanently separate Central and Eastern Europe from the Allies, but to prevent them from discriminating against the Reich. On April 6 and again on September 27, Wilson repudiated the idea of a negotiated settlement. In order to obtain peace, the Central European powers would have to accept the entire American program, which was restated at Mount Vernon on July 7. In particular, Germany would have to repudiate the Bucharest and Brest-Litovsk treaties, including their economic provisions, as well as the unequal treaties it contemplated with Belgium and Poland. Wilson told the British in August 1918 that he fully intended to use the "economic weapon" in order to achieve peace and the transformation of Germany. But he reacted strongly when Lloyd George suggested on July 31 that the Allies and United States should retain their wartime economic cooperation after the war and include harsh economic terms against Germany in the peace treaty. For President Wilson, permanent discrimination against Germany was out of the question once it had reformed itself and accepted the new world order.

Thus there was no American opposition to the Allies' suggestion at the time of the Armistice that the blockade of Germany should continue until the peace treaty was signed. And the American delegation in Paris wholly concurred with the British and French when they suggested that Germany unilaterally grant the most-favored-nation treatment to the Allies for five years. The most-favored treatment applied to Allied exports and in general to all matters of economic interest, such as transportation, investments, taxation, and patents. German properties in Allied countries could also be expropriated. The economic section of the treaty was remarkably similar to the resolutions of the Allied Economic Conference of June 1916! Since article 280 of the treaty allowed the League of Nations to extend the validity of all five-year economic clauses, the victorious powers retained the possibility of a long-term and crippling discrimination against Germany.

But President Wilson, not wanting the Allies alone to dictate their policy, intended to participate fully in the League of Nations and the Reparations Commission. He intended to adjust the reparations payments and the eventual termination of the treaty's five-year economic clauses to both the development of world economy and the democratic transformation of Germany. He did not intend to use the reparations and economic sections of the treaty as a permanent means to reduce German power, regardless of Germany's internal and external changes. Wilson agreed with the Allies' – in my view false – diagnosis that Germany's trade practices were unfair, and he agreed with the harsh economic terms they wrote into the treaty. But for Wilson these terms were of a transitory nature. His aim was not to punish Germany, but to redeem it. His late conversion to Open Door was, to a large extent, the consequence of this aim.

Note to Chapter 15

This contribution is based on my book, *L'Or et le Sang: Les buts de guerre économiques de la Première Guerre mondiale*. Paris, 1989.

16

German Disappointment and Anti-Western Resentment, 1918–19

Peter Krüger

I

When the former president of the United States, Woodrow Wilson, was at death's door in the beginning of February 1924, Gustav Stresemann, the German foreign minister, instructed the German ambassador to Washington to refrain from any official expression of condolence in case of Wilson's death. As a result, after Wilson had died on February 3, the German Embassy caused a scandal by doing nothing, not even lowering their flag to half-mast.[1] This happened during the early stage of the investigations and deliberations of the Dawes committee, which was dealing with the thorniest postwar problem: reparations. It was one of the decisive turning points for Germany in the 1920s, and the outcome of the deliberations depended above all else on the attitude of the Americans.[2] Nevertheless, with respect to the main trend of the nationalist public in Germany, which was inimicably opposed to and full of resentment towards all those it held responsible for the Treaty of Versailles, Stresemann joined, or at least did not resist, the nearly irrational, narrow-minded demonstration of introverted nationalism against Wilson. Although there were a few commentators in Germany who tried to be fair with Wilson, the majority remained prejudiced and, repeating the stereotypes of 1919, characterized Wilson as stubborn and self-righteous, as a hypocrite and traitor, as someone who ruined Germany by repudiating his own promises and principles at the Paris Peace Conference.[3]

Arthur Young, an unofficial State Department observer of the Dawes committee's activities, experienced a similar attitude in personal discussions with German businessmen. He particularly mentioned the reproaches levied by Carl Duisberg, one of the most influential leaders of Germany's chemical industry, against Wilson a few days after his death. "All in all, he gave a real demonstration of Prussianism," Young noted, revealing the American prejudice that Prussia was the root of all evil. His

Notes to Chapter 16 can be found on page 334.

comment on the entire affair was: "The Germans are always clumsy, and especially so in critical times."[4] Certainly, the statements by the German businessmen were, in general, more moderate and sometimes more sympathetic towards the United States than those prevailing in public opinion.[5] However, these various groups converged on one fundamental point: their dislike of Wilson and his policy towards the Reich in 1918–19. Although the dividing line in German public life was convoluted, with several twists and turns, the more pragmatic and realistic people, particularly among the businessmen who needed the American connection, distinguished between Wilson and the United States. On the other hand, a strong minority combined, in a kind of cumulative effect, their aversion to Wilson with that to American civilization as a whole.[6]

To this strong but by no means uniform resentment against Wilson should be added another dimension: the remarkable preservation of such resentment over time. The propagation of anti-Wilson feelings won a certain support and established a tradition in convincing the Germans that the Reich was crushed and almost permanently ruined by the Western powers in general and the United States in particular. The National Socialists took advantage of such emotions to deepen the impression of decay, corruption and weakness of the Weimar Republic. In the early period of the *Nationalsozialistische Deutsche Arbeiterpartei*, some of their leading members, especially Joseph Goebbels, volubly promoted the traditional contempt for rotten Western civilization, a contempt widespread in intellectual circles, their vehement rejection and hatred of liberalism, even their sometimes eccentric penchant for Russia, and pushed to an extreme their separation of law and morality from "realistic" power politics.[7] Later on, the National-Socialists painted the Weimar Republic in the darkest colors possible in order to present the allegedly unprecedented national revival and reconstruction under their rule to their best advantage. In his address of 30 January 1943, on the occasion of the tenth anniversary of Hitler's accession to power (and during the catastrophe of Stalingrad), Hermann Göring stressed "the dissembling, mendacious promises" that, together with the cowardly, treacherous mind of German leaders, had caused the ending of the fight in 1918.[8] This was another version of the "stab in the back" myth that was already popular throughout Germany. Göring tried to refurbish these memories to help mobilize the Germans for total war and to summon up all their strength. A situation like that of October-November 1918 had to be avoided at all costs, and the Germans had to demonstrate what they were capable of achieving if they did not listen to people like Wilson. National-Socialist propaganda was thought so efficient that some American experts on Germany, advising their government on counter-propaganda, assumed a surprisingly defensive attitude in referring to Wilson and his peace program. In April 1942 the political scientist James K. Pollock, later one of the leading instructors of officers selected to build up occupational administration in Germany, was asked by the War Department to write a memorandum on German and American war propaganda. His confidential memorandum of 29 April 1942 included the advice that they should give Germans some hope in order to strengthen their resistance against Hitler and concrete assurances that the United States government intended "to restore the world, including Germany, to economic and political health." These assurances, Pollock thought, ought to be based on the Atlantic Charter. Pollock also considered it a good idea, however, to avoid mentioning Wilson's peace program, the Fourteen Points. But if a reference to them proved necessary, it should be emphasized that only three of the fourteen points had been broken – and even they had not been broken by the Americans in the first place. [9]

These statements were a tribute to Germany's deeply entrenched image of Wilson and his responsibility for the Treaty of Versailles. But in addition, they followed the genuine American tradition of criticizing Wilson. They indicate a feeling that some of the German reproaches had not been totally wrong, and that the Americans, for the sake of effective propaganda, should pass over this chapter in history in silence. But Pollock himself had some political roots in Wilsonism, especially in the idea that a close connection between domestic reform and a just, cooperative international order should be established in Germany after the war – at the second attempt since the first had proved a failure in 1919. He suggested, therefore, that Germans should be persuaded to return to a liberal tradition and to remember the alternative they had not taken in World War I: "We might well develop the line that Germany could have saved itself great grief in 1918 if it had yielded earlier to the suggestions of liberal German leaders for a reform of its political system."[10] Here, finally, the small group of German Wilsonians, hidden among the liberals, entered the picture. When the terms imposed on Germany were published, the President of the United States, Woodrow Wilson, became the main target of fierce and limitless attacks by the German public.

II

Why did Wilson provoke such emotions, disgust and in some cases even hatred in Germany? Why was the group of his followers so small? Why did endorsement of his ideas, for some time a distinct and prominent part of German political rhetoric, decrease so rapidly that it was ultimately expressed in a rather furtive manner, if at all? This was the more surprising since it was obvious that a determined support of Wilson's plans for a new international order beyond the peace treaties, would be highly rewarding for both German foreign policy and the German economy.

The facts are well-known, the interpretations too. During the last part of World War I, when the collapse of Germany was imminent, the last imperial government, the reform cabinet of Max Prince of Baden, was successful with a diplomatic coup. The request for an armistice was not sent to the Allies, but to Wilson, which made him in effect the mediator between Germany and the Allied powers in the fundamental question of the basis of the peace treaty to be concluded as quickly as possible. What was intended to, and did, induce Wilson to play the mediator was the statement that Germany accepted Wilson's peace program, particularly the Fourteen Points, as the foundation for future peace.[11]

In its precarious situation, Wilson's program was less detrimental to Germany than the demands of France or the United Kingdom. So the unexpected situation occurred that the German government was the first foreign government to accept the Wilson doctrine. This was predominantly a diplomatic action taken for tactical reasons. Nevertheless, it went beyond tactical concerns. The center-to-left coalition, which had formed in the fall of 1916 and assumed power in October 1918, advocated a peace of understanding. By 1917, they had already agreed with Wilson's general principles. This coincided with a broader current: the orientation towards the United States in political and economic matters. Cultivating a closer relationship, which was seen as being in the interest of both countries, and Wilson's existence were independent elements. It took into account the United States' rise to the status of world power, its special position vis-à-vis the Allies, its power to counteract France and Britain in more than just the peace conference, its economic strength, and its interest in a stable Europe and in a strong partner there. It was evident that the Germans wished to become the European partner of the United States. In spite of some rivalries, this idea of a close relationship between Germany and the United States although not dominant, had already been a part of German foreign policy before 1914.[12]

Wilson, however, was president and, for better or for worse, personified the American peace policy. Whether or not they liked it, the Germans, therefore, had to adjust their policy and, to a certain extent, their language to Wilson's peace program. As a result, there were not just two factions[13] in regard to Germany's special relationship with Wilson but three: Those who were more or less inclined to take up Wilson's ideas of a new international order (a small group, although reaching to the highest ranks of political leadership in 1918–19); those realists, many of whom were in the economic sector, who were interested basically in a closer relationship with the United States as a pre-condition of the reconstruction of Germany as a great power, but who showed no particular interest in Wilson's plans; and finally, those who disliked or hated Wilson, American civilization, the United States' overwhelming power, and Germany's dependence on them. These three factions, although for quite different reasons, united for a short time by committing themselves and Germany's fate to Wilson's Fourteen Points.[14]

The real problem was not the doubtful, incoherent, opportunistic, short-lived, and in any case strange amalgamation of new devotees of Wilson, but the highly unrealistic interpretations in Germany's favor of Wilson's peace program and of the international constellation that was being voiced everywhere in the country, from the political authorities to the newspapers. High expectations and the charged atmosphere of domestic turmoil, uncertainty and pressure from the victors produced a situation in which political bargaining, decisions and compromises in preparing for peace – and especially in preparing for the peace conference itself – were subjected to a fundamental test by German politicians and public opinion. It was a test of right or wrong, good or evil, and what was put to the test was both Wilson's principles of peace as the Germans wanted to conceive them – and Wilson himself.

This maladjustment had dangerous consequences during the peace conference, culminated in Scheidemann's cabinet refusing to sign the peace treaty, and put a heavy burden on German foreign policy. When the peace terms of 7 May 1919 became known, the disaster was inevitable. The storm of indignation again united unholy alliance of both the Right and the Left. Most Germans did not understand the sudden shift from the expectation of certain victory to crushing defeat and the breakdown of the old political order. For several months during the armistice period, they lived in a dreamland, and the government's propaganda could have been understood as a preparing for mass opposition to any peace treaty not compatible with German expectations. Now all hopes of getting off lightly ended in a shock of disillusionment, which gave rise to an outburst of nationalistic protest. Obviously this was a bad start for a new era, and it proved to be an almost unbearable burden for the future republic. The advocates for the old order, however, could exploit this mood. To be sure, the protest was directed against all victors and people regarded as responsible for the outcome, especially German socialists, democrats, republicans, and first of all, Wilson.

The Treaty of Versailles included questionable and unwise terms dealing with frontier questions, reparations, foreign trade, and German responsibility for the war. Wilson had to compromise on several points, and sometimes did not adequately respond to the challenges of the peace conference and the situation in Europe. But he was fairly successful, and the peace treaty contained vital elements for a new and promising international order. A great majority of the German people, however, refused to examine properly the terms of the peace as well as Wilson's share in formulating them and his role at the peace conference. Condemnation prevailed from the outset of the discussion on the conditions of peace, and it is hard to see what concessions by the victors would have satisfied the Germans. Protest was understandable and, to a certain extent, reasonable, even as a tactical means of supporting the German delegation at Versailles. But German protest was dangerous; it was emotional and grossly exaggerated, and partly resulted from a serious lack of political realism, partly from an unscrupulous demagogic rhetoric.

The storm of indignation, that outburst of boundless protest which broke out in Germany was, I think, an expression of the sudden disillusionment of an introvert nation. Not just for the rightists was the Treaty of Versailles a fraud and deception, but Wilson was a swindler and hypocrite, and the way Germany was treated was incredibly unjust. Stresemann had always been convinced of the United States' importance for Germany, but he had expected a dictated peace and was suspicious of Wilson. His nationalistic rhetoric bloomed. He characterized the peace terms as politically sadistic, the greatest swindle history had ever seen, and a death sentence for Germany.[15] Compared to this, the statement by the banker Paul von Schwabach was moderate. In 1915 he had cautioned against breaking ties with the United States for both economic reasons and because of the important political and moral position of the United States in the world. As early as January 1919 Schwabach emphasized the binding character of the Fourteen Points, saying that abandoning this basis of peace would be a breach of faith. His remarks became stronger in later years.[16]

The conservatives felt justified in their distrust of and aversion to President Wilson. They had never actually believed that he would support the peace terms that would meet German requirements, although for tactical reasons they had agreed to comply with Wilson's peace program. As matters stood, this peace program provided the most favorable platform from which to fight for a moderate peace treaty and what was then called Germany's rights. The conservatives hoped that they could take advantage of this vital issue for their own political purposes, and that the German people, united in national protest against the enemy, would pave the road to the recovery of German conservatism.[17] The deep disappointment with Wilson and the peace treaty would bring many people back to the right-wing parties and organizations, thus considerably deepening the gulf between the German political and social tradition and the

Western principles of organizing a modern society. Wilson's international-al order and Western parliamentary democracy would be averted at the same time.

More pragmatic and open-minded politicians, industrialists and busi-nessmen, many of whom had representatives in the oversized German delegation of Versailles, expressed harsh criticism and protested against Wilson's failure. They continued, however, to advocate for close rela-tions with the United States as the only way of improving Germany's political and economic situation.[18] Whereas the rightists accused Wilson of having deceived the Germans, frustrated leftists accused him of having betrayed not only the Germans but his own principles as well. The small group of sincere German pacifists were deeply affected and desperate, but they, as for example one of their leaders, a member of the National Assembly, the historian Ludwig Quidde, neither insulted nor verbally abused Wilson. They did, however, protest and bewail the contrast between his words and deeds. But in joining the common predictions that Germany was being exposed to ruin, that her young democracy was in danger of strangulation, and that the new, just world order was doomed to failure if such a peace treaty were put into effect, they expressed their patriotism too and were loyally keeping in line with gov-ernmental tactics.[20]

As a result of the raised expectations and the highly equivocal, incon-sistent German attitude, the Germans were on the edge of an abrupt and drastic change of mind in regard to Wilson: from hosanna to crucify him! This tense situation had far-reaching consequences. The Germans sub-jected Wilson – and the victors in general – to a severe and, strictly speaking, absurd test on the issue of making peace. When it was not passed in a manner that satisfied the Germans, Wilson was condemned. His plans for a new international order and the principles of Western lib-eral democracy were also discredited, at least in the views of a majority of the Germans. The alarming reaction contributed strongly to the difficult start of the Weimar Republic and the socio-psychological obstacles to transforming the Reich into a republic with a political system and social structure similar to those found in the West. Moreover, the heavy nationalistic burden made the pursuit of a conciliatory and cooperative foreign policy extremely arduous.

Anti-American, and anti-Western resentment in general, were finally advancing, although it is necessary to distinguish between the spheres of politics and cultural affairs. In cultural questions, a consciousness of a common European tradition – as opposed to the American way of life – prevailed. In the political sphere, however, the collective experience and heavily biased memories of 1919 proved an almost insurmountable barrier to all efforts to open Germany to Western political thinking and practice – and often ended up in a cloud of nationalistic rhetoric. Nevertheless, what the National Assembly, with its strong republican majority, accomplished was in fact a constitution of the classical Western type, despite the apathy of the people and the uncompromising rejection of the Right, who considered the new constitution consistently "un-German."[20] In general, the cliché of Wilson's fraud was merged into one impression with the traditional prejudices against "perfidious Albion" and crafty French politicians. At least in the large right wing of the political spectrum, there was no doubt that diplomacy and compromise had something to do either with being cheated or with surrendering and renouncing legitimate German rights. As applied to domestic affairs, therefore, the parliamentary system was not only considered "un-German" but corrupt, selfish and an impediment to strong national leadership. On the other hand, this increased the striving for rearmament and "real" great power status for the Reich in order to get its claims accepted. Under these circumstances, it was not surprising that a precise and thorough understanding of American politics became particularly difficult. This leads, finally, to the deeper reasons for German indignation and protest in 1919.

III

Some of the deeper reasons for the vehement expression of disappointment in Germany over Wilson's policy lie in the past. In spite of a long-lasting coherence in the complex German attitude towards the United States[21] it seems appropriate to distinguish between the immediate past of the peace-making period, the exceptional case of World War I, and the time before 1914. Going backwards step by step into the past may help to clarify the reasons for German resentment.

World War I very quickly created the previously unknown situation in which the United States was an alarming presence within the German sphere of action. What once had received limited contact and controversy, now became matters of vital importance and consequence to Germany. The war greatly intensified fears and hopes, for which Wilson was like a distorting mirror. The moment of truth brought about by the war prompted confessions and reactions for and against the United States. The German conservatives were immediately suspicious and refused violently to recognize Wilson as the mediator of peace, especially during the peace soundings in 1916–17. They felt the rising of an immense threat: the unique though well-known combination of American goals for a new international order and foreign democratic reform. Not only would the German conservatives' understanding of foreign policy as power politics and freedom of action be destroyed by Wilson's ideas for peace and a just international order, but such a peace would strengthen and encourage all kinds of progressives in Germany, thus undermining the traditional social and political order that was the basis of conservative privileges and dominant position. In particular, Wilson's distinction between the German regime and the German people attacked the roots of power of the German Right, who tried to counter this attack, with some success, by discrediting their adversaries as some kind of "fifth column" of Wilson.[22]

Nobody could ignore the overwhelming strength of the new American world power, which continued to grow despite some foolish German attempts to ridicule Wilson and the Americans and to minimize the danger of the United States' going to war. Therefore, not just the conservatives, but the right-wing Social Democrat Südekum stated: "Today America is the worst of our enemies" doing violence to Europe.[23] Spoken in September 1918, these were the traditional fears of a disunited and helpless Europe at the mercy of new world powers. For conservative politicians, the United States had no business being in Europe. In the fall of 1917, Count Westarp appealed to the German people to demonstrate their contempt for Wilson's hypocrisy and malice, for a man they had never liked and who tried to drive a wedge between the Hohenzollern dynasty and the German people.[24] Such vituperative attacks were similar to those of 1919.

Germany, on the other hand, had to fulfill her own mission in defending her unique culture and traditional order against the flood of Western capitalism, materialism and superficial civilization based on featureless masses. During the war, particularly in 1917–18, anti-Western feeling focused on the United States because American foreign policy was influenced by a genuine missionary drive. In drawing conclusions from the situation, right-wing politicians reinforced their desperate efforts to build up a nearly self-sufficient German block in continental Europe, to ward off Western intervention and economic influence, and to drastically reduce Germany's participation in the world economy. The ideological revival of Johann Gottlieb Fichte's *Geschlossener Handelsstaat* underscored this mood.[25] Unlike the development in German politics, however, more liberal principles prevailed within the German business community, which, in its majority, never agreed to Germany's leaving the already highly integrated world market. This basic decision was hotly contended during the war, but clear.[26]

As a result, the dividing line between Germany and the United States also ran through German society. Again it was apparent that the United

States provided a medium, a challenge or a platform for the fighting of fundamental controversies over siding with or against American – and Western – political and economic principles.

All of this reveals some reasons for the German attitude underlying the excited mood in 1919. It was influenced by a strong reaction to the threat of lasting restraints on Germany's traditional foreign policy as well as to deep changes in the political system. Perhaps the most important prerequisite for the outbreak of collective anger was the Reich's dependency on Wilson's good will at the end of the war, even when his enemies reluctantly acquiesced in accepting his peace program. But the overwhelming majority of the Germans interpreted it very much in Germany's favor. Their demands for a "true" Wilson peace were neither modest nor fair and became a test of Wilson's "sincerity." When he failed to meet their unrealistic expectations, their reactions were supported by disappointment and indignation, boundless and outrageous. But Wilson's conservative adversaries in Germany went far beyond the usual criticism; they now tried to erase from memory their own momentary compliance – the result of their determination to prevent the worst in the time of total defeat – with Wilson's ideas. Agreeing with those ideas had never been sincere.

Swimming on the wave of general indignation, the German Right wanted to deny their own failure and responsibility by making Wilson the scapegoat for all of Germany's misfortunes. This was the real meaning of the seemingly simple accusation that Wilson had betrayed the Germans by persuading them to lay down their arms and place their confidence in him. Stating that there was no German defeat without Wilson thus acquired another meaning; it was another "stab in the back" by Wilson. The real enemy, however, was Western civilization in general and American political and economic principles in particular; because Wilson was their exponent, to discredit one was to discredit all three.

One more step back into the past may round off my attempts to show, one, that there was a long-term problem and, two, that the 1919 outburst of public indignation, which would last until 1945, indicated that this problem had reached its critical stage. Although the pro-Western forces should not be underestimated, the problem was the conservative German's aversion to the political and social principles of the West and even to its life-style.

In the last decade of the nineteenth and the beginning of the twentieth century – a period of breathtaking industrial advance, rapid change, imperialistic expansion, and new social and cultural movements as well as intensified, polarized conflicts at home and abroad – tensions between the United States and Germany were increasing, especially on economic matters detrimental to the interests of conservative landowners.[27] The dispatches from the well-informed American embassy in Berlin illustrate the growing animosity of German public opinion towards the United States. Although the agrarian interest was the original driving force of this animosity, the issue was soon extended and changed. This is the interesting point: The arch-conservatives, "reactionary to an incredible degree" (26 April 1898), saw the economic basis of their status and influence being undermined. Moreover, American diplomats observed that German conservatives felt pressured about domestic issues – and therefore "engaged in what they almost consider a struggle for their own existence as well as that of the German and Prussian states" – and were "bitterly anti-American and feared that Germany might become dependent economically on the United States" (15 December 1899). They were strengthening their effectiveness so that "the organization of the League (*Bund der Landwirte*) surpasses that of any other German political body with the possible exception of the Social Democratic Party" (12 February 1902). The conservatives, more than others, stressed the increasing world influence of the United States in spreading democratic principles and restricting German movement. Moreover, the Americans were blamed for threatening Germany's political and social order.[28]

Here we have a conflict between two different political systems. The defensive mood of the conservatives transformed it into an outright refusal of general Western influence.[29] This coincided and sometimes merged with a broader current of cultural protest against modern industrial civilization and above all in the huge public debate on Germany's future fought out on the issue of agricultural versus industrial nation.[30] It was American modernity, success and dynamic force that made the United States the preferred target of German anti-Western attacks, which used the rather crude weapon of slandering American culture.

Finally, a far more subtle and thoughtful version of this animosity and criticism of some Western developments that was occurring on the academic level should be mentioned. In his inaugural address to the Prussian Academy of Sciences on 30 June 1887, Gustav Schmoller, the celebrated head of the Historical School of German economists, announced his ambitious program to totally separate German economics from "the dogmatism" of the British and French philosophy of utility (*Utilitätsphilosophie*), and to reestablish German economics on the basis of economic history.[31] This was neither shallow anti-Western resentment nor connected with anti-Americanism. Schmoller clearly recognized the growth and future importance of the United States, and his empirical and historical approach influenced the development of American economics and social science for some time.[32] But his program and outstanding position in Germany had a greater significance than being at the core of his famous controversy on methods with Carl Menger: it advanced a tendency, in fact, to separate German political economy from that of the Western countries. The impulse to historicize academic disciplines within the special atmosphere and nationalistic excitement at the time of William II made them susceptible to ideological influences, which called for a unique German cultural development opposed and superior to that of the West. Such thinking remained in the background during normal times, but escalated into producing extreme reactions in times of crisis, like World War I.

Notes to Chapter 16

1. Politisches Archiv des Auswärtigen Amts, Bonn, Abteilung III, Politik 2 Vereinigte Staaten, Beiheft Flaggenzwischenfall; Manfred Berg, *Gustav Stresemann und die Vereinigten Staaten von Amerika: Weltwirtschaftliche Verflechtung und Revisionspolitik 1907–1929* (Baden-Baden, 1990), pp. 237–40.

2. Werner Link, *Die amerikanische Stabilisierungspolitik in Deutschland 1921–32* (Düsseldorf, 1970), pp. 241–314; Peter Krüger, *Die Außenpolitik der Republik von Weimar* (Darmstadt, 1985), pp. 218–47.

3. Ernst Fraenkel, "Das deutsche Wilsonbild," *Jahrbuch für Amerikastudien* 5 (1960), pp. 83–86.

4. Arthur N. Young, Diary 1923–24 (Arthur N. Young Collection, Box 1, Hoover Institution Archives, Stanford, CA.), 4 and 9 February 1924.

5. Max M. Warburg, *Aus meinen Aufzeichnungen* (Private print, New York, 1952).

6. Peter Berg, *Deutschland und Amerika 1918–1929: Über das deutsche Amerikabild der zwanziger Jahre* (Lübeck and Hamburg, 1963), chapters 1 and 2; Klaus Schwabe, "Anti-Americanism within the German Right 1917–1933," *Amerikastudien* 21 (1976), pp. 89–108.

7. Hans Hecker, *"Die Tat" und ihr Osteuropa-Bild 1909–1939* (Köln, 1974); Joseph Goebbels, *Die Zweite Revolution* (Zwickau, 1926), p. 47: "Darum schauen wir nach Rußland, weil es am ehesten mit uns den Weg zum Sozialismus gehen wird. Weil Rußland der uns von der Natur gegebene Bundesgenosse gegen die teuflische Verseuchung und Korruption des Westens ist." For important general analysis of such attitudes, see: Richard Löwenthal, *Der romantische Rückfall* (Stuttgart, 1970).

8. *Völkischer Beobachter*, 3 February 1943.

9. Pollock Papers, Box 19, Folder 15 (Bentley Historical Library, Ann Arbor, University of Michigan).

10. Pollock Papers, ibid.

11. Klaus Schwabe, *Woodrow Wilson, Revolutionary Germany, and Peace-making* (Chapel Hill, 1985); Krüger, *Außenpolitik*, pp. 31–58.

12. Hans W. Gatzke, *Germany and the United States. A Special Relationship?* (Cambridge, MA, 1980); Reiner Pommerin, *Der Kaiser und Amerika: Die USA und die Politik der Reichsleitung 1890–1917* (Köln and Wien, 1986).

13. Fraenkel, *Wilsonbild*.

14. Peter Krüger, *Deutschland und die Reparationen 1918/19* (Stuttgart, 1973), pp. 51–57, 74–91, 128–31.

15. Manfred Berg, *Stresemann*, pp. 123–128; Fraenkel, *Wilsonbild*, pp. 81–92; Peter Berg, *Amerika*, pp. 19–33.

16. Paul H. von Schwabach, *Aus meinen Akten* (Private print, Berlin, 1927), pp. 284, 373, 442.

17. See for instance: Kuno Graf von Westarp, *Deutschlands Zukunftsaufgaben in der auswärtigen Politik*, Deutschnationale Flugschriften 24 (Address to the party congress of the DNVP, 12–13 July 1919).

18. Link, *Stabilisierungspolitik*, introduction; Peter Berg, *Amerika*, pp. 96–132.

19. Here I differ from the interpretation of Fraenkel, *Wilsonbild*, p. 88.

20. Gerhard Anschütz in: *Der deutsche Föderalismus. Die Diktatur des Reichspräsidenten*, Veröffentlichungen der Vereinigung der deutschen Staatsrechtslehrer 1 (Berlin and Leipzig, 1924), pp. 22, 24, 25.

21. Sources: Ernst Fraenkel, Amerika im Spiegel des deutschen politischen Denkens (Köln and Opladen, 1959).

22. Count Westarp on 10 October 1917, in the *Reichstag; Verhandlungen des Reichstags: Stenographische Berichte*, vol. 310, pp. 3837–8; Kuno Graf von Westarp, *Zwei Gedenktage in schwerer Zeit* (Berlin, 1916); Fraenkel, *Wilsonbild*, pp. 69–74; Werner Link, "Demokratische Staatsordnung und außenpolitische Orientierung. Die Einstellung zu den USA als Problem der deutschen Politik im 20. Jahrhundert," in Lothar Albertin, Werner Link, eds., *Politische Parteien auf dem Weg zur parlamentarischen Demokratie in Deutschland* (Düsseldorf, 1981), pp. 63–65.

23. *Der Interfraktionelle Ausschuß 1917/18*, vol. 2, Quellen zur Geschichte des Parlamentarismus und der politischen Parteien, Erste Reihe 1 (Düsseldorf, 1959), p. 485 (6 September 1918).

24. Cf. n. 22.

25. Peter Theiner, "'Mitteleuropa'- Pläne im Wilhelminischen Deutschland," in Helmut Berding (Hg.), *Wirtschaftliche und politische Integration in Europa im 19. und 20. Jahrhundert* (Göttingen, 1984), pp. 136–48; Hermann Lübbe, *Politische Philosophie in Deutschland* (München, 1974), pp. 193–205; but cf., among others, Karl Diehl, *Deutschland als geschlossener Handelsstaat* (Stuttgart and Berlin, 1916).

26. Georges-Henri Soutou, *L'or et le sang: Les buts de guerre économiques de la Première Guerre mondiale* (Paris, 1989), pp. 847–48.

27. Alfred Vagts, *Deutschland und die Vereinigten Staaten in der Weltpolitik* (New York, 1935); Pommerin, *Kaiser*.

28. National Archives, Washington D.C., Microfilm 44, rolls 83 (7 January 1898), 84 (3 February and 26 April 1898), 86 (29 October 1898), 90 (15 December 1899), 94 (12 December 1901, 12 February 1902); Link, "Staatsordnung," pp. 64–65.

29. See in general Henning Köhler, ed., *Deutschland und der Westen* (Berlin, 1984); Johann Baptist Müller, *Deutschland und der Westen* (Berlin, 1989).

30. Kenneth Barkin, *The Controversy over German Industrialization, 1890–1902* (Chicago, 1970).

31. *Sitzungsberichte der Königlich Preußischen Akademie der Wissenschaften zu Berlin 33* (Berlin, 1887), p. 638. There was a certain tradition of skepticism towards western ideas or even anti-western resentment from Fichte to Sombart.

32. Joseph Dorfman, "The role of the German Historical School in American Economic Thought," *American Economic Review* 45/2 (1955), pp. 17–28; Jurgen Herbst, *The German Historical School in American Scholarship* (Ithaca, NY, 1965).

17

Imperialism and Revolution: Wilsonian Dilemmas

Lloyd E. Ambrosius

There is a notable consensus among the authors of the four contributions on Germany and the United States in the era of World War I relating to imperialism and revolution. Lloyd C. Gardner, Laura Garcés, Georges-Henri Soutou, and Peter Krüger all share several key assumptions in their otherwise different historical approaches to the subject.

Focusing on national states in world affairs, these scholars acknowledge the pervasive influence of nationalism in the early twentieth century. They recognize that national perceptions or biases were extremely influential in the United States and Germany during this era.[1] A statesman such as President Woodrow Wilson drew upon his own national experience to interpret – or frequently misinterpret – the behavior of his counterparts in other lands. This limitation, which also afflicted leaders in Germany, was typical of international politics, which, after all, involved relations among nations.

Gardner, Garcés, Soutou, and Krüger appreciate, moreover, the complex interdependence between internal and external affairs in the modern world.[2] All of them recognize that domestic factors influenced the foreign policies of the great powers and that international affairs impacted the developments at home in any particular nation. None interpret international politics in the traditionally narrow framework of diplomatic or military history. Some of these authors attribute greater importance to internal versus external factors, but none believes in the primacy of either domestic or foreign affairs to the exclusion of the other.

These historians recognize as well that a comprehensive study of international politics must include socioeconomic and cultural dimensions.[3] It must encompass more than diplomacy and warfare between states. At stake in the relationship between the United States and Germany during the era of World War I were their longstanding interests and values, not merely their leaders' current policies. Differences between their nations' economic systems and political cultures prevented American and Ger-

Notes to Chapter 17 can be found on page 346.

man statesmen from even comprehending the other's position, thereby limiting leeway in seeking accommodations.

Gardner, Garcés, Soutou, and Krüger understand that the United States had emerged as a powerful modern nation by the early twentieth century. It had achieved sufficient power to influence the future course of world affairs. Drawing upon a capitalist economy and a democratic culture, President Wilson could project American values and institutions abroad to an extent unprecedented in the history of the United States. A great power on the rise, it had become a decisive factor in the balance among European empires. The Eurocentric world of the previous four centuries would shift in favor of the United States, making the twentieth century genuinely "the American age."[4]

Furthermore, these four historians adopt perspectives on the subject of imperialism and revolution that presuppose that these were phenomena occurring outside the United States. They examine European imperialism and revolutions in Mexico, Russia, and Germany. In this context, they analyze the American response to foreign empires and revolutions. These scholars overlook the imperial and revolutionary character of the United States itself. This nation appeared as an emerging great power, with enormous economic and military strength, but not like empires elsewhere. Nor were the revolutionary aspects of American political culture noted as such by them. Neglecting to compare the United States with other empires, or to recognize its revolutionary ideals and behavior, the authors implicitly subscribe to the myth of American exceptionalism.[5] They avoid direct comparisons that might stress similarities between the United States and other great powers.[6]

A central problem that all four historians address was that of the connection between national self-determination and world order. In an era of war and revolution, Wilson sought both change and stability in international relations.[7] He faced the dilemma of balancing each nation's right to determine its own destiny with all other nations' needs to protect their stakes in the world order as well as their own separate interests. This was a problem for all nations, not just the United States or Germany.

Lloyd C. Gardner focuses directly on this problem. Wilson, he correctly understands, wanted to foster both self-determination and world order. The president, however, faced the difficulty that these two goals might be either complementary or contradictory. As Gardner notes, while nineteenth-century liberalism had stressed self-determination, twentieth-century liberalism would shift toward world order with more intervention by government. In making this transition, Wilson sought to strike a balance between fragmentation and regimentation.[8] He advocated moderate reform at home in order to preserve liberalism, recognizing, moreover, that its ultimate success in the United States depended upon its acceptance abroad.

As Gardner more fully explains in *Safe for Democracy*, Wilson wanted to create a new world order that would protect democracy and capitalism from dangers on the Right and the Left. Toward that end he had become a progressive reformer. He had witnessed the failure of empires even before World War I generated revolutions in Eastern and Central Europe. Mexico and China already challenged the president to find a middle road between reactionary imperialism and radical revolution. Seeking to identify moderate leaders who would exercise national self-determination in ways acceptable to the United States, and to exclude from power others who rejected his intervention, Wilson also endeavored to protect these countries from European or Japanese imperialism. He later adopted this same approach toward Russia, Austria-Hungary, and Germany.[9]

Domestic and foreign affairs were inextricably linked in the twentieth century. In *Safe for Democracy*, Gardner observes that "perhaps the most difficult problem Wilson poses for the historian is how to reconcile his openness to seeking change, as in Mexico and China, with his consistent fear of radicalism in domestic politics." Wilson's new world order, which culminated in the League of Nations, promised a solution to internal as well as external dangers. Not only would it replace imperialism, it would also guard against radicalism by facilitating liberal reform within nations. Thus, Gardner further observes, "the League would have a tremendous impact on the success or failure of domestic political institutions as the contradictions of the industrial age drove nation after nation toward some form of the New Nationalism or socialism."[10]

Presupposing American exceptionalism, the president did not regard U.S. intervention abroad as imperialism. While criticizing the imperial ambitions of other great powers and also the special interests of reactionary Americans in Mexico, China, or later in Russia, he never recognized that his pursuit of a new world order involved U.S. hegemony.[11] He saw it, instead, as an alternative to imperialism and radicalism, both of which seemed to deny the authentic expression of national self-determination. The potential contradiction between world order and national self-determination apparently disappeared. Wilson assumed that, if given the opportunity, the people of any land would prefer political and economic institutions like those of the United States. In this framework, promoting American values abroad was consistent with the principle of self-determination. To those who shared Wilson's perspective, his reformist program apparently reconciled self-determination and world order.[12]

Gardner recognizes potential conflicts between national self-determination and world order. He perceives this Wilsonian dilemma from a revisionist perspective. In the case of the Austro-Hungarian empire, he notes that the competing claims of subject peoples were not adequately taken into account by either Wilson or his friend and adviser Edward M. House. Application of the principle of self-determination in the Habsburg empire might threaten the new world order that they hoped to create.

Betty Miller Unterberger, too, recognizes this Wilsonian dilemma in *The United States, Revolutionary Russia, and the Rise of Czechoslovakia*.[13] But rather than accept Gardner's conclusion that the president's vision was flawed, she endeavors to finesse the problem. Like Wilson, she defines self-determination in different ways at different times. At first, it meant autonomy for subject peoples within the Habsburg empire. Even as late as the Fourteen Points, after the United States had declared war against Austria-Hungary, the president refrained from advocating independence for the various nationalities. Only at the war's end did he finally recognize Czechoslovakia and other new nations emerging from the empire's collapse. Unterberger reconciles Wilson's commitments to both democracy and international security by identifying self-determination with his position at any given time. His vision of a new world order anticipated that all nations might come together in harmony. In her Wilsonian perspective, the dilemma that Gardner stresses between self-determination and world order virtually disappears. By definition, albeit changing definitions, it ceases to be a problem.[14]

Laura Garcés examines the Wilsonian dilemma relative to the Mexican revolution. Like Gardner, she emphasizes the linkage not only between domestic and foreign affairs, but also between war and revolution. Wilson confronted the dangers in Mexico of both European imperialism and radical revolution. Great Britain and Germany sought to exploit the chaotic situation to gain advantages for themselves at the expense of the United States. Their imperial ambitions challenged the Monroe Doctrine. Responding to revolution and imperialism in Mexico, Wilson endeavored to foster a new world order that affirmed national self-determination.

In pursuit of the potentially contradictory goals of order and self-determination, Wilson experienced what Garcés calls "an American dilemma." The more he intervened in Mexico to guide its revolution away from radicalism toward acceptable reform, the more the United States encountered resistance from various Mexican factions. As nationalists, the Mexicans wanted to have their own revolution. Despite differences among Francisco Madero, Victoriano Huerta, Venustiano Carranza, and Francisco "Pancho" Villa, all of them shared a common Mexican antipathy toward U.S. hegemony. From the perspective of American exceptionalism, Wilson misunderstood Mexican nationalism and exaggerated European influences in Mexico. In his view, imperialism and revolution combined there to challenge the Monroe Doctrine. Garcés agrees with Gardner's summary of the problem: "European imperialism produced the injustices that led to revolution; Latin American revolution produced intervention and imperialism."[15] This Wilsonian dilemma was a prime example of the modern world's complex interdependence.

Dangers from Europe threatened to spread into the Western Hemisphere. In 1917, as the United States prepared for war against Germany, Wilson apprehended the possibility of German conspiracy in Mexico. The Zimmermann telegram appeared to prove such a menace.[16] The United States refused, however, to sacrifice its own interests in Mexico to discourage that nation's possible alignment with Germany. When Carranza's government announced a new constitution in 1917, Americans resisted any surrender of their claims to Mexico's subsoil resources, especially petroleum. Rather than understand Mexico's new constitution as a nationalist expression of self-determination, Wilson viewed it as possible evidence of German intrigue. Mexican self-determination was acceptable only within the limits that he set for world order.

Wilson's Pan-Americanism affirmed the principle of national self-determination and heralded a new world order. In his mind, these goals were not contradictory because he presupposed U.S. hegemony. His vision of world order, which would culminate in the League of Nations, anticipated the worldwide extension of Pan-Americanism. As Garcés notes, in common with other historians, the president advocated the globalization of the Monroe Doctrine.[17] He wanted all nations, like those in the Western Hemisphere, to exercise self-determination. They might even undertake revolutions as long as these followed the middle road toward democracy and capitalism. Rejecting the European extremes of radicalism and imperialism, Wilson espoused what Emily S. Rosenberg calls "the ideology of liberal-developmentalism."[18]

This Wilsonian ideology affirmed American exceptionalism and, paradoxically, used it as the standard for judging other nations. As Rosenberg notes, "liberal-developmentalism merged nineteenth-century liberal tenets with the historical experience of America's own development, elevating the beliefs and experiences of America's unique historical time and circumstance into developmental laws thought to be applicable everywhere."[19] From a similarly critical perspective, Gardner notes ideological constraints on Wilson's response to the Mexican revolution: "What Mexico had to have, therefore, was an American revolution, if it was to break free from foreign economic dominion, avoid a violent lurching back and forth between reaction and anarchy, and, most important, not set the wrong precedent as the world moved out from under the shadow of the dying imperial order."[20] In short, other nations such as Mexico needed American-style revolutions to enable them to exercise their national self-determination in a manner acceptable to the United States in a new world order.

Georges-Henri Soutou explores this Wilsonian dilemma in his contribution on the American perspective toward German economic war aims during the First World War. Like Garcés, who observes mutual misunderstandings between Mexicans and Americans, he studies the growing hostility between the United States and Germany. Created for political as well as economic reasons, Germany's *Mitteleuropa* appeared to Wilson as an ever increasing threat to world order. It challenged his vision of a world order that embraced the Open Door policy.

Tracing the changes in American foreign economic policy from bilateralism in 1913 to multilateralism in 1917, Soutou notes the connection between this development and the American decision for war against Germany. Wilson at first concentrated on trade in the Western Hemisphere, but then shifted toward the worldwide extension of the Open Door. Proceeding from an "economic Monroe Doctrine" to an Atlantic system, which would link the United States with Western Europe, the president envisaged an economic order that rejected the partition of the world. His alternative vision of equal commercial opportunities for all nations confronted Mitteleuropa. Wilson expressed this goal as the third of his Fourteen Points, making it an integral part of his new world order. Linked to the League of Nations, the Open Door promised equal status for all nations within the new order.[21]

By the end of World War I, as Soutou notes, Wilson wanted the universal application of the Open Door. In Germany, as in Mexico, this Wilsonian order promised economic as well as political self-determination, but with restrictions. A reformed Germany could participate in the world economy, but only if it accepted the Open Door rules and transformed its political system. While such changes appeared to Wilson as a way to redeem rather than punish Germany, it amounted to an American-style revolution – although Soutou does not label it as such. Until the Germans suffered military defeat in 1918, they eschewed this alternative to their Mitteleuropa. They preferred their own self-determination to Wilson's capitalist and democratic world order.

Focusing on American foreign economic policy, Soutou neglects cultural factors beyond those of the political economy. The Open Door, which originated with reference to China, expressed cultural values as well as economic interests. Wilson's response to German economic war aims during World War I reflected tensions similar to those in his East Asian policy. Beyond equal economic opportunities for the United States, the president favored China's territorial integrity and political independence. He reluctantly recognized special Japanese interests in East Asia even when these only marginally threatened the commercial and financial interests of the United States.

Wilson's political commitment to China, although related to the Open Door, emerged more from the "missionary mind" in the United States than from economic interests. The Protestant missionary movement, concentrating on China since the 1890s, influenced Wilson's decisions in 1913 to denounce President William Howard Taft's "dollar diplomacy" and to recognize the new Chinese republic, and two years later to oppose Japan's Twenty-one Demands. American cultural values, beyond those of political economy, shaped Wilson's concept of the Open Door. His commitment to China and antipathy toward Japan went well beyond the economic interests of American merchants and bankers.[22]

Wilson's liberal internationalism, which culminated in the League of Nations as well as the related concept of the Open Door, expressed the modernist impulse of American culture in the early twentieth century. As a great power on the rise, the United States hoped to spread its civilization around the world; it wanted to export more than agricultural and industrial goods. The Protestant missionary movement exemplified this modernist thrust. Protestant Americans pursued a civilizing and evangelizing mission during this era that, as William R. Hutchison notes, amounted to "a moral equivalent for imperialism."[23] They identified Christianity with Americanism. Wilson, a devout Presbyterian, as well as his secretaries of state, William Jennings Bryan and Robert Lansing, shared this ideology. From these cultural roots came their style of missionary diplomacy, which they expressed in the globalization of the Monroe Doctrine and the Open Door.[24]

Wilson summarized his political philosophy in a brief article, "The Road Away From Revolution," published in *Atlantic Monthly*, in 1923. As a scholar, he had once intended to write a magnum opus on this subject. A poor substitute, this article was all the ailing former president could manage. Nevertheless, it reiterated the key elements in his ideology. He identified democracy, capitalism, and Christianity as the essence of "modern civilization" and offered these as the political, economic, and cultural answer to the Russian revolution. In his judgment, the United States was "a Christian civilization," not just "the greatest of democracies." Moreover, he believed that "the world has been made safe for democracy." Capitalism, however, was still insecure. To counter the Bolshevik attack on this economic system, further reform was needed to overcome the problem of reactionary special interests. The root of this problem was spiritual. The United States needed to reform itself by implementing "a Christian conception of justice." It could be saved only by "the spirit of Christ."[25]

Within the framework of American exceptionalism, Wilson never acknowledged the imperial and revolutionary implications of the "modern civilization" that he heralded. His vision of a new world order combined democracy, capitalism, and Christianity as the alternative to European imperialism and radical revolution. From other perspectives, however, this modernist impulse constituted an American form of political, economic, and cultural imperialism. Although quite different from Bolshevism, it also threatened the old order with revolution. Gardner, Garcés, and Soutou, like Wilson, do not label the modernist impulse of the United States as either imperialism or revolution. Although critical in other ways, they implicitly accept American exceptionalism as the ideological framework for analyzing Wilson's statecraft during World War I.[26]

Peter Krüger, too, avoids categorizing the United States as an imperial or revolutionary power. He does not compare European and American forms of imperialism or revolution in his contribution on Germany's postwar disappointment with the United States. Krüger recognizes, however, the modernist impulse that Wilson epitomized. He understands that Germany's resentment toward the United States expressed a cultural protest against modern civilization.

As Krüger observes, German nationalism asserted itself in an increasingly strong aversion to Wilson after World War I. Only a small faction inside Germany identified at this time with his liberalism. Others, notably businessmen and their political allies, nominally accepted his promise of a new world order for practical reasons. They might embrace the Fourteen Points as long as they could interpret them in their own way. But in their subsequent disappointment, they aligned with a third faction, which held a deep antipathy toward Wilson in particular and American civilization in general. This broad anti-Western coalition resisted the Wilsonian program of domestic reform and international cooperation. The reconstruction of Germany and its integration into the League of Nations on Wilson's conditions were unacceptable to the vast majority of Germans. Eventually, this anti-Western resentment furnished the basis for the emergence of National Socialism and the triumph of Adolf Hitler.[27]

The Treaty of Versailles revealed the gulf between German and Western expectations. At the time of the armistice in 1918, the middle group of Germans embraced Wilson's Fourteen Points for practical reasons and seemed to agree with the small faction of genuine German liberals. But when the peace treaty required more sacrifices than these Germans ever expected, their disappointment produced anti-Western resentment. Their sense of betrayal by Wilson reflected a serious lack not only of political realism, but also of commitment to his political and social values. After 1919 this middle group increasingly joined German conservatives in asserting what Krüger calls "introverted nationalism." They denounced the democracy and capitalism of modern Western society and the apparently superficial civilization that undergirded this political and economic system. Wilson served as the scapegoat for these German nationalists in their disillusionment.[28]

Krüger notes that Germany's postwar resentment focused on the United States because Wilson's foreign policy expressed "a genuine missionary drive." This modernist impulse created a dividing line in German society between those few who shared the president's goals of democratic reform and world order, on one side, and the vast majority who rejected these changes, on the other. This cultural gulf within Germany, and, even more, between German nationalism and Western civilization, linked internal and external affairs in a net of complex interdependence.

Protestant Americans, William R. Hutchison observes in *Errand to the World*, impacted international politics with their cultural imperialism. Aggressive activism of American missionaries evoked a negative reaction from Europeans during this era. The modernist impulse of Wilsonian Americanism provoked this same reaction from German nationalists. Krüger's perceptive analysis of the roots of Germany's anti-Western resentment after World War I illustrates Hutchison's point: "American-European tensions, though they have been passed over very lightly in most histories of the missionary and ecumenical movements, had a bearing on the misunderstandings that led to the First World War, and then to the tragically incomplete reconciliation after 1918."[29] The cultural gulf between Germans and Americans contributed to mutual misunderstandings in international politics. In other words, from the perspective of German conservatives, the United States was itself a revolutionary and imperial power at this time.

Taken together, the contributions of Gardner, Garcés, Soutou, and Krüger reveal various facets of imperialism and revolution during the era of World War I. They recognize nationalism as a pervasive influence in both the United States and Germany. Given the complex interdependence of the modern world, internal and external factors were intertwined in the actions and reactions on both sides of the Atlantic. Cultural as well as politico-military and socioeconomic factors within nations shaped their involvement in world affairs. Out of the national experience of the United States, Wilson projected the ideals and practices of democracy, capitalism, and Chrisitianity as the basis for a new world order. Advocating the globalization of the Monroe Doctrine and the Open Door, he hoped to reform the Old World and thereby to protect the United States against the dangers of European imperialism and radical revolution. The president encountered the dilemma, however, of reconciling this new world order with national self-determination. As all four historians observe, Wilson never resolved this dilemma. It remained to confound his successors throughout the twentieth century.

Notes to Chapter 17

1. E. J. Hobsbawm, *Nations and Nationalism Since 1780: Programme, Myth, Reality* (Cambridge, 1990), pp. 101–62, observes that nationalism reached its apogee during this era.

2. Robert O. Keohane and Joseph S. Nye, *Power and Interdependence*, second edition (Glenview, IL, 1989), introduces the concept of "complex interdependence" to explain transnational relations. This concept emphasizes what I describe in Lloyd E. Ambrosius' *Woodrow Wilson and the American Diplomatic Tradition: The Treaty Fight in Perspective* (Cambridge, 1987), as the paradoxical reality of pluralism and interdependence in the modern world.

3. Ideology and culture in international history, in addition to politico-military and socioeconomic factors, are emphasized by Michael H. Hunt, *Ideology and U.S. Foreign Policy* (New Haven, 1987); *idem*, "Ideology," and Akira Iriye, "Culture and International History," *Explaining the History of American Foreign Relations*, eds., Michael J. Hogan and Thomas G. Paterson, (Cambridge, 1991), pp. 193–201, 214–25.

4. Walter LaFeber, *The American Age: United States Foreign Policy at Home and Abroad since 1750* (New York, 1989), uses this term for the eighteenth and nineteenth centuries as well.

5. The myth of American exceptionalism, having shaped the origins of the social sciences and historiography in the United States at the beginning of the twentieth century, has continued to exert a pervasive influence in these disciplines even among scholars who somewhat reject it. See especially Dorothy Ross, *The Origins of American Social Science* (Cambridge, 1991); David W. Noble, *The End of American History: Democracy, Capitalism, and the Metaphor of Two Worlds in American Historical Writing, 1880–1980* (Minneapolis, 1985); and Peter Novick, *That Noble Dream: The "Objectivity Question" and the American Historical Profession* (Cambridge, 1988), pp. 61–132.

6. The United States does not appear as an exceptional nation, exempt from decline, in Paul Kennedy, *The Rise and Fall of the Great Powers: Economic Change and Military Conflict from 1500 to 2000* (New York, 1987). Like other great powers, it has experienced "relative decline" in the late twentieth century, despite its continuing status as the preeminent world power.

7. Robert Gilpin, *War and Change in World Politics* (Cambridge, 1981), examines the problem of stability and change relative to war. Wilson offered the concept of "international social control" as his solution to this global problem. For my critique of this concept in his pursuit of "progressive order," see Lloyd Ambrosius, "Woodrow Wilson and the Quest for Orderly Progress," in *Traditions and Values: American Diplomacy, 1965–1945*, ed., Norman A. Graebner (Lanham, MD, 1985), pp. 73–100; idem, *Woodrow Wilson and the*

American Diplomatic Tradition, pp. 1–14, passim; idem, *Wilsonian Statecraft: Theory and Practice of Liberal Internationalism during World War I* (Wilmington, DE, 1991), pp. 1–33.

8. Barry D. Karl, *The Uneasy State: The United States from 1915 to 1945* (Chicago, 1983), pp. 1–79, examines the tensions between centralization and decentralization in this era, developing this theme in both domestic and foreign affairs. I stress the paradoxical reality of interdependence and pluralism in the modern world, using these concepts to analyze this problem in *Woodrow Wilson and the American Diplomatic Tradition*.

9. Lloyd C. Gardner, *Safe for Democracy: The Anglo-American Response to Revolution, 1913–1923* (New York, 1984).

10. Gardner, *Safe for Democracy*, p. 104; Lloyd C. Gardner, *A Covenant with Power: America and World Order from Wilson to Reagan* (New York, 1984), pp. 3–28.

11. I emphasize Wilson's pursuit of U.S. hegemony through the creation of the League of Nations in *Woodrow Wilson and the American Diplomatic Tradition*.

12. See, for example, Frederick S. Calhoun, *Power and Principle: Armed Intervention in Wilsonian Foreign Policy* (Kent, OH, 1986).

13. Betty Miller Unterberger, *The United States, Revolutionary Russia, and the Rise of Czechoslovakia* (Chapel Hill, 1989).

14. For my critique of Unterberger's book, see Lloyd E. Ambrosius, "Wilsonian Self-Determination," *Diplomatic History* 16 (Winter 1992), pp. 141–48.

15. Lloyd C. Gardner, "Woodrow Wilson and the Mexican Revolution," in *Woodrow Wilson and a Revolutionary World, 1913–1921*, ed., Arthur S. Link (Chapel Hill, 1982), p. 22.

16. The most detailed account of U.S.-European relations toward the Mexican revolution is Frederich Katz, *The Secret War in Mexico: Europe, the United States, and the Mexican Revolution* (Chicago, 1981).

17. Laura Garcés, *La Mondialisation de la Doctrine Monroe à l'Ere Wilsonienne* (Lausanne, 1988); Kurt Wimer, "Woodrow Wilson and World Order," *Woodrow Wilson and a Revolutionary World*, pp. 146–73; Mark T. Gilderhus, *Pan American Visions: Woodrow Wilson in the Western Hemisphere, 1913–1921* (Tuscon, 1986); Ambrosius, *Woodrow Wilson and the American Diplomatic Tradition*, pp. 15–50.

18. Emily S. Rosenberg, *Spreading the American Dream: American Economic and Cultural Expansion, 1890–1945* (New York, 1982), pp. 7–13.

19. Rosenberg, *Spreading the American Dream*, p. 7.

20. Gardner, *Safe for Democracy*, p. 62.

21. This contribution derives from Georges-Henri Soutou, *L'Or et le Sang: Les Buts de Guerre Économiques de la Première Guerre Mondiale* (Paris, 1989).

22. James Reed, *The Missionary Mind and American East Asia Policy, 1911–1915* (Cambridge, MA, 1983); Jane Hunter, *The Gospel of Gentility: American Women Missionaries in Turn-of-the-Century China* (New Haven, 1984); Michael H. Hunt, *The Making of a Special Relationship: The United States and China to 1914* (New York, 1983), pp. 258–98; Warren I. Cohen, *The Chinese Connection: Roger S. Greene, Thomas W. Lamont, George E. Sololsky and American-East Asian Relations* (New York, 1978), pp. 1–87; Noel H. Pugach, *Paul S. Reinsch: Open Door Diplomat in Action* (Millwood, NY, 1979).

23. William R. Hutchison, *Errand to the World: American Protestant Thought and Foreign Missions* (Chicago, 1987), pp. 91–124; idem, *The Modernist Impulse in American Protestantism* (Cambridge, MA, 1976).

24. Ambrosius, *Wilsonian Statecraft*, pp. 10–13; John M. Mulder, *Woodrow Wilson: The Years of Preparation* (Princeton, 1978); Garcés, *La Mondialisation de la Doctrine Monroe*, pp. 98–110. Other recent studies that emphasize Wilsonian missionary diplomacy include Kendrick A. Clements, *William Jennings Bryan: Missionary Isolationist* (Knoxville, 1982) and Klaus Schwabe, *Woodrow Wilson, Revolutionary Germany, and Peacemaking, 1918–1919: Missionary Diplomacy and the Realities of Power* (Chapel Hill, 1985).

25. Woodrow Wilson, *The Public Papers of Woodrow Wilson: War and Peace*, eds., Ray Stannard Baker and William E. Dodd (New York, 1927), 2:536–39. See also August Heckscher, *Woodrow Wilson: A Biography* (New York, 1991), pp. 133–34, 650, 658–59, 666–67.

26. For European perspectives on America as a metaphor, or the modernist impulse toward Americanization of the Old World, see C. Vann Woodward, *The Old World's New World* (New York, 1991).

27. See also Peter Krüger, *Die Aussenpolitik der Republik von Weimar* (Darmstadt, 1985); idem, *Versailles: Deutsche Aussenpolitik zwischen Revisionismus und Friedenssicherung* (München, 1986).

28. For German views of Wilson, see also Peter Berg, *Deutschland und Amerika, 1918–1929* (Lübeck and Hamburg, 1963), pp. 9–47.

29. Hutchison, *Errand to the World*, p. 129.

Discussion

The session on "Imperialism and Revolution," which was chaired by Werner Link, focused on the years 1917 through 1919. A broad spectrum of issues was raised in the papers of Laura Garcés, Lloyd Gardner, Peter Krüger, and Georges-Henri Soutou. The debate initiated by these four contributions concentrated on the following issues: Woodrow Wilson's foreign policy perspectives and his presence at the Paris Peace Conference, the revolutionary challenges in both Europe and Mexico, the importance of the Monroe Doctrine in German-American relations, inconsistencies of self-determination and Wilson's concept of a new world order, the German problem and the changing perceptions of Wilson's peace terms within Germany. During the conference Lloyd Ambrosius gave a commentary on all four contributions, which are published in this volume. Fortunately, Professor Ambrosius did not hesitate to expand his commentary when this was suggested by the editor. However, the expanded version, printed in this volume under the title "Imperialism and Revolution: Wilsonian Dilemmas," is much more than just a commentary on the presentations by Garcés, Gardner, Krüger and Soutou. Ambrosius' contribution also reflects the major points of the discussion during the conference.

A second extensive commentary, entitled "Wilson, Versailles and the German Problem," was given at the conference by Klaus Schwabe. He began with some remarks on the kind of challenge the Mexican Revolution presented to Wilson. As far as the United States perception of Germany's role in Mexico was concerned, Schwabe suggested differentiating between Wilson and his advisors. Unlike Lansing, for example, Wilson seemed to have a more detached view concerning German activities in Mexico. At the center of Schwabe's commentary were the German problem in Wilson's peace strategy and the changing perceptions on both the American and the German sides. In Schwabe's opinion, Germany tended to overemphasize the American influence at the Paris Peace Conference. This was a misperception that contributed to the kind of disillusionment mentioned by Peter Krüger. Having been defeated most Germans hoped that American politicians intended to contain Allied ambitions to completely control Germany. Some Germans even thought that American influence at the Paris Peace Conference would be strong enough to dictate peace terms to all Europeans. This turned out to be an illusion. Schwabe confirmed that Wilson had to compromise at Versailles, but Schwabe left no doubt that the developments within Germany contributed to Wilson's harsh approach to the German problem and his justification of the severe character of the Versailles Treaty. The German people who had supported the Emperor up to the very end of the war, Wilson felt, deserved no better. Unfortunately, a written version of Schwabe's oral presentation could not be completed in time to be published here. Therefore, those readers interested in Schwabe's extensive research and writings on Wilson and the German problem may wish to consult Schwabe's publications on the subject, namely: *Deutsche Revolution und Wilson-Frieden: Die amerikanische und deutsche Friedensstrategie zwischen Ideologie und Machtpolitik* (Düsseldorf, 1971); English translation: *Woodrow Wilson, Revolutionary Germany, and Peacemaking 1918–1919: Missionary Diplomacy and the Realities of Power* (Chapel Hill, NC, 1985); "U.S. Secret War Diplomacy, Intelligence, and the Coming of the German Revolution in 1918: The Role of Vice Consul McNally" in *Diplomatic History* 16 (1992): 175–200.

None of the participants expected the conference to solve the Wilsonian dilemmas. However, the discussion made it evident that interpreting German-American relations in the crucial years from American intervention into World War I and the Paris Peace Conference in bilateral terms is insufficient. It is necessary to put the bilateral American-German relationship into a broader framework with a global perspective. Again, Latin America and the Monroe Doctrine turned out to be important examples for the necessity of a multilateral approach in the interpretation of American-German relations.

PART V

Isolation or Reconstruction?

18

German and American Concepts to Restore a Liberal World Trading System after World War I

Elisabeth Glaser-Schmidt

For German-American economic relations and commercial politics, the aftermath of World War I brought about a confusing and paradoxical situation.[1] The exigencies of readjusting the war economies to "normalcy" strengthened leanings toward economic nationalism on both sides, which aggravated the problems in bilateral commercial relations that existed before the war.[2] But the peace settlement also provided an opportunity for new departures since the power relationship between the two countries was changed and clarified: the United States could set new premises for a liberal world trading system and international economic cooperation. The chief needs in this regard were financial arrangements to enable a flow of funds to fields of investment, diplomatic readjustments of commercial policy, and corresponding domestic decisions in regard to tariff and currency attunements.

While the readjustment of international finance after the war has been addressed widely by historians, the restructuring of foreign trade regimes between Germany and the United States has suffered from relative neglect.[3] The foreign commercial-policy relationship between Germany and the United States had a threefold significance for the postwar international system: (1) it was a blueprint for further bilateral arrangements and thus established premises for a new international commercial system; (2) it supplemented diplomatic negotiations in other fields and thus created important preconditions for establishing mutual confidence, and (3) it fixed new rules for the exchange of goods and services in an attempt to facilitate international economic reconstruction. The postwar international system was characterized by a strong interdependence of political, economic, and commercial factors that had become even more significant than in prewar years. The inherent requirements proved difficult to harmonize. The political needs were, for the most part, met by a liberal diplomacy that was practiced by both sides. However, serious contradictions between protectionism and economic liberalism developed with the economic performance of the new system.

Analyzed in the context of commercial policy during the interwar period, the term "liberal" refers to lines of conduct aimed at nondiscrimination and the creation of a new framework of international capitalistic growth. Outlining German and American attempts to restructure commercial policy in the years between 1920 and 1924, this paper will argue that liberal commercial diplomacy was circumscribed by serious conflicts in the economic sphere concerning governmental economic policy, industrial competition, and protectionism. These tensions effectively hampered the execution of both German and American plans in regard to rules of international commerce. Thus the term "liberal commercial policy" is in part a misnomer. It is valid only for certain aspects of the commercial diplomacy of both powers, but cannot be applied to the postwar international commercial order in toto as it evolved in 1924–25. That system, which was created by the German-American treaty of commerce in 1923 and the Dawes Plan in 1924, aimed to facilitate reconstruction and stability for the ensuing period. Nevertheless, it rested on a basic misunderstanding about how to solve problems of international economic competition. Paradoxically, it had to be complemented by those economic conditions it meant to create.

Problems arising from economic rivalry between the two industrial powers can be traced back to prewar differences. Although a treaty regulated commercial relations between Germany and the United States, growing symptoms of mutual protectionism and differing interests in foreign trade set the tone in economic relations.[4] These substantial frictions concerning the economic relationship between the competing industrial export nations could not be alleviated, since they constituted a part of a growing antagonism between the two powers, emanating from conflicting designs in regard to their respective positions in world politics. After the United States had entered the war in 1917, mutual trade diminished and then stopped completely. The disposition of German property in the United States cumulated the list of problems to be solved after 1918. The sequestration of German property by the Wilson Administration stripped the Reich of a potential means to make up for its current account deficit with the United States after the war. Liberal groups in Germany soon recognized the need for a new design of bilateral relations that included as key elements a more liberal trading system and mutual cooperation. But bilateral contacts concerning questions of economic policy could not precede a general peace settlement.[5]

The commercial clauses of the Versailles treaty created a new basis for German-American relations. The treaty was to remain the central point of reference for bilateral ties until 1924–25, even though the United States did not become a formal party to it. The Reich was obliged to grant unilateral most-favored-nation status to the Allied and Associated Powers. In addition, the peace regime restricted Germany's right to revise its tariff rates for imports. Successive German governments and liberal economic experts considered this order of things, coupled with the obligation to pay reparations, to be both politically and economically unjust. President Woodrow Wilson's Fourteen Points were viewed by many as a cynical deception. Clearly, both German and American liberal concepts for a future world-trading system developed along Wilsonian principles, emphasizing equality of treatment, but because the United States did not ratify the Treaty of Versailles, these plans could not be realized in the near future.[6]

Until peace was concluded between Germany and the United States in 1921, most officials in the Wilson administration showed little interest in German-American commercial cooperation. Contrary to German economic experts, some economists in the American delegation in Paris stressed the educational effects of the commercial clauses of the treaty.[7] John Foster Dulles, at that time working as a lawyer for Sullivan and Cromwell in 1921, seeking to solve prewar German property claims, advised the incoming Republican administration that the economic provisions of the treaty seemed rather beneficial for American interests, especially in regard to the legal status of sequestered German holdings.[8] The State Department formulated the American agenda for a treaty of peace with Germany, demanding equal rights under the Versailles system: "we should negotiate a new treaty that should in the first place provide for our obtaining the same treatment that is to be given to Allied and Associated Powers under the Versailles Treaty, and in the next place ensure that neither our citizens nor our trade shall be discriminated against. These two matters are obviously closely related and are reciprocal."[9] The peace treaty between Germany and the United States incorporated the first provision, and thus gave the United States the stronger position for future negotiations on a new commercial agreement.[10] Moreover, the American government insisted that the German ratification of the peace treaty should precede discussions about a new commercial instrument.[11] Thus the Treaty of Berlin essentially predetermined the superior position of the United States in regard to future commercial negotiations.[12]

Although the American aims for a treaty of peace with Germany reflected certain conceptions about commercial policy, a comprehensive design for a postwar foreign commercial scheme developed only gradually. American government circles had recognized early that economic planning would be an important factor in determining international trade politics in the period after the war. It was, in the words of an official in the Bureau of Foreign and Domestic Commerce (BFDC), "second in importance only to the actual winning of the war."[13] Nevertheless, no significant steps in regard to commercial planning for the postwar world were taken during the last two years of the Wilson administration. The reason for this, as Robert Lansing observed, was that the ratification of the Versailles treaty formed a prerequisite for effective cooperation between Washington and American business.[14]

Even before the conclusion of the peace, some American business leaders had recognized that the economic results of the war necessitated drastic changes in American foreign economic policy. Several speakers at the convention of the National Foreign Trade Council in May discussed the new status of the United States as a creditor nation in the international economy. It seemed simple enough to arrive at the necessary conclusions from that assessment, but proved harder to draw the practical consequences; the United States had to increase imports. The surplus of goods thus generated there had to be directed into the Far East or South America. Excess capital had to be invested permanently in those European countries that could not pay for American imports by their own exports.[15] Since there existed no domestic consensus about the future course of American foreign policy, the Wilson administration could implement only some of the necessary prerequisites. Nondiscrimination of American commerce, which already had become one of the main American concerns during the war, remained the most important point on the agenda for postwar commercial policy planning. The need to defend American rights concerning foreign trade and investment abroad soon became clear, since the British manifested strong leanings toward imperial preference. Besides, France was continuing its economic war against Germany by trying to weaken German import controls under the guise of clauses 264–67 of the Versailles treaty. Both powers obstructed American requests to trade on an equal footing in the former German colonies. The danger that separate spheres of influence would be created in important economic regions of the world loomed large.[16]

The task of securing further recognition of the principles of nondiscrimination and of developing general rules for a future world-trading system fell to the Harding administration. In the first years of the Republican regime, foreign economic policy-planning was hampered by the fact that questions of foreign economic policy became a point of jurisdictional controversy between the Departments of State and Commerce, as well as the Tariff Commission. Herbert Hoover, the new Secretary of Commerce, strove to become the most efficient champion for the preservation of domestic financial stability and American rights in foreign commerce.[17]

Crucial decisions were made in the context of the 1922 tariff revision, one of the key items in the Republican agenda for domestic economic policy of the Republican party. William S. Culbertson, chairman of the Tariff Commission, formulated the plan to use the new tariff as an efficient weapon against foreign trade discrimination. Acting in close cooperation with the State Department, he succeeded in shaping important provisions of the tariff according to his concepts: the articles allowing for reciprocity and tariff bargaining embodied in the original bill were replaced by a broad provision for flexible penalty duties. With this he established the principles of general equality of treatment and the unconditional use of the most-favored-nation clause as a rule in American commercial policy. Special bilateral tariff concessions were abolished.[18] Culbertson then proposed corresponding changes in American commercial diplomacy. He pointed out to Secretary of State Charles E. Hughes that international recognition of the principles of nondiscrimination and equality of treatment could be obtained only by negotiating new bilateral commercial treaties. The State Department formally adopted this principle in the following year. Thus, by the end of 1922, the political foundations for a new system of commercial policy had been laid. Its purpose consisted in ensuring appropriate returns for the fittest competitor in world trade.[19]

The consequences of the inherent contradictions between economic exigencies and policy principles became obvious in the case of the Reich. At least on the surface, Germany's political and economic system seemed more adversely affected by the war's economic sequelae than did that of the United States. Until 1925 German commercial policy was mainly determined by resentment against the Versailles treaty. German public sentiment almost unanimously opposed the economic clauses of that settlement. Received opinion held that foreign unilateral transfers could only be made if the Reich obtained the maximum foreign-exchange returns for exports. The melody was played in an all-but-chaotic situation that reflected bureaucratic and ideological rivalries within and between the Foreign Office (AA) and the Economics Ministry (RWM). In the AA, a special division for foreign trade, the *Außenhandelsstelle*, was established, only to be dissolved in October 1921.[20]

From 1919 until 1925, the wish to regain commercial sovereignty determined official German commercial policy. This led to a demand for freedom of commerce and the claim to recover the prewar most-favored-nation status. The power to control imports arriving through the areas occupied by the French constituted another desideratum.[21]

Carl-Ludwig Holtfrerich, Hermann-Josef Rupieper, and others have described a variety of efforts to circumvent and fight the restrictions of the economic settlement that accompanied these political initiatives. Both the German government and German industrial leaders tried to evade the regulations of the treaty by different means. In the Federation of German Industries (RDI), Hermann Bücher advocated cheap German exports as a form of economic warfare. The Reich tried without much success to keep out Allied imports by imposing customs calculated on a gold-basis.

In 1921 the German government imposed a rigid system of foreign trade controls (*Außenhandelskontrolle*).[22] The initial motives for this step were largely pragmatic. The new scheme aimed at preventing exports of domestically needed goods and at regulating export prices so as to establish an "appropriate relation" between export prices and the exchange rate of the German mark. A complicated and not always efficient system was installed that worked mainly through agencies established by German industry. The latter subsequently started to use the control rules as measures of administrative protectionism. Officials in the AA seemed ambivalent toward foreign trade controls. Although apparently they never criticized that system openly, the ministry tried to tone down arguments for granting or withholding import or export permits. This was done in order to avoid any foreign reactions that could endanger German claims for a more liberal system of foreign commerce and an expansion of German trade.[23]

The founding and administering of foreign trade controls has to be viewed as a means to adapt to the economic crisis that was triggered by inflation. Large parts of the German government bureaucracy and the German public viewed the underlying causes of the decline of the German currency as rooted in the foreign economic constraints imposed on Germany by the Versailles treaty. Thus, long-term planning for a new foreign trade policy constituted a prominent and widely propagated aim of German foreign policy, while short-term measures were subject to the exigencies of currency depreciation. The AA and the RWM designed a more liberal commercial policy, although the latter institution held foreign trade controls in a higher esteem than the AA, owing to its inclination toward a planned economy.[24] Karl Ritter and Franz von Schönebeck,[25] who were to become key decision-makers in the realm of German foreign economic policy, emphasized from early on the need to reintegrate Germany into the world economy by means of a liberal trade policy governed by the most-favored-nation principle. In December 1920 Schönebeck outlined in two memoranda what was to become the official guideline of German commercial policy. He called for more provisional commercial agreements, which should precede long-term treaties with the important countries. While admitting the present necessity of foreign trade restrictions, he asked for the termination of all government controls as soon as economic conditions permitted it. With regard to future German commercial policy, Schönebeck advised a return to the dual principles of furthering German exports and protecting domestic industries. He emphasized that the promotion of foreign trade had gained high priority since the war.[26]

By 1924–25 these principles largely superseded the commercial policy regime of the first years of the Weimar Republic. Foreign trade controls did become a controversial issue; they were reduced in 1923 and largely abolished in 1924.[27] The provisional commercial treaties that the German government concluded in 1920 and the following year with Czechoslovakia and the Kingdom of Yugoslavia reflected the principles of German commercial policy that had evolved from German opposition to the Versailles treaty.[28] At the Brussels and Genoa conferences, the delegations of the Reich presented German foreign trade maxims as official demands aimed at revising the economic clauses of the peace order.[29] Thus, on the surface, Germany's demands for a liberal commercial policy neatly supplemented the American agenda, but it took the French occupation of the Ruhr in 1923 to create something resembling a community of interest regarding the political implementation of those principles.

Parallel to the formulation of commercial policy maxims, basic economic conflicts developed between Germany and the United States that reduced the chances of a true commercial rapprochement. For the American government, the problems of economic development and foreign trade policy pointed to the need for international cooperation and protection of the domestic economy.[30] These requirements were hard to harmonize, however; in addition, they partly contradicted the war debtors' commercial-policy agenda for the United States as a creditor nation. In spite of plans for a liberal commercial diplomacy, protectionism was soon accepted in the United States as well as in Germany as a quick solution for the ills of postwar economic readjustment. This process can only be explained in the context of economic problems associated with the reparations issue and the German inflation.[31]

The development of German-American trade in the years after World War I has been described elsewhere and need not to be discussed in detail here, but its impact on economic planning is relevant. The assessment of the postwar economic situation in both countries and its consequences for a future commercial policy took longer than the quick resumption of the transatlantic exchange of goods.[32] An analysis of German-American trade statistics for the years 1919 to 1924 illustrates the pervasive instability which from 1924–25 onward evolved into marked conflicts. Despite a considerable flow of American imports to the Reich, Germany was unable to recover its prewar position as exporter of goods to the United States.[33] Nevertheless, the Reich ranked as an important market for American raw materials and agricultural goods in the first years after the war.[34] Those articles were needed in Germany to such an extent that the 1913-level of American exports was reached and surpassed in 1921. This was caused partly by the fact that the United States now supplanted Russia as an exporter of food to Germany.[35] Therefore, and as long as the German hyperinflation discouraged sufficient domestic production, agricultural protectionism which had formerly constituted a prominent theme in German-American trade quarrels, ceased to be an issue. Given the rapid depreciation of the German currency, only American loans could finance the Reich's imports from the United States, either in the form of short-term acceptance credits, by American private loans to German cities, or by German re-exports in a kind of direct exchange.[36]

German exports to the United States boomed in the hyperinflation years 1922–1923.[37] But even in 1923, when Germany sold goods for $161 million to the United States, the level of prewar exports was not

Table 1: German exports to the United States(=G), American exports to Germany (=U.S.), 1913, 1919–1924, in millions of dollars[39]

	1913	1919	1920	1921	1922	1923	1924
G:	184	11	89	80	117	161	139
U.S.:	332	93	311	372	316	317	440

Table 2: Selected German exports to the United States, 1922–1925, in millions of dollars[40]

	1922	1923	1924	1925
Cotton Goods	12	17	12	14
Toys, including dolls	6	7	4	3
Table and kitchen glassware	2	2	0.5	0.4

reached. After the stabilization of the German currency and the Dawes Plan, the German balance of payments depended more on exports than the American economy; thus, the prewar pattern of trade rivalries came into existence again. Germany's weakened position as a seller in the international market became obvious with the stabilization of the mark in 1924. Then the impact of the Fordney-McCumber tariff became apparent too.[38] The question of how Germany could adjust her negative trade balance with the United States thus remained unresolved.

From 1920 to the beginning of 1923, American attitudes in regard to commercial policy toward Germany changed considerably, as the unstable state of German-American trade relations constantly modified the American assessment of the situation. The State Department reacted initially with sympathy when learning about the Reich's foreign commercial policy quandaries. German plans to collect customs duties on a gold-basis met approval, because that scheme would "afford Germany an opportunity to conserve her resources for her own industrial rehabilitation."[41] Subsequently however, as some German politicians tried to exploit American signs of sympathy, Ellis Loring Dresel, the first American commissioner to Germany, reacted with pungent criticism concerning the excessively self-serving character of German foreign trade controls.[42] His complaints were justified, since import controls from 1920 to 1921 evolved into a system of outright protection.[43] Dresel reported in December 1921 that decisions concerning the granting of import-permits were made according to the wishes of the industries in question. A representative of the German iron industry later admitted that import controls had sought "to keep out of Germany all imports which could not be justified on economic motives." In those branches of German industries that were affected by American industrial imports, a phobia of American economic efficiency developed together with a marked tendency toward industrial protectionism, which became an issue after 1924.[44]

Faced with German intransigence in the reparations question during the spring of 1921, the State Department recognized increasingly that the Reich's expressions of mutual economic dependency signified only German wishes for American cooperation against France. Consequently, it became clear that Germany's economic potential should be circumscribed rather than built up by unilateral American actions. A memorandum for Hughes explained that new approach: "even our selfish trade interests will be better served by the economic revival of all of Europe, possibly through real reparation payments, than through a rapid revival of German prosperity at the expense of world prosperity."[45] While officials in the State Department kept these opinions to themselves, Hoover told a member of the German embassy flatly that the United States was in no way economically dependent on exports to Europe and that America showed no material but merely a sentimental interest in the reparations question.[46]

Subsequent to these signs of estrangement at the diplomatic level, strong anti–German protectionist impulses arose. That process should be understood as a consequence of the recession that took place in the United States from 1921 to 1922. The slump in the United States occurred concomitant to a fall in the total value of American exports from an all-time high of $8.2 billion in 1920 to $4.4 billion in 1921 and to $3.8 billion in 1922. These figures point to the international state of the depression.[47] The financial crisis in Germany which grew severe from 1921 onwards, added to the specter of economic threats originating abroad, as it reduced the dollar valuation of German exports.

American reports from the Reich reflected the ambiguity of German economic development after 1920. On the one hand, Dresel stressed the precarious character of the German economic and financial situation and the need for a more active role of the United States.[48] On the other hand, Charles E. Herring, commercial attaché in Berlin, reported that owing to German subsidies and industrial consolidation, Germany enjoyed for the time being certain competitive advantages.[49] As soon as German industrial leaders and officials of the RWM became aware of American attacks against German subsidies, they took pains to prove that the German government subsidized food prices for social reasons merely.[50] At the same time, the AA sought to downplay profitable German business activities.[51] But official representations did not lead to much. With reports about growing German competition abroad, the Department of Commerce pointed to "the constant recurrence of the question of German competition." Comparing German and American exports to third countries in the years 1920 and 1921, the BFDC noted that German competition was considerably affecting the export trade of the United States.[52]

The Emergency Tariff of 1921 had by then embodied prevalent protectionist impulses in the United States.[53] Its successor, the 1922 Fordney-McCumber measure, contained several important flexible provisions. A general increase of rates, however, constituted its main feature. The new duties figured much higher than those proposed by advocates of the new liberal commercial policy. Here the basic contradiction in American commercial policy became apparent: its underlying philosophy regarded a stable interior structure of wages and prices as a precondition to domestic economic efficiency and competitive performance abroad. That constellation in any case could only be preserved by protecting the American industry against cheap-currency imports. Hoover understood this well and accordingly embraced tariff safeguards as the preferable means to regulate international economic problems.[54]

Not surprisingly, the preparation and discussion of the tariff bill gave occasion to strong complaints about German competition. American trade experts correctly assessed German dumping as a symptom of the ills of inflation.[55] According to Otto Wiedfeldt, the new ambassador to Washington, the extent of anti-German feeling forbade any action by the embassy against the raising of tariff rates which were apt to curtail German exports to the United States. Hyperinflation began after June 1922, and with that official representations in opposition to American demands for protection became futile anyway.[56] Complaints about the contemplated schedules thus became a chore of German business circles.[57]

While the tariff as it was enacted did not discriminate against any specific country, it included some provisions which were de facto directed against German imports. For the controversial item of dyes,[58] the protective assessment in American valuation was retained. A member of the Bureau of Foreign and Domestic Commerce explicitly acknowledged that the purpose of the new law was to keep out many products formerly imported from Europe.[59] Nevertheless, an increase in German exports except for dyes took place in 1923. But this tendency figured solely as a result of the rapid depreciation of the mark, which more than made up for tariff increases.[60] The protectionist character of American commercial policy led to reactions in Germany that lent support to those officials who advocated higher German tariff rates. This process set the agenda for future tariff conflicts. Hermann Davidsen, the AA's expert for economic relations with the United States, argued in a memorandum for Ritter that the American tariff did not discriminate specifically against Germany, "what of course the German duties for agricultural products will not do in regard to the U.S." He then stated that the new American tariff rates particularly affected German industry. In his view, the handling of provisions for the marking of goods constituted a thorny aspect of administrative protectionism. In this regard even the French seemed more cooperative than the United States.[61]

The American decision to protect domestic industries from German competition formed part of an international process. In 1921, in addition to several other tariff measures, the British parliament passed a "Safeguarding of Industries Act," which was directed chiefly against German imports. Protectionist tariffs against German imports were also enacted in France and Belgium and were contemplated in Sweden. When the United States as the most solvent world power joined the movement for industrial protectionism, it introduced a modicum of flexibility and reviewing of procedures into tariff scheduling. Even though America seemed moderate when viewed in international comparison, the subsequent administration of the new tariff regime was characterized by burdensome bureaucratic procedures. Congress passed the Fordney-McCumber Bill at the heyday of European postwar inflation and thus reacted to corresponding American concerns. By 1924–25 that purpose was to a considerable extent outdated and ensuingly failed to meet the needs of America's most important trade partners, Britain and Germany.[62]

Already by 1923 it had become obvious that protectionist tariffs formed only a stopgap measure that, by itself, could not solve the problem of German underselling of American goods. With German inflation worsening, it was widely recognized in the Harding administration that currency fluctuations in Europe were the main reason for the unstable condition of American foreign trade. American exports were also affected. When the State Department admonished Dresel in November 1920 that "the great desirability that Germany should be enabled to take American surplus, cotton etc. . . should be borne in mind," the American commissioner responded by stressing that American raw materials could be sold only in a very limited amount in Germany since the international purchasing power of the mark was diminishing. Consul Verne Richardson repeated this assessment in 1923: "The truth is, no matter how anxious German importers may be to handle American goods and to reap rich profits on their sale, it is absolutely impossible for them to do so, so long as for every dollar's worth they buy, an equivalent in mark of not less than 20–25 thousand [marks] must be spent. . . ."[63]

German industrial competition remained a central issue when the discussion in Washington shifted to the financial rehabiliation of Europe. Hoover noted in his famous memorandum on financial reconstruction in Europe to the president that the efforts of the German government to secure fiscal stability in Germany had been defeated. A combination of state subsidies, enormously increased government payrolls, and the activities of the "industrial group," which dominated the German economy and wrecked all plans of proper taxation, had caused this state of affairs. Reparations constituted a main part of the problem, but could only be dealt with when the other problems indicated were solved. Hoover emphasized that in the present situation Germany was able to compete with the entire world because of temporarily reduced costs of manufactured production. He insisted that inflation had transferred property values to holders of equity, including the "industrial group."[64] This assessment of the internal and external results of German inflation indicated the need to regulate German industrial development and curb excessive German competition and thus set the agenda for American stabilization policy.

In spite of the commercial barriers imposed by inflation and corresponding protectionist reactions, German and American business leaders tried to foster mutual trade. They addressed some of the most urgent problems even before official relations were reestablished. Werner Link has described the agreements between business groups that were concluded between 1920 and 1924. These compacts sought to solve the problems of German competition in a cooperative manner and aimed to reopen and broaden channels of commerce. The most important accords were those between the AEG and General Electric (GE), Siemens and Westinghouse, and the shipping accords between the German Hapag and the Harriman interests.[65] Besides rapidly smoothing business relations, the contacts between the AEG and GE in 1920 and the Hapag-Harriman agreement reflected the common interest in making the Soviet Union accessible as a market and a field of investment.[66] Apart from the establishing of a German shipping enterprise with the help of American capital, these designs did not yield instant results. The hesitant beginnings for German-American cooperation in Russia soon broadened to semi-official planning. They illustrate the mutual interests of German and American leaders in redirecting the flow of German products to regions that did not possess competing industries. This project sought to eliminate a major quandary of the postwar world trading system.

The initiative for these plans came mainly from Max Warburg and Walther Rathenau. In 1921 they pointed out to Dresel that it seemed desirable to combine American capital and German skills and expertise to open the Soviet Union.[67] Their ideas met with considerable interest not only from Dresel, but also in the State Department and the BFDC. American flirting with that scheme came to a sudden end, however, when in December Hoover decided against the idea, apparently without having consulted anybody. His reasonings, which emphasized the advantages of direct trade with Russia, met no formal opposition from the State Department. Nevertheless his conduct left the impression of serious bureaucratic differences concerning German and European stabilization. Fred M. Dearing, the Assistant Secretary of State, reacted angrily to Hoover's decision: "We had also in mind . . . that the United States will derive an important and direct economic benefit not only from the rehabilitation of Russia but also from the rehabilitation of Germany. The shortsightedness of any policy which does not provide a fair opportunity for Germany to reestablish herself economically need hardly be demonstrated. . . . It would appear . . . that the Department of Commerce has decided upon definite policies involving our foreign relations and that in doing so it has not considered it necessary or advisable to consult the Department of State in any way."[68]

The dissent between the two main foreign economic policy-making bodies did not terminate official American interest regarding future cooperation with Germany in the Soviet Union. Rather, both departments followed a policy of watch-and-wait concerning German economic activities in this field. But the impact of the quarrel, together with American disenchantment about Rapallo,[69] terminated the chances of establishing mutually advantageous collaboration in the Soviet Union in the near future. In addition, Rathenau's assassination removed one of the main protagonists of this course from the scene.[70] Further plans for mutual cooperation concerning Russia and capital investments in Eastern Europe were delayed by the French occupation of the Ruhr and the American policy of non-recognition.[71]

Official German obstinacy obstructed another initiative that was meant to further business cooperation with the aim to reintegrate Germany into international commercial planning. The episode illustrates the extent to which "questions of honor" prevented even the AA from adopting pragmatic positions that could regain Germany's international credibility. When Edward Filene, the planner and coorganizer of the International Chamber of Commerce (ICC), proposed in 1920 that Germany should become a member of that body, he was rebuked rather undiplomatically by the Undersecretary for Economic Questions in the AA, Adolf von Boyé. After the beginning of informal contacts between the German Embassy and the central bureau of the ICC in Paris, the AA insisted with increasing firmness that the government and the Deutsche Industrie und Handelstag (DIHT) reconsider its position. But German officials even then stalled, because in its 1922 congress the ICC had adopted the position that reparations were an obligation with moral character. The DIHT demanded an official repudiation of that principle as a precondition for joining the ICC. It took until 1925 to resolve this dispute.[72]

Despite these varying conflicts in the economic sphere, liberal commercial diplomacy still seemed to be the best strategy to advance American commercial policy aims and also to contribute to a solution of the intricate questions of Germany's future economic status and reparations payments.[73] Informal talks for a new commercial treaty between Germany and the United States began in October 1921. Negotiations were soon stalled, however, because Hughes decided that an agreement regulating American war claims from Germany should have priority. Since the future course of American commercial policy had not been determined conclusively, this happened to be a convenient position. Moreover, the American government did not particularly care whether there was such a treaty or not, but knew perfectly well that the Germans would like to have one, as Castle pointed out to Dresel. The German government seemed, indeed, mostly for political and revisionist reasonings, the more eager party to conclude a treaty with the United States. A commercial agreement would lead to more intimate relations with the power the Reich sought cooperation with, and also accord Germany the most-favored-nation status in international trade, thus circumscribing the economic clauses of the Versailles treaty.[74] With the conclusion of the mixed-claims agreement in August 1922, serious negotiations became possible. The American ambassador Alanson Houghton pointed out to the State Department that renewed talks about a commercial treaty seemed a necessity. This was the time to respond to the obvious German interest in American friendship. Hughes' economic advisers recognized that this situation presented an opportunity to conclude a treaty of commerce with Germany that would embody the unconditional most-favored-nation clause. Contrary to Castle's assessment, the bureaucracy in Washington grasped clearly the economic importance of this move.[75] After the necessary consultations within the Harding administration and the rather time-consuming drafting of the new model treaty, formal negotiations with Wiedfeldt began in July 1923.[76]

As Link and Buckingham have shown, the weak position of Germany enabled the Department of State to incorporate all substantial principles of the new American commercial policy into the treaty. Only some of the German counter-proposals were met. The State Department renounced the American right to most-favored-nation status in regard to commercial concessions Germany had accorded France in the Ruhr, and yielded in minor details. Correspondingly, Germany had to make major concessions by relinquishing the options of preferential agreements outside the scope of the unlimited most-favored-nation clause or a customs union with Austria.[77] The unconditional most-favored-nation clause was included in the treaty as the guiding principle of American commercial policy. This denied the original German wish for a merely reciprocal version. In addition, the AA accepted liberal regulations in regard to the right of foreign corporations to establish themselves. The State Department excluded all options to link most-favored-nation treatment to tariff rates and thus secure a lower tariff for German imports.[78]

The German-American treaty of amity and commerce was signed on 8 December 1923. The United States thus tried to establish the American version of liberal trade as the leading principle for the world trading system. This meant that American commercial policy, with all its contradictory assumptions, including both protectionism and nondiscrimination as guiding principles, would serve as a pattern for future international commercial cooperation. After 1924–25 it became evident that, given the specter of further tariff and trade conflicts, the German-American accord alone could not provide universal acceptance of the new principles. This danger was conveniently overlooked in 1923. The treaty united Germany and the United States in a community of interest against French commercial policy, which did not provide for most-favored-nation treatment.[79]

The signing of the instrument constituted a diplomatic victory for Germany, since it sanctioned the attempts to breach the commercial restrictions of the Versailles treaty. These aspects were strongly emphasized by Stresemann. For the new chief of the AA, the commercial treaty formed a substantial first success, despite the fact that its completion was overshadowed by German indiscretions. More importantly, the accord documented the chances for future German-American political cooperation. A closer association with America became the guiding principle of Stresemann's revisionist foreign policy.[80] Thus the treaty ended a period of instability in the political sphere of German-American commercial relations. Subsequent problems arising with the ratification debates in both countries (which is outside of the time period treated here) illustrate, however, that the agreement just imposed a new framework over a fragile structure without solving the basic economic conflicts.

The new commercial scheme governing German-American relations was supplemented in 1924 by the political and economic regime underlying the Dawes Plan.[81] While the treaty concluded in 1923 officially recognized the need for nondiscrimination and commercial equality for Germany, the report of the committee of experts set up a provisional solution for the problem of reparations. Incidentally, it also addressed the two major issues which had characterized German-American commercial relations in the previous years: The exigency to promote German exports and thus to continue attempts to liberalize the world trading system, and the necessity to curtail excessive German competition in the world market. The lack of adequate mechanisms to enforce these aims emanated from the basic conception of the Dawes Plan, which was meant to solve the international financial and political crisis that characterized the reparations question after the French occupation of the Ruhr. The 1924 financial project aimed at making means and ends meet by creating the basic preconditions for international economic normalcy. Apart from regulating reparations payments in kind by the Reich, it refrained from taking further measures that would have interfered directly with German foreign trade.

American reactions to the occupation of the Ruhr also reflected the rationale of promoting economic and financial reform. The imperative of American foreign economic policy in the second half of 1923 sought to save opportunities for American investments in German industry and above all to keep the German economy from collapsing. According to the State Department, this aim was to be achieved by promoting a currency reform as a precondition to recovery.[82] To that extent, the experts' plan worked. On the other hand, it merely included an outline for a possible solution in regard to Germany's trade relations with the world; Costigliola has shown that Owen D. Young, the leading figure in the American group of the committee of experts and the mastermind of the plan, wanted to use reparations for the economic recovery of Germany in the first phase. Parallel to this, capital investments in underdeveloped regions should promote German foreign trade. Young also regarded German reparation payments as a means to limit the competitive advantages that Germany had gained by hyperinflation. Hoover had already emphasized that this development had eliminated the largest part of Germany's debts.[83] Thus German entry into the American system of liberal trade, nondiscrimination and equal opportunity had to be preceeded by the elimination of her undue competitive advantages. At J. P. Morgan's and by others, the contradictory character of the assumptions concerning Germany's capacity to earn an export surplus in the light of previous experience were clearly recognized. Nevertheless, this inconsistency seemed to constitute a matter of minor importance in comparison to the political impact of the plan.[84]

The new principles for economic and commercial policy that were designed to regulate German-American relations in 1923–24 represented merely political experiments aimed at a new world-trading system. As a result of the power structure in the years after World War I, this novel commercial system evolved mainly out of American conceptions. One of its underlying assumptions resulted from a common German-American interest in nondiscrimination and liberal commercial policy. A protectionist high-tariff policy on the American side and a strong similar tendency in German trade regime, however, impaired this version of commercial liberalism. This situation reflected current economic rationales meant to mitigate the ills of postwar depression, inflation, and international competition. The tendency of this continuing pattern of conflicting economic schemes tended to hamper foreign trade expansion. The lack of basic agreements concerning the integration of France and the Soviet Union into the new commercial system added to its deficiencies. Thus, the decisions made in 1923–24 formed only blueprints for future developments, sponsored by those who possessed the necessary knowledge and had the will to effect essential changes, but who in the face of adverse economic and political developments lacked the power to convert their plans into reality.

Notes to Chapter 18

1. Research for this paper was partly financed by the Deutsche Forschungsgemeinschaft and the German Marshall Fund of the United States.

2. The subject of German-American economic relations before World War I is treated by Ragnhild Fiebig-von Hase, "Die deutsch-amerikanischen Wirtschaftsbeziehungen, 1890–1914, im Zeichen von Protektionismus und internationaler Integration," *Amerikastudien* 33 (1988), pp. 329–57.

3. Werner Link, *Die amerikanische Stabilisierungspolitik in Deutschland, 1921–1932* (Düsseldorf, 1970) remains the most exhaustive study of German-American political as well as economic relations. Similar themes for the latter part of the interwar period are covered by Hans-Jürgen Schröder, *Deutschland und die Vereinigten Staaten, 1933–1939* (Wiesbaden, 1970). The financial diplomacy leading to the Dawes Plan has been examined by Stephen A. Schuker, *The End of French Predominance in Europe: The Financial Crisis of 1924 and the Adoption of the Dawes Plan* (Chapel Hill, NC, 1976). Important aspects of German-American financial relations are treated by Carl-Ludwig Holtfrerich, *The German Inflation, 1914–1923* (Berlin/New York, 1986); and by the same author, "Amerikanischer Kapitalexport und Wiederaufbau der deutschen Wirtschaft 1919–1923 im Vergleich zu 1924–1929," *Vierteljahrschrift für Sozial- und Wirtschaftsgeschichte* 64 (1977), pp. 497–529. For an assessment of American-European cooperation, see Michael Hogan, *Informal Entente: The Private Structure of Cooperation in Anglo-American Economic Diplomacy* (Columbia, MO/London, 1970); Melvyn P. Leffler, *The Elusive Quest: America's Pursuit of European Stability and French Security, 1919–1933* (Chapel Hill, NC, 1979); and Frank Costigliola, *Awkward Dominion: American Political, Economic, and Cultural Relations with Europe, 1919–1933* (Ithaca, NY/London, 1984). In the last several years a growing interest in commercial foreign policy as an independent variable in international relations during the interwar period has developed: See Dirk Stegmann, "Deutsche Zoll- und Handelspolitik 1924/5–1929 unter besonderer Berücksichtigung agrarischer und industrieller Interessen," in Hans Mommsen, Dietmar Petzina and Bernd Weisbrod, eds., *Industrielles System und politische Entwicklung in der Weimarer Republik* (Düsseldorf, 1974), pp. 499–513; Carl-Ludwig Holtfrerich, "Deutscher Außenhandel und Goldzölle 1919–1923," in Gerald D. Feldman, Carl-L. Holtfrerich, Gerhard A. Ritter and Peter Christian Witt, eds., *Die Anpaßung an die Inflation* (Berlin 1986), pp. 472–84; Olof Åhlander, *Staat, Wirtschaft und Handelspolitik: Schweden und Deutschland, 1918–1921* (Lund, 1983); Carl-Ludwig Holtfrerich, "U.S. Economic (Policy) Development and World Trade during the Interwar Period Compared to the Last Twenty Years," in Ivan T. Berend and Knut Borchardt, eds., *The Impact of the Depression of the 1930's and its Relevance for the Contemporary World:* Comparative studies prepared for the A/5 Session of the 9th International Economic History Congress, 24–29 August 1986, Bern (Budapest, 1986), pp. 61–81; Wilfried Feldenkirchen, "Deutsche Zoll- und Handelspolitik 1914–1933," in *Die Auswirkungen von Zöllen und anderen Handelshemmnissen auf Wirtschaft und Gesellschaft vom Mittelalter bis zur Gegenwart*, Vierteljahresschrift für Sozial- und Wirtschaftsgeschichte, Beiheft no. 80 (Stuttgart, 1987), pp. 328–57; Jürgen Bellers, *Außenwirtschaft und politisches System der Weimarer Republik* (Münster, 1988). A useful summary of economic research can be found in Jeffrey A. Frieden and David A. Lake, eds., *International Political Economy: Perspectives on Global Power and Wealth* (New York, 1991).

4. Fiebig-von Hase, *Wirtschaftsbeziehungen* (cf. n. 2).

5. For German concepts regarding a liberal commercial policy at the end of the war, see Leo Haupts, *Deutsche Friedenspolitik 1918–19* (Düsseldorf, 1976), pp.100–38; for the term "economic experts" see Peter Grupp, *Deutsche Außenpolitik im Schatten von Versailles, 1918–1920* (Paderborn, 1987), pp. 44–45.

6. Moritz Bonn, "Undatierte Aufzeichnung zu einer Kritik der alliierten Friedensbedingungen aus den von Wilson entwickelten Gedankengängen," *Moritz Bonn Papers*, Bundesarchiv Koblenz (BA).

7. Memorandum from Allyn Abbott Young for Thomas W. Lamont, 5 April 1919, *Records of International Conferences, Commissions and Expositions*, RG 256, Inquiry Docu-

ments, Economic Division, Document No. 256, National Archives (NARS); for other American views which were more critical see Hermann-Josef Rupieper, *The Cuno Government and Reparations* (The Hague, 1979), p. 5.

8. Dulles to Hoover, 5 April 1921 and 7 April 1921, *Herbert C. Hoover Papers*, Commerce Papers (Hoover CP), 3256, Herbert C. Hoover Presidential Library, West Branch, Iowa.

9. Unsigned memorandum, 22 June 1921, *General Records of the Department of State*, RG 59, Decimal File (DF) 763.72119/11887, NARS; the history of the German-American Treaty of Peace is discussed more fully in my contribution *"Von Paris nach Berlin. Überlegungen zur Neugestaltung der deutsch-amerikanischen Beziehungen in der Ära Harding,"* in Norbert Finzsch, Hermann Wellenreuther, eds., *Liberalitas: Festschrift für Erich Angermann* (Stuttgart, 1992), pp. 319–42.

10. Link, *Stabilisierungspolitik* (cf. n. 3), pp. 89–100; for the German position, see *Akten der Reichskanzlei, Die Kabinette Wirth I und II*, vol. 1 (Boppard, 1974), pp. 143–43, 192.

11. Unsigned and undated memorandum, ca. 8 November 1921, Akten zur Deutschen Auswärtigen Politik (ADAP), vol. A V (Göttingen, 1987), pp. 210–24; Link, *Stabilisierungspolitik* (cf. n. 3), p. 100.

12. Costigliola, *Dominion* (cf. n. 3), pp. 77–80.

13. B.S. Cutler to Lansing, 2 September 1918, *DF* 600.001/568.

14. Lansing to Wilson, 15 August 1919, *DF* 600.001/872.

15. E.L. Bogart to Secretary of State, 18 June 1920, *DF* 600.1115/211.

16. Carl P. Parrini, *Heir to Empire: United States Economic Diplomacy, 1916–1923* (Pittsburgh, 1969), pp. 221–225, deals mainly with reactions to these developments in American business circles. For the attitude in the Department of State, see Wallace to the Secretary of State, 3 March 1920, and unsigned and undated memorandum of the Department of State relating thereto, *DF* 662.003/11.

17. Joseph Brandes, *Herbert Hoover and Economic Diplomacy: Department of Commerce Policy* (Pittsburgh, 1962), pp. 63–64, and passim; William J. Barber, *From the New Era to the New Deal: Herbert Hoover, the Economists, and American Economic Policy, 1921–1933* (Cambridge, MA, 1985), p. 31.

18. The shaping of the Fordney-McCumber Tariff is broadly discussed in Parrini, *Heir*, pp. 227–34 (cf. n. 16); Leffler, *Elusive Quest* (cf. n. 3), pp. 45–48; Joan Hoff Wilson, *American Business and Foreign Policy, 1920–1933* (Lexington, KY, 1971), pp. 80–87; William S. Culbertson, *International Economic Policies* (New York, 1925), pp. 141–47.

19. The protectionist features of the Fordney-McCumber tariff are discussed below. Culbertson's views and his cooperation with the Department of State are amply documented in the department's files. See Culbertson to Dearing, 16 July 1921, *DF* 611.003/835 and the final draft of the State Department for the defensive provisions of the tariff bill, undated, 611.003/838; Office of the Economic Adviser to Harrison, 20 October 1922, ibidem, /1188; Culbertson to Hughes, 31 May 1922, *DF* 611.0031 /155, and 14 December 1922, *Papers Relating to the Foreign Relations of the U.S.* (Foreign Relations), 1923, vol. 1, 121–126; memorandum of the Office of the Economic Adviser, 22 August 1923, ibidem, /file 200. For differing views of Hoover and the Bureau of Foreign and Domestic Commerce, see Hoover to Harding, 1 August 1921, *Hoover CP*, President Harding; and minutes of a meeting of officials from the Department of State, the Department of Commerce, and the Tariff Commission, 2 May 1921, *DF* 600.003/841; Peter Buckingham, *International Normalcy* (Wilmington, DE, 1983), pp. 157–61, with a good discussion of Culbertson's views.

20. See Peter Krüger's assessment of the work of the AA, "Struktur, Organisation und Wirkungsmöglichkeiten der leitenden Beamten des auswärtigen Dienstes 1921–33," pp. 101–69, especially 157, in Klaus Schwabe, ed., *Das diplomatische Korps* (Boppard, 1985); Kurt Doß, *Das deutsche Auswärtige Amt im Übergang vom Kaiserreich zur Weimarer Republik* (Düsseldorf, 1977), pp. 216–305; P.G. Lauren, *Diplomats and Bureaucrats: The First Institutional Responses to Twentieth Century Diplomacy in France and Germany* (Stanford, CA, 1976), pp. 169–76; for the RWM, see Eckhard Wandel, *Hans Schäffer* (Stuttgart, 1974), pp. 51–52, and passim.

21. Peter Krüger, *Die Außenpolitik der Republik von Weimar* (Darmstadt, 1985), pp. 92–94; AA to Sthamer, 25 February 1920, *ADAP*, vol. A III (Göttingen, 1985), pp. 86–90.

22. Rupieper, *Cuno* (cf. n. 6), p. 33; Holtfrerich, *"Deutscher Außenhandel und Goldzölle"* (cf. n. 3); AA to Sthamer, 25 February 1920, (cf. n. 21); regarding foreign trade control, see Gerald D. Feldman, *Iron and Steel in the German Inflation, 1916–1923* (Princeton, NJ, 1977), pp. 191–208; Bellers, *Außenwirtschaftspolitik und politisches System* (cf. n. 3), pp. 195–202.

23. Maximilian von Löhr to RWM, 1 November 1919, *AA files*, Unterstaatssekretär W 1066–2, Politisches Archiv des Auswärtigen Amtes, Bonn (PA).

24. See Wandel, *Schäffer* (cf. n. 20), p. 52, regarding viewpoints in the RWM.

25. As undersecretary in the AA from 1922 onward, Ritter was responsible for economic foreign policy and reparations; von Schönebeck served as the director of the foreign-trade division (Abteilung II) in the RWM.

26. Secret memorandum by Schönebeck, 25 November 1920 "Leitsätze für die Außenhandels- und Zollpolitik der nächsten Zukunft," *RWM* files 20351, pp. 131–143, *Zentrales Staatsarchiv Potsdam* (ZStA); see also Schönebeck's secret memorandum "Künftige Außenhandels- und Zollpolitik und die Handelsverträge," 11 December 1920, ibidem, pp. 101–129; for Ritter, see Striemer to Ritter, 23 January 1923 and Ritter's reply, *AA files*, Sonderreferat Wirtschaft (SW), Handel 6, Bd. 1, PA. See also Åhlander, *Staat, Wirtschaft und Handelspolitik* (cf. n. 3), pp. 197–203, who, however, overemphasizes the role of the reparations question in Schönebeck's decisions.

27. Feldman, *Iron and Steel*, (cf. n. 22), pp. 197–208; Feldenkirchen, *"Deutsche Zoll- und Handelspolitik 1914–1933"* (cf. n. 3), pp. 338–39.

28. Krüger, *Außenpolitik* (cf. n. 21), pp. 113–15; see also the list of the commercial treaties of Germany with foreign countries "Übersicht über die handelspolitischen Beziehungen des Auslandes zum Deutschen Reiche," 1 June 1922, *AA files*, SW, Handel 13, Handelsvertragsverhältnis zu Deutschland, vol. 2.

29. Entwurf von Richtlinien für die Delegierten zur Brüssleler Sachverständigenkonferenz.[3 December 1920], *Akten der Reichskanzlei: Das Kabinett Fehrenbach* (Boppard, 1972); Carole Fink, *The Genoa Conference* (Chapel Hill, NC/London, 1984), pp. 249–51; protocol of the cabinet meeting in Genoa, 17 April 1922, *Akten der Reichskanzlei, Die Kabinette Wirth I und II*, vol. 2, pp. 708–09.

30. Hogan, *Informal Entente* (cf. n. 3), pp. 29–37; Leffler, *Elusive Quest* (cf. n. 3), pp. 10–41; Costigliola, *Awkward Dominion* (cf. n. 3) pp. 96–110; see esp. Hoff-Wilson, *Business* (cf. n. 18), pp. 65–100, regarding the contradictions in American commercial policy.

31. Carl-Ludwig Holtfrerich, *Inflation* (cf. n. 3), pp. 136–54; Bruce Kent, *The Spoils of War: The Politics, Economics and Diplomacy of Reparations 1918–1932* (Oxford, 1989), pp. 45–242; Schuker, *End of French Predominance* (cf. n. 3), pp. 14–28, and passim, has pointed out that the reparations question constitutes an important political factor to explain German hesitancy to stop the inflation. See also by the same author, "Finance and Foreign Policy in the Era of the German Inflation: British, French, and German Strategies for Economic Reconstruction after the First World War," in Otto Büsch and Gerald D. Feldman, eds., *Historische Prozesse der Deutschen Inflation, 1914–1924: Ein Tagungsbericht* (Berlin, 1978), pp. 343–62.

32. As Link has shown, German-American trade was resumed even before trade prohibitions of the Trading-with-the Enemy Act had been officially ended in July 1919: See Link, *Stabilisierungspolitik* (cf. n. 3), pp. 58–63.

33. See table 1 (t 1), infra. For the problems arising in regard to the interpretation of German statistics, see Holtfrerich, *German Inflation* (cf. n. 3), p. 207.

34. Link, *Stabilisierungspolitik* (cf. n. 3), pp. 58–76; Holtfrerich, *German Inflation* (cf. n. 3), pp. 207–9; from the same author: *"Amerikanischer Kapitalexport"* (cf. n. 3). The state of German-American trade relations is documented in an unsigned memorandum "Die Wirtschafts beziehungen zwischen Deutschland und den Vereinigten Staaten von Amerika," 18 July 1921, *Akten der Reichskanzlei*, R 43 I, 101, BA.

35. U.S. Dept. of Commerce, Commerce Reports 1922 (Washington D.C., 1923), pp. 463–65.

36. Mainly unmanufactured American cotton was exchanged against processed cotton goods from Germany. RWM to Minister of Finances, 3 March 1920, *AA files* 4548, pp. 179–84, ZStA; regarding American credits to finance German imports, see Holtfrerich, *Kapitalexport* (cf. n. 3), pp. 503–12.

37. Regarding Walther Rathenau's expectations for better prospects for industrial exports in the light of inflation, see Stephen A. Schuker, *American "Reparations" to Germany, 1919–1933: Implications for the Third-World Debt Crisis* (Princeton, NJ, 1988), p. 21.

38. See table 2 (t 2) regarding the impact of the tariff and stabilization; as to how the tariff affected German imports to the United States, see Memorandum from Hermann Davidsen for Ritter, 17 July 1924, *AA files* 47486, ZStA; for a different view see Malcolm E. Falkus: "U.S. Economic Policy and the 'Dollar Gap' of the 1920's," *Economic History Rev.* 24, pp. 599–623, esp. pp. 614–15.

39. The figures are from Bureau of the Census, ed., *Historical Statistics of the U.S: Colonial Times to 1970* (Washington, D.C., 1976), series u–327 and u–345.

40. The figures are calculated from the statistics for merchandise imports from foreign countries in *Foreign Commerce and Navigation of the U.S.,* 1922–1925 (Washington D.C., 1923–26). Although the goods named in table 2 may not be representative for German imports as a whole, they illustrate the impact of the American tariff and currency stabilization in Germany on German specialty exports. Iron, steel, and chemical exports were omitted since these were heavily impaired by the Ruhr crisis.

41. In regard to the collection of customs on a gold-basis, see Holtfrerich, "*Goldzölle,*" (cf n. 3); Frederick Simpich to Secretary of State, 6 February 1920, *DF* 862.51/1262; the quote is from Alvey Adee to Norman Davis, 21 February 1920, *DF* 662.003/12a.

42. Dresel to Dulles, 29 November 1920, *Ellis Loring Dresel Papers*, Houghton Library, Harvard University; for Count Ernst von Reventlow's attempt to convince Dresel that it would be in the United States' own interest to resist alleged British attempts to reduce Germany to one of Great Britain's commercial dependencies, see paraphrase of a letter from Dresel, 7 March 1920, *Records of the Bureau of Accounts*, NARS, RG 39, County Files G 110 17–1.

43. Impulses to protect the German industry against foreign attempts to acquire shares and thus a controlling interest in German key-industries have been described by Gerald D. Feldman, "Foreign Penetration of German Enterprises after the First World War: The Problem of 'Überfremdung'," in Alice Teichova (ed.), *Historical Studies in International Business* (Cambridge, England/New York, 1989), pp. 87–110.

44. Dresel to Secretary of State, 8 December 1920, *DF* 862.50/468; the quote is from Clemens Klein, *Die Aussenhandelsstelle für Eisen- und Stahlerzeugnisse* (Berlin, 1924), p. 8 (translation is mine); Kraft-Pflug-Industrie to Reichsministerium of Ernährung und Landwirtschaft, 5 April 1923, *AA files* 45531, pp. 21–38, ZStA.

45. Memorandum for the secretary, unsigned, 24 March 1921, *DF* 462.00R29/563; see also Link, *Stabilisierungspolitik* (cf. n. 3), p. 57.

46. Lang to AA, 3 February 1922, *AA files* 44356, p. 38, ZStA.

47. U.S. Department of Commerce: *Commerce Yearbook 1922* (Washington D.C., 1923), pp. 3–5, 451.

48. Dresel to Grew, 16 January 1921, *Dresel P*; Dresel to Castle, 31 March 1921, ibid.; Dresel to Lodge, 6 January 1921, ibid. Regarding similar views of Alanson B. Houghton, see Hermann-Josef Rupieper, "Alanson B. Houghton. An American Ambassador in Germany, 1922–1925," *International History Review* 1.4 (1979), pp. 490–508.

49. BFDC memo for Hoover about report from Herring, 21 June 1921, *Hoover CP* 4239; see also report of Maurice Parmelee, 28 February 1921, about the consolidation in German industry, *DF* 862.60/38.

50. Memorandum by Rudolf Schneider about production costs in German industries in English translation, file 23, box 108, non commodity operations files, central correspondence files, *Records of the U.S. Tariff Commission*, RG 81, NARS.

51. AA to Reichsbund der Deutschen Industrie and to Deutsche Industrie und Handelstag, 18 April 1921, *AA files* 44154, p. 12, ZStA. For figures regarding the German currency depreciation, see Holtfrerich, *German Inflation* (cf. n. 3), Table 1, p. 15.

52. Memorandum of Julius Klein for Christian Herter, 2 May 1922, *Hoover CP* 4249; Department of Commerce: Export Trade of the United States and Germany. 24 April 1922, *Trade Information Bulletin* No. 21, p. 16; see also Link, *Stabilisierungspolitik*, (cf. n. 3), pp. 72–3.

53. Frank W. Taussig, *The Tariff History of the United States* (New York, 1931), pp. 451–53.

54. Costigliola, *Awkward Dominion* (cf. n. 3), p. 101; Hoff-Wilson, *Business* (cf. n. 18), pp. 82–85; Leffler, *Quest* (cf. n. 3), pp. 49–50. A case for the protectionist tendencies in American tariff policy in the twenties has been made by Holtfrerich: "*U.S. Economic (Policy) Development*" (cf. n. 3); Hoover to Thomas W. Page, 29 November 1921, *Hoover CP*, Tariff-U.S. Tariff Commission.

55. Department of Commerce, German Reparations, Budget, and Foreign Trade. *Trade Information Bulletin* 40, 26 June 1922 (Washington, D.C., 1922), pp. 17–24.

56. Wiedfeldt to AA, 14 June 1922, and Ernst Wagemann, RWM, to AA, 22 August 1922, *AA files* 47483, pp. 86–87, 155, ZStA.

57. Kempff to AA, 5 May 1921, *AA files* 47481, p. 27, ZStA; Geheimrat von Reiswitz an Rhenania, Verein Chemischer Fabriken, 8 April 1922, *AA files* 47482, pp. 237–38; Wiedfeldt to AA, 5 December 1922, *AA files* 47484, p. 138.

58. This aspect will be treated in a forthcoming article.

59. Hoff-Wilson, *Business* (cf. n. 18), p. 84; Hohn to Domeratzky, Memorandum "Effect of the New Tariff," 29 September 1922, *Hoover CP* , Tariff 1922, June-December.

60. U.S. Department of Commerce, *Commerce Yearbook 1923* (Washington D.C., 1925), pp. 522–23.

61. Davidsen to Ritter, 17 July 1924, *AA files* 47486, ZStA.

62. Bernd Dohrmann, *Die englische Europapolitik in der Wirtschaftskrise 1921–1923* (München/Wien, 1980), pp. 45–55; Åhlander, *Staat, Wirtschaft und Handelspolitik* (cf. n. 3), pp. 329–37. For a sharp critique of American protectionism see, in addition to the titles mentioned in n. 54, Gilbert Ziebura, *Weltwirtschaft und Weltpolitik 1922/24–1931* (Frankfurt, 1984), pp. 64–67.

63. Norman Davis to American Embassy Paris, for Dresel, 20 November 1920, *DF* 862.50/419 a; Dresel to Secretary of State, 1 December 1920, ibid., /file 420; report by Consul Verne Richardson: "Why Germany Cannot Buy American Goods," ibid. /file 496.

64. "Memorandum on the Major Questions before the Proposed Economic Conference in Europe," attached to Hoover to Harding, 4 January 1922, *Warren G. Harding Papers*, LC, reel 131; Costigliola, *Awkward Dominion* (cf. n. 3), p. 100.

65. Link, *Stabilisierungspolitik* (cf. n. 3), pp. 67–73; regarding American wishes to limit German competition, ibid., pp. 69–70; K.G. Frank to Carl F. von Siemens, 11 June 1920, File La 827, *Siemens Archives*, Munich; regarding the Hapag-Harriman agreement, see the undated memorandum of Dr. Wilhelm Berne, *AA files*, Unterstaatssekretär Wirtschaft, 10, 1074/1, PA.

66. Copy of a letter from William Meinhardt dated 2 September 1920, describing a talk between Gerard Swope, A.W. Burchard and Carolan, File La 827, *Siemens Archives*; Heinz-Hellmut Kohlhaus, *Die Hapag, Cuno und das Deutsche Reich 1920 bis 1933* (PhD Dissertation, Hamburg, 1952), pp. 90–94.

67. Dresel to Secretary of State, 1 February 1920, Country file G 110–17–1, *RG 39*, and 2 February 1920, *DF* 862.51/1271; Dresel to Henry Cabot Lodge, 6 January 1921, *Dresel P.* A similar plan had been contemplated in the AA at the end of 1920, see Aufzeichnung des Wirklichen Legationsrats Hermann Bücher, 18 December 1920, *ADAP* Vol. A IV (Göttingen, 1986), pp. 164–66.

68. Hughes to Hoover, 3 November 1921, *Foreign Relations*, 1921, vol. 2, 785, with memorandum of division of Russian affairs, ibid.; Hoover to Hughes, 6 December 1921, ibid., 787; Hughes to Hoover, 27 December 1921, ibid., 790; the quote is from memorandum of Assistant Secretary of State for Hughes, 12 December 1921, *DF* 661.6215/1; see also Link, *Stabilisierungspolitik* (cf. n. 3), pp. 117–18.

69. For an American assessment of Rapallo, see James A. Logan to Harrison, 28 April 1922, Reparation Commission-Genoa Conference, *Records of International Conferences, Commission, and Expositions*, RG 43, NARS.

70. After the end of the Genoa conference Hughes demonstrated skepticism concerning a quick reestablishment of economic ties with Russia. Hughes to Harding, 20 May 1922, *Hughes Papers*, Roll 27; regarding consultations between Houghton and Rathenau as to chances of capital investments in the Soviet Union, see Houghton to Castle, 19 June 1922 and 8 July 1922, *William R. Castle P*, G-51, Herbert Hoover Presidential Library, West Branch, Iowa.

71. Houghton to State Department, 31 October 1923, with two memoranda about talks between Senator Robert La Follette and Felix Deutsch about Russia, *DF* 862.50/520.

72. Memorandum by von Boyé about a discussion with Filene, 19 August 1920, *AA files*, SW, Handel 20a, Bd. 1; the remaining correspondence relating to the German entry into the ICC can be found ibidem, in vols. 2–5.

73. A detailed discussion of the genesis of the treaty can be found in Link, *Stabilisierungspolitik* (cf. n. 3), pp. 101–05, 190–99; and Buckingham: *Normalcy* (cf. n. 19), pp. 161–64. As far as not indicated otherwise, I have drawn my information concerning the negotiations leading to the treaty of commerce from them.

74. Confidential draft of a commercial treaty with the U.S., undated, *AA files* 44427, pp. 312–16, ZStA; minutes of the discussion between representatives of the various departments about the treaty draft held on 24 October 1921, ibidem, pp. 37–41; the paraphrase is from Castle to Dresel, 1 February 1922, *Dresel P*; on the American assessment of German interest in a treaty see also William Coffin to Secretary of State, 6 February 1922, *DF* 611.6231/166.

75. Houghton to Castle, 6 June 1922, Castle P, G–51; Houghton to Secretary of State, 11 August 1922, and attached memorandum of Wallace McClure, 12 August 1922, *DF* 611.6231/file 175; memorandum of the Division of West European Affairs, 2 August 1922, ibidem, /file 164. Already in 1921, the Solicitor in the Department of State had advocated the rewriting of the treaty of commerce between Germany and the United States as well as of other treaties. See memorandum by Fred. K. Nielsen for Hughes, 24 May 1921, *DF* 711.62119/119.

76. Memoranda of the Office of the Economic Adviser, 6 July 1923 and 11 July 1923, *DF* 611.0031/190 and 193; Wiedfeldt to AA, 28 July 1923, *AA files* 44428, p. 9; the negotiations are summarized from the American perspective in an undated memorandum (ca. 1925) of the West European Division, Negotiation of Commercial Treaty with Germany, *DF* 611.6231/242.

77. Regarding American views about German-Austrian relations in 1919, see Klaus Schwabe, *Woodrow Wilson, Revolutionary Germany, and Peacemaking, 1918–1919* (Chapel Hill, NC, 1985), pp. 241–43.

78. See note 73; for the German perspective, see minutes of conference about the commercial treaty with the United States on 10 November 1921, *AA files* 44427, pp. 69–76; Wiedfeldt to AA, 8 December 1923, *AA files* 44428, pp. 335–41 ZStA; undated memorandum about the treaty, ibid., pp. 482–98; Stresemann to Wiedfeldt, 30 November 1923, *AA files*, Büro RM, Vereinigte Staaten von Nordamerika, vol. 3, PA; the text of the treaty can be found in *Foreign Relations*, 1923, vol. 2, pp. 29–46.

79. Regarding the problems of German-French and American-French commercial relations, see Schuker, *End of French Predominance*, pp. 222–29, 359–73 (cf. n. 3); Leffler, *Quest*, (cf. n. 3), pp. 52–53, and passim.

80. Manfred Berg, *Gustav Stresemann und die Vereinigten Staaten von Amerika: Weltwirtschaftliche Verflechtung und Revisionspolitik 1907–1929*. (Baden-Baden, 1990), p. 157 and passim; Stresemann's article for the Berliner Tageblatt, Die Vereinigten Staaten von Amerika und Europa, 8 December 1923, *Stresemann Papers*, vol. 5, PA.

81. For the evolution of the Dawes-Plan see Link, *Stabilisierungspolitik* (cf. n. 3), pp. 201–337; Schuker, *End of French Predominance* (cf. n. 3); Costigliola, *Awkward Dominion* (cf. n. 3), pp. 111–26; for a discussion of recent research about the reparations problem, see Jon Jacobson, "The reparation settlement of 1924," in Gerald D. Feldmann, Carl-Ludwig

Holtfrerich, Gerhard A. Ritter, Peter Christian Witt (eds.), *Konsequenzen der Inflation* (Berlin, 1989), pp. 79–108.

82. Memorandum by Dr. Walther about a visit of the American commercial attaches in Berlin and Paris, 18 June 1923, *AA files* 43814, pp. 130–33, ZStA; memorandum of Office of the Economic Adviser: Preliminary Analysis of Economic Aspects of Proposed Reparation Conference and their Bearing upon Selection of American Representatives, 31 October 1923, *DF* 462.00R296/81; Werner Link, "Die Ruhrbesetzung und die wirtschaftspolitischen Interessen der USA" *Vierteljahreshefte für Zeitgeschichte* 17 (1969), pp. 372–82, and from the same author "Die Vereinigten Staaten und der Ruhrkonflikt" in Klaus Schwabe, (ed.) *Die Ruhrkrise 1923: Wendepunkte der internationalen Beziehungen nach dem Ersten Weltkrieg* (Paderborn, 1985), pp. 39–51.

83. Costigliola, *Awkward Dominion* (cf. n.3), pp. 116–19; see also Costigliola, "The United States and the Reconstruction of Germany," *Business Hist. Rev.* 50 (1976), pp. 477–502, see esp. pp. 487–88; Houghton to Hughes, 19 February 1924, *Hughes P*, roll 28, with an enthusiastic assessment of Young's concept; memorandum of Meinhardt about a conversation with Young in Paris, dated 15 January 1924, *AA files*, Wirtschaft Reparation, Friedensvertrag allg. 13 geheim, PA; Goldsmith to Christian Herter, undated, *Hoover CP* 4330, accession from the *Leonard Ayres P*, LC, Box 4.

84. Alan Goldsmith to Herter, 4 February 1924, 9 March 1924, Accession from Ayres P in *Hoover CP* 4330; two unsigned memoranda about the Dawes Report, 17 April 1924 and 1 May 1924, *Thomas W. Lamont P*, 176, 8 and –9, Baker Library, Harvard; see also Leffler, *Elusive Quest* (cf. n. 3), p. 103.

19

Origins of American Stabilization Policy in Europe: The Financial Dimension, 1918–1924

Stephen A. Schuker

During World War I, the United States burst suddenly upon the world stage as an economic and financial superpower. In the history of modern industrial societies, war or diplomatic crisis has often served to focus public consciousness on a dramatic shift in the global balance of forces. Almost invariably, longer-term evolution in the international economy prepares the way for each diplomatic revolution. It is common for a declining power to adjust awkwardly to the portents of decline. It is equally common for an emerging hegemon to lack the outlook and political institutions that might help it to function effectively as a stabilizer of the international system. Periods of rapid change thus carry with them the seeds of instability – as the history of the 1990s will undoubtedly remind us in ways that we still cannot foresee.

The United States, the emerging hegemon of the 1920s, could not and did not return to prewar "isolation." Leaders in both government and finance made strenuous efforts to promote European economic reconstruction from the devastation of war. Yet inevitably, the shapers of economic strategy in Washington and Wall Street pursued this policy within the limits of national interest as they perceived it. Unlike their successors after World War II, they did not generally consider the health of the American economy and polity to depend in the first instance on European recovery. And given the relative self-sufficiency of the United States, there remained even after 1919 something to be said for a policy of limited involvement in parochial European concerns.

American prosperity before World War I had derived from exploitation of the domestic market – the largest free-trade area in the world. The United States had pulled ahead of Great Britain and even Germany before World War I in part through the application of advanced science and engineering knowledge to processes at the cutting edge of the indus-

Notes to Chapter 19 can be found on page 403.

trial revolution – especially in the electrical, chemical, and motor-car industries. But the nation had also prospered by the application of innovative management techniques to capital-intensive, energy-consuming industries using continuous-batch technology (for example, primary metals, packaged foods, petroleum, transportation equipment, and machinery manufacture). In those sectors, giant integrated firms could achieve efficiency through mass production, mass distribution, and mass marketing precisely because of the size, homogeneity, and accessibility of the home market.[1] While some of the largest firms, particularly in the extractive industries, relied on raw materials from abroad, and others had begun to seek markets outside the country before 1914, they generally remained less focused on the international economy than comparable businesses in Great Britain or Germany.[2]

On the eve of war, the United States alone produced 35.8 percent of world manufactures – almost the equivalent of British, German, and French output combined.[3] The United States had drawn even with Germany and was closing fast on Great Britain in percentage share of world exports.[4] Yet because of the sheer size of the American economy, exports and imports together still amounted to scarcely 10 percent of Gross National Product, compared with a third or more for the country's principal European competitors. Moreover, American involvement in the European economy had diminished since the turn of the century. In the nineteenth century, the principal industrial countries had figured as each other's best customers. That pattern had slowly begun to change. Increasingly, American firms targeted Latin America and Asia as their principal future growth markets.[5] Although 60 percent of American exports still went to Europe in 1913, the United States already drew fully 52 percent of its imports from other continents.[6] Americans clung to a tradition as old as the Republic, as Washington had put it in his Farewell Address, of avoiding entanglement in "the toils of European ambition, rivalship, interest, humor or caprice." Because American economic ties to the old Continent remained relatively limited before 1914, policymakers had as yet little reason to reexamine conventional attitudes.

The outbreak of World War I posed two serious obstacles to continued U.S. trade with Europe and reinforced the secular tendency toward diversification of the country's foreign economic ties. The high-cost American merchant marine had the capacity to service less than 10 percent of the nation's ocean-going commerce, and the European belligerents who had traditionally carried American goods did not merely make war upon each other's shipping, but also restricted their own merchant fleets to transporting vital military supplies. American exporters had also heretofore relied on the London City for financial accommodation. The disruption and subsequent regulation of British money markets left them without the customary means to finance foreign trade not relevant to the British war effort. After some false starts, the Wilson administration found a solution for both problems. Following a long debate over the propriety of public authorities entering the shipping business in competition with private enterprise, Congress agreed in September 1916 to create an Emergency Fleet Corporation with the mission of building tonnage for a five-year period; at the same time it set up a permanent U.S. Shipping Board to operate the fleet and regulate the industry.[7] Meanwhile, various branches of government took steps to alleviate the shortage of trade finance. The Federal Reserve Act of 1913 had for the first time allowed American banks to discount commercial acceptances and to establish branches overseas. To facilitate those developments, among other purposes, the Webb-Pomerene Act of 1918 exempted exporters from the strictures of the anti-trust laws. While the Europeans pursued their fratricidal war, the United States took advantage of their preoccupations to extend the "Open Door" in Latin America and to undermine the banking and trade dominance of all the belligerents in previously sheltered third markets.[8]

The several agencies involved in foreign trade expansion did not coordinate their efforts, and administration figures differed among themselves about how aggressively to challenge other powers. Edward N. Hurley, the outspoken and tough-minded nationalist who headed the Shipping Board, contemplated using the expanded merchant fleet after hostilities ended in Europe to corner strategic raw materials and to launch a scarcely veiled trade war against Great Britain. Secretary of Commerce William Redfield, a convinced free-trader, warned by contrast that "the law of grasp and gouge is not the law of business permanence." Commerce, as he high-mindedly defined it, represented "mutual exchange to mutual benefit and not a species of industrial war."[9] Yet whichever strategy of trade promotion the U.S. government ultimately embraced, it could draw on more sophisticated institutional supports than had obtained prior to 1914. The Wilson administration vastly expanded the research function of the Bureau of Foreign and Domestic Commerce and set in place a wider network of commercial attachés than had existed before the war.[10]

While Wilson appointees lavished more attention on both institutional supports and the substantive content of foreign economic policies than had previous administrations, the president's attitude toward the European conflict turned paradoxically almost entirely on politics. As is now well known, Wilson led the country into belligerency largely because of German violations of neutral rights, and in particular because of unconditional submarine warfare. Even those of his advisers, like Colonel Edward House and Secretary of State Robert Lansing, who took a broader view of the potential threat to American national security, gave little thought at first to the long-term financial consequences of American participation in the struggle overseas. They did not dwell on the responsibilities that would follow the nation's abrupt transformation into the world's leading creditor power. And the international bankers, foreign-trade lobbyists, and munition makers to whom economic determinists of the 1930s ascribed such awesome and malevolent powers exercised virtually no influence on the determination of European policy.[11]

When America declared war on Germany in April 1917, the Allies had virtually exhausted their ability to borrow on private U.S. financial markets. They had to petition for direct loans from the U.S. Treasury and for the broadest collaboration of official Washington in the procurement and organization of shipping, munitions, foodstuffs, and other logistic aid.[12] The British and French missions that came to Washington as petitioners declared their situation desperate. The administration could have taken advantage of the opportunity to secure far-reaching political concessions. Indeed, Secretary of the Treasury William McAdoo explicitly wished to do so. McAdoo prepared a draft note asking for British assurances about the size of their postwar navy, their intention to make preferential trade arrangements, and their territorial war aims. But neither Lansing nor House favored using loans as a political club. President Wilson, in a celebrated pronouncement, took their side against his own son-in-law, at least as a matter of tactics. "England and France have not the same views with regard to peace that we have by any means," the president wrote to House. "When the war is over, we can force them to our way of thinking, because by that time they will, among other things, be financially in our hands; but we cannot force them now, and any attempt to speak for them or to speak our common mind would bring on disagreements which would inevitably come to the surface in public and rob the whole thing of its effect."[13]

Over the course of the next two years, the Treasury lent over $10 billion to the European Allies – an amount that constituted fully 40 percent of the entire American national debt after the war. The Treasury raised the money by selling bonds publicly in small denominations. At the time, the Liberty and Victory bond drives stood as an unprecedented achievement. Nevertheless, they stored up trouble for the future.

Traditionally, only a narrow stratum of plutocrats had purchased government bonds. In 1917, therefore, Treasury officials had good reason to fear that they could not raise the stupendous sums required for the prosecution of hostilities against Germany through routine operations on the money markets. They solved the problem through a patriotic appeal. Millions of simple Americans who never before in their lives had bought securities of any sort now pledged their savings through local banks or wage check-offs to help whip "Kaiser Bill."[14] These same people – voters and taxpayers innocent of high finance – would not understand why their bonds subsequently depreciated in the high-rate environment after the war or why the European Allies refused to repay in a straightforward manner the sums they had unambiguously pledged to repay.[15] For twenty years to come, the public and Congressional consensus that foreign governments should honor their just debts would constrict the ability of successive administrations to take a broad-minded approach to European affairs. While the battle raged, however, officials on both sides studiously avoided general discussion of American-European financial relations. The Treasury and the British and French negotiating missions focused all their attention on comparatively technical points: the availability of standard monthly purchasing allotments, the limitations on dollar expenditures for non-American supplies, the employment of Treasury funds to support foreign exchange, whether public monies could be used to repay the overdraft on Wall Street bank loans predating American belligerency, and whether the British would have to pledge as security the private investments of their citizens in the United States.[16] The political reckoning would come after the restoration of peace.

★   ★   ★

Strange as it would later appear, the United States government developed no detailed economic war aims in 1917–18. Nor did officials in any agency elaborate concrete plans for Washington to take the lead in reconstructing Europe after the war. But failure to plan did not betoken an absence of policy. It served, rather, as a reaffirmation of widely-held, often reflexive American assumptions about the proper way to organize the international economy. An end to intrusive government controls, the restoration of free-market principles, and extension of the Open Door for trade everywhere represented the very embodiment of policy. Administration officials could anticipate various difficulties from the Allies as well as from the Germans in implementing such a liberal trading system.

From the start of the conflict, German civilian leaders from Bethmann Hollweg down, as well as their counterparts in the military and the great industrial associations, had worked out detailed schemes for perpetuating the economic dominance of the Reich over *Mitteleuropa* and, indeed, over the whole area from the Atlantic to the Caucasus. Admittedly, these schemes drew their impetus from political and racialist rather than pure-

381

ly economic assumptions. Hard-nosed businessmen pointed out frequently that autarky would not work. They noted also that the Reich had relatively little to gain from a customs union with the backward Habsburg realms. Still, the grandiose nature of German ambitions, insofar as they became known, frightened the Allies badly. Allied planners had a healthy respect for the superior efficiency of German business and labor before the war. They nursed the anxiety that, even if the Reich failed to prevail on the battlefield, their countries might fall behind afterward in the race for international markets on a level playing field. At the Paris Economic Conference held in June 1916, the British and French, with the tacit consent of the Italians and Russians, devised their own program for a war after the war. That program called for permanent discrimination against German trade and, at least in the French view, postulated the exclusionary pooling of raw materials among the victors. Although the British backed off from the Paris resolutions and pursued a more ambiguous policy after Lloyd George replaced Asquith in December 1916, French Commerce Minister Clémentel continued singlemindedly to press for the perpetuation of inter-Allied controls over shipping, food, and other key resources through the 1918 Armistice and beyond.[17] American officials reacted with consternation to Clémentel's vision. They would have none of it.

Secretary Lansing warned the president in June 1916, at a time when the United States remained neutral, that the Paris resolutions might at once prolong the war and disrupt American commerce. The secretary feared that trade discrimination could well leave the United States suspended between two warring blocs and without access to the markets of protected colonial empires.[18] Although Wilson declined to organize a combination of neutrals as Lansing had suggested, he spoke out repeatedly against postwar trade discrimination after the United States entered the conflict. In his reply to the pope's peace initiative in August 1917, Wilson registered his formal opposition to "the establishment of selfish and exclusive economic leagues;" indeed, only upon Colonel House's urging did he scale down his denunciation of such combinations to "inexpedient" rather than "childish."[19] And in his Fourteen Points address of January 1918, the president threw down the gauntlet to protectionists at home as well as abroad by calling for "the removal, so far as possible, of all economic barriers and the establishment of an equality of trade conditions among all the nations consenting to the peace and associating themselves for its maintenance."[20]

For Wilson, a global political order resting on democratic values and a commercial regime guaranteeing equality of opportunity formed part of a single integrated vision. The president saw no contradiction between

America's wartime political alliances and the economic underpinnings of his program for a better world. A cynic might observe that, at least in the short run, the Open Door best served the interests of the most technologically advanced powers. American commercial and financial interests thus stood in potential contradiction to the wartime political lineup. Equality of trade would favor both the United States and Germany more than it would help France and Great Britain, for, if the latter nations remained closer to the United States in political culture, they nonetheless followed a flatter path of economic growth.

Diplomacy, however, does not take place at this level of abstraction, especially during wartime. Neither Wilson nor his chief advisers worked out a program of specific economic aims (aside from temporary measures designed to win the war) that would give tangible form to the generalizations articulated by the president in his public addresses.[21] The "Inquiry," which House organized under the leadership of his brother-in-law Sidney Mezes in the fall of 1917 to study postwar problems, scarcely considered questions of economic policy.[22] House and Mezes had a vague preliminary discussion with Professor Frank Taussig, chairman of the Tariff Commission, and Taussig subsequently sent Wilson a memorandum arguing that the United States should avoid economic alliances, oppose trade preferences especially in the British Dominions, and adopt a flexible tariff system that compelled all trade partners to accord the U.S. most-favored-nation treatment.[23] Wilson seemed to agree, although he ordered no bureaucratic amplification of the position. In the course of 1918, the president repeatedly told the French, who to his exasperation affected not to understand, that he would neither pool raw materials, share general war costs, nor countenance any economic war after the war.[24] But he elaborated no positive alternative, except for a return to international laissez-faire. In fact, until he arrived in Paris in January 1919 the president did not expect the peace conference to deal with economic questions at all. The delegates, he believed, should confine themselves to determining the political, geographic, and ethnic settlement. "Distinct economic problems," he insisted, "if worked out by international conferences at all, will necessarily be worked out by special bodies to whom the peace conference will delegate their consideration."[25]

Colonel House, who had a better sense of practical diplomacy than his chief, sought to bring over Assistant Secretary Russell C. Leffingwell, the intellectual eminence of the Treasury Department, to coordinate the American financial and economic position in Paris. But Carter Glass, who had just succeeded McAdoo as secretary of the treasury, decided that he could not spare Leffingwell. The American economic group, as it finally took shape over several weeks in response to perceived need, included a number of able people, among them Vance McCormick of the War Trade Board, Bernard Baruch of the War Industries Board, Assistant Secretary Norman Davis and the Morgan financier Thomas W. Lamont as representatives of the Treasury, and, around the penumbra, Herbert Hoover as head of the American Relief Administration.[26] Yet the group lacked central direction or leadership. It engaged the interest of the president only sporadically. And it necessarily responded to particular issues as they arose in an ad hoc manner.[27]

A first and characteristic dispute arose in October 1918 over the advisability of continued American participation in the Allied Maritime Transport Council and other inter-Allied boards that supervised food, raw materials, and energy distribution. Hoover wanted to close down the inter-Allied agencies forthwith and to pursue a unilateral American policy; after some indecision, Wilson followed the counsels of McCormick and Baruch to maintain cooperation with the Allies until the peace conference concluded its work. But Hoover returned to the charge in early 1919. He accused the Europeans of using the blockade apparatus to stymie American agriculture and to force down the price of surplus pork products. The British particularly irritated him by cynically declining to make food and shipping available to the former enemy powers without a guarantee that the corresponding payment would enjoy priority over reparations that would largely benefit France. After much acrimony, the parties stumbled into a messy interim compromise. The blockade of Germany continued although with appreciable modification; the War Finance Corporation advanced export credits that sustained Allied demand for Midwestern pork at the expense of the American taxpayer; and Hoover won a relatively free hand to conduct relief operations in Central and Eastern Europe with the twin objectives of fighting Bolshevism and bolstering American farm prices.[28]

The president, meanwhile, focused his attention throughout the conference on one main objective: to create a viable League of Nations and thus to establish an international "concert of right" in place of the balance of power. To achieve this objective – however illusory it would later prove to be – Wilson had perforce to compromise on a variety of economic as well as territorial issues. Georges-Henri Soutou rightly observes that, in shaping the economic clauses of the treaty, Wilson met Allied desiderata for the harsh treatment of Germany more fully than one might have anticipated given his reputation as an ideologue. After initially demanding a fixed sum for reparations that fell definitely within German capacity to pay, American negotiators agreed to leave to a politicized Reparation Commission the task of determining German obligations. They conceded also that these obligations would include pensions as well as material damages. In practice, including pensions changed only the distribution and not the amount of the indemnity, since the Germans could scarcely be required to pay more than they had the capacity to transfer. Nevertheless, as politically sensitive observers realized, increasing the nominal bill could not fail to produce bitterness in the Reich and to hold up acceptance of a practical settlement. Finally, the Americans agreed, against their better judgment, to incorporate in the treaty a number of discriminatory economic clauses, among them the provision that Germany grant most-favored-nation treatment to the Allies without reciprocity for five years.[29]

U.S. negotiators drew the line, however, at Allied attempts to secure war-debt cancellation and to transfer the cost of paying reparation to the American investor and taxpayer. In the early part of the conference, the fatuous French finance minister, Louis-Lucien Klotz, floated a scheme for pooling all war costs, thinly veiled as a "Financial League of Nations." Then, toward the end of the proceedings, the highly nationalistic British Treasury operative, John Maynard Keynes, drew up an equally ingenuous plan to funnel American taxpayer resources to Europe by means of a "guarantee" of German reparation payments to the Allies. The U.S. Treasury stood firm against all such contrivances. The president and Secretary Glass reiterated that they had no authority to discuss foreign loans in Paris. Assistant Secretary Leffingwell dismissed the Keynes plan as "preposterous." Great Britain would undoubtedly stand a better chance of regaining its prewar position as the central intermediary in world banking, shipping, and insurance if it could throw the major burden of underwriting European reconstruction upon the United States. But what reason did Washington have for facilitating such a maneuver?

American officials on the scene plainly understood that in order to overcome bottlenecks the war-ravaged Continent required credits for raw materials, transport equipment, and agricultural machinery. They could see with their own eyes that factories and houses had to be rebuilt in the French and Belgian war zones, that defeated Germany desperately needed working capital, and that the Habsburg Successor States could scarcely hope to master hyperinflation without help in establishing sound currencies.[30] But the political preparation that allowed the Truman administration to contemplate massive aid programs for Europe after World War II had not taken place in 1917–18. The public at home felt that it had already contributed enough. As Leffingwell put it, the American people believed that they had "performed heroic deeds and borne great sacrifices" to save Europe from "annihilation by the Hun." They would interpret any call for a taxpayer-financed reconstruction program as an overweening attempt by Europeans to take advantage of their generosity. The Treasury had secured permission to meet the Allies' most pressing needs during the Armistice period only by dint of an intensive lobbying effort. The Europeans failed utterly to grasp the public mood or to understand the partisan temper of the Republicans who had won control of Congress in the mid-term elections of November 1918.[31]

Over the next decade, both the Allied governments and European private financiers would nevertheless propose innumerable variants on the Klotz plan or the Keynes plan. The idea that the innumerate American taxpayer would consent to write a blank check for European reconstruction proved enormously seductive. Some schemes contemplated the cancellation of war debts "all around" – as if, for example, American claims on Britain and British claims on the defunct czarist government represented obligations of equal worth. Other schemes assumed that German reparations bonds could be"commercialized"in large quantities and sold to American investors. Proposals that varied enormously in sophistication and political intent revolved around one common principle. The United States should extend massive public or private credits to Germany so that, if that country defaulted on reparations, Americans would be left holding the bag. In drafting the president's rejection of the Keynes plan, Thomas Lamont voiced the objection that Washington and Wall Street would repeatedly make in succeeding years to pleas for American loans to rehabilitate German finance: "How can anyone expect America to turn over to Germany in any considerable measure new working capital to take the place of that which the European nations have determined to take from her?"[32] Putting it another way, Assistant Secretary Norman Davis explained to the president a few months later what Britain and France hoped to achieve: "While the Allies have never bluntly so stated, their policy seems to be to make Germany indemnify them for having started the war and to make us indemnify them for not having entered the war sooner."[33]

While unwilling to fall in with these machinations, both the American economic group at the peace conference and Treasury officials back in Washington sought to harness private capital and export interests to satisfy Europe's concrete requirements. The operative question, as Leffingwell expressed it, was not "whether America will help," but whether the Europeans possessed "adaptability enough and vigor enough to work out some business transactions and [to] interest American businessmen in their financial and economic restoration."[34] In mid-May, Lamont explored the ground with his British and French negotiating partners, Robert Brand and Jean Monnet. He disabused his colleagues of the fantasy that the president would seek an unencumbered $3 billion appropriation from Congress, but recommended that each European country draw up a list of its practical needs. Wall Street stood ready to found a series of industry-based export corporations to meet those needs; Lamont hoped that the War Finance Corporation would help by discounting exporter bills and that the Treasury would facilitate private credit by extending war-risk insurance. He asked with seeming innocence only that the British and French cooperate in stabilizing weak currencies and commit themselves to finance their own exports.[35]

When Lamont completed his consultations and filled in the details in June 1919, however, it quickly emerged that the proposition came with political strings attached. The sticking point was not money, but power. America offered funds for European reconstruction; in return it wanted new ground rules for world finance and trade. J. P. Morgan and his partner Harry Davison had already organized the twenty leading bankers of the country and contacted the key export industries (steel, copper, cotton, grain, and machinery). This group planned to found a giant trading corporation prepared to supply ample credit for three years. It suggested that each participating European country form a corresponding organism to block out national requirements and to provide a triple guarantee of repayment from importers, banks, and the respective governments. Morgan partner E. R. Stettinius would open an office in Paris to coordinate European demands and to channel them efficiently to New York. The proposed administrative structure thus served as a rough precursor of the post–World War II Marshall Plan.

In 1919, however, the Americans posed several significant conditions. They would stand, first of all, on Open Door principles. "We are not asking tariff favors, nor concessions, for ourselves," noted Lamont, "but if we find that we are going to be treated on a less-favored-nation basis and that the credits that we grant are going to be turned around and used against us, then of course we shall gracefully withdraw." Moreover, American credits would be made available only for the purchase of American goods; if the British, for example, needed liquidity beyond that, they would have to sell their overseas securities to United States citizens. Finally, and not least important, Wall Street sought a worldwide British-American financial condominium. Lamont attempted to sugarcoat the pill: "America has ample credit resources, Great Britain has wonderful credit machinery all over the world. Why not make a combination of the two?" Americans would like to acquire a half-interest in British banks throughout the Far East and Latin America. If the English-speaking peoples became partners instead of rivals, they could both make a lot more money. They might seize the opportunity also to "establish such a rapprochement that the world could never shake us out of peace and into war."[36]

Given the terms on offer, the British quickly lost their enthusiasm for comprehensive schemes designed to foster European economic reconstruction. Keynes sniffed dismissively that British banks "wanted to run their own business and didn't want any interference from outside." Spokesmen for the City observed that Britain ran a serious trade deficit; it could not extend significant credits to others before getting the costs of domestic production down. The financial press expressed the view that the Continental states exhibited such diverse needs that no all-embracing organization could solve their problems. The president of the Board of Trade and the chancellor of the exchequer remained studiously evasive. The French made clear that they would not stand for American dictation concerning their discriminatory tariff structure. By the end of August 1919, Harry Davison reported from New York that the "psychological moment" for action had passed. Widespread sentiment in favor of deflation had developed in the United States. Politicians outside the great financial centers proclaimed that hothoused demand for U.S. foodstuffs and manufactures overseas would inevitably defeat efforts to bring down the high cost of living at home.[37] The attempt to coordinate European reconstruction in a grand manner thus fizzled out ignominiously. Business and financial interests on both sides of the Atlantic were left to work out mutually advantageous arrangements on an individual basis.

Meanwhile, the United States also limited its participation in the formal structure of treaty enforcement. President Wilson had intended at first to maintain a high profile on the boards and commissions that would implement the economic provisions of the peace. But when the Senate rejected the Treaty of Versailles, the administration reversed field. It consented to leave only an unofficial observer on the interim Reparation Commission. Secretary Lansing counseled American diplomats to stick to normal diplomatic channels. "Our people," he explained sententiously, "are tired out with the bickering and petty quarrels."[38]

Of course, the form of American participation in the structure of treaty enforcement had little ultimate significance. What particular reservations the Senate might express to articles of the League Covenant remained similarly unimportant. In the long run, whether the American people saw permanent involvement in European affairs as vital to the national interest mattered more than specific institutional arrangements. Would the world's leading creditor power work constructively to restore stability by taking part in an ongoing process of diplomatic and economic problem-solving? The wisest and most sophisticated Americans who contemplated postwar problems understood this to be the central issue.

Governor Benjamin Strong of the New York Federal Reserve renewed his ties to European central bankers in the summer of 1919 and lobbied strenuously for creative American statesmanship to spur reconstruction along generous lines. Secretary of Commerce Redfield hailed the Morgan-Davison scheme and warned that Treasury foot-dragging might lead to a collapse of the export trade. The partners of the House of Morgan, who increasingly assumed the mantle of moral leadership on Wall Street, sought to nurture the affinities forged in wartime among financiers in the three main Allied countries and to expand the network of private bankers dedicated to cooperative endeavor worldwide.[39] Colonel House, though spurned as an adviser by Wilson, worked with the British and French ambassadors to find an accommodation that would allow the mild reservationists in the Senate to vote for ratification of the Versailles treaty.

President Wilson, however, forbade all talk of compromise. At a crucial juncture, a stroke impaired the president's judgment and reinforced his rigidity of character. The changes that Senator Henry Cabot Lodge and other mild reservationists insisted on would still have permitted the United States to play a constructive part in the League and European affairs generally. But Wilson preferred to see the treaty doomed and the Covenant rejected rather than accept the slightest alteration in his handiwork. Even before his stroke, Wilson got so caught up in the treaty fight that he had little time to contemplate the mundane problems of economic recovery. Afterward, the unedifying quarrel over treaty ratification created a wave of public revulsion against any sort of participation in European affairs. Wilson, in his disappointment and bitterness, curiously shared in that revulsion. If the American people would not meet their moral obligations through the League, he deemed no lesser efforts worthwhile.[40] Moreover, the president remained largely incapacitated; a nonentity took over the State Department in early 1920; and the key officials at the Treasury drifted away to the private sector. For almost eighteen months, the United States lacked a government capable of taking the initiative in international affairs. While bureaucrats continued to transact routine business, for all intents and purposes the United States had no comprehensive European stabilization policies until the Harding administration took office in the spring of 1921.

★　　★　　★

In the absence of presidential leadership, foreign-trade interests fell back on variants of the June 1919 Morgan-Davison plan for privately sponsored export organizations. Just before Christmas 1919, Congress authorized two types of foreign-trade financing corporations under the so-called Edge Amendment to the Federal Reserve Act. The legislation authorized nationally chartered banks to combine in setting up foreign acceptance banks. Such organizations would grant short-term acceptance credits and thus free American exporters from exclusive dependence on British or Continental accommodation to finance foreign trade. Even more important, the Edge Act allowed Federal Reserve member banks to set up long-term investment corporations that could raise capital by selling debentures to the public. The sponsors hoped in the first instance that Edge Act corporations would tap the wartime savings of the American people in order to keep exports flowing until European customers had restored their purchasing power. Beyond that, they nurtured a larger ambition. In the days of high imperialism, European financiers had frequently structured loans so that borrowers had to purchase capital goods from the lending country. American competitors had lost out. Under the right circumstances, Edge corporations might turn the tables. They could promote infrastructure development overseas while imposing the proviso that credit recipients give preference to American suppliers. The National Foreign Trade Council and the American Bankers Association debated the prospects enthusiastically at their conventions in 1920 and 1921. Visions of sugarplums to come alleviated the habitual solemnity of those occasions.[41]

Hardly anything came of all the talk. In order to break the inflationary spiral, the Federal Reserve hiked interest rates at the end of 1919. The bond market collapsed. Within a few months the American economy slid into a depression – as severe in many respects as the downturn of 1929–31. The depression did not end until the summer of 1921.[42] In these circumstances, no one cared to tie up speculative capital. Neither existing banks nor potential purchasers of debentures showed the slightest willingness to shoulder the risks associated with Edge corporation investments. Paul Warburg of Kuhn, Loeb & Co., who had a particular interest in promoting trade with Germany and not coincidentally in restoring the fortunes of M. M. Warburg & Co., the family bank in Hamburg, achieved some success in financing the export of raw materials through his International Acceptance Bank.[43] Two other Edge banks also began to offer short-term trade accommodation on a modest scale. Even so, New York never created an acceptance market in the 1920s that could compete on equal terms with the London City. Meanwhile, the efforts of the National City Bank to extend its network of overseas branches in order to service American business encountered similar difficulties and, especially in Latin America, failed to supplant the British banks already in place.[44]

American producers of wheat, cotton, pork, tobacco, copper, oil, and fertilizer scrambled to find one method or another that would permit them to unload their surpluses in Europe so long as domestic markets remained in the doldrums. More often than not, they had to bear part of the credit risk themselves. Holtfrerich points out that speculative purchases of mark-denominated securities and currency by American citizens amounted to $770 million in 1919–23. This sum almost covered direct American exports to Germany, which amounted to $951 million over the same period. (Additional goods undoubtedly passed through neutral ports before the signature of a separate peace between Washington and Berlin in July 1921.) In practice, American exporters or financial intermediaries left mark credits on deposit in Berlin banks, and then lost their entire equity when the Reich embarked on hyperinflation in 1922–23.[45] While Holtfrerich notes philosophically that countercyclical German demand for raw materials and foodstuffs helped pull the United States out of the 1920–21 depression, giving away their goods for free is scarcely what American exporters sought to achieve by commerce promotion schemes.

During the 1920s European critics frequently charged the United States with refusing to accept its implicit responsibilities as a creditor power to stabilize the global system of trade and exchange. Leading contemporary economic historians still echo this criticism.[46] The prevailing interpretation holds that, after the immediate postwar crisis had passed, the United States prevented European countries from reaching equilibrium in their international accounts by raising tariffs, running an outsized trade surplus, insisting on war-debt collection beyond the debtors' capacity to pay, and providing insufficient long-term funding to meet Europe's capital needs. Whatever validity the explanation may have for the persistence of the Great Depression in the 1930s, it does not fit the available statistical evidence for the first postwar decade.

The huge trade surpluses that America enjoyed in 1919–21 (averaging $2.981 billion annually) melted away rapidly thereafter. Led by the new consumer industries (automobiles, radio and telephone, synthetic textiles, and household appliances) now reaching the high point of their product cycles, the country registered enormous gains in productivity. But exports failed to keep pace with domestic prosperity. From 1921 to 1925, Gross National Product leaped ahead almost 9 percent annually. Exports, however, increased at the modest rate of 2.5 percent annually.[47] The trade surplus for the whole period of the Fordney-McCumber tariff regime, 1922 to 1930, averaged a mere $720 million per year. This small margin proved insufficient to cover the deficit on such invisibles as shipping and insurance, tourist travel abroad, and remittances home by immigrants (the latter almost entirely to Europe). After approximately breaking even in 1922, the United States ran a combined loss on commodity trade and current invisibles in every year but one from 1923 through the devaluation of the dollar in 1933. The combined loss under the Fordney-McCumber tariff regime (1922–30) averaged $216 million annually.[48] These results hardly reflect a prohibitive tariff policy on the part of the United States.[49]

The legislative history of tariff legislation serves further to correct the traditional picture. The Emergency Tariff Act of May 1921 was only a temporary measure targeted to fight the postwar farm depression. It imposed specific anti-dumping levies in order to block the import of agricultural commodities from countries with depreciated currencies, but it did not affect European manufactured goods. The Fordney-McCumber Tariff, which took effect in September 1922, raised rates appreciably above the 1913 Underwood Tariff on certain high-profile dutiable imports, yet left a significant "free" list. Hence average rates on all imports nudged up just a few percentage points over the old Underwood rates and remained comfortably below the levels that had prevailed from the time America became an industrial powerhouse up to 1913.[50] In any case, in the minds of the State Department and Tariff Commission officials who fashioned the underlying basis for the Fordney-McCumber legislation, the rates that Congressional logrollers imposed for particular products mattered less than general tariff philosophy. Progressives in both parties, from the Taft administration onward, had championed a flexible bargaining tariff formulated along scientific lines. The Fordney-McCumber Act translated their aspirations into law. The act paved the way for new trade treaties based on the unconditional most-favored-nation principle, in other words the generalization of negotiated trade preferences to all. The president now had a bargaining tool with which to fight British imperial-preference arrangements and the notorious French "two-column" system, which applied discriminatory maximum levies against nations that failed to provide special advantages for French exports on a bilateral basis.[51]

Germany, of all the industrialized nations, treated the new American tariff philosophy with the least disdain. The German-American trade treaty of December 1923 marked a major step toward reconciliation of the two erstwhile opponents. The U.S. Senate, despite theoretical adherence to the Open Door, in practice demanded a preference for American shipping, and this embarrassing intrusion of pressure-group politics stalled the treaty until Berlin conceded the point in February 1925.[52] Generally speaking, however, the United States and Germany found a common interest in seeking equality of trade opportunity during the middle 1920s, especially in Latin America and the rest of the developing world. On the other hand, Britain, France, and the minor European colonial powers sought to maintain discriminatory preferences wherever they could, and toward the end of the decade German businessmen also began to complain that owing to American manufacturing efficiency the Open Door worked against them.[53] It is true that the flexible provisions of the Fordney-McCumber Act failed to operate well in practice. The cost-of-production standard for rate adjustment did not allow the Tariff Commission sufficient latitude to recommend decreases. Still, if worldwide protectionism continued to impede the flow of trade in the 1920s, the fault did not lie one-sidedly with the United States.

Even Americans who embraced political isolation in the 1920s tended to believe that a peaceful and prosperous world lay in the national interest. Beyond that moral and sentimental concern, international bankers and exporters frequently argued that the United States had a more specific stake in the adjustment of European postwar disputes and the stabilization of currencies because the economic recovery expected to follow would expand the market for American products. The results did not fully justify those hopes from the standpoint of narrow self-interest.[54]

After the mid-decade reparation settlement and the growth in central-bank cooperation, some American industries (especially in the automotive and electrotechnical fields) succeeded in penetrating markets in Europe and even in establishing subsidiaries there. American firms in the electrical, automotive, chemical, and steel industries reached licensing agreements and exchanged equity interests especially with their German partners, although it remains doubtful whether cooperation between businessmen exerted as much influence on political relations as certain scholars have claimed.[55] However, Europeans increasingly resented the American business invasion and attempted to resist it by copying New World techniques of standardization and rationalization.

In two related areas, European recovery actually reduced the opportunities for American exports. The abrupt end to the war left the world with a colossal oversupply of merchant shipping capacity. Freight rates plummeted. The high-cost American merchant marine could not meet the competition after the withdrawal of government subsidies in 1920, and within a few years three-quarters of American goods again moved in foreign bottoms.[56] The precipitous fall in shipping rates also rendered it economical for Europeans to buy off-season grain from Australia and Argentina instead of storing U.S. grain year-round, with the attendant losses from rodents and weather. As Europeans became more prosperous, moreover, they ate more meat and less bread. Under these circumstances, American farmers who had borrowed at usurious wartime rates from undercapitalized local banks in order to expand wheat production on the thin topsoil of the Western Plains had no chance whatever of restoring profitability.[57] In the long run, they had to go out of business. Since the conclusion was politically unpalatable, the American farm lobby continued throughout the decade to embellish schemes for dumping surpluses overseas. But the hope of finding a solution to the American farm crisis in Europe figured from the outset as a mirage.

Americans, in short, had good reasons to promote European recovery and financial stabilization. But those reasons were as much political and ethical as narrowly economic. After a period of drift, the Republican administration that came to power in March 1921 gradually developed a program for prudent reengagement in Europe insofar as public sentiment permitted it. The chief strategists of Harding foreign policy sought first of all to encourage the Allies to fund their war debts on reasonable terms, while concomitantly they tried to sway Congress to a more charitable view of fairness. Despite failure to ratify the Versailles treaty, they maintained unofficial representation on the Reparation Commission. At crucial junctures, they cautiously offered the unofficial good offices of the United States in order to achieve an equitable reparations compromise. Such a settlement, as they saw it, would restrict payments to German capacity to pay and promote reintegration of the Reich into the global economy, while providing reconstruction funds within those limits to assist the victims of wartime aggression. Both Harding and his principal cabinet officers also emphasized naval and land disarmament as a pathway to peace; somewhat naïvely, they believed that a reparations settlement between Germany and France would facilitate radical disarmament across the whole European continent. Finally, they expected that such a settlement would pave the way for restoring sterling to par and ultimately stabilizing Continental currencies on some variant of the prewar gold standard, with the dollar serving as the principal reserve currency. Settlement of reparations and stabilization of currencies would in turn create sufficient confidence so that Americans would voluntarily recycle their capital surpluses to meet Europe's needs on a profitable business basis. While Wilsonian internationalists considered their successors pusillanimous in the face of public opinion, the program as such did not lack ambition.[58] Yet as Secretary of Commerce Herbert Hoover emphasized in early 1922, the United States could if necessary "reestablish its material prosperity and comfort without European trade." The administration had no reason to sacrifice its domestic agenda if European statesmen declined to cooperate along constructive lines. The same sense of detachment inspired President Coolidge's reaction when it appeared that Germany might disintegrate following the collapse of "passive resistance" to the Ruhr occupation in September 1923: "I do not feel that if certain people in Germany act foolishly, the result is going to be the downfall of civilization, as some people seem to think."[59]

In the fall of 1919, the Treasury had accorded the Allies a three-year respite in the payment of interest on their wartime obligations. The Wilson administration had no wish to press European governments while they grappled with the problems of post-Armistice adjustment. But Congress displayed no inclination to extend the moratorium past its expiration date in October 1922. Loans to foreign governments associated with the United States in the prosecution of the world war made up 40 percent of the entire Federal debt. The American taxpayer, for whom the exactions of the income tax still represented a novelty, vociferously demanded relief. Veterans agitated for a bonus. Citizens who had acquired Liberty bonds in the flush of patriotic enthusiasm now complained that their holdings stood below par. Hence the Treasury turned a deaf ear to the clamor from the other side of the Atlantic for what was euphemistically called writing down the world balance sheet.

The self-appointed financial authorities who composed the Amsterdam Memorial in January 1920 and who delivered homilies to each other at the League-sponsored Brussels Conference in October of that year acted from a variety of motives. The neutrals who took the lead wished to recoup commercial loans and sustain their profits on trade with the Reich by stigmatizing "political" debts as counterproductive; the German-Americans who operated behind the scenes perceived an opportunity to undermine reparations; while some bankers, in the London City and elsewhere, genuinely aimed to foster recovery by advertising the dangers of fiscal inflation. Almost to a man, however, these experts assumed that Europeans could not generate the requisite capital through their own labor and savings and would have to obtain funds on concessionary terms from Washington or New York. Many assumed an aggressive tone. The time had come, argued John Maynard Keynes, fresh from his polemical success with *The Economic Consequences of the Peace*, to speak out boldly and to "stop humbugging with the Americans." From New York, the like-minded Paul Warburg proclaimed it "a mortification and a crime" that the United States had not followed the "dictate of humanity" and put its shoulder to the wheel.[60] This sort of overheated rhetoric did not play well either in Washington or Peoria as America entered a depression of its own and business failures multiplied because of restrictions on domestic credit.

In the spring of 1920, Assistant Treasury Secretary Albert Rathbone had canvassed intergovernmental debt issues with Sir Basil Blackett, his opposite number in Whitehall. While some Continental states suffered from genuine liquidity problems, no one could doubt that the British, with their bulging portfolio of foreign assets, could make good on their wartime loans if only they wished to do so. Blackett agreed tentatively to fund the British debt on normal commercial terms. But Prime Minister Lloyd George vetoed the deal and maneuvered instead to embarrass the United States into unilateral cancellation. Some Foreign Office sharpers apparently hoped to win forgiveness by trading away the Anglo-Japanese alliance. In any event, a deadlock ensued.

Andrew Mellon, the Republican secretary of the treasury, attempted to break the impasse in 1921 by action on two fronts simultaneously. He again invited the British to send a funding mission without reference to the Continental debts. At the same time, he asked the Congress for authority to fix terms of repayment as the Treasury thought best, and even to accept German reparation bonds in exchange for Allied obligations if that should prove expedient.[61] Congress, however, refused to play along. A number of indiscreet statements by visiting European politicians and bankers reinforced the distemper on Capitol Hill. As Maurice Casenave, former chief of the French economic mission in New York, presciently observed, the war-debt issue became "like the clerical question used to be" in the French Chamber – a matter certain to be dragged into everything, whether the ostensible issue at stake was tariff revision, tax reduction, or the soldiers' bonus.[62] After months of wrangling, Congress set up a World War Foreign Debt Commission in January 1922 to conduct refunding negotiations. On this body, designees of the House and Senate stood watch to ensure that their colleagues from the executive branch did not give away too much. The law directed the commission to require a minimum 4.25 percent interest rate. This rate compared favorably with the 7 percent that sovereign borrowers had to pay on Wall Street, but left little leeway for disguised cancellation.

Meanwhile, in May 1921 the European Allies had imposed the London Schedule of Payments on Germany. The Reparation Commission sought to reconcile inflated public expectations in the recipient countries with the limited capacity of the Weimar Republic to extract payment from a resentful citizenry through financial slight-of-hand. The London Schedule set the theoretical German debt at 132 milliard gold marks (roughly $33 billion), divided into three sets of bonds. For the moment, however, the Reich would have to pay interest and amortization only on the first two *tranches*, totalling 50 milliard gold marks. American experts at the 1919 peace conference had calculated that Germany could shoulder a burden of 60 milliards; hence in practice the London Schedule fell within the range that moderates had earlier thought reasonable. To be sure, the Reich remained legally obligated to service an additional 82 milliards of "C-bonds" if the Reparation Commission determined that it had become sufficiently prosperous to do so. But, as the Belgian prime minister pointedly remarked, when the commission printed up those debentures, it could "stick them in a drawer without bothering to lock up, for no one would be tempted to steal them." In fact, the C-bonds constituted a reserve of funny-money that its originators hoped the Americans might ultimately accept in substitution for the Allied war debts. The true reparations annuity amounted to approximately 5.37 percent of German national income in 1921 – a considerable charge, but not an impossible one for a nation possessed of sufficient political and economic discipline to limit consumption and facilitate the transfer.[63]

Yet the pivotal issue of will to pay remained. Weimar politicians lacked both the inclination and the power to enforce the requisite discipline. Capital and labor would neither abate their distributional struggle nor accept the consequences of the lost war. The government in Berlin stoked the fires of inflation by avoiding serious taxation and dispensing fiscal largesse on a massive scale. Americans and other foreigners unwittingly subsidized the maneuver by speculating in depreciating mark notes and securities. Thus, despite all rhetorical complaints about the reparations burden, the net flow of capital ran strongly toward the Reich and financed a considerable import surplus.[64]

Reparations diplomacy in 1922 turned on the conditions that would allow, induce, or force Germany (depending on one's point of view) to stabilize its currency and meet its external obligations. The Germans insisted on a long reparations moratorium before subjecting themselves to the rigors of stabilization. The French, who suspected their neighbors across the Rhine of using inflation as a diplomatic weapon, demanded control of the customs and other productive guarantees. The British, preoccupied by stagnation in the so-called depressed areas, sought to link a German moratorium with a general scheme for writing down the world's balance sheet at the expense of the United States. His Majesty's government declared in the Balfour note of August 1922 that it would seek to collect only enough from Germany and its Continental debtors together as proved necessary to pay the United States. Not surprisingly, the Harding administration reacted with fury at this artless endeavor to blacken America before the bar of world opinion. Robert Brand of Lazard's London branch summed up the resulting situation for the acting British foreign secretary: "What with the French determination to get impossible sums from Germany, the American determination not to agree to cancellation of debts . . . until Europe behaves, . . . and the general cloud of prejudice and misunderstanding in which the whole question can be involved, it seems to me that Bernard Shaw may be right, and that the democracies of the world have created a machine which they are not clever enough to run."[65]

Shaw, as usual, confirmed his reputation for cleverness, but he missed the larger issues at stake. The reparations controversy assumed much greater significance than the uninitiated observer might conclude from monitoring the wrangling over coal quotas or the dispute about shipment of telegraph poles. When rejecting the Versailles treaty, the United States Senate had also allowed the proposed Anglo-American guarantee of French security to lapse.[66] Franco-British conflict over colonial and naval matters imposed further strains on the solidarity of the democracies. With token support from East European nations whose armies scarcely mattered in the larger scheme of things, France emerged virtually alone to uphold the edifice of European security established in 1919. In addition to the devastation of its ten northeastern departments, France suffered from a backward manufacturing structure, an outmoded tax system, and a potential labor shortage. Germany, despite its losses and disabilities, continued to enjoy pride of place as the most advanced industrial power on the Continent. In the natural course of events, the Reich would eventually regain the military hegemony that it had enjoyed prior to the war. Still, if France received the coal, coke, and capital to which it claimed entitlement on reparation account, that country might aspire to make a sufficient leap forward industrially to balance Germany in some respects. At the least, it could hope to maintain somewhat longer the security position sustained for the nonce by paper treaty texts. While the French took care to keep their reparation claims and their security aims juridically distinct, an implicit linkage subsisted. Reparations emerged as the chief bone of contention in the Franco-German struggle for political and economic dominance in Europe. It marked, in short, the continuation of war by other means.[67]

The British war debt to the United States played a similar, if more symbolic, role. British obligations under the Mellon-Baldwin agreement of January 1923 came to just over a fifth of the annuity owed by Germany under the London Schedule of Payments. The sum due equaled a levy of a mere 0.8 percent annually on Britain's existing overseas investment portfolio. Capacity to pay therefore hardly entered into the equation. And transfer posed no difficulty. As the chancellor of the exchequer informed the cabinet in June 1922, the problem was "not how to find the dollars, but simply how to persuade our own people to pay the taxation involved in the transfer of the dollars to the Exchequer's control."[68] Yet on the expediency of settling with America, the London policy-making elite divided. Bankers in the City and Atlanticists in Whitehall thought that funding the debt would help bring the United States back as a stabilizing force into European diplomacy, promote economic growth on the Continent, and thereby revive markets for crucial British exports. The anti-American faction countered that payment would shift the tax burden from the New World to the Old and, in the long run, reduce the ability of British manufacturers and bankers to compete with their American rivals in the third world. While the quantitative effects on the balance of payments did not bulk very large, the debt issue served as a convenient focus of anger for Britons who resented the fact that the upstart Americans had gained the upper hand in the struggle for global financial supremacy. Thus the permanent under secretary of the Foreign Office found the American demand for funding "incredibly mean and contemptible." And certain Treasury hardliners, though they lost the battle in 1922–23, nurtured such a sense of grievance that in 1931 they preferred to see the gold-exchange standard collapse rather than suffer the system of "political" debt remittances to continue.[69]

But these problems lay in the future. The United States brought sufficient pressure to bear so that the British dispatched a funding mission that settled the debt at the beginning of 1923. The World War Foreign Debt Commission exceeded its instructions and offered relatively generous terms. The British agreement, which became the model for the 1925–26 agreements with the Continental nations, offered a concessionary interest rate and a sixty-two year payment schedule that mounted by degrees. In effect, the British received an immediate 35.1 percent reduction of the bill. The French, Belgians, and Italians would later obtain forgiveness of between 63.3 percent and 81.5 percent of prior obligations.[70] Since no insiders expected debt payments to continue after the Liberty Bonds became fully amortized in 1947, the American negotiators in practice made even greater concessions than these figures imply.

However, American attempts to encourage a reparations compromise without offering a direct linkage to war debts did not yield success in 1922. Werner Link points out that the government of the Reich, despite its disappointment with President Wilson at the peace conference, continued to cultivate American interest in a democratic, peacefully-inclined Germany and to invite mediation by Washington in the reparations dispute. Certain "Easterners" in the *Auswärtiges Amt* preferred an alliance of the revisionist powers or at least a policy of balancing east and west. Some businessmen, like Hugo Stinnes, flirted with the notion of improving relations with France as the initial step in creating a transmogrified Continental bloc. At every critical juncture, however, the responsible authorities in Berlin sought to play the American card. Thus in April 1921 Foreign Minister Walther Simons appealed for American arbitration with a view to staving off the London Schedule of Payments.

In December 1922 Chancellor Wilhelm Cuno followed the promptings of the U.S. ambassador and proposed a nonaggression pact as France prepared to occupy the Ruhr. And again, in 1923–24, Gustav Stresemann made a particular show of cooperating with the Dawes Committee as the best way of mobilizing Anglo-American pressure to force France out of that region.[71]

It does not reciprocally follow, however, that American leaders sympathized with German attempts to evade their reparations obligations. Certain ethnic groups (especially German- and Irish-Americans) that had borne the afflictions of wartime chauvinism instinctively sided with the underdog, but "hyphenate Americans" did not constitute an important constituency for the Harding or Coolidge administrations. To be sure, Secretary of State Charles Evans Hughes proclaimed in his New Haven speech of December 1922: "We do not wish to see a prostrate Germany. There can be no economic recuperation in Europe unless Germany recuperates."[72] Yet neither did Washington or Wall Street envisage such recuperation at the sole expense of those entitled to receive reparations. Instead, policymakers and bankers alike fastened on the notion of "capacity to pay" as a stratagem to bring about a settlement tolerable – if not acceptable – to both sides.

The administration made a first effort to bring about such a settlement in June 1922 by prompting J. P. Morgan to serve on a Bankers Committee to pass on preconditions for a German stabilization loan. The point, as Morgan partner Dwight Morrow expressed it, was to find a way "to make France recede from an indefensible position with regard to reparations which will be compatible with the dignity of a great nation which contributed so much to the winning of the war and which bore so much of the suffering of the war."[73] French Premier Raymond Poincaré refused, however, to accept the committee's finding that a reparations moratorium would have to precede a stabilization loan. All through the summer and fall of 1922, Secretary Hughes looked for a propitious moment to try again. The Balfour note, unfortunately, touched off a firestorm of disapproval in the United States and limited his maneuvering room. At the end of December, Allied unity broke down. The Cuno government perceived an opportunity to mount an open revolt against reparations and the Versailles treaty generally. The French, although fearful of the consequences, saw no choice but to occupy the Ruhr as a sanction. With time running out, Hughes proposed an expert committee of businessmen to look into German capacity to pay. But the proposal came too late to stem the rush of events. French soldiers marched; the German government, with a fine sense for the budding discipline of public relations, organized what it denominated "passive resistance."

Ten months later came a chance for the American secretary of state to try again. Passive resistance in the Ruhr broke down in September 1923, but the French found the attempt to collect reparations through physical occupation frustrating. Moreover, the effort strained French finances and attracted the unwelcome attention of bear speculators against the franc. This time, Poincaré had no effective choice but to accept the Hughes plan for an economic inquiry with the widest possible mandate.

In theory, the Dawes Committee comprised a group of independent financiers and businessmen. These experts would examine the conditions necessary to stabilize the German currency and balance the budget of the Reich. In practice, committee members kept in close touch with their governments and attempted to cut a political deal with enough of a scientific aura to garner public approval. Owen D. Young, the chief American negotiator, defined the objective by using the homely expression of an upstate New York neighbor who had come to buy a cow: they aimed to fashion a settlement "most too dear to take and most too cheap to leave."[74] In this respect, the committee succeeded brilliantly, in part by avoiding the touchy issue of the total sum owed by Germany. It focused instead on an annuity schedule that would rise gradually until it reached 2.5 milliard gold marks (as it turned out, 3.12 percent of German national income at factor cost) in 1929. None of the European governments really liked the Dawes Report, yet none dared publicly to oppose it. The French, having called in J. P. Morgan & Co. to rescue them from a run on the franc in March 1924, could no longer pursue a unilateral policy. British Treasury officials fulminated behind closed doors about the Americans' "beastly plan" and the dangers inherent in stabilizing the Deutsche Mark on the dollar; still, MacDonald's Labour government could not recede from its ostensible commitment to international collaboration. Stresemann and his colleagues in the German cabinet schemed to demand another reduction in the bill as soon as they decently could, but for the moment saw the plan as a convenient lever to pry the French out of the Ruhr. And so, under the watchful eye of American officials who – in deference to domestic isolationists – affected to be present by happenstance, the European nations reached a reparations settlement at the London Conference of July-August 1924.[75]

Paradoxically, the American bankers who had served the Allied cause most faithfully between 1914 and 1918 now imposed conditions for the loan required by the Dawes Plan that turned the balance of power decisively in Germany's favor. J. P. Morgan & Co., as a result of its public-spirited leadership during the war, largely set the tone for Wall Street. And in view of public opposition to official entanglement in European affairs, private bankers came by default to exercise tremendous power.

The Morgan partners worried greatly about the resulting problem of public accountability. Under the circumstances, however, they had to reconcile as best they could the national interest in pacifying Europe with their specific business concerns. Their primary responsibility lay in ensuring the safety of bonds syndicated by the firm. Thomas Lamont and Russell Leffingwell, the leading partners at Morgan corner, claimed with apparent sincerity that they favored the largest possible reparations figures: "Our sympathies are all for making Germany pay to the last drop." At the same time, they cautioned that Germany could "not sell bonds secured by the proceeds of the next military invasion of the Ruhr."[76] At the London Conference, Lamont therefore worked with Montagu Norman of the Bank of England to scrap the powers of the Reparation Commission. The bankers demanded an assurance that, if Germany defaulted again, France would not resort to sanctions without first obtaining Allied unanimity and the acquiescence of bondholder representatives. Moreover, France had to agree not merely to evacuate the Ruhr, but also to maintain the original Versailles timetable for evacuation of the Rhineland. At a stroke, the French in effect bargained away both the right to take future sanctions and the chief territorial guarantee of their security.

The London Conference thus marked the end of a system based on compulsion under the Versailles treaty. It opened the way for the reintegration of Germany as an equal partner in European affairs. For several years it appeared that American stabilization policy would have a beneficent effect. American loans poured into Germany and produced an improvement in living conditions and public amenities. Britain returned to the gold-exchange standard. The Continental countries followed its lead. Central bankers organized a cooperative network to manage the international monetary system. The Western powers agreed at Locarno to a non-aggression pact along the Rhine. Although this opened the way to German revisionism in the East, optimists who lacked a direct stake in Eastern Europe indulged the hope that change might take place in that far-away region through a process of mutual accommodation. But the American policy of financial stabilization without political participation could not accomplish certain things. It could not bring domestic stability to Germany or avert the fragmentation of its party system. It could not alter the passionate consensus in the Reich for territorial revision of the peace treaties. It could not satisfy the frantic French search for security. It did not attenuate the national ambitions and cultural conflicts that opposed France to Germany and Great Britain to the United States. Thus the stability of the middle 1920s proved, perhaps necessarily, ephemeral.

While history teaches no simple lessons, this is an instructive moment to review the history of American-European relations after World War I. Once again, to paraphrase Emerson, events are in the saddle and ride mankind. Within a short span of years, the United States has lost its creditor position. It has returned to the debtor status that it occupied throughout the 19th century. American productivity growth has fallen sharply in relative terms. The dollar has begun to yield its position as the principal reserve currency. The end of American dominance of multilateral financial institutions may very well follow. The creation of a unified European market in 1992 and the restoration of a united Germany as the dominant power within that market bid fair to revolutionize recent power relationships between Europe and the United States. The consequences for NATO have already become apparent.[77] As Germany and the European Community take their place in the "common European house" whose foundations are now under preliminary construction, we may look back to the 1920s in order to gauge the peculiar fragility and malleability of European-American ties. It is yet to be seen whether the sense of common problems and common destiny, anticipated by a mere handful of visionaries in the 1920s, then fashioned into a solid edifice by the purposive statesmen of the 1940s, can possibly survive the vicissitudes of the 1990s.

Notes to Chapter 19

1. Alfred D. Chandler, Jr., *The Visible Hand: The Managerial Revolution in American Business* (Cambridge, MA, 1977), pp. 285–376; David Landes, *The Unbound Prometheus: Technological Change and Industrial Development in Western Europe from 1750 to the Present* (Cambridge, England, 1969), pp. 231–358.

2. Mira Wilkins, T*he Maturing of Multinational Enterprise: American Business Abroad from 1914 to 1970* (Cambridge, MA, 1974).

3. Werner Link, *Die amerikanische Stabilisierungspolitik in Deutschland 1921–32* (Düsseldorf, 1970), p. 53.

4. Gerd Hardach, *The First World War, 1914–1918* (Berkeley, CA, 1977), p. 5.

5. David Kennedy, *Over Here: The First World War and American Society* (New York, 1980), p. 298.

6. Hardach, *The First World War*, p. 5.

7. Kennedy, *Over Here*, pp. 301–5; Georges-Henri Soutou, *L'Or et le sang: Les buts de guerre économiques de la Première Guerre mondiale* (Paris, 1989), pp. 310–12; Jeffrey J. Safford, *Wilsonian Maritime Diplomacy, 1913–1921* (New Brunswick, NJ, 1978).

8. Soutou, *L'Or et le sang*, pp. 324–30; Carl Parrini, *Heir to Empire: United States Economic Diplomacy, 1916–1923* (Pittsburgh, PA, 1969), pp. 19–29.

9. Quoted in Kennedy, *Over Here*, pp. 308, 330–31.

10. Burton I. Kaufman, *Efficiency and Expansion: Foreign Trade Organization in the Wilson Administration, 1913–1921* (Westport, CT, 1974).

11. Ernest R. May, *The World War and American Isolation, 1914–1917* (Cambridge, MA,

1959); Arthur S. Link, *Wilson the Diplomatist: A Look at His Major Foreign Policies* (Chicago, IL, 1965).

12. Kathleen Burk, B*ritain, America and the Sinews of War, 1914–1918* (Boston, MA, 1985), pp. 99–136; also André Kaspi, *Le Temps des américains 1917–18* (Paris, 1976).

13. Wilson to House, 21 July 1917, quoted in Ray Stannard Baker, *Woodrow Wilson, Life and Letters*, 8 vols. (Garden City, NY, 1927–39), 7:180; excellent discussion in Kennedy, *Over Here*, pp. 320–22.

14. For data on the complexities of raising loans through mass public subscription, see Boxes 174–186 and especially Box 552 (Liberty Loan file), William Gibbs McAdoo Papers, Library of Congress, Washington, DC.

15. Benjamin Rhodes, "The United States and the War Debt Question, 1917–1934," Ph.D. diss., University of Colorado, 1965; Ellen Schrecker, *The Hired Money: The French Debt to the United States, 1917–1929* (New York, 1979).

16. Burk, *Britain, America and the Sinews of War*, pp. 197–220.

17. The definitive work is Soutou, *L'Or et le sang*. See also Fritz Fischer, *Griff nach der Weltmacht* (Düsseldorf, 1961); the postwar work by the French commerce minister, Etienne Clémentel, *La France et la politique économique interalliée* (Paris, 1931); and the insightful analysis of Clémentel's strategy by Marc Trachtenberg, *Reparation in World Politics: France and European Economic Diplomacy, 1916–1923* (New York, 1980), pp. 1–27.

18. Parrini, *Heir to Empire*, pp. 21–22; Kennedy, *Over Here*, pp. 308–11.

19. Charles Seymour, ed., *The Intimate Papers of Colonel House*, 4 vols. (Boston, MA and New York, 1926–28), 3:162–65.

20. House, who considered territorial and commercial greed the two twin causes of war, argued explicitly for tariff reduction as well as for the elimination of artificial trade restrictions. Wilson, who feared the reaction of high-tariff forces in the Senate, nevertheless agreed at length to tackle the issue discreetly. See Seymour, *Intimate Papers*, 3:326–27; also Soutou, *L'Or et le sang*, p. 540.

21. Soutou, *L'Or et le sang*, pp. 540–42.

22. Lawrence E. Gelfand, *The Inquiry: American Preparations for Peace, 1917–1919* (New Haven, CT, 1963).

23. Soutou, *L'Or et le sang*, pp. 542–48.

24. See the numerous reports from French High Commissioner André Tardieu and Ambassador Jules Jusserand to Clémentel in Nos. 1217–1219 ("Entente économique entre les Alliés. L'arme économique: le contrôle des matières premières"), Série A-Guerre, Ministère des Affaires Etrangères, Paris.

25. Wilson to Charles C. McCord, 22 November 1918, quoted in Arthur Walworth, *America's Moment, 1918: American Diplomacy at the End of World War I* (New York, 1977).

26. See Bernard Baruch, *The Making of the Reparation and Economic Sections of the Treaty* (New York, 1920); Edward M. House and Charles Seymour, eds., *What Really Happened at Paris* (New York, 1921); and Philip Mason Burnett, ed., *Reparation at the Paris Peace Conference from the Standpoint of the American Delegation*, 2 vols. (New York, 1940).

27. The so-called President's Committee of Economic Advisers, constituted in January 1919, met periodically for lunch, but kept no formal minutes or records; see, however, on its activities, Vance McCormick's "Diary," Sterling Library, Yale University, New Haven, CT (microfilm copy in the Harvard College Library).

28. Walworth, *America's Moment*, pp. 210–48; Walworth, *Wilson and His Peacemakers: American Diplomacy at the Paris Peace Conference, 1919* (New York,1986), pp. 89–90, 157–61; Francis William O'Brien, ed., *Two Peacemakers in Paris: The Hoover-Wilson Post-Armistice Letters, 1918–1920* (College Station, TX, 1978).

29. Soutou, *L'Or et le sang*, pp. 836–43; also Walworth, *Wilson and His Peacemakers*, pp. 163–80, 398–408; and Trachtenberg, *Reparation in World Politics*, pp. 29–98.

30. See the Lamont-Davis "Memorandum on the Financial Situation in Europe," 13 May 1919, prepared for discussion both with their own delegation and with Robert Brand and Jean Monnet, their French and British colleagues on the Supreme Economic Council, in Box 18, Hon R.H. Brand Papers, Bodleian Library, Oxford University.

31. Stephen A. Schuker, *The End of French Predominance in Europe* (Chapel Hill, NC,

1976), esp. pp. 176–77; Walworth, *America's Moment*, pp. 244–47. See also the extensive correspondence of Leffingwell in Washington with Lamont and Davis in Paris in Box 16A, Norman H. Davis Papers, Library of Congress, (especially Leffingwell to Davis, 7 May 1919). For an insightful examination of British strategy, see J.A. Hemery, "The Emergence of Treasury Influence in British Foreign Policy, 1914–1921," Ph.D. diss., University of Cambridge, 1988. On the domestic issues that had proven decisive in the 1918 U.S. elections, see Seward W. Livermore, *Politics is Adjourned: Woodrow Wilson and the War Congress, 1916–1918* (Middletown, CT, 1966), pp. 169–247.

32. Woodrow Wilson to Prime Minister David Lloyd George, 5 April 1919, Box 16A, Davis Papers.

33. Norman Davis to Wilson, 21 February 1920, copy in U.S. Senate, 67th Cong., 2nd Session, Committee on Judiciary, *Loans to Foreign Governments*, Document No. 86 (Washington, DC, 1921).

34. Leffingwell to Davis, 7 May 1919, Box 16A, Davis Papers.

35. Brand notes on a conversation with Lamont and Monnet, 15 May 1919, Box 18, Brand Papers.

36. Lamont to Brand, 10 June 1919, Box 12, Brand Papers.

37. Eugene Meyer (War Finance Corporation) to Brand, 1 July and 6 August; Brand to Sir Auckland Geddes, 2 July; Board of Trade to Brand, 4 July; Frank Altschul (Lazards-New York) to Brand, 22 August; Brand to Altschul, 25 August; Brand to Meyer, 1 October 1919, Boxes 12 and 16, Brand Papers.

38. Lansing to John W. Davis, 18 November 1919, quoted in Walworth, *Wilson and His Peacemakers*, pp. 293, 554.

39. Lester V. Chandler, *Benjamin Strong, Central Banker* (Washington, DC, 1958), pp. 141–48; Michael J. Hogan, *Informal Entente: The Private Structure of Cooperation in Anglo-American Economic Diplomacy, 1918–1928* (Columbia, MO, 1977), pp. 31–33; Kathleen Burk, "The House of Morgan in Financial Diplomacy, 1920–1930," in B.J.C. McKercher, ed., *The Struggle for Supremacy: Aspects of Anglo-American Relations in the 1920s* (Edmonton, Alberta, 1990); Ron Chernow, *The House of Morgan* (New York, 1990), pp. 206–10.

40. Walworth, *Wilson and His Peacemakers*, pp. 528–56; Lloyd E. Ambrosius, *Woodrow Wilson and the American Diplomatic Tradition: The Treaty Fight in Perspective* (New York, 1987). On the relative flexibility of the mild reservationists, see also William C. Widenor, *Henry Cabot Lodge and the Search for an American Foreign Policy* (Berkeley and Los Angeles, 1980), pp. 300–48.

41. Parrini, *Heir to Empire*, pp. 72–137; Hogan, *Informal Entente*, pp. 34–37.

42. Milton Friedman and Anna Jacobson Schwartz, *A Monetary History of the United States, 1867–1960* (Princeton, NJ, 1963), pp. 221–44; Chandler, *Benjamin Strong, Central Banker*, pp. 149–87.

43. James P. Warburg, "History of the Warburg Family," pp. 33–65, unpublished Mss., Paul Warburg Papers, Sterling Library, Yale University, New Haven, CT.

44. Parrini, *Heir to Empire*, pp. 101–37.

45. Carl-L. Holtfrerich, "Amerikanischer Kapitalexport und Wiederaufbau der deutschen Wirtschaft 1919–1923 im Vergleich zu 1924–1929," revised version in Michael Stürmer, ed., *Die Weimarer Republik: Belagerte Civitas* (Königstein/Ts., 1980), pp. 131–57 [now available also as "U.S. Capital Exports to Germany 1919–1923 Compared to 1924–1929," in *Explorations in Economic History* 23 (1986), pp. 1–32]. For statistical information, see also League of Nations, *Europe's Overseas Needs 1919–1920 and How They Were Met* (Geneva, 1943); and for a conceptual overview, M.E. Falkus, "United States Economic Policy and the 'Dollar Gap' of the 1920's," *Economic History Review* 24 (November 1971): 599–623.

46. See, for example, Charles P. Kindleberger, *The World in Depression* (Berkeley, CA, 1973), esp. pp. 19–57, 291–308.

47. Bureau of the Census, *Historical Statistics of the United States, Colonial Times to 1970*, 2 vols. (Washington, DC, 1975), 1:887, cited and interpreted by Kennedy, *Over Here*, pp. 342–43.

48. See the balance of payment statistics and analysis in Stephen A. Schuker, *American*

"Reparations" to Germany, 1919–33: Implications for the Third-World Debt Crisis, Princeton Studies in International Finance 61 (Princeton, NJ, 1988), pp. 92–97.

49. For a sophisticated restatement of the traditional view, which I seek to undermine here, see Carl-L.Holtfrerich, "The Grown-up in Infant's Clothing: The U.S. Protectionist Relapse in the Interwar Period," Working Paper No. 19, John F. Kennedy-Institut für Nordamerikastudien (Abteilung für Wirtschaft), Freie Universität Berlin (Berlin, 1989).

50. See Robert Pastor, *Congress and the Politics of U.S. Foreign Economic Policy* (Berkeley, CA, 1980), p. 78 (Table 3).

51. Parrini, *Heir to Empire*, pp. 212–47; Melvyn P. Leffler, *The Elusive Quest: America's Pursuit of European Stability and French Security, 1919–1933* (Chapel Hill, NC, 1979), pp. 43–53; also, for a chronologically wider perspective, Sidney Ratner, *The Tariff in American History* (New York, 1972).

52. Werner Link, *Die amerikanische Stabilisierungspolitik in Deutschland*, pp. 190–99, 324–37.

53. Schuker, *American "Reparations" to Germany*, pp. 98–99.

54. Frank Costigliola, *Awkward Dominion: American Political, Economic, and Cultural Relations with Europe, 1919–1933* (Ithaca, NY, 1984), pp. 140–66.

55. Link, *Die amerikanische Stabilisierungspolitik in Deutschland*, pp. 367–81, 593–617; note also the more pointed formulation of the argument in Link's essay, "Die Beziehungen zwischen der Weimarer Republik und den USA," in Michael Stürmer, ed., *Die Weimarer Republik: Belagerte Civitas*, pp. 63–92.

56. Kennedy, *Over Here*, p. 339.

57. Prescient observers came to understand this at the time. See, notably, the correspondence of Eugene Meyer as Commissioner of the Farm Loan Bureau under President Coolidge, in Boxes 245, 247–48, Meyer Papers, Library of Congress, Washington, DC. For retrospective confirmation, see Wilfrid Malenbaum, *The World Wheat Economy, 1885–1939* (Cambridge, MA, 1953).

58. See, among other works, Leffler, *The Elusive Quest*, pp. 30–81.

59. Hoover Memorandum on the Genoa Conference, 4 January 1922, Box 21, Secretary of Commerce–Official Papers, Herbert Hoover Presidential Library, West Branch IA, also cited in Leffler, *The Elusive Quest*, p. 81; Coolidge statement in William R. Castle Diary, 25 September 1923, Houghton Library, Harvard University, Cambridge, MA, also cited in Dieter B. Gescher, *Die Vereinigten Staaten von Nordamerika und die Reparationen 1920–1924* (Bonn, 1956), p. 193.

60. John Maynard Keynes to Robert Brand, 30 December 1919, Box 20; Paul Warburg to Brand, 22 March 1920, Box 22 (Amsterdam/Brussels Conference files), Brand Papers, Bodleian Library, Oxford.

61. Stephen A. Schuker, "American Policy toward Debts and Reconstruction at Genoa," in Carole Fink, Axel Frohn, and Jürgen Heideking, eds., *Genoa, Rapallo, and the Reconstruction of Europe in 1922* (New York, 1991), pp. 95–122; also Roberta A. Dayer, "The British War Debts to the United States and the Anglo-Japanese Alliance, 1920–1923," *Pacific Historical Review* 45 (November 1976): 569–95; and Benjamin F. Rhodes, "Reassessing Uncle Shylock: The United States and the French War Debt, 1917–1929," *Journal of American History* 55 (March 1969): 787–803.

62. Casenave to M. Vignon, chef de cabinet to President Alexandre Millerand, 21 July 1921, Box 5, Folder 8, Louis Loucheur Papers, Hoover Institution, Stanford, CA.

63. Schuker, *American "Reparations" to Germany*, pp. 16–19; Trachtenberg, *Reparation in World Politics*, pp. 193–211; Sally Marks, "The Myths of Reparations," *Central European History* 11 (September 1978): 231–55. For Belgian Premier Georges Theunis's witticism, see his memorandum of 30 August 1923, "A propos de l'article de M. Tardieu," Série Politique Nr. 10.074, Ministère des Affaires Etrangères et du Commerce Extérieur, Brussels.

64. Carl-L. Holtfrerich, "Internationale Verteilungsfolgen der deutschen Inflation 1918–1923," *Kyklos* (1977, No. 2): 271–92; Schuker, *American "Reparations" to Germany*, pp. 106–14.

65. Brand to the Earl of Balfour, 4 August 1922, Box 93, Brand Papers.

66. Louis A.R. Yates, *The United States and French Security, 1917–1921* (New York, 1957).

67. Schuker, *The End of French Predominance in Europe*, pp. 3–28; also Schuker, "Frankreich und die Weimarer Republik," in Stürmer, *Die Weimarer Republik*, pp. 92–112.

68. Chancellor of the Exchequer memorandum, "British Debt to the United States," 8 June 1922, C.P. 4020, CAB 24/137, Public Record Office, Kew.

69. For the views of the permanent under secretary, see Sir Eyre Crowe minute, 18 May 1922, FO 371/8191: N4766/646/38, Public Record Office. For Treasury attitudes in 1931, note among other works Roberta Allbert Dayer, *Finance and Empire: Sir Charles Addis, 1861–1945* (New York, 1988), pp. 209–30; also Diane B. Kunz, *The Battle for Britain's Gold Standard in 1931* (London, 1987). Some Treasury officials of the 1920s generation held the United States in such contempt that they failed to succumb even to the "hands-across-the-sea" atmosphere of World War II. Sir Otto Niemeyer, for example, rejected a State Department contract in the 1950s with a Latin expletive: "Am I thy servant's dog, that I should do such a thing! [Quid enim sum servus tuus canis, ut faciam istam rem?]" (Niemeyer to Maurice Frère, 10 September 1953, Folder 82, Frère Papers, Archives générales du royaume, Brussels).

70. Commerce Department "Memorandum on War Debt Settlement," June 1926, U.S. State Department, 800.51W89/283, Record Group 59, National Archives, Washington, DC.

71. Link, *Die amerikanische Stabilisierungspolitik in Deutschland*, pp. 44–52, 176–188, 203–314; similar interpretation in Peter Krüger, *Die Aussenpolitik der Republik von Weimar* (Darmstadt, 1985).

72. *Foreign Relations of the United States, 1922*, 2 vols. (Washington, DC 1938), 2:201.

73. Dwight Morrow to Thomas W. Lamont, 1 May 1922, Box 113/14, Lamont Papers, Harvard Business School, Boston, MA.

74. Josephine Young Case and Everett Needham Case, *Owen D. Young and American Enterprise* (Boston, MA, 1982), p. 282.

75. Schuker, *The End of French Predominance*, pp. 171–382; Jacques Bariéty, *Les Relations franco-allemandes après la première guerre mondiale, 10 novembre 1918–10 janvier 1925* (Paris, 1977), pp. 425–756. For a discussion of British–American conflict over the appropriate currency (the dollar or sterling) on which to stabilize the mark, see Hans Otto Schötz, *Der Kampf um die Mark 1923/24: Die deutsche Währungsstabilisierung unter dem Einfluß der nationalen Interessen Frankreichs, Großbritanniens und der USA* (Berlin and New York, 1987), pp. 100–175.

76. Lamont and Leffingwell to Morgan, Harjes & Cie., 1 April 1924; Leffingwell memorandum, 26 July 1924, quoted in Schuker, *The End of French Predominance*, pp. 275, 306.

77. On these themes, see among other works David Calleo, *The Imperious Economy* (Cambridge, MA, 1982), and *Beyond American Hegemony: The Future of the Western Alliance* (New York, 1987); Benjamin M. Friedman, *Day of Reckoning: The Consequences of American Economic Policy under Reagan and After* (New York, 1988); and Carl-L. Holtfrerich, "Reaganomics und Weltwirtschaft," Working Paper No. 21, John F. Kennedy-Institut für Nordamerikastudien (Abteilung für Wirtschaft), Freie Universität Berlin (Berlin, 1990).

20

Trade, Debts, and Reparations: Economic Concepts and Political Constraints

Manfred Berg

At the end of World War I, the new republican government of Germany and leading representatives of German industry and finance launched a political offensive for a peace settlement that would allow for Germany's reintegration into a liberal world economy.[1] While most of those who spoke in favor of economic liberalism truly believed that cooperation among the former belligerent nations was imperative on behalf of the victors and vanquished alike, their political interests were plain to see: the Germans dreaded continued economic warfare by the Allies and wished to avert peace conditions that would burden them with high reparation demands and discriminate against their trade. Moreover, since fears of socialism had not calmed down entirely, a swift integration into a liberal, capitalist, international system also promised safeguards against domestic radicalism – except that only a non-socialist Germany could attract the foreign capital and credits necessary for economic rehabilitation. Finally, the firm conviction that the recovery of war-stricken Europe depended on German production and consumption nourished the hope of exploiting Germany's industrial potential in becoming a great power again even after military defeat. As U.S. President Woodrow Wilson had called explicitly for the removal of economic barriers and equality of trade in his Fourteen Points, which Germany had accepted as the basis for peace negotiations, it was only natural to seek American support. Even when the Treaty of Versailles, which had left open the reparation bill and imposed trade discriminations violating letter and spirit of the Wilson program, had dashed German hopes, the belief that Germany's significance for the world economy necessitated a revision of the peace settlement – and that the United States as the leading world power and champion of liberal capitalism was a natural partner in this process – remained a guiding principle of German foreign policy.[2]

Notes to Chapter 20 can be found on page 414.

Beyond the ubiquitous rhetoric of free trade and economic cooperation, however, traditional rivalries and protectionism persisted between
previous Allies and enemies during the postwar period, as the highly
instructive papers by Elisabeth Glaser-Schmidt and Stephen A. Schuker
demonstrate. While the Germans made much of an alleged German-
American interest in restoring a liberal world economy, they did not
hesitate to resort to trade restrictions and controls when they were
deemed expedient. Contrary to what Germany believed, U.S. policymakers cared far less about German recovery and far more for domestic
prosperity, which was not, as Schuker points out, vitally dependent on
foreign trade. A successful rehabilitation of Germany was even regarded
as a potential threat to American commercial interests, and cheap German exports subsidized by inflation were viewed with outright disfavor.
Nonetheless, in principle, American political and business leaders accepted Germany's key role in the reconstruction of Europe and cherished
far-reaching expectations for future commerce. Glaser-Schmidt observes
that U.S. exports to Germany surpassed their prewar level in 1921, when
their volume increased to $372 million from $311 million in the previous year. During the same period the total value of American exports
plummeted to $4.3 billion from $8.2 billion, with only two countries,
Germany and Mexico, exempted from the general decline.[3] However
exceptional this situation might have been, such figures underscored the
U.S. observers' assessment that Germany would be an excellent market
for American goods if only inflation could be halted and the political
uncertainties resulting from the reparation impasse could be removed.[4]
In general, the Germans were correct in assuming that American economic interests in Germany constituted a political asset. Flawed attempts
to coopt the U.S. Government by surprise, like the desperate appeal to
President Warren Harding for arbitration in the reparation crisis of April
1921, would, however, merely deter the Americans from adopting a
more active role in European affairs.

Economic cooperation depended heavily on existing political conditions. Glaser-Schmidt concludes correctly that the political and economic cooperation with the United States which the Germans hoped for did
not materialize before 1923. The foundation of a close relationship
between Germany and the United States – the Treaty of Commerce and
the Dawes Plan – was laid after Gustav Stresemann took charge of German foreign policy in the summer of 1923. These events were far from
coincidental. Despite his nationalist background, Stresemann had developed a generally correct assessment of American interests and was prepared to meet the requirements for reestablishing international tranquility and prosperity.[5] While his rhetoric on the Bolshevik menace and Ger-

many's pivotal importance in the world economy differed little from his predecessors, his actions during 1923–24 sufficiently persuaded the Americans that Germany would be a reliable partner under his leadership. The cessation of passive resistance in September 1923, the stabilization of the Reichsmark, his unambigous support for the work of the Dawes Committee, and his firm stance in the domestic quarrels over the Dawes Plan convinced the Americans that the German government was finally willing to meet the political and economic conditions for U.S. participation in solving the reparations problem. The political benefits for German revisionism that Stresemann and his associates expected from close cooperation with the United States would materialize during the ensuing years.

The restoration of a liberal world trading order crucially affected the ubiquitous problem of international debts, since payment of both inter-allied war loans and German reparations could only be expected if world trade expanded. As Glaser-Schmidt underscores at the end of her paper, however, the conflicting goals of increasing Germany's export revenues to facilitate reparation payment and restricting German competition were never adequately reconciled. Indeed, this problem – that a continuous and substantial transfer of reparations was only possible if the creditors opened their markets to German goods – has troubled economic experts and historians since the Paris Peace Conference. It also has been considered frequently as a key impediment to a genuine solution.[6] It certainly was not by chance that the framers of the Dawes Plan put it at the center of their scheme. Schuker, however, has never assigned much relevance to this problem. In his paper, he contends that Germany's capacity to pay depended simply on "sufficient political and economic discipline to limit consumption and facilitate the transfer," but Weimar politicians lacked this discipline and embarked on various evasive strategies.[7] It is understood that Germans, for propaganda reasons, habitually exaggerated the economic burden of reparations. Yet, aside from questioning to what extent a real transfer of purchasing power between reparation debtors and creditors would have been possible without damaging either's economy, reparations always remained basically a political obligation. As Carl-Ludwig Holtfrerich has argued, there can be a political inability to serve foreign debts even if the economic capacity seems assured theoretically.[8] The political capacity of the Weimar Republic to pay reparations was not solely limited by its unwillingness, but by grave political and social constraints as well. Social progress was the only ground on which the Republic could hope to achieve legitimacy, and those who struggled for its survival could hardly be expected to sacrifice their domestic aims to the service of foreign debts that most Germans disdained as tributes imposed by relentless victors. If, as Schuker convincingly argues, American public opinion precluded a more generous policy toward interallied debts, this argument applies even more to Germany, where *Erfüllungspolitiker* risked more than their political future. The assassinations of Matthias Erzberger and Walther Rathenau made this painfully clear.

The political character of reparations also makes questionable calling the C-bonds of the London schedule of payments (nominally 82 billion Reichmarks) "funny-money." True, their actual service was, at best, a remote possibility, but they still offered an easily available lever for all future reparation talks.[9] In the negotiations about the Dawes Plan, France's insistence on the 132 billion figure prevented a final reparation bill from being fixed, and again in 1928–29, French Prime Minister Raymond Poincaré resurrected the C-bonds when the revision of the Dawes Plan and the evacuation of the Rhineland came to the agenda of international politics. Besides being diplomatic bargaining assets, the large nominal figures of the London schedule were meant to soothe public demands for high sums so that the illusion that somebody would eventually pay the bill for the war could be retained. France, in particular, hoped either to make the Germans pay large sums or to trade these claims to the United States for the cancellation of debts. Paradoxically, such numbers also helped to reassure American bondholders that the Allies would be able to honor their obligations. It also permitted the Harding administration to adopt a tough stand on the issue of war debts – an important reason why American leaders had no interest in seeing Germany relieved of her reparation burden. Unfortunately, the political usefulness of high figures did not render them any more realistic.

The impact of public opinion as a constraint for international debt policies, which Schuker discusses for the United States but somewhat neglects for Germany, needs more comparative research, particularly as to how policymakers met this challenge or even tried to manipulate it. Did they merely respond to pressure, or did "the political spokesmen of the wealthy classes" resort to "financial demagoguery" in order to avoid telling their clients the truth about the financial consequences of the war?[10] In either case, the yearning of American taxpayers for fiscal "normalcy" that was guiding their attitude toward debt cancellation was certainly shared by their European counterparts, who, with some justification, could point to the burdens and hardships they had endured during the war. But even if the U.S. administration had been both willing and able to persuade the American public to take a more lenient view on "burden sharing," the possible beneficial effects still remain in doubt. American financial stabilization – as Schuker is right to remind us –

could not solve the basic domestic and international conflicts that troubled the continent after the Great War. And although the European
nations were constantly trying to coopt the United States for political and
economic purposes, they did not want America to be the supreme arbiter
of their affairs. The times for a Pax Americana had not yet arrived.

History teaches no simple lessons, but some analogies may be useful.
With the demise of communism and the break-up of the Soviet Union,
the leading economic powers of the world are once more confronted
with the task of integrating a former "enemy" into a liberal world economy and coping with enormous international debts, which most likely
will never be fully paid. Will the Western powers live up to their praised
liberal principles and open their markets for Eastern Europe, or will they
fall back into narrow self-interest and protectionism? Will their popula-
tions and taxpayers be prepared to pay for a transfer of wealth with the
vague hope of ensuing political stabilization?

While there remains a large gap between the rhetoric and practice of
free trade, some current political conditions for a successful approach
appear more favorable than in the 1920s. Unlike World War I, the Cold
War did not leave bitterness and resentment between the former adversaries, but a feeling that Western Europe cannot be secure and prosperous with the former Eastern bloc in political turmoil and economic distress. Until recently, there has been a widespread consensus among the
Western political elite that the cost of the Cold War was a necessary
price to pay for peace. What is needed now is an equally solid consensus
that a comparable effort is required to overcome the consequences of the
East-West conflict. The urgent need for economic assistance, at least, is
uncontested, and few people will deny that the financial and political
capacity of former Eastern bloc countries to pay foreign debts is unlikely
to permit more than token acknowledgements – especially since the
political resolve of the creditors to collect debts will surely be affected by
the fact that some of the major debtors possess nuclear weapons.

Nevertheless, if there is a lesson to be learned from the 1920s, it is that
stabilization requires a concerted effort by all major industrialized nations
and cannot be left to a single hegemon. Just as the United States was
expected to perform miracles in the 1920s,[11] many people in Eastern and
Western Europe, the United States, and Japan believe that, due to her
political interests and geographical proximity to Eastern Europe, Germany alone must manage the formidable economic and social problems
left by communism. As the unexpectedly grave problems of German
reunification have clearly demonstrated, this is a task far beyond her economic ressources and political influence.

Notes to Chapter 20

1. For German peace preparations cf. Leo Haupts, *Deutsche Friedenspolitik, 1918–19* (Düsseldorf, 1976); Peter Krüger, *Die Außenpolitik der Republik von Weimar* (Darmstadt, 1985), pp. 65–77.

2. This conviction formed the core of Gustav Stresemann's foreign political concept. Manfred Berg, *Gustav Stresemann und die Vereinigten Staaten von Amerika. Weltwirtschaftliche Verflechtung und Revisionspolitik 1907–1929* (Baden-Baden, 1990), pp. 94ff.; also cf. my comparison of Stresemann and Rathenau, in "Germany and the United States: The Concept of World Economic Interdependence," in *Genoa, Rapallo, and European Reconstruction in 1922*, ed. by Carole Fink, Axel Frohn, and Jürgen Heideking (Cambridge University Press, 1991), pp. 77–93; for a general overview cf. Werner Link, *Die amerikanische Stabilisierungspolitik in Deutschland, 1921–1932* (Düsseldorf, 1970), pp. 38ff.

3. *Historical Statistics of the United States: Colonial Times to 1970* (Washington D.C., 1976), series U 317–334. Exports to Mexico only increased to $222 million from $208.

4. See for example the report by U.S. Consul Richardson of 13 October 1922: "Germany as a Present Day Market for American Goods," National Archives Washington, D.C., Record Group 59 662.111/-.

5. Cf. Berg, *Gustav Stresemann und die Vereinigten Staaten*, pp. 123–227.

6. Cf. Bruce Kent, *The Spoils of War: The Politics, Economics and Diplomacy of Reparations 1918–1932* (Oxford, 1989), pp. 2–4; Derek H. Aldcroft, *Die zwanziger Jahre: Von Versailles zur Wall Street, 1919–1929* (München, 1978), pp. 108–09; Peter Krüger, "Das Reparationsproblem in fragwürdiger Sicht. Kritische Überlegungen zur neuesten Forschung," in *Vierteljahrshefte für Zeitgeschichte* 29 (1981), pp. 21–47.

7. Cf. Stephen A. Schuker, *The End of French Predominance in Europe: The Financial Crisis of 1924 and the Adoption of the Dawes-Plan* (Chapel Hill, 1976), p. 186; idem, *American "Reparations" to Germany, 1919–1933: Implications for the Third World Debt Crisis*, Princeton Studies in International Finance 61 (Princeton, 1988).

8. Cf. Holtfrerich's review of Schuker's *American "Reparations" to Germany*, in *Historische Zeitschrift* 251 (1990), pp. 468–71.

9. Cf. Krüger, *Außenpolitik*, p. 130, n. 107.

10. Cf. Kent, *The Spoils of War*, pp. 17–55, 44.

11. Cf. Frank C. Costigliola, *Awkward Dominion: American Political, Economic, and Cultural Relations with Europe, 1919–1933* (Ithaca, 1984), pp. 167–83.

21

The Limits of American Stabilization Policy in Europe

Michael Behnen

Stephen Schuker focused on the question: What were the origins of American stabilization policy in Europe? But he also described some of the main features and effects of reconstruction policy prior to the Dawes Plan. Before going into the details, I should like to recall that there were different aspects of reconstruction policy: financial and commercial, which I want to call direct instruments of reconstruction; and political, ideological, and military aspects, which may be described as indirect. These different aspects of reconstruction were more often than not intertwined. What they have in common is that they reacted to the multilateral political and economic framework established in Paris in 1919.

All attempts at bilateral analysis must keep in mind another point: the difference between "merely" financial or economic issues, in the United States and Germany for example, and the problem of security, first of all in Germany, but also in France. The guidelines for the U.S. stabilization policy ignored the importance of this security problem for France and Germany. Between 1921 and 1925, the currency disputes between the United States and Great Britain concerning the British adoption of the American gold standard created grave obstacles for attaining one of the main goals of the American reconstruction policy, i.e., reintegrating Germany into a prosperous Europe on a so-called open door, capitalist basis as a precondition for achieving the ultimate aim of furthering and extending trade relations between the United States and all major European countries.

What were the features and instruments of the U.S. reconstruction policy just after the end of the war? Let me first of all turn to the priority the U.S. administration assigned to economic matters. In this field, in my opinion, there existed no decisive differences between the Wilsonians and the Republicans. The American politicians among the Wilsonians, whom historians like Michael Hogan called "cooperationalists," adhered to a very simple and insufficient explanation of the outbreak of World War I, and they drew conclusions from this explanation regarding future U.S. economic policy. These "cooperationalists" explained the outbreak of the war in 1914 with commercial imperialism, especially between Great Britain and Germany, which escalated into political and military conflict. According to this interpretation, the European powers ignored the basic law of economic interdependence, which implied the existence and maintainance of an open international market.

The Paris Economic Conference in 1916 concluded with the Allies' determination to renew the policy of commercial imperialism after the war. Along these lines, Bernard Baruch, for example, advocated "wider trade aiming at the diminishing of military conflicts and social unrest" (23 October 1918). Otherwise, he thought, the industrial inequalities would result in revolutions or new wars. A second element of the future reconstruction policy emerged as early as 1919. Since economic instability in Europe would lead to depression in the United States, Thomas W. Lamont and Norman Davis thought it inevitable that "this will generate industrial and political revolutions" (memorandum, May 1919).

Thus American stabilization concepts were based on the conviction that a "unity of action" was indispensable. "Unity of action" meant limited government loans organized by the Treasury and long term financing by a consortium of European bankers, supervised by the Treasury, that would oversee reproductive, industrial, and commercial projects only. Herbert Hoover as secretary of commerce later added two more important clauses: no discriminatory tariffs and support for a liberal reparation settlement.

During the Paris Peace Conference, the American economic and financial concepts were based on a narrow concept of international trade relations. My question is this: Did the "cooperationalists'" interpretation of escalating commercial conflicts leading to the outbreak of World War I later hinder them from recognizing the serious consequences of some of the clauses of the Treaty of Versailles, such as the inclusions of pensions and other well-known discriminatory clauses (Germany granted most-favoured-nation treatment to the Allies without reciprocity for 5 years)? Schuker mentions this point, but he does not ask which American business interests received what concessions. From the beginning in 1921, the American reconstruction policy mixed commercial and financial with political considerations, with the effect that the American stabilization policy continually moved further and further away from Wilson's Fourteen Points. The allusion in the Lamont and Davis memorandum of May 1919 to the "bolshevist danger" – reduced to the ad hominem argument directed against Wilson: "political revolution" – was added to the other motives of this policy.

Also, one of the main features of the U.S. reconstruction policy was the lack of Anglo-American cooperation on financial and currency matters. In my opinion, Schuker could and might admit that this was one of the major reasons for increased tensions in 1923 between Germany and the Allies, with its well-known consequences for the German middle classes.

The currency issue is of particular importance because it reveals that the reconstruction policy was aimed first of all at the financial and commercial predominance of the United States – and this clearly meant U.S. economic nationalism. The adoption of the gold standard on American terms in 1925, however, ended the fight between two different forms of financial imperialism, a fight the Bank of England and Lloyd George wanted to win at the Genoa Conference of 1922 with the establishment of a commercial and financial community led by London. Of course, the question of the war debt continued to plague Anglo-American rivalry. It made the British ambassador to Washington, Auckland Geddes, complain in 1921: "they treat us as a vassal state so long as the debt remains unpaid."

After surveying the key political issues, such as the war debts, reintegration of Germany, naval and land disarmament after a reparation settlement between Germany and France, Schuker emphasizes that, shortly after coming to power, the Republican administration "developed a prudent program for reengagement in Europe . . . to promote European recovery and stabilization. . . . But those reasons were as much political and ethical as narrowly economic." It is unclear to me what the term "ethical" means in this context. And if those standards were little more than business standards, what were they like?

Another point: In evaluating the Dawes Plan, Schuker writes that it "turned the balance of power decisively in Germany's favor." He draws our attention to the fact that American bankers, especially J. P. Morgan & Co., imposed loan conditions that led to unfavorable political results in France. The Morgan partners "had to reconcile as best they could the national interest in pacifying Europe with their specific business concerns." You may guess my argument. We are in need of further enlightenment about the proper definitions and the adequate criteria of both terms – of national interest and of "business concerns" – if we are to understand the Republican stabilization policy up until 1924. Who defined national interest, for example, in financing Fascist Italy? We might also ask in which distinct but hidden areas of the U. S. reconstruction policy with respect to stabilization purposes (like armament) may we assume or prove the existence of a consistent, productive, and continuous collaboration between the government and business community, culminating in the well-known activities of people like the "private statesman" T. W. Lamont, one of the Morgan partners?

Providing that sufficient empirical datas illustrating the cooperation between the U. S. banking community and the Republican administration are available, we need not be content with Schuker's relatively pessimistic judgement at the end of his paper, where he points to the American stabilization policy's refusal to commit U. S. foreign policy to particular aims: "Thus the stability of the middle 1920s proved perhaps necessarily ephemeral." We may call it "non-isolationism" or "financial interventionalism" or "independent internationalism." The problem of evaluating both the political and the financial substance and the effects of the U. S. stabilization policy must be solved by examining closely the procedure of giving loans to and promoting trade in every European country.

In my opinion, the American stabilization policy towards Central and West European countries depended clearly on one fundamental issue until 1924: maintaining the freedom of action vis-à-vis domestic financial and commercial constraints. The national interest of the United States as the ideological basis of the manifold stabilization and reconstruction policies lacked an adequate and comprehensive political goal. I agree with Stephen Schuker when he points to the war-debt settlement with Great Britain, which became the model for the following agreements with other European countries, as containing "relatively generous terms." But as a part of the stabilization policy, these settlements were ambivalent, serving the American interest as well as the national economies of particular European countries with either democratic or fascist constitutions.

Discussion

The discussion, which was chaired by Joan Hoff-Wilson, made it quite clear that no one was prepared to defend the thesis that the United States policy toward Europe could still be interpreted as isolationism. The session's title, "Isolation or Reconstruction?", was therefore not seen as an alternative in the interpretation of Washington's policy. There was general agreement that reconstruction had to be seen as the dominant theme of American policy towards Europe and vis à vis Germany. This was also true for Germany's postwar policy. For the defeated Germany reconstruction was of vital importance both in terms of economic reconstruction at home and as a means to regain world power-status in the international system.

Following the papers by Elisabeth Glaser-Schmidt and Stephen Schuker, and the respective commentaries by Michael Behnen and Peter Berg, most discussion participants dealt either directly or indirectly with various economic implications of American and German post-World War I policies: economic conditions in both the United States and Germany, the interpretation of the respective national interests, the significance of a liberal world order for the United States as well as for Germany, the interdependence of economics and politics.

As far as the interrelationship of economics and politics was concerned, there was no consensus as to when one should talk about economic or political priorities. Werner Link, for example, challenged Stephen Schuker's assessment that political reasons were more important than the economic motives for the policy of stabilization in Europe. Link conceded that this might be "a correct objective judgement" from a historical perspective, but thought that the "perceptions of the actors" changed the way things looked. By the end of the 1920s, Owen D. Young, for example, had completely shifted to an "economic primacy concept" when he wrote in a letter of 17 February 1930: "One of the greatest assurances of peace in the world is the economic integration of the world. We shall never have in my judgement political integration until after we have first had economic integration. Economics must lead and politics must follow." Link thought that for the 1920s a priority, or even a "primacy of economics," was characteristic. However, the economic dimension had been overemphasized by most decision-makers, while the military security dimension had been underestimated, due to "a complete misperception on the American side as far as German policy is concerned." When the Americans thought they could use Germany in fostering European disarmament, they did not realize that this was instead an armament policy.

Other participants in the discussion raised the question as to whether an analysis of American stabilization policy could be limited to the years between 1919 and 1924. The goals and limits of American stabilization policy in Germany during the early 1920s had to be contrasted with the dissolution of American-German parallelism in the early 1930s, suggested many participants.

Edward Crapol went a step further and proposed that most problems of the 1920s, for two reasons, had to be interpreted in an even broader framework and on the background of developments in the United States since the Civil War. Many economic issues of the 1920s had to be seen in the context of continuity rather than as specific post-World War I problems; overproduction in agriculture was cited as one example. Such a long-range perspective, Crapol argued, would also offer insight into the nature of America's rise as a leading world power. What bothered him most as a historian was the idea – as expressed in Stephen Schuker's paper and by other participants – that the United States "all of a sudden, in the context of World War I, burst upon the stage as an economic and financial superpower." One needed to avoid the impressions that "there is a vacuum" and that "the United States never made any efforts to gain great power status or secure an empire either before 1914 or after World War I." Crapol drew attention to the papers of the first session and reemphasized that America's rise to world power status "is the process of a long historical continuity in the nineteenth century," and that the "American historical rise to super power status" did not "just occur miraculously in 1914 or in 1917." In this connection Crapol also reminded the audience of the achievements of American historiography since the 1960s. He explicitly mentioned William Appleman Williams' *The Tragedy of American Diplomacy*, first edition (New York, 1959) and Walter LaFeber's *The New Empire: An Interpretation of American expansion 1860–1890* (Ithaca, NY, 1963). Crapol expressed his impression that the works of these and other revisionists had not yet been integrated into most of the papers presented at the conference.

Such a longe-range perspective as suggested by Edward Crapol is certainly useful in understanding the motives and interests of American stabilization policy in Europe after World War I. Germany became the cornerstone of this policy, and during the 1920s there emerged a close

German-American cooperation. But why did American stabilization policy in Europe fail? Who is to be held resspsonsible? As to the limits and ultimate failure of American stabilization schemes during the Great Depression, a broad spectrum of elements was discussed. Due to the key importance of the reparation problem, it was repeatedly referred to during the discussion. Gerald Feldman emphasized "the terribly destructive role of reparations" for both Germany's domestic development and for the international system.

In addition, one should take into account various inconsistencies in both Germany and the United States. The question was raised as to whether the liberal capitalist system referred to by Elisabeth Glaser-Schmidt and others should not more correctly be described as "economic nationalism of a very egoistic sort" (Ragnhild Fiebig-von Hase). Joan Hoff-Wilson gave examples of various inconsistencies in American policy, which manifested themselves in the person of Herbert Hoover. She then cited the Fordney-McCumber Tariff, which also "contained a bundle of contradictions" in the sense that the flexible provisions could have been used to lower as well as to raise tariffs – the protectionist element supplemented by another potential. The third example Joan Hoff-Wilson mentioned was the American position towards the Dawes Plan and the Young Plan. While the United States did not officially participate in these plans, they "unofficially" guaranteed the respective loans. In this context Lloyd Gardner referred to American reactions to the Keynes plan of 1919 to exemplify American opposition to state loans.

But could a more coherent American stabilization policy have been more successful? Stepen Schuker was quite pessimistic, emphasizing German domestic problems. The so-called stable period of the Weimar Republic, the several years after the adoption of the Dawes plan in 1924, had to be regarded as "an unbalanced and disturbed society," and "these problems came from within" because the distribution conflict in Germany could not be solved. People used reparations as an "excuse" not to face the German domestic social problem. Gerd Hardach added that German policy at that time "was on a double standard." The defeat of 1918 had never been accepted politically; therefore, all solutions offered by Germany "were half-hearted."

Given the structural defects of American reconstruction policy in Europe and the problems Washington faced in Germany, any historical analysis of American-German relations during the 1920s must come to the conclusion that there existed virtually no safeguards to protect the German-American parallelism of the 1920 against its fast dissolution during the Great Depression in the early 1930s.

Some participants compared American reconstruction policy of the

1920s and the dissolution of German-American cooperation during the Great Depression with Washington's post-World War II policy, demonstrating that the former lacked cultural and diplomatic initiatives. Hartmut Lehmann and Stephen Schuker mentioned the European Recovery Program, pointing out that the whole Marshall Plan strategy was more successful because it was better able to integrate economic and political aims and because it was supplemented by American cultural initiatives, which it had lacked in the 1920s. Of course, the international system had changed completely during the 1930s and early 1940s. After World War II, Americans grasped that engagement in Europe could not be limited to economic means. This, however, was also a result of the experience of the 1920s when "economic engagement was the only possibility," when "achievements for the economic international order seemed to be like a last hope," as Gerald Feldman and Peter Krüger formulated in complete agreement with all participants.

22

1917 Reconsidered

Erich Angermann

When I began thinking about this lecture, I quickly realized that I was in a position similar to that of the Chinese historian who prefaced his lecture on present day China with a brief survey of his country's ten-thousand-year history – and never got to the subject! I could do better. I could bore you with an endless summary of the historiography on the origins of World War I, pepper it with a rehash of the events leading up to the beginning of the War, and, for good measure, toss in a summary of what my learned colleagues will present in their sessions of this conference. I would have strained your patience beyond endurance, and such a scholastic marathon, of course, would have ruined the reception after my talk. Therefore, I will do something different. I will shock you with some reflections on the rather loose correlation between the historians' findings and the public's reaction to the events of the year 1917.

You might wonder why a historian, a master of his art, whose age declares him familiar with the methodologies of his field, whose fervor has mellowed through his encounters with quantification, hermeneutics, and sundry theories of history, proposes to shock you. You might suspect some nightmarish experience behind it all. And you would be right, of course. Indeed, the problem has nightmarish proportions, for I intend nothing less than to reflect on the difficult relationship between the state of the art on a given problem and the foggy, curiously undefinable, and indistinct notions and reactions of the public to the same problem at both that time and today.

The public, of course, cherishes the belief that historians working in their ivory towers are oblivious to what they, the public, find interesting and exciting. Although this is often true, it highlights the importance of my problem: the relationship between the wine produced by historians in God's vineyards and the tasting and enjoying of that wine by the connoisseur, the public. As laborers in the vineyard – as producers, you might say – it behooves historians to try to improve the quality as well as the sale of their products. This also implies that historians have to

Notes to Chapter 22 can be found on page 435.

observe carefully how people receive, think about, taste, and enjoy their products. To focus on the year 1917 is probably as rewarding as tasting a Lafite 1961. The latter is a fine choice for its richness and full-bodied smoothness; the former a fitting example for its many confusing, inter-twined developments, events, strange mixture of mentalities, and curi-ously complex power interests.

Let me be a bit more specific. When I began thinking about this sub-ject two years ago, it seemed both attractive and handy. Attractive because its dignity, complexity, and forceful dynamics could, like a woodcut, be reduced to a basic yet richly textured structure; and handy because I could omit historical details and focus on the social and cultural undercurrents, flavor, and colorful paraphenalia of the period – since everyone would already be familiar with the course of events. Alas, the dramatic events in Eastern Europe during the last two years have affect-ed every part of the world. They have affected, too, our hitherto unquestioned views and interpretations of the year 1917. What seemed legitimate then is now questionable, what seemed to be received wisdom then is now subject to our doubts, what seemed logical then may now seem irrational. These changes demand a new and careful scrutiny of old and familiar notions, interpretations, and ideas on the period surround-ing 1917.

We are familiar with the basic decisions and events of 1917 – they are in every textbook – but let me recall the highlights. The drama opened with the crashing collapse of czaristic Russia in March 1917, which fol-lowed in the wake of the terrible hunger crisis of the preceding winter, of other shortages, of military defeats, and of poor military leadership. The axis powers, no less authoritarian, rushed to join Russia's fate. After Emperor Franz Joseph's death on 21 November 1917, Austria, exhaust-ed from the pyrrhic victories on the Isonzo and in Rumania and Galicia, unable to integrate its individual territories into a new federation, and without profiting from turning Poland into a monarchy, hurried gloomily on to its own disintegration and utter ruin. Although Imperial Germany demonstrated an incredible fighting spirit, particularly in the sea battle at Skagerrak (31 March 1917) and in the horrible battles of Verdun, in Flanders, and in the Champagne, these battles, fought with newly developed, deadly weapons like poison gas, flame-throwers, and tanks, neither perfected the blockade of England nor led to the decisive military successes so badly needed. Thus, after the failure of the Pope's, the axis powers', and President Wilson's (21 December 1917) peace ini-tiatives, the "Third OHL" (as the newly appointed supreme command was called) of Hindenburg-Ludendorff was faced with a military stale-mate as the result of a deteriorating supply situation in all countries participating in this war and a sagging war moral, decided for quick and decisive action to grasp the last chance for a *Siegfrieden*. In order to break the stalemate and end the war both quickly and satisfactorily, Germany plunged into a series of ill-conceived adventures.

The first of these adventures began on 30 January 1917 with the foundation of the Universum Film AG (UFA). The intention was to use the newly invented cinema for propaganda purposes and to boost German war moral. These efforts, however, did not get beyond its infancy during the war. The following day the OHL began its second adventure. It forced the reluctant imperial government to approve the OHL's request for unlimited submarine warfare against the United States. This senseless decision practically pushed that country into the war. Finally, the third, last, and at the time least noted adventure occurred when the OHL helped an obscure professional revolutionary named Vladimir Il'ic Ul'janov, called Lenin, return to Petrograd from exile in Zurich in order to speed up the destabilization process of the quickly disintegrating Russian Republic, which most unreasonably was, in the eyes of the OHL, still bent on continuing its war against Germany. Let me invoke for you the scene that has been so lovingly fabricated by writers, filmmakers, and television producers of the great, good, and modest Lenin as he crossed Germany in the beginning of April 1917.[1] How, with a few close and trusty friends, his steely will, and a fierce determination to force his luck and overcome all obstacles, he staged – for the best of his fatherland, of course, and only in the interest of the oppressed proletariate – the "Great Socialist October Revolution" (6–7 November 1917) in Russia, grasped absolute power, and thus made a beginning for the world revolution.

One wonders whether it was Hegel's *List der Idee* that designated the Third OHL as the instrument for revolutionizing our century. Did the *Weltgeist* lend a helping hand in realizing the visions of Alexis de Tocqueville, Constantin Frantz, and other nineteenth-century writers concerned about the emergence of powers on the fringes of the European power system, Russia and America, into world or "super" powers?[2] Whatever timetable the *Weltgeist* had destined for the world, the much closer timing of the OHL rested on wrong premises, which became clear soon enough. The OHL had based its timetable on a prediction that it could break the so-called hunger-blockade with unlimited submarine warfare; only this, so the argument went, would decisively improve German supply. Since all participants in this war were supposedly tired of war as well as poorly supplied, these successes would, so the OHL said, tip the scale in favor of Imperial Germany.

None of these predictions materialized. Shifting much needed supplies and forces from the eastern to the western front took much longer than anticipated – actually until the signing of the peace treaty of Brest-Litowsk on 3 March 1918. This also meant that these forces arrived too late to secure decisive victories in the west. Unlimited submarine warfare, on the other hand, neither broke the blockade nor supplied Germany with much needed raw material and goods. Thus, the OHL's three adventures produced but one decisive result: the United States' entry into the war on the side of the Allied powers. That entry boosted the Allies' war moral immediately, although it took some time to affect the military situation.

Another failure of the OHL during 1917 had equally serious consequences. The OHL and the German government were so preoccupied with military considerations and organizing the war economy that they both constantly overlooked the vital political, psychological, and ideological ramifications of these decisions. The OHL did not realize that the failure to win decisive military breakthroughs, together with the mounting and increasingly irreplacable losses of lives, rapidly deteriorating food supplies, and Germany's worsening military situation, fostered increasing war weariness and doubts about a glorious end of the war. In addition, Germany's political and military will to resist became increasingly affected by peace propaganda, the Soviet Russian revolutionary example, and Lenin's claim to spread the Soviet Revolution to the world. You will not be surprised that German public opinion, on the whole unified before 1917, now became deeply divided. The war consensus of all political parties, formed in 1914, began to crumble at the same time the political and military failures produced a new discussion of war aims. As a result, a newly forged majority in the Imperial Diet passed – on 19 July 1917, under the leadership of Matthias Erzberger – peace resolutions. Far from uniting the people, however, these resolutions heightened the resistance of those political groups that were against both peace and reconciliation. Even worse, these opposers of concession, conciliation, and peace, led by the *Vaterlandspartei*, gained enough leverage not only to prevent the conclusion of a moderate peace with Soviet Russia but to dictate to that country the peace of Brest-Litowsk (3 March 1918). This created a most unfortunate precedent for the peace negotiations later that year.

The Allied powers were of course not free from similar influences and afflictions. France, Italy, and Great Britain, too – the latter additionally troubled by serious revolutionary unrest in Ireland – had to survive severe leadership crises in 1917. However, it does make a difference whether people are faced with a steadily deteriorating military, economic, and political situation or have to live through dire times with the cheerful prospect of gaining in military might due to the United States' entry into the war – even if it took some time for the American soldiers to have an impact on the war. I should add, too, that French as well as British leadership proved more energetic and more determined than that of the axis powers. In critical situations even marginal factors can become decisive. The historian Friedrich Meinecke – no sharp observer, but with an astute historical perspective – noted with desperation after the United States' entry into the war that now the last vestiges for a *Versöhnungsfriede* had vanished: "World peace will now probably be transformed into a world revolution."[3] Let me add however that Meinecke's thoughts differ more with Lenin's expectations than they – for terminological reasons – seem to do.

These remarks bring us back to the two main events that structured the fundamental and secular break of the year 1917 and to which all other developments and events are but partly harmonious and partly dissonant commentaries: the United States' entry into the War, which decided the winners, and the Russian Revolution. America viewed the war as a fight between darkness and light, as a battle between good and evil, in which America aimed "to make the world safe for democracy" against the autocratic powers of militarism and monarchy. This is our first main theme. The second is the Russian Revolution of February 1917, which seemed to be clothed in democracy. The West noted the destruction by Lenin's "Great Socialistic October Revolution" only *after* Lenin and the Bolsheviks had secured absolute and totalitarian power in all key areas. The historian Erwin Hölzle, a remnant of the Third Reich, interpreted the year 1917 as a clash of two "world revolutions," that of the Bolsheviks with the older by more than two centuries American Revolution. This suggestion foreshadowed certain hypotheses of Ernst Nolte.[4] Although Hölzle's interpretation suggests some interesting arguments, it seems to me rather absurd. For the American Revolution wanted to *demonstrate* to the world the practicability of its values, although these principles did exercise some destructive influence on the rest of the world, while the revolutionary principles of Lenin and Stalin *actively* and *destructively* strove to revolutionize the world. Certain structural similarities do not provide sufficient ground for an equation of both revolutions.

And yet, is it not possible that this bundle of horrible events, which the British summarily named "The Great War," with all its gruesome, inhumane experiences, created a new world filled with turbulent emotions, which rudely propelled the generation of 1917 out of its bourgeois, proletarian, or aristocratic self-defined complacency and forced it, after decades of seemingly endless human progress, to stare once more into the abyss of what human ingenuity can do for its own destruction?

And does it not seem possible that this trauma prepared – no, sensitized and made receptive – a people who had lived through the horrors of war for new ideas, fresh concepts, and radical thoughts? Could these experiences not have brightened their eyes and cleansed their ears so that they would finally be able to appreciate the formerly rejected prewar radical anti-establishment intellectual movements as well as demands of earlier reforming and protesting groups both set within established intellectual contexts? If it is not possible to proclaim the dawn of a radical new beginning, as some in 1914 did in their frenzy, and if it is not realistic to expect a unified reaction to the experiences of the war, is it not at least feasible and reasonable to expect many to have formulated a new and restructured world view, which was so desperately needed in the face of – as Hermann Broch so clearly saw – the crumbling, disintegrating collapse of all hitherto accepted values? If we cannot find new and definitive philosophical systems and structures, should we not at least be able to discover and feel powerful forces emanating from a newly created magnetic field?

You will have noticed, ladies and gentlemen, that I have progressed from rather carefully phrased descriptive statements to even more cautiously formulated questions. The more I have thought about my subject, the more insistently did these questions push themselves into the foreground. I have reached a point where I can no longer ignore these questions. Yet neither my knowledge nor my scholarly ethos permit me to transform these questions into hypotheses. My curiosity about these phenomena was aroused by the observation that the two dominant events of the crisis year 1917 – the American entry into the war and the Russian Revolution – were perceived by contemporaries and later commentators, irrespective of their subjective perspectives and sympathies, as evidently "normal" consequences of the First World War and its social and political conditions. They saw them as natural results of preconditions, interests, and events, and understood them as results of historical events that an intelligent mind could rationally deduce from those events. In doing so contemporaries and later commentators were suggesting that rationality still reigned supreme. They ignored Friedrich Nietzsche, Henri Bergson, expressionism, and other irrational thought systems that had already proclaimed the end of the bourgeois belief in rationality and the possibility of calculating the future.

Let me clarify my meaning by recalling some of these developments. Surely, most Americans joined President Woodrow Wilson, as they had joined Wilson's predecessor, Theodore Roosevelt, in his frenzied proclamation of a millennial Armageddon and in seeing the Great War, which they were forced to enter in 1917, as a fight between good and evil, as a fight for democracy, liberty, and self-determination against autocracy, militarism, and oppression. To Americans this was a familiar view. They interpreted the entry into this war as they did the American intervention in the Mexican Revolution (1913–1917). Both decisions were logical consequences of the Progressive movement's reforms, and both would end in a "Peace without Victory" – remember Friedrich Meinecke! – and in a new world order culminating in a general council of nations (*Völkerbund*).

The German emperor was actually not unfamiliar with such thoughts, as his correspondence with Houston Stewart Chamberlain in January 1915 shows:

"Der Krieg ist der Kampf zwischen zwei Weltanschauungen; der germanisch-deutschen für Sitte, Recht, Treu und Glauben, wahre Humanität, Wahrheit und echte Freiheit, gegen . . . Mammonsdienst, Geldmacht, Genuß, Landgier, Lüge, Verrrat, Trug und nicht zuletzt Meuchelmord! Diese beiden Weltanschauungen können sich nicht 'versöhnen' oder 'vertragen', eine muß *siegen*, die andere muß *untergehen*! Solange muß *gefochten* werden! . . . Jetzt wird es dem deutschen Michael mit einemmal klar, daß der Kampf für ihn zum *Kreuzzug* geworden und daß er jetzt St. Michael geworden ist."

To which Chamberlain replied:

"daß es im tiefsten Grund der Krieg des Judentums und des ihm naheverwandten Amerikanertums um die Beherrschung der Welt ist . . . Es ist der Krieg der modernen mechanischen 'Zivilisation' gegen die uralte heilige ewig in Neugeburt befindliche 'Kultur' auserlesener Menschenrassen."[5]

Both of course knew of Wilson's casual remark of 1915, which the British had so bitterly resented, that "England is fighting our Fight."[6] Yet there was certainly no doubt where American sympathies really were. Besides, the United States could not ignore the economic risks they had taken in supporting the Allied powers. America's national interests demanded the prevention of a crushing military defeat of the Allied powers as well as the preservation of existing European power relations – but this argument also held true for the opposing side. Americans saw their expectations realized: the necessary economic and military means were, albeit slowly but effectively, mobilized. The victory of the Allied powers was but a matter of time. That the United States was unable to secure a just peace had been the result of forces beyond their control; it nevertheless generated a general disappointment. For America, the "New Order" for Europe was tinctured with too many destructive features. The United States, therefore, retreated from Europe and abandoned their newly discovered responsibilities.

To a large extent these developments were shaped by the explosive dynamics emanating from a revolutionizing Russia, which culminated in Lenin's Bolshevik coup d'état. Its tactical perfection, its organizational accomplishments, its ruthless realization, its hard-nosed pursuit of a peace policy in blatant disregard of all contrary considerations, and, finally, its world-encompassing revolutionary expansionism defied all rational understanding of bourgeois analysis and thinking. Yet its logical and flexible agility to plan, its straight-forward tactical approach to solve problems, and its ability to produce results – in all these characteristic features it discovered itself as the legitimate child of bourgeois rational thought. No wonder that Lenin's revolution soon became the much hated and feared, but admired blueprint for a successful, modern social revolution. And such it has remained right down to our times. Not only Marxists and believers in Lenin cherished this blueprint, but even historians of admittedly critical abilities subscribed to it.

Let me cite Eberhard Kolb, my esteemed colleague at Cologne, as a most respectable and surely unbiased witness. Kolb described the revolutionary events of November 1918 which spilled over from Russia, as a *"steckengebliebene Revolution,"* an "unfinished Revolution," because the movement had failed to thoroughly democratize all political and social structures. Moreover, so he added, a divided Social Democratic Party had lacked the stamina, *"der jungen Republik den Stempel prononciert sozialdemokratischer Staats- und Gesellschaftsvorstellungen aufzuprägen."*[7] It seems, however, to me that it is a rather too simple procedure, to consider only the Marxist-Leninist revolution as a *completed* revolution, and thus proclaim it the yardstick against which other revolutions are measured. After all, the majority of the Social Democratic Party considered itself to be a democratic party whose government represented all the people. The "Majority Social Democrats," therefore, viewed the revolutionary forces with considerable reserve because they were not only frightened by a civil war triggered by the Bolsheviks, but also by the continuation of the Allied blockade to starve Germany, for there was no help to be expected from Soviet Russia. To blame these politicians under these circumstances for sticking to their democratic ideals, as well as for a lack of revolutionary zeal and unscrupulous use of power, strikes me as a bit unreasonable! Even Lenin, who surely tolerated no opposition against priority of political domination, stooped to use, albeit for pragmatic reasons, the competence of pre-revolutionary elites when he thought it worthwhile for attaining Bolshevik goals, despite the fact that his power and position was much stronger than that of any German party at the time.

Let me finally ask which of the revolutions of modern times did not eventually get bogged down and lose its momentum, was blocked by counterrevolutionary forces, by the inbuilt dynamics of the revolutionary process itself, by a multitude of problems requiring immediate and urgent attention, not to speak of foreign, geopolitical, economic, ideological and other inhibiting factors? We need not even be too particular about the puzzling interaction of revolutionary forces and counterforces in order to realize how unsatisfactory it is to proclaim the Marxist-Leninist revolution a model for all other revolutions. Skillfully using the push it received from its stunning successes, from its supposedly successful fundamental social changes, and from its role as a paradigm for a communist revolution of the world – at the same time the capitalist system demonstrated its failure in the great economic collapse – Lenin's revolution and its offsprings in other countries were for two generations considered the blueprint for a successful dawn of the coming socialist millennium. Since then that glossy picture has received its scratches through news about unnecessary cruelties and killings, widespread starvation periods and serious supply shortages, and its all-pervading dishonesty as well as its political inflexibility and lack of administrative competence. In the light of glasnost and perestroika, and its effects on the image of Lenin's revolution, we have to radically question this traditional all-encompassing argument: should we not ask whether the period of World War I does not offer still other types of revolutions than those triggered by the American entry into the war and by Lenin's revolution in Russia? Is it not indeed likely that such questions might suggest a new over-all interpretation for the whole period?

How did, for example, artists, writers, and other intellectuals react to the horrors of the First World War, which after 1915 surpassed all previous known forms of mass-brutality and mass-killings while inventing ever new forms of dispatching people as it went on? Diaries, correspondences, and other writings offer numerous reflections to these atrocities, that I was unable to sample and analyze. Let me just indulge in a little spontaneous name-calling – which I will slightly bias in favor of Krefeld – to illustrate my point. Recall T. S. Eliot's *The Waste Land*, written in 1917 under the influence of Ezra Pound, as a bitter reaction to the murderous battle at the Somme, but published five years later. Remember Ernest Hemingway's novel *A Farewell to Arms* published in 1929, but based on Hemingway's own experiences in the war. And Erich Maria Remarque's *Im Westen nichts Neues*, published the same year, or Ernst Jünger's *Im Stahlgewitter*, which came out in 1920, two years before his *Krieg als inneres Erlebnis*. In the year 1917 Igor Stravinsky set Charles Ramuz' charming, yet cheeky *Geschichte vom Soldaten* to music. But expressionist paintings and writings probably offer the most direct reactions to the war. Although a number of these artists, like August Macke and Franz Marc, did not survive it, other artists' participation in the war was rather slight. I am thinking for instance of Heinrich Nauen or Heinrich Campendonk. To me the strongest reflections on the brutalities and cruelties of the war are conveyed by Otto Dix's "Totentanz anno 1917" and his many other etchings. Yet many other artists, like Käthe Kollwitz, Ernst Barlach, Max Beckmann, Max Ernst, and George Grosz, could also be cited for their reflections on the war. How far did all of these artists travel down the road from the disciplined sketching, crisp lines, and warm coloring of Cézanne to the demolition of clear lines in cubism and futurism, to the destruction of the concrete figure and the discovery of the abstract in the paintings of Wassily Kandinsky, from the homely fulsome vivacious persons of prewar paintings to the shadowy, horrid cry of bereavement in Edvard Munch's paintings!

It is almost impossible to find a general pattern in all of these reactions to the First World War. We finally stumble again into the methodological problems I have mentioned in the beginning. Let me once again quote Hermann Broch:

> was ist ein historisches Ereignis? was ist die historische Einheit? oder noch weiter gefaßt: was ist ein Ereignis überhaupt? welche Auslese ist erforderlich, damit Einzelfakten sich zur Einheit eines Ereignisses zusammenfügen?

If we focus on those reactions we have just mentioned, the general pattern could be baptized the "possibility to realize things" (*Machbarkeit der Sachen*), about which among others Hans Freyer in his *Theorie des gegenwärtigen Zeitalters* in 1955 talked.[8] With this label Freyer and I mean a thoroughly rationalized and mechanized environment that is hostile to life, kills all spontaneity, and suffocates all critical thinking. Such an environment – I am of course referring to the modern, highly organized industrial society – leaves humankind helpless and degrades people to objects. Men and women can react to such an environment only with anxiety the more so, the more perfect, the more efficient such an environment gets itself organized. Never was such organized efficiency more brutally realized and experienced than in the big battles of Verdun, in the Champagne, and in Flanders, where killing went hand in hand with a systematic destruction of the countryside, an unscrupulous sacrifice of *Menschenmaterial* was perfected with guns of hitherto unknown efficiency to kill, with tanks (Somme 1916), with lurid mass-produced weaponry designed to kill ever larger numbers of soldiers with smoother efficiency and effectiveness, with flame-throwers and other products of industrial mass production – what a strange "economy of scale"! Wilhelm Lamszus had already in 1912 anticipated this development:

It is as if the scythe of death was consigned to the rubbish heap, as if it became a machinist. . . . So be it; I've stood up to my neck in it. We will be by technologists, by machinists, transported from life to death. And as buttons and pins are fabricated in a large-scale operation, so are cripples and corpses.[9]

Indeed, one needs to imbibe quite a lot of Ernst Jünger's "heroic nihilism" (*heroischem Nihilismus*) to be able to recognize something other than naked cynicism against human life in these events, recognize something that draws on the contemporary reliance and confidence, that everything is possible, deduces its practicability, and justifies its legitimacy. Those cursed — or should I say blessed? — with large doses of sensibility and sensitivity, who survived the horrors of war, survived it with a broken heart and a barren soul while others suffered from these memories for the rest of their lives. Yet the more robust and stronger, while equally defending themselves against a rationalistic worldview, began after the War to invent heroic legends about the Great War. They thus helped to prevent others from drawing the necessary consequences from this war for our culture.

Although we are but at the beginning of raising new questions, I have reached the end of my argument. Of course I could go on for hours, yet for the best of all of us and for the sake of a joyous reception after this talk, let me conclude by phrasing the basic problem that has so insistently pushed itself onto the foreground during my work on this lecture: did the year 1917 experience any decisions of secular importance and significance? Did people at that time and since not rather remain tied and glued to old established concepts, models, ideologies, and cultural values, and thus lose the chance for a thorough new beginning? It is of course possible that Luther's *Verstocktheit* offers one key for a deeper understanding of the unproductiveness of this great and eventful period, this year 1917. Luther's term means a stubborn holding on to the belief that everything is possible, that everything can be done. It therefrom derives its ethical legitimacy. Thus America's impressive achievements in entering the World War I could only produce a "lost generation" and intellectual rejection. Russian revolutionaries experienced the fruitless fight for a new society in a similar vein; Kandinsky, Chagall, and Majakowsky soon distanced themselves from these efforts whose intellectual shallowness are so obvious today. Yet not only they, but Europeans in a narrower sense, too, did not find the path to a better and more human society.

A Note on Sources:

To burden my sketchy observations with a scholarly apparatus would be absurd. Therefore, I will not mention the many handbooks and scholarly books published on the subject. The following titles, which are of course but an arbitrary selection, are cited because I found reading them helpful and stimulating. This is especially true for the work of the British writer Paul Johnson, *Modern Times: The World from the Twenties to the Eighties* (New York, 1983). For the larger political context, cf. e.g. Heinz Gollwitzer, *Geschichte des weltpolitischen Denkens*, 2 vols. (Göttingen, 1972/1982), Karl Dietrich Bracher, *Die Krise Europas, 1917–1975*, – Propyläengeschichte Europas, vol. 6 (Frankfurt a.M., 1977), and *Zeit der Ideologien. Eine Geschichte des politischen Denkens im 20. Jahrhundert* (Stuttgart, 1982), as well as James Joll, *Die Ursprünge des ersten Weltkriegs* (Munich, 1988). There is much of value in Klaus Vondung, ed., *Kriegser- lebnis: Der Erste Weltkrieg in der literarischen Gestaltung und symbolischen Deutung der Nationen* (Göttingen, 1980), as well as in August Nitschke, Gerhard A. Ritter, Rüdiger vom Bruch, eds., *Jahrhundertwende: Der Auf- bruch in die Moderne, 1880–1930* (Reinbek near Hamburg, 1990). I found reading Modris Ekstein, *Tanz über Gräben: Die Geburt der Moderne und der Erste Weltkrieg* (Reinbek near Hamburg, 1990) (original Ameri- can edition: *Rites of Spring. The Great War and the Birth of the Modern Age* [1989]) a disappointing experience. On the nations involved in World War I and their relations with each other, cf. Henry F. May, *The End of American Innocence: A Study of the First Years of Our Own Time 1912–1917* (New York, 1959), and with stronger emphasis on the war as a radical turning point Stuart I. Rochester, *American Liberal Disillusionment in the Wake of World War I* (University Park, PA, 1977), Neil A. Wynn, *From Progressivism to Prosperity: World War I and American Society* (New York/London, 1986), David M. Kennedy, *Over Here: The First World War and American Society* (New York/Oxford, 1980). The European scene and Europe's international relations are analysed for example by Peter Graf von Kielmansegg, *Deutschland und der Erste Weltkrieg* (Stuttgart, 2nd ed., 1980), by Eberhard Kolb, *Die Weimarer Republik*, – Oldenbourg Grundriß der Geschichte, vol. 16 (München/Wien, 2nd ed., 1988), N. Gordon Levin, Jr., *Woodrow Wilson and World Politics: America's Response to War and Revolution* (New York, 1968), John Lewis Gaddis, *Russia, the Soviet Union and the United States: An Interpretative His- tory* (New York, 2nd ed., 1990), Dietrich Geyer, *Die Russische Revolu- tion. Historische Probleme und Perspektiven*, – Kleine Vandenhoeck-Reihe, 1433 (Göttingen, 4th ed., 1985), Helmut Altrichter, *Staat und Revolution in Sowjetrußland 1917–1922/23*, – Erträge der Forschung, vol. 148 (Darmstadt, 1981), and Raymond Poidevin, Jacques Bariéty, *Frankreich und Deutschland. Die Geschichte ihrer Beziehungen, 1815–1975* (München, 1982).

Notes to Chaper 22

1. Cf. Emil Belzner, *Die Fahrt in die Revolution, oder Jene Reise. Ade-mémoire* (Munich, 1969).

2. Cf. Geoffrey Barraclough, "Europa, Amerika und Rußland in Vorstellung und Denken des 19. Jahrhunderts," *Historische Zeitschrift*, vol. 203 (1966), 280–315, and Heinz Gollwitzer, *Geschichte des weltpolitischen Denkens*, 2 vols. (Göttingen, 1972–1982).

3. Cf. Friedrich Meinecke, *Autobiographische Schriften*, ed. Eberhard Kessel, *Werke*, vol. 8 (Stuttgart, 1969), 276ff, quote on 312.

4. Cf. Erwin Hölzle, "Die amerikanische und die bolschewistische Weltrevolution," in *Weltwende 1917: Monarchie – Weltrevolution – Demokratie*, ed. Hellmuth Rössler (Göttingen, 1965), 169–184, and Ernst Nolte, *Deutschland und der Kalte Krieg* (Munich, 1974).

5. Houston Steward Chamberlain, *Briefwechsel 1882–1924 und Briefwechsel mit Kaiser Wilhelm II.*, vol. 2, ed. P. Pretzsch (Munich, 1928), 250ff. I am grateful to John Röhl for drawing my attention to this letter on 8 September 1989.

6. Joseph R. Conlin, *The Morrow Book of Quotations in American History* (New York, 1984), 320.

7. Eberhard Kolb, "1918/1919: Die steckengebliebene Revolution," in *Wendepunkte deutscher Geschichte 1848–1945*, ed. Carola Stern, Heinrich A. Winkler (Frankfurt a. M., 1979), 87–109, quotation on 105.

8. Hans Freyer, *Theorie des gegenwärtigen Zeitalters* (Stuttgart, 1955), esp. 15ff.

9. Quoted in *Kriegserlebnis. Der Erste Weltkrieg in der literarischen Gestaltung und symbolischen Deutung der Nationen*, ed. Klaus Vondung (Göttingen, 1980), 101.

Notes On Contributors

LLOYD E. AMBROSIUS, Professor of History at the University of Lincoln-Nebraska.

ERICH ANGERMANN, Professor Emeritus of Anglo-American History at the University of Cologne.

MICHAEL BEHNEN, Professor of Modern and Contemporary History at the University of Göttingen.

MANFRED BERG, Research Fellow at the German Historical Institute, Washington, DC.

EDWARD P. CRAPOL, Professor of History at the College of William and Mary, Williamsburg, Virginia.

REINHARD R. DOERRIES, Professor of Foreign Studies in the Faculty of Economics and Social Science at the University of Erlangen-Nürnberg.

GERALD D. FELDMAN, Professor of History at the University of California, Berkeley.

RAGNHILD FIEBIG-VON HASE, Institute of Anglo-American History at the University of Cologne.

PAUL FINKELMAN, Associate Professor of History at Virginia Polytechnic Institute and State University, Blacksburg.

NORBERT FINZSCH, Professor of Modern History at the University of Hamburg.

LAURA GARCÉS, Washington, DC.

LLYOD C. GARDNER, Charles and Mary Beard Professor of History at Rutgers University, New Brunswick, New Jersey.

ELISABETH GLASER-SCHMIDT, Research Fellow at the German Historical Institute, Washington, DC.

ROBERT E. HANNIGAN, Senior Lecturer in History at Suffolk University, Boston.

GERD HARDACH, Professor of Economic History at the University of Marburg.

CARL-LUDWIG HOLTFRERICH, Professor of Economic History at John F. Kennedy Institute for North American Studies of the Free University Berlin.

PETER KRÜGER, Professor of Modern History at the University of Marburg.

JOAN HOFF-WILSON, Professor of History at the University of Indiana, Bloomington.

DAVID M. KENNEDY, William Robertson Coe Professor of History and American Studies at Stanford University.

RAIMUND LAMMERSDORF, Assistant Professor at the John F. Kennedy Institute for North American Studies of the Free University Berlin.

HARTMUT LEHMANN, Director, German Historical Institute, Washington, DC.

WERNER LINK, Professor of Political Science at the University of Cologne.

WOLFGANG J. MOMMSEN, Professor of History at the University of Düsseldorf.

JÖRG NAGLER, Research Fellow at the German Historical Institute, Washington DC, and Visiting Professor at the University of Maryland, College Park.

ELLIOTT SHORE, Director of the Historical Studies – Social Science Library at the Institute of Advanced Studies, Princeton.

HANS-JÜRGEN SCHRÖDER, Professor of Contemporary History at the University of Giessen.

STEPHEN A. SCHUKER, currently William V. Corcoran Professor in Modern European History at the University of Virginia, Charlottesville.

KLAUS SCHWABE, Professor of American History at the Technical University Aachen.

GEORGES-HENRY SOUTOU, Professor of Contemporary History at the University of Paris-Sorbonne.

MARIA STURM, Institute of Anglo-American History at the University of Cologne.

FRANK TROMMLER, Professor of German and Comparative Literature at the University of Pennsylvania, Philadelphia.

HERMANN WELLENREUTHER, Professor of History at the University of Göttingen.

Select Bibliography

Compiled by Elisabeth Laube

The bibliography is not limited to a strictly bilateral approach for the interpretation of German-American relations. It also includes references to works that help to better understand both the emergence of German-American conflicts during the early 20th century and the origins of German-American cooperation during the 1920s.

Adams, Henry M. "Recall of the Attachés. An Episode in German-American Relations, December 1915," *Historische Mitteilungen* 2 (1989): 61–77.

Ambrosius, Lloyd E. "Wilson, the Republicans, and French Security after World War I," *Journal of American History* 59 (1972): 341–352.

Ambrosius, Lloyd E. "Wilson, Clemenceau and the German Problem at the Paris Peace Conference of 1919," *Rocky Mountain Social Science Journal* 12 (1975): 69–79.

Ambrosius, Lloyd E. "The Orthodoxy of Revisionism: Woodrow Wilson and the New Left," *Diplomatic History* 1 (1977): 199–214.

Ambrosius, Lloyd E. "Secret German-American Negotiations during the Paris Peace Conference," *Amerikastudien/American Studies* 24 (1979): 288–309.

Ambrosius, Lloyd E. "Ethnic Politics and German-American Relations after World War I: The Fight over the Versailles Treaty in the United States," in Hans L. Trefousse (ed.), *Germany and America: Essays on Problems of International Relations and Immigration* (New York, 1980), 29–40.

Ambrosius, Lloyd E. "Woodrow Wilson and the Quest for Orderly Progress," in Norman A. Graebner, ed., *Traditions and Values: American Diplomacy, 1865–1945* (Lanham, MD, 1985).

Ambrosius, Lloyd E. "Die deutsch-amerikanischen Beziehungen von Versailles bis zur Machtergreifung," in Detlef Junker, ed., *Deutschland und die USA, 1890–1985* (Heidelberg, 1985), 17–26.

Ambrosius, Lloyd E. *Woodrow Wilson and the American Diplomatic Tradition: The Treaty Fight in Perspective* (Cambridge, 1987).

Ambrosius, Lloyd E. *Wilsonian Statecraft: Theory and Practice of Liberal Internationalism during World War I* (Wilmington, DE, 1991).

Ambrosius, Lloyd E. "Wilsonian Self-Determination," *Diplomatic History* 16 (1992): 141–148.

Angermann, Erich. "Ein Wendepunkt in der Geschichte der Monroe-Doktrin und der deutsch-amerikanischen Beziehungen: Die Venezuelakrise von 1902/03 im Spiegel der amerikanischen Tagespresse," *Jahrbuch für Amerikastudien* 3 (1958): 22–58.

Anderson, Stuart. *Race and Rapprochement: Anglo-Saxonism and Anglo-American Relations, 1895–1904* (East Brunswick, NJ, 1968).

App, Austin J. "German-Americans and Wilson's Peace-Making," *Social Justice Review* 56, no. 3 (1963): 93–96, 107; no. 4, 126–130; no.5, 166–171.

Artaud, Denise. "Die Hintergründe der Ruhrbesetzung 1923. Das Problem der interalliierten Schulden," *Vierteljahrshefte für Zeitgeschichte* 27 (1979): 241–259.

Aubitz, Shawn/Gail F. Stern. "Ethnic Images in World War I Posters," *Journal of American Culture* 9, no. 4 (1986): 83–98.

Bade, Klaus J. "Emigration to the United States and Continental Immigration to Germany in the Late Nineteenth and Early Twentieth Centuries," *Central European History* 13 (1980): 348–377.

Baecker, Thomas. *Die deutsche Mexikopolitik 1913/14* (Berlin, 1971).

Baecker, Thomas. "Blau gegen Schwarz. Der amerikanische Kriegsplan von 1913 für einen deutsch-amerikanischen Krieg," *Marine-Rundschau* 69 (1972): 347–360.

Baecker, Thomas. "Das deutsche Feindbild in der amerikanischen Marine 1900–1914," *Marine-Rundschau* 70 (1973): 65–84.

Baecker, Thomas. "Deutschland im karibischen Raum im Spiegel amerikanischer Akten (1898–1914)," *Jahrbuch für Amerikastudien* 19 (1974): 167–237.

Baecker, Thomas. *The Lusitania Disaster. An Episode in Modern Warfare and Diplomacy* (New York, 1975).

Baecker, Thomas. "Mahan über Deutschland," *Marine-Rundschau* 73 (1976): 10–19; 86–102.

Barraclough, Geoffry. "Europa, Amerika und Rußland in Vorstellung und Denken des 19. Jahrhunderts," *Historische Zeitschrift* 203 (1966): 280–315.

Baumgarten, Otto. *Das Echo der alldeutschen Gefahr in Amerika* (Jena, 1917).

Beale, Howard Kennedy. "Theodore Roosevelt, Wilhelm II und die deutsch-amerikanischen Beziehungen," *Die Welt als Geschichte* 15 (1955): 155–187.

Beale, Howard. *Theodore Roosevelt and the Rise of America to World Power*, 2nd. ed. (Baltimore, MD, 1962).

Beck, Earl R. *Germany Rediscovers America* (Tallahassee, FL, 1968).

Berg, Manfred. *Gustav Stresemann und die Vereinigten Staaten von Amerika. Weltwirtschaftliche Verflechtung und Revisionspolitik 1907–1929* (Baden-Baden, 1990).

Berg, Peter. *Deutschland und Amerika 1918–1929. Über das deutsche Amerikabild der zwanziger Jahre* (Lübeck, 1963).

Berghahn, Volker R. *Der Tirpitz-Plan. Genesis und Verfall einer innenpolitischen Krisenstrategie unter Wilhelm II.* (Düsseldorf, 1971).

Berghahn, Volker R. *Rüstung und Machtpolitik. Zur Anatomie des "kalten Krieges" vor 1914* (Düsseldorf, 1973).

Berghahn, Volker R. *Germany and the Approach of War in 1914* (London, 1973).

Bergsträsser, Arnold. "Zum Problem der sogenannten Amerikanisierung Deutschlands," *Jahrbuch für Amerikastudien* 8 (1963): 13–23.

Bernstein, Barton J./Franklin A. Leib. "Progressive Republican Senators and Imperialism, 1898–1916," *Mid-America* 50 (1968): 163–205.

Bernstorff, Graf Johann-Heinrich. *Deutschland und Amerika. Erinnerungen aus dem fünfjährigen Kriege* (Berlin, 1920).

Bingham, Hiram. *The Monroe Doctrine. An Obsolete Shibboleth* (New Haven, CT, 1913).

Birnbaum, Karl E. *Peace Moves and U-Boat Warfare: A Study of Imperial Germany's Policy towards the United States, April 18, 1916 – January 9, 1917* (Hamden, CT, 1970).

Blaich, Fritz. *Amerikanische Firmen in Deutschland, 1890–1918. US-Direktinvestitionen im deutschen Maschinenbau* (Wiesbaden, 1984).

Blake, Nelson M. "Ambassadors to the Court of Theodore Roosevelt," *American Heritage* 7, no. 2 (1956): 20–25; 96–99.

Bonadio, Felice A. "The Failure of German Propaganda in the United States, 1914–1917," *Mid-America* 41 (1959): 40–57.

Bourne, Kenneth. *Britain and the Balance of Power in North America, 1815–1908* (Berkeley, CA, 1976).

Braeman, John. "American Foreign Policy in the Age of Normalcy: Three Historiographical Traditions," *Amerikastudien/American Studies* 26 (1981): 125–158.

Bridges, Lamar W. "Zimmermann Telegram: Reactions of Southern, Southwestern Newspapers," *Journalism Quarterly* 46 (1969): 81–86.

Brocke, Bernhard vom. "Der deutsch-amerikanische Professorenaustausch. Preußische Wissenschaftspolitik, internationale Wirtschaftsbeziehungen und die Anfänge einer deutschen auswärtigen Kulturpolitik vor dem Ersten Weltkrieg," *Zeitschrift für Kulturaustausch* 31 (1981): 128–182.

Brooks, Sidney. *American Aid to Germany, 1918–1925* (New York, 1943).

Buckingham, Peter H. *International Normalcy. The Open Door with the Former Central Powers, 1921–29* (Wilmington, DE, 1983).

Burchell, R.A. "Did the Irish and German Voters Desert the Democrats in 1920? A Tentative Statistical Answer," *Journal of American Studies* 6 (1972): 153–164.

Burner, David. "Brakeup of the Wilson Coalition of 1916," *Mid-America* 45 (1963): 18–35.

Burnham, Walter Dean. "Political Immunization and Political Confessionalism: The United States and Weimar Germany," *Journal of Interdisciplinary History* 3 (1972): 1–30.

Calhoun, Frederick S. *Power and Principle: Armed Intervention in Wilsonian Foreign Policy* (Kent, OH, 1986).

Calleo, David P. *The German Problem Reconsidered. Germany and the World Order, 1871 to the Present* (Cambridge, 1978).

Campbell, A.E. *Britain and the United States, 1895–1903* (London, 1960).

Campbell, Charles S. *Anglo-American Understanding, 1898–1903* (Baltimore, MD, 1957).

Campbell, Charles S. *From Revolution to Rapprochement. The United States and Great Britain, 1783–1900* (New York, 1974).

Challener, Richard. *Admirals, Generals, and American Foreign Politics, 1898–1914* (Princeton, NJ, 1973).

Charles, Heinrich. *The Commercial Relations between Germany and the United States* (New York, 1907).

Child, James Clifton. "German-American Attempts to Prevent the Exportation of Munitions of War, 1914–1915," *Mississippi Valley Historical Review* 25 (1938): 351–368.

Child, James Clifton. *German-Americans in Politics 1914–1917* (New York, 1939).

Clements, Kendrick A. *William Jennings Bryan: Missionary Isolationist* (Knoxville, TN, 1982).

Clement, Wilhelm. "Die Monroedoktrin und die deutsch-amerikanischen Beziehungen im Zeitalter des Imperialismus," *Jahrbuch für Amerikastudien* 1 (1956): 153–167.

Clifford, John. "Admiral Dewey and the Germans, 1903: A New Perspective," *Mid-America* 49 (1967): 214–220.

Cohen, Warren I., ed., *Intervention 1917: Why America Fought* (Boston, 1966).

Cohen, Warren I. *The American Revisionists: The Lesson of Intervention in World War I* (Chicago, 1967).

Cooper, John Milton. *The Vanity of Power: American Isolationism and the First World War, 1914–1917* (Westport, CT, 1969).

Costigliola, Frank C. "The United States and the Reconstruction of Germany in the 1920s," *Business History Review* 50 (1976/77): 477–502.

Costigliola, Frank C. *Awkward Dominion. American Political, Economic, and Cultural Relations with Europe, 1919–1933* (Ithaca, NY, 1984).

Craig, Gordon A. "Transatlantische Perspektiven," in Walter Hofer, ed., *Europa und die Einheit Deutschlands. Eine Bilanz nach 100 Jahren* (Cologne, 1970), 285–303.

Crapol, Edward P./Howard Schonberger. "The Shift to Global Expansion, 1865–1900," in William A. Williams, ed., *From Colony to Empire. Essays in the History of American Foreign Relations* (New York, 1972), 135–202.

Crapol, Edward P. *America for Americans: Economic Nationalism and Anglophobia in the Late Nineteenth Century* (Westport, CT, 1973).

Cuddy, Edward. "Pro-Germanism and American Catholicism, 1914–1917," *Catholic Historical Review* 54 (1968): 427–454.

Davis, Gerald H. *The Diplomatic Relations between the United States and Austria-Hungary, 1913–1917* (Diss. Vanderbilt Univ., 1959).

Davis, Calvin DeArmond. *The United States and the Second Hague Peace Conference. American Diplomacy and International Organization 1899–1914* (Durham, NC, 1975).

Davis, Gerald H. "The 'Ancona' Affair: A Case of Preventive Diplomacy," *Journal of Modern History* 38 (1966): 267–277.

Dehio, Ludwig. *Deutschland und die Weltpolitik im 20. Jahrhundert* (Wien, 1955).

Deike, Gertrud. *Das Amerikabild der deutschen öffentlichen Meinung 1898–1914* (Diss. Hamburg, 1956).

Dobbert, G.A. "German-Americans Between New and Old Fatherland, 1870–1914," *American Quarterly* 19 (1967): 663–680.

Doerries, Reinhard R. "Amerikanische Außenpolitik im Karibischen Raum vor dem Ersten Weltkrieg," *Jahrbuch für Amerikastudien* 18 (1973): 62–77.

Doerries, Reinhard R. "Imperial Berlin and Washington: New Light on Germany's Foreign Policy and America's Entry into World War I," *Central European History* 11 (1978): 23–49.

Doerries, Reinhard R. "The Politics of Irresponsibility: Imperial Germany's Defiance of United States Neutrality during World War I," in Hans L. Trefousse, ed., *Germany and America: Essays on Problems of International Relations and Immigration* (New York, 1980), 3–20.

Doerries, Reinhard R. "Empire and Republic: German-American Relations Before 1917," in Trommler/McVeigh, *America and the Germans*, vol. 2, 3–17.

Doerries, Reinhard R. *Washington-Berlin 1908/17. Die Tätigkeit des Botschafters Johann Heinrich Graf von Bernstorff in Washington vor dem Eintritt der Vereinigten Staaten von Amerika in den Ersten Weltkrieg* (Düsseldorf, 1975); revised edition: *Imperial Challenge. Ambassador Count Bernstorff and German-American Relations, 1908–1917* (Chapel Hill, NC, 1989).

Duff, John B. "German-Americans and the Peace, 1918–1920," *American Jewish History Quarterly* 59 (1970): 424–444.

Dülffer, Jost. *Regeln gegen den Krieg? Die Haager Friedenskonferenzen von 1899–1907 in der internationalen Politik* (Berlin, 1981).

Eichhoff, Jürgen. "The German Language in America," in Trommler/McVeigh, *America and the Gemans*, vol. 1, 223–240.

Epstein, Fritz T. "Germany and the United States: Basic Patterns of Conflict and Understanding," in George L. Anderson, ed., *Issues and Conflicts: Studies in Twentieth Century American Diplomacy* (Lawrence, KS, 1959).

Esslinger, Dean R. "American, German and Irish Attitudes toward Neutrality, 1914–1917," *Catholic Historical Review* 53 (1967): 194–216.

Esthus, Raymond A. "The Changing Concept of the Open Door Policy, 1899–1910," *Mississippi Valley Historical Review* 46 (1959): 435–454.

Esthus, Raymond A. *Theodore Roosevelt and International Rivalries* (Waltham, MA, 1970).

Falk, Karen. "Public Opinion in Wisconsin during Wolrd War I," *Wisconsin Magazine of History* 25 (1942): 389–407.

Feldman, Gerald D. *Army, Industry and Labor in Germany, 1914–1918* (Princeton, NJ, 1966).

Feldman, Gerald D. *Iron and Steel in the German Inflation, 1916–1923* (Princeton, NJ, 1977).

Feldman, Gerald D. *The Great Disorder: Politics and Society in the German Inflation, 1914–1924* (Oxford, 1991).

Fernandez, Ronald. "Getting Germans to Fight Germans: The Americanizers of World War I," *Journal of Ethic Studies* 9 (1981): 53–68.

Fiebig-von Hase, Ragnhild. *Lateinamerika als Konfliktherd der deutsch-amerikanischen Beziehungen, 1890–1903*, 2 vols.(Göttingen, 1986).

Fiebig-von Hase, Ragnhild. "Die deutsch-amerikanischen Wirtschaftsbeziehungen 1890–1914 im Zeichen von Protektionismus und internationaler Integration," *Amerikastudien/American Studies* 33 (1988): 329–357.

Fiebig-von Hase, Ragnhild. "Amerikanische Friedensbemühungen in Europa, 1905–1914," in *Liberalitas. Festschrift für Erich Angermann zum 65. Geburtstag*, ed. by Norbert Finzsch and Hermann Wellenreuther, with the assistance of Manfred F. Boemeke and Marie-Luise Frings (Stuttgart, 1992), 285–318.

Fischer, Fritz. *Germany's Aims in the First World War* (New York, 1967).

Fischer, Fritz. *War of Illusions: German Policies from 1911 to 1914* (Boston, MA, 1976)

Fisk, George M. "German-American 'most-favored nations' Relations," *Journal of Political Economy* 2 (1903): 220–236.

Fisk, George M. "German-American Diplomatic and Commercial Relations. Historically Considered," *American Monthly* 25 (1902): 323–328.

Forndran, Erhard. "Kontinuitäten und Veränderungen in den transatlantischen Beziehungen seit 1918," in Manfred Knapp, ed., *Transatlantische Beziehungen. Die USA und Europa zwischen gemeinsamen Interessen und Konflikt* (Stuttgart, 1990), 9–36.

Forndran, Erhard. *Die Vereinigten Staaten von Amerika und Europa: Erfahrungen und Perspektiven transatlantischer Beziehungen seit dem Ersten Weltkrieg* (Baden-Baden 1991).

Forstmeier, Friedrich. "Deutsche Invasionspläne gegen die USA um 1900," *Marine-Rundschau* 58 (1971): 344–351.

Fowler, James H. "Tar and Feather Patriotism: The Suppression of Dissent in Oklahoma during World War I," *Chronicles of Oklahoma* 61 (1978): 409–430.

Fraenkel, Ernst. "Das deutsche Wilsonbild," *Jahrbuch für Amerikastudien* 5 (1960): 66–120.

Freytag, Dirk. *Die Vereinigten Staaten auf dem Weg zur Intervention. Studien zur amerikanischen Außenpolitik 1910–14* (Heidelberg, 1971).

Friedberg, Aaron L. *The Weary Titan. Britain and the Experience of Relative Decline, 1895–1905* (Princeton, NJ, 1988).

Garcés, Laura. *La Mondialisation de la Doctrine Monroe à l'Ere Wilsonienne* (Lausanne, 1988).

Gardner, Lloyd C. "American Foreign Policy, 1900–1921: A Second Look at the Realist Critique of American Diplomacy," in Barton J. Bernstein, ed., *Towards a New Past: Dissenting Essays in American History* (New York, 1969).

Gardner, Lloyd C., ed., *Wilson and Revolutions: 1913–1921* (Philadelphia, PA, 1976).

Gardner, Lloyd C. "Woodrow Wilson and the Mexican Revolution," in Arthur S. Link, ed., *Woodrow Wilson and a Revolutionary World, 1913–1921* (Chapel Hill, NC, 1982), 3–48.

Gardner, Lloyd C. *A Covenant with Power: America and World Order from Wilson to Reagan* (New York, 1984).

Gardner, Lloyd C. *Safe for Democracy: The Anglo-American Response to Revolution, 1913–1923* (New York, 1984).

Gatzke, Hans W. "The United States and Germany on the Eve of World War

I," in Imanuel Geiss/Bernd-Jürgen Wendt, eds., *Deutschland in der Weltpolitik des 19. und 20. Jahrhunderts* (Düsseldorf, 1973), 271–286.

Gatzke, Hans W. *Germany and the United States. A "Special Relationship?"* (Cambridge, MA, 1980).

Geiss, Imanuel. *German Foreign Policy, 1871–1916* (Boston, MA, 1976).

Gerard, James W. *My Four Years in Germany* (New York, 1917).

Gerhards, Josef Werner. *Theodore Roosevelt im Urteil der deutschen öffentlichen Meinung 1898–1914* (Diss. Mainz, 1962).

Gescher, Dieter Bruno. *Die Vereinigten Staaten von Nordamerika und die Reparationen 1920–1924. Eine Untersuchung der Reparationsfrage auf der Grundlage amerikanischer Akten* (Bonn, 1956).

Gilderhus, Mark T. *Pan American Visions: Woodrow Wilson in the Western Hemisphere, 1913–1921* (Tuscon, AZ, 1986).

Glaser-Schmidt, Elisabeth. "Von Versailles nach Berlin: Überlegungen zur Neugestaltung der deutsch-amerikanischen Beziehungen in der Ära Harding," in *Liberalitas. Festschrift für Erich Angermann zum 65. Geburtstag,* ed. by Norbert Finzsch and Hermann Wellenreuther, with the assistance of Manfred F. Boemeke and Marie-Luise Frings (Stuttgart, 1992), 319–342.

Glasrud, Clarence A., ed., *A Heritage Deferred: The German-Americans in Minnesota* (Moorhead, MI, 1981).

Goldberger, Ludwig Max. *Das Land der unbegrenzten Möglichkeiten: Beobachtungen über das Wirtschaftsleben der Vereinigten Staaten von Amerika* (Berlin, 1903).

Goldberger, Ludwig Max. "Die amerikanische Gefahr," *Preußische Jahrbücher* 120 (1905): 1–33.

Gottschall, Terrell Dean. *Germany and the Spanish-American War: A Case Study of Navalism and Imperialism, 1898* (Diss. Washington State University, 1981).

Gottwald, Robert. *Die deutsch-amerikanischen Beziehungen in der Ära Stresemann* (Berlin, 1965).

Grupp, Peter. *Deutsche Außenpolitik im Schatten von Versailles, 1918–1920* (Paderborn, 1987).

Hale, William H. "Thus Spoke the Kaiser: The Lost Interview which Solves an International Mystery," *Atlantic Monthly* 153 (1934): 513–523, 696–705.

Hammerstein, Notker. *Deutschland und die Vereinigten Staaten von Amerika im Spiegel der führenden politischen Presse Deutschlands, 1898–1906* (Diss. Frankfurt/M., 1956).

Hannigan, Robert E. "Reciprocity 1911: Continentalism and American Weltpolitik," *Diplomatic History* 4 (1980): 1–18.

Hardach, Gerd. *Weltmarktorientierung und relative Stagnation. Währungspolitik in Deutschland 1924–1931* (Berlin, 1976).

Hardach, Gerd. *The First World War, 1914–1918* (Berkeley, CA, 1977).

Haupts, Leo. *Deutsche Friedenspolitik 1918–19* (Düsseldorf, 1976).

Heideking, Jürgen. *Aeropag der Diplomaten. Die Pariser Botschafterkonferenz der alliierten Hauptmächte und die Probleme der europäischen Politik 1920–1931* (Husum, 1979).

Heinemann, Ulrich. *Die verdrängte Niederlage. Politische Öffentlichkeit und Kriegsschuldfrage in der Weimarer Republik* (Göttingen, 1983).

Hendrickson, Embert J. "Roosevelt's Second Venezuelan Controversy," *Hispanic American Historical Review* 50 (1970): 482–498.

Herwig, Holger H./David F. Trask. "Naval Operation Plans between Germany and the United States of America. 1898–1913," *Militärgeschichtliche Mitteilungen* no. 2 (1970): 1–32.

Herwig, Holger H. *Politics and Frustration: The United States in German Naval Planning, 1889–1941* (Boston, 1976).

Herwig, Holger H. "German Imperialism and South America Before the First World War: The Venezuelan Case 1902/03," in Rußland-Deutschland-Amerika. Festschrift für Fritz T. Epstein zum 80. Geburtstag, ed. by Alexander Fischer et al.(Wiesbaden, 1978), 117–130.

Herwig, Holger/David M. Trask, "Naval Operations Plans between Germany and the USA, 1898–1913: A Study of Strategic Planning in the Age of Imperialism," in Paul M. Kennedy, ed., *War Plans and the Great Powers 1880–1914* (Boston, 1979).

Hillgruber, Andreas. *Deutschlands Rolle in der Vorgeschichte der beiden Weltkriege. Die deutsche Frage in der Welt* (Göttingen, 1967).

Hirsch, Felix. "Stresemann, Ballin und die Vereinigten Staaten," *Vierteljahrshefte für Zeitgeschichte* 3 (1955): 20–35.

Hogan, Michael J. *Informal Entente: The Private Structure of Cooperation in Anglo-American Economic Diplomacy, 1918–1928* (Columbia, MO, 1977).

Holsinger M. Paul. "The Oregon School Bill Controversy, 1922–1925," *Pacific Historical Review* 37 (1968): 327–341.

Holtfrerich, Carl-Ludwig. "Amerikanischer Kapitalexport und Wiederaufbau der deutschen Wirtschaft 1919–23 im Vergleich zu 1924–29," *Vierteljahrschrift für Sozial- und Wirtschaftsgeschichte* 64 (1977): 497–529.

Holtfrerich, Carl-Ludwig. *Die deutsche Inflation, 1914–1923. Ursachen und Folgen in internationaler Perspektive* (Berlin, 1980).

Hunt, Michael H. *Ideology and U.S. Foreign Policy* (New Haven, CT, 1987).

Jäger, Wolfgang. *Historische Forschung und politische Kultur in Deutschland. Die Debatte 1914–1980 über den Ausbruch des Ersten Weltkrieges* (Göttingen, 1984).

Joll, James. *The Origins of the First World War* (New York, 1984).

Jonas, Manfred. "Mutualism in the Relations between the United States and the Early Weimar Republic," in Hans L. Trefousse, ed., *Germany and America: Essays on Problems of International Relations and Immigration* (New York, 1980), 41–53.

Jonas, Manfred. *The United States and Germany. A Diplomatic History* (Ithaca, NY, 1984).

Jonas, Manfred. "Deutschland und die USA im Kaiserreich 1890–1918," in Detlef Junker, ed., *Deutschland und die USA, 1890–1985* (Heidelberg, 1985), 4–16.

Jones, John Price. *The German Secret Service in America 1914–1918* (Boston, 1918).

Junker, Detlef, ed., *Deutschland und die USA, 1890–1985* (Heidelberg, 1985).

Kabisch, Thomas R. *Deutsches Kapital in den USA. Von der Reichsgründung bis zur Sequestierung (1917) und Freigabe* (Stuttgart, 1982).

Karl, Barry D. *The Uneasy State: The United States from 1915 to 1945* (Chicago, 1983).

Katz, Friedrich. *The Secret War in Mexico: Europe, the United States, and the Mexican Revolution* (Chicago, 1981).

Kaufmann, Burton I. *Efficiency and Expansion. Foreign Trade Organization in the Wilson Administration 1913–1921* (Westport, CT, 1974).

Keim, Jeanette. *Forty Years of German-American Political Relations* (Philadelphia, PA, 1919).

Kennedy, David M. *Over Here: The First World War and American Society* (New York, 1980).

Kennedy, Paul. *The Samoan Tangle: A Study in Anglo-German-American Relations, 1878–1900* (New York, 1974).

Kennedy, Paul. *The Rise of the Anglo-German Antagonism, 1860–1914* (London, 1980).

Kennedy, Paul. "The Kaiser and German Weltpolitik: Reflections on Wilhelm II's Place in the Making of German Foreign Policy," in John C. Röhl/N. Sombart, eds., *Kaiser Wilhelm II: New Interpretations* (New York, 1982).

Kennedy, Paul. "The Tradition of Appeasement in British Foreign Policy, 1865–1939," in Paul Kennedy, *Strategy and Diplomacy, 1870–1945. Eight Studies* (London, 1983).

Kennedy, Paul. "British and German Reactions to the Rise of American Power," in Roger J. Bullen et al., eds., *Ideas into Politics: Aspects of European History, 1880–1950* (London, 1984), 15–24.

Kennedy, Paul. *The Rise and Fall of the Great Powers: Economic Change and Military Conflict from 1500 to 2000* (New York, 1987).

Kerr, Thomas J. "German-Americans and Neutrality in the 1916 Elections," *Mid-America* 43 (1961): 95–105.

Koehane, Robert O./Joseph S. Nye. *Power and Interdependence*, 2nd ed. (Glenview, IL, 1989).

Kraus, Herbert. *Die Monroedoktrin in ihren Beziehungen zur amerikanischen Diplomatie und zum Völkerrecht* (Berlin, 1913).

Kreider, John Kenneth. *Diplomatic Relations between Germany and the United States 1906–1913* (Diss. Univ. of Pennsylvania, 1969).

Krüger, Peter. *Deutschland und die Reparationen 1918/19* (Stuttgart, 1973).

Krüger, Peter. "Friedenssicherung und deutsche Revisionspolitik. Die deutsche Außenpolitik und die Verhandlungen über den Kellogg-Pakt," *Vierteljahrshefte für Zeitgeschichte* 22 (1974): 227–257.

Krüger, Peter. *Die Außenpolitik der Republik von Weimar* (Darmstadt, 1985).

Krüger, Peter. *Versailles: Deutsche Außenpolitik zwischen Revisionismus und Friedenssicherung* (München, 1986).

Krüger, Peter. "Zwei Epochen: Erfolg und Mißerfolg amerikanischer Einwirkung auf den Verfassungswandel in Deutschland nach dem Ersten und Zweiten Weltkrieg," in *Wandel und Kontinuum. Festschrift für Walter Falk zum*

65. Geburtstag, ed. by Helmut Bernsmeier/Hans-Peter Ziegler (Frankfurt/ M., 1992), 295–322.

Kunz-Lack, Ilse. *Die deutsch-amerikanischen Beziehungen 1890–1914* (Stuttgart, 1935).

LaFeber, Walter. *The New Empire. An Interpretation of American Expansion, 1860–1898* (Ithaca, NY, 1963).

LaFeber, Walter. *The American Age: United States Foreign Policy at Home and Abroad since 1750* (New York, 1989).

Leffler, Melvyn P. "Political Isolationism, Economic Expansionism, or Diplomatic Realism? American Policy toward Western Europe, 1921–1933," *Perspectives in American History* 8 (1974): 413–468.

Leffler, Melvyn P. *The Elusive Quest: America's Pursuit of European Stability and French Security 1919–1933* (Chapel Hill, NC, 1979).

Levin, N. Gordon. *Woodrow Wilson and World Politics. America's Response to War and Revolution* (New York, 1968).

Leussner, Hermann. *Ein Jahrzehnt deutsch-amerikanischer Politik, 1897–1906* (München, 1928).

Link, Arthur S. *Wilson the Diplomatist: A Look at His Major Foreign Policies* (Chicago, IL, 1965).

Link, Werner. "Die Außenpolitik der USA 1919–1933. Quellen und neue amerikanische Literatur," *Neue Politische Literatur* 12 (1967): 343–356.

Link, Werner. "Die Ruhrbesetzung und die wirtschaftspolitischen Interessen der USA," *Vierteljahrshefte für Zeitgeschichte* 17 (1969): 372–382.

Link, Werner. *Die amerikanische Stabilisierungspolitik in Deutschland 1921–32* (Düsseldorf, 1970).

Link, Werner. "Zum Problem der Kontinuität der amerikanischen Deutschlandpolitik im 20. Jahrhundert," in Manfred Knapp, ed., *Die deutsch-amerikanischen Beziehungen nach 1945* (Frankfurt/New York, 1975), 86–131.

Link, Werner. "Demokratische Staatsordnung und außenpolitische Orientierung: Die Einstellung zu den USA als Problem der deutschen Politik im 20. Jahrhundert," in Lothar Albertin/Werner Link, eds., *Politische Parteien auf dem Weg zur parlamentarischen Demokratie in Deutschland. Entwicklungslinien bis zur Gegenwart* (Düsseldorf, 1981), 63–89.

Link, Werner. "Die Vereinigten Staaten und der Ruhrkonflikt," in Klaus Schwabe, ed., *Die Ruhrkrise 1923. Wendepunkt der internationalen Beziehungen nach dem Ersten Weltkrieg* (Paderborn, 1985), 39–51.

Livermore, Seward W. *Politics is Adjourned: Woodrow Wilson and the War Congress, 1916–1918* (Middletown, CT, 1966).

Luebke, Frederick C. *Bonds of Loyalty: German-Americans in World War I* (DeKalb, IL, 1974).

Luebke, Frederick C. "Images of German Immigrants in the United States and Brazil, 1890–1918: Some Comparisons," in Trommler/McVeigh, *America and the Germans*, vol. 1, 207–220.

Margulies, Herbert F. "The Election of 1920 in Wisconsin," *Wisconsin Magazine of History* 41 (1957): 15–22.

Marks, Sally/Denis Dulude. "German-American Relations 1918–1921," *Mid-America* 53 (1971): 211–226.

May, Ernest R. *The World War and American Isolation, 1914–1917* (Cambridge, MA, 1959).

McDougall, Walter A. *France's Rhineland Diplomacy 1914–1924. The Last Bid for a Balance of Power in Europe* (Princeton, NJ, 1978).

McNeill, William C. *American Money and the Weimar Republic. Economics and Politics in the Era of the Great Depression* (New York, 1986).

Meyer, Henry Cord. *Mitteleuropa in German Thought and Action, 1815–1945* (The Hague, 1955).

Meyer, Henry Cord. *Five Images of Germany* (Washington, DC, 1960).

Möckelmann, Jürgen. *Deutsch-amerikanische Beziehungen in der Krise. Studien zur amerikanischen Politik im Ersten Weltkrieg* (Frankfurt/M., 1967).

Mommsen, Hans et al., eds., *Industrielles System und politische Entwicklung in der Weimarer Republik* (Düsseldorf, 1974).

Mommsen, Wolfgang J., ed., *Der moderne Imperialismus* (Stuttgart, 1971).

Mommsen, Wolfgang J./Jürgen Osterhammel, eds., *Imperialism and After. Continuities and Discontinuities* (London, 1986).

Nelson, Keith. "What Colonel House Overlooked in the Armistice," *Mid-America* 51 (1969): 75–91.

Noble, David W. *The End of American History: Democracy, Capitalism, and the Metaphor of Two Worlds in American Historical Writing, 1880–1980* (Minneapolis, 1985).

O'Grady, Joseph P., ed., *The Immigrants' Influence on Wilson's Peace Policies* (Lexington, KY, 1967).

Parrini, Carl. *Heir to Empire: United States Economic Diplomacy, 1916–1923* (Pittsburgh, PA, 1969).

Parsons, Edward B. "The German-American Crisis of 1902–03," *Historian* 33 (1971): 436–452.

Parsons, Edward B. *Wilsonian Diplomacy. Allied-American Rivalries in War and Peace* (St. Louis, MO, 1978).

Perkins, Bradford. *The Great Rapprochement: England and the United States, 1895–1914* (New York, 1968).

Pletcher, David M. *The Awkward Years. American Foreign Relations under Garfield and Arthur* (Columbia, MO, 1961).

Pommerin, Reiner. "Die Gründung des Germanischen Museums an der Harvard Universität. Zur Geschichte der Kulturpolitik in den USA unter Wilhelm II," *Archiv für Kulturgeschichte* 61 (1979): 420–430.

Pommerin, Reiner. *Der Kaiser und Amerika* (Köln, 1986).

Prager, Ludwig. *Die Handelsbeziehungen des Deutschen Reiches mit den Vereinigten Staaten von Amerika bis zum Ausbruch des Weltkrieges im Jahre 1914. Dazu ein*

Nachtrag über die Entwicklung der Verhältnisse in der Nachkriegszeit bis 1924 (Weimar, 1926).

Read, James M. *Atrocity Propaganda, 1914–1919* (New Haven, CT, 1941).
Remak, Joachim. "Trouble at Manila Bay: The Dewey-Diederichs Incident," *American-German Review* 23, no. 5 (1957): 17–19, 27.
Rich, Norman. "Eine Bemerkung über Friedrich von Holsteins Aufenthalt in Amerika," *Historische Zeitschrift* 186 (1958): 80–86.
Rippley, La Vern J. "Ameliorated Americanization: The Effect of World War I on German-Americans in the 1920s," in Trommler/ McVeigh, *America and the Germans*, vol. 2, 232–242.
Rock, Stephen R. *Why Peace Breaks Out. Great Power Rapprochement in Historical Perspective* (Chapel Hill, NC, 1989).
Rogon, Michael. "Max Weber and Woodrow Wilson: The Iron Cage in Germany and America," *Polity* 3 (1971): 557–575.
Rohwer, Jürgen. "Kriegsschiffbau und Flottengesetze um die Jahrhundertwende," in Herbert Schottelius/Wilhelm Deist, eds., *Marine und Marinepolitik im kaiserlichen Deutschland, 1871–1914* (Düsseldorf, 1972), 211–235.
Rosenberg, Emily S. *Spreading the American Dream: American Economic and Cultural Expansion, 1890–1945* (New York, NY, 1982).
Rupieper, Hermann J. "Allanson B. Houghton. An American Ambassador in Germany," *International History Review* 1 (1979): 490–508.

Scheiber, Harry N. *The Wilson Administration and Civil Liberties, 1917–1921* (Ithaca, NY, 1960).
Schieber, Clara E. *The Transformation of American Sentiment toward Germany, 1870–1914* (New York, 1923).
Schmidt, Gustav, ed., *Konstellationen internationaler Politik 1924–1932. Politische und wirtschaftliche Faktoren in den Beziehungen zwischen Westeuropa und den Vereinigten Staaten* (Bochum, 1983).
Schmidt, Henry J. "The Rhetoric of Survival. The Germanist in America from 1900 to 1925," in Trommler/McVeigh, *America and the Germans*, vol. 2, 204–216.
Schötz, Hans Otto. *Der Kampf um die Mark 1923/24: Die deutsche Währungsstabilisierung unter dem Einfluß der nationalen Interessen Frankreichs, Großbritanniens und der USA* (Berlin, 1987).
Schröder, Hans-Jürgen. "Ökonomische Aspekte der amerikanischen Außenpolitik 1900–1923," *Neue Politische Literatur* 17 (1972): 298–321.
Schröder, Hans-Jürgen. "Zur politischen Bedeutung der deutschen Handelspolitik nach dem Ersten Weltkrieg," in Gerald D. Feldman et al., eds., *Die deutsche Inflation. Eine Zwischenbilanz* (Berlin, 1982), 233–251.
Schüddekopf, Otto-Ernst. *Die Stützpunktpolitik des Deutschen Reiches, 1890–1914* (Berlin, 1941).
Schuker, Stephen A. *The End of French Predominance in Europe. The Financial Crisis of 1924 and the Adoption of the Dawes Plan* (Chapel Hill, NC, 1976).
Schuker, Stephen A. "Finance and Foreign Policy in the Era of the German

Inflation: British, French, and German Strategies for Economic Reconstruction after the First World War," in Gerald D. Feldman/Otto Büsch, eds., *Historische Prozesse der deutschen Inflation, 1914–1924* (Berlin, 1978), 343–361.

Schuker, Stephen A. "American 'Reparations' to Germany, 1919–1933," in Gerald D. Feldman, ed., *Die Nachwirkungen der Inflation auf die deutsche Geschichte 1924–1933* (München, 1985), 335–384.

Schuker, Stephen A. *American "Reparations" to Germany, 1919–1933. Implications of the Third World Debt Crisis* (Princeton, NJ, 1988).

Schuker, Stephen A. "American Policy toward Debts and Reconstruction at Genoa, 1922," in Carole Fink/ Axel Frohn/Jürgen Heideking, eds., *Genoa, Rapallo, and the Reconstruction of Europe in 1922* (New York, 1992), 95–130.

Schwabe, Klaus. "Die amerikanische und die deutsche Geheimdiplomatie und das Problem eines Verständigungsfriedens im Jahre 1918," *Vierteljahrshefte für Zeitgeschichte* 19 (1971): 1–32.

Schwabe, Klaus. "Woodrow Wilson and Germany's Membership in the League of Nations," *Central European History* 8 (1975): 3–22.

Schwabe, Klaus. *Woodrow Wilson: Ein Staatsmann zwischen Puritanertum und Liberalismus* (Göttingen, 1971).

Schwabe, Klaus. *Der amerikanische Isolationismus im 20. Jahrhundert. Legende und Wirklichkeit* (Wiesbaden, 1975).

Schwabe, Klaus. "Anti-Americanism within the German Right 1917–1933," *Amerikastudien/American Studies* 21 (1976): 89–108.

Schwabe, Klaus. "America's Contribution to the Stabilization of the Early Weimar Republic," in Hans L. Trefousse (ed.), *Germany and America: Essays on Problems of International Relations and Immigration* (New York, 1980), 21–28.

Schwabe, Klaus. "The United States and the Weimar Republic: A 'Special Relationship' that Failed," in Trommler/McVeigh, *America and the Germans*, vol. 2, 18–29.

Schwabe, Klaus. *Woodrow Wilson, Revolutionary Germany, and Peace-Making, 1918–1919* (Chapel Hill, NC, 1985); revised edition of *Deutsche Revolution und Wilson-Frieden. Die amerikanische und deutsche Friedensstrategie zwischen Ideologie und Machtpolitik 1918/19* (Düsseldorf, 1971).

Schwabe, Klaus. "U.S. Secret War Diplomacy, Intelligence, and the Coming of the German Revolution in 1918: The Role of Vice Consul McNally," *Diplomatic History* 16 (1992): 175–200.

Scott, Clifford H. "Assimilation in a German-American Community: The Impact of World War I," *Northwest Ohio Quarterly* 52 (1980): 153–165.

Shore, Elliott, *The German-American Radical Press: The Shaping of the Left Political Culture, 1850 to 1940* (Urbana, IL, 1992).

Simon, Matthew/David E. Novack. "Some Dimensions of the American Commercial Invasion of Europe, 1871–1914," *Journal of Economic History* 24 (1964): 591–508.

Skaggs, William H. *German Conspiracies in America. From an American Point of View by an American* (London, 1915).

Small, Melvin. "The United States and the German 'Threat' to the Hemisphere, 1905–1914," *The Americas* 28 (1972): 252–270.

Smith, Joseph. *Illusions of Conflict: Anglo-American Diplomacy toward Latin America, 1865–1896* (Pittsburgh, PA, 1979).

Snell, John L. "Wilson on Germany and the Fourteen Points," *Journal of Modern History* 26 (1954): 364–369.

Soutou, Georges–Henri. *L'Or et le Sang: Les Buts de Guerre Économique de la Première Guerre Mondiale* (Paris, 1989).

Spitzer, H.M. "German's Attack on America," *South Atlantic Quarterly* 43 (1944): 292–303.

Steuerwald, Ulrich. *Der amerikanische Weltkriegsroman 1919–1939* (Bern, 1965).

Strickland, Charles F. "American Aid to Germany, 1919 to 1921," *Wisconsin Magazine of History* 45 (1961/62): 256–270.

Theiner, Peter. "'Mitteleuropa'- Pläne im Wilhelminischen Deutschland," in Helmut Berding, ed., *Wirtschaftliche und politische Integration in Europa im 19. und 20. Jahrhundert* (Göttingen, 1984), 136–148.

Totten, Christine M. "Elusive Affinities: Acceptance and Rejection of the German-Americans," in Trommler/McVeigh, *America and the Germans*, vol. 2, 185–203.

Trachtenberg, Marc. *Reparation in World Politics: France and the European Economic Diplomacy, 1916–1923* (New York, 1980).

Trefousse, Hans L., ed., *Germany and America: Essays on Problems of International Relations and Immigration* (New York, 1980).

Trommler, Frank/Joseph McVeigh, eds., *America and the Germans. An Assessment of a Three-Hundred-Year History*, 2 vols. (Philadelphia, PA, 1985) – cited Trommler/McVeigh. *America and the Germans.*

Trommler, Frank. "The Rise and Fall of Americanism in Germany," in Trommler/McVeigh, *America and the Germans*, vol. 2, 332–342.

Urban, Henry F. "Die Monroe-Doktrin," *Die Zukunft* 31 (1900): 202–206.

Vagts, Alfred. *Deutschland und die Vereinigten Staaten in der Weltpolitik*, 2 vols., (New York, 1935).

Vagts, Alfred. "Hopes and Fears of an American-German War, 1870–1915," *Political Science Quarterly* 54 (1939): 514–535.

Vagts, Alfred. "Die Vereinigten Staaten und das Gleichgewicht der Mächte," in Alfred Vagts. *Bilanzen und Balancen. Aufsätze zur internationalen Finanz und internationalen Politik*, ed. by Hans-Ulrich Wehler, (Frankfurt/M, 1979), 161–192.

Vann Woodward, C. *The Old World's New World* (New York, 1991).

Walworth, Arthur. *America's Moment, 1918: American Diplomacy at the End of World War I* (New York, 1977).

Walworth, Arthur. *Wilson and His Peacemakers: American Diplomacy at the Paris Peace Conference, 1919* (New York, 1986).

Wandel, Eckhard. *Die Bedeutung der Vereinigten Staaten von Amerika für das deutsche Reparationsproblem, 1924–29* (Tübingen, 1971).

Ward, Robert D. "The Origin and Activities of the National Security League, 1914–1919," *Mississippi Valley Historical Review* 47 (1960): 51–65.

Wehler, Hans-Ulrich. *Der Aufstieg des amerikanischen Imperialismus* (Göttingen, 1974, 2nd ed., 1987).

Wilkins, Mira. *The Maturing of Multinational Enterprise: American Business Abroad from 1914 to 1970* (Cambridge, MA, 1974).

Williams, William A. *The Roots of the Modern American Empire. A Study of the Growth and Shaping of Social Consciousness in a Market Place Society* (New York, 1969).

Williams, William A., ed., *From Colony to Empire: Essays in the History of American Foreign Relations* (New York, 1972).

Wimer, Kurt. "Woodrow Wilson and World Order," in Arthur S. Link, ed., *Woodrow Wilson and a Revolutionary World, 1913–1923* (New York, 1984), 146–173.

Wittke, Carl. "American Germans in Two World Wars," *Wisconsin Magazine of History* 17 (1943): 6–16.

Wittke, Carl. *The German Language Press in America*, (Lexington, KY, 1957).

Index

Index